Lecture Notes in Computer Science 12383

More information about this subseries at http://www.springer.com/series/7409

Guojun Wang · Bing Chen ·
Wei Li · Roberto Di Pietro ·
Xuefeng Yan · Hao Han (Eds.)

Security, Privacy, and Anonymity in Computation, Communication, and Storage

SpaCCS 2020 International Workshops
Nanjing, China, December 18–20, 2020
Proceedings

Springer

Editors
Guojun Wang ⓘ
Guangzhou University
Guangzhou, China

Wei Li ⓘ
Computer Science
Georgia State University
Atlanta, GA, USA

Xuefeng Yan
Nanjing University of Aeronautics
and Astronautics
Nanjing, China

Bing Chen ⓘ
Nanjing University of Aeronautics
and Astronautics
Nanjing, China

Roberto Di Pietro ⓘ
College of Science and Engineering
Qatar Foundation Education City
Doha, Qatar

Hao Han ⓘ
Nanjing University of Aeronautics
and Astronautics
Nanjing, China

ISSN 0302-9743   ISSN 1611-3349 (electronic)
Lecture Notes in Computer Science
ISBN 978-3-030-68883-7   ISBN 978-3-030-68884-4 (eBook)
https://doi.org/10.1007/978-3-030-68884-4

LNCS Sublibrary: SL3 – Information Systems and Applications, incl. Internet/Web, and HCI

This Springer imprint is published by the registered company Springer Nature Switzerland AG
The registered company address is: Gewerbestrasse 11, 6330 Cham, Switzerland

Preface

A very warm welcome to the 13th International Conference on Security, Privacy and Anonymity in Computation, Communication and Storage (SpaCCS 2020), held in Nanjing, China during December 18–20, 2020. SpaCCS 2020 was hosted by Nanjing University of Aeronautics and Astronautics and co-organized by Key Lab of Information System Requirement, Jiangsu Computer Society, and Collaborative Innovation Center of Novel Software Technology and Industrialization.

SpaCCS 2020 and its associated symposiums and workshops provide a forum for researchers and practitioners around the world to gather and share their research findings, ideas, and emerging trends in the research fields of computation, communication, and storage, with regard to security, privacy, and anonymity aspects of computer systems and networks. The previous SpaCCS conferences were successfully held in Atlanta, USA (2019), Melbourne, Australia (2018), Guangzhou, China (2017), Zhangjiajie, China (2016), Helsinki, Finland (2015), Beijing, China (2014), Melbourne, Australia (2013), Liverpool, UK (2012), and Changsha, China (2011).

The workshop program this year consisted of seven symposiums and workshops that covered a broad range of research topics on security, privacy, and anonymity in computation, communication, and storage, namely:

(1) The 11th International Workshop on Trust, Security and Privacy for Big Data (TrustData 2020)
(2) The 10th International Symposium on Trust, Security and Privacy for Emerging Applications (TSP 2020)
(3) The 9th International Symposium on Security and Privacy on Internet of Things (SPIoT 2020)
(4) The 6th International Symposium on Sensor-Cloud Systems (SCS 2020)
(5) The 2nd International Workshop on Communication, Computing, Informatics and Security (CCIS 2020)
(6) The 1st International Workshop on Intelligence and Security in Next Generation Networks (ISNGN 2020)
(7) The 1st International Symposium on Emerging Information Security and Applications (EISA 2020)

SpaCCS 2020 symposiums and workshops attracted 131 submissions from many different countries. All submissions were reviewed by at least three experts with relevant subject matter expertise. Based on the recommendations of the reviewers and subsequent discussions of the program committee members, 48 papers were selected for oral presentation at the conference and inclusion in this Springer LNCS volume (i.e., an acceptance rate of 36.6%). In addition to the technical presentations, the program includes a number of keynote speeches by world-renowned researchers. We would like to thank the keynote speakers for their time and willingness to share their expertise with the conference attendees.

This event would not have been possible without the contributions of many experts who volunteered their time and energy. We would like to thank the symposium and workshop organizers for their hard work in soliciting high-quality submissions, assembling the Program Committee, managing the peer-review process, and planning the symposium and workshop agenda. We would also like to acknowledge the strong support of the Organizing Committee of SpaCCS 2020, and in particular the Steering Chairs, Prof. Guojun Wang from Guangzhou University, China, and Prof. Gregorio Martinez from University of Murcia, Spain, for guiding the entire process of the conference. We also would like to offer our gratitude to General Chairs, Prof. Zhiqiu Huang, Prof. Zhipeng Cai, Prof. Xuefeng Yan, and Prof. Aniello Castiglione, for their tremendous support and advice in ensuring the success of the conference. Thanks also go to: Program Chairs, Guojun Wang, Bing Chen, Wei Li and Roberto Di Pietro; Workshop Chair, Ryan Ko; Local Organizing Committee Chairs, Hao Han, and Kun Zhu; Publicity Chairs, Xin Li, Alberto Huertas, Shuhong Chen, Marco Guazzone, Yan Huang, and Weizhi Meng; and Conference Secretariat, Liming Fang.

Finally, we thank you for contributing to and participating in the SpaCCS 2020 conference and hope you found the conference a stimulating and exciting forum! Hopefully, you also enjoyed the beautiful city of Nanjing, China!

December 2020

Guojun Wang
Bing Chen
Wei Li
Roberto Di Pietro
Xuefeng Yan
Hao Han

Organization

TrustData 2020 Organizing and Program Committees

General Chairs

Qin Liu	Hunan University, China
Arun Kumar Sangaiah	Vellore Institute of Technology, India
Wei Chang	Saint Joseph's University, USA

Program Chairs

Jiankun Hu	UNSW Canberra at the Australian Defence Force Academy, Australia
Isaac Agudo	University of Málaga, Spain

Program Committee (in alphabetical order)

Habtamu Abie	Norwegian Computing Center/Norsk Regnesentral, Norway
Salima Benbernou	Université Paris Descartes, France
Christian Callegari	The University of Pisa, Italy
Wei Chang	Saint Joseph's University, USA
Anupam Chattopadhyay	Nanyang Technological University, Singapore
John A. Clark	University of York, UK
Alfredo Cuzzocrea	University of Calabria and ICAR-CNR, Italy
Sabrina De Capitani di Vimercati	Università degli Studi di Milano, Italy
Yucong Duan	Hainan University, China
Sheikh M. Habib	Technical University of Darmstadt, Germany
Ching-Hsien Hsu	Asia University, Taiwan
Hai Jiang	Arkansas State University, USA
Vana Kalogeraki	Athens University of Economics and Business, Greece
Ryan Ko	University of Queensland, Australia
Ruggero Donida Labati	Università degli Studi di Milano, Italy
Xin Liao	Hunan University, China
Giovanni Livraga	Università degli Studi di Milano, Italy
Haibing Lu	Santa Clara University, USA
Joon S. Park	Syracuse University, USA
Roberto Di Pietro	Hamad Bin Khalifa University, Qatar
Vincenzo Piuri	Università degli Studi di Milano, Italy
Imed Romdhani	Edinburgh Napier University, UK

Bimal Roy	Indian Statistical Institute, India
Jun Shen	University of Wollongong, Australia
Dimitris E. Simos	SBA Research, Austria
Chao Song	University of Electronic Science and Technology of China, China
Chang-ai Sun	University of Science and Technology Beijing, China
Yuanyuan Sun	Huazhong University of Science and Technology, China
Luis Javier García Villalba	Universidad Complutense de Madrid, Spain
Yunsheng Wang	Kettering University, USA
Mingzhong Wang	University of the Sunshine Coast, Australia
Yongdong Wu	Institute for Infocomm Research, Singapore
Hejun Wu	Sun Yat-sen University, China
Muneer Masadeh Bani Yassein	Jordan University of Science and Technology, Jordan
Sherali Zeadally	University of Kentucky, USA

Publicity Chairs

Weiwei Chen	Hunan University, China
Bo Ou	Hunan University, China

Webmaster

Yuzhu Ning	Hunan University, China

Steering Committee

Jemal H. Abawajy	Deakin University, Australia
Isaac Agudo	University of Málaga, Spain
Jose M. Alcaraz Calero	University of the West of Scotland, UK
Jiannong Cao	Hong Kong Polytechnic University, Hong Kong
Raymond Choo	The University of Texas at San Antonio, USA
Minyi Guo	Shanghai Jiao Tong University, China
Jiankun Hu	UNSW Canberra at the Australian Defence Force Academy, Australia
Konstantinos Lambrinoudakis	University of Piraeus, Greece
Jianhua Ma	Hosei University, Japan
Peter Müller	IBM Zurich Research Laboratory, Switzerland
Indrakshi Ray	Colorado State University, USA
Bhavani Thuraisingham	The University of Texas at Dallas, USA
Guojun Wang	Guangzhou University, China
Jie Wu	Temple University, USA
Yang Xiang	Swinburne University of Technology, Australia
Laurence T. Yang	St. Francis Xavier University, Canada

Kun Yang   University of Essex, UK
Wanlei Zhou   City University of Macau, Macau

TSP 2020 Organizing and Program Committees

General Co-chairs

Xiaodong Lin   University of Guelph, Canada
Khalid Alharbi   Northern Border University, Saudi Arabia

Program Co-chairs

Imad Jawhar   Al Maaref University, Lebanon
Deqing Zou   Huazhong University of Science and Technology,
                             China

Publicity Chairs

Can Wang   Griffith University, Australia
David Zheng   Frostburg State University, USA
Dawei Li   Montclair State University, USA
Wei Chen   InterDigital Communications, Inc., USA

Program Committee Members

Mingwu Zhang   Hubei University of Technology, China
Haitao Lang   Dept. Physics & Electronics, China
Yunsheng Wang   Kettering University, USA
Yaxiong Zhao   Google Inc., USA
Xuanxia Yao   University of Science and Technology Beijing, China
Xiaojun Hei   Huazhong University of Science and Technology,
                             China
Ying Dai   Temple University, USA
Youwen Zhu   Nanjing University of Aeronautics and Astronautics,
                             China
Huan Zhou   China Three Gorges University, China
Xin Li   Nanjing University of Aeronautics and Astronautics,
                             China
Chao Song   University of Electronic Science and Technology
                             of China, China
Chi Lin   Dalian University of Technology, China
Lin Ye   Harbin Institute of Technology, China
Xiaofeng Ding   Huazhong University of Science and Technology,
                             China
Guangzhong Sun   University of Science and Technology of China, China

Yanghua Xiao	Fudan University, China
Toon De Pessemier	Ghent University, Belgium
Filipa Peleja	Yahoo Research Barcelona, Spain
Ricky J. Sethi	Fitchburg State University, USA
Ed Fernandez	Florida Atlantic University, USA
Pouya Ostovari	San José State University, USA
Abdessamad Imine	University of Lorraine, France

Web Chair

Mingmin Shao	Hunan University, China

Steering Committee

Wenjun Jiang (Chair)	Hunan University, China
Laurence T. Yang	St. Francis Xavier University, Canada
Guojun Wang	Guangzhou University, China
Minyi Guo	Shanghai Jiao Tong University, China
Jie Li	University of Tsukuba, Japan
Jianhua Ma	Hosei University, Japan
Peter Müller	IBM Zurich Research Laboratory, Switzerland
Indrakshi Ray	Colorado State University, USA
Kouichi Sakurai	Kyushu University, Japan
Bhavani Thuraisingham	The University of Texas at Dallas, USA
Jie Wu	Temple University, USA
Yang Xiang	Swinburne University of Technology, Australia
Kun Yang	University of Essex, UK
Wanlei Zhou	University of Technology Sydney (UTS), Australia

SPIoT 2020 Organizing and Program Committees

Program Chairs

Marios Anagnostopoulos	Norwegian University of Science and Technology (NTNU), Norway
Constantinos Kolias	University of Idaho, USA

Program Committee

Afrand Agah	West Chester University of Pennsylvania, USA
Cataldo Basile	Politecnico di Torino, Italy
Dan Garcia-Carrillo	University of Murcia, Spain
Dimitris Geneiatakis	Joint Research Centre, European Commission, Belgium

Vasileios Gkioulos	Norwegian University of Science and Technology (NTNU), Norway
Hsiang-Cheh Huang	National University of Kaohsiung, Taiwan
Youssef Iraqi	Khalifa University of Science, Technology and Research, UAE
Georgios Karopoulos	National and Kapodistrian University of Athens, Greece
Riccardo Lazzeretti	Sapienza University of Rome, Italy
Wissam Mallouli	Montimage, France
Daisuke Mashima	Advanced Digital Sciences Center, Singapore
Sofia Anna Menesidou	Ubitech Ltd., Greece
Weizhi Meng	Technical University of Denmark, Denmark
Juan Pedro Muñoz-Gea	Universidad Politécnica de Cartagena, Spain
Christoforos Ntantogian	University of Piraeus, Greece
Dimitrios Papamartzivanos	Ubitech Ltd., Greece
Rodrigo Roman	University of Málaga, Spain
Corinna Schmitt	Bundeswehr University Munich, Germany
Asaf Shabtai	Ben-Gurion University of the Negev, Israel
Georgios Spathoulas	University of Thessaly, Greece
Angelo Spognardi	Sapienza Università di Roma, Italy
Zisis Tsiatsikas	University of the Aegean, Greece
Corrado Aaron Visaggio	University of Sannio, Italy
Lanier A. Watkins	The Johns Hopkins University, USA
Keping Yu	Waseda University, Japan
Peng Zhou	Shanghai University, China

Steering Committee

Georgios Kambourakis (Chair)	European Commission, Joint Research Centre (JRC), Italy, and University of the Aegean, Greece
Guojun Wang (Chair)	Guangzhou University, China
Mauro Conti	University of Padua, Italy
Hua Wang	Victoria University, Australia
Vasilis Katos	Bournemouth University, UK
Jaime Lloret Mauri	Polytechnic University of Valencia, Spain
Yongdong Wu	Institute for Infocomm Research, Singapore
Zhoujun Li	Beihang University, China

SCS 2020 Organizing and Program Committees

General Chairs

Tian Wang	Huaqiao University, China
Ying Ma	Xiamen University of Technology, China
Yang Liu	Beijing University of Posts and Telecommunications, China

Program Chairs

Hongning Dai   Macau University of Science and Technology, Macau
Md Zakirul Alam Bhuiyan   Fordham University, USA

Program Committee

A. M. A. Elman Bashar   Plymouth State University, USA
Dapeng Qu   Liaoning University, China
Deze Zeng   The University of Aizu, Japan
Dongxiao Yu   Shandong University, China
Guangsheng Feng   Harbin Engineering University, China
Guisong Yang   University of Shanghai for Science and Technology,
                               China
Haiping Huang   Nanjing University of Posts and Telecommunications,
                               China
Hao Yang   Tsinghua University, China
Kai Liu   Chongqing University, China
Kashif Sharif   Beijing Institute of Technology, China
Lin Cui   Jinan University, China
Mande Xie   Zhejiang Gongshang University, China
Peiyin Xiong   Hunan University of Science and Technology, China
Peng Liu   Hangzhou Dianzi University, China
Ruiyun Yu   Northeastern University, China
Tang Liu   Sichuan Normal University, China
Weiping Zhu   Wuhan University, China
Wenzheng Xu   Sichuan University, China
Xiaopeng Fan   Chinese Academy of Sciences, China
Xiaoyu Wang   Nanjing University, China
Xiaoyu Zhu   Central South University, China
Xuxun Liu   South China University of Technology, China
Yang Liu   Beijing University of Posts and Telecommunications,
                               China
Ying Ma   Xiamen University of Technology, China
Yong Xie   Xiamen University of Technology, China
Yongxuan Lai   Xiamen University, China
Yucong Duan   Hainan University, China
Yunjian Jia   Chongqing University, China
Zeyu Sun   Luoyang Institute of Science and Technology, China
Zhong Li   Donghua University, China

Publicity Chairs

Arun Kumar Sangaiah   Vellore Institute of Technology (VIT), India
Shaohua Wan   Zhongnan University of Economics and Law, China
Youke Wu   Huaqiao University, China

Steering Committee

Jiannong Cao (Chair)	The Hong Kong Polytechnic University, Hong Kong
Xiaojiang Chen	Northwest University, China
Kim-Kwang Raymond Choo	The University of Texas at San Antonio, USA
Mianxiong Dong	Muroran Institute of Technology, Japan
Wei Dong	Zhejiang University, China
Xiao-Jiang Du (James)	Temple University, USA
Guangjie Han	Hohai University, China
Weijia Jia	Beijing Normal University & UIC, China
Kuan-Ching Li	Providence University, Taiwan
Qing Li	City University of Hong Kong, Hong Kong
Limin Sun	Institute of Information Engineering, Chinese Academy of Sciences, China
Guojun Wang	Guangzhou University, China
Hongyi Wu	Old Dominion University (ODU), USA
Yang Xiao	The University of Alabama, USA

CCIS 2020 Organizing and Program Committees

Program Chairs

Yongjun Ren	Nanjing University of Information Science & Technology, China
Chunhua Su	The University of Aizu, Japan

Publicity Chairs

Xin Li	Nanjing University of Aeronautics and Astronautics, China
Weizhi Meng	Technical University of Denmark, Denmark

Publication Chairs

Tao Peng	Guangzhou University, China
Xiaofei Xing	Guangzhou University, China

Registration Chair

Chunpeng Ge	Nanjing University of Aeronautics and Astronautics, China

Program Committee

Daojing He	Wuhan University, China
Shouling Ji	Zhejiang University, China
Weizhi Meng	Technical University of Denmark, Denmark
Jiang Xu	Nanjing University of Information Science & Technology, China
Yuxiang Wang	Nanjing University of Information Science & Technology, China
Jian Zhang	Nanjing University of Information Science & Technology, China
Xuejie Zhang	Hohai University, China

Workshop Secretariat

Liming Fang	Nanjing University of Aeronautics and Astronautics, China

Web Chair

Ran Wang	Nanjing University of Aeronautics and Astronautics, China

ISNGN 2020 Organizing and Program Committees

Program Chairs

Hao Han	Nanjing University of Aeronautics and Astronautics, China
Kun Zhu	Nanjing University of Aeronautics and Astronautics, China

Program Committee

Dinh Thai Hoang	University of Technology Sydney, Australia
Fei Shen	Chinese Academy of Sciences, China
Tung Nguyen	Intelligent Automation, Inc., USA
Meng Han	Kennesaw State University, USA
Fengyuan Xu	Nanjing University, China
Ed Novak	Franklin and Marshall College, USA
Yifan Zhang	Binghamton University, USA
Chiu C. Tan	Temple University, USA
Xin Li	Nanjing University of Aeronautics and Astronautics, China
Bo Sheng	University of Massachusetts Boston, USA

Workshop Secretariat

Liming Fang　　　　　　　　Nanjing University of Aeronautics and Astronautics, China

Web Chair

Ran Wang　　　　　　　　Nanjing University of Aeronautics and Astronautics, China

EISA 2020 Organizing and Program Committees

General Chairs

Liqun Chen　　　　　　　　University of Surrey, UK
Kazumasa Omote　　　　　University of Tsukuba, Japan

Program Chairs

Weizhi Meng　　　　　　　Technical University of Denmark, Denmark
Jiageng Chen　　　　　　　Central China Normal University, China
Kuan-Ching　　　　　　　Providence University, Taiwan

Program Committee

Gergely Biczók　　　　　　Budapest University of Technology and Economics, Hungary
Rongmao Chen　　　　　　National University of Defense Technology, China
Chen-Mou Cheng　　　　　Kanazawa University, Japan
Changyu Dong　　　　　　Newcastle University, UK
Yunhe Feng　　　　　　　University of Washington, USA
Stefanos Gritzalis　　　　　University of Piraeus, Greece
Debiao He　　　　　　　　Wuhan University, China
Yousef Al Hammadi　　　　UAE University, United Arab Emirates
Shoichi Hirose　　　　　　University of Fukui, Japan
Julian Jang-Jaccard　　　　Massey University, New Zealand
Costas Lambrinoudakis　　University of Piraeus, Greece
Wenjuan Li　　　　　　　Hong Kong Polytechnic University, China
Giovanni Livraga　　　　　University of Milan, Italy
Mohammad Mamun　　　　National Research Council Canada, Canada
David Naccache　　　　　　ENS, France
Javier Parra-Arnau　　　　Karlsruhe Institute of Technology, Germany
Josef Pieprzyk　　　　　　CSIRO/Data61, Australia
Jun Shao　　　　　　　　Zhejiang Gongshang University, China
Je Sen Teh　　　　　　　Universiti Sains Malaysia, Malaysia

Qianhong Wu	Beihang University, China
Zhe Xia	Wuhan University of Technology, China
Jingfang Xu	Central China Normal University, China
Wun-She Yap	Universiti Tunku Abdul Rahman, Malaysia

Publicity Chairs

| Zhe Xia | Wuhan University of Technology, China |
| Chunhua Su | The University of Aizu, Japan |

Steering Committee

Jiageng Chen	Central China Normal University, China
Liqun Chen	University of Surrey, UK
Steven Furnell	University of Plymouth, UK
Anthony T. S. Ho	University of Surrey, UK
Sokratis K. Katsikas	Norwegian University of Science and Technology, Norway
Javier Lopez	University of Málaga, Spain
Weizhi Meng	Technical University of Denmark, Denmark

Contents

**The 6th International Symposium on Sensor-Cloud
Systems (SCS 2020)**

The 1st International Symposium on Emerging Information Security and Applications (EISA 2020)

The 11th International Workshop on Trust, Security and Privacy for Big Data (TrustData 2020)

EDC: An Edge-Oriented Dynamic Resource Configuration Strategy

Lei Wei[1], Weiwei Miao[2], Zeng Zeng[2], Hesheng Sun[3], and Zhuzhong Qian[3(✉)]

[1] State Grid Jiangsu Electric Power Co. Ltd., Nanjing 210024, China
[2] State Grid Jiangsu Electric Power Co. Ltd. Information and Telecommunication Branch, Nanjing 210024, China
[3] Department of Computer Science and Technology, Nanjing University, Nanjing 210023, China
qzz@nju.edu.cn

Abstract. With the development of machine learning technology, various applications have different requirements for computing power, network bandwidth, delay limit and Quality of Service (QoS). Existing research usually focuses on a single type of service without considering the characteristics of different services. However, in the real life, the application requirements for edge computing are often diversified. This paper considers how to allocate bandwidth and computing power for applications with different types of requirements and characteristics in a real edge environment, so as to obtain the best QoS for heterogeneous applications while balancing the long-term-time-delay. Through the Lyapunov optimization method, the long-term time-delay constraints can be converted into online problems, which will be solved using current known information without requiring future information. Then the Karush-Kuhn-Tucker (KKT) condition is used to solve the current online optimization problem, and the expected goal of real-time scheduling of current network bandwidth resources to minimize the delay is achieved. We evaluate the performance of our proposed edge-oriented dynamic resource configuration (EDC) strategy using trace-driven experiments. The results show the integrated performance of the heterogeneous inference model within our system is improved by about 10.3%, while the average latency is reduced by about 33.7%.

Keywords: Edge computing · Resource configuration · Machine learning

1 Introduction

With the popularity of cloud computing technology, a large number of computing tasks are implemented in the cloud [9]. From individuals to enterprises, people upload their own business to the cloud for processing, which brings great convenience to people's life. In addition, with the development and progress of machine learning technology, the upload and download speed of large-scale data

© Springer Nature Switzerland AG 2021
G. Wang et al. (Eds.): SpaCCS 2020, LNCS 12383, pp. 3–14, 2021.
https://doi.org/10.1007/978-3-030-68884-4_1

has become a key factor because the application of machine learning in the cloud requires a lot of data. The most widely used machine learning applications such as computer vision [5], mobile augmented reality [10] obtain the optimal model through a big data set, and then are widely deployed in various applications. But the upload and download of the data takes a lot of time causing the long cumulative delay, which is a crucial problem for many applications that cannot be ignored [3] in cloud computing diagram.

In order to solve the problems such as QoS degradation caused by delay, researchers from academia and industry have proposed many ways to offload tasks to the edge for computing, such as fog computing [7], edge cloud and cloudlet [13]. Although their names are different, they all belong to the paradigm of edge computing, which is being widely used in industrial production [8], agricultural planting and people's daily life [4]. Due to the low latency of edge computing, it has been applied in many edge scenarios and has also received huge investment from many companies [1].

However, most of these studies only focus on one type of application, without considering the variety and heterogeneity of applications on the edge, which are far from reality [2]. In order to deal with the heterogeneity of application types and the diversity of resource constraints in the edge system [12], this paper considers how to allocate bandwidth and computing power for applications with different types of requirements and characteristics in a real edge environment [3], so as to obtain the best QoS for heterogeneous applications while balancing the long-term-time-delay [6]. Our main contributions are summarized as follows:

This article abstracts these elements into mathematical conditions and expresses them with an optimization problem. We proposed an edge-oriented dynamic resource configuration (EDC) strategy which realizes bandwidth resource allocation and allocation according to user needs. This paper firstly proves the applicability of Lyapunov's method theoretically, and at the same time shows that the algorithm has a good effect compared with other algorithms through simulation trace-back experiments.

2 Problem Model and Formulation

2.1 System Model

Suppose that there are a total of K terminals in an edge computing system, represented by the set $U = \{1, 2, \ldots, K\}$, the terminal needs to collect data to execute different edge inference models, suppose the set of these models is $M = \{0, 1, \ldots, N\}$, where the model labeled 0 represents the inference model deployed in the cloud. The model can only be executed at the edge or the cloud.

Assuming that the scheduling interval is discrete, that is, resources will be reassigned once in each scheduling slot. Assuming that the time of resource scheduling is $t \in \{1, \ldots, T\}$, we set only one task to be executed during one scheduling interval. Use $x_{k,t}^i$ to represent the edge inference model assigned to the user k at the scheduling time t. When $x_{k,t}^i = 1$, it means that the model is selected, and 0 means that the model is not selected, then the model selection variables' limit are defined as

$$x_{k,t}^i = \{0,1\}, k \in U, i \in M, t \in \{1, \dots, T\} \tag{1}$$

2.2   Utility Model

Record that the amount of data collected by each terminal is r_0, the sampling rate of the data uploaded to the cloud or edge by the terminal is r_k. r_0 is determined by the terminal itself, and the operator can determine the data sampling rate according to the bandwidth allocated to each user. Obviously, the data uploaded by the terminal cannot exceed the data collected by itself, so $r_k \in \{0,1\}$.

Assuming that for the application executed by the current edge computing system, there are N different inference models on the edge server, the total amount of data received by the inference model is $r_0 * r_k$, and the relationship between the execution effect and the amount of data r_k is defined as

$$a_{k,t}^i = \epsilon_1(i)(1 - c_0 e^{-\frac{r_0 r_k}{c_1}}), k \in U, i \in M \backslash \{0\}, t \in \{1, \dots, T\} \tag{2}$$

Where $\epsilon_1(i) \in (0,1)$ represents the influence factors of different models. $1 - c_0 e^{-\frac{r_0 r_k}{c_1}}$ represents the relationship between the execution effect of the model and the amount of data. It is an increasing function, which means the larger the amount of data, the better the execution effect.

The cloud computing resources are more abundant and can implement a more powerful reasoning model. Assuming that the cloud execution effect impact factor is 1, that is, $\epsilon_1(0) = 1$, the relationship between the execution effect of the reasoning model and the amount of calculation can be obtained as

$$a_{k,t}^i = \epsilon_1(i)(1 - c_0 e^{-\frac{r_0 r_k}{c_1}}), k \in U, i \in M, t \in \{1, \dots, T\} \tag{3}$$

2.3   Resource Constraints Model

Assuming that the total storage resources on the edge server is C, and assuming that the benchmark storage consumed by the model that requires more space is c_0, then the storage resources required by each model are $\epsilon_2(i)c_0$.

Assuming that all data passes through the network access point and then is distributed to the edge server and cloud server by the network access point, use B_t^e to indicate the bandwidth of the edge server, and B_t^0 to indicate the total amount of the network access point. And $b_{k,t}$ means the bandwidth allocated to each user, because model 0 represents the version calculated on the cloud, so the model version number executed at the edge starts from 1. Then the bandwidth limit for edge servers is defined as

$$\sum_{k=1}^{K} \sum_{i=0}^{N} x_{k,t}^i b_{k,t}^i = B_t^0, k \in U, t \in \{1, \dots, T\} \tag{4}$$

2.4   Real-Time Requirements Analysis

Real-time limitations are reflected in two aspects: one is that the data sampling rate of different terminals at each moment cannot exceed the bandwidth limit; the other is that the average delay of the system cannot exceed the user's tolerance, that is, the overall average delay is less than L_m. Use τ to indicate the duration of each scheduled time slot. Then there are the following requirements for the amount of data,

$$r_0 r_k \leq b_{k,t}\tau, k \in U, t \in \{1, \ldots, T\} \tag{5}$$

In addition, for task types with high real-time requirements and a large amount of data, there should be no delay in the entire task duration. In order to describe this limitation, the average delay in each scheduling slot is required to be less than a preset delay L_m. For the edge server, the delay consists of two parts, one part is the transmission delay, and the other part is the delay caused by the calculation s_i, where s_i represents the calculation time required by different models on the edge server. If the model is placed on the edge to execute, due to relatively insufficient computing resources and close to the terminal, the transmission delay and the delay caused by the calculation are mainly considered. The transmission delay is $\frac{x_{k,t}^i r_0 r_k}{b_{k,t}}$, that is, the total amount of data divided by time, so the total delay is

$$\sum_{i=1}^{N} \left(\frac{x_{k,t}^i r_0 r_k}{b_{k,t}} + x_{k,t}^i s_i \right) \tag{6}$$

If computing is performed in the cloud, then the propagation delay caused by distance needs to be considered, and the powerful computing power of the cloud makes the computing delay much smaller than the propagation delay. At this time, the propagation delay and transmission delay are mainly considered, so the delay limited condition is defined as

$$\left(\frac{x_{k,t}^0 r_0 r_k}{b_{k,t}} + x_{k,t}^0 L_c \right) \tag{7}$$

where L_c represents propagation delay from local to cloud. Integrating the delay caused by the two parts of cloud and edge computing, the real-time constraint can be expressed as

$$\lim_{T \to +\infty} \frac{1}{KT} \sum_{t=0}^{T} \sum_{k=1}^{K} \left[\left(\sum_{i=1}^{N} \frac{x_{k,t}^i r_0 r_k}{b_{k,t}} + x_{k,t}^i s_i \right) + \left(\frac{x_{k,t}^0 r_0 r_k}{b_{k,t}} + x_{k,t}^0 L_c \right) \right] < L_m \tag{8}$$

2.5   Problem Formulation

The first is the user's decision variable x, the user chooses the reasoning model and execution area for solving the problem; the second is the bandwidth allocation vector b; the third is the user's data size r.

The goal is to achieve the best overall execution effect rather than the best in a single scheduling time slot, so the final optimization problem is how to make the average execution utility in all scheduling time slots optimal. So the optimization objective function is defined as

$$P_0 : \max_{x,b} \quad \lim_{T \to \infty} \frac{1}{T} \sum_{t=0}^{T} \frac{1}{K} \sum_{k=1}^{K} w_k \sum_{i=0}^{N} x_{k,t}^i a_{k,t}^i \tag{9}$$

$$\text{s.t.} \quad (1),(2),(11),(4)-(8) \tag{10}$$

3 Details of EDC Algorithm

3.1 Long-Term Constraint Transformation

First, we record the delay of each user at the scheduling time t as $l_{k,t}$, then

$$l_{k,t} = \sum_{i=1}^{N} \frac{x_{k,t}^i r_0 r_k}{b_{k,t}} + x_{k,t}^i s_i + \left(\frac{x_{k,t}^0 r_0 r_k}{b_{k,t}} + x_{k,t}^0 L_c \right) \tag{11}$$

The main challenge in solving problem P is that the constraints Eq. 8 are long-term. In order to deal with this problem, the Lyapunov optimization method is introduced to convert the long-term problem into real-time constraints, and a virtual queue is constructed for each user.

$$q_k(t+1) = \max \{q_k(t) + l_{k,t} - L_m, 0\}, k \in U \tag{12}$$

Equation 12 indicates the cumulative delay of the user k at time $t+1$. At the current scheduling time t, the size of this queue is known, that is, the network operator knows the size of $q_k(t)$ at the current scheduling time t. If the amount of data uploaded by the terminal is increased indefinitely, then this queue will grow indefinitely, so it is very necessary to keep this queue stable. In other words, the user's virtual delay queue is stable, indicating that the delay has not accumulated, which means that the terminal's real-time performance is satisfied. This function is a piecewise function, which is difficult to handle. A quadratic Lyapunov function $L(q_k(t)) = \frac{1}{2} q_k(t)^2$ is introduced to represent the measurement of the cumulative delay of the queue. For wireless access points, the cumulative Lyapunov offset of the entire system is:

$$\Delta(q(t)) = \sum_{k=1}^{K} E\left[L\left(q_k(t+1)\right) - L\left(q_k(t)\right) \mid q_k(t) \right] \tag{13}$$

The offset $\Delta(q(t))$. It indicates the expected value of the change of the Lyapunov function every time a scheduling time slot passes. The smaller the value, the more stable the virtual queue, and the lower the delay experienced by the terminal. Our goal is to find a reasonable bandwidth and data volume configuration so that the real-time performance of the system can be met. Record the weighted sum of the execution effect of the inference model of each user in each scheduling slot as

$$a_t = \frac{1}{K} \sum_{k=1}^{K} w_k \sum_{i=0}^{N} x_{k,t}^i a_{k,t}^i, t \in \{1, \ldots, T\} \tag{14}$$

According to this stability condition and the expectation of the final execution effect of the model, we can get a Lyapunov cumulative and penalty term function:

$$\Delta(q(t)) - V \cdot E[a_t \mid q_1(t), \ldots, q_k(t)] \tag{15}$$

where the positive number V is used to balance the weight of the execution effect relative to the delay.

According to Eq. 15, at this time, $\Delta(q(t))$ still contains the term $q_k(t+1)$, which is unknown at the current scheduling time t, so it is necessary to reconsider $\Delta(q(t))$. When processing is performed, the current known information can be used to indicate the cumulative delay. According to Lyapunov's optimization method, an upper bound constructed by known information can be found at this time to replace $\Delta(q(t))$. It can be expressed as the following Theorem 1:

Theorem 1. *For the value of $\Delta(q(t))$ obtained by any bandwidth configuration method, the following inequality holds*

$$\Delta(q(t)) \leq B + \sum_{k=1}^{K} q_k(t) E\left[(l_{k,t} - l_{k,\max}) \mid q_1(t), \ldots, q_k(t)\right] \tag{16}$$

where $B = \frac{1}{2}\sum_{k=1}^{K} (l_{k,\max} - L_m)^2$ is a constant. And $l_{k,\max} = \max_{t \in \{1,\ldots,T\}} \{l_{k,t}\}$ indicates the maximum delay of each user.

Proof. According to Eq. 15

$$\Delta(q(t)) = \sum_{k=1}^{K} E\left[L(q_k(t+1)) - L(q_k(t)) \mid q_1(t), \ldots, q_k(t)\right]$$

$$= \frac{1}{2} E\left[\sum_{k=1}^{K} (q_k^2(t+1) - q_k^2(t)) \mid q_1(t), \ldots, q_k(t)\right]$$

$$\leq \frac{1}{2} E\left[\sum_{k=1}^{K} \left((q(t) + l_{k,t} - L_m)^2 - q(t)^2\right) \mid q_1(t), \ldots, q_k(t)\right] \tag{17}$$

$$= \frac{1}{2} \sum_{k=1}^{K} (l_{k,t} - l_m)^2 + \sum_{k=1}^{K} q_k(t) E\left[(l_{k,t} - L_m) \mid q_1(t), \ldots, q_k(t)\right]$$

$$\leq B + \sum_{k=1}^{K} q_k(t) E\left[(l_{k,t} - L_m) \mid q(t)\right]$$

Therefore, according to the upper bound of $\Delta(q(t))$, we can transform the problem P_0 and omit the constant term in the upper bound, then the problem is transformed into P_1

$$P_1 : \max_{x,b} \quad \sum_{k=1}^{K} q_k(t) \cdot l_{k,t} - V \cdot E\left[a_t \mid q_1(t), \ldots, q_k(t)\right] \tag{18}$$

$$\text{s.t.} \quad (1), (2), (4) - (8) \tag{19}$$

Algorithm 1: Parameter Decision Algorithm

Input: $\epsilon_1(i), \epsilon_2(i), i \in M, L_m, c_0, C, \tau$

Output: $r_{k,t}$

1 **while** $\sum_{k=1}^{K} \sum_{i=1}^{N} x_{k,t}^i \epsilon_2(i) c_0 > C$ **do**

2 | Randomly select a user to change its reasoning model $x_{k,t}^i$;

3 **end**

4 let $r'_{k,t} = R_l = r_{k,t-1}, R_r = 1, b_{k,t} = b_{k,t-1}$;

5 **while** $r'_{k,t} r_0 \leq b_{k,t} \tau$ **do**

6 | $r_{k,t} = r'_{k,t}$;

7 | $r'_{k,t} = \frac{1}{2}(R_l + R_r)$;

8 | According to Eq. 24 calculate the end users' allocated bandwidth $b_{k,t}$;

9 | **if** $\sum_{k=1} K \sum_{i=1} N x_{k,t}^i b_{k,t} > B_t^e$ **then**

10 | | For the end users that selects the edge as the model execution area, randomly selects part (a preset proportion) and puts it into the cloud for execution, then **goto** Step. 2;

11 | **end**

12 | $R_l = r_{k,t}$;

13 **end**

3.2 Resource Configuration

According to the condition Eq. 3, no matter which model is selected, the larger the amount of data uploaded by the terminal, the better the execution effect of the model. Therefore, for the current moment, we can divide the optimization goal into two parts. The first part is to maximize the data sampling rate, and the second part is to find out how to configure the bandwidth of each terminal according to the current data volume. So we can express this non-integer programming problem as P_2:

$$P_2 : \max_{x,b} \quad \sum_{k=1}^{K} q_k(t) \cdot l_{k,t} - V \cdot E\left[a_t \mid q_1(t), \ldots, q_k(t)\right] \tag{20}$$

$$\text{s.t.} \quad (6) - (8) \tag{21}$$

This is a multi-objective optimization problem, and the two optimization objectives restrict each other through the condition 5. If the terminal data sampling rate is too large, the allocated bandwidth cannot achieve the large amount of data uploaded; the selected data amount is small, and the optimal model execution effect cannot be achieved. Generally speaking, the multi-objective optimization problem is more difficult to solve, but for this problem, the optimization form of the second optimization objective is simple and can be used.

The basic idea is to first assume that the terminal selects the largest amount of data to upload each time, that is, let $r_k = 1$. So the minimum bandwidth allocation method at this time can be found out, and then compare whether the bandwidth allocation can carry the amount of data uploaded by the terminal according to the condition Eq. 5. The specific details is shown in Algorithm. 1

When we get the amount of data uploaded by the terminal, we can directly use the KKT condition to solve the bandwidth allocation, as shown in problem P_3

$$P_3 : \max_{x,b} \quad \left(\sum_{k=1}^{K} q_k(t) \cdot l_{k,t}, -r \right) \tag{22}$$

$$\text{s.t.} \quad (6) - (8) \tag{23}$$

And the solution to this problem is

$$b_{k,t}^* = \frac{\sqrt{\left(\sum_{i=0}^{N} x_{k,t}^i r_0 r_k \right) \cdot q_k(t)}}{\sum_{k=1}^{K} \sqrt{\left(\sum_{i=0}^{N} x_{k,t}^i r_0 r_k \right) \cdot q_k(t)}} B_t^0 \tag{24}$$

Now we have a specific method for bandwidth allocation, but this result is also limited by the Eq. (7). We consider this question in the selection of model execution area. If the total allocated bandwidth exceeds the range that the edge server can do, part of the model will be executed in the cloud. This part of the algorithm will be described in the next section.

4   EDC Performance on Simulation Experiments

In this section, we evaluated our proposed **EDC algorithm** through simulation experiments, and compared it with other algorithms. We simulated an edge computing system with a total of 100 terminals, and a total of 25 different inference models, of which 3 models were deployed in the cloud and 22 models were deployed on the edge server for image or video stream inspection.

We quoted the conclusions of existing studies [11] and described the influence function of the amount of data on the effect of the inference model $h(r_k)$. Since the size of the reasoning model has a significant relationship with its execution effect and calculation time, and it is also very closely related to the hardware. In order to simplify the processing, we normalize it, and use the parameters ϵ_2 and s to describe the execution effect of the reasoning model impact factor and processing task calculation time.

We selected four existing bandwidth allocation algorithms for comparison:

Average-Bandwidth: The bandwidth is allocated to these users on average, and the sample rate of the data uploaded by the users will take into account the current real-time requirements.

Max-Data: Based on the fair bandwidth allocation algorithm, only the amount of bandwidth allocated by the system, the corresponding amount of data is uploaded. And all the bandwidth of the allocated area is used as much as possible.

Delay-Optimal: The core idea is to have the lowest delay, a model with poor reasoning ability but short calculation time will be chosen firstly.

Max-Effective: According to the current accumulated delays of different users, the scheduler selects the terminal with the higher accumulated delay to allocate more bandwidth to it, and then selects the model with better effect as much as possible.

4.1   How EDC Ensured Low Latency

The algorithm mainly uses two mechanisms to balance the low-delay requirements of the system and the performance requirements of the system at each scheduling time. **Cloud-Edge collaboration mechanism:** As shown in Fig. 1, the impact of bandwidth resources on the selection model is described. When the total bandwidth is getting higher and the edge bandwidth resources are limited, the algorithm will automatically choose to upload more models to the cloud for execution, and simulate the experiment The results show that about 20% of the terminals will choose to execute the model in the cloud in the stable phase. **Real-time bandwidth allocation mechanism:** As shown in Fig. 2, when bandwidth resources are relatively tight, the average delay will be relatively large, and the maximum cumulative delay of users will increase accordingly. At

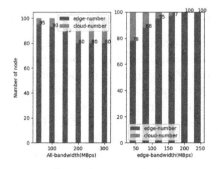

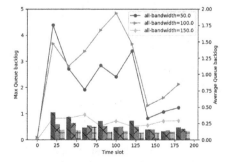

Fig. 1. Proportion of edge nodes   **Fig. 2.** Delay-queue fluctuation

this time, the algorithm will allocate relatively large bandwidth to these users with corresponding large cumulative delay in order to balance these users, so as to stabilize the overall delay of the system.

4.2   The Influence of Hyperparameters

Step size: When the step size is large, the time needed to reach the optimal solution is very short. However, when the step size is too large, it will cause continuous fluctuations in the subsequent scheduling time, so that we can not find the optimal solution. In our experiment, which was shown in Fig. 3, we choose the step size $\iota = 0.1$ to have the most suitable effect. **Stop threshold:** When the threshold value is large, the model update speed is very slow. This is because the execution effect change is less than the threshold value at multiple consecutive scheduling moments. In fact, it stays on a local optimal solution. When the threshold is too small, as shown in Fig. 4, it will cause large fluctuations in the execution effect, so the final selection of the threshold $\delta = 0.0035$ is more appropriate. **Maximum delay limit:** As shown by the yellow line in Fig. 5, when the average maximum delay limit is too low, in order to ensure real-time requirements, the system has to sacrifice the requirements for execution effect. Therefore, excessive real-time requirements will greatly reduce the execution effect of the system. We discover $L_m = 1.4$ is suitable for our experiments.

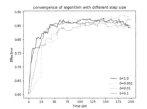
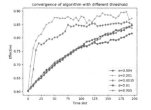
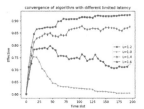

Fig. 3. Step-size influence   **Fig. 4.** Stop-threshold influence   **Fig. 5.** L_m influence

4.3   Comparison of Different Algorithms

We mainly compare the pros and cons of different algorithms from three aspects, the average user delay at each moment, the maximum delay, and the weighted sum of model execution effects. All the algorithms participating in the comparison will choose a model with a lower data sampling rate and a shorter calculation time during the initialization phase to meet real-time requirements.

The green lines in Figs. 6, 7 and 8 represent Our algorithm EDC. In the initial stage, due to the small cumulative delay, EDC alogorithm tends to be a radical data upload strategy. It can be seen from Fig. 7 that the execution volatility of EDC algorithm is much smaller than other bandwidth allocation algorithms, and the volatility is only about 50% higher than the delay-optimal algorithm, and this fluctuation range is completely acceptable for the maximum delay of the entire system.

Finally, As shown in Figs. 6, 7 and 8, the performance of the inference model for end users within the system is improved by about 10.3%, while the average latency is reduced by about 33.7%.

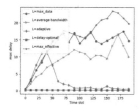 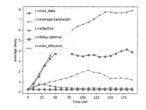 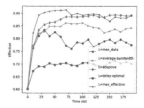

Fig. 6. Maximum-delay fluctuation

Fig. 7. Average-delay fluctuation

Fig. 8. Utility varietu

5 Conclusion

This paper formalized a cloud-side collaborative model reasoning system with multiple resource constraints, using the Lyapunov method to transform the long-term constraint mechanism into sub-problems that can be solved based on known information. Then an adaptive real-time bandwidth allocation algorithm EDC is proposed. Finally, the performance of the inference model for end users within the system is improved by about 10.3%, while the average latency is reduced by about 33.7%.

Acknowledgments. This work is supported by the Science and Technology Project of State Grid Corporation of China (Research on Key Technologies of Edge Intelligent Computing for Smart IoT System, No. 5210ED209Q3U).

References

1. Snapdragon 8 series mobile platforms. [EB/OL]. https://www.qualcomm.com/products/snapdragon-8-series-mobile-platforms
2. Aazam, M., Huh, E.N.: Fog computing micro datacenter based dynamic resource estimation and pricing model for IoT. In: 2015 IEEE 29th International Conference on Advanced Information Networking and Applications, pp. 687–694. IEEE (2015)
3. Barbera, M.V., Kosta, S., Mei, A., Stefa, J.: To offload or not to offload? The bandwidth and energy costs of mobile cloud computing. In: 2013 Proceedings IEEE INFOCOM, pp. 1285–1293. IEEE (2013)
4. Bonomi, F., Milito, R., Zhu, J., Addepalli, S.: Fog computing and its role in the internet of things. In: Proceedings of the First Edition of the MCC Workshop on Mobile Cloud Computing, pp. 13–16 (2012)
5. Goodfellow, I., et al.: Generative adversarial nets. In: Advances in Neural Information Processing Systems, pp. 2672–2680 (2014)

6. Hochreiter, S., Schmidhuber, J.: Long short-term memory. Neural Comput. **9**(8), 1735–1780 (1997)
7. Hu, W., et al.: Quantifying the impact of edge computing on mobile applications. In: Proceedings of the 7th ACM SIGOPS Asia-Pacific Workshop on Systems, pp. 1–8 (2016)
8. Mahgoub, A., Tarrad, N., Elsherif, R., Ismail, L., Al-Ali, A.: Fire alarm system for smart cities using edge computing. In: 2020 IEEE International Conference on Informatics, IoT, and Enabling Technologies (ICIoT), pp. 597–602. IEEE (2020)
9. Manning, C., Schutze, H.: Foundations of Statistical Natural Language Processing. MIT press, Cambridge (1999)
10. Mnih, V., et al.: Human-level control through deep reinforcement learning. Nature **518**(7540), 529–533 (2015)
11. Neely, M.J.: Stochastic network optimization with application to communication and queueing systems. Synth. Lect. Commun. Netw. **3**(1), 1–211 (2010)
12. Satyanarayanan, M., Bahl, P., Caceres, R., Davies, N.: The case for VM-based cloudlets in mobile computing. IEEE Pervasive Comput. **8**(4), 14–23 (2009)
13. Taleb, T., Samdanis, K., Mada, B., Flinck, H., Dutta, S., Sabella, D.: On multi-access edge computing: a survey of the emerging 5G network edge cloud architecture and orchestration. IEEE Commun. Surv. Tutorials **19**(3), 1657–1681 (2017)

The Future Prospects of Adversarial Nets

Muhammad Sohaib Yousaf[1] ⓘ, Shazia Riaz[1] ⓘ, Saqib Ali[1,2](✉) ⓘ,
Shuhong Chen[2] ⓘ, and Guojun Wang[2](✉) ⓘ

[1] Department of Computer Science, University of Agriculture,
Faisalabad 38000, Pakistan
{2019ag2623,2018ag4549,saqib}@uaf.edu.pk
[2] School of Computer Science, Guangzhou University, Guangzhou 510006, China
{saqibali,shuhongchen,csgjwang}@gzhu.edu.cn

Abstract. Machine learning has obtained remarkable achievement in longstanding tasks in various domains of artificial intelligence. However, machine learning certainly has some security threats, such as adversarial examples that hamper the machine learning models from correctly classifying the data. The adversarial examples are minor perturbations in the actual inputs to detract the model from its original task. Adversarial Attacks and their defenses are found in parallel when it comes to the literature of machine learning adversaries. In this paper, we have tried to inspect the adversarial attack types and their defenses by comprehensively classifying different techniques.

Keywords: Adversarial examples · Machine learning · Poisoning · Adversarial training · Adversarial defense mechanism

1 Introduction

The availability of large amount of data outsourced in the cloud has increased the popularity of machine learning models. The automation of machines has made them highly vulnerable to external attacks. These attacks can be of any type such as attacks on the privacy leakage of outsourced data [26], adversarial attacks, evasion or inference attack, etc. All these types of attacks can force the machine learning models to misclassify or misbehave to the environment where the model has to perform the classifying task [1]. One of such attacks is the adversarial attack in which the input is perturbed to fool the machine learning model. The model can be deceived to an extent that it will classify a horse to a motorbike. Perturbation in the input is the amalgamation of a minor value that does the trick for the adversary. This minor value is denoted by epsilon ϵ in the machine learning field and the minor change in the input is termed as a perturbation. The term perturbation is used in a negative sense as it is used to dupe the models and drive the machines to flop.

Unlike the previous concept, the new development in this field argues that a little change in the inputs is going to change the output up to a great extent [24].

© Springer Nature Switzerland AG 2021
G. Wang et al. (Eds.): SpaCCS 2020, LNCS 12383, pp. 15–26, 2021.
https://doi.org/10.1007/978-3-030-68884-4_2

Great research has been done in this field in the previous years, but the reality is that the expansion in the machine learning field is inversely proportional to the steadfastness and reliability of the models developed in this respect. The reason behind this issue is the defenses, developed against malicious perturbations did not hold good, rather these defenses showed incorrect and vague evaluations [7]. Several of the findings have been deduced so far. One of them is the realization of the adversarial inputs to get good hold at one model will also have an effective gesture on the other models to malign the outputs of the other models as well for which the adversarial input is not made [15].

The objective of this paper includes a systematic explanation of the adversarial attacks and their defenses in a comprehensive way. The paper discusses the techniques that are used to generate the adversarial attacks and their defenses by discussing the theoretical as well as their implementation in detail. The paper also includes the classification of various techniques that are employed to either generate the adversaries or in the creation of their defenses. Moreover, this work investigates the advantages and shortcomings of these proposed methods and also suggests future directions that can be augmented by the researchers.

The paper is organized as follows. Section 2 describes contemporary adversarial attacks and their classification. The adversarial defenses are discussed in Sect. 3. Finally, the Sect. 4 concludes the paper.

2   Contemporary Adversarial Attacks and Their Classification

The term adversarial example was coined to generate some noise in the actual input and deceive the machine learning model. Adversarial attacks can be categorized as either black-box or white box attacks. The white box attacks can be describe as the attacks where the adversary has to get complete knowledge of the internal structure of machine learning model. Hence the attack example is constructed on the basis of this information. While on the other hand the black box attacks are those in which the adversary has no knowledge about the internal structure rather the attack is generated in target model disguise. In black box attacks a local substitute model is trained by querying the target model. Detail of some famous adversarial attacks is given below.

2.1   Fast Gradient Sign Method (FGSM)

A contemporary approach to the renowned adversarial examples attacks was the Fast Gradient Sign Method (FGSM). Goodfellow et al. [9] proposed a framework on the linearization of the cost function. The method worked on two different types of models one of which was generative adversarial model G that worked on creating the adversarial examples while the other model i.e., the distributive model D worked to guess whether the input came from examples generation model G or clean data. The framework worked by learning the generator distribution p_g from the original data x. There is a noise variable $p_z(z)$ that generates the noise distribution p_g. The generative model G maps to the data space function G $(z; \theta_g)$. It is a differentiable function which is represented by a multilayer perceptron having parameters θ_g. The other multilayer perceptron D(x; θ_d) outputs the single scalar. D(x) worked on the probability that x input came from the data than p_g as shown in Fig. 1.

Train D for maximizing the probability for assigning the correct label for both training examples and samples from G. Simultaneously, it trained G for minimizing log(1-D(G(z))).

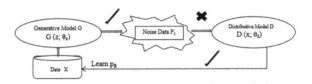

Fig. 1. Fast gradient sign method

J(θ, x, y) was the cost function for training, and J was used for the training of the model f around the training point x. Here in this approach the x corresponded to the actual input while there was an epsilon ϵ value added to the x input and it resulted in the formation of the x* value that was off-course an adversarial input example, the approach could be understood by the following equation.

$$\overrightarrow{x}^* \leftarrow x + \varepsilon. \bigtriangledown_{\overrightarrow{x}} J(f, \theta, \overrightarrow{x}) \tag{1}$$

The minute ϵ value was the parameter that controlled the magnitude of the perturbation. Like Szegedy et al. [24], Goodfellow et al. [9] focused on the more effectiveness of minute change in the actual input so that the attack remained un-detective for most of the defensive models. In this equation ϵ refers to the parameter which controlled the magnitude of the infiltration, which was decided to be included in the input.

2.2 Carlini and Wagner (C&W)

An approach was given by Carlini and Wagner [7] to overcome the defensive distillation developed against the adversarial perturbations. The methodology behind this adversarial attack was to form three types of attacks against the defense mechanisms i.e., L2, L0, and L∞ attacks as shown in Fig. 2. In the first step, the neural network was properly trained. After that, it computed the softmax and soft training labels by applying the network to each of them in the training data set. From these attacks, it could be deduced that the adversarial attack L2 used a minimum Delta value while the L0 type of attack was considered as non-differentiable and did not suit to the gradient descent. In the same way, the L∞ behaved almost the same in case of the gradient descent to the L2 attack but unlike the L2 attack, it was a differentiable attack. The C&W attack could be categorized in the white box configuration because the adversary should know the internal structure of the model before the example generation similarly should also know the parameters required to generate the adversarial examples.

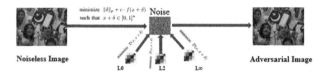

Fig. 2. Carlini and Wagner attack

2.3   Projected Gradient Descent (PGD)

PGD was introduced to overcome the shortcomings of FGSM method by introducing the negative loss function. The idea was floated by Madry et al. [18]. The PGD method was a slightly sophisticated method as compared to the FGSM as the former was just a single step process to generate the adversaries while the latter is a multi-step process. The experiments were developed on two different data sets i.e., MNIST and CIFAR-10. The target value was to compute the L∞ gradient descent in the X + S space from where the initial values were randomly taken. The epsilon ϵ value was kept smaller than a certain value and repeats to find out the maximum loss of the machine learning model. As shown in Fig. 3(a) where four projections were shown that iterate randomly and start from a random position and pass through different gradients to get the gradient which incurred the maximum loss. Figure 3(b) show a single gradient projection that tries to target the desired value.

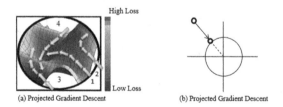

(a) Projected Gradient Descent   (b) Projected Gradient Descent

Fig. 3. The PGD method

2.4   Low Memory-BFGS

The LM-BFGS technique on adversarial examples was one of the pioneer works which was done by Szegedy et al. [24]. In this technique, the author named the small perturbations as adversarial examples. The basic philosophy behind this technique was the utilization of maximum stimulation on a random basis rather than on a natural basis in inspecting the properties of $\varphi(x)$. It is shown in the figure below where Fig. 4(a) used the image projection on a random basis while in the Fig. 4(b) used natural projection to make the analysis. The author assumed that the random direction shows very similar semantically interpretable properties. However, the technique utilized $I_c \ \varepsilon \ R^m$ was a clean image. To compute the perturbation $\rho \ \varepsilon \ R^m$, that was a slight change in the actual input.

$$\min_{\rho} \|\rho\|_2 \quad s.t. C(I_c + \rho = \ell; I_c + \rho \ \varepsilon \ [0,1]^m \tag{2}$$

Here ℓ denote the image label while $C(.)$ was a deep neural network classifier. A critical limitation of the L-BFGS is its implementation with small datasets as it consisted of the limited memory. The L-BFGS/LM-BFGS method was also considered as the white box attack because in this method the adversary has some internal knowledge of the internal structure as well as its parameters.

(a) Maximum stimulation on random basis direction

(b) Maximum stimulation on the natural basis direction

Fig. 4. The basic philosophy of L-BFGS

2.5 Iterative Least Likely Class Method

Kurakin et al. [15] worked on this idea of getting the input from physical world where the perturbations could not be seen directly. The technique worked in the idea of Goodfellow et al. [9] in 2014 which was considered as fast adversaries' generated method. The methodology worked by adding the noise to the input iteratively until an adversarial example would be generated as depicted in Fig. 5. Hence there was a drawback to this approach that it only worked on small datasets like MNIST and CIFAR-10. The basic iterative method included a clip function to alter the pixel values but up to a limited extent.

$$X_0^{adv} = X, \quad X_{N+1}^{adv} = Clipx_{,e} X_N^{adv} - \alpha sign(\nabla_X J(X_N^{adv}, yLL)) \tag{3}$$

In each iteration a minute change was made to limit the step size small. The new method was called the iterative least-likely class method. In this method the previous approach was revised as it iteratively used to adjust the value of epsilon ϵ. As discussed earlier the BIM was a variation of the FGSM, so its black box implementation can be made.

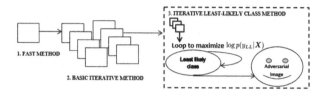

Fig. 5. Adversarial examples in the physical world

3   Adversarial Defenses

To make the machine learning models robust in the true sense and resistant against adversarial attacks, researchers are taking a keen interest in designing models containing proper defense mechanisms to detect and reduce adversarial examples. But these defense mechanisms are in the developing stage and are not much robust against these attacks. Every attack is followed by a defense mechanism and in the same way, for every defense strategy, there is an attack following it. However, some certified robust techniques have also been proposed in the literature to fight against adversarial attacks.

3.1   Taxonomy of Adversarial Defense Mechanisms

Defense against adversarial attacks can be characterized in different ways. Researchers adopted several approaches to categorize them. We divide these into two broad categories, i.e., reactive defense and proactive defense.

State of the art adversarial defense mechanisms are classified into these main categories as shown in Table 1.

Table 1. Taxonomy of adversarial defense mechanism in machine learning

Adversarial defense strategies	
Reactive Defense	Proactive defense
Input preprocessing	Universal defense techniques
Data compression techniques	Defensive distillation
Dimensionality reduction	Adversarial training
Defense for data poisoning attacks	GAN based techniques
Gradient obfuscation techniques	Stochastic activation pruning
	Differential privacy as defense mechanism

Reactive Defense: In this approach, the attack designer works with the machine learning model designer to investigate the vulnerabilities of the model.

After the model is developed, the attacker scrutinizes its defense mechanism and formulates an adversarial response to alleviate this defense. Based on information gathered from different iterations of the above attack-defense process, the machine learning model designer augments the model with the required functionality to cope with these types of attacks as presented in Fig. 6(a).

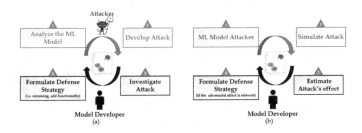

Fig. 6. Theoretical framework of reactive and proactive defenses [5]

Input Preprocessing: Preprocessing of input data is a popular defense mechanism. In [11], the researchers augmented the training data of the DNN model F with non-differentiable preprocessor G(.). Model F(G(.)) trained on transformed input does not undergo differentiable behavior in terms of x, making the adversarial examples failed to harm the DNN model predictions. Buckman et al. [6] introduced the concept of thermometer encoding. It is based on the discretization of input pixels to map them with multidimensional vector, the vector is used as a thermometer. The authors used a discretization preprocessor for this purpose and later on, the DNN model is trained on it.

Data Compression Techniques: Generally, most of machine learning model datasets consist of JPG images. Ghahramani et al. [14] investigates the effect of JPG compression on the performance of machine learning models in terms of their prediction accuracy. They found that in FGSM perturbations, compression does not much affect the classification accuracy of the model. Likewise, some researchers employed an ensemble-based method to study the consequences of compression on JPEG images as a countermeasure against FGSM attacks. Data compression defense techniques can be helpful to some extent as more compression effects the performance of the classifier in terms of prediction accuracies.

Dimensionality Reduction: Another method that is widely used as a defense against adversarial examples is dimensionality reduction. Among the techniques used for dimensionality reduction, "Principal Component Analysis" is the more famous one. For example, Bhagoji et al. [4] enhance the performance and flexibility of machine learning models by exercising the Principal Component Analysis and data 'anti-whitening' techniques to reduce the high dimensionality of input data these models.

Defense for Data Poisoning Attacks: Data poisoning attacks tries to change the statistical properties of training samples [23]. The attacker tries to extract a percentage of α of training samples of original dataset χ to create a new dataset χ_p

$$|\chi_p| = \alpha|\chi| \tag{4}$$

The technique used to defend these attacks is called the data sanitization technique, which separated the adversarial examples from the training set. The model designer trains the model using original samples as well as poisoned samples. The loss function calculated for the machine learning model decides whether attack or defense is successful.

Gradient Obfuscation Techniques: Gradient information of the model is mostly exploited to generate attacks. Shaham et al. [21] develop a framework by applying efficient optimization techniques to enhance the steadiness of neural network models. They tried to limit the loss function of adversarial example during parameter updating in the backpropagation process. The minimization-maximization method is used to implement the approach, which makes it difficult to generate new adversarial examples Gradient obfuscation techniques are still exposed to different attacks crafted in literature [3]. The problem with these techniques is that they cannot guarantee the removal of adversarial examples but, simply fool the adversary.

Proactive Defense: In proactive defense the developer of the machine learning model proposes the defense techniques in advance of the occurrence of attack, by inspecting the susceptibilities and loopholes of the model, from where the adversary can get access to damage the model's output predictions Fig. 6(b).

Defensive Distillation: Defensive distillation is proposed in [12] where the training method aims to decrease the size of the DNN model by transferring the knowledge of a lager DNN to a smaller one by the distillation process. Inspired by this technique, Papernot et al. [19] reformulates a defensive distillation technique that is robust against adversarial perturbation, i.e., Szegedy's L-BFGS attack, FGSM, or DeepFool. It trains the base model as well as the distilled model by using a similar DNN model architecture. They train the original model f on a given training set (x,y) with softmax layer temperature adjusted at T and calculate the probabilities produced by f(x). Then they trained another DNN model f^d on the training set (x, f(x)) sampled from f with the same softmax temperature T. This new model f^d is named as a distilled model. The working of defensive distillation is shown in Fig. 7. It is observed that, as compared to the original distillation model, the defensive distillation is more resistant to adversarial attacks by extracting knowledge from its own structures.

Adversarial Training: Adversarial training was the first strategy to guard against adversarial examples, devised by Goodfellow et al. [10]. In this technique, machine learning models as trained on a hybrid dataset consisting of original as well as of adversarial samples to enhance their robustness. The inclusion of adversarial examples with a true label (X', Y) in the dataset will instruct the model to classify X' as Y. In this way, the classifier will truly classify labels of

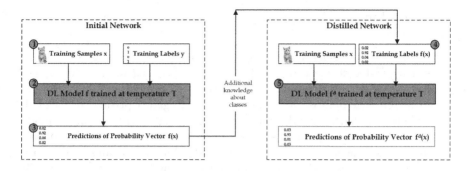

Fig. 7. Defensive distillation mechanism

unseen adversarial examples. Adversarial examples X' for training dataset are produced by non-targeted FGSM as shown in the equation below.

$$X' = \epsilon sign(\nabla_X L(\theta, X, Y)) \tag{5}$$

To scale the adversarial training model to larger datasets, its training procedure is modified in scaled adversarial training by using batch normalization [13]. They demonstrated that batch normalization will help to enhance the performance of the training process of adversarial training techniques. Later on, ensemble adversarial training was proposed by Tramer et al. [25] which supplements the training process of adversarial training by using the perturbed training data transferred from other models.

GAN-based Techniques: The pioneers of Generative Adversarial Networks are Goodfellow et al. [9]. They introduced this approach to semantically enhance the performance of machine learning models. Later on, Lee et al. [17] presented GAN based defense model as a robust defense mechanism to mitigate adversarial attacks i.e., FGSM attacks. The proposed model accurately classifies both original images and adversarial images. The same GAN based approach is used in [22] to repair the contaminated images. In this approach, the generator component of GAN is used to restore the infected images.

Stochastic Activation Pruning: Dhillon et al. [8] proposed a defense technique, "Stochastic activation pruning", in which nodes of each layer during forwarding propagation pass of the DNN model are dropped out stochastically. The hidden layers activation adaption effects the classification probabilities of the output, at the same time it enhances the robustness of the technique.

Universal Defense Techniques: Sometimes the universal defense approach was utilized to rectify the perturbed input. They employed pre input layer, perturbation rectifying network (PRN) in the model to deal with contaminated input. The training datasets for both PRN and targeted models are characterized by the same distribution. PRN is trained using the same parameters of base model [2]. The input samples are first passed through PRN before the input layer of the targeted model to identify the contaminations depending on the output of the rectifying unit.

Differential Privacy Defense Techniques: Recently, adversarial attacks are addressed by Differential Privacy (DP). Machine learning models are trained using large scale datasets containing sensitive user information. Thus, the privacy of this sensitive data is much more important against privacy attacks [20]. DP techniques are characterized by adding noise during the training of the model at a certain stage to maintain the privacy of data. Lecuyer et al. [16] proposed an innovative approach "Pixel DP" as certified robustness against adversarial attacks. PixelDP autoencoder can be appended at the beginning of nonmodifiable networks as a robust defense mechanism against any norm-based attacks. It adds a noise layer in the architecture of the machine learning model to generate the random outputs, which leverages the DP on prediction probabilities without altering the model accuracy on prediction results. PixelDP training is analogous to usual deep learning model training using similar loss and optimizer of the original model. It differs in the calculation of pre noise layers bounding it to the sensitivity of p-norm input deviations. The output Q(.) is given by the following equation.

$$Q(.) = h(g(.)) \tag{6}$$

Where g is prior to noise layer calculation and h denotes calculations in the next layers producing Q(.) as shown in Fig. 8.

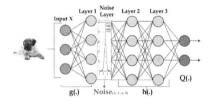

Fig. 8. Architecture of PixelDP approach

4   Conclusion

Our work describes the major adversarial attacks and defenses in a novel form as these techniques are not only classified but also represented graphically. Here we suggested, the generation of such models that not only keep the optimization but also tune the performance of models. The creation of more generalized models helps out to a great deal when it comes to taking care of the optimization problem. Orthodox models cannot help out in defending against various types of hybrid attacks. Similarly, the local smoothness and clean toy problems do not put a smart impact when it comes to the generation of adversarial examples and their defenses. It is better to align the adversarial examples with their defenses but try to develop such examples and defenses that should have their independent goals so that the defense against some developed adversarial example should be harder to find. Some other guidelines are there as well, on the basis of which effective models can be developed that exhibit a chronic impact on defenses. Adversarial examples become treacherous whose reverse engineering is not possible or hard to engineer. Similarly, those adversarial attacks prove to be lethal which are nontransferable from model to model.

Acknowledgments. This work was supported in part by the National Natural Science Foundation of China under Grant 61632009, in part by the Guangdong Provincial Natural Science Foundation under Grant 2017A030308006, in part by the High- Level Talents Program of Higher Education in Guangdong Province under Grant 2016ZJ01.

References

1. Ahmad, U., Song, H., Bilal, A., Alazab, M., Jolfaei, A.: Secure passive keyless entry and start system using machine learning. In: Wang, G., Chen, J., Yang, L.T. (eds.) SpaCCS 2018. LNCS, vol. 11342, pp. 304–313. Springer, Cham (2018). https://doi.org/10.1007/978-3-030-05345-1_26
2. Akhtar, N., Liu, J., Mian, A.: Defense against universal adversarial perturbations. In: Proceedings of the IEEE Conference on Computer Vision and Pattern Recognition (CVPR), June 2018
3. Athalye, A., Carlini, N., Wagner, D.A.: Obfuscated gradients give a false sense of security: circumventing defenses to adversarial examples. CoRR abs/1802.00420 (2018). http://arxiv.org/abs/1802.00420
4. Bhagoji, A.N., Cullina, D., Mittal, P.: Dimensionality reduction as a defense against evasion attacks on machine learning classifiers. arXiv preprint arXiv:1704.02654, vol. 2 (2017)
5. Biggio, B., Roli, F.: Wild patterns: len years after the rise of adversarial machine learning. Patt. Recogn. **84**, 317–331 (2018)
6. Buckman, J., Roy, A., Raffel, C., Goodfellow, I.: Thermometer encoding: one hot way to resist adversarial examples. In: International Conference on Learning Representations (2018)
7. Carlini, N., Wagner, D.: Towards evaluating the robustness of neural networks. In: 2017 IEEE Symposium on Security and Privacy (SP), pp. 39–57 (2017)
8. Dhillon, G.S., et al.: Stochastic activation pruning for robust adversarial defense. arXiv e-prints arXiv:1803.01442, March 2018
9. Goodfellow, I., et al.: Generative adversarial nets. In: Ghahramani, Z., Welling, M., Cortes, C., Lawrence, N.D., Weinberger, K.Q. (eds.) Advances in Neural Information Processing Systems 27, pp. 2672–2680. Curran Associates, Inc. (2014)
10. Goodfellow, I.J., Shlens, J., Szegedy, C.: Explaining and harnessing adversarial examples. arXiv e-prints arXiv:1412.6572, December 2014
11. Guo, C., Rana, M., Cisse, M., van der Maaten, L.: Countering adversarial images using input transformations. arXiv e-prints arXiv:1711.00117 (Oct 2017)
12. Hinton, G., Vinyals, O., Dean, J.: Distilling the knowledge in a neural network. arXiv e-prints arXiv:1503.02531, March 2015
13. Ioffe, S., Szegedy, C.: Batch normalization: accelerating deep network training by reducing internal covariate shift. arXiv e-prints arXiv:1502.03167, February 2015
14. Dziugaite, G.K., Ghahramani, Z., Roy, D.M.: A study of the effect of JPG compression on adversarial images. arXiv e-prints arXiv:1608.00853, August 2016

15. Kurakin, A., Goodfellow, I., Bengio, S.: Adversarial machine learning at scale. arXiv e-prints arXiv:1611.01236, November 2016

16. Lecuyer, M., Atlidakis, V., Geambasu, R., Hsu, D., Jana, S.: Certified robustness to adversarial examples with differential privacy. In: 2019 IEEE Symposium on Security and Privacy (SP), pp. 656–672 (2019)

17. Lee, H., Han, S., Lee, J.: Generative adversarial trainer: defense to adversarial perturbations with GAN. arXiv e-prints arXiv:1705.03387, May 2017

18. Madry, A., Makelov, A., Schmidt, L., Tsipras, D., Vladu, A.: Towards deep learning models resistant to adversarial attacks. arXiv e-prints arXiv:1706.06083, June 2017

19. Papernot, N., McDaniel, P., Wu, X., Jha, S., Swami, A.: Distillation as a defense to adversarial perturbations against deep neural networks. In: 2016 IEEE Symposium on Security and Privacy (SP), pp. 582–597 (2016)

20. Quinlan, M., Zhao, J., Simpson, A.: Connected vehicles: a privacy analysis. In: Wang, G., Feng, J., Bhuiyan, M.Z.A., Lu, R. (eds.) SpaCCS 2019. LNCS, vol. 11637, pp. 35–44. Springer, Cham (2019). https://doi.org/10.1007/978-3-030-24900-7_3

21. Shaham, U., Yamada, Y., Negahban, S.: Understanding adversarial training: Increasing local stability of supervised models through robust optimization. Neurocomputing **307**, 195–204 (2018)

22. Shen, S., Jin, G., Gao, K., Zhang, Y.: APE-GAN: adversarial perturbation elimination with GAN. arXiv e-prints arXiv:1707.05474, July 2017

23. Steinhardt, J., Koh, P.W.W., Liang, P.S.: Certified defenses for data poisoning attacks. In: Guyon, I., Luxburg, U.V., Bengio, S., Wallach, H., Fergus, R., Vishwanathan, S., Garnett, R. (eds.) Advances in Neural Information Processing Systems 30, pp. 3517–3529. Curran Associates, Inc. (2017)

24. Szegedy, C., et al.: Intriguing properties of neural networks. arXiv e-prints arXiv:1312.6199, December 2013

25. Tramèr, F., Kurakin, A., Papernot, N., Goodfellow, I., Boneh, D., McDaniel, P.: Ensemble adversarial training: attacks and defenses. arXiv e-prints arXiv:1705.07204, May 2017

26. Zhang, Q., Liu, Q., Wang, G.: A privacy-preserving hybrid cooperative searching scheme over outsourced cloud data. In: Wang, G., Ray, I., Alcaraz Calero, J.M., Thampi, S.M. (eds.) SpaCCS 2016. LNCS, vol. 10066, pp. 265–278. Springer, Cham (2016). https://doi.org/10.1007/978-3-319-49148-6_23

Secure Cross-Domain Data Sharing Technology Based on Blockchain

Manchao Zhang$^{(\boxtimes)}$, Hong Zhu, and Kai Jiang

Nanjing Research Institute of Electronic Engineering, Nanjing 210007, China
3194352184@qq.com

Abstract. Considering the difficulties of cross-domain data sharing and secure access tracking between multiple organizations, this paper proposes a cross-domain data sharing model based on blockchain and the features of cloud computing storage; puts forward a data sharing protocol via digital digest matching algorithm. By matching information within digital digest, this protocol can realize the restricted sharing of data while protecting data privacy. This paper also proposes a multi-level, secure storage architecture for data according to authorization, introduces a method for adding heterogeneous data to the chain, develops a data access mechanism and a privacy protection mechanism, and provides a solution for data storage and trusted sharing in untrusted environments.

Keywords: Blockchain · Consortium blockchain · Secure sharing · Immutability · Cloud platform

1 Introduction

With the rapid development of information technology, collaboration between institutions and organizations increasingly relies on information systems, and the key to inter-organization collaboration lies in cross-domain data sharing, which is limited by multiple factors. The difficulties of data sharing are as follows. First, various types of data are managed and operated by different entities, between which there is no trust mechanisms. Without the intervention of a third party, it is difficult to realize cross-domain data sharing. Second, lacking of secure data sharing mechanisms and credible tracking and tracing methods may lead to security problems, such as data loss, data tampering, privacy leakage and so on.

Blockchain is a distributed ledger that stores sequenced transaction records, with the features of decentralization, traceability and immutability [1]. As a peer-to-peer network, the blockchain is essentially a decentralized public ledger. Anyone have the rights to verify this ledger, while no individual actors can take control of it. Blockchain provides a reliable method for information and value exchange in untrusted networks. In the blockchain system, participants update the ledger together. Since the state of the blockchain can only be modified in accordance with strict rules and consensus, the transaction data are immutable, which forms the basis of a decentralized trust mechanism.

Considering the difficulties of cross-domain data sharing between multiple organizations, this paper proposes a cross-domain data sharing model based on blockchain, puts forward a mechanism for protecting data privacy, and provides a solution for data storage and trusted sharing in untrusted environments.

© Springer Nature Switzerland AG 2021
G. Wang et al. (Eds.): SpaCCS 2020, LNCS 12383, pp. 27–38, 2021.
https://doi.org/10.1007/978-3-030-68884-4_3

2 Secure Cross-Domain Data Sharing Model

With regards to the fully decentralized public chain, any user can access and exit the network at any time and check the data on the chain, which does not meet the requirements of security and confidentiality, and the excessive number of nodes will seriously affect the efficiency of information release and transmission. Therefore, based on consortium blockchain technology, this paper proposes a cross-domain data sharing model, which makes full use of the consortium blockchain featuring high availability, high performance, programmability, information security, immutability and traceability [2–5]. Moreover, leveraging the computing and storage advantage of cloud platform, this paper solves the problems of low efficiency of cross-domain data sharing, weak protection and tracking, as is shown in Fig. 1.

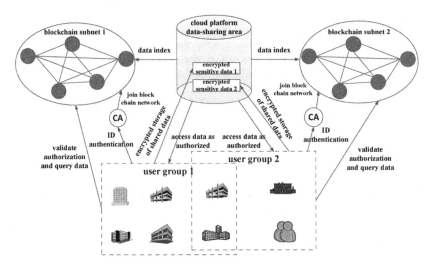

Fig. 1. Cross-domain data sharing model based on blockchain

The blockchain-based cross-domain data sharing model mainly consists of three parts: cross-domain user groups, blockchain networks and shared data areas based on cloud platforms. Either be data providers or data users, user groups join the blockchain network after identity authentication as nodes of the blockchain network. The data provider selects the sensitive data for sharing, and stores those data on the cloud platform after encryption, while the blockchain network only stores the index information. Users finally acquire the data on the cloud by retrieving the index information on the blockchain. The blockchain leverages a distributed ledger to record all the data sharing records. In order to make the model work effectively, it is necessary to study the cross-domain networking technology of blockchain and build a consortium blockchain for cross-domain data sharing. It is also required to develop data storage architecture of the model to achieve secure and efficient access to sensitive data, study cross-domain data sharing mechanism, design data sharing process, etc.

3   Building Consortium Blockchain

3.1   Technical Architecture

As shown in Fig. 2, the technical architecture of consortium blockchain consists of infrastructure layer, blockchain platform layer and blockchain application layer.

Infrastructure layer provides physical resources and computing drivers for the upper layer as the fundamental support for the blockchain system, including computing, storage, network and identity.

Blockchain platform layer serves as the core engine of blockchain. Its basic components provide the communication mechanism, database and password bank for the blockchain system network. The ledger is responsible for collecting transactions, packaging them into blocks, verifying the authenticity and linking the validated blocks into chains. Consensus ensures that data record is consistent across the network. The smart contract layer implements, compiles and deploys the business logic of the blockchain system in the form of code to complete the conditional triggering and automatic execution under established rules. The interface is mainly used to package functional modules and provides a simple way of invocation for the application layer. System management is in charge of the managing other parts in the blockchain architecture, while operation and maintenance is responsible for the daily operation and maintenance of the blockchain system.

Blockchain application layer is based on the blockchain engine with different business scenarios. It builds trusted applications across departments, organizations and levels, such as cross-domain data sharing and reliable management of data.

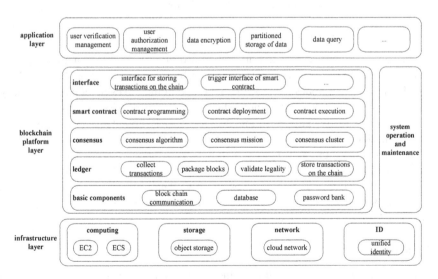

Fig. 2. Technical architecture of the blockchain

3.2   Topology

Figure 3 shows the consortium blockchain topology for cross-domain data sharing. Each member constructs its own nodes to form consortium blockchain network according to their roles and responsibilities, and preserves the shared data through the entire life cycle.

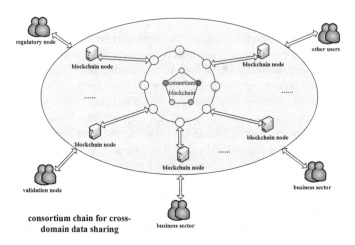

Fig. 3. Consortium blockchain topology for cross-domain data sharing

The functions of each node are designed as follows:

1. Data business sector node

The business sector is connected to the consortium blockchain network as an accounting node, links the ledger data generated by the system to the chain for consensus. Business sector nodes are at the initial phase of the life cycle of electronic data. In the data production phase, they are solidified and synchronized to all consortium blockchain nodes for backup, ensuring that the data is immutable. Meanwhile, the consensus mechanism is used to synchronize the data to the validation node for online real-time validation at the first time, ensuring the authenticity and legality of the data for subsequent usage.

The validated electronic data involves sensitive data of the business sector, which confines to the internal server. The data are required to be indexed by hash digest before stored on the chain via smart contract.

2. Validation node

The validation node is connected to the consortium blockchain network as an accounting node, responsible for online real-time validation of the data on the chain.

Validation requires the original information of the encrypted data on the chain, which is stored on the internal server. Via dedicated encrypted channel or encrypted communication protocol with the authorization from the data user, original data can be transmitted and acquired to verify the authenticity and validity of the data on the chain. After validation, data can be stored on the chain via smart contract. Compared with the data from the internal centralized system of the business sector, data on the blockchain are much more credible, and it is easier to provide validation information.

On the consortium blockchain, multiple validation nodes can be set as appropriate. Joint validation from several parties will improve the credibility of data while increasing the cost of operation and maintenance.

3. Regulatory node

The regulatory agency is connected to the consortium blockchain network as a regulatory node. Since sensitive data sharing requires regulation from relevant departments, the consortium blockchain must be regulated as well. Implementing all regulatory functions according to requirements, the regulatory node can automatically perform regulatory functions by deploying smart contracts in each node. The supervisory node is equivalent to the manager of the consortium blockchain. By assigning the regulatory node with the highest authority, regulation across the entire consortium blockchain can be fulfilled.

4. Other user nodes

Other users are linked to the consortium blockchain network as accounting nodes. Each user designs system functions and smart contracts in accordance with unified standards and participates in the constructing the business framework of the entire consortium blockchain. The consortium blockchain network formed by several business sectors contributes to the unification of business rules within the industry, and the unified data sharing rules will make the regulatory work more fair and smooth, which helps to break down the barriers of cross-domain data verification and audit.

4 Cross-Domain Data Storage Architecture Based on Blockchain

4.1 Data Storage Architecture Based on Cloud Platform

In order to improve the performance of blockchain and the efficiency of cross-domain sensitive data sharing, the storage architecture of blockchain data is developed on the basis of a cloud platform [6, 7]. A common data sharing area is established based on the cloud platform. The business sector providing the data encrypts the sensitive data to be shared and uploads it to the cloud, while the index information of the data, including users, authorization, storage address, data description and so on, is published to the blockchain network for storage. The overall architecture of the data storage is demonstrated in Fig. 4.

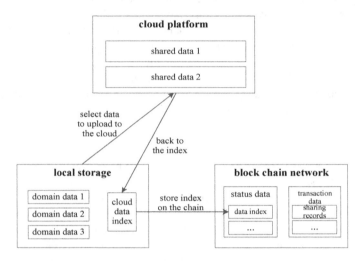

Fig. 4. Data storage architecture of blockchain based on a cloud platform

4.2   Conventional Methods for Linking Data to the Chain

Mainly dealing with text data, conventional blockchain or validation chain generates checksum via hash encryption, and then determines whether the data has changed by comparing the hash checksums. Due to the decentralized feature of the blockchain, each node must preserve the whole ledger data, thus resulting in great storage and communication cost. This also makes it difficult for conventional blockchain systems to store a large amount of heterogeneous and morphological data. The conventional methods for linking data to the chain mainly include content validation and hash validation.

Content validation refers to directly linking the content to the blockchain. However, the storage space on the blockchain is precious and limited, so the content is generally not too large. For example, so far we have found that applications operating on blockchain often referred to as "smart contract". Generally, smart contract is not powerful, and the amount of its code is low after compiling. Less function means less code, and less code means less space, all of which is to save space on the blockchain. Because of the public transparency of the blockchain, directly linking the content to the chain means that the content is public. Therefore, it may be appropriate for making some statements and claiming copyright, but not for the text with large amount of content or the content with privacy requirements.

Hash validation means saving the hash value of a file and storing it on the chain. The hash value of a file, also known as the "digital fingerprint', can be obtained by hashing the file's contents. Since the length of hash value is relatively limited, for example, the hash value of content with tens of thousands of words is only a 256-bit character, such content can be easily stored on the chain. One can verify whether the file content has been altered by means of hash validation. For instance, after the hash value of a certain file is stored on the block chain, we retrieve this file and hash its content. If the hash value is consistent with that stored on the chain, the content is considered credible without being altered and vice versa. This can prevent software from being planting malicious virus. A company can put the "digital fingerprint" of its self-developed software on the blockchain, and users can verify whether the "digital fingerprint" has been altered by softwares downloaded from various sources. If there are any changes, may be a virus or Trojan has planted into the software, and it is no longer safe. However, this scheme can only work out if the file has been altered, without knowing what the original text really is.

4.3   Linking Heterogeneous and Morphological Data to the Chain

In addition to conventional text data, a large amount of unstructured data, such as images, audio or video, has been accumulated in the business system. The effective use of these data is of great significance to the business. For example, unstructured documents such as contract documents or signing certificates can be used as evidence to help us figure out responsibilities and facilitate auditing.

Due to the technical principles and mechanisms, blockchain is not applicable for storing unstructured data. The traditional solution in the industry is to upload data to the cloud, and then upload the checksum to the block chain. This solution poses several problems, like insufficient business continuity and easy to be altered in the process of linking the validated data to the chain. By monitoring object storage changes via Lambda functions, it enables automatically triggering the data validation and linking the data track to the chain, ensuring business continuity of linking the unstructured data to the chain, so as to automatically link data to the chain after uploading data to the cloud, making it more convenient and reliable for linking unstructured data to the chain. (See Fig. 5).

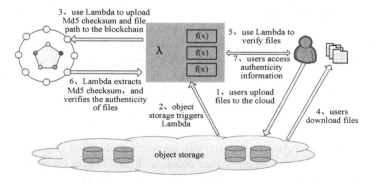

Fig. 5. Unstructured data processing view of blockchain-as-a-service

5   Sensitive Data Sharing Mechanism Based on Blockchain

5.1   Analysis and Design of Typical Data Sharing Processes

The typical pattern of "request + response" for cross-domain sensitive data sharing is applied. To simplify the process, we assume that data provider A and data requester B participate in data sharing. The data provider stores data index and provides real data, and verifies the authorization of data sharing request. The data requester requests permission to access data from a data provider. As shown in Fig. 6, the overall data sharing process can be divided into three phases: creating index for shared data, data query and data acquisition.

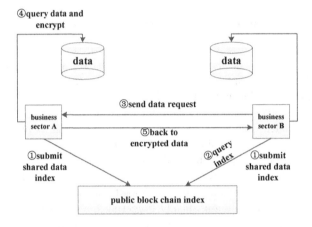

Fig. 6. Data sharing process based on blockchain

Creating Index for Shared Data. This phase encrypts the original data via a hashing algorithm to guarantee the security of the data. Generally, the index for shared data mainly consists of private key signature, public key data, hash value of the data, description of principal data and its hash value. Creating index for shared data follows four steps. First, the members determine and select the shared data by themselves. Second, hash the shared data and create index based on it. Third, encrypt the data index via the key. The above steps imply that only the same set of keys can access the corresponding data. Fourth, recreate data index after uploading data to the blockchain network. This step consists of four tasks: receiving the request packet, verifying the signature, creating new index and forming a chain. In addition, members can query and download the index for shared data but not delete or change the related content.

Data Query. Upon receiving a data request, members should first confirm the release of data index, and find the required data index, and then extract the principal information for corresponding ciphertext. After that, users can upload ciphertext and inquire via the platform. Moreover, users can query according to ciphertext and download the required data index files. Users can acquire the complete index record by means of above methods. The index record does not consist of data provider, authorization and detailed description other than real data.

Data Acquisition. Data is acquired through the following steps. First, via the service address acquired during the data query phase, the user accesses this address. Second, the user sends the information request packet including public key, private key and principal ID value, and waits for the reply from the data owner. Third, the data owner confirms the identity of the data requester via public key information and sends response. Then, the relevant data is extracted according to the requirements of the requester, the private key is used to sign the data, and the public key is applied to encrypt the data. Fourth, after receiving the data packet, the requester will verify the data source, decrypt the data packet and extract the data. After that, the user will compare the hash value of the index with that of data to further verify the authenticity of data.

5.2   A Mechanism for Ensuring Secure Sharing of Sensitive Data

Data Confidentiality Mechanism. The data confidentiality mechanism requires that the data are encrypted before storage, so that only specific users can have access to it. After sharing, the data requester can only browse partial data. To view and process relevant data, the requester has to go through the system-specific interface [8–11]. The requester must use the correct identity to acquire all the data loading and browsing permissions as data can't be used out of the system. In order to avoid data leakage, data backup and replication are not allowed, and data processing by the requester must be completed in this system.

Ownership Certification Mechanism. The ownership certification mechanism aims to generate a permanent ownership certificate by giving digital signatures to the data via SM2 algorithm. Digital signatures generated by SM2 algorithm can't be compromised or altered, which ensures that the original owner of sensitive data can be traced back even after multiple flows. With SM2 algorithm, if sensitive data is forwarded, the system can't change the original owner's signature, instead it keeps the record by adding more signatures. It is quite difficult for the traditional certification mechanism to determine the original owner of the data if the data is settled. The owner certification mechanism solves this problem.

Credit Validation Mechanism. Like other distributed systems, there are some problems with this system, such as hacking, security vulnerability, software errors, transmission errors and network delays. Meanwhile, affected by decentralization, the system is also prone to malicious nodes and data divergence. In order to avoid these potential problems and ensure the uniqueness of each node block information, the system should establish a unified credit validation mechanism. There are five common consensus mechanisms for now, namely dBFT, Pool, DPOS, POS and POW. Compared with the rest consensus mechanisms, dBFT has the advantages of high throughput, high speed and final validation. From the perspective of function, dBFT requires more than two-thirds of consent to generate data index. If not reached, the consensus has to be re-initiated. dBFT serves as the core of the overall process, which directly determines the formation of data index block. To be specific, the data provider proposes a request for adding data index, and reaches a consensus to generate the corresponding data index block. Before linking to the blockchain, the generation process and data format has to be verified via hash.

Two-Way Anonymity Mechanism. Although the transaction records on the blockchain only consist of public information such as the public key of both parties, hash value, principal content description and principal ID, the third party can still figure out the data usage from the above information. Therefore, the system adopts a two-way anonymity mechanism, and protects the privacy of both parties to the greatest extent via hash processing of relevant data. In comparison to other algorithms, a hashing algorithm features by irreversibility, strong collision, avalanche effect, output of a fixed-length and fast calculation speed. From the perspective of the effect of hashing algorithm, the system processes the signature and principal information of the sharing participants, generates the hash value to replace the actual content, in order to protect the privacy of the information.

Decentralized Sharing Mechanism. The sensitive data sharing system based on blockchain is isolated from shared data, and the stored data index only consists of private key signature, public key data, hash value, principal data description and so on, which fundamentally enhances the security of shared data. At the same time, in order to prevent data from settling, this system adopts decentralized sharing mechanism, aiming to provide sharing channel, query and payment service for both parties. By means of asymmetric encryption technology, this mechanism can realize peer-to-peer data transmission and further ensure the security of shared data. At present, elliptic curve algorithm and international RSA algorithm are two mainstream algorithms of asymmetric encryption technology. As one of the elliptic curve algorithms, SM2 algorithm has advantages in performance and security. Considering the speed of encryption and security, this system adopts SM2 algorithm, which helps realize peer-to-peer transmission between transaction participants and effectively guarantee the security of transaction data.

5.3   Private Data Access Mechanism Based on Layered Encryption

The private data access mechanism based on layered encryption is shown in Fig. 7.

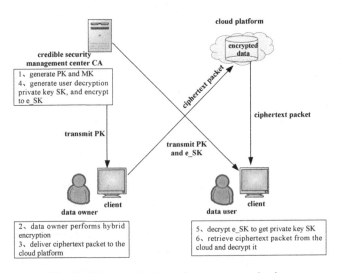

Fig. 7. Diagram of private data access mechanism

First, the credible security management center CA performs initialization and generates the system public key PK and the system master key MK. The CA issues PK for all the users in the system, while MK is secretly kept by CA. After data owner generates private data, which will be categorized into three security levels as low, mid and high, those data will be encrypted via symmetric encryption algorithm, and kept integral by HMAC algorithm. Then, attribute-based layered encryption will be applied to encrypt 3 symmetric keys and HMAC keys. By formatting, ciphertext packet will be generated and stored in the cloud platform. CA grants an attribute set for data user and generates private key SK. The data user requests e_SK from CA and decrypts it to SK, retrieves the ciphertext packet from the platform, and tries to obtain the corresponding part of user private data after decryption.

6 Conclusion

With the features of traceability, immutability and chain protection, block chain is well-suited for cross-domain data accessing and secure sharing between multiple nodes in untrusted environments. Combing on-chain and off-chain storage, this paper proposes a data sharing model with safety and high performance, enabling the user to control the data while ensuring the security of data calculation and sharing, significantly enhances the credibility and security of data sharing, and thus provides a solution for data storage and credible sharing in untrusted environments.

References

1. Yang, B., Chen, C.: Principle, Design and Application of Blockchain. China Machine Press, Beijing (2017)
2. Liu, A., Du, X., Wang, N., et al.: Research progress of blockchain technology and its application in information security. J. Softw. 29(7), 2092–2115 (2018)
3. Zhao, M., Zhang, L., Qi, J.: A framework of trusted services management based on blockchain in social Internet of Things. Telecommun. Sci. 33(10), 19–25 (2017)
4. Lee, H., Ma, M.: Blockchain-based mobility management for LTE and beyond. In: Wang, G., Feng, J., Bhuiyan, M., Lu, R. (eds.) Security, Privacy, and Anonymity in Computation, Communication, and Storage, SpaCCS 2019. Lecture Notes in Computer Science, vol. 11611, pp. 36–49. Springer, Cham (2019)
5. Wang, H., Wu, T.: Cryptography on the blockchain. J. Nanjing Univ. Posts Telecommun. (Nat. Sci. Ed.) 37(6), 61–67 (2017). (in Chinese)
6. Zheng, Z.H., Zhang, M.Q., Wang, X.A.: Identity based proxy re-encryption scheme for secure cloud data sharing. Comput. Eng. Appl. 33(11), 3450–3454 (2016). (in Chinese)
7. Liu, J., Wang, Z., Lian, X., et al.: Buffer queue technology for cloud storage hierarchical service. Command Inf. Syst. Technol. 9(5), 96–100 (2018)
8. Zhu, L.H., Gao, F., Shen, M., et al.: Survey on privacy preserving techniques for blockchain techniques. Comput. Eng. Appl. 54(10), 2170–2186 (2017). (in Chinese)

9. Zyskind, G., Nathan, O.A., et al.: decentralizing privacy: using blockchain to protect personal data. In: IEEE Security and Privacy Workshop, pp. 180–184. IEEE Computer Society (2015)

10. Do, H.G., Ng, W.K.: Blockchain- based system for secure data storage with private keyword search. In: IEEE World Congress on Service, pp. 90–93. IEEE (2017)

11. Min, X., Du, K., Dai, Y.: Electronic certification sharing platform based on blockchain technology. Command Inf. Syst. Technol. **8**(2), 47–51 (2017)

The 10th International Symposium
on Trust, Security and Privacy
for Emerging Applications (TSP 2020)

Microservice-Oriented Edge Server Deployment in Cloud-Edge System

Yang Dai[1], Songyun Wang[1], Xilong Wang[2], and Xin Li[2(✉)]

[1] Jiangsu Frontier Electric Co. Ltd., Nanjing 211102, China
[2] Nanjing Univeristy of Aeronautics and Astronautics, Nanjing 210016, China
`lics@nuaa.edu.cn`

Abstract. With the advent of the fifth generation communication system (5G), edge computing has been more widely used. In edge computing, in order to maximize the use of resources, and to deal with the computation request as soon as possible, the layout and allocation of edge server is particularly important. Due to the unpredictability of user behavior, a new problem appeared that is how to arrange each edge server in the appropriate location and then reasonably allocate the spare computing resources after the user makes a request so that the request can be processed within a certain time. In this paper, we design a server deployment mechanism for edge computing – a high response ratio computing resource scheduling mechanism for edge computing and the problems encountered in edge computing. At the same time, this paper implements a set of simulation prototype system of edge computing, and simulates the service request and server resource allocation in edge computing. Through the simulation results, this paper analyzes the reasons for the failure of the edge computing request. It is verified that the mechanism designed in this paper has good effects on alleviating and smoothing the number of failed edge service requests and improving the overall edge server processing efficiency.

Keywords: Edge computing · Server deployment · Cloud computing

1 Introduction

5G network architecture is driven by business, and its core idea is to meet the needs of different users and different industries for mobile network in a new way of information interaction. The emergence of 5G will fully cloud the Internet and strengthen the 5G network institutions to meet the needs of 5G technology to carry a large number of different types of businesses [1]. Under the background of 5G era, many emerging industries and high-end technologies have high demands for network delay, data reliability and privacy, which traditional cloud computing model cannot meet. Edge computing aims to solve the problems of high latency, high energy consumption and difficult privacy protection in cloud computing. Edge computing also can reduce the cost in some business

© Springer Nature Switzerland AG 2021
G. Wang et al. (Eds.): SpaCCS 2020, LNCS 12383, pp. 41–52, 2021.
https://doi.org/10.1007/978-3-030-68884-4_4

deployments. Edge computing gives up the resources to obtain computing data from cloud computing center, instead, it uses edge servers that deployed near users' mobile devices for computing, and replaces the original cloud computing center with edge grid [2]. Therefore, in edge computing, how to reasonably deploy edge server is the key.

Because edge nodes are deployed on the edge side, there are usually only a virtualized resource pool composed of several servers, but various types of terminal devices are connected to the edge platform through the edge side. Therefore, generally speaking, the pressure of resource shortage on the edge side is relatively high. . In many scenarios such as medical, industrial, and Internet of Vehicles, many terminals and sensors are connected to the edge platform through the network. Put forward higher requirements for edge cloud. The central cloud exists to manage multiple edge clouds and provide sufficient virtualization resources for the edge clouds. And because the central cloud is composed of a large number of server virtualization, it can provide persistent storage and provide resources for applications that require large amounts of calculation, such as big data applications Hadoop, Spark, artificial intelligence applications Tenseflow, etc.

With the advent of 5G, the question of how to place edge computing servers has become a hot topic. This problem requires a placement strategy to provide a reasonable solution for the placement of edge servers. Most of the researches are based on the assumption that the edge servers have been placed, and through some strategy, the computing work is distributed from the cloud to the edge servers [3–5]. The placement of the edge servers has not been fully studied, it requires a placement strategy to provide a reasonable solution for the placement of edge servers. However, the user's requirements and resource constraints on the computing resources make a great limitation on the placement strategy. How to place the server in order to solve or reduce the data transmission delay in the network and improve the utilization of the limited resources is a very challenging work. Calculating the location of the server on the edge, and the number of places placed in each location, both are problems that the placement strategy needs to solve. Different edge server deployment schemes will have a great impact on the computing efficiency. In the research on the problem of optimizing the average response time of service request and minimizing the server deployment and configuration cost, most scholars mainly use mathematical model, optimization algorithm and other methods to conduct in-depth research on the server deployment.

In this paper, we design a server deployment mechanism for edge computing and the problems encountered in edge computing – a high response ratio computing resource scheduling mechanism for edge computing. The main contributions of this paper are as follows:

(1) A prototype system is implemented to simulate the service request and server resource allocation of edge computing.
(2) Based on the simulation results of the existing algorithms, we propose a new service request scheduling method in edge computing server. Experimental results show that this method can significantly reduce the number

of redirection of user requests during processing, so as to greatly reduce the transmission delay, increase the processing efficiency and improving the user experience.

The rest of this paper is organized as follows. In Sect. 2, we define the problem of edge server deployment. In Sect. 3, two edge server deployment algorithms are introduced and the edge computing service resource allocation strategy we proposed with high response ratio priority is presented. The prototype system is shown in Sect. 4. Experimental results for validation and evaluation are given in Sect. 5. Section 6 discusses related works and conclusions will be drawn in Sect. 7.

2   Problem Descripition of Edge Server Deployment

Edge server deployment problem, that is, how to deploy the server in the case of limited server resources to get the most benefits. The benefits here can be translated into the ratio of the number of services that can be processed to the number of all services in the server scope. These server resources include the collaboration of computing, storage, network, virtualization and other infrastructure resources provided by edge nodes for value-added network services, as well as the life cycle of edge node devices themselves Management collaboration.

The topology of edge network can be represented by $G(V,E)$. Suppose that the total amount of load in the service scope of current network access point i is O, and the total amount of current resources of this network access point is U. The collection of network access points can be expressed as V = $\{i, i = 1,2...,V\}$, the network access point High-speed link can be represented as set E. We also define that the edge server is deployed to the edge network with the set C = j, j = 1,2...,k. There are two basic guidelines for deploying edge servers in edge networks:

(1) Each edge server can only be deployed to one service access point;
(2) Each service access point can only connect directly to one edge server.

Indicator variable $I_{i,j}$ is used to indicate whether edge server j corresponds to network access point i. If the edge server j corresponds to network access point i, $I_{i,j} = 1$; otherwise, $I_{i,j} = 0$. For each packet delivered to network access point i, if access point i is idle, the packet will be transmitted directly; otherwise, the packet will join the queue of service request data waiting to be transferred. Each network access point delivers packets in the transmission queue to the next network access point until it reaches the edge server serving it. B represents the total amount of resources required by the service. Whenever the service is transferred to the access point, compare this amount with the total amount of current server resources P. If B is less than P, update U to U-B, otherwise transmission cannot be executed. $P_{m,n}^i$ indicates whether the service request data from the service scope of network access point m passes through network access point i, Assume that the edge server of the service request service from network access point m is deployed at network access point n. If network access point i is on the path, then $P_{m,n}^i = 1$, otherwise $P_{m,n}^i = 0$. $v_{j,i}$ indicates whether the service from the scope of the network access point i is served by the edge server j. If it is, $v_{j,i} = 1$, else $v_{j,i} = 0$.

All service requests to network access point i come from two ways: 1) Service requests from mobile devices within the communication range of network access point i; 2) Service requests from mobile devices within the communication range of other network access points but require routing redirection through network access point i. Therefore, the following formula can be used to describe the number of service requests on network access point i:

$$S = \sum_{n,m \in V} \sum_{j \in C} (I_{m,j} v_{j,n} P_{m,n}^i) \tag{1}$$

From the perspective of the whole edge server access system, the service request data sent by all mobile devices enters the edge server access system through their adjacent network access point, and processed eventually when the service request reaches the edge server that provides service for it.

In a given edge network, we define how to optimally deploy k edge servers to maximize the number of efficient processing services in the entire network. So we set the initial resource amount to T. The optimal deployment of k edge servers in the edge network is defined as follows:

$$max\left(\frac{\sum_{n,m \in V} \sum_{j \in C} (I_{m,j} v_{j,n} P_{m,n}^i)}{O}\right) \tag{2}$$

$$\sum_{j \in C} I_{i,j} = 1, \forall i \in V \tag{3}$$

$$\sum_{i \in V} I_{i,j} = 1, \forall j \in C \tag{4}$$

$$\sum_{i \in V} I_{i,j} = 1, \forall U \leq T \tag{5}$$

Knapsack problem is a NP - complete problem of combinatorial optimization. Our problem can be classified as a Knapsack problem: Given certain server resources, each service has its own load and value. Under the condition of limited server resources, how to deploy (optimal deployment) can get the maximum value (maximum service processing efficiency). According to the definition of the Knapsack problem, the problem can be expressed as:

$$max \sum_{j=1}^{n} p_j x_j \tag{6}$$

subject to

$$\sum_{j=1}^{n} w_j x_j \leq W, x_j \in \{0, 1, ..., b_j\} \tag{7}$$

As mentioned above, we think we can describe the edge server deployment problem as a Knapsack problem for discussion.

3   Edge Server Deployment Algorithm

This section firstly introduces the edge server deployment algorithm based on enumeration method and the approximate optimal edge server deployment algorithm based on ranking [6]. After the deployment of edge server, we propose an optimization strategy of edge computing service resource allocation with high response ratio and priority for the utilization of edge server resources.

3.1   Edge Server Deployment Algorithm Based on Enumeration Method

Firstly, three metrics are given to evaluate the deployment plan: the rate at which the service handles requests effectively, the number of redirection to other edge server, and the utilization of the edge server resources. Enumeration Method lists the deployment plans of all edge servers, then calculates the values of the three metrics under each plan, and then compares the best deployment plan. For each deployment plan, the following algorithm is designed to transfer the service requests of all edge devices to each edge server reasonably: firstly, an empty set G is defined to record the requests from mobile devices that have obtained the edge server services; Then, they are sorted according to the current load of all edge servers. Starting from the server with the smallest load, the requests of devices closest to the edge server and not within the range of data acceptance in set G are sent to the edge server for service, and the service in set G is updated. Then the remaining services are processed in the order of load from small to large. After all processing is completed, the scope of processing is expanded until the scope is extended to the entire service area, that is, the service scope is identified as H.

3.2   An Approximate Optimal Edge Server Deployment Algorithm Based on Ranking

The basic idea of this algorithm is to obtain F network access points with the highest fitness as the deployment location of F edge servers. Fitness is obtained by a joint assessment of several attributes that affect the services that the edge server provides to the user.

The algorithm first evaluates the connection properties of each service network access point. Each service in the network access point's near-center property can show it's average distance to the edge of the network, higher degree of centricity means the edge server may be within the same distance connection to other more edge server, the shorter the distance will lead to smaller service request access delay, so service network access points have a higher degree of centricity and edge server is more suitable for deployment. When all of the mobile service request routing to provide service for the server, the edge of each through the network to the path of the access point number reveals the network access point node needs to transmit data arrival rate, the more after the node routing path means that the node is congestion, the request data in the waiting time is long, the mediation centricity and load centricity can very well to this feature.

After analyzing the attributes of each network access points, the algorithm will be every step of the current edge server deployed on the edge of the network in the rest of the influence into account, including two parts, the first is each service network access point and the average distance between the edge of the currently deployed server, the second is on the edge of the currently deployed server services, each service network access point of service request data arrival rate. On the one hand, in order to prevent all the edge servers from being concentrated in a small area, the further away from the currently deployed edge servers is the more appropriate network access point for the remaining optional deployment of the next edge server. On the other hand, in order to reduce the average access delay of edge servers, network access points with high average service request arrival rate are more eligible to be selected as the next edge server to be deployed. In each iteration, the algorithm selects the most appropriate network access point to deploy the next edge server. After k iterations, the algorithm will get k locations that are most suitable for deploying edge servers.

3.3 Optimization Strategy of Edge Computing Service Resource Allocation

Both of the above algorithms are about how to deploy the edge server to the most appropriate location, while the processing of service requests in the edge server is a first-come-first-served strategy. When implemented in our proposed prototype, we felt there was room for optimization. Inspired by the operating system's high response ratio priority scheduling, we propose an optimization strategy for resource allocation of edge computing services based on high response ratio priority.

The specific method is to assign the corresponding response ratio to the service request when the edge server receives the edge service request. This value is used to sort the requests when the server receives the service requests. The server will receive the first service request first, and reject the next one and send the relocation. Therefore, the response ratio used in this paper is defined as:

$$p = \frac{T - N * \theta}{T_{max}} \tag{8}$$

Where T represents processing time required for the current service, N represents the number of times the service is redirected, T_{max} represents the maximum service processing time in queue, and θ represents an initial predetermined ratio. Obviously, the more time a service takes to process a request, the larger its initial response ratio is, but as the number of redirects increases, the response ratio gradually decreases. Therefore, the smaller the response ratio defined in this article, the higher the priority, will be prioritized and will be received and processed by the server.

4   Prototype System

In this section we will introduce a prototype system for simulating service requests and resource allocation in edge computing.

The service request and resource allocation process in edge computing is divided into the following four steps:

(1) Initialize the global clock, and initialize the edge server according to the number of edge servers preset by simulation, including its computing resources, memory resources and bandwidth resources, and its positioning parameters. The capability of edge system server is reflected by its computing resources, memory resources and bandwidth resources. The prototype system assumes that each edge server has the same properties and values at time t_0. A random algorithm is used to generate a preset edge server in a two-dimensional matrix representing coordinates.

(2) Before the simulation time t_n arrives, all servers synchronize the global clock. For each edge server, the current queue of service requests is traversed. If the service requests in the queue are redirected more than the number of times the emulation is scheduled, the service is removed; or the service request is redirected to another server. At the same time, the new service request is randomly generated and inserted into the service request queue in the whole system according to the predetermined parameter ratio. Synchronously updates the list and status of service requests for all servers.

(3) At the time of t_n, firstly, each edge server processes the service request it is currently processing and responds to the newly generated service request. Each server first traverses the service queue that it is processing to determine whether the service has been processed under the current clock. Secondly, each server traverses the current list of service requests, responds to the user service requests within its own processing scope, and judges whether the service requests can be accepted for processing. If the processing conditions cannot be met, the redirection times of the service request plus 1 and it will be thrown, randomly thrown to the next edge server; If the processing conditions are met, the processing is carried out.

(4) After completing all the work at the time of t_n, return to the first step of the simulation process and start the simulation of the next time slice until the simulation times reach the predetermined times of the system.

5   Experimental Comparison and Simulation Results

Based on our prototype system, we set three metrics to reflect the processing of edge requests.

Effectively processed edge service's ratio.

$$S = F/N \tag{9}$$

Where F represents the number of successfully processed edge service requests, while N represents the total number of edge service requests

The average number of redirection processed by an edge service.

$$Arg(C) = [Sum(N_s)]/N \tag{10}$$

Where $Sum(N_s)$ is the sum of service redirection for all edge requests.
Resource utilization efficiency of edge servers. The prototype system evaluates the usage of three types of resources respectively. For one type of resources, such as the utilization rate of computing resources, the following methods are used to calculate:

$$\sum_n \frac{\sum_t C_i/C}{T}/n \tag{11}$$

Where Ci is the computing resources used by a server in a certain time, C is the total computing resources of the server, T is the total number of time slices, and n is the total number of servers.

Using our prototype system, we respectively carried out experiments on the Enumeration method mentioned in the third section above and the algorithm in [6], and finally replaced their resource scheduling method with the high-response-to-priority scheduling method proposed in this paper.

Table 1 shows the main setting of parameters in the system during the experiment. ServerNum represents the total numbers of the servers. RequestLimits represents limitation of request numbers. RejectReqCountLimit represents the maximum of Rejection. RunTime represents the number of times of system simulation.

Table 1. Parameters in system.

ServerNum	RequestLimits	RejectReqCountLimit	RunTime
30	30	10	1000

Experimental results of first-in-first-out scheduling strategy are shown in Figs. 1, 2 and 3. It illustrates the feasibility of the prototype system. At the same time, the experimental comparison results of the original algorithm in [6] and the high-response-to-priority scheduling are shown in Fig. 4, 5 and Fig. 6, where the red line represents the high-response ratio priority scheduling algorithm, and the blue line represents the method mentioned in [6]. In the experiment, the θ is set to 6.

After comparison, it is not difficult to see that there is no significant difference in server request processing rates as shown in Fig. 4. Figure 6 shows that with the exception of a few errors at the beginning of the experiment (possibly due to the random generation of the service), the average level of the server's calculated resource utilization is approximately 80%, similar to that of the high-response-to-first algorithm. Figure 5 shows the redirection numbers comparison. From the figure, it is obvious that the gap between the two method is large. With

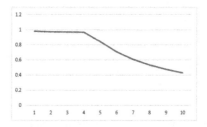

Fig. 1. Effective request rate versus request generation rate.

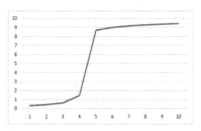

Fig. 2. The number of times an edge service request is redirected.

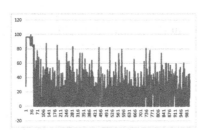

Fig. 3. Computing resource utilization of edge servers.

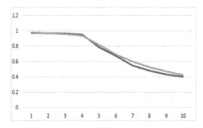

Fig. 4. The ratio of the two methods is compared.

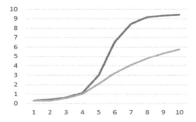

Fig. 5. The redirection times of the two methods are compared. (Color figure online)

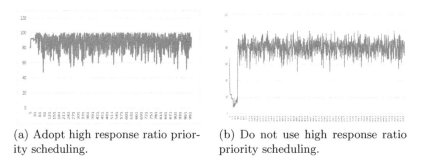

(a) Adopt high response ratio prior-   (b) Do not use high response ratio
ity scheduling.   priority scheduling.

Fig. 6. Edge servers computing resource utilization comparisons

the increase of the number of processing services, the adoption of the algorithm based on high response ratio priority can significantly reduce the number of redirection of user requests in the process, thus greatly reducing the transmission delay, increasing the processing efficiency and improving the user experience.

6   Related Works

There have been many achievements in the research of edge server deployment algorithm. The following are some mainstream deployment algorithms. L. Zhao et al. proposed an optimal layout algorithm based on enumeration algorithm and a near-optimal layout algorithm based on divide and conquer [7]. This paper first proposed the concept of how to push the service from the cloud center to the edge of the grid, so as to minimize the effect of average data transmission. Through the enumeration algorithm, all the deployment plans of K edge computing servers in the edge grid were enumerated, and the average data flow of each placement case was evaluated.

The nearly optimal layout algorithm based on divide and conquer (DCNOPA) is also a common deployment algorithm [8]. Divide and conquer the server placement problem by splitting the edge servers into multiple clusters, each of which deploys a virtual server replica. The original problem is then divided into multiple optimal locations to find a copy of the virtual server for each cluster.

There are also deployment strategies designed from optimization algorithms. Zichuan Xu et al. studied the placement of edge servers in large-scale wireless metropolitan area networks, which studied the placement of edge servers with limited cost and budget [9]. Yali Zhao et al. of Beijing University of Posts and Telecommunications proposed an edge server placement algorithm MIP based on mixed integer programming [10], and regarded the placement system of edge computing server as a network structure. Multi-objective optimization algorithm is used to solve the problem of server deployment.

When considering the deployment of edge server, this paper focuses on the scheduling of edge service requests after the deployment of edge server, and designs a resource scheduling method of edge server based on high response ratio priority. The two modules of edge computing server deployment and the allocation of computing resources in edge computing are aimed at the problem of more effective placement of edge servers and more reasonable allocation of computing resources and tasks in the case of existing limited resources.

The above researches have improved the resource allocation problem of edge computing to some extent and greatly reduced the pressure on the cloud, but there are still some deficiencies. Not all of them can be applied in the actual situation, mainly reflected in the following aspects: some tasks are inconvenient to be divided into different machines for processing, and the time consumed by re-integration after segmentation should also be taken into account. In addition, the existing researches, such as using enumeration method to get its optimal solution, which would originally take a lot of time. Once the number of mobile terminals and edge computing servers is large, and the mobile terminals are always in a moving state, then it is necessary to use the enumeration algorithm to calculate again, this time complexity is quite high, and will greatly increase the time consumption.

7 Conclusion

The problem of edge computing server deployment is to deploy edge servers more effectively and allocate computing resources and tasks more reasonably under the existing limited resources. The main contribution of this paper is to realize a prototype system for the simulation of edge computing, and based on the analysis of the simulation of the existing algorithm, a new service request scheduling method based on high response ratio edge computing server is proposed. The simulation experiment results show that the proposed method is effective, especially in reducing the number of service redirection. In future work, we can find better algorithms based on these studies, or use a combination of these technologies to further reduce the total energy consumption and improve the transmission efficiency.

Acknowledgments. This work is supported in part by the National Key R&D Program of China under Grant 2019YFB2102002, in part by the National Natural Science Foundation of China under Grant 61802182.

References

1. Loghin, D., Ramapantulu, L., Teo, Y.M.: Towards analyzing the performance of hybrid edge-cloud processing. In: 2019 IEEE International Conference on Edge Computing, pp. 87–94 (2019)
2. De Nitto Personè, V., Grassi, V.: Architectural issues for self-adaptive service migration management in mobile edge computing scenarios. In: 2019 IEEE International Conference on Edge Computing, pp. 27–29 (2019)
3. Kim, Y.H., Lim, E.J., Cha, G.I., Bae, S.J.: A design of resource fault handling mechanism using dynamic resource reallocation for the resource and job management system. In: 2015 17th International Conference on Advanced Communication Technology (ICACT), pp. 701–705 (2015)
4. Chouhan, S.: Energy optimal partial computation offloading framework for mobile devices in multi-access edge computing. In: 2019 International Conference on Software, Telecommunications and Computer Networks, pp. 1–6 (2019)
5. Fernando, N., Loke, S.W., Rahayu, W.: Computing with nearby mobile devices: a work sharing algorithm for mobile edge-clouds. IEEE Trans. Cloud Comput. **7**(2), 329–343 (2019)
6. Lovén, L., et al.: Scaling up an edge server deployment. In: 2020 IEEE International Conference on Pervasive Computing and Communications Workshops, pp. 1–7 (2020)
7. Ding, Y., Liao, G., Liu, S.: Virtual machine placement based on degradation factor ant colony algorithm. In: 2018 13th IEEE Conference on Industrial Electronics and Applications, pp. 775–779 (2018)
8. Flores, H., Tran, V., Tang, B.: PAM & PAL: policy-aware virtual machine migration and placement in dynamic cloud data centers. In: IEEE INFOCOM 2020 - IEEE Conference on Computer Communications, pp. 2549–2558 (2020)
9. Xu, Z., Liang, W., Xu, W., Jia, M., Guo, S.: Efficient algorithms for capacitated cloudlet placements. In: IEEE Transactions on Parallel and Distributed Systems, vol. 27(10), pp. 2866–2880 (2016)
10. Shao, X., Hasegawa, G., Kamiyama, N., Liu, Z., Masui, H., Ji, Y.: Joint optimization of computing resources and data allocation for mobile edge computing (MEC): an online approach. In: 2019 28th International Conference on Computer Communication and Networks, pp. 1–9 (2019)

QoS-Aware Dynamical Resource Scheduling in Cloud Data Centers

Kaidi Wu[1], Lei Wang[1], Huijie Li[2], and Xin Li[2(✉)]

[1] Nanjing Research Institute of Electronic Engineering, Nanjing 210007, China
[2] Nanjing University of Aeronautics and Astronautics, Nanjing 210016, China
lics@nuaa.edu.cn

Abstract. In order to improve the utilization rate of cloud computing resources within the data center, the scheduler dynamically allocates resources according to the load of each node and migrates virtual
machines. Virtual machine migration is one of the effective ways to realize the dynamic allocation of resources, and virtual machine migration
will cause a certain quality of service interference to the services carried
on it. We analyze the impact of virtual machine migration on service
quality, study the problems of virtual machine migration timing, migration objects and migration destination, targeted optimization strategies,
established an evaluation model of the impact of migration mechanism
on service quality. Based on this, an effective dynamic resource scheduling strategy is proposed. Experimental results show that compared with
the existing online migration strategy, our model can reduce unnecessary
migration by about 33% on average while reducing migration costs by
30%. In addition, our proposed resource scheduling strategy solves the
problem of insufficient resources during the subsequent migration of a
heavily loaded virtual machine.

Keywords: Cloud computing · Virtualization · Dynamic resource
scheduling · Virtual machine migration · Quality of service

1 Introduction

Cloud computing is an increase, use, and delivery model of Internet-based related
services, usually involving the provision of dynamically scalable and often virtualized resources over the Internet [1]. Resource scheduling is an important
research direction of cloud computing. It is a process of resource adjustment
between respective users in a certain resource environment according to the
rules of resource use [2]. In recent years, virtualization technology has become
the core technology of cloud data centers [3]. Virtual machine online migration
technology can migrate computer systems in the cloud data center to another
physical machine or data center without interrupting application services [4].
This feature greatly improves the dynamic resource allocation capability of the
cloud data center [5].

© Springer Nature Switzerland AG 2021
G. Wang et al. (Eds.): SpaCCS 2020, LNCS 12383, pp. 53–64, 2021.
https://doi.org/10.1007/978-3-030-68884-4_5

The migration of a virtual machine refers to migrating the entire virtual machine's operating environment from one physical node to another physical node, thereby reducing the load on the host machine and achieving load balancing of the virtual machine. There are two ways to migrate: First: During the migration process, the applications running on the virtual machine will be interrupted, which we call offline migration. Second: During the migration process, the applications running on the virtual machine can continue to run without being affected Interference, we call it online migration [6]. In this paper, we mainly consider online migration of virtual machines. The online migration of virtual machines is shown in Fig. 1.

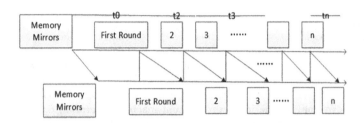

Fig. 1. Virtual machine online migration diagram.

However, the migration of virtual machines will cause a certain quality of service interference to the services carried on it [7]. In this paper, we analyze the impact of virtual machine migration on service quality, establish an evaluation model of the impact of migration mechanism on service quality, and propose an effective dynamic resource scheduling mechanism based on this [8].

Our main contributions in this paper are as follows:

- We have established an evaluation model of the impact of migration mechanism on service quality based on the impact of virtual machine migration on service quality;
- We propose an effective dynamic online capital virtual machine migration model, our model can reduce unnecessary migration by about 33% on average while reducing migration costs by 30%;
- Our proposed resource scheduling strategy solves the problem of insufficient resources during the subsequent migration of a heavily loaded virtual machine.

The rest of the paper is organized as follows. We mainly introduce the background technology of virtual migration and the motivation of our strategy in Sect. 2. We introduce our decision model and placement strategy for virtual machine migration in Sect. 3. We introduce our predictive migration strategy for sensitive applications with high service quality in Sect. 4. We conducted a performance evaluation of our model in Sect. 5, and we summarized the related work in Sect. 6. Finally, the conclusion is given in Sect. 7.

2   Background

As one of the effective methods of dynamic resource scheduling [9], virtual machine migration is of great significance for the establishment of a dynamically scalable large green data center [10]. In this paper, we focus on virtual machine placement technology to improve the service quality of dynamic resource scheduling in cloud data centers. It mainly solves the following three problems: first, the migration trigger strategy based on prediction; second, the decision model of virtual machine migration; third, the placement strategy of virtual machines with probability.

2.1   Migration Triggering Strategy Based on Prediction

The current mainstream migration trigger strategy is still the simplest trigger mechanism. When a virtual machine migration request is made, the virtual machine migration is performed [11]. This simple triggering strategy will lead to the migration of virtual machines only when the instantaneous load peak is higher than the threshold, which in turn causes frequent migration of virtual machines, which has a great impact on the quality of service [12]. Therefore, this paper proposes a prediction-based triggering strategy for virtual machine migration, to ensure that a small instantaneous load peak will not trigger unnecessary migration. And it can also achieve a basic prediction of future load, giving a reference to the target machine with high migration priority. As far as possible, before the arrival of load fluctuations that continue to exceed the threshold, the destination machine should be migrated in advance to avoid the impact of service quality caused by the load above the threshold.

2.2   Virtual Machine Placement Strategy with Probability

At present, there are many researches on the placement of virtual machines. The PMapper model mentioned above and the virtual machine placement technology under the high availability target, as well as the network-aware virtual machine placement technology have made detailed migrations of virtual machines in different situations Research, it is difficult for us to surpass them. However, these methods lack the possibility of reserving the adaptation destination for subsequent source hosts. Therefore, this article will propose a virtual machine placement strategy with probability, hoping to optimize it on the basis of existing research and maximize load balancing in the virtual computing system.

3   Migration Triggering Strategy Based on Prediction

The traditional triggering strategy for virtual machine migration refers to immediately assessing the load changes according to the load of the source host, so as to determine whether to perform virtual machine migration. Our proposed migration strategy for virtual machines does not immediately migrate when the load of the virtual machine is too heavy, and only when the load exceeds the threshold for a certain period of time. This ensures that there is no needless migration due to transient overload. In this section, we will introduce the process of proposing a migration trigger strategy based on prediction.

3.1   Virtual Machine Migration Priority

For different applications running on virtual machines, due to their different priority requirements for service quality. Therefore, the application classification will be based on the sensitivity of different applications to interrupts:

– The highest priority of migration L_1: This type of program can be defined as an application that is suspended in a virtual machine or occupies only a small amount of resources. When a migration demand arises, the source host where it is located is preferentially migrated.
– Migration sub-priority L_2: This type of program can be defined as an application that does not communicate in real time or has little interaction with the user, such as some download tools, background updates, etc. When a migration requirement arises, the source where it is migrated second is given priority hosts.
– Low-priority migration L_3: This type of program can be defined as an application with a high degree of interaction with users, such as communication, games, and some websites. When a migration requirement arises, the source host where it is located is migrated.

3.2   Migration Triggering Strategy Based on Prediction

Aiming at the existing trigger migration strategy based on threshold only [13], we propose a more optimized solution. That is, when the load of the virtual machine is too heavy, the migration is not performed immediately, and the migration is performed only when the load exceeds the threshold for a certain period of time. This ensures that there is no needless migration due to transient overload. Through this triggering strategy, we can avoid migration caused by instantaneous peaks. Reduce the impact of service quality due to frequent migration.

This paper uses the autoregressive model $AR(n)$ in time series prediction technology [14] to predict the load value. The model uses n past observations arranged in time series to make predictions about the future. For example, the observed load value sequence: $y_1, y_2 \ldots y_{n-1}$. For this given time series, use the p-order autoregressive model $AR(n)$ to predict the load value yt at time t, and the formula 1 is as follows:

$$Y_t = \phi_1 y_{t-1} + \phi_2 y_{t-2} + \ldots + \phi_p y_{t-p} + \xi \tag{1}$$

Among them, ξ is an independent and identically distributed random variable; ϕ_p is a time series parameter.

At time t, the virtual machine load exceeds the threshold and the predicted data $y_{t+1}, y_{t+2} \ldots y_{t+n}$ is obtained. If there are k sets of data greater than the threshold, we will migrate the virtual machine. If multiple virtual machines are running on a physical machine, our triggering strategy can be adjusted to migrate the virtual machines in the physical machine when $\sum_{i=1}^{N} *y_i t$ is greater than or equal to the total load Y of the physical machine.

4   Decision Model and Placement Strategy for Virtual Machine Migration

In this section, we will analyze the key parameters that affect the performance of virtual machine migration in virtual machine online migration. We establish a decision model for virtual machine migration and combine the model to give a placement strategy for virtual machines to achieve load balancing and ensure service quality.

4.1   Key Parameters of Virtual Machine Migration

In paper, the migration costs of virtual machines with different loads are obtained through experiments. As shown in Table 1, five different loads are running in five virtual machines. When virtual machines are migrated, the total amount of data transmission and energy consumption have different migration costs, because of the different costs, resulting in different impacts on service quality.

Table 1. Virtual machine migration cost.

Load	Downtime	Complete time	Data transfer volume
idle Linux	23 ms	15 s	1026 MB
dbench	124 ms	21 s	1283 MB
TPC-C	25 ms	15 s	1081 MB
linpack	914 ms	49 s	3270 MB
SPECweb	1200 ms	53 s	3610 MB

As shown in Table 2, the key parameters and meanings of virtual machine online migration are defined. Suppose that the online migration needs to be iterated for n rounds, the amount of data transmitted in each round is V_i ($0 < = i < = n$), and the time required for each round of transmission is T_i. V_0 is the size of the virtual machine memory image, T_0 is the time it takes to transfer the virtual machine memory image, and T_i is the time to transfer the dirty pages generated during the previous round of pre-copy, then the amount of data transferred in each round can be expressed as formula 2:

$$V_i = \begin{cases} V_{mem} & i = 0 \\ D * T_{i-1} & i > 0 \end{cases} \tag{2}$$

Table 2. Virtual machine online migration parameter table

Notations	Abbreviation
V_{mem}	The size of the virtual machine memory image during migration
V_{mig}	Total network data transmission volume during migration
T_{mig}	Total migration time
T_{down}	Downtime during migration
R	Memory transfer speed during migration
D	The generation speed of dirty pages in memory during migration

The time for each round of transmission can be expressed as formula 3:

$$T_i = \frac{D * T_{i-1}}{R} = \frac{D_i * V_{mem}}{R^{i+1}} \tag{3}$$

Use λ to express the ratio of the memory dirty page generation speed to the memory transfer speed, as shown in formula 4:

$$\lambda = \frac{D}{R} \tag{4}$$

Combined with the above formula, the amount of network transmission data for each round can be converted into formula 5:

$$V_i = D * \frac{V_{mem}}{R} * \lambda^{i-1} = V_{mem} * \lambda^i \tag{5}$$

Cumulatively, the total network data transmission during the migration process can be expressed as formula 6:

$$V_{mig} = \sum_{i=1}^{N} V_i = V_{mem} * \frac{1 - \lambda^{n+1}}{1 - \lambda} \tag{6}$$

Downtime can be expressed as formula 7:

$$T_{down} = T_n + T_{resume} \tag{7}$$

where T_n is the time during which the dirty pages of the memory were generated during the last round of copying, T_{resume} is the time required for the virtual machine to resume running on the destination machine, and the time deviation of its recovery on different virtual machines is very small, which can be set to a certain value. T_n can be expressed as formula 8:

$$T_n = \frac{V_{mem} * \lambda}{R} \tag{8}$$

4.2   Decision Model for Virtual Machine Migration

In order to minimize the migration cost, we give an optimal decision model, we consider all migration performance and migration priority to select the target virtual machine, as shown in formula 9:

$$C(VM_i) = a' * T_{down} + b' * T_{mig} + c' * V_{mig} + d' * L_i \tag{9}$$

$C(VM_i)$ represents the selection of the target machine. Among them, T_{down}, T_{mig}, V_{mig} can be converted into polynomials containing V_{mem} by the above formula, and finally we can simplify it to formula 10:

$$C(VM_i) = a * V_{mem} * k + b * L_i \tag{10}$$

Among them, a and b are the weight coefficients of each performance index, and the sum of a and b is equal to 1. L_i is the migration priority. The value of k is as the formula 10:

$$k = \frac{R+1}{R} * \frac{1 - \lambda^{n+1}}{1 - \lambda} + \frac{\lambda^n}{R} \tag{11}$$

4.3   Virtual Machine Placement Strategy

Current virtual machine placement strategies lack the possibility of reserving the adaptation destination for subsequent source hosts [14]. To an adapted destination machine, which can not be migrated, affecting the quality of service.As the formula 11 shows ,we suppose the CPU utilization of node V_i is u_i, let node weight $w_i = 1 - u_i$, the forwarding probability p_i of node V_i is:

$$p_i = \frac{w_i}{\sum_{i=1}^{N} w_i} \tag{12}$$

After the destination machine triggers a migration, we use a random number between $[0, 1]$. Then determine which destination machine is in the probability range according to the random number, thereby determining the destination machine for migration. In this way, we can let the destination machines with smaller loads have a greater probability of selection. And the destination machines with heavy loads also have a certain probability to become candidate destination machines. Therefore, when the migration occurs, all candidate destination machines may become the definite migration destination machine. To maximize the load balance of the data center, it also provides the possibility of the optimal destination machine for the virtual machine with large load demand.

In addition, if there is no destination machine that meets the VM_i migration conditions, then we have to return to the selection strategy, adjust the weighting factor, and replace the source host until the migration is successful.

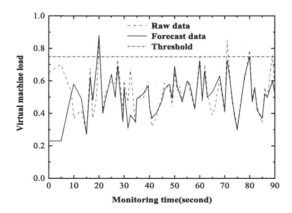

Fig. 2. Performance results of predictive migration strategies.

5   Performance Evaluation

5.1   Performance Evaluation of Predictive Migration Strategies

As shown in Fig. 2, We give the actual value of the CPU utilization sequence detected within a time period (0.65, 0.70, 0.4, 0.85, 0.6, 0.5, 0.45, 0.65, 0.75, 0.4, 0.8). And we set the trigger threshold of the virtual machine is 0.75, and the established prediction model is $AR(8)$. Based on the above 10 sets of data, we can conduct simulation experiments. The experimental results can be seen that at t equals {8, 20, 30, 60, 70, 80}, the actual data all exceed the threshold, but at t equals {8, 20, 30, 80}, the prediction-based triggering strategy predicts that the physical machine load is on a downward trend, which can avoid 4 unnecessary migrations. But the threshold-based triggering strategy will trigger migrations at the above 6 moments, resulting in frequent migrations Happening. From the above experiment data, compared with OpenStack native online migration strategy, we can reduce unnecessary migration by about 60%.

As shown in Fig. 3. We use high-quality-of-service sensitive virtual machine migration for predictive migration. Given the actual value of the CPU utilization sequence detected within a time period (0.30, 0.50, 0.45, 0.70, 0.55, 0.70, 0.65, 0.80, 0.85, 0.60, 0.65), the trigger value is 0.75, and the time interval is set to 5 Unit time to predict the load value. The simulation experiment results at t equals 35, we predict that the load will exceed the threshold at t equals 40. Since the application on this virtual machine is highly sensitive to the quality of service, we will perform the test on the virtual machine. Migration to ensure its load balance and reduce the impact on service quality. From the actual data, when t equals 40, the CPU utilization has indeed exceeded the threshold. By predicting the migration, the effect of service quality due to overload is effectively reduced.

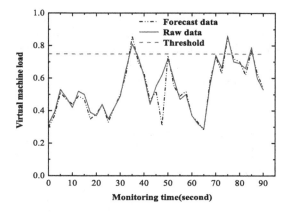

Fig. 3. Performance results for high-quality service-sensitive applications.

5.2   Performance Evaluation of Virtual Machine Migration Decision Model

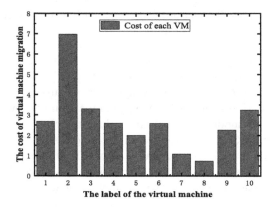

Fig. 4. Virtual machine migration cost.

For all virtual machines running on the physical machine, we must first sample the dirty page rate of the memory (that is, the dirty page generation speed), combined with historical information, we can get the current memory dirty page rate, the system data transmission The speed is fixed, so we can get the ratio λ of the dirty page generation speed to the memory transfer speed. And calculate the migration priority of the application. When all input parameters are known, we can get the best candidate source host VM_i through our decision model. We can get the migration cost of each virtual machine as shown in Fig. 4.

As shown in the Fig. 4, we test the results of the virtual machine migration decision model given above based on the historical data of 10 virtual machines.

We compare the virtual machine No. 2 with the virtual machine No. 8 and the cost is almost 10 times the difference. Through the above experimental data, we can see that when our decision model is used, we can obtain the optimal migration candidates, minimize the cost of migration, and greatly reduce the impact of virtual machine migration on service quality.

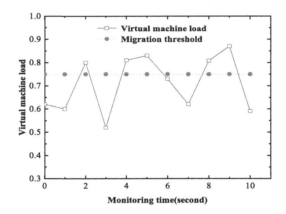

Fig. 5. Load fluctuations for virtual machine migration.

In addition, we compared our decision model with the current threshold-based triggering strategy and the migration strategy without a decision model: within a certain time T_0, with the change in load caused by the migration, the virtual machine Migration, performance comparison is shown in the Fig. 5: results show that our model can not only reduce unnecessary virtual machine migration by about 33%, but also reduce migration costs by 30%. It is consistent with the distribution probability calculated before. Therefore, the above method can not only find a suitable destination machine, but also provide the possibility of an optimal destination machine for a virtual machine with a large load demand later.

6   Related Work

There are three main solving algorithms for the current placement problem of virtual machines: First-Fit Decreasing (FFD) [15], Best-Fit [16] and Worst-Fit [17]. The existing PMapper model uses the FFD algorithm to determine the placement of virtual machines, and by continuously giving optimal solutions to deal with the placement of virtual machines to achieve load balancing. The virtual machine placement technology under the high-availability target focuses on the availability of the target machine, so that each source host to be migrated can find a certain target machine that can be normal. In addition, there is a Network-Aware virtual machine placement technology [18], which focuses on considering that the virtual machine will continue to receive dirty page information during migration, so it needs to be placed dynamically. However, these algorithms lack the possibility of reserving the adaptation destination for subsequent source hosts.

7   Conclusion

In cloud data centers, we usually use dynamic resource scheduling to manage massive amounts of data, and one of the commonly used dynamic resource scheduling methods is the virtual machine real-time migration technology studied in this paper. In order to reduce the impact of uploading applications and improve service quality during virtual machine migration, this paper proposes a prediction-based virtual machine triggering strategy, which can reduce unnecessary migration by about 33% quality of service. The decision model of virtual machine migration proposed by us can reduce the migration cost by up to 90%. At the same time, the probabilistic virtual machine placement strategy we proposed provides a possibility for subsequent virtual machines that occupy a large amount of resources to still have the optimal target machine selection, this is of practical significance for improving the overall resource utilization of the data center in a production environment.

Acknowledgments. This work is supported in part by the National Key R&D Program of China under Grant 2019YFB2102002, in part by the National Natural Science Foundation of China under Grant 61802182.

References

1. Shen, J., Zhou, T., Chen, X., Li, J., Susilo, W.: Anonymous and traceable group data sharing in cloud computing. IEEE Trans. Inf. Forensics Secur. **13**(4), 912–925 (2018)
2. Ling, L., Xiaozhen, M., Yulan, H.: CDN cloud: a novel scheme for combining CDN and cloud computing. In: 5th International Conference on Modelling, Identification and Control, vol. 01, pp. 687–690 (2013)
3. Ma, K., Yang, B.: Live data replication approach from relational tables to schema-free collections using stream processing framework. In: 10th International Conference on P2P, Parallel, Grid, Cloud and Internet Computing, pp. 26–31 (2015)
4. Pagani, S., Shafique, M., Khdr, H., Chen, J.-J., Henkel, J.: seBoost: selective boosting for heterogeneous manycores. In: Hardware/Software Codesign and System Synthesis, pp. 104–113 (2019)
5. Jianhong, M., Bangbang, R.: Strategies of controller selection balance for cloud data center network. Command Inf. Syst. Technol. **10**(4), 96–100 (2017)
6. Mizusawa, N., Kon, J., Seki, Y., Tao, J., Yamaguchi, S.: Performance improvement of file operations on OverlayFS for containers. In: IEEE International Conference on Smart Computing, pp. 297–302 (2018)
7. Li, B., Zhang, W., Gu, X., Cong, L.: Research on the production scheduling for automobile parts based on hybrid algorithm. In: 5th International Conference on Intelligent Human-Machine Systems and Cybernetics, vol. 2, pp. 267–270 (2013)

8. Wendi, C., Shaojie, M., Ran, D.: Generation and deployment technology for cloud simulation test environment. Command Inf. Syst. Technol. 10(3), 37–40 (2019)
9. Wu, X., Deng, S.: Research on optimizing strategy of database-oriented GIS graph database query. In: IEEE International Conference on Cloud Computing and Intelligence Systems, pp. 305–309 (2018)
10. Jangra, A., Kumar, A.: Dynamic prioritization based efficient task scheduling for grid computing. In: 2nd International Conference on Information Management in the Knowledge Economy, pp. 150–155 (2013)
11. Zhang, L., Han, T., Ansari, N.: Renewable energy-aware inter-datacenter virtual machine migration over elastic optical networks. In: IEEE 7th International Conference on Cloud Computing Technology and Science, pp. 440–443 (2015)
12. Li, Z.: Time synchronization method for cloud computing server clusters. Command Inf. Syst. Technol. 9(4), 63–67 (2017)
13. Filho, M.C.S., Monteiro, C.C., Inácio, P.R.M., Freire, M.M.: Approaches for optimizing virtual machine placement and migration in cloud environments: a survey. J. Parallel Distrib. Comput. 111, 222 (2018)
14. Heikkilä, M., Rättyä, A., Pieskä, S., Joni Jämsä, J.: Security challenges in small- and medium-sized manufacturing enterprises. In: 3rd International Symposium on Small-scale Intelligent Manufacturing Systems, pp. 25–30 (2020)
15. Aldahari, E.: Dynamic voltage and frequency scaling enhanced task scheduling technologies toward green cloud computing. In: International Conference on Computational Science and Intelligence, pp. 20–25 (2016)
16. Bożejko, W., Chaczko, Z., Nadybski, P., Wodecki, M.: Contemporary Complex Systems and Their Dependability 761, 74 (2018)
17. Lv, L., Liang, Q.: Communication-aware container placement and reassignment in large-scale internet data centers. IEEE J. Sel. Areas Commun. 37(3), 540–555 (2019)
18. Zhao, H., Wang, Q.: VM performance maximization and PM load balancing virtual machine placement in cloud. In: 2020 20th IEEE/ACM International Symposium on Cluster, Cloud and Internet Computing, pp. 857–864 (2020)

BinSEAL: Linux Binary Obfuscation Against Symbolic Execution

Ruizhe Qin[1,2(✉)] and Hao Han[1,2(✉)]

[1] College of Computer Sciences and Technology, Nanjing University of Aeronautics and Astronautics, Nanjing, China
{qrzbing,hhan}@nuaa.edu.cn
[2] Collaborative Innovation Center of Novel Software Technology and Industrialization, Nanjing 211106, China

Abstract. With the development of the software industry, the competition between software protection and cracking has become increasingly fierce, and corresponding protection and cracking methods have emerged in endlessly. Nowadays, most hackers need reverse engineering coupled with static analysis to perform cracking. Software protection is usually prevented from being cracked or maliciously reused through program obfuscation. Opaque predicates have been proposed for program obfuscation in recent years. The main approaches are to add condition branches with bogus program paths whose execution is unknown before runtime. Unlike those approaches, we propose a new obfuscation method dubbed BinSEAL in this paper by converting direct function calls of a program into indirect ones and using opaque predicates to obfuscate the target addresses. We implement BinSEAL and publish a toolset that can automatically transform Linux COTS binaries into obfuscated ones without requiring binary reconstruction. Evaluation results show that our method can resist certain static analysis such as symbolic execution.

Keywords: Control flow · Code obfuscation · Opaque predicate · Symbolic execution · Software security

1 Introduction

Driven by such a huge benefit, commercial software has always been the hardest hit by software cracking and malicious reuse. In order to prevent hackers from reverse engineering commercial software, people introduce obfuscation into commercial software. Although obfuscation does not completely prevent the malicious cracking of commercial software by hackers, but it can turn the attack process into a very time-consuming and costly job, which can allow software publishers to generate sufficient revenue during this period to maintain profitability.

In recent literature, most of work focused on static analysis and program obfuscation with source code. But in many cases, we can only obfuscate binary

© Springer Nature Switzerland AG 2021
G. Wang et al. (Eds.): SpaCCS 2020, LNCS 12383, pp. 65–76, 2021.
https://doi.org/10.1007/978-3-030-68884-4_6

rather than source code, so we need a binary-oriented obfuscation method that can resist static analysis. Another issue of existing obfuscation is that they do not clearly define in how they resilient against reverse engineering techniques such as static analysis, dynamic analysis.

Hence, we propose a technique that can prevent symbolic execution in this paper, which is the most effective static analysis from inferring correct control flow graph (CFG). Our basic idea is to insert opaque predicates in the binary code instead of the source code to obfuscate the direct call, thereby preventing static analysis and symbolic execution. Existing methods add branches to the program to let static method confuse. We propose a new idea that we not only add branches, but also make function jump address more complex. Several challenges should be tackled in the workflow, like binary rewrite revolves some hard problems, and it is complex to determine whether the logic is correct after code insertion.

We implement BinSEAL and its source code is available for downloading in GitHub (https://github.com/nuaa-s3lab/BinSEAL). Our contributions are as follows:

1. We firstly use opaque predicates to serially obfuscate code for direct calls (such as function calls). Because the existing obfuscation work is not enough to obfuscate function calls, so we add opaque predicates to confuse direct calls.
2. We provide a set of toolkit BinSEAL to directly obfuscate the Linux binary code, do not depend on specific hardware, and do not need to provide the source code of the program. There is currently no similar tool.
3. We evaluated the BinSEAL with several experiments. Results show that Bin-SEAL can resist code detection based on static analysis, prevent the establishment of control flowcharts, and prevent the detection of antivirus software to a certain extent.

2   Related Work

Popov et al. [8] proposed to transform unconditional jumps into traps that generate signals, and then they used signal processing mechanisms to implement the semantics of unconditional jumps. Polymorphic obfuscation generates multiple obfuscated versions of the protected program by introducing some randomization mechanism in the obfuscation. Lin et al. [5] proposed to generate different data structure layouts during each compilation process, and randomly reorder the data for polymorphic obfuscation. ProGuard et al. [9] have used vocabulary obfuscation as the default obfuscation scheme for Android programs.

Lexical obfuscation will turn meaningful symbols into meaningless symbols. Control flow obfuscation increases the ambiguity of control flow in various ways. Mu et al. [7] proposed a ROPOB with control flow flattening, which turns a control flow with multiple branches into a linear control flow.

Nowadays, people devote them to prevent advanced static analysis. Xu et al. [13] designed an obfuscation method against LOOP [6] based on o-LLVM.

In addition, Balachandran et al. [1] found that control instructions (such as jmp) are important information for reverse analysis, and they suggested replacing such instructions with mov and other instructions. Dolan verified that the mov instruction after the introduction of control instructions such as indexed addressing data is Turing complete [4], which means that we can implement all machine instructions with only mov. Xu et al. [14] proposed Bi-opaque predicates, which concludes a new opinion about opaque predicates and provides a obfuscator template based on o-LLVM. People can add opaque predicates according to that template. Seto et al. [10] proposed a new low-overhead opaque predicates using bit operations, and achieve good results against symbolic execution engine. Zobernig et al. [15] found that opaque predicates are effective in two situations, which provide new ideas for the accurate definition of opaque predicates. Suk et al. [11] presented a module that prevents deobfuscation through code tampering (preventive obfuscation) at the source code level, which is the first to demonstrate the necessity of source-level optimization and control-flow reconstruction empirically.

However, most of the method above do obfuscation on source code level.

3 System Design

Our goal is to convert ELF Files to Opaque-Predicate-Obfuscated ones, whose control flow information has been concealed, so that static de-obfuscation methods will fail to construct the control flow graph. Obfuscated files are semantically equal to the origin ones. In this section we will give an overview of our method.

This workflow is shown as Fig. 1 and our approach is consists of five major steps:

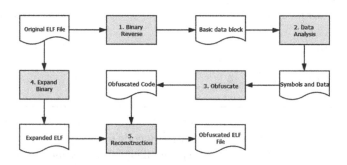

Fig. 1. System workflow of BinSEAL

1. Parsing ELF to several basic blocks.
2. Parsing basic blocks to find needed symbols and data.
3. Generate obfuscated code with opaque predicates.
4. Expand original ELF file.
5. Insert obfuscated code into data section to reconstruct ELF file.

The workflow is straightforward. According to experiments in paper [10], symbolic execution on binary is harder than on source code. So our work is aimed at obfuscating binary files under Linux(ELF files). At first, we disassemble ELF files into several blocks to analysis. The format of ELF is clear, we will get several sections, here we call them basic blocks.

Next, we search contents in basic blocks, find useful data to be obfuscated in ELF, such as function symbols, direct calls, string data, etc. Most of current work on binary is based on x86 architecture, which is about to be replaced by x64. Comparing with x86, x64 has a larger addressable space and more complex features. Our work supports x64 binary files under Linux.

Then we can choose obfuscation method to obfuscate obtained data. To obfuscate binary, we can obfuscate control flow [2], layout [9], data [3], etc. We use the opaque predicate in control flow obfuscation to obfuscate the direct call. Opaque predicates, which can resist static analysis effectively, are popular in recent years. But in recent years, people can easily remove opaque predicates through machine learning [12] and other methods because opaque predicates do not really change control flow.

We have further improved on the basis of opaque predicates and obfuscate direct calls, which damage origin control flow, can prevent static analysis tools such as IDA Pro and angr from establishing control flow graphs.

Listing 1 shows an example of simple program. We can find a direct call points to add function in Fig. 2a, which is the control flow graph generated by angr. But after obfuscation in Fig. 2b, the control flow graph is more complex, and we can not find the direct call points to add function, which will prevent symbolic execution.

Listing 1. A simple code sample

```
int add(int a, int b) {
    return a + b;
}
int main() {
    int a = 1, b = 2;
    return add(a, b);
}
```

After that, we need to generate assembly code that contains opaque predicates. Unlike high-level languages, obfuscation code in assembly need more select and test to strike a balance between space efficiency and time efficiency. Since various data of binary is determined, we also need to modify binary file to insert obfuscation code. Generally speaking, we can reversely expand the text section or forward expand the data section of the binary file. In the process of modifying binary, we also have to ensure that the original data of binary like strings, global variable, etc. is not damaged.

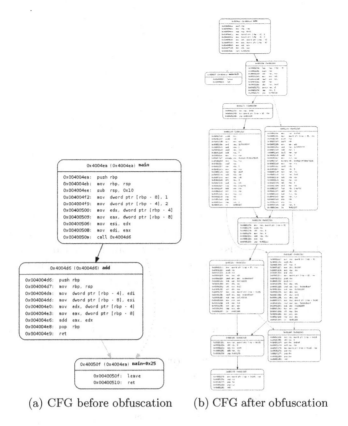

(a) CFG before obfuscation   (b) CFG after obfuscation

Fig. 2. Illustration of Obfuscation in CFG

4   Implementation

We design our method as a tool, called BinSEAL, which takes an ordinary 64-bit ELF file as input and an Opaque-Predicated-Obfuscated ELF file with the same semantic as output.

Direct Call Finder. We use objdump to find all direct calls in the binary. Our goal is to edit all direct call and make them point to parasite code we obfuscated, so in direct call finder, we scan all Elf files to save some useful information like Elf Header, Program Header, etc. as Fig. 3.

Opaque Predicates Generate. In this paper, we choose opaque predicate as the obfuscation algorithm. The characteristic of opaque predicates is that known properties of predicate obfuscated by the obfuscator are difficult to be known during anti-aliasing. Invariant opaque, which predicates are opaque predicates that output true values for any input predicates are selected for concatenation.

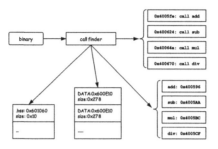

Fig. 3. Direct call finder

Generally speaking, opaque predicate needs to verify the input, because it is always a constant truth, so no matter what value is input will not change its output. Since this article confuses direct calls in binary, we can assume that the input is a function call parameter. In the x86-64 architecture, Linux will call the register to pass parameters in the order rdi, rsi, rdx, rcx, r8, r9. More than 6 parameters will be passed through the stack.

We use opaque predicate concatenation method to confuse the direct call. As shown in Fig. 4, origin direct function call will now jump to new position after obfuscation process. Each opaque predicate will process rax to a certain extent, and finally piece together the return address.

Insert Obfuscated Code. We use data segment injection to insert obfuscated code. On systems that do not have the NX bit set, such as 32-bit Linux systems, code on data segment is executable. In 64-bit Linux system, we can set executable permissions on data segment. Figure 5 shows the effect of data segment injection. Since the structure of the binary file will be destroyed when the data segment is injected, we will use the previously saved information in direct call finder.

5   Evaluation

It is important to test BinSEAL's performance, so we design a series of experiments on it. We tested BinSEAL with GNU Core Utilities, and succeed to obfuscate them and evaluate BinSEAL in three aspects, including control flow concealing, VirusTotal obfuscate test and program overhead on space and time. Our experiments are performed on Ubuntu 16.04 LTS x64, with 4G memory and kernel version - 4.15.

5.1   Control Flow Concealing

We design two experiments in this example. Listing 1 shows a code example of the function call, and the direct call is a call to the add function.

Binary control flow graph (CFG) generated by angr generating sample code is shown in Fig. 2a. We let angr start to establish the control flow graph from

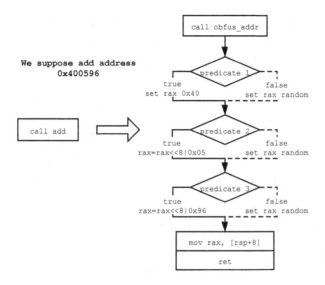

Fig. 4. Logic of obfuscated code

the main function. Angr will split the assembly into basic blocks and identify all the instructions for jumps and function calls, and finally establish a complete program control flow graph. The basic block in assembly refers to the instruction sequence that ends with direct or indirect jump instructions such as jmp, jcc, call, and ret in the assembly code. In our schematic diagram, the running process of the entire function can be parsed into three basic blocks. Obviously, main will return after calling the add function.

In control flow concealing, we also use the GNU Core Utilities to test the obfuscation ability of BinSEAL. We chose Coreutils because it is open source and widely used in Linux systems to facilitate experiments.

There is no standard for obfuscation strength. Since the content of this article is for the obfuscation of control flow, we evaluate the intensity of obfuscation by detecting the effectiveness of control flow hiding before and after obfuscation.

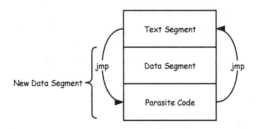

Fig. 5. data segment injection

We analyze the test program before and after obfuscation from the perspective of the reverser to evaluate the obfuscation ability of BinSEAL.

In function call concealing, control flow graph generated after obfuscation is shown in Fig. 2b. After we obfuscate the program, the basic blocks become disordered, and the edge pointing to the add function can no longer be found in the figure, which shows that BinSEAL can indeed prevent the establishment of the program control flow graph in reverse engineering.

Coreutils obfuscation experiment can be seen from Table 1 that the number of nodes after obfuscation has increased compared to before obfuscation, which is obvious because the obfuscation code we introduced contains multiple nodes; the static analysis after obfuscation has significantly reduced edges.

Table 1. Coreutils evaluation for nodes, edges and crossings

Coreutils	Nodes			Edges			Crossings		
	Before	After	Inc	Before	After	Dec	Before	After	Dec
echo	138	187	49	181	61	120	213	120	93
uname	149	202	53	203	51	142	324	138	186
pwd	169	234	65	255	79	176	537	366	171
md5sum	172	233	71	335	60	275	554	127	427
cat	204	280	76	475	131	344	2,179	890	1,289
date	221	303	82	564	104	460	1,416	471	945
df	327	461	134	1,152	362	790	10,082	13,081	−2,999
ls	413	554	141	1,361	394	977	7,022	8,389	1,367
mv	502	689	187	2,745	581	2,164	26,563	24,992	1,571
cp	532	732	200	3,052	676	2,376	32,900	31,947	−953

This proves that BinSEAL is effective in establishing a control flow chart against static analysis. But for the number of cross-references, the data before and after obfuscation cannot fully reflect the characteristics: in most cases, the number of them is reduced, but for a small number of examples, the number of them is increased. We speculate that it may be due to the large number of cross-references in the obfuscated code we introduced. In summary, BinSEAL is very effective in hiding the control flow, and it can prevent the establishment of the program control flow chart by the static analysis tool to a great extent.

5.2 Resistance to Static Analysis

In this section, we will obfuscate some existing viruses, and verify whether they can be detected by antivirus software in order to evaluate the resistance of BinSEAL to static analysis. We use viruses in this experiment because we assume that existing antivirus software use static analysis to detect viruses, so that we can use the number of viruses detected to determine how BinSEAL works after obfuscation. By selecting several virus samples and obfuscating, we detect how the antivirus software can detect and kill the virus after the obfuscation control flow. VirusTotal is a well-known malware analysis service provider and also provides free analysis services.

We obfuscate the virus separately, set the address of the direct call location to 0, obfuscation with UPX, obfuscation with no file execution experiment. For the reason that BinSEAL edit direct call at the first step, we set direct call address to 0x0 to test how antivirus software detect virus.

Table 2 shows the experimental results of VirusTotal. In the table, name is short of Virus name. For example, BA.bx-0083 is short of Backdoor.Agent.bx-0083. In this experiment, we use ten types Virus. In other columns, "call 0" means we set all direct call address to 0x00000000, "BinSEAL+FA" means we use BinSEAL and Fileless execution. Obviously, due to the obvious characteristics of viruses, BinSEAL only obfuscates direct calls.

Table 2. Static Analysis Test (Detected/Not Detected)

Name	Nothing	BinSEAL	call 0	BinSEAL+UPX	BinSEAL+FE
BA.bx-0083	29/59	4/59	9/61	7/59	0/59
BG.a-1b44	34/58	27/59	26/60	10/60	0/58
BG.a-1d38	38/58	27/59	30/60	9/60	0/60
BG.bj-0f65	35/57	27/60	29/60	10/60	0/60
BG.bj-0fc5	36/58	28/59	29/60	10/60	0/60
BS.t-00f9	19/55	8/60	7/60	7/60	0/60
BT.bh-0fc8	38/58	28/60	29/59	11/60	0/60
EC.a-0f58	23/57	15/60	16/60	error	0/60
LSD.BA-1b46	15/55	3/60	3/60	4/60	0/60
TA.dp-0b5f	41/60	10/60	23/59	9/59	0/60
TW.a-0b93	32/58	4/60	7/60	6/60	0/60
RTBCM.b-0a6d	21/56	20/60	21/60	8/60	0/60

BinSEAL does not significantly affect the detection results. Some results are greatly reduced, it may be caused by obfuscation that changes part of the code characteristics. BinSEAL is successful in obfuscating control flow because we have not destroyed too much feature, anti-virus software do not just pass control flow detection when detecting viruses, so detected numbers are not change enough. After UPX packing, the detection ability of antivirus software has decreased significantly. We used fileless execution technique to modify virus program to prevent antivirus software's UPX-unpacked technique, and none of them can detect any virus program after fully editing. Experiment shows that BinSEAL can interfere with the detection of antivirus software to a certain extent.

5.3   Obfuscation Overhead

Space overhead and time overhead are also characteristics that significantly affect the program. If the code we insert is too large, the original program will swell; if the time overhead is too large, it will affect the daily use of users.

In space overhead experiment, we still use Coreutils as an example to compare the overhead before and after obfuscation.

Table 3. Space overhead (byte)

Coreutils	Nothing	BinSEAL	Up size	bss size	Act size	Ratio (%)
echo	31,376	52,009	20,633	416	20,217	64.43
uname	31,440	53,831	22,391	416	21,975	69.89
pwd	31,472	57,672	26,200	416	25,784	81.92
md5sum	43,792	70,650	26,858	488	26,370	60.21
cat	52,080	86,782	34,702	2,472	32,230	61.88
date	68,464	105,838	37,374	456	36,918	53.92
df	97,912	158,947	61,035	2,728	58,307	59.55
ls	126,584	198,871	72,287	3,432	68,855	54.39
mv	130,488	225,246	94,758	1,584	93,174	71.40
cp	151,024	253,485	102,461	3,720	98,741	65.38

Table 3 shows the space overhead of Coreutils before and after obfuscation. We used the data segment injection, which will be affected by the bss segment: in the actual environment, different compilers compile the program with different optimization methods to address and make different operations. If we do not reserve space for the bss segment, the operation of the bss segment at runtime will destroy the code we injected.

BinSEAL significantly increases the file space overhead. The best case increased by 53%, and the worst case increased by 81%. In BinSEAL, obfuscated code with a fixed length is generated for the addresses that are directly called. The size of code in BinSEAL is 1458 bytes and will rapidly expand when there are more nodes. Increased space overhead can cause a greater burden on reverse engineering, the reverse is also a burden for the obfuscator.

Time experiment will test the sort tool in Coreutils. The sort tool is a sorting tool in Coreutils, which contains a large number of direct call operations such as function calls, which is very suitable for testing time overhead. The data of the sort tool used in time overhead before and after obfuscation is shown in Table 4. We perform sorting tests on separately generating 5000000, 10000000, 20000000 and 40000000 numbers and letters.

Table 4. Sort utility

	Nodes	Edges	Crossings	Size (byte)
Before	403	2,253	9,666	110,040
After	558	431	10,444	184,371

Table 5 shows the time spent in the sorting algorithm before and after the obfuscation. Unsurprisingly, due to the large volume of obfuscated code we inserted and the large space overhead, the time overhead is also high. In the case where the sort tool frequently makes function calls, the time cost is greatly expanded, and even reaches 120% to 130%. Once users encounters time-sensitive computing operations, consumed time may be increase significantly.

Table 5. Time overhead (second)

	5,000,000	10,000,000	20,000,000	400,000,00
Before	4.327	8.828	20.394	37.851
After	9.670	19.440	44.061	89.29
Increased time	5.343	10.612	23.667	51.439
Increase ratio	123.48	120.20	116.04	135.89

6   Conclusion

In this paper, we designed BinSEAL, a method of obfuscation that is directly applied to binary for control flow. In the experiment, space-time overhead may be the most important issue but it is hard to solve, and space overhead can be solved through code compression or code reuse. Some predicate implementations are inefficient in different architecture, so improper selection of opaque predicate compounds may also reduce the security of opaque predicates. Finally, we discussed the currently popular dynamic execution solution to the opaque predicate problem.

Acknowledgements. We sincerely thank reviewers for their insightful feedback. This work was supported in part by NSFC Award #61972200.

References

1. Balachandran, V., Emmanuel, S.: Software code obfuscation by hiding control flow information in stack. In: 2011 IEEE International Workshop on Information Forensics and Security, pp. 1–6. IEEE (2011)

2. Collberg, C., Thomborson, C., Low, D.: A taxonomy of obfuscating transformations (1997)
3. Collberg, C., Thomborson, C., Low, D.: Breaking abstractions and unstructuring data structures. In: Proceedings of the 1998 International Conference on Computer Languages (Cat. No. 98CB36225), pp. 28–38. IEEE (1998)
4. Dolan, S.: MOV is Turing-complete. Cl. Cam. Ac. Uk, pp. 1–4 (2013)
5. Lin, Z., Riley, R.D., Xu, D.: Polymorphing software by randomizing data structure layout. In: Flegel, U., Bruschi, D. (eds.) DIMVA 2009. LNCS, vol. 5587, pp. 107–126. Springer, Heidelberg (2009). https://doi.org/10.1007/978-3-642-02918-9_7
6. Ming, J., Xu, D., Wang, L., Wu, D.: LOOP: logic-oriented opaque predicate detection in obfuscated binary code. In: Proceedings of the 22nd ACM SIGSAC Conference on Computer and Communications Security, pp. 757–768 (2015)
7. Mu, D., Guo, J., Ding, W., Wang, Z., Mao, B., Shi, L.: ROPOB: obfuscating binary code via return oriented programming. In: Lin, X., Ghorbani, A., Ren, K., Zhu, S., Zhang, A. (eds.) SecureComm 2017. LNICST, vol. 238, pp. 721–737. Springer, Cham (2018). https://doi.org/10.1007/978-3-319-78813-5_38
8. Popov, I.V., Debray, S.K., Andrews, G.R.: Binary obfuscation using signals. In: USENIX Security Symposium, pp. 275–290 (2007)
9. ProGuard: Shrink, obfuscate, and optimize your app (2020). https://developer.android.com/studio/build/shrink-code
10. Seto, T., Monden, A., Yücel, Z., Kanzaki, Y.: On preventing symbolic execution attacks by low cost obfuscation. In: 2019 20th IEEE/ACIS International Conference on Software Engineering, Artificial Intelligence, Networking and Parallel/Distributed Computing (SNPD), pp. 495–500. IEEE (2019)
11. Suk, J.H., Lee, Y.B., Lee, D.H.: SCORE: source code optimization & reconstruction. IEEE Access **8**, 129478–129496 (2020)
12. Tofighi-Shirazi, R., Asavoae, I.M., Elbaz-Vincent, P., Le, T.H.: Defeating opaque predicates statically through machine learning and binary analysis. In: Proceedings of the 3rd ACM Workshop on Software Protection, pp. 3–14 (2019)
13. Xu, D., Ming, J., Wu, D.: Generalized dynamic opaque predicates: a new control flow obfuscation method. In: Bishop, M., Nascimento, A.C.A. (eds.) ISC 2016. LNCS, vol. 9866, pp. 323–342. Springer, Cham (2016). https://doi.org/10.1007/978-3-319-45871-7_20
14. Xu, H., Zhou, Y., Kang, Y., Tu, F., Lyu, M.: Manufacturing resilient bi-opaque predicates against symbolic execution. In: 2018 48th Annual IEEE/IFIP International Conference on Dependable Systems and Networks (DSN), pp. 666–677. IEEE (2018)
15. Zobernig, L., Galbraith, S.D., Russello, G.: When are opaque predicates useful? In: 2019 18th IEEE International Conference on Trust, Security and Privacy in Computing and Communications/13th IEEE International Conference on Big Data Science and Engineering (TrustCom/BigDataSE), pp. 168–175. IEEE (2019)

Location Based Communication Privacy in Internet of Vehicles Using Fog Computing

Muhammad Arif[1], Jianer Chen[1], Pin Liu[2], and Guojun Wang[1(✉)]

[1] School of Computer Science, Guangzhou University, Guangzhou 510006,
Guangdong, China
`arifmuhammad36@hotmail.com`, {`jianer,csgjwang`}`@gzhu.edu.cn`
[2] School of Computer Science and Engineering,
Central South University, Changsha 410083, Hunan, China
`jiandanglp@csu.edu.cn`

Abstract. In the Vehicular Ad-hoc Networks (VANETs), a vehicle or the vehicle driver could be perceived and followed by listening in its inquiries (e.g., reference points) by an enemy, since these quires contain individual data and information, for example, the questions and area of the vehicle. This attack prompts dangers on the vehicles area protection. The current arrangements, practices anonymizer, a Third Trusted Party (TTP) in the middle of the LBS and the vehicles. The addition of the TTP shifts the imperilled element from the LBS to the Anonymizer, with respect to security hazard, and with the endangered anonymizer, the vehicles or vehicles drivers related information will likewise be in danger. In this paper, we think of productive area based correspondence protection in VANETs communication. In which, we utilize the Fog Computing (FC) alongside TTP calculation and data perturbation. Before sending the inquiry to the TTP first we anonymizes the communication information by utilizing data perturbation. Then, we utilize the Adaptive Interval Cloaking Algorithm (AICA) as TTP to handle the ideal question from vehicles to LBS. In this paper, we provide the double communication privacy based on data perturbations and AICA. Subsequent to accepting the prepared inquiry from the LBS, the TTP sends the outcomes back to the drives, where the vehicle drivers finds their ideal results. The results shows that the proposed method save the security area dependent on the questions at the low correspondence and computational expense.

Keywords: VANETs · Communication · Privacy · Fog computing · Data perturbation

1 Introduction

Vehicular Ad-hoc Networks (VANETs) is a strategy to build the security of the roads. VANETs is normally realistic through correspondences either between

G. Wang et al. (Eds.): SpaCCS 2020, LNCS 12383, pp. 77–90, 2021.
https://doi.org/10.1007/978-3-030-68884-4_7

two vehicles (V2V), or between a vehicle and a framework (V2I). Vehicles can communicate cautioning messages and traffic the executives directions in the vehicular condition to raise driver's consciousness of conceivable travel dangers. As far as solace and comfort of travellers, vehicles can likewise trade, for instance, sight and sound with different vehicles in the system [3].

Since the quantity of mishaps and unsatisfied clients in vehicular systems are impressively expanding; presently, the principle worry in this field is to improve the street security and guarantee traveller compost, which are reachable by insightful transportation frameworks. Albeit numerous specialized endeavours have been completed to accomplish the objectives of VANETs, it despite every-thing displays a few drawbacks. For example, since the versatility of vehicles is moderately high, it loads on the administration obliged inter-changes and prompts a significant expense communication [4, 6, 7] (Fig. 1).

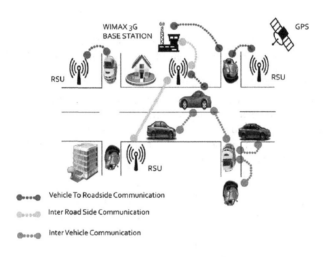

Fig. 1. VANETs architecture [4].

Because of the extraordinary highlights of the vehicular condition, the applied advancements just as the reasonable security model have the crucial part to improve the well-being of the travellers. From innovation vantage point, Cisco (2012) created Fog Computing (FC) as a world view that expands distributed computing and administrations to the edge of the system rather than altogether in the cloud [2]. Moreover, haze processing is a promising strategy for to satisfy VANETs prerequisites.

For instance, FC offers a speedy response to hidden gadget. It additionally diminishes the weight on the cloud and offers the capacity to investigate the FC stream continuous with the cloud, [18]. As per [18], FC is a reasonable strategy to build the well-being administrations and improve traffic the board which both require neighbourhood data and ongoing handling. Because of the upsides of edge area, FC has capacity to help applications with low dormancy necessities,

[27]. Henceforth, in this work, haze processing is receive ed as a solid stockpiling of neighbourhood data of the vehicular condition [5,9].

The remaining part of the paper is distributed as, in Sect. 2 we discussed about the related work. Section 3 is about the system methodology. Section 4 is related to the results an analysis, and at the end we provide the conclusions of the research work.

2 Related Work

The Fog Computing (FC) based system design is another world view that can give calculation, correspondence, arrangement, stockpiling, control, and deal with the significant highlights, including low reaction inertness, area mindfulness and geographic dispersion [21,23], between the Internet and the terminal gadgets. The FC nodes situated at the edge of the FC systems administration can speak with the enormous number of self-sorted out decentralized cell phones. Additionally, the portable hubs can team up with one another by means of the FC hubs. There are a few essential administrations remember for the FC organizing. For instance, basic measure of storage is completed at or close by the end client as opposed to putting away in the enormous scope server farm. fog nodes play out a lot of correspondence at or close to the end-client rather than through the spine arrange [12,24].

Since key administrations were done, the fog hub in the systems administration should go about as a switch for its Neighbours and adjust to the portability of the hub. Crowd sensing vehicle organize is a launch of VANETs [8,10]. Thusly, the standards utilized in VANETs could be the reason for the FC based crowd sensing vehicle systems [33]. In mist organizing, the information gathered by the sensor are sent to the system edge gadgets, switches for preparing as opposed to sending to the cloud workers. Along these lines, the mist processing system with a low transmission capacity is viable to diminish the traffic information. Besides, the mist processing limits the dormancy and improves the nature of administration. The haze registering decreases the traffic information to the cloud and not defer the calculation and correspondence because of the haze hubs are put close to information source. The new haze based figuring world view upholds heterogeneity including passageways, edge switches, and end client gadgets. It can give focal points in advertising, amusement, individual versatile figuring, and different applications [25].

Luan et al. [26] presented a disseminated mist registering framework where the haze workers were conveyed in appropriated way by isolated proprietor's work. The RSUs who has a similar mystery key with the vehicle can make any phony verifications. Open key-based conventions can accomplish the non-deniability property when computerized signature-based vehicle verification system is utilized. The above reasons and exploration hole spurred us to build up another protection safeguarding haze based protocol that can be utilized in the vehicular crowd sensing system. The most concerning issue of the client is the danger of security spillage in VANETs. In haze registering, the calculations of protection saving are run among the haze hubs and the cloud, on the grounds that there is no issue of calculation, preparing, and capacity for the two sides, and these are adequate. Furthermore, the running calculations are asset denied at end gadget, they normally gather the information for the end gadgets, for the protection safeguarding at the FC hubs the homomorphic encryption is utilized for the preservation of the security without the unscrambling. For the factual and accumulation vary entail security is applied to approval of non-presentation of protection of a discretionary and clashing single passage in informational index.

3 Methodology

The proposed methodology is based on three steps. The first step is based on Fog Computing (FC) the purpose of FC is to handle the information at locale level, it also provide the internal security and privacy and efficient storage processing, which reduces the time for information processing. Second step is related to data perturbation and last step is related to third trusted party in which we anonymize the data for VANETs communication. We provide the double anonymization privacy for communication in the VANETs. The flow diagram is given below (Fig. 2).

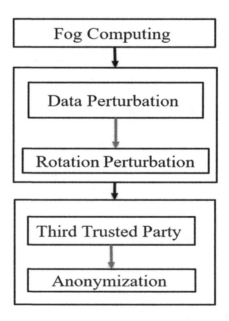

Fig. 2. Proposed method flow diagram.

3.1   Fog Computing (FC)

As of late, FC has become a functioning cloud-related exploration territory. It was joined by Cisco in 2012 [11]. It is an all-inclusive world view of distributed computing where system edge is utilized for information preparing and benefits in opposition to the current procedure in which this is totally done in the cloud. It offers some advertisement vantages in correlation with customary frameworks as area mindfulness, portability backing and low inertness can be accomplished by utilizing haze design which in the long run puts the haze hubs closer to end clients. Haze processing additionally joins centre cloud administrations. It changes traditional server farms into heterogeneous and dispersed stages also. Along these lines, mist registering underpins the uses of web of things in vehicular systems, entertainer/sensor systems and modern robotics that require the preparing of setting mindfulness and delicate postponements [14]. The purpose of FC is to handle the information at locale level, it also provide the internal security and privacy and efficient storage processing, which reduces the time for information processing (Fig. 3).

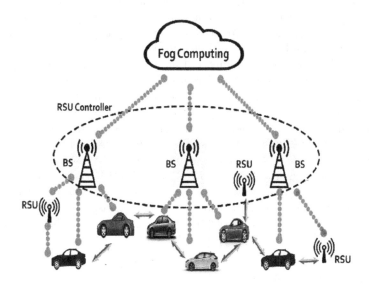

Fig. 3. VANETs communication through fog computing.

3.2   Data Perturbation Technique

An information annoyance technique can be essentially portrayed as follows. Before the information proprietors distribute their information, they change the information in specific approaches to mask the sensitive data while saving the specific information property that is basic for constructing significant information mining models. Irritation procedures need to deal with the intrinsic compromise between protecting information security and saving information utility, according to vague information for the most part decreases information utility [1].

Perturbation procedures are regularly assessed with two essential measurements: level of privacy assurance and level of model-explicit information utility safeguarded, which is frequently measured by the loss of precision for information grouping and information bunching. An extreme objective for all information bother calculations is to streamline the information change supportive of cess by expanding both information protection and information utility accomplished. In any case, the two measurements are normally speaking to two clashing objectives in many existing irritation procedures [19]. Information security is generally estimated by the trouble level in assessing the first information from the annoyed information. Given an information bother technique, the more elevated level of trouble where the first qualities can be assessed from the irritated information, the more significant level of information protection this strategy upholds [16].

The inborn relationship betweens the information protection and the information utility raises various significant issues with respect to how to locate a correct harmony between the two measures. In synopsis, we recognize three significant structure standards for multiplicative information annoyances. To begin with, saving the mining undertaking and model-explicit information properties is basic for giving better quality assurance on both security and model exactness. Second, it is helpful if information annoyance can adequately safeguard the undertaking/model-explicit information utility data, and maintain a strategic distance from the requirement for creating special mining calculations that can utilize the irritated information as arbitrary noise expansion requires. Third and in particular, in the event that one can build up an information irritation technique that doesn't instigate any lost of mining-task/model explicit information utility, this will empower us to zero in on improving annoyance calculations by amplifying the degree of information protection against assaults, which at last prompts better generally nature of both information security and information utility.

3.3   Rotation Perturbation

In this technique the estimation of the two properties in the network is pivoted yet the significance of the worth is secured. The pair of characteristics is first chosen then the worth distortion strategy is applied for those qualities [15]. Assume unique dataset have d section and N records then it is spoken to as X dn, the revolution irritation of dataset X will be characterized as $G(X) = RX$, where Rdd is an arbitrary pivot orthonormal network [17]. which has following properties.

The lattice R_{dd} is an orthonormal grid [30], which has following properties. Let R^T speak to the translate of R, r_{ij} speak to the (i, j) component of R, and

i be the identity lattice. The lines and sections of R are orthonormal, i.e., for any segment j,

$$\sum_{i=1}^{d} r_{ij}^2 = 1 \tag{1}$$

and for any two sections j and k, $j \neq k$, and

$$\sum_{i=1}^{d} r_{ij} r_{ij} = 0 \tag{2}$$

A comparative property is held for lines. This definition induces that

$$R^T R = RR^T = I \tag{3}$$

It likewise infers that by changing the request for the lines or sections of a symmetrical network, the subsequent framework is as yet symmetrical. An irregular orthonormal network can be productively created following the Haar dispersion [32]. A key component of revolution change is that it safeguard the Euclidean separation of multi-dimensional focuses during the change. Let x^T speak to the render of vector x, and $||x|| = x^T x$ speak to the length of a vector x. By the meaning of pivot network, we have

$$||Rx|| = ||x|| \tag{4}$$

Correspondingly, inward item is additionally invariant to revolution. Let $(x, y) = x^T y$ represent the internal result of x and y. We have,

$$(Rx, Ry) = x^T R^T Ry = (x, y) \tag{5}$$

When all is said in done, revolution likewise saves the mathematical shapes, for example, hyperplane and hyper bended surface in the multidimensional space [15]. We saw that since numerous classifiers search for mathematical choice limit, for example, hyperplane and hyper surface, pivot change will protect the most basic data for some, characterization models. There are two different ways to apply turn annoyance. We can either apply it to the entire dataset X [15], or bunch segments to sets and apply variant pivot bothers to various sets of sections [28].

3.4   TTP Architecture

A TTP the specific areas from customers, obscures the areas, and sends the obscured areas to the worker. Furnish ground-breaking security ensures with great administrations. The TTP, going about as a moderate level between the vehicle and the LBS. In this dad per we utilize Adaptive-Interval Cloaking Algorithms as a TTP engineering. This architecture is a concentrated confided in element which is answerable for social affair and providing the necessary security for every vehicle in the system. TTP got the specific location from the vehicles

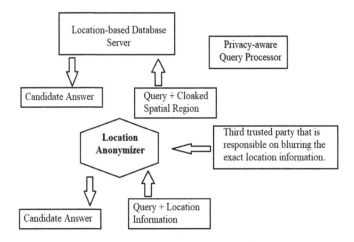

Fig. 4. Third trusted party architecture [29].

and hazy spots the area and sends to the LBS. It additionally furnishes ground-breaking protection ensure with top notch administrations. Least spatial territory requirements and k namelessness has been helps by the Adaptive-Interval Cloaking Algorithms [20] (Fig. 4).

3.5 Anonymizing Location Information

In our framework model, the vehicles corresponds with outside administrations through a focal secrecy worker that is essential for the confided in processing base. In an initialization stage, the hubs will set up a verified and scrambled association with the secrecy worker. At the point when a portable hub sends position and time data to an outer help, the namelessness worker decodes the message, eliminates any identifiers, for example, organize addresses, and annoys the position information as per the accompanying shrouding calculations to diminish the re-identification hazard. In addition, the namelessness worker goes about as a blend switch [13], which haphazardly reorders messages from a few versatile hubs, to keep a foe from connecting ingoing and active messages at the obscurity worker. At last, the obscurity worker advances the message to the outside assistance. For planning the bother calculations, we start with the assumption that the secrecy worker knows the current situation all things considered. The subject's portable hubs could intermittently refresh their position data with the anonymizer. k-Anonymous Location Information While namelessness is etymologically characterized as "being anonymous" or "of obscure initiation", data security scientists decipher it from a more grounded perspective [20].

Designed by [31], we consider a subject as k-mysterious regarding area data, if and just if the area data introduced is indistinct from the area data of at any rate k 1 different subjects. Unless in any case expressed, we accept that area data incorporates fleeting information (i.e., when the subject was available at the area). All the more explicitly, area data is spoken to by a tuple containing three spans ($[x1, x2], [y1, y2], [t1, t2]$). The spans $[x1, x2]$ and $[y1, y2]$ portray a two dimensional region where the subject is found. $[t1, t2]$ portrays a time frame during which the subject was available in the region. Note that the spans speak to vulnerability ranges; we just realize that eventually in time inside the fleeting stretch the subject was available sooner or later of the territory given by the spatial stretches. Consequently, an area tuple for a subject is k-mysterious, when it portrays the area of the subject, yet in addition the locations of k 1 different subjects. As such, k_1 different subjects likewise probably been available in the region and the timespan portrayed by the tuple. As a rule, the bigger the secrecy set k is, the higher is the level of namelessness. Accordingly, we will quantify the level of secrecy.

3.6   Adaptive-Interval Cloaking Algorithms

At the age of shrouded locale, Gruteser and Grunwald have proposed a versatile stretch Adaptive-Interval Cloaking Algorithms [20]. Their algorithm starts with the root hub of the record tree and partitions the region around the ensured subject until the quantity of subjects in the territory falls underneath k. At that point the calculation restores the parent quadrant as the shrouded district. We embrace this calculation to produce the shrouded territory that is utilized in our arrangement implementation. A realistic representation of versatile span shrouding calculation. In this test, we accept that every one of the hubs $R13, R14, R11, R12, R8, R9, R10$ contain a solitary client. At the point when $k = 5$ and the secured client is situated in hub $R11$, the calculation partitions the zone until it arrives at quadrant R4 which has less subjects than 5. The calculation at that point restores the shrouded district $R1$ which is the parent quadrant of $R4$.

The key thought hidden this calculation is that a given level of namelessness can be kept up in any area—paying little mind to populace thickness—by diminishing the exactness of the uncovered spatial information. To this end, the calculation picks an adequately huge territory, with the goal that enough different subjects possess the region to fulfil the namelessness imperative. The ideal level of secrecy is determined by the boundary k_{min}, the base worthy namelessness set size. Besides, the calculation takes as data sources the current situation of the requester, the directions of the territory secured by the anonymity worker, and the current places of every single other vehicle/subjects in the region.

The spatial discretization calculation that recognizes an adequately enormous territory for a given k_{min}. In run-down, the calculation is inspired by quad tree calculations [22]. It partitions the zone around the subject's position until the quantity of subjects in the territory falls underneath the imperative k_{min}. The past quadrant, which despite everything meets the imperative, is then returned. A symmetrical way to deal with spatial shrouding is fleeting shrouding. This technique can uncover spatial directions with more precision, while diminishing the exactness in time. The key thought is to postpone the solicitation until k_{min} vehicles have visited the territory decided for the requester. The spatial

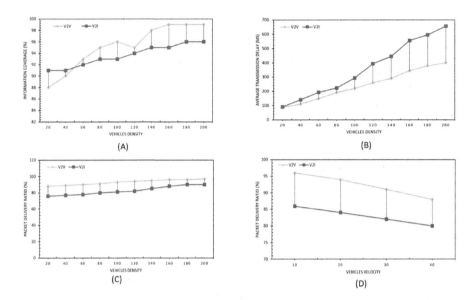

Fig. 5. (A) Information versus vehicle density in VANETs, (B) Average information transmission versus vehicle density in VANETs, (C) Information delay ratio versus vehicle density in VANETs, (D) Information delay ratio versus vehicle velocity in VANETs.

shrouding calculation is altered to take an extra spatial goal boundary as info. It at that point decides the observing zone by isolating the space until the predefined goal is reached. The calculation screens vehicle developments over this region. When k_{min} various vehicles have visited the territory, a period span $[t1, t2]$ is figured as follows: $t2$ is set to the current time, and $t1$ is set to the hour of solicitation short an arbitrary shrouding factor. The zone and the time span are then returned.

4   Results and Analysis

For assessment, we utilized OMNeT++, VEINS, and SUMO to plan the recreation. SUMO was utilized to represent traffic development on streets associated with VEINS by means of Transmission Control Protocol (TCP) attachment, while the development of vehicles was reflected in OMNeT++. VEINS incorporates usage of IEEE 1609.4 and IEEE 802.11p correspondence principles. The reproduction was rehashed multiple times, and the midpoints were accounted for. In our reproductions we just spotlight on V2V and V2I correspondence in the VANETs. In the experiments we only focus on information transmission, average information delay with resect to the vehicles, we also computed the success rate and accuracy of information delivered to the vehicles.

Data inclusion Information inclusion is characterized as the quantity of vehicles getting an emergency information in a vehicular system including N vehicles.

As such, it is the absolute geological region secured by an emergency information. Figure 5(A) delineates a correlation of EM inclusion territory between the V2V and V2I. For the V2V, the inclusion zone at first increments with expanding vehicle thickness yet begins diminishing as the vehicle thickness arrives at 200 vehicles for every km. This is because of the way that with expanding vehicle density, more postponements are acquired in view of blockage. In contrast with V2I, the V2V performs better in a thick domain. With vehicle thickness somewhere in the range of 75 and 125 for every km, the V2V displays more inclusion region looked at V2I. As a demonstrative measure, at 200 vehicles for every km, we watch 9.7% more inclusion territory contrasted with V2I.

Transmission postpone Transmission delay is the measure of time needed to send a whole EM to different vehicles. Figure 5(B) shows the normal transmission delay regarding vehicle thickness. V2I requires calculation on each hub because of its probabilistic sending approach, and thus, experiences extra postponement. This post-pone increments with expanding vehicle thickness. Besides, V2I expects vehicles to send packets to their neighbouring vehicles, causing clog in a thick system, high bundle misfortune, and regular retransmissions. On account of V2I, vehicles spread EMs with high likelihood to vehicles farther separated. Along these lines, this likelihood to advance a message increments directly with expanding separation, prompting the transmission storm issue due to the quantity of repetitive messages. The proposed strategy brings about diminished transmission delays by 14%, 25.7%, and 4.4%.

Packets Drops Ratio (PDR) is the proportion of the quantity of parcels sent by the source vehicle to the number of bundles got at the following bounce objective vehicle. Figure 5(C) shows the impact of expanding vehicle thickness on PDR. In the V2V, at first, when the system inclusion is low, a few messages neglect to convey. Be that as it may, with expanding vehicle sparsity, PDRs are improved. The outcome shows V2I with the most reduced PDR followed by V2V. In general, the V2V shows 5.5%, 19%, and 41% improvement in PDRs contrasted with V2I. Figure 5(D) shows the effect of speed on PDR. The proportion is acceptable at lower speeds, however decays as the vehicles quicken. This decrease is because of the way that high versatility diminishes organize lifetime.

Figure 6(A) shows the normal transmission delay as for vehicle thickness at various guide spans. With shorter guide spans, more messages are generated on the system, which builds the system blockage and unfavourably impacts the EM transmission delay. Figure 6(B) and (C) show the effect on PDR with differing vehicle thickness and speed, individually. In the two cases, the PDRs are brought down when guides are created all the more much of the time.

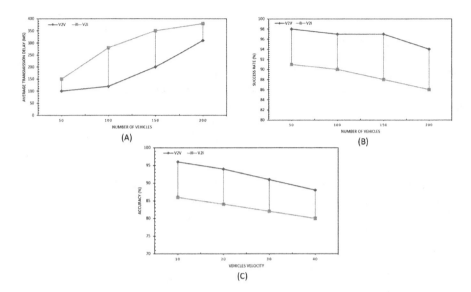

Fig. 6. (A) Average information delay ratio versus vehicles in VANETs, (B) Success rate versus number of vehicles, (C) Accuracy versus vehicles velocity in VANETs.

5   Conclusions

In this paper we proposed a productive strategy wherein we protect the communication privacy in the VANETs. So as to safeguard the both V2V and V2I correspondence privacy, we give the double mode protection. In this, we utilized the FC and data perturbation and after that the anonymization algorithm which is called Adaptive Interval Cloaking Algorithm (AICA). The purpose of FC is manage the information at local level, vehicles can share the different types of information at locally, it reduce the processing and computation time, it also provide the efficient storage and privacy for vehicles information in the VANETs. Besides, we utilized AICA as TTP, yet this TTP doesn't have a clue about the genuine area of the vehicle driver because we applied data perturbation method on information generated by the vehicles in the VANETs. We applied data perturbation to make sure that the information related the vehicle or vehicle driver are secured, because some time we can not confide in the TTP, in light of the fact that, this might be undermined, and the delicate data will uncover. Furthermore we send all these data to TTP and TTP anonymized the inquiry and send to the LBS, and get the ideal outcomes from the LBS and send back to the vehicles or vehicles drive to achieve the desired results.

Acknowledgments. This work was supported in part by the National Natural Science Foundation of China under Grant 61632009 and Grant 61872097, in part by the Guangdong Provincial Natural Science Foundation under Grant 2017A030308006, and in part by the High-Level Talents Program of Higher Education in Guangdong Province under Grant 2016ZJ01.

References

1. Agrawal, D., Aggarwal, C.C.: On the design and quantification of privacy preserving data mining algorithms. In: Proceedings of the Twentieth ACM SIGMOD-SIGACT-SIGART Symposium on Principles of Database Systems, pp. 247–255 (2001)
2. Arif, M., Wang, G.: Cloud-based service oriented architecture for social vehicular ad hoc network communications. Int. J. Commun. Netw. Distrib. Syst. **24**(2), 143–166 (2020)
3. Arif, M., Wang, G., Balas, V.E.: Secure VANETs: trusted communication scheme between vehicles and infrastructure based on fog computing. Stud. Inf. Control **27**(2), 235–246 (2018)
4. Arif, M., Wang, G., Balas, V.E., Geman, O., Castiglione, A., Chen, J.: SDN based communications privacy-preserving architecture for VANETs using fog computing. Veh. Commun. **26**, 100265 (2020)
5. Arif, M., Wang, G., Bhuiyan, M.Z.A., Wang, T., Chen, J.: A survey on security attacks in VANETs: communication, applications and challenges. Veh. Commun. **19**, 100179 (2019)
6. Arif, M., Wang, G., Chen, S.: Deep learning with non-parametric regression model for traffic flow prediction. In: IEEE 16th International Conference on Dependable, Autonomic and Secure Computing, 16th International Conference on Pervasive Intelligence and Computing, 4th International Conference on Big Data Intelligence and Computing and Cyber Science and Technology Congress (DASC/PiCom/DataCom/CyberSciTech), pp. 681–688. IEEE (2018)
7. Arif, M., et al.: SDN-based VANETs, security attacks, applications, and challenges. Appl. Sci. **10**(9), 3217 (2020)
8. Arif, M., Wang, G., Peng, T.: Track me if you can? Query based dual location privacy in vanets for V2V and V2I. In: 17th IEEE International Conference on Trust, Security and Privacy in Computing and Communications/12th IEEE International Conference On Big Data Science And Engineering (TrustCom/BigDataSE), pp. 1091–1096. IEEE (2018)
9. Arif, M., Wang, G., Peng, T., Balas, V.E., Geman, O., Chen, J.: Optimization of communication in VANETs using fuzzy logic and artificial bee colony. J. Intell. Fuzzy Syst. 1–13 (2020, preprint)
10. Arif, M., Wang, G., Wang, T., Peng, T.: SDN-based secure VANETs communication with fog computing. In: Wang, G., Chen, J., Yang, L.T. (eds.) SpaCCS 2018. LNCS, vol. 11342, pp. 46–59. Springer, Cham (2018). https://doi.org/10.1007/978-3-030-05345-1_4
11. Bonomi, F., Milito, R., Zhu, J., Addepalli, S.: Fog computing and its role in the internet of things. In: Proceedings of the First Edition of the MCC Workshop on Mobile Cloud Computing, pp. 13–16 (2012)
12. Bylykbashi, K., Qafzezi, E., Ikeda, M., Matsuo, K., Barolli, L.: Fuzzy-based driver monitoring system (FDMS): implementation of two intelligent FDMSs and a testbed for safe driving in VANETs. Future Gener. Comput. Syst. **105**, 665–674 (2020)
13. Chaum, D.L.: Untraceable electronic mail, return addresses, and digital pseudonyms. Commun. ACM **24**(2), 84–90 (1981)
14. Chen, C.M., Huang, Y., Wang, K.H., Kumari, S., Wu, M.E.: A secure authenticated and key exchange scheme for fog computing. Enterp. Inf. Syst. 1–16 (2020). https://doi.org/10.1080/17517575.2020.1712746

15. Chen, K., Liu, L.: A random rotation perturbation approach to privacy preserving data classification (2005)
16. Chen, K., Liu, L.: A survey of multiplicative perturbation for privacy-preserving data mining. In: Aggarwal, C.C., Yu, P.S. (eds.) Privacy-Preserving Data Mining. Advances in Database SystemsAdvances in Database Systems, vol. 34, pp. 157–181. Springer, Boston (2008). https://doi.org/10.1007/978-0-387-70992-5_7
17. Chen, K., Sun, G., Liu, L.: Towards attack-resilient geometric data perturbation. In: Proceedings of the 2007 SIAM International Conference on Data Mining, pp. 78–89. SIAM (2007)
18. Dastjerdi, A.V., Buyya, R.: Fog computing: helping the internet of things realize its potential. Computer **49**(8), 112–116 (2016)
19. Evfimievski, A., Gehrke, J., Srikant, R.: Limiting privacy breaches in privacy preserving data mining. In: Proceedings of the Twenty-second ACM SIGMOD-SIGACT-SIGART Symposium on Principles of Database Systems, pp. 211–222 (2003)
20. Gruteser, M., Grunwald, D.: Anonymous usage of location-based services through spatial and temporal cloaking. In: Proceedings of the 1st International Conference on Mobile Systems, Applications and Services, pp. 31–42 (2003)
21. Han, M., Liu, S., Ma, S., Wan, A.: Anonymous-authentication scheme based on fog computing for VANET. PLoS One **15**(2), e0228319 (2020)
22. Hjaltason, G.R., Samet, H.: Ranking in spatial databases. In: Egenhofer, M.J., Herring, J.R. (eds.) SSD 1995. LNCS, vol. 951, pp. 83–95. Springer, Heidelberg (1995). https://doi.org/10.1007/3-540-60159-7_6
23. Khattak, H.A., Islam, S.U., Din, I.U., Guizani, M.: Integrating fog computing with VANETs: a consumer perspective. IEEE Commun. Stan. Mag. **3**(1), 19–25 (2019)
24. Liu, K., Xiao, K., Dai, P., Lee, V., Guo, S., Cao, J.: Fog computing empowered data dissemination in software defined heterogeneous vanets. IEEE Trans. Mobile Comput. (2020). https://doi.org/10.1109/TMC.2020.2997460
25. Lu, R., Liang, X., Li, X., Lin, X., Shen, X.: EPPA: an efficient and privacy-preserving aggregation scheme for secure smart grid communications. IEEE Trans. Parallel Distrib. Syst. **23**(9), 1621–1631 (2012)
26. Luan, T.H., Cai, L.X., Chen, J., Shen, X., Bai, F.: VTube: towards the media rich city life with autonomous vehicular content distribution. In: 8th Annual IEEE Communications Society Conference on Sensor, Mesh and Ad Hoc Communications and Networks, pp. 359–367. IEEE (2011)
27. Ning, Z., Huang, J., Wang, X.: Vehicular fog computing: enabling real-time traffic management for smart cities. IEEE Wirel. Commun. **26**(1), 87–93 (2019)
28. Oliveira, S.R.M., Zaïane, O.R.: Achieving privacy preservation when sharing data for clustering. In: Jonker, W., Petković, M. (eds.) SDM 2004. LNCS, vol. 3178, pp. 67–82. Springer, Heidelberg (2004). https://doi.org/10.1007/978-3-540-30073-1_6
29. Poolsappasit, N., Ray, I.: Towards achieving personalized privacy for location-based services. Trans. Data Priv. **2**(1), 77–99 (2009)
30. Sadun, L.A.: Applied Linear Algebra: The Decoupling Principle. American Mathematical Society, Providence (2007)
31. Samarati, P., Sweeney, L.: Protecting privacy when disclosing information: k-anonymity and its enforcement through generalization and suppression (1998)
32. Stewart, G.W.: The efficient generation of random orthogonal matrices with an application to condition estimators. SIAM J. Numer. Anal. **17**(3), 403–409 (1980)
33. Vaquero, L.M., Rodero-Merino, L.: Finding your way in the fog: towards a comprehensive definition of fog computing. ACM SIGCOMM Comput. Commun. Rev. **44**(5), 27–32 (2014)

The 9th International Symposium on Security and Privacy on Internet of Things (SPIoT 2020)

The Theory and Practice of Magic Hash Based Attacks on Lightweight Cryptographic Hash Functions in Complex IoT Environments

Norbert Tihanyi[1,2]([⊠]) and Bertalan Borsos[1]

[1] Faculty of Informatics, Eötvös Loránd University (ELTE), Budapest, Hungary
tihanyi.pgp@gmail.com, bertalanborsos@gmail.com
[2] xen1thLabs, Level 15, Aldar HQ, Abu Dhabi, United Arab Emirates
norbert.tihanyi@digital14.com
https://www.digital14.com

Abstract. In this paper a new type of application layer attack against complex IoT environments is presented which is based on unsafe type-casting and loose comparisons. We describe the concept of magic hashes and explain why they are relevant in IoT platforms from a security point of view. We focus our efforts on lightweight cryptographic hash functions which can be potential candidates for future IoT applications and embedded systems. We present the first known magic hashes for lightweight cryptographic hash function families PHOTON, QUARK and SPONGENT which were designed for constrained environments such as IoT devices. With this, we aim to create a reference point not only for further scientific research but also for practical testing of the above mentioned systems. We also run through calculations on the estimated amount of computation necessary to find hashes with the required characteristics and compare these estimates with empirical results. We conclude with an assessment on the feasibility of finding additional magic hashes with our current computational possibilities.

Keywords: IoT security · Lightweight cryptography · Hash functions · Magic hashes · Loose comparison

1 Introduction

The number of connected devices worldwide is expected to grow exponentially to more than 70 billion by 2025. Simultaneously, the number of use cases for these devices is also growing (cars, pacemakers, refrigerators, fans, lights etc. [1,2]). We can communicate with smart devices and control them using applications, or evaluate values originating from different devices. This can be summarized as the Internet of Things (IoT). The word IoT can be defined as a pervasive and ubiquitous network which enables monitoring and control of the physical environment by collecting, processing, and analyzing the data generated by sensors

© Springer Nature Switzerland AG 2021
G. Wang et al. (Eds.): SpaCCS 2020, LNCS 12383, pp. 93–107, 2021.
https://doi.org/10.1007/978-3-030-68884-4_8

or smart objects [3]. In a complex environment where a high number of embedded systems are connected to each other the protection of each device is key. One of the biggest security-related threats for IoT systems is that these connected devices can become targets of cyberattacks. Quite frequently IoT devices are connected to critical back-end systems such as SCADA, power grid or water distribution control systems. The potential of attacks against these infrastructures is underestimated [4], and most of the classical cyberattacks can be performed much more easily on these infrastructures. To name a few relevant examples, Constantinos et al. analyzed the Mirai botnet and its variants which targeted IP cameras and home routers [5]. This is a good example of a distributed denial of service attack using IoT devices. Jonathan Petit and Steven E. Shladover analyzed the threats on autonomous automated vehicles and cooperative automated vehicles [6] which are gaining more popularity nowadays. Patric Nadert et al. used machine learning techniques to detect cyber attacks against water distribution systems [7]. C. Tranchita et al. evaluated the power systems security with regard to cyberattacks [8].

In most cases IoT devices used in these environments are low-cost RFID tags and sensors which do not have the same processing power or memory capabilities as other computerized systems, hence standard cryptographic primitives are not suitable for IoT endpoints. Lightweight cryptography (LWC) is commonly defined as cryptography for constrained environments including RFID tags, sensors, contactless smart cards and similar devices [9]. In lightweight cryptography a number of key algorithms are known that can be used in embedded devices. Due to the diverse nature of IoT devices, a key challenge in the design of IoT systems is ensuring appropriate device identification and authentication. In a complex IoT environment a sensor is identified by a unique ID (access token) and the IoT Management Platform (IMP) is responsible for identifying every sensor. Data is not collected or analyzed from unauthenticated sensors. IMP's are using standard cryptographic primitives and IoT endpoints are using lightweight cryptographic protocols. Complex IoT environments are a good example of the healthy symbiosis of lightweight cryptography and general purpose IT security. Using strong cryptographic protocols is often considered a satisfactory security control, and in many cases, other security aspects are ignored [10].

The focus and scope of this paper is to show a new type of application layer attack against IoT environments, a so-called "type-juggling" attack on lightweight cryptographic hash functions. Type-juggling attacks rely on certain programming languages dynamically deciding what variable type to cast variables as at comparison time and in some cases this can be used to bypass identification or authentication mechanisms. Type-juggling vulnerabilities using classical cryptographic hash functions have been well known in the security community since 2011. However, for lightweight cryptographic hash functions this is not the case. In this paper we are looking to raise the awareness of IoT developers and the research community regarding this vulnerability through real life case studies. To the best of our knowledge prior to this publication this type of program behavior has not been documented in scientific literature and the threat has not been analyzed in the context of IoT systems. The main contributions of this paper can be summarized as follows:

1. Introducing the concept of type-juggling attacks against IoT systems that are using lightweight cryptographic hash functions and formally defining "magic hashes" (Sect. 2).
2. Presenting our own case study on bypassing sensor identification using the concept of magic hashes (Sect. 3).
3. Using a supercomputing cluster we calculated the first known magic hashes for some of the state of the art lightweight cryptographic hash functions: PHOTON, QUARK and SPONGENT which are potential candidates that will be used in future IoT embedded devices (Sect. 4).

2   The IoT Development Landscape

There are several open-source IoT platforms on the market that are designed for data collection, processing, visualization, and device management. These platforms provide a graphical user interface and make it easy for the operators to observe the status of different IoT systems, interact with the IoT devices, and receive alarms indicating abnormal behavior. Without loss of generality some widely used ones are Zetta, Node-RED or Thingsboard. There are also multiple programming engines for IoT such as JerryScript [11] which is an ultra-lightweight (runs on devices with less than 64 KB of RAM and less than 200 KB of flash memory) JavaScript engine for IoT. CylonJS is a JavaScript framework for robotics, physical computing, and IoT. Ruff is a JavaScript runtime specialized in IoT development and PHPoC (PHP on Chip) is a programming language and an IoT hardware platform. These are all different purpose dashboards or programming engines for IoT systems.

2.1   Implicit Type Conversions

The common thing in all of the above mentioned IoT platforms is that they are built on JavaScript, NodeJS or PHP. All three of these languages are using implicit type conversion and unlike C for example, they do not store values in fixed type variables. Variables are interpreted as belonging to a certain type only when they are used so the actual data being stored can be cast to different variable types. Implicit conversion means a type conversion that happens without explicitly being specified or called for by the user, essentially a conversion handled solely by the inner logic of the language. Such behavior can often be challenging to handle properly even for proficient developers of the language [12,13].

In PHP, NodeJs or JavaScript there are two different operators when it comes to comparisons between constants and variables. These two different operators are called strict comparison and loose comparison, sometimes referred to as type-unsafe and type-safe comparison with the operator symbols being == and ===, respectively. Strict comparison is labeled as "identical" meaning the comparison of two variables or values is only going to be true if their value and also their type is the same. For example, 1 is equal only to 1 (i.e. 1===1) and true is equal only to true (i.e "true"==="true"), however, true is not equal to 1 (i.e true ≠ 1), etc. For loose comparisons this is not necessarily true and some results can indeed be surprising, such as true equal to 1 (i.e. true ==1), or an empty array is equal to 0 (i.e: [ ] == 0). This becomes even more interesting if a string begins with the integer 0 followed by a single e and then an arbitrary number of additional decimal digits (e.g: 0e9172723). These kind of strings are interpreted as scientific notation representations of large integers and all these numbers are equivalent to 0 in the engine's eyes. To be more precise 0e91727233 will be interpreted as $0 \times 10^{91727233} = 0$.

This kind of representation can lead to the unexpected behavior of applications. Importantly, this specific pattern of characters can occur in the hexadecimal string representation of hash digests. This difference between == and === in NodeJS can be observed in Algorithm 1.

Algorithm 1. IMPLICIT TYPE CASTING IN NODEJS

```
1: const c = require('crypto');
2: let str ="240610708";
3: HASH1=c.createHash('md5').update(str).digest("hex");
4: console.log(HASH1);
5: if (0e10==HASH1) console.log("Magic hash, loose comparison");
6: if (0e10===HASH1) console.log("Magic hash, strict comparison");
7: let str2 ="anystring";
8: HASH2=c.createHash('md5').update(str2).digest("hex");
9: console.log(HASH2);
10: if (0e10==HASH2) console.log("Regular hash, loose comparison);
11: if (0e10===HASH2) console.log("Regular hash, strict comparison");
```

Output:
0e462097431906509019562988736854
Magic hash, loose comparison
d6ec7d099972cc954151c53e857b0362

The condition in line number 5 and line number 10 should behave the same, however, this is not the case. The condition in line 5 evaluates to true while the one in line 10 comes back as false. As we can see the MD5 digest of 240610708 is 0e462097431906509019562988736854. NodeJS coverts this number to 0 when using the == operator instead of === and this leads to the condition evaluating to true. The comparison operator will treat it as decimal 0 ($0e46209743 = 0 \times 10^{46209743} = 0$). In line number 6 the same condition evaluation is false, because of the strict comparison being used. This is even more conspicuous in the PHP language as we can see in Algorithm 2.

Algorithm 2. IMPLICIT TYPE CASTING IN PHP

```
1: $str1 = md5('240610708');
2: $str2 = md5('QNKCDZO');
3: echo $str1;
4: if ($str1 == $str2) echo "Magic hash, loose comparison";
5: echo $str2;
6: if ($str1 === $str2) echo "Magic hash, strict comparison";
```

Output:
0e462097431906509019562988736854
Magic hash, loose comparison
0e830400451993494058024219903391

The core issue here is that the implementation uses the type unsafe comparison variant of the language. The 240610708 and QNKCDZO strings would have an md5 digest of the discussed form - starting with zeroes followed by an e and then decimal digits only - and would be interpreted as integer 0, so in line number 4 the if condition evaluates to true.

2.2 Magic Hashes

This language specific behaviour is a classical example of "type juggling" and has been used and exploited in practice in conjunction with some well known classical cryptographic hash functions such as MD5 or SHA1.

In 2011 Gregor Kopf from the Ruhr-Universität Bochum noted that the type unsafe comparison of PHP can be used against standard cryptographic hash functions [14]. In 28 February, 2014 Michal Špaček aka @spazef0rze announced on Twitter that he had found two different strings whose MD5 digests are equivalent using type-unsafe comparison.

$$md5('240610708') == md5('QNKCDZO')$$

These were the first example strings for standard cryptographic hash functions. We call these strings magic strings and the output or digest is referred to as a magic hash. To be more precise we can define magic hashes as follows:

Definition 1. *Let S^* denote the set of arbitrary length strings and let H_n be an arbitrary cryptographic hash function with a digest size of n in hexadecimal string representation. Then, for any $s \in S^*$ for which $f(s)$ is a string of the form $0^l e[0-9]^{n-l-1}$, where $0 \leq l \leq n-2$ we say that s is a magic string for the hash function H_n and $f(s)$ is a magic hash.*

2.3 Practical Examples of Magic Hash Based Vulnerabilities

In December 2014 Dec Jos Wetzels found one of the first 'type juggling' vulnerabilities in the Humhub 0.10 application. Since then numerous web applications have been reported to contain magic hash based type juggling vulnerabilities. For example Teclib GLPI before 9.4.1.1 is affected by a PHP type juggling vulnerability allowing bypass of authentication (CVE-2019-10231). In rare cases, a PHP type juggling vulnerability in centreonAuth.class.php in Centreon Web before 2.8.27 allows attackers to bypass authentication mechanisms (CVE-2018-21020). YOURLS through 1.7.3 is affected by a type juggling vulnerability in the API component that can result in login bypass (CVE-2019-14537). The list is endless for standard web applications. As more and more vulnerabilities were reported the research community became increasingly interested in magic hashes for other hash functions like the SHA family. In 2015 Michael A. Cleverly announced on Twitter [15] that he had found a magic hash for SHA-1 namely for 10932435112 we have 0e077669150041331763470558650263311692244. The first magic hashes larger than 200 bits in size were announced by Norbert Tihanyi on Twitter in June 2019 [16] and July 2019 [17] respectively. For SHA-224(10885164793773) and SHA-256(34250003024812) we have magic hashes. These two strings were the first known magic hashes for the SHA-2 family.

2.4   The Probability of Finding Magic Hashes

In order to understand the distribution of magic hashes we first revisit some underlying connected topics. One of the key characteristics of hash functions that is often mentioned is the avalanche effect, the attribute that suggests - loosely speaking - that even the smallest change in the input will result in a completely different digest with no observable connection to the previous one. Even though not definitively proven, this is expected to be true for all cryptographic hash functions. This would also mean that the outputs, the digests of such a hash function are uniformly distributed in the sense that choosing a random input would produce an output that is equally likely to have any of the 16 possible symbols in any of its positions when represented as a hexadecimal string. In other words, given a randomly chosen input string s and hash function H_n with a digest size of n in hexadecimal string representation, all 16^n outputs $H_n(s)$ have an equal probability. Under this assumption, considering the discrete nature of the problem calculating the probability that given a randomly chosen s input string and a hash function H_n we get a magic hash as output is fairly straightforward and can be considered a Bernoulli trial for our goals and purposes.

The number of possible magic hashes for H_n can be calculated in the following way:

$$M(H_n) = \sum_{i=0}^{n-2} 10^i \qquad (1)$$

We will denote the probability of a single input mapping to a magic hash in a hash function of length n - under the assumption that said function produces images in a uniformly distributed way - with p_n. Considering that according to the definition of a magic hash we can have any number of zeroes in the first positions as long as they are followed by an e and only numbers afterwards, p_n can be calculated in the following way.

$$p_n = \frac{M(H_n)}{16^n} \tag{2}$$

For an 80 bit hash length (20 characters in hexadecimal string representation) this would mean that the probability of finding a magic hash is as follows.

$$p_{20} = \frac{\sum_{i=0}^{18} 10^i}{16^{20}} = \frac{1 + 10 + ... + 10^{18}}{16^{20}} \approx 0.0000009 \tag{3}$$

This probability is quite low and it is easy to see that it will converge to zero with increasing n. We can also note that since we are interested in finding the first hash digest with the magic hash properties the expected value for the required number of attempts - with the random variable following a geometric distribution - is $\frac{1}{p_n}$.

In our practical approach a brute force method was used, simply using randomly chosen inputs, avoiding using the same input twice. As according to our assumption of uniformity there is no difference between inputs, an instinctive heurism is using integers starting from one. As the number of attempts increases so does our chance of finding an input that maps to a magic hash. As we are interested only in finding a single digest with the desired attributes, this can once again be calculated with elementary methods. The inverse probability of a single attempt not yielding a favorable result is $1 - p_n$ for a hash function of length n digest size and the probability of not finding any magic hashes after m attempts is simply $(1 - p_n)^m$. Based on this our probability $q_{m,n}$ will denote the chance of finding a magic string for a hash function of length n digest size after m attempts, which once again holds only under the assumption that the hash function in question produces outputs in a uniformly distributed way. This can be calculated as

$$q_{m,n} = 1 - (1 - p_n)^m = 1 - \left(1 - \frac{M(H_n)}{16^n}\right)^m \tag{4}$$

meaning that for our example of an 80 bit hash function, after performing 5000000 random input operations we would be finding a magic hash with a probability of

$$q_{5000000,20} = 1 - ((1 - p_{20})^{5000000}) \approx 0.9899 \tag{5}$$

In order to find a magic hash with an 90% probability for a 256 bit hash function one would need to try approximately 2.4 quadrillion hashes. Using a device that is able to calculate one million hashes/sec it would require 76 years to find a magic hash. Reaching 99.99% probability with the same architecture would take more than 300 years.

3   Magic Hashes in IoT Systems

Type-unsafe comparisons and magic hashes can prove to be problematic in more complex setups as well. As we noted in the introduction many IoT platforms are using NodeJS, PHP or JavaScript where type-unsafe comparison can be a problem. Node tampering, Side Channel attacks and other "device-close" attacks take place in the Perceptual layer. Node jamming, RFID spoofing and DOS attacks against sensors take place in the Network Layer. "Magic Hash Type-juggling" based on type-unsafe comparisons is a new attack type in the IOT context which belongs to the Application layer. To the best of our knowledge this type of attack has never been used against IoT environments.

3.1   The Odd One Out

We are going to present a short case-study adopted from a real penetration test and cryptanalysis of an IoT environment conducted by the authors in the middle of 2019. There is an IMP and there are connected sensors. The IMP authenticates and identifies sensors by calculated cryptographic hash digests. Calculated hashes are stored in a reference database. In our particular case the IMP is using PHP and the IoT sensors are able to calculate a 128 bit lightweight cryptographic hash function. The hash function which the sensors are using is the PHOTON lightweight cryptographic hash function, namely PHOTON/128/16/16. There are many connected sensors in the system and hence there are many digests in the reference database. If a sensor's calculated hash digest can be found in the database then the sensor is identified as part of the IoT environment.

There is a sensor in the reference database with ID#-47736359. Its calculated PHOTON/128/16/16 hash is 0e7362880619456377800530456862224[1]. The sensor can not be impersonated by other sensors unless there is a hash collision. During the investigation we have identified that the IMP is using type-unsafe comparison and we were able to replace the valid sensor with a malicious one. The attacker needs to find a number whose PHOTON/128/16/16 digest is a magic hash. One can observe that for the string 1270404878 we have 0e93678765974947902859284322793. Because of the type-unsafe comparison the IMP accepted our malicious sensor as an authenticated one.

One can see in Fig. 1 that there are two sensors in the reference database, a malicious one (red) and the original one (green). At comparison time both digests were interpreted as $0 \times 10^{93678765} = 0 \times 10^{73628806} = 0$ and were deemed identical by the system.

$$\text{0e93678765974947902859284322793 } == $$
$$\text{0e7362880619456377800530456862224}$$

This very short case study inspired us to find different magic hashes for different lightweight cryptographic hash functions. These magic hashes can be used to identify type-juggling vulnerabilities in IoT platforms and can be used as reference hashes by the research community in the future. In the next chapter we will present the first known magic hashes for the PHOTON hash family, QUARK hash family and SPONGENT hash family. These lightweight cryptographic hash

---

[1] PHOTON-128(47736359) = 0e7362880619456377800530456862224.

functions are frontrunners for implementation in future IoT systems as they were specifically designed for such constrained environments.

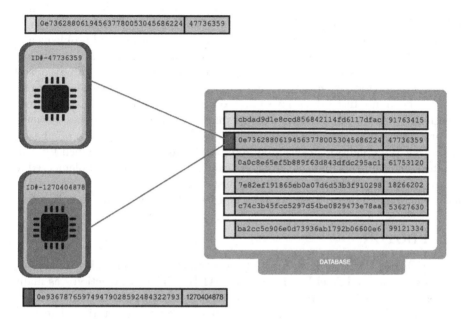

Fig. 1. Malicious sensor with magic hash ID using the PHOTON/128/16/16 lightweight cryptographic hash algorithm. (Color figure online)

4   Computational Results

In this section, we present the numerical results of our computations. As the operations we are performing are essentially a really high number of hash operations, we have to take into consideration the fact that the speed of one hashing - the atomic unit of our calculations - depends heavily on the implementation. In the following section we first present the hash functions we have been working with, then introduce three different hardware environments before calculating how much time each hash variant approximately requires for a magic hash so that these can later be compared to empirical results of actual runs.

4.1   Lightweight Hash Functions

In recent years we witnessed a bloom in the IoT and embedded systems industry and it is only natural that cryptography, a vital component of any security sensitive computer system, has to evolve and keep up with new trends. With the emergence of lightweight cryptography we are witnessing exactly this [18].

However, as lightweight primitives have to be designed with special constraints, some tradeoffs have to be accepted. One of the primary differences one has to deal with is that classical cryptographic primitives usually use a lot of processing power and storage space, none of which is of abundance in a constrained environment like embedded systems and IoT devices. Thus, new primitives had to be created in order to come up with solutions that tackle the original problems and provide alternatives to classical primitives with as little compromise as possible. Surveying recent developments in lightweight cryptography is definitely out of scope for this paper, even only for hash functions, but papers with exactly this goal can be found. Instead, we give a brief description of the three hash functions mentioned earlier without attempting to analyze their exact properties, however we present specific computational results for each. We would like to emphasize again that these lightweight cryptographic hash functions are designed for constrained environments and they are good candidates that will be implemented in future IoT devices and other embedded systems, so the practical usage of these hash functions are more likely as more and more IoT devices are emerging.

4.2   PHOTON

The PHOTON family of hash functions was originally introduced by Jian Guo, Thomas Peyrin, and Axel Poschmann in 2011 [19]. The construction - as many others in lightweight cryptography - follows the sponge design for domain extension and combines it with an AES-like internal unkeyed permutation. The algorithm is very close to being optimal in compactness, reaching around 1120 gate equivalence for 64 bit collision resistance security, while still maintaining good performance in terms of speed and resource consumption. The different members of the family are identified by the triplet $n/r/r'$, where n is the output size, while r and r' denote the input and output bitrate, respectively. At the time of its introduction, five different variants of PHOTON were presented, PHOTON-80/20/16, PHOTON-128/16/16, PHOTON-160/36/36, PHOTON-224/32/32 and PHOTON-256/32/32.

4.3   QUARK

Similarly relying on the sponge construction but using a core permutation inspired by previous primitives to optimize for resource consumption, the QUARK family - introduced in 2012 by Aumasson et al [20] - consists of three members, u-Quark, d-Quark and s-Quark. Similarly to their particle physics counterparts, u-Quark is the "lightest" of the three, followed by d-Quark and then s-Quark. A notable design decision for Quark was the idea to separate the length of the hash function output from the security level, effectively proposing a tradeoff of security level for efficiency. This resulted in the digest sizes of the Quark variants set to more unconventional values, 136, 176 and 256 bits respectively.

4.4   SPONGENT

Introduced in 2011 by Bogdanov et al. [21], the SPONGENT family of hash functions ensures security against some of the most common attacks by using a PRESENT-type primitive. Simultaneously, one of the most attractive qualities of SPONGENT is its flexibility allowing for many different modifications and variants tailored to different purposes. Originally thirteen instances were proposed with five different digest sizes of 88, 128, 160 224 and 256 bits.

4.5   Hardware Details

We used three different computer environments that we will be referring to as Environment A, B, C. Environment A is a regular Mid 2015 MacBook Pro laptop equipped with 2.8 GHz Intel Core i7 4980HQ CPU and 16 GB of RAM. Environment B is a medium class server machine equipped with 2 Xeon E5-2650 v4 2.2 GHz CPU having 24 cores and 48 threads as well as 64 GB of RAM. All lightweight cryptographic magic hashes larger than 128 bits are calculated by the ATLAS Supercomputing Cluster operating in the Eötvös Loránd University denoted by Environment C. The architecture consists of one dedicated Headnode and 44 Computing nodes. The most important characteristics of ATLAS are the following:

1. 88x Intel® Xeon® E5520 Nehalem Quad Core 2.26 GHz Processor with 8 MB cache (HyperThreading ON)
2. 1056 Gbyte RAM

Each Nehalem Quad core CPU has 4 physical cores with SSE extension. Each node has 2×36.256 GFLOP/sec peak performance. There are 44 computing nodes which contain 88 physical CPUs. The total number of physical cores is 352 (4×88). The peak performance of the ATLAS Computing Cluster is $72.512 \times 44 = 3190.528$ GFLOP/sec. FLOPS are calculated with the following formula:

$$\text{FLOPS} = \text{cores} \times \text{GHz} \times 2(\text{SIMD double prec.}) \times 2(\text{MUL}, \text{ADD})$$

Lightweight cryptographic hash functions are not implemented for GPU's like classical hash functions, so calculating lightweight magic hashes is more time consuming than classical ones. For QUARK, PHOTON and SPONGENT the exact hash/sec speed can be seen in Table 1, Table 2 and Table 3 respectively.

Using the $q(m, n)$ function one can see that calculating magic hashes for 256 bit hashes without GPU implementation is far beyond our capacity. For example finding a magic hash with a probability of 90% for the 256 bits s-quark using the ATLAS super cluster takes approximately 143 years:

$$\frac{2400000000000000}{530300 * 3600 * 24 * 365} \approx 143.51 \tag{6}$$

One can see that GPU-based implementations of classical hash functions far outperform the speed of lightweight hash functions. Finding a magic hash for

Table 1. 3 QUARK variant reference code speed

QUARK	Environment A (≈80 GFLOP/sec)	Environment B (≈256 GFLOP/sec)	Environment C (≈3190 GFLOP/sec)
u-136	≈10.400 hash/sec	≈33.200 hash /sec	≈414.700 hash/sec
d-176	≈13.300 hash/sec	≈42.600 hash /sec	≈530.300 hash/sec
s-256	≈13.300 hash/sec	≈42.600 hash/sec	≈530.300 hash/sec

Table 2. 5 PHOTON variant reference code speed

PHOTON	Environment A (≈80 GFLOP/sec)	Environment B (≈256 GFLOP/sec)	Environment C (≈3190 GFLOP/sec)
80	≈1.920.000 hash/sec	≈6.144.000 hash/sec	≈74.820.000 hash/sec
128	≈985.000 hash/sec	≈3.152.000 hash/sec	≈38.415.000 hash/sec
160	≈1.240.000 hash/sec	≈3.968.000 hash/sec	≈48.360.000 hash/sec
224	≈685.000 hash/sec	≈1.192.000 hash/sec	≈26.715.000 hash/sec
256	≈1.280.000 hash/sec	≈4.096.000 hash/sec	≈49.920.000 hash/sec

Table 3. 13 SPONGENT variant reference code speed

SPONGENT	Environment A (≈80 GFLOP /sec)	Environment B (≈256 GFLOP/sec)	Environment C (≈3190 GFLOP/sec)
88-080-008	≈32.000 hash/sec	≈102.400 hash/sec	≈1.276.000 hash/sec
88-176-088	≈47.100 hash/sec	≈150.700 hash/sec	≈1.878.100 hash/sec
128-128-008	≈11.700 hash/sec	≈37.400 hash/sec	≈466.500 hash/sec
128-256-128	≈32.000 hash/sec	≈102.400 hash/sec	≈1.276.000 hash/sec
160-160-016	≈13.300 hash/sec	≈42.600 hash/sec	≈530.300 hash/sec
160-160-080	≈40.000 hash/sec	≈128.000 hash/sec	≈1.595.000 hash/sec
160-320-160	≈16.600 hash/sec	≈53.300 hash/sec	≈662.000 hash/sec
224-224-016	≈6400 hash/sec	≈20.400 hash/sec	≈255.200 hash/sec
224-224-112	≈22.800 hash/sec	≈73.100 hash/sec	≈909.100 hash/sec
224-448-224	≈21.000 hash/sec	≈67.300 hash/sec	≈837.300 hash/sec
256-256-016	≈4.400 hash/sec	≈14.200 hash/sec	≈175.400 hash/sec
256-256-128	≈22.200 hash/sec	≈71.100 hash/sec	≈885.200 hash/sec
256-512-256	≈16.000 hash/sec	≈51.200 hash/sec	≈638.000 hash/sec

SHA-256 is possible using GPU optimized software such as a modified hashcat implementation, but this is not the case for lightweight hash functions. This is the reason that finding magic hashes for lightweight cryptographic hash functions is exponentially harder. However using the ATLAS Computing Cluster we were able to find magic hashes for many different lightweight hash functions, using the non-optimized reference codes of said functions.

Table 4. Calculated magic hashes for Lightweight cryptographic hash functions

Hash type	Magic string	Magic hash
PHOTON-80/20/16	F0I	0e742747199306221255
	Ac63aMnO	0e455521882400797795
	sMZn	0e977811982162876671
	82831	0e667377751846732418
PHOTON-128/16/16	pbdKH?5A	0e01272354457603977680080446960
	47736359	0e73628806194563778005304568622
	TkF(b!l6Pb	0e19417881953241143501203734071
PHOTON-160/36/36	tFJpIXP/	0e5455980179041901489142712643887148232
	eCyX4OPGVNa	0e9739672685729188402065320672680996900
U-QUARK-136	ZundPwf9iBo?	0e13325335111606651366127869934432
	kVL5]YHd')2w	0e55928919040627575902775991439254
SPONGENT-88/80/8	Wmoq1Brofz55	0e8260948788020034453
	59901852	0e1648384782564041117
	ElNx.Lst	0e1632089404941014430
SPONGENT-88/176/88	jL)F%PSM6znt	0e95054134193703151156
	29356510	0e30248137769278438830
	2qO2rw	0e01207343331608349073
SPONGENT-128/128/8	9cCmdzELvp	0e1962246407195858479222590408
	-s-X)vN%Bx	0e4282866883777316744819628127
SPONGENT-128/256/128	QN4xgJKX2O	0e09093110521911601787466702324
	Tu(rNbj4TQ	0e39091216258486456461174806397
	T7y%!stmL'	0e36670351308357323770738742717

4.6   The First Known Magic Hashes for Lightweight Hash Functions

One of the main contributions of this paper is to present calculated magic hashes for the research community. Using the following magic hashes as reference it is possible to identify type-juggling vulnerabilities in different IoT environments. In this section we present the first known magic hashes for PHOTON, QUARK and SPONGENT lightweight cryptographic hash functions. These magic hashes can be seen in Table 4. To the best of our knowledge prior to this publication no magic hashes are calculated for lightweight cryptographic hash functions.

5   Conclusion

The sensor identification bypass technique that we just presented in Sect. 3 has many different variations applicable to different fields of the IoT world. Type-juggling based security issues have been identified several times in the last decade, however these were mostly revolving around web applications written in PHP and authentication schemes using the MD5 hash algorithm, the combination of which provided an environment where calculating these special hash values or even using a precomputed magic hash often resulted in a login bypass. This paper defined magic hashes formally, a concept well known in the security community, but was never investigated in scientific literature especially not for lightweight cryptographic hash functions and IoT systems. The focus area - lightweight hash functions - was more thoroughly explored, presenting the first ever calculated example magic hashes for the most promising lightweight hash functions: PHOTON, QUARK and SPONGENT. At the same time the probability and expected resource cost of finding these special values for them and other variants were calculated. These values can serve as a benchmark for further research and at the same time as a reference point for testing for vulnerabilities of this type. In order to highlight the practical relevance of an attack based on magic hashes an example scenario was presented and live IoT codebases were tested in order to measure how frequently type-unsafe comparison operators are used in real life IoT applications. The authors would like to note that by simply using the type safe variant of comparison operators in affected languages the entire problem can be prevented. However, this would require practitioners of these languages to follow strict coding practices which are difficult to realize in real life. Based on the overall results we conclude that magic hash based vulnerabilities are likely in IoT infrastructures, sensor networks and similar constructions making use of lightweight cryptographic hash functions and the magic values identified during this research can effectively be used to test for and validate such issues.

We urge the IT security community to search for magic hashes for other lightweight cryptographic hash functions so that these values can be used as reference in the future.

Acknowledgments. The authors would like to thank Axel Poschmann for his insightful comments. We would also like to thank Eötvös Loránd University for the opportunity to use the ATLAS Super Cluster.

References

1. Al-Fuqaha, A., Guizani, M., Mohammadi, M., Aledhari, M., Ayyash, M.: Internet of things: a survey on enabling technologies, protocols, and applications. IEEE Commun. Surv. Tutor. **17**(4), 2347–2376 (2015)
2. Dorsemaine, B., Gaulier, J.P., Wary, J.P., Kheir, N., Urien, P.: Internet of Things: a definition & taxonomy. In: 2015 9th International Conference on Next Generation Mobile Applications, Services and Technologies, pp. 72–77. IEEE (2015)
3. Xu, Z., Li, X.: Secure transfer protocol between app and device of internet of things. In: Wang, G., Atiquzzaman, M., Yan, Z., Choo, K.-K.R. (eds.) SpaCCS 2017. LNCS, vol. 10658, pp. 25–34. Springer, Cham (2017). https://doi.org/10.1007/978-3-319-72395-2_3
4. Stellios, I., Kotzanikolaou, P., Psarakis, M., Alcaraz, C., Lopez, J.: A survey of IoT-enabled cyberattacks: assessing attack paths to critical infrastructures and services. IEEE Commun. Surv. Tutor. **20**(4), 3453–3495 (2018)
5. Kolias, C., Kambourakis, G., Stavrou, A., Voas, J.: DDoS in the IoT: Mirai and other botnets. IEEE Comput. **50**(7), 80–84 (2017)

6. Petit, J., Shladover, S.E.: Potential cyberattacks on automated vehicles. IEEE Trans. Intell. Transp. Syst. **16**(2), 546–556 (2015)
7. Nader, P., Honeine, P., Beauseroy, P.: Detection of cyberattacks in a water distribution system using machine learning techniques. In: Sixth International Conference on Digital Information Processing and Communications (ICDIPC), Beirut, pp. 25–30 (2016)
8. Tranchita, C., Hadjsaid, N., Torres, A.: Overview of the power systems security with regard to cyberattacks. In: 2009 Fourth International Conference on Critical Infrastructures, Linkoping, pp. 1–8 (2009)
9. Panasenko, S., Smagin, S.: Lightweight cryptography: underlying principles and approaches. Int. J. Comput. Theory Eng. **3**(4), 516–520 (2011)
10. Schneier, B.: Cryptographic design vulnerabilities. IEEE Comput. **31**(9), 29–33 (1998)
11. Garrin, E., Lee, S., Ayrapetyan, R., Shitov, A.: Ultra lightweight JavaScript engine for internet of things. In: SPLASH Companion: Companion Proceedings of the 2015 ACM SIGPLAN International Conference on Systems. Software for Humanity, Programming, Languages and Applications (2015)
12. Pradel, M., Sen, K.: The good, the bad, and the ugly: an empirical study of implicit type conversions in JavaScript. In: 29th European Conference on Object-Oriented Programming (ECOOP 2015) (2015)
13. Eshkevari, L., Dos Santos, F., Cordy, J.R., Antoniol, G.: Are PHP applications ready for hack? In: 2015 IEEE 22nd International Conference on Software Analysis, Evolution, and Reengineering (SANER) (2015)
14. Kopf, G.: Non-obvious bugs by example. In: 9th CCONFidence Conference (2011)
15. Cleverly, M.A.: https://twitter.com/macleverly/status/597969666598801409, May 2015 Twitter announcement
16. Tihanyi, N.: https://twitter.com/TihanyiNorbert/status/1138075224010833921, June 2019 Twitter announcement
17. Tihanyi, N.: https://twitter.com/TihanyiNorbert/status/1148586399207178241, July 2019 Twitter announcement
18. Mckay, K., Bassham, L., Turan, M., Mouha, N.: Report on Lightweight Cryptography NISTIR 8114 (2017)
19. Guo, J., Peyrin, T., Poschmann, A.: The PHOTON family of lightweight hash functions. In: Rogaway, P. (ed.) CRYPTO 2011. LNCS, vol. 6841, pp. 222–239. Springer, Heidelberg (2011). https://doi.org/10.1007/978-3-642-22792-9_13
20. Aumasson, J.-P., Henzen, L., Meier, W., Naya-Plasencia, M.: QUARK: a lightweight hash. J. Cryptol. **26**(2), 313–339 (2012). https://doi.org/10.1007/s00145-012-9125-6
21. Bogdanov, A., Knežević, M., Leander, G., Toz, D., Varıcı, K., Verbauwhede, I.: SPONGENT: a lightweight hash function. In: Preneel, B., Takagi, T. (eds.) CHES 2011. LNCS, vol. 6917, pp. 312–325. Springer, Heidelberg (2011). https://doi.org/10.1007/978-3-642-23951-9_21

Efficient Public Key Cryptography Scheme with Equality Test for Heterogeneous Systems in IIoT

Abdelrhman Hassan[1], Rashad Elhabob[2], Umar Ibrahim[1], and Yong Wang[1(✉)]

[1] School of Computer Science and Engineering, University of Electronic Science and Technology of China, Chengdu 611731, China
cla@uestc.edu.cn
[2] School of Information and Software Engineering, University of Electronic Science and Technology of China, Chengdu 610054, China

Abstract. Industrial Internet of Things (IIoT) incorporates various varieties of smart devices and communication technologies that allow organizations to move from conventional industries to smart industries. IIoT provides cost-saving and collaboration since it relies on the availability, flexibility, and powerful processing capabilities of the cloud server. Considering the cloud's untrusted nature, it is essential to protect the IIoT data before uploading it to the server. However, encryption yields a further critical issue. Due to the "All-or-Nothing" decryption characteristic, it is impractical for the users of another public-key cryptosystem to download all the data stored on the server to obtain their needs. In resolving this issue, this paper proposes Efficient Public-Key Cryptography with Equality Test scheme for Heterogeneous Systems (PKC-ET-HS). The PKC-ET-HS scheme incorporates the notions of Certificateless Public-Key Encryption with Equality Test (CL-PKE-ET) as well as the Identity-Based Encryption with Equality Test (IBE-ET). The scheme enables the cloud server to check whether two ciphertexts having their encryptions performed under a heterogeneous systems contain identical messages. Moreover, in the Random Oracle Model (ROM), the modified Bilinear Diffie-Hellman Intractable (mDBHI) assumption is stated to construct the security of the suggested scheme. Ultimately, the performance evaluation authenticates that the suggested scheme is practicable and convenient for IIoT environments.

Keywords: Industrial Internet of Things · Cloud computing · Equality test for heterogeneous systems · Public-key cryptography

1 Introduction

Recently, as part of the Internet of Things (IoT) [1,2], the Industrial Internet of Things (IIoT) has emerged rapidly, which is looking at industrial applications. IIoT is an advanced heterogeneous network that incorporates numerous

G. Wang et al. (Eds.): SpaCCS 2020, LNCS 12383, pp. 108–121, 2021.
https://doi.org/10.1007/978-3-030-68884-4_9

actuators, sensors, or smart devices connecting to the Internet through the wireless communication technologies [3]. These devices can frequently accumulate and exchange data with humans to support more comfortable services such as production control, device maintenance, etc. [4]. Besides enhancing the manufacturing performance, IIoT dramatically decreases the operational expenses and capital compared with traditional industries. Nevertheless, with the massive increase of data in IIoT, the storage, and processing of a big data remain a significant challenge [5]. Fortunately, cloud computing is a viable solution [6], as it takes and advantage of powerful processing capability, unlimited virtual storage, high availability, and low cost. In cloud-assisted IIoT [4], the massive accumulated data is uploaded to the cloud server. The cloud then enhances the IIoT data processing and transmission as well as permits a reliable computing services to users regardless of locations and time constraints.

Although the incorporation of IIoT and cloud computing provides tremendous business advantages and technical benefits, it inherits various security and privacy challenges that hinder the widespread deployment and adoption of the cloud-assisted IIoT. Since the cloud is deemed untrusted, it is challenging to communicate private data to the cloud without prior protection [7]. Encryption then outsourcing is an ideal method to protect the confidentiality of data [8]. However, this method hinders the availability of IIoT data, as it is difficult to search for encrypted data. In an attempt to handle this impairment, Boneh et al. [9] suggested a Public-Key Encryption with Keyword Search (PKE-KS) scheme to support search functionality on the encrypted data without decrypting it. Nevertheless, the scheme is only functioning effectively with the ciphertexts encrypted with the same public-key. Yang et al. [10] designed a PKE scheme supporting the Equality Test known as (PKE-ET) which permits users to perform the equality test on encryptions with the identical public-key as well as those encrypted with different public keys. Obviously, their scheme suffered from the certificate management problems due to conventional Public-Key Infrastructure (PKI). Ma et al. [11] presented an IBE-ET scheme incorporating the notions of the PKE-ET and the Identity-Based Cryptosystem (IBC). This technique was a step forward in that the user's identity was used as his public-key and thus eliminated the certificates management problem in [10]. However, the scheme experience difficulties with the key escrow problem. To solve this problem, Al-Riyami et al. [12] came up with the concept of CertificateLess Public-Key Cryptography (CL-PKC). With the CL-PKC scheme, the private keys of users were kept in two folds, with one-fold in the user's possession and the other in the custody of the Key Generator Center (KGC). KGC then does not have a way to acquire user's data which makes it secure. Based on the idea of Certificateless Encryption (CLE), Qu et al. [13] presented the notion of Certificateless Public Key Encryption with Equality Test (CL-PKE-ET). Taking an exact look at these schemes, one can conclude that these techniques are effective in situations where the public-key cryptography is the same; in other words, homogeneous in nature. Practically, the cloud-assisted IIoT including various cryptosystems and the above schemes are not suitable for heterogeneous cloud-assisted IIoT environment. To address this issue, we suggest a PKC-ET-HS scheme to provide efficient search functionality for heterogeneous systems in the IIoT. Considering a typical scenario of the IIoT environment in a nutshell where the smart sensors frequently gather the IIoT data from the manufacturing department and then transmit it via the internet to the cloud server to be accessible elsewhere (as illustrated in Fig. 1). Particularly, since the IBE system is a one of the few technologies that can achieve user identity authentication and secure data transmission over the networks, sensors usually choose to use the IBE system to encrypt data. To avoid the key escrow problem of the IBE, most users use the CLE-cryptosystem to encrypt their data. When a user wishes to search on remote encrypted data, the user uses his public key to create a trapdoor and convey it to the cloud. By utilizing its massive storage capacity and computing capabilities, the cloud can proceed with the test and sends the result back to the user.

Fig. 1. An application scenario for IIoT.

The contribution of this work is summarized as follows:

1. We introduce the definition and security model of the PKC-ET-HS by integrating the notions of the IBE-ET and CL-PKE-ET cryptosystems. The PKC-ET-HS allows the server to check the equality of two different ciphertexts belonging to IBE and CLE cryptosystems.
2. We present the construction of PKC-ET-HS scheme based on the bilinear pairing, and based on ROM, we state the security of PKC-ET-HS to be equal to the mBDHI assumption.
3. The experimental results shows that the PKC-ET-HS scheme outperforms the other similar schemes, which make it suitable for the IIoT environment.

2   Related Work

Yang et al. [10] proposed a PKE-ET scheme to permit the server to check if two identical or different ciphertexts encapsulate the same plaintext. Accordingly, Tang [14] proposed FG-PKE-ET scheme that incorporate fine grained authorization with equality test. The scheme permits only two users to process the equivalence test. Furthermore, another scheme was designed by Tang, known as all-or-nothing PKE-ET [15]. The refined scheme can decide who would have a permission to perform the equality test. Ma et al. [16] devised PKE-DET scheme that incorporates a PKE with delegated equality test. Thereafter, a scheme that involved authorized equality test i.e. PKE-AET was designed in [17]. However, as the basis of PKE-ET, PKI system will cause certificate management problems which greatly increase the overhead of the system [18]. As an extension of this work, the identity-based encryption put forward as shown in [11,18,19] to handle the limitations of PKE-ET scheme. Noticeably, the ID-based scheme confronted difficulties due to the key escrow problem [5]. A new research direction was introduced by Qu et al. [13]. The idea incorporates the certificateless public-key cryptography with equality test. Based on this idea, various CL-PKE-ET schemes have been presented such as [4,5,20]. Taking a clear look at all the above mentioned works, one can conclude that these scheme are effective in a situation where the public-key is same which make them unsuitable for heterogeneous IIoT environment. To enable the cloud to perform the equivalence test between two different ciphertexts belong to different cryptosystems, there is a need to construct an efficient and secure scheme that supports a heterogeneous equivalence test.

In solving the above problem, the recent work on heterogeneous equivalence test has hence sprouted as shown by [3,21–23]. Elhabob et al. [21] proposed a hybrid scheme that incorporates the CLE system and PKI systems to support a heterogeneous equality test. The scheme enables the server to check whether two ciphertexts encryptions belong to different cryptosystems encapsulating the identical message. Similarly, the work in [22] presented a heterogeneous equality test scheme in which a user of the CLE and IBE systems can transmit messages to each other. Another heterogeneous equality test scheme proposed in [23] integrates the PKI and IBE systems supporting heterogeneous equality test in IoT environments. Further, inspired by the idea of signcryption with heterogeneous systems proposed in [24], Xiong et al. [3] designed a signcryption with equivalence test scheme for heterogeneous systems in IIoT environment. Nevertheless, due to many pairing operations, these schemes are still inefficient and unsuitable for the cloud-assisted IIoT environments, whereas the lightweight IIoT devices have a limited computing power, network bandwidth, capacity, and battery lifetime.

3   Definition

3.1   Preliminaries

Bilinear Map. Considering two additive and multiplicative cyclic groups $\mathbb{G}_1$ and $\mathbb{G}_2$ with the same prime order p, respectively; P is a generator of group $\mathbb{G}_1$. $e : \mathbb{G}_1 \times \mathbb{G}_1 \to \mathbb{G}_2$ is a bilinear map if the following properties hold:

1. Bilinearity: $\forall R, S \in \mathbb{G}_1$, and $a, b \in \mathbb{Z}_p^*$, $e(aR, bS) = e(R, S)^{ab}$.
2. Non-degeneracy: $\forall R \in \mathbb{G}_1$, $e(R, R) \neq 1 \in \mathbb{G}_2$.
3. Computability: $\forall R, S \in \mathbb{G}_1$, $e(R, S)$ can be computed.

Hardness Problem. Provided by the groups $\mathbb{G}_1$ and $\mathbb{G}_2$ with the same prime order p, respectively; P is a generator of group $\mathbb{G}_1$; and $e : \mathbb{G}_1 \times \mathbb{G}_1 \to \mathbb{G}_2$ is an admissible bilinear map. Given $< P, aP, b >$, then computes $e(P, P)^{\frac{1}{a+b}}$, where $a, b \in \mathbb{Z}_p^*$ [25].

3.2 System Model

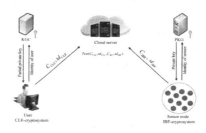

Fig. 2. A system model for PKC-ET-HS

The system model for PKC-ET-HS is illustrated in Fig. 2. It composes of following parties, KGC, PKG, cloud server, sensor node, and authorized user. The parties of the system work as follows: Regarding the CLE-cryptosystem, an authorized user submits his identity to the KGC, then KGC respond with corresponding partial private-key to the user. Similarly, the sensor node received the private-key after submits the identity to the PKG. Then, both an authorized user and sensor node calculate the trapdoors td_{CLE} and td_{IBE}, respectively. The sensor node uses its private-key to encrypt the data and convey it along with td_{IBE} to the cloud. When authorized user wishes to return such data, he generates a query trapdoors td_{CLE} and conveys it to the cloud server. Then, the cloud performs the test equivalence on td_{CLE} and td_{IBE}, considering different cryptosystems and sends the results to the authorized user.

3.3 Security Model

According to [13, 26] we define the One-Way Chosen Ciphertext Attack (OW-CCA) opposed to the adversary in PKC-ET-HS scheme. We denote by PKC-ET-HS-CLC to the case that users related to the CLE-cryptosystem, and PKC-ET-HS-IBE to those who are related to the IBE cryptosystem.

Definition 1: Regarding the security of PKC-ET-HS-CLE scheme, we consider $Type_1$ and $Type_2$ adversaries. The adversary $Type_1$ denoted as $\mathcal{A}_1$ adversary who is ables to modify any user's public-key, but cannot returns the master private-key. The adversary $Type_2$ denoted as $\mathcal{A}_2$ can access the system's private-key, but cannot be able to replace the user's public-key.

Game-1: Given λ as a security parameter, the adversary $\mathcal{A}_1$ and the challenger $\mathcal{C}$ play the following game:

1. **Setup:** $\mathcal{C}$ establishes the public parameters $parms_{CLE}$ and master private-key mpk. Eventually, $\mathcal{C}$ retrieves $parms_{CLE}$.
2. **Phase 1:** $\mathcal{A}_1$ is permitted to make the below queries:

- *Partial private-key queries(ID_i):* $\mathcal{C}$ submits ID_i to $\mathcal{A}_1$.
- *Private-key queries (ID_i):* $\mathcal{C}$ submits sk_{CLE_i} to $\mathcal{A}_1$.
- *Public-key queries(ID_i):* $\mathcal{C}$ submits pk_{CLE_i} to $\mathcal{A}_1$.
- *Replace public-key queries:* $\mathcal{C}$ replaces pk_{CLE_i} of a user with pk'_{CLE_i}.
- *Decryption-queries:* It run by $\mathcal{C}$ in **CLE-Decrypt**(C_i, sk_{CLE_i}), where sk_{CLE_i} is a private-key corresponds to ID_i. Lastly, $\mathcal{C}$ submits M_i to $\mathcal{A}_1$.
- *Trapdoor queries:* C establishes tdr_{CLE_i} and tdr_{IBE_j} using **CLE-Trapdoor** and **IBE-Trapdoor** algorithms, respectively. Lastly, C gives tdr_{CLE_i} and tdr_{IBE_j} to A_1.

3. **Challenge:** $\mathcal{C}$ selects a message $M \in \{0,1\}^n$ randomly, the challenge identity ID_ξ, and computes $C' = (ID_\xi, M)$. Lastly, $\mathcal{C}$ submits C' to $\mathcal{A}_1$.
4. **Phase 2:** The response of $\mathcal{C}$ to $\mathcal{A}_1$ in similar to that in **Phase 1** except on the ground that:
   - ID_ξ should not appear in *Private-key queries.*
   - If the public-key corresponded to (ID_i) is replaced, the ID_ξ should not appear in the *Partial private-key queries.*
   - (ID_ξ, C') should not appear in *Decryption-queries*
5. **Guess:** $\mathcal{A}_1$ returns M', and wins if $M = M'$. The $\mathcal{A}_1$'s advantage is given as follows: $Adv^{OW-CCA,PKC-ET-HS-CLE}_{PKC-ET-HS,\mathcal{A}_1}(\lambda) = \Pr[M = M']$.

Game-2: Given the security parameter λ, the adversary $\mathcal{A}_2$ and the challenger $\mathcal{C}$ play the following game:

1. **Setup:** $\mathcal{C}$ establishes the public parameters $parms_{CLE}$ and master private-key mpk. Finally, $\mathcal{C}$ sends $parms_{CLE}$ and mpk to $\mathcal{A}_2$.
2. **Phase 1:** $\mathcal{A}_2$ makes queries as in **Game-1** except the *Partial private-key queries* and *Replace public-key queries* is not considered.
3. **Challenge:** $\mathcal{C}$ chooses $M \in \{0,1\}^n$ randomly, and calculates $C' = $ **CLE-Encrypt**(ID_ξ, M). Lastly, $\mathcal{C}$ submits C' to $\mathcal{A}_2$.
4. **Phase 2:** The response of $\mathcal{C}$ to $\mathcal{A}_2$ is similar to that in **Phase 1:** except on the ground that ID_ξ did not query in *Private-key queries*, and (ID_ξ, C') did not query in *Decryption-queries.*
5. **Guess:** $\mathcal{A}_2$ returns M', and wins if $M = M'$. The $\mathcal{A}_2$'s advantage is given as follows: $Adv^{OW-CCA,PKC-ET-HS-CLE}_{PKC-ET-HS,\mathcal{A}_2}(\lambda) = \Pr[M = M']$.

Definition 2: The PKC-ET-HS-IBE scheme is OW-ID-CCA secure if for any OW-ID-CCA adversary $\mathcal{A}$ has a non-negligible advantage.

1. **Setup:** provided with λ as a security parameter, $\mathcal{C}$ executes the algorithm **Setup**. Then, $\mathcal{C}$ give the $parms_{IBE}$ to $\mathcal{A}$ and stores the mpk secret.
2. **Phase 1:** $\mathcal{A}$ has a permission to make the following queries:
   - *Key-generation queries:* $\mathcal{C}$ runs **IBE-PKG** and submits dk_{IBE} to $\mathcal{A}$.
   - *Decryption-queries(ID_i, C_i):* $\mathcal{C}$ runs **IBE-Decrypt**, and sends M to $\mathcal{A}$.
   - *Trapdoor queries:* C establishes tdr_{CLE_i} and tdr_{IBE_j} using **CLE-Trapdoor** and **IBE-Trapdoor** algorithms, respectively. Eventually, C submits tdr_{CLE_i} and tdr_{PKI_j} to A.

3. **Challenge:** $\mathcal{C}$ selects M randomly, and computes
$C^* = $ **IBE-Encrypt**(ID^*, M). $\mathcal{C}$ sends the challenge ciphertext C^* to $\mathcal{A}$.
4. **Phase 2:** $\mathcal{C}$ replies to $\mathcal{A}$ in similar way as in **Phase 1** except on the constraints that ID^* should not appear in *Key generation queries*, and (ID^*, C^*) should not appear in *Decryption-queries*
5. **Guess:** $\mathcal{A}$ retrieves M' and wins if $M = M'$. The advantage of $\mathcal{A}$ is given as follows: $Adv_{PKC-ET-HS,\mathcal{A}}^{OW-CCA,PKC-ET-HS-IBE}(\lambda) = \Pr[M = M']$.

4   The Construction of the PKC-ET-HS Scheme

In this section, we first define the algorithms of the PKC-ET-HS scheme. Then, we present the concrete construction of the proposed scheme. Table 1 provides a detailed description of the notations used in the paper.

Table 1. The summery of notations.

Notation	Description
H_i	A one way hash functions, where $(1 \leq i \leq 4)$
mpk	A master private-key
$parms$	The public parameters
D_{ID}	A partial private-key in CLE system
pk_{ID}	A user public-key in CLE system
sk_{CLE}	A user private-key in CLE system
dk_{IBE}	A receiver's decryption-key in IBE system
$\oplus$	The bitwise XOR operation
$\|$	The concatenation operation
$\mathbb{F}_q$	The finite field with primary order q

4.1   Definition

The algorithms of the PKC-ET-HS scheme are defined as follows:

1. **Setup:** It takes a security parameter λ as input, and outputs the system parameters, the public parameters $parms$ and a master private-key mpk.
2. **CLE-PKG:** The following algorithms generate the private-key of the CLE-cryptosystem:
   - **Partial private-key:** It runs by KGC. Given $parms$, mpk and the user's identity ID as input, it returns the Partial private-key D_{ID}.
   - **User-key generation:** It runs by the user, given $parms$, and ID as input, it returns a user-key pk_{ID}.

- **Assign private-key:** It runs by the user, given $parms$, D_{ID}, and pk_{ID} as inputs, it outputs a user's private-key sk_{CLE}.
3. **CLE-Trapdoor:** It takes as input sk_{CLE} of the CLE-cryptosystem, and returns a Trapdoor tdr_{CLE}.
4. **IBE-PKG:** It generates a private-key of the IBE users. The IBE user sends his identity ID to the PKG. Then, the PKG generates the corresponding decryption-key dk_{IBE} and sends it back to the user.
5. **IBE-Trapdoor:** It takes as input sk_{IBE} of the IBE-cryptosystem, and returns a Trapdoor tdr_{IBE}.
6. **CLE-Encrypt:** It execute by the CLE users. It takes a message M and receiver's public key pk_{ID}, it returns the ciphertext C.
7. **CLE-Decrypt:** It runs by the CLE users. It takes as inputs a ciphertext C and the secret-key sk_{CLE}, and returns the plaintext M. Else, it returns $\perp$.
8. **IBE-Encrypt:** It execute by the IBE users. Provided by a message M and receiver's identity ID, it returns the ciphertext C.
9. **IBE-Decrypt:** It runs by the IBE users. It takes as inputs C, and the receiver's decryption-key dk_{IBE}, and returns M. Else, it returns $\perp$.
10. **Test-algorithm:** It runs by the cloud server. It takes C_{CLE} and tdr_{CLE} of the user in the CLE-cryptosystem, as well as C_{IBE} and tdr_{IBE} of the user in the IBE-cryptosystem as inputs. Then, it returns 1 if C_{CLE}, and C_{IBE} encapsulate the same message. Else, it returns $\perp$.

4.2   Concrete Construction

1. **Setup:** Provided by λ, the algorithm **Setup:** performs the following:
   - Creates a groups $\mathbb{G}_1$ and $\mathbb{G}_2$ of prime order p, $e : \mathbb{G}_1 \times \mathbb{G}_1 \rightarrow \mathbb{G}_2$ is an admissible bilinear map, and a random generators $P \in \mathbb{G}_1$
   - Selects the hash functions: $H_1 : \{0,1\}^n \rightarrow \mathbb{Z}_p^*$, $H_2 : \mathbb{G}_1 \rightarrow \mathbb{Z}_p^*$, $H_3 : \mathbb{G}_2 \rightarrow \{0,1\}^{n+l}$, $H_4 : \mathbb{G}_2 \rightarrow \mathbb{Z}_p^*$. Where, $n = |\mathbb{G}_1|$ and $l = |\mathbb{Z}_p^*|$.
   - Selects $x, x' \in \mathbb{Z}_p^*$ and set the public-keys $P_{pub} = xP, P'_{pub} = x'P$.
   - Finally, publishes the parameters:
     $parms = \{p, P, \mathbb{G}_1, \mathbb{G}_2, e, H_1, H_2, H_3, H_4, P_{pub}, P'_{pub}\}$.
2. **CLE-PKG:** The algorithm creates the public-key and the private-key. It performs as follows:
   - *Partial private-key:* provided by a string $ID \in \{0,1\}^*$, calculates $h_{ID} = H_1(ID)$ and *Partial private-key:* $D_{ID} = (D_1, D_2) = (\frac{1}{h_{ID}+x}P, \frac{1}{h_{ID}+x'}P)$.
   - *User-key generation:* The algorithm takes $parms$ and D_{ID} as input, then chooses $s_{ID} \in \mathbb{Z}_p^*$, and produces the public-key as:

$$pk_{ID} = (pk_1, pk_1) = (s_{ID}(h_{ID} + P_{pub}), s_{ID}(h_{ID} + P'_{pub})).$$

   - *Assign private-key:* It takes $parms$, and D_{ID}, and s_{ID} then produces the full private-key, $sk_{CLE} = (sk_1, sk_2) = (\frac{1}{s_{ID}+h_1}D_1, \frac{1}{s_{ID}+h_2}D_2)$, where, $h_1 = H_2(pk_1), h_2 = H_2(pk_2)$.

3. **CLE-Trapdoor:** It takes sk_i from the user U_i in CLE-cryptosystem as input, and outputs a Trapdoor $tdr_{CLE} = sk_2 = \frac{1}{s_{ID}+h_2}D_2$.

4. **IBE-PKG** The user of IBE-cryptosystem submits his identity ID to its **IBE-PKG** which calculates $h_{ID} = H_1(ID)$. Then, it calculates $dk_{IBE} = (dk_1, dk_2) = (\frac{1}{h_{ID}+x_1}P, \frac{1}{h_{ID}+x_2}P)$.

5. **IBE-Trapdoor:** It takes sk_{IBE} from the user of IBE-cryptosystem as input, and outputs a Trapdoor $tdr_{IBE} = dk_2 = \frac{1}{h_{ID}+x_2}P$.

6. **CLE-Encrypt:** It takes a message $M \in \{0,1\}^n$, ID, $pk_{ID} = (pk_1, pk_2)$ as inputs and works as follows:
   - Chooses a two random numbers $r_1, r_2 \in \mathbb{Z}_p^*$.
   - Calculates $C_1 = r_1(pk_1 + h_1(h_{ID}P + P_{pub}))$, $C_2 = r_2(pk_2 + h_2(h_{ID}P + P'_{pub}))$, $C_3 = (M \parallel r_2) \oplus H_3(g^{r_1})$, $C_4 = (m \cdot r_2) \cdot H_4(g^{r_2})$, $m = H_1(M)$.

7. **CLE-Decrypt:** It takes C and private-key sk_{CLE} of the user in **CLE** cryptosystem, and returns the message M by performs the following:
   - Calculates $(M \parallel r_2) = C_3 \oplus H_3(e(C_1, sk_1))$.
   - Verifies $C_2 = r_2(pk_2 + h_2(h_{ID}P + P'_{pub}))$ and $\frac{C_4}{H_1(M).r_2} = H_4(e(C_2, sk_2))$. If the verifies hold, it retrieves 1, else it retrieves $\perp$.

8. **IBE-Encrypt:** It takes the $M \in \{0,1\}^n$, ID, and the randoms $r_1, r_2 \in \mathbb{Z}_P^*$ as inputs. and works as follows:
   - Calculates the ciphertext $C_1 = r_1(h_1(h_{ID}P + P_{pub}))$, $C_2 = r_2(h_2(h_{ID}P + P'_{pub}))$, $C_3 = (M \parallel r_2) \oplus H_3(g^{r_1})$, $C_4 = (m \cdot r_2) \cdot H_4(g^{r_2})$, $m = H_1(M)$.

9. **IBE-Decrypt:** It takes dk_{IBE} of the user in IBE-cryptosystem and the ciphertext C as input, and performs the following:
   - Calculates $(M \parallel r_2) = C_3 \oplus H_3(e(C_1, dk_1))$.
   - Verifies $C_2 = r_2(h_2(h_{ID}P + P'_{pub}))$ and $\frac{C_4}{H_1(M).r_2} = H_4(e(C_2, dk_2))$. If the verifies hold, it retrieves M. Else, it retrieves $\perp$.

10. **Test-algorithms:** $Test_1(C_i, td_{CLE}, C_j, td_{IBE})$ Suppose there is a tow users U_i and U_j of the PKC-ET-HS. Suppose that U_i uses a CLE-cryptosystem and U_j uses IBE-cryptosystem, with their corresponding ciphertext C_i and C_j respectively. The Test algorithms are constructed as fallows:

$$Y_i = e(td_{CLE_i}, C_{i,2}) = e(sk_{i,2}, C_{i,2}), = e(sk_{i,2}, r_{i,2}(pk_{i,2} + h_{2_i}(h_{ID_i}P + P'_{pub}))),$$

$$= e((\frac{1}{s_{ID_i} + h_{2_i}})D_2, r_{i,2}(pk_{i,2} + h_{2_i}(h_{ID_i}P + P'_{pub}))), = e((\frac{1}{s_{ID_i}} + h_{2_i})D_2,$$

$$r_{i,2}(s_{ID_i}(h_{ID_i}P + P'_{pub})) + h_{2_i}(h_{ID_i}P + P'_{pub}))),$$

$$= e((\frac{1}{s_{ID_i} + h_{2_i}})D_2, r_{i,2}(h_{ID_i}P + P'_{pub})(s_{ID_i} + h_{2_i}))),$$

$$= e((\frac{1}{h_{ID_i} + x'})P, r_{i,2}(h_{ID_i}P + P'_{pub})), = e(P, r_{i,2}P) = g^{r_{i,2}}.$$

$$Z_i = \frac{C_{i,4}}{H_4(e(td_{CLE_i}, C_{i,2}))} = \frac{(m_i \cdot r_{i,2}) \cdot H_4(g^{r_{i,2}})}{H_4(g^{r_{i,2}})} = m_i \cdot r_{i,2}.$$

$$Y_j = e(td_{IBE_j}, C_{j,2}) = e(dk_{j,2}, C_{j,2}), = e(dk_{j,2}, r_{j,2}(h_{ID_j} \cdot P + P'_{pub})),$$

$$= e(\frac{1}{h_{ID_j} + x_2})P, r_{j,2} \cdot (h_{ID_j} \cdot P + x_2 P)),$$

$$= e(\frac{1}{h_{ID_j} + x_2}P, r_{j,2} \cdot P \cdot (h_{ID_j} + x_2))) = e(P, P)^{r_{j,2}} = g^{r_{j,2}}.$$

$$Z_j = \frac{C_{j,4}}{H_4(e(td_{IBE_i}, C_{i,2}))} = \frac{(m_j \cdot r_{j,2}) \cdot H_4(g^{r_{j,2}})}{H_4(g^{r_{j,2}})} = m_j \cdot r_{j,2}.$$

The *Test* returns 1, if $(Y_i)^{Z_j} = (Y_j)^{Z_i}$. Else, it returns $\perp$.

5   Security Analysis

The security proof of the suggested scheme is similar to that in [13] and [26]. The theorems is given as follows:

Theorem 1: Suppose that the mBDHI problem is hard and H_1, H_2, H_3, H_4 are random oracles. The suggested PKC-ET-HS-CLE is OW-CCA secure under the ROM. Suppose the $Type_1$ adversary $\mathcal{A}_1$ has advantage ϵ' versus PKC-ET-HS-CLE scheme. Also suppose that $\mathcal{A}_1$ makes Q_{pk} public-key queries, Q_{sk} private-key queries, Q_{psk} partial private-key queries, Q_{tr} Trapdoor-queries, Q_{rpk} replace public-key queries, Q_{dec} decryption-queries, Q_{H_1} hash-queries to H_1, and Q_{H_3} hash-queries to H_3. Thus, there exist $\mathcal{B}_1$ algorithm which solve the mDBHI problem with an advantage of at least:

$$\epsilon' \geq \frac{\epsilon}{Q_{H_3} + 2Q_{H_4}}(1 - \frac{Q_d}{2^\lambda})^{Q_{psk} + Q_{sk} + Q_{tr}}$$

Theorem 2: Suppose that the mBDHI problem is hard and H_1, H_2, H_3, H_4 are random oracles. The suggested PKC-ET-HS-CLE is OW-CCA secure under the ROM. Suppose the $Type_2$ adversary $\mathcal{A}_2$ has an advantage ϵ'' versus PKC-ET-HS-CLE scheme. Also suppose that $\mathcal{A}_2$ makes Q_{pk} public-key queries, Q_{sk} private-key queries, Q_{tr} trapdoor-queries, Q_{dec} decryption-queries, Q_{H_1} hash-queries to H_1, and Q_{H_3} hash-queries to H_3. Thus, there exit $\mathcal{B}_2$ algorithm which solve the mDBHI problem with an advantage of at minimum:

$$\epsilon'' \geq \frac{\epsilon}{Q_{H_3} + 2Q_{H_4}}(1 - \frac{Q_{dec}}{2^\lambda})^{Q_{sk} + Q_{tr}}$$

Theorem 3: Suppose that the mBDHI problem is hard and H_1, H_2, H_3, H_4 are random oracles. The suggested PKC-ET-HS-IBE is OW-ID-CCA secure under the ROM. Suppose that there is OW-ID-CCA adversary $\mathcal{A}$ has an advantage $\varepsilon(\lambda)$ versus PKC-ET-HS-IBE scheme. Also suppose that $\mathcal{A}$ makes Q_e key-generation queries, Q_{tr_IBE} trapdoor-queries, Q_{dec} decryption-queries, Q_{H_1} hash-queries to H_1, and Q_{H_3} hash-queries to H_3. Thus, there exist $\mathcal{B}$ algorithm that solve the mDBHI problem with an advantage of at minimum, $\varepsilon(\lambda)/e(Q_e + Q_{tr} + Q_{dec} + 1)$.

Proof: Due to the limited number of pages, the interested refers are invited to look at the references [13, 20, 26] for more details about the security proof.

6   Performance Analysis

6.1   Implementation Details

In the experiment, we use the Pairing-Based Cryptography (PBC) library [27]. Because we consider the equality test in heterogeneous systems, we implement our scheme and the schemes in [3, 21–23]. We run the experiment on a PC with Intel(R) Core(TM) i7-7700 CPU @3.60 GHz and 8 GB RAM, and with Windows10 pro 64-bit OS. We used C++ with 64-bit version to run the program as well as we utilized $Type_A$ pairings constructed from the curve $z^2 = x^3 + x$ over a finite field $\mathbb{F}_q$. Moreover, we realized 1024-bit of RSA security levels. The time of the bilinear pairing operation BP is set to 11.370 ms (milliseconds) and for the exponentiation operations Exp_1 and Exp_2 is tuned to 5.378 and 1.369 ms, respectively, in the experiment simulation. Eventually, we have the size of $\mathbb{G}_1$, $\mathbb{G}_2$, and $\mathbb{Z}_p$ are 128 bytes, 128 bytes and 20 bytes, respectively.

Table 2. Comparisons of the communication and computation cost.

Scheme	$|CT|$	Encryption	Decryption	Test
[3]	$3\mathbb{G}_1 + 2\mathbb{Z}_p$	$2Exp_2$	$3BP + Exp_2$	$4BP + 4Exp_2$
[21]	$3\mathbb{G}_1 + \mathbb{Z}_p$	$5Exp_1$	$2BP + 2Exp_1$	$3BP + Exp_1$
[22]	$3\mathbb{G}_1 + \mathbb{Z}_p$	$2BP + 5Exp_1$	$2BP + 2Exp_1$	$4BP$
[23]	$3\mathbb{G}_1 + \mathbb{Z}_p$	$5Exp_1$	$2BP + 4Exp_1$	$3BP + Exp_1$
PKC-ET-HS	$2\mathbb{G}_1 + 2\mathbb{Z}_p$	$2Exp_2$	$2BP$	$2BP + 2Exp_2$

Legends: $|CT|$ is a size of the ciphertext, respectively; Exp_1 and Exp_2 are the exponentiation operations in $\mathbb{G}_1$ and $\mathbb{G}_2$, respectively; BP is the pairing operation.

6.2   Communication and Computation Comparisons

Table 2 and Fig. 3(a) show the communication cost of the PKC-ET-HS scheme compared with other similar schemes. It can be seen that the PKC-ET-HS scheme has a smaller ciphertext size than [3, 21–23]. In addition, Table 2 and Fig. 3(b) show that it accomplishes better computation cost than all other schemes under experiments. This is because our construction is free from pairing during the encryption phase, while it only requires two pairing operations during the decryption and testing phases.

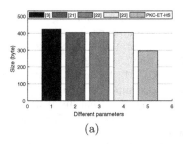 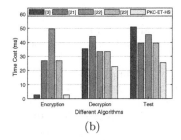

(a)   (b)

Fig. 3. Communication and computation cost of different works.

7   Conclusion

In this paper we proposed an efficient equality test scheme for the heterogeneous systems. The equality test in the suggested scheme is heterogeneous such that the cloud server can check the equality of two ciphertexts under the CLE-cryptosystem and IBE-cryptosystem. Moreover, Basing on the random oracle model, the security of the proposed scheme is reduced to the modified Diffie-Hellman assumption. The experiment analysis showed that our proposed scheme is efficient and more convenient than other's similar scheme. The future work includes the construction of a heterogeneous scheme that supports the test authorization to enhance users' privacy.

Acknowledgments. This work is supported by the National Key Research and Development Program of China (Grant No. 2018YFB0804702).

References

1. Long, J., Zhang, K., Wang, X., Dai, H.-N.: Lightweight distributed attribute based keyword search system for internet of things. In: Wang, G., Feng, J., Bhuiyan, M.Z.A., Lu, R. (eds.) SpaCCS 2019. LNCS, vol. 11637, pp. 253–264. Springer, Cham (2019). https://doi.org/10.1007/978-3-030-24900-7_21
2. Hassan, A., Liu, F., Wang, F., Wang, Y.: Secure image classification with deep neural networks for IoT applications. J. Ambient Intell. Human. Comput. 1–19 (2020). DOIurl10.1007/s12652-020-02565-z
3. Xiong, H., et al.: Heterogeneous signcryption with equality test for IIoT environment. IEEE Internet Things J. (2020). https://doi.org/10.1109/JIOT.2020.3008955
4. Elhabob, R., Zhao, Y., Sella, I., Xiong, H.: An efficient certificateless public key cryptography with authorized equality test in IIoT. J. Ambient Intell. Human. Comput. **11**, 1065–1083 (2020). https://doi.org/10.1007/s12652-019-01365-4
5. Elhabob, R., Zhao, Y., Sella, I., Xiong, H.: Efficient certificateless public key cryptography with equality test for internet of vehicles. IEEE Access **7**, 68957–68969 (2019). https://doi.org/10.1109/ACCESS.2019.2917326

6. Al-Nadwi, M.M.K., Refat, N., Zaman, N., Rahman, M.A., Bhuiyan, M.Z.A., Razali, R.B.: Cloud enabled *e*-glossary system: a smart campus perspective. In: Wang, G., Chen, J., Yang, L.T. (eds.) SpaCCS 2018. LNCS, vol. 11342, pp. 251–260. Springer, Cham (2018). https://doi.org/10.1007/978-3-030-05345-1_21

7. Peng, K., Zheng, L., Xu, X., Lin, T., Leung, V.C.M.: Balanced iterative reducing and clustering using hierarchies with principal component analysis (PBirch) for intrusion detection over big data in mobile cloud environment. In: Wang, G., Chen, J., Yang, L.T. (eds.) SpaCCS 2018. LNCS, vol. 11342, pp. 166–177. Springer, Cham (2018). https://doi.org/10.1007/978-3-030-05345-1_14

8. Raeini, M.G., Nojoumian, M.: Privacy-preserving big data analytics: from theory to practice. In: Wang, G., Feng, J., Bhuiyan, M.Z.A., Lu, R. (eds.) SpaCCS 2019. LNCS, vol. 11637, pp. 45–59. Springer, Cham (2019). https://doi.org/10.1007/978-3-030-24900-7_4

9. Boneh, D., Di Crescenzo, G., Ostrovsky, R., Persiano, G.: Public key encryption with keyword search. In: Cachin, C., Camenisch, J.L. (eds.) EUROCRYPT 2004. LNCS, vol. 3027, pp. 506–522. Springer, Heidelberg (2004). https://doi.org/10.1007/978-3-540-24676-3_30

10. Yang, G., Tan, C.H., Huang, Q., Wong, D.S.: Probabilistic public key encryption with equality test. In: Pieprzyk, J. (ed.) CT-RSA 2010. LNCS, vol. 5985, pp. 119–131. Springer, Heidelberg (2010). https://doi.org/10.1007/978-3-642-11925-5_9

11. Ma, S.: Identity-based encryption with outsourced equality test in cloud computing. Inf. Sci. **328**, 389–402 (2016)

12. Al-Riyami, S.S., Paterson, K.G.: Certificateless public key cryptography. In: Laih, C.-S. (ed.) ASIACRYPT 2003. LNCS, vol. 2894, pp. 452–473. Springer, Heidelberg (2003). https://doi.org/10.1007/978-3-540-40061-5_29

13. Qu, H., Yan, Z., Lin, X.J., Zhang, Q., Sun, L.: Certificateless public key encryption with equality test. Inf. Sci. **462**, 76–92 (2018)

14. Tang, Q.: Towards public key encryption scheme supporting equality test with fine-grained authorization. In: Parampalli, U., Hawkes, P. (eds.) ACISP 2011. LNCS, vol. 6812, pp. 389–406. Springer, Heidelberg (2011). https://doi.org/10.1007/978-3-642-22497-3_25

15. Tang, Q.: Public key encryption supporting plaintext equality test and user-specified authorization. Secur. Commun. Netw. **5**(12), 1351–1362 (2012)

16. Ma, S., Zhang, M., Huang, Q., Yang, B.: Public key encryption with delegated equality test in a multi-user setting. Comput. J. **58**(4), 986–1002 (2015)

17. Huang, K., Tso, R., Chen, Y.C., Rahman, S.M.M., Almogren, A., Alamri, A.: PKE-AET: public key encryption with authorized equality test. Comput. J. **58**(10), 2686–2697 (2015)

18. Elhabob, R., Zhao, Y., Eltayieb, N., Abdelgader, A.M., Xiong, H.: Identity-based encryption with authorized equivalence test for cloud-assisted IoT. Cluster Comput. **23**, 1085–1101 (2020). https://doi.org/10.1007/s10586-019-02979-1

19. Wu, L., Zhang, Y., Choo, K.K.R., He, D.: Efficient and secure identity-based encryption scheme with equality test in cloud computing. Future Gener. Comput. Syst. **73**, 22–31 (2017)

20. Hassan, A., Wang, Y., Elhabob, R., Eltayieb, N., Li, F.: An efficient certificateless public key encryption scheme with authorized equality test in healthcare environments. J. Syst. Archit. **109**, 101776 (2020). https://doi.org/10.1016/j.sysarc.2020.101776

21. Elhabob, R., Sella, I., Zhao, Y., Zhu, G., Xiong, H.: A heterogeneous systems public key encryption with equality test in smart city. In: Proceedings of The 18th International Conference on Electronic Business (ICEB), Guilin (2018)

22. Elhabob, R., Zhao, Y., Sella, I., Xiong, H.: Public key encryption with equality test for heterogeneous systems in cloud computing. KSII Trans. Internet Inf. Syst. (TIIS) **13**(9), 4742–4770 (2019)
23. Elhabob, R., Zhao, Y., Hassan, A., Xiong, H.: PKE-ET-HS: public key encryption with equality test for heterogeneous systems in IoT. Wirel. Pers. Commun. **113**, 313–335 (2020)
24. Saeed, M.E.S., Liu, Q., Tian, G., Gao, B., Li, F.: HOOSC: heterogeneous online/offline signcryption for the internet of things. Wirel. Netw. **24**(8), 3141–3160 (2018)
25. Chen, L., Cheng, Z.: Security proof of Sakai-Kasahara's identity-based encryption scheme. In: Smart, N.P. (ed.) Cryptography and Coding 2005. LNCS, vol. 3796, pp. 442–459. Springer, Heidelberg (2005). https://doi.org/10.1007/11586821_29
26. Boneh, D., Franklin, M.: Identity-based encryption from the weil pairing. In: Kilian, J. (ed.) CRYPTO 2001. LNCS, vol. 2139, pp. 213–229. Springer, Heidelberg (2001). https://doi.org/10.1007/3-540-44647-8_13
27. Lynn, B., et al.: The Stanford pairing based crypto library (2006). http://crypto.stanford.edu/pbc/. Accessed 27 March 2013

The Dark (and Bright) Side of IoT: Attacks and Countermeasures for Identifying Smart Home Devices and Services

Ahmed Mohamed Hussain[1(✉)], Gabriele Oligeri[2], and Thiemo Voigt[1]

[1] Department of Information Technology, Uppsala University, Uppsala, Sweden
ahmed.hussain.7023@student.uu.se
[2] Division of Information and Computing Technology (ICT),
College of Science and Engineering (CSE), Hamad Bin Khalifa University (HBKU),
Doha, Qatar

Abstract. We present a new machine learning-based attack that exploits network patterns to detect the presence of smart IoT devices and running services in the WiFi radio spectrum. We perform an extensive measurement campaign of data collection, and we build up a model describing the traffic patterns characterizing three popular IoT smart home devices, i.e., Google Nest Mini, Amazon Echo, and Amazon Echo Dot. We prove that it is possible to detect and identify with overwhelming probability their presence and the services running by the aforementioned devices in a crowded WiFi scenario. This work proves that standard encryption techniques alone are not sufficient to protect the privacy of the end-user, since the network traffic itself exposes the presence of both the device and the associated service. While more work is required to prevent non-trusted third parties to detect and identify the user's devices, we introduce *Eclipse*, a technique to mitigate these types of attacks, which reshapes the traffic making the identification of the devices and the associated services similar to the random classification baseline.

Keywords: Internet of Things · Machine learning · Security · Privacy · Cyberphysical systems

1 Introduction

Security and privacy of communications are of paramount importance given the growing number of user devices connected to the Internet. Indeed, the number of smart devices is exponentially growing around the world, and the vast majority of today's network traffic is encrypted to guarantee the security and privacy of the communications. Recently, encrypted network traffic classification has emerged as a technique to detect and identify traffic patterns although being anonymized by one or more encryption layers [1–3]. The same techniques have

© Springer Nature Switzerland AG 2021
G. Wang et al. (Eds.): SpaCCS 2020, LNCS 12383, pp. 122–136, 2021.
https://doi.org/10.1007/978-3-030-68884-4_10

been successfully adopted for drones [4] and cryptojacking detection [5]. The main idea behind traffic classification is to characterize the network traffic flow according to statistical features independently of the information that can be retrieved from the packet headers, such as network and physical layer addresses. Standard features can be packet size and interarrival times between consecutive packets, while more advanced features take into account statistics such as mean and variance computed over sequences of consecutive packets. While HTTPS and VPN services protect the end user from adversaries willing to exfiltrate information from the content of the packet, traffic patterns are very difficult to hide without affecting services' performance. Moreover, the wireless scenarios considered in this paper make such attacks even more effective and efficient. Indeed, due to its intrinsic broadcast nature, wireless communications can be easily eavesdropped without the consent of the user, and an adversary can exploit the traffic pattern generated by users to infer either the devices they have at home or the services they are using. This presents major issues for the users' privacy, not just because non-trusted third parties can infer the user behavior, but also detect the presence of specific devices to target in subsequent attacks.

Contribution. We propose a methodology based on machine learning classification to detect and identify the presence of smart devices and their running services in the WiFi radio spectrum. We tested our approach against three different smart devices, i.e., Google Nest, Google Chromecast, Amazon Echo and Amazon Echo Dot, and three popular services, i.e., Music, YouTube and News streaming. We proved that the aforementioned devices and services are affected by a critical privacy leakage since they allow not-authorized third parties to detect their presence even in the case of standard multi-layer encrypted streams such as WPA and HTTPS. Additionally, we construct and release the data-set[1] associated with each service and device used in this paper. This paper proves that the most commonly used smart devices in the market and their related services can be easily detected with overwhelming probability (>0.99) from a crowded WiFi link. We provide deep statistical insights about the traffic characterization, we show how standard machine learning techniques can be used to detect the presence of the devices. Finally, we introduce a mitigation technique called "Eclipse", which reshapes the traffic making the identification of the devices and the associated services similar to a random guess.

Paper Organization. The remainder of this paper is organized as follows: Sect. 2 summarizes recent contributions in the field of encrypted traffic classification, while Sect. 3 illustrates our assumptions and the adversary model. Our measurement setup and data collection procedures are introduced in Sect. 4, while Sect. 5 introduces the statistical analysis and reports the performance of our device identification methodology. Section 6 shows the results of our detection algorithm when considering a crowded WiFi link, and Sect. 7 discusses

---

[1] https://github.com/AMHD/The-Dark-and-Bright-Side-of-IoT-Dataset.

countermeasures against our attack. Finally, Sect. 8 tightens conclusions and draws some future work.

2 Related Work

Msadek et al. [6] proposed to fingerprint and map IoT devices to their associated encrypted traffic flow using machine learning. They assumed that the adversary is capable of passively collecting the traffic generated from the IoT devices through monitoring the gateway or a compromised IoT device. The data-set used in their analysis [7] constituted of seven different categories. The adversary in their study is remote and capable of obtaining the bidirectional flows generated by the devices. They reported the performance from five different classification algorithms, where *Adaboost* [8] outperformed with 95.5% accuracy in identifying the type of the device. However, their analysis did not focus on either applications or services these devices are running.

Shahid et al. [2] presented a machine learning-based approach to identify the type of four different IoT devices connected to the network, by analyzing the bidirectional flows. From the first N packets exchanged between the internet and IoT devices, they extracted two features: packet size and inter-arrival times. Devices were connected to an access point and traffic between the access point and internet is redirected through a Raspberry Pi for capturing packets. Different supervised machine learning algorithms were used for classification, best performance has been achieved using Random Forest with 99.9% accuracy. Their methodology involves collecting the data from an intermediate communication node (Raspberry Pi) and not directly from the wireless radio spectrum as we do.

Santos et al. [9] used a data-set that was collected within a smart campus [10]. The total number of IoT and non-IoT devices in this data-set is 18. The considered features were maximum packet size in the forward direction, source port, destination port, and average packet size. They were able to identify each device network traffic flow, with 99% of accuracy by using the Random Forest algorithm. Even in this case study, the authors were able to distinguish devices, but not the application run by the device itself.

Sivanathan et al. [10] considered a data-set collected over a period of three weeks, for more than 20 IoT devices such as cameras, lights, appliances, and health monitors. They extracted features such as data rates and burstiness, activity cycles, and signaling patterns. By exploiting the aforementioned features, they were able to distinguish IoT from non-IoT traffic, furthermore identifying specific IoT devices with about 95% accuracy. Similarly to previous related work, this contribution focuses on the device but not on the applications run by the device.

Jackson and Camp [11] investigated the performance of six different supervised machine learning algorithms to infer information from encrypted TCP packets. They were able to identify encrypted information/request[2] exchanged

---

[2] Such as: "Alexa, turn off the light".

between the Alexa cloud service and the Echo device by only looking at the request packets exchanged. They adopted three different feature vectors: TCP-trace Features Vector [12], Histogram Feature Vector, and Combined Feature Vector. They were able to achieve an accuracy of more than 93% using the Random Forest algorithm for each of the features vectors. Data collection set-up in this study involves an intermediate communication node (computer) and not directly from the wireless radio spectrum as we propose in this paper.

Trimananda et al. [13] developed a tool that fingerprints generated traffic by smart home IoT devices when switched on or off, through analyzing the initial exchanged packets. This solution is effective only at the startup process, while it does not provide any guarantees when the eavesdropped packets comes from an arbitrary point of the stream.

Valdez et al. [14] focused on the identification and classification of IoT devices network traffic, while being encrypted. Leveraging the identify key features of the TLS handshake protocol, they were able to build a model that is capable of identifying 71 IoT devices, with an accuracy over 90%.

Different methods has been proposed in literature to prevent traffic detection, most notably: traffic and packet *padding* [15,16], traffic *morphing* [17], and *frequency hopping*. These techniques do mitigate the traffic pattern, but mainly focusing only on one feature (notably packet size). On the other hand, the *Leaky Bucket* algorithm can be used to mitigate the pattern created by the interarrival times by reshaping the traffic at a constant rate.

3   Adversarial Model

The main reason for performing this attack on the WiFi link, is due to the effectiveness and how easy it is to sniff (collect) the traffic from the WiFi spectrum between the access point and devices without the need to be connected to any of the sending/receiving parties. In this attack, we are particularly interested in services that generates Quality of Service (QoS) traffic, as it generates large number of packets exchanged between the devices and the access point, unlike switching on/off IoT devices.

Our adversary model features two essential characteristics: *stealthy* and *resource constrained*. Indeed, we assume that our adversary is able to eavesdrop and collect 802.11 radio messages (WiFi) from a remote location, even far away from the target user depending on the receiving capabilities of his equipment. Figure 1 wraps up our assumption on the adversarial model. We consider a general user case scenario, where the user enjoys different IoT/smart devices connected to the Internet. The aforementioned devices provide different smart services such as news reading and music streaming by resorting to the user's voice commands. The voice command is detected and processed by the smart device, and in turn, sent to the cloud service. Subsequently, the cloud service replies to the smart device with the answer that (in this work) consists of an audio stream.

We assume the adversary is sitting far away from both the device and the WiFi access point, but still, he can eavesdrop and collect the WiFi radio messages. In particular, our adversary model takes into account the stream of messages from the cloud to the device (ingoing flow). For each eavesdropped message, the adversary records only the packet size and the time at which the packet is received.

We stress that our analysis is powerful even in the presence of a user able to anonymize all the messages, e.g., by sanitizing all the information related to source and destination IP/MAC addresses. Although we recognize that this will require the deployment of ad-hoc protocols able to guarantee the message delivery between the smart device and the WiFi access point, we do assume the worst possible conditions from the adversary perspective, i.e., our adversary will not resort to standard techniques to infer on the service/device such as port scanning or MAC addressing manufacturer mapping.

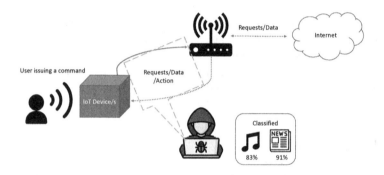

Fig. 1. Adversary model considered in this work.

4   Measurement Set-Up and Data Collection

In this section, we introduce our measurement set-up by considering both the hardware and the software tools we adopted.

Hardware–Smart Devices. Our smart home set-up consists of three smart home devices: *Amazon Echo, Amazon Echo Dot, Google Chromecast*, and *Google Nest Mini*. These devices are distributed in different places and connected to a D-Link router (1200AC) via WiFi.

Adversary–Hardware. We adopted an Alfa Card (AWUS036NH) for capturing the traffic by switching to *monitor mode*, and therefore, collecting all the over-the-air data traffic.

Adversary–Software. We consider a standard Linux distribution (Kali Linux), and the tools *airodump-ng/Wireshark* for collecting and logging the WiFi packets. Finally, we adopted *MATLAB 2019b* for data preprocessing and classification.

Data Collection. We would like to stress that we resort to MAC addresses to select the traffic of the smart devices and generate the ground truth with the machine learning algorithms. As it will be clear in the following sections, the classification will be independent of the aforementioned information, while being rooted only on features like packet size, interarrival times and statistical computations derived from them.

The data collection has been performed accordingly to the following procedure:

1. We adopted *airodump-ng* to identify the victim access point and the devices connected to it.
2. Identifying information such as MAC addresses and WiFi channel used by the devices in the network.
3. Setting the Alfa card channel to the one used by the smart device.
4. Using either *TCPDump* or *Wireshark* for traffic collection and filtering out the traffic generated from the access point to each of the IoT device, using the MAC address obtained from step 1.
5. Extract the time and packet size associated with each over-the-air message.

The traffic forwarded by the access point to each of the smart devices is collected over approximately 8 h of continuous news and music streaming. In our set-up, we ensure that no other devices are connected to the network other than the IoT devices. The total number of packets forwarded by the WiFi access point to each device is approximately 280,000 for each service. In total, the overall data-set size sums up to 1,680,000 packets of streaming news on amazon echo and echo dot and streaming music on echo, echo dot, and google nest mini.

5   Data Processing, Statistics, and Device Identification

In this section, we provide the analysis, methodologies and techniques we adopted for *pre-processing* and *classifying* the collected traffic.

Pre-processing. The raw reception times and packet sizes are extracted from the traces. Inter-arrival times are calculated as $T_{x+1} - T_x$, where T_{x+1} is the time of the packet $x + 1$ that is received after packet x. After this preliminary computation, 8 different features are computed considering different *window sizes* from the inter-arrival times and packet sizes.

Different statistical features have been adopted in the literature to uniquely identify patterns from encrypted traffic [9,11,18]. In this work, we consider 8 statistical features: standard deviation, sum, variance, maximum, minimum, mean, median, skewness, and kurtosis. These features are extracted by using a sliding window technique, where a window of N adjacent massages is considered for the computation of the aforementioned statistics.

Classification. Machine learning algorithms facilitates its capabilities to identify and distinguish unique patterns from the used features (interarrival times and packet sizes), which result in identifying services and devices more accurately. The vast majority of our results adopts the *Random Forest* algorithm for all our tests being the best performer from related works in the literature [2,6,9–11,18]. We consider the following configuration for the random forest algorithm: **k-folds = 15, number of trees/bags** = 30. All classes have been balanced to ensure that the number of samples is equal among all the traces.

5.1   Interarrival Times Analysis

In this section, we show the performance of the random forest classifier considering only one feature, i.e., the interarrival time between consecutive packets. For each device and service, we extracted and analyzed the inter-arrival times as reported in Fig. 2, which shows the interpolated inter-arrival times for the three devices and two services (except Google Nest Mini running one service). Although the samples have similar patterns, the interpolating polynomial functions have distinct patterns meaning that each service on each device can be potentially identified by just comparing the interarrival times.

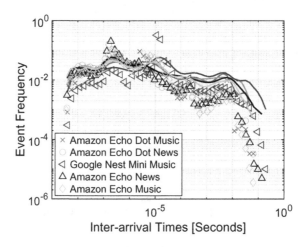

Fig. 2. Probability distribution function associated with the interarrival times (seconds).

Classification. We consider a naive approach and perform the classification of the encrypted traffic by resorting only to the interarrival times achieving an accuracy of about 33.59%. Subsequently, we considered the previously introduced statistical features computed from the inter-arrival times using the *sliding window* technique. The window size has been set between 20 to 340 packets. Figure 3(a) shows the accuracy of the random forest algorithm as a function of the window size. We observe that the trend of the accuracy saturates when it reaches the value of 200 being equivalent to about 80 s. We highlight that we choose the shortest window size (with the highest possible accuracy), in this case 200 packets, to guarantee the shortest detection delay. Figure 3(b) shows the confusion matrix for the previously considered five classes, i.e., Amazon Echo Dot Music (ED Music), Amazon Echo Dot News (ED News), Amazon Echo Music (Echo Music), Amazon Echo News (Echo News), Google Nest Music (GN Music), while the total number of samples is 2330. We considered the Random Forest algorithm and the 8 statistical features previously introduced, estimated over a window size of 200 samples that is sufficient and leads to an accuracy of 84.5%.

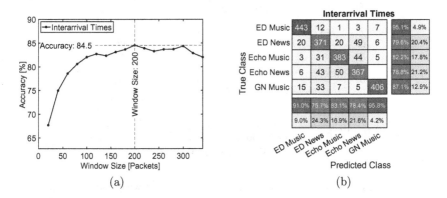

(a)   (b)

Fig. 3. Random Forrest Classifier performance: (a) Accuracy as a function of Window Size. (b) Confusion Matrix associated with window size of 200 and 8 statistical features.

5.2   Packet Size Analysis

Packets sizes can be easily extracted and used directly for analysis (to identify the existence of a unique pattern) and classification. Figure 4 shows the packet size analysis as a function of the five classes considered in this paper. We observe that the frequency associated with the packet size is very different among the five considered categories, in particular when considering packet sizes larger than 800 bytes.

Classification. As a baseline scenario, we consider the Random Forest algorithm and only the packet size feature. As for the previous case (interarrival times), such configuration gives us very poor performance, i.e., the accuracy achieved is 0.33. Therefore, we consider 8 statistical features computed using the sliding window technique with a range between 20 and 340 subsequent packets. Figure 5(a) shows the accuracy of the Random Forrest algorithm as a function of the packet size considering different window sizes. The highest accuracy achieved is approximately 0.755, using a window size of 320 packets being equivalent to about 130 s. Figure 5(b) shows the confusion matrix for the previously considered five classes, i.e., Amazon Echo Dot Music (ED Music), Amazon Echo Dot News (ED News), Amazon Echo Music (Echo Music), Amazon Echo News (Echo News), Google Nest Music (GN Music), where the total number of samples is 1455. We considered the Random Forest algorithm and the 8 statistical features previously introduced estimated over a window size of 320 samples.

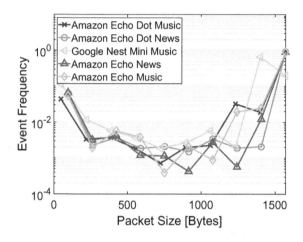

Fig. 4. Probability distribution function associated with packet sizes.

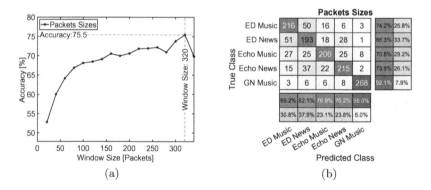

Fig. 5. Random Forrest Classifier performance: (a) Accuracy as a function of Window Size. (b) Confusion Matrix associated with window size of 320 and 8 statistical features.

5.3   Packet Size and Interarrival Times

In this section, we consider the combination of packet size and interarrival times, by combining all the statistical features previously computed together, i.e., 8 for the packet size and 8 for the interarrival time for a total of 16 values. As for the previous cases, we consider the Random Forest algorithm and a sliding window spanning between 20 and 340. Figure 6(a) shows the accuracy as a function of the window size considering a total of 16 features. The accuracy saturates to the value of about 0.86 without any major improvement when the window size is becoming greater than 180 being equal to 80 s. While Fig. 6(b) shows the confusion matrix (with a total of 2585 samples) associated with the performance of the Random Forest algorithm when considering 16 statistical features computed from both packet size and interarrival time as previously described.

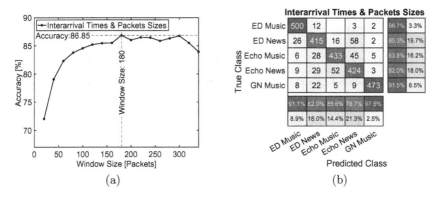

(a)   (b)

Fig. 6. Random Forrest Classifier performance: (a) Accuracy as a function of Window Size. (b) Confusion Matrix associated with window size of 180 and 16 statistical features.

6   Device and Service Detection in the Wild

While in the previous sections we focus on devices and services identification, in this section, we show the performance of the Random Forrest classifier to detect the presence of the considered smart devices and services running, from a crowded WiFi traffic. The noise is collected from an environment where different number of users are connected to the same access point. The noise includes different types of packets, such DNS queries, ACK, ICMP, HTTP, HTTPs, QoS. As previously considered, we start our analysis by providing a statistical description of the WiFi traffic we collected from a crowded place. Firstly, we faced a class imbalance problem; indeed, the WiFi trace collected from the wild is much larger than the one collected from the devices. In order to make the comparison fair, we divided the WiFi trace in chunks of the same size of the trace collected from each device associated with each service, once detecting the device type. In the case of having two devices of the same type running the exact same service within the WiFi channel, the classifier will match and classify both devices to the same class. We applied the previously introduced methodology and we trained a model to identify each of the 5 classes, i.e., Amazon Echo Dot (Music), Amazon Echo Dot (News), Amazon Echo (Music), Amazon Echo (News), Google Nest Mini (Music), against the WiFi collected from the crowded place. Finally, we tested the model with independent traces taken from the previous 5+1 classes of traffic. We run the classifiers on each chunk and we averaged the final results. Table 1 shows the results associated with the detection of each of the device/service previously considered assuming a window size of 180 samples. We report performance in terms of True Positive Rate (TPR), False Positive Rate (FPR) and Accuracy. Our results show that performance is striking and our approach can easily detect a smart device and the associated service from a generic encrypted WiFi link.

Table 1. Performance for devices/services detection

Device	Service	TPR	FPR [$\cdot 10^{-4}$]	Accuracy
Amazon Echo Dot	Music	0.9988	3.4	0.9992
	News	0.9996	7.9	0.9994
Amazon Echo	News	0.9996	2.7	0.9996
	Music	0.9998	3.6	0.9997
Google Nest Mini	Music	0.9995	9.2	0.9997

Comparison with Other Adversarial Models. Other attacks introduced in literature focus on using either raw or statistical features extracted from multiple information found in the exchanged packets such as (but not limited to) port number, packet direction, round trip time (RTT), inter-packet time (IPT), and other none-encrypted information. Our attack only leverages the two aforementioned features, interarrival times and packet size. Table 2 shows the comparison between our solution and the most representative in the literature in terms of type of device, technology, connectivity, attack strategy and capability to classify the application associated to the eavesdropped traffic. We remark that this contribution is the first to deal with encrypted traffic classification over a wireless link and considering only one flow direction, i.e., from the AP to the IoT device(s). Previous work [10] considered the same problem but taking into account a wired link making their scenarios (wired) not comparable with ours (wireless)—the wireless scenario being more challenging, indeed the adversary can be stealthier since he might hide himself behind obstructions, while the radio link is characterized by delays and jitters that make the classification process more difficult, but as we proved in this paper, achievable with overwhelming probability. Moreover, to the best of our knowledge, other contributions do not differentiate between services and devices, while in our analysis we provide the likelihood to detect a specific device, and subsequently, to identify the provided service.

Table 2. Comparison of our approach with other solutions.

Ref.	WiFi devices only	Remote attack	Services classification	Single direction flow
[6]	✗	✓	✗	✗
[2]	✗	✗	✗	✗
[9]	✗	✓	✗	✗
[10]	✗	✓	✓	✗
[11]	✓	✓	✓	✗
Our approach	✓	✓	✓	✓

7   Our Countermeasure: Eclipse

In the following, we propose an effective and efficient solution to the aforementioned attack. Our intuition is that encrypted network traffic classification can be made (arbitrary) less effective if the features characterizing the different traffic flows are reshaped, thus becoming similar. Indeed, the performance of the attack can be significantly mitigated if the adversary is not able to build a ground-truth related to the device/service traffic. We propose a simple but effective solution we name *Eclipse*. Eclipse is implemented in the WiFi access point as a proxy between the Internet traffic (wired) and the wireless connections between the WiFi access point and the IoT devices (recall Fig. 1). We adopt our previously introduced classification methodology by taking into account 16 total features (8 for the packet size and 8 for the interarrival time), considering a window size of 180 packets.

Interarrival Time and Packet Size Reshaping. We implement the traffic reshaping for both the packet size (as previously discussed) and for the interarrival times, i.e., by introducing random delays in the packet forwarding. Figure 7 shows the classification accuracy as a function of the introduced (maximum) delay. We observe how the overall accuracy drops from about 85% to about 20% by rescheduling the packets with a (maximum) delay of 0.5 ms. We highlight that training a new model with the reshaped traffic is useless since the features are no more biased towards a specific class (traffic flow), thus making the training (on the reshaped traffic) completely ineffective.

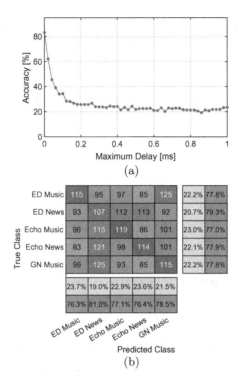

Fig. 7. (a) Classification accuracy as a function of the introduced mitigation method. (b) Confusion Matrix associated with the obscured data.

8   Conclusion

In this paper, we have presented a methodology to identify and classify popular smart devices and related streaming services by adopting standard machine learning algorithms. Our approach is based on extracting and detecting network patterns (features) such as packet size and interarrival times and the related statistics. We prove that our attack is feasible and can detect and identify smart devices with probabilities, about 0.99 and 0.86, respectively. We have proved that, contrary to the common belief, multi-layer encryption does not solve the problem of privacy, highlighting that smart devices require additional attention to guarantee the privacy of the end-user. Finally, we proposed a novel mitigation technique that prevents the identification of the traffic pattern by reshaping both the packet size and the inter-arrival times. Our findings prove that reshaping the packet size, e.g., setting all the packets to the same size, is completely ineffective to hide the presence of a specific flow, while introducing (small) random delays in the packet forwarding process makes the identification of the flow comparable to the random classification baseline.

Acknowledgments. This publication was made possible by NPRP grants NPRP12S-0125-190013 and NPRP12C-0814-190012 from the Qatar National Research Fund (a member of Qatar Foundation). The findings achieved herein are solely the responsibility of the authors.

References

1. Li, W., Moore, A.W.: A machine learning approach for efficient traffic classification. In: 2007 15th International Symposium on Modeling, Analysis, and Simulation of Computer and Telecommunication Systems, pp. 310–317. IEEE (2007)
2. Shahid, M.R., Blanc, G., Zhang, Z., Debar, H.: IoT devices recognition through network traffic analysis. In: 2018 IEEE International Conference on Big Data (Big Data), pp. 5187–5192. IEEE (2018)
3. Sivanathan, A., Sherratt, D., Gharakheili, H.H., Sivaraman, V., Vishwanath, A.: Low-cost flow-based security solutions for smart-home IoT devices. In: 2016 IEEE International Conference on Advanced Networks and Telecommunications Systems (ANTS), pp. 1–6. IEEE (2016)
4. Sciancalepore, S., Ibrahim, O.A., Oligeri, G., Di Pietro, R.: PiNcH: an effective, efficient, and robust solution to drone detection via network traffic analysis. Comput. Netw. **168**, 107044 (2020). http://www.sciencedirect.com/science/article/pii/S1389128619311764
5. Caprolu, M., Raponi, S., Oligeri, G., Di Pietro, R.: Cryptomining makes noise: a machine learning approach for cryptojacking detection. https://arxiv.org/abs/1910.09272
6. Msadek, N., Soua, R., Engel, T.: IoT device fingerprinting: machine learning based encrypted traffic analysis. In: 2019 IEEE Wireless Communications and Networking Conference (WCNC), pp. 1–8. IEEE (2019)
7. UNSW Sydney: IoT traffic analysis. https://iotanalytics.unsw.edu.au/. Accessed Feb 2020
8. Jan, T.: Ada-boosted locally enhanced probabilistic neural network for IoT intrusion detection. In: Barolli, L., Javaid, N., Ikeda, M., Takizawa, M. (eds.) CISIS 2018. AISC, vol. 772, pp. 583–589. Springer, Cham (2019). https://doi.org/10.1007/978-3-319-93659-8_52
9. Santos, M.R., Andrade, R.M., Gomes, D.G., Callado, A.C.: An efficient approach for device identification and traffic classification in IoT ecosystems. In: 2018 IEEE Symposium on Computers and Communications (ISCC), pp. 00 304–00 309. IEEE (2018)
10. Sivanathan, A., et al.: Characterizing and classifying IoT traffic in smart cities and campuses. In: 2017 IEEE Conference on Computer Communications Workshops (INFOCOM WKSHPS), pp. 559–564. IEEE (2017)
11. Jackson, R.B., Camp, T.: Amazon echo security: machine learning to classify encrypted traffic. In: 2018 27th International Conference on Computer Communication and Networks (ICCCN), pp. 1–10. IEEE (2018)
12. Lazarevic, A., Ertoz, L., Kumar, V., Ozgur, A., Srivastava, J.: A comparative study of anomaly detection schemes in network intrusion detection. In: Proceedings of the 2003 SIAM International Conference on Data Mining, pp. 25–36. SIAM (2003)
13. Trimananda, R., Varmarken, J., Markopoulou, A., Demsky, B.: PingPong: packet-level signatures for smart home device events. arXiv preprint arXiv:1907.11797 (2019)

14. Valdez, E., Pendarakis, D., Jamjoom, H.: How to discover IoT devices when network traffic is encrypted. In: IEEE International Congress on Internet of Things (ICIOT), pp. 17–24 (2019)
15. Chen, S., Wang, R., Wang, X., Zhang, K.: Side-channel leaks in web applications: a reality today, a challenge tomorrow. In: 2010 IEEE Symposium on Security and Privacy, pp. 191–206. IEEE (2010)
16. Sun, Q., Simon, D.R., Wang, Y.-M., Russell, W., Padmanabhan, V.N., Qiu, L.: Statistical identification of encrypted web browsing traffic. In: Proceedings 2002 IEEE Symposium on Security and Privacy, pp. 19–30. IEEE (2002)
17. Hafeez, I., Antikainen, M., Tarkoma, S.: Protecting IoT-environments against traffic analysis attacks with traffic morphing. In: IEEE International Conference on Pervasive Computing and Communications Workshops (PerCom Workshops), pp. 196–201 (2019)
18. Acar, A., et al.: Peek-a-Boo: I see your smart home activities, even encrypted! In: Proceedings of the 13th ACM Conference on Security and Privacy in Wireless and Mobile Networks, pp. 207–218 (2020)

Study of Transparent File Encryption Technology on Android Platform

Yongzhong Li[✉], Shipeng Zhang, and Yi Li

School of Computer, Jiangsu University of Science and Technology,
Zhenjiang 212003, China
liyongzhong61@163.com

Abstract. Aiming at the data security problem of Android platform, a transparent encryption system based on file filter driver is designed and implemented, according to the technology of file transparent encryption and decryption system based on hook transparent encryption technology and file filtering driven transparent encryption technology used on windows platform. This system is different from the traditional APP development method of Android system. By intercepting the system call function and using the secret-key converted from the host MAC address, the encryption and decryption algorithm is written into the kernel, which fundamentally guarantees the security of user information. At the same time, the user's security experience is improved by putting authentication on the screen unlocking. The system design and implementation are described in this paper from system requirement analysis to overall design and detailed design of each module. Android application development technology and cross-compiling principle are used in the coding process. The system test results show that the system can effectively transparently encrypt files and protect the privacy of mobile files.

Keywords: Android · Data security · Transparent encryption · Privacy preservation

1 Introduction

As an open source mobile development platform, Android has been supported by mobile phone users and developers all over the world. In May 2017, at the 2017Google Developers Conference, Google announced that the number of smartphones using Android has reached 2 billion, close to one third of the world's population. However, while people enjoy the convenience brought by mobile phones, as an important data carrier of daily life and work, their security problems are becoming increasingly prominent.

At present, file transparent encryption technology has become increasingly mature. However, it is mostly used in Windows platform, and the application market for Android mobile phone file encryption software is uneven, and users are required to enter passwords to verify every time they encrypt and decrypt files, which greatly reduce the encryption efficiency and user experience. A transparent encryption system based on Android file filter driver is designed in this paper. In the kernel layer, the

G. Wang et al. (Eds.): SpaCCS 2020, LNCS 12383, pp. 137–145, 2021.
https://doi.org/10.1007/978-3-030-68884-4_11

encryption and decryption algorithm are written into the kernel by intercepting system calls, so as to improve user experience and encryption efficiency. The system's authentication is placed in the screen lock.

2 Android System Architecture

Android system architecture is based on the Linux kernel and is bottom-up structure [1]. It is mainly divided into four layers, as shown in Fig. 1, the Linux Kernel layer, the Library layer, the Application Framework layers and the Application layer. The Linux kernel layer provides the underlying drivers for various hardware of Android devices, such as display driver, audio driver, etc. The system runtime layer mainly provides the main features support for Android system through some C/C++ libraries, such as SQLite library, etc. The application framework layer mainly provides various APIs that may be used to build applications. Application Programming Interface (API); the application layer includes all applications installed on mobile phones [2].

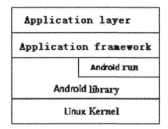

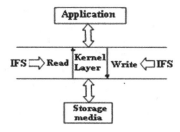

Fig. 1. Android system architecture   **Fig. 2.** Transparent encryption

3 Principle of Transparent Encryption Technology

Transparent encryption refers to the process of encrypting and decrypting files without changing the user's operating habits. It is a passive compulsory encryption technology [3], which is insensitive to users. When the user opens or edits the specified file, the system will automatically encrypt the unencrypted file and decrypt the encrypted file. Encrypted files leave the current usage environment, which can not automatically decrypt and protect the contents of files.

Transparent encryption technology can be divided into user-mode implementation and kernel-mode implementation according to the location of implementation. They correspond to the two main transparent encryption technologies, namely hook transparent encryption and file filter-driven transparent encryption. According to encryption efficiency, hook encryption technology encrypts the whole file in the application layer, and encrypts and decrypts the file relatively slowly. Driving transparency technology encrypts and decrypts the file dynamically in the driver layer, which has high efficiency. So file filter-driven transparent encryption is used in this paper.

3.1   File Filter Driven Transparent Encryption Technology

File Driver Encryption (IFS) technology is based on Windows File System Filter Driver (IFS) technology [5], which works in the kernel layer of Windows. Without affecting the upper and lower interfaces, it can intercept all file system requests, so that new functions can be added without modifying the upper software or the lower driver, as shown in Fig. 2 [4]. It is characterized by high encryption efficiency and security, but the technical threshold is high. It is necessary to understand the Windows system kernel in depth and difficult to develop. All tables and figures with text only should be boxed in; i.e., a box should be drawn around the table or figure either by hand with a ruler or with a draw facility on.

4   Design and Implementation of Transparent File Encryption System

4.1   Overall Design

This system is a transparent file encryption system based on Android platform. It mainly completes the encryption and decryption of specified files, and takes into account the user's good experience, so as to ensure the personal information security of Android users.

The frame design of the whole system is shown in Fig. 3.

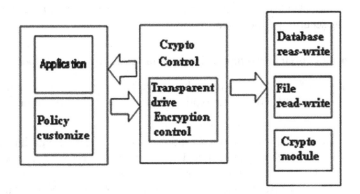

Fig. 3. System overall design framework

The system uses MVP (Model, View, Presenter) framework. Model (model) receives the control information from the controller, completes the operation of reading and writing files and encryption and decryption. View (user interface) mainly realizes the interaction with users and updates the user's encryption policy customization to relevant database items. Presenter is responsible for logical processing, customizing and updating the monitoring list according to the user's encryption strategy, monitoring and accepting the data read and write operations applied in the list, and passing the information to Model. MVP is evolved from MVC framework [6]. It cuts off the connection between View and Model, makes View interact only with Presenter, increases readability and reusability, and reduces the cost of later testing and maintenance [7].

In the choice of encryption algorithm, we chose the currently popular encryption algorithm AES and the encryption algorithm SM4 independently developed by China. The reason for making these two choices is mainly considering the following reasons:

1) The reason why AES is selected as the encryption algorithm is because AES encryption algorithm is one of the most popular algorithms in symmetric encryption, and it replaced the original DES encryption algorithm. For now, AES is still a primary consideration in some encryption scenarios. At least for now, the AES encryption algorithm does not show a decline, nor does it show obvious problems in security;

2) The reason why I chose AES as the encryption algorithm for this design made in this article and developed a similar function using SM4, mainly considering that SM4 is an encryption algorithm independently developed by China. The emergence of encryption algorithms such as SM4 independently developed by China is an essential measure to ensure the security of encryption algorithms.

The system authenticates the user through screen lock when the mobile phone starts. When the system intercepts the user to read the file, it calls the function module of the kernel to decrypt the ciphertext, and then transmits the decrypted plaintext to the application layer for the user to read. When the system intercepts the user to write the file, it stores the plaintext encryption on the storage device to improve the user experience and security performance.

4.2   Design and Implementation of Encryption and Decryption Module

The performance of the encryption module affects the security of the transparent encrypted file system [8]. For the encryption algorithm, we have made the following two choices.

AES. AES is known as the advanced encryption standard. The AES algorithm requires a 128-bit or 16-byte length of plaintext, and the length of the secret key can be divided into 128-bit, 192-bit, or 256-bit (16, 24, or 32 bytes) [9]. The AES encryption process involves four operations: AddRoundKey, SubBytes, ShiftRows, and MixColumns. The decryption process is the corresponding inverse operation of the encryption [10]. Figure 4 shows the working flow chart of the encryption module.

SM4. Similar to DES and AES algorithms, the SM4 algorithm is a block cipher algorithm. The packet length is 128 bits, and the key length is also 128 bits. The encryption algorithm and the key expansion algorithm both use 32 rounds of non-linear iterative structure, and encrypt operations are performed in units of words (32 bits). Each iteration operation is a round of transformation function F. In SM4, the structure of the encryption algorithm and the decryption algorithm are the same, except that the round key used is opposite, where the decryption round key is the reverse order of the encryption round key.

Regardless of whether AES encryption algorithm or SM4 encryption algorithm is used, the functions we want to achieve are consistent. Figure 4 shows the workflow diagram of the encryption module.

The mac address is unique to a terminal device, so the mac address is used as the encryption and decryption key. By reading the MAC address of the Android terminal, after a series of replacement transformations and other operations, it is transmitted to the encryption algorithm of the kernel module as the encryption key of the current device. Among them, accessing the MAC address of the Android terminal requires reading the address under / sys / class / net / wlan0. Therefore, each terminal has its own unique key. If the terminal is changed, the files of the local terminal will not be able to view. The function plays a vital role in protecting the privacy of mobile files.

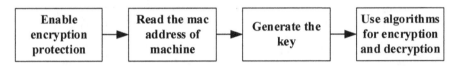

Fig. 4. Workflow of encryption module

4.3   Design and Implementation of the Whole System

The whole design module of the system is divided into application layer module and kernel module. The application layer module mainly completes the function of customizing encryption strategy and interacting with users; the kernel module completes the functions of monitoring, encryption and decryption, data reading and writing according to the setting of application module.

The overall design flow chart of the system is shown in Fig. 5. After the system starts to run, the user carries out the "policy customization" operation at the user level, enters the kernel layer after the policy formulation, and monitors the reading and writing operations of the files. In order to read a file, the first step is to determine whether the file is an open encrypted protected file. If it is, it decrypts and passes the data to the user; if it is to write a file, it is still necessary to determine whether the file is an open encrypted file, and if it is, it is encrypted and writes the data to the database or SD card. If the read-write operation file is not the file protected by the policy, then the normal read-write operation can be carried out.

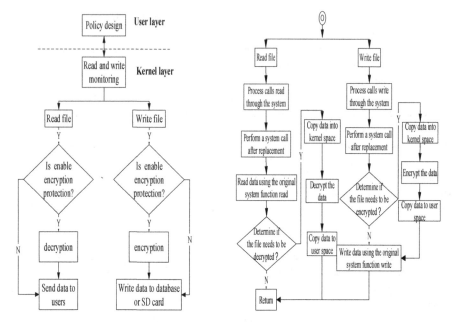

Fig. 5. The overall design flow of the system   **Fig. 6.** The Design flow of kernel module

4.4   Design and Implementation of Kernel Module

System calls under Linux are implemented with soft interrupts. The interrupt program handles different system calls according to the system call number. Through the soft interrupt program, the program will be trapped in the kernel space for system call processing. In addition, Linux provides a program that can load kernel modules, namely LKM (Loadable Kernel Module), which is mainly used to dynamically extend the functions of the Linux kernel [11]. Figure 6 shows the workflow diagram of the kernel module.

When run the process of writing files, the encryption process, is executed, the interception system calls write. At this run point, the kernel module gets the file name and structure. Comparing with the file name and file structure in the encryption strategy formulated by the application layer, if the file name and file structure match, the data will be copied to the kernel space, and AES symmetric encryption operation is performed on the data through the pre-written encryption function. The key is obtained from the application layer and encrypted. Then the file is copied to the user space, and the data is written into the storage medium by calling the original system function write. If the current operation of the file is not specified in the encryption policy, the normal file write operation is run.

When the read file operation is performed, the interception system calls read. Get the file name and structure of the file currently operating in the kernel module.

Comparing with the file name and file structure in the encryption strategy formulated by the application layer, if the file name and file structure match, the file will be copied to the kernel space and decrypted. After the plaintext data is transferred to the kernel space, if the current operation file is not specified in the encryption policy, the file reading operation will be performed normally.

5 System Testing

The system is installed on API18 simulator and successfully implements the transparent encryption function of txt and doc file format on SD card. After the encryption is successful, the files can be viewed normally at the local terminal. Replacing the terminal and viewing it on the PC and another mobile phone is random code, thus completing the privacy protection of Android mobile phone files, as shown in Fig. 7, 8, 9, 10, 11 and 12.

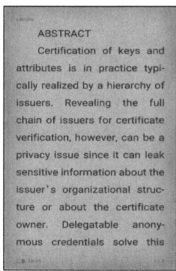

Fig. 7. The encrypted TXT on local terminal   **Fig. 8.** The encrypted TXT file on PC

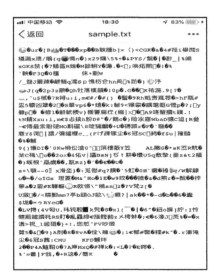

Fig. 9. The encrypted TXT file on another terminal

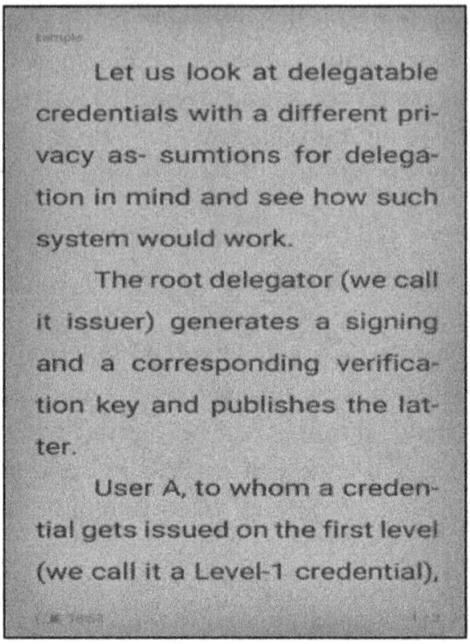

Let us look at delegatable credentials with a different privacy as- sumtions for delegation in mind and see how such system would work.

The root delegator (we call it issuer) generates a signing and a corresponding verification key and publishes the latter.

User A, to whom a credential gets issued on the first level (we call it a Level-1 credential),

Fig. 10. The encrypted doc file on local terminal

Fig. 11. The encrypted doc files on PC

Fig. 12. The encrypted doc files on another terminal

6 Conclusion

According to the test results, when the encryption is completed, the files can be viewed normally on the local mobile phone after the authentication of screen lock, but not in other environments. The transparent encryption function of files under Android platform has been successfully implemented. The system uses file filtering to drive transparent encryption technology. By intercepting system calls and using keys converted from MAC address of host computer, the encryption and decryption algorithm is written into the kernel. In the process of encryption, the plaintext of files only appears in the kernel layer, which has the characteristics of security, stability and efficiency. However, the software user interface for this system can also be beautified, and the type of file data for encryption protection can also be increased, which will become the next research content.

References

1. Ma, L., Gu, L., Wang, J.: Research and development of mobile application for android platform. Int. J. Multimedia Ubiq. Eng. **9**(4), 187–198 (2014)
2. Enck, W., Ongtang, M., McDaniel, P.: Understanding android security. IEEE Secur. Priv. **7** (1), 50–57 (2009)
3. Yang, D., Peng, Y., Fang, Z.: The application of transparent decryption in trusted storage of electronic documents. Electron. Sci. Technol. **4**(04), 147–150 (2017)
4. Wang, Q., Zhou, Q., Liu, Y.: Research on file system transparent encryption techniques. Comput. Technol. Dev. **20**, 147–150 (2010)
5. Liu, W., Li, D.: A file protection scheme based on the transparent encryption technology. In: 2018 IEEE International Conference of Safety Produce Informatization (IICSPI), pp. 793–795 (2018)
6. Lin, Y.: Application of MVVM design pattern and MVP design pattern based on ZK. J. Chongqing Univ. Arts Sci. (Nat. Sci. Ed.) **72–74**, 78 (2010)
7. Zeng, L.: Application research of MVP for android. Comput. Eng. Softw. **2016**(06), 75–78 (2016)
8. Fu, C.: Design of transparent encryption system for documents based on windows kernel. J. Chongqing Univ. Educ. **28**, 171–173 (2015)
9. Nawaz, Y., Wang, L., Ammour, K.: Processing analysis of confidential modes of operation. In: International Conference on Security, Privacy and Anonymity in Computation, Communication and Storage (SpaCCS), pp. 98–110 (2018)
10. Qiu, P., Wang, D., Lv, Y., et al.: Voltjockey: breaching trustzone by software-controlled voltage manipulation over multi-core frequencies. In: Proceedings of the 2019 ACM SIGSAC Conference on Computer and Communications Security (CCS), pp. 195–209 (2019)
11. Salman, H., Uddin, M.N., Acheampong, S., et al.: Design and implementation of IoT based class attendance monitoring system using computer vision and embedded linux platform. In: Workshops of the International Conference on Advanced Information Networking and Applications (AINA), pp. 25–34 (2019)

SCPAC: An Access Control Framework for Diverse IoT Platforms Based on OAuth2.0

Tong Ye⬤ and Yi Zhuang$^{(\boxtimes)}$⬤

College of Computer Science and Technology, Nanjing University
of Aeronautics and Astronautics, Nanjing 211100, China
{yetong, zyl6}@nuaa.edu.cn

Abstract. With the emergency of the Internet of Things in all walks of life, its security problems are getting more attention. Different devices need to access users' data from different platforms. However, as different platforms are developed based on different security architectures, when the security policies of different platforms are supposed to be composed, it will result in new vulnerabilities and bring security risks. To address this problem, a new cross-domain access control framework based on OAuth 2.0 is proposed in this paper. The framework realizes secure and flexible management of authentication and authorization of cross-platform access control. The security domain token is used for entities to access and share the resources of each security domain, which solves the cross-domain security problem. The proposed approach is formally modeled in Coq theorem prover, and the results show that the proposed access control mechanism satisfies the security properties.

Keywords: Access control · OAuth 2.0 · Internet of Things · Security · Cross-domain · Formal method · Coq

1 Introduction

Internet of Things (IoT) [1] is a kind of network that connects electronic equipment with Internet for information exchange and communication, so as to realize intelligent identification, positioning, tracking, monitoring and management. It has been applied in all walks of life to improve productivity and efficiency. As a result, global companies like Google and Amazon have been researching and developing IoT related products (such as sensors and IoT devices). Gartner predicts that 14.2 billion connected IoT devices will be used by 2019 and this number will reach 25 billion by 2021 [2]. However, the Internet of Things still faces great challenges in terms of interoperability, security and privacy protection [3]. Different from the traditional information management, the Internet of Things usually collects users' personal privacy data automatically from the devices. As a result, it is necessary to provide users with adequate management and control of automatic data flow. There are many devices in the Internet of Things platforms. Different devices need to access users' information from different platforms. In this aspect, the access control mechanism is particularly important. OAuth2.0 protocol [4] is an open industry standard authorization protocol. Nowadays, it has become the most widely used approach for authentication and third-party

G. Wang et al. (Eds.): SpaCCS 2020, LNCS 12383, pp. 146–157, 2021.
https://doi.org/10.1007/978-3-030-68884-4_12

authorization in Web environment [5]. Many famous companies (such as Google and Facebook) use OAuth2.0 to support their access control services. However, as most IoT platforms are developed by their own security approaches, when considering inter-operability, these methods will be composed and result in new vulnerabilities, which can lead to huge security risks.

In fact, traditional access control systems based on OAuth2.0 cannot interoperate with each other, as OAuth2.0 is based on single client and single server. So its application in IoT environment needs to enhance its interoperability as well as security. Some existing approaches have extended OAuth2.0. However, these approaches are more or less insufficient in security aspect.

We propose a secure interoperable access control framework, namely, SCPAC (Secure Cross-Platform Access Control) for IoT environment. First, we analyze the requirements of access control framework in the environment of Internet of things. Based on the analysis of the requirements, we propose an interoperable mutual authentication authorization access framework based on OAuth 2.0. The framework realizes the flexible management of data flow and insure the security of uses' information.

The main contributions of this paper are as follows:

(1) We propose a security-enhanced access control framework based on OAuth 2.0 to realize cross-domain authentication and authorization;
(2) We propose a mutual authentication and authorization approach for entities to access and share various resources (such as data and services) by using the security token in each security domain;
(3) We formalize and verify the proposed OAuth-based security mechanism in the widely used Coq theorem prover. This approach can help to find errors of security mechanisms in the design phase.

The structure of the rest of this paper is as follows: In Sect. 2, we introduce the related research work; In Sect. 3, we analyze the security requirements of access control mechanisms in the Internet of Things environment. We give the proposed cross-domain access control framework for diverse IoT platforms; The formal modeling and verification of the authorization and authentication process based on OAuth2.0 are carried out in Coq theorem prover in Sect. 4; Sect. 5 gives the conclusion and the work in future.

2 Related Work

The Internet of things environment is composed of heterogeneous devices, which constantly exchange information and are widely accessed through networks. This requires the establishment of a flexible, lightweight and adaptable access control mechanism to deal with the heterogeneity of Internet of Things devices, while ensuring reliable communication between trusted devices. Oauth2.0 is an industry standard protocol in the field of authorization. It replaces the original OAuth protocol created in 2006, and focuses more on the simplicity and convenience of client development. It can provide specific authorization flow for web applications, desktop applications, mobile smart devices and home devices. It has been widely used by major Internet companies as a standard protocol of authorization and authentication. With the explosive growth of intelligent devices connected through the Internet of Things, data sharing between IoT devices from different platforms has become a common scenario. However, at present, there is no universally recognized secure and lightweight cross-platform access control mechanism to realize secure data sharing of IoT devices from different platforms.

The widely used access control models are Role-Based Access Control(RBAC) [6], Attribute-Based Access Control (ABAC) [7], Capability-Based Access Control (Cap-BAC) [8], Organization-Based Access Control (OrBAC) [9] and Trust-Based Access Control (TBAC). RBAC specifies the access permissions to resources according to roles, but it has the problem of role explosion. In traditional RBAC model, roles are organized in a static hierarchy. However, smart city scenarios contain some roles that cannot be organized in a static hierarchy. As a result, RBAC cannot meet the dynamic needs of the IoT. Moreover, RBAC is designed for single server, and it cannot deal with the cross-application scenarios. Researches have been done to improve traditional RBAC model. Chen proposed a RBAC model across multiple collaborative IOT servers [10], which uses the trust evaluation (TE) algorithm to evaluate the reliability of IOT devices. The trust evaluation algorithm includes local trust evaluation, actual trust evaluation algorithm and collaborative trust evaluation. To grant permissions dynamically according to context conditions (for example, body sensor data), Kayes *et al.* proposed a context aware access control method [11] which dynamically specifies the context role according to the relevant context conditions obtained from the information provided by the IoT. They also proposed an ontology-based dynamic context role modeling method and access control strategy.

In order to solve the weakness of RBAC model in highly distributed network environment, many researches introduce Attribute-Based Access Control (ABAC) into the IoT to solve the problem of role explosion. ABAC grants or denies access requests to resources by evaluating the properties (for example, object, topic, action, and environment) of various entities. ABAC model provides fine-grained access control by making decisions based on the inherent characteristics of any entity. Xu *et al.* Proposed an attribute-based cloud access control system of the IoT [12]. They introduced an effective attribute-based revocable encryption scheme to provide effective management to data. This system can deal with the key revocation of malicious users as well as the unexpected key exposure of honest users. Combined the attribute-based access control model (ABAC) with the OM-AM (Objective, Model, Architecture, and Mechanism) four layer model [6], Sifou *et al.* proposed a new model [13], which uses XACML (eXtensible Access Control Markup Language) as the description language of access control strategy, and uses the access based encryption model (ABE) to encrypt storage Data in the cloud. Bouanani *et al.* extended ABAC model and proposed a two-layer access control model PerBAC [14] which includes abstract layer and concrete layer. Abstract layer includes logical attributes with multiple conditions, while concrete layer contains physical attributes. If the attributes of the concrete entity (subject, object or action) describe the corresponding abstract entity (role, view or action), the former will match the latter automatically. This model has better dynamic performance and is more suitable for the IoT environment. Ouechtati *et al.* [15] proposed an access control framework, which integrates user behavior and risk assessment into ABAC model to enhance access control in the IoT environment. The framework aims to adapt system faults, resource changes and user requirements dynamically.

However, the disadvantage of these methods is that decision-making needs complex calculation, which is not suitable for IoT nodes with limited resources. With the increasing number of devices, the consistency of cross-domain attributes will significantly increase the workload and complexity of policy management. Because the RBAC model and ABAC model have more or less defects when applied to the IoT environment, many researchers began to introduce CBAC into the IoT. In the CBAC model, each subject is associated with a list of capabilities representing its access rights to all objects. Marian *et al.* proposed a lightweight CBAC mechanism LCAP [16], which uses symmetric key to encrypt tokens to reduce the energy consumption of limited devices which makes it more suitable for the IoT environment. Imane *et al.* proposed an access control model called SmartOrBAC [17]. This model enhances the existing Organization-Based Access Control model (OrBAC) and adapts it to the IOT environment. SmartOrBAC divides the problem into different functional layers, and then schedules and allocates computing tasks to devices. In addition, they proposed a specific solution to solve the cross-domain cooperation problem.

Though a great amount of research work has been done in the area of access control of IoT and some significant contributions have been made to improve access control in smart city environments, there are still many issues such as enabling cross-application access control in smart city environment, designing high-confidence framework to secure information flow, modeling and verification of high-confidence city IoT access control mechanism.

To fill the research gaps, we propose an access control mechanism, namely SCPAC, which is able to handle the heterogeneous data sources coming from different IoT platforms, and display a secure access to users. The proposed solution aims to fulfill the security requirements in mutiple-party data sharing in the IoT environment. We conduct a theoretical analysis through formal modeling and verification to validate the correctness and effectiveness of the proposed method. Results show that the proposed method can ensure the confidentiality and integrity of users' information on each platform and realize convenient and secure cross-platform access control.

3   The Proposed Framework

In this section, we analyze the security requirements of access control mechanisms in the Internet of Things environment. We introduce the security domain, and give the illustration of the proposed cross-domain access control framework for diverse IoT platforms.

3.1 Security Requirements of Access Control Mechanisms in IoT Environment

This paper refers to the existing research study [18] of IoT and analyzes the existing security problems. Based on which, we summarize the following security requirements of access control mechanisms in IoT environment:

1) **Lightweight:** The computing resources and energy of devices in the IoT environment are often limited, so the security policies applied to these devices should be lightweight.

2) **Generality:** The application scenarios involved in the IoT environment are changeable. General authorization access mechanisms, such as smart city scenarios, require fine-grained access control, while smart home scenarios require coarse-grained access control.

3) **Interoperability:** Authorization management of user resources in IoT application scenarios often involves IoT devices and applications on more than one platform, and the traditional single client and single authorization server access control mechanism is no longer applicable. Enhancing the interoperability of platform devices and realizing access control across heterogeneous IoT platforms are the main security requirements of the access control mechanisms for IoT environment.

4) **Cross-Domain Security:** In cross-platform authorization and authentication, each platform, as an independent and autonomous security domain, applies different security policies and authorization access mechanisms. Cross-domain security aims to achieve mutual trust and mutual access between different platforms across security domains.

5) **Mutual Authentication:** The authorization server verifies the identity of the client by authenticating the client (the client must prove the secret or private key material that the client has rights), and verifies the access rights applied for, so as to offer the authorization service. The client authenticates each entity it interacts with to prevent unauthorized disclosure of private information. As cross-platform authorization and authentication are involved, mutual authentication between authorization servers of different platforms is also necessary.

6) **Information Transmission Security:** In the process of authorization and authentication, the information is transmitted through the public channel. Information transmission security requires that the attacker cannot eavesdrop on the information of the public channel to realize man-in-the-middle attack, replay attack, etc., which requires the confidentiality and integrity of data in the transmission process, as well as the anonymity and untraceability of both parties involved in authentication.

3.2 Overview of the Proposed Framework

Usually, the traditional OAuth2.0 protocol is often used for single client and single server authorization and authentication. However, in the IoT environment, it is necessary to realize third-party access control which is also referred to as interoperability between platforms. In most existing approaches, a platform serves as a user agent for the third-party authorization that can be interoperated by customers. However, the third-party user login of other platforms through forwarding violates the fundamental design principle of security. To address this problem, in this paper, original OAuth2.0 protocol is extended to support cross-domain access control among multiple IoT platforms. We propose a security-enhanced cross-domain access control framework, namely, SCPAC, based on OAuth2.0. As shown in Fig. 1, each IoT platform is regarded as an independent and autonomous security-domain, which is denoted as Domain N. The security domain includes authorization server and resource server. The authorization server processes authorization requests and conducts authentication by issuing authorization code. Each platform has one or more resource servers which store the resource data of users.

In Fig. 1, we introduce a virtual authorization management layer to evaluate the trust of entities. This helps to make sure whether the entity has enough credibility to get access to the resource data of users. The trust degree has an initial value, and each successful access control event will increase the credibility of the entities. As a general approach, we don't specify the calculation approach of the trust degree, it can be specified according to application scenarios. The topic of trust assessment is out of range of this paper, we recommend that readers refer to advanced trust assessment approaches introduced in [19] and [20].

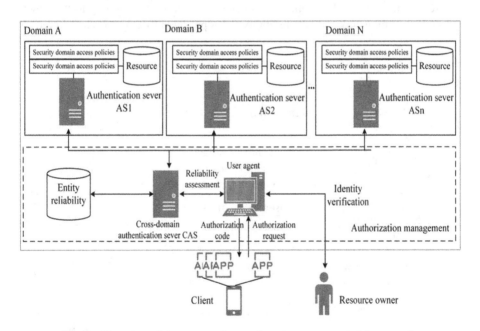

Fig. 1. Overview of the proposed cross-domain access control framework.

3.3 Security-Enhanced Mutual Authentication and Authorization Procedure Based on OAuth2.0

In this paper, the traditional OAuth2.0 protocol is extended to support mutual authorization and authentication of multiple parties. The proposed authentication and authorization process is shown in Fig. 2. The steps of the proposed procedure are as follows (Note that (A), (B), (C), (D), (E) represent messages transmitted between entities):

Step 1: The client sends authorization request which is denoted as (A) in Fig. 2 to the user agent. (A) consists of the following information: client ID and secret & redirect URI & ID of multiple domains requested to be accessed;

Step 2: The user agent forwards the authorization request (A) to the trust management server, which maintains a trust list of domains and devices. Then the sever replies whether the client and domain are trusted or not;

Step 3: The trust management server forwards the authorization request (A) to the authorization server of each domain to obtain (B), the access permission of the resource owner;

Step 4: The trust management server forwards the authorization request (A), authorization permission (B) and client trust authentication result (D) to the authorization server of each domain according to the ID of the domain. After which, the server performs authorization;

Step 5: Mutual authentication is carried out between the domains. The domain sever is responsible to decide whether to trust the other domain according to their own security requirements and the credibility proof provided by authorization server. In

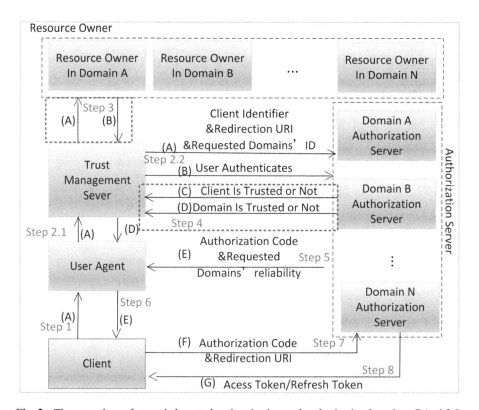

Fig. 2. The procedure of extended mutual authentication and authorization based on OAuth2.0.

each security domain, the server which is trusted by all other authorization servers, is responsible for generating (E) authorization codes and tokens. And then it forwards the message (E) to user agents;

Step 6: The user agent forwards (E) domain credibility and authorization code to the client;

Step 7: The client can choose whether to continue the authorization process according to the domain's trust degree. If it continues, it will forward the authorization code and redirection URI to the authorization server;

Step 8: The server generates the token that can access multiple domains requested by the user, and issues the token to the client, so the user can access data from multiple platforms by using the one token at a same time.

4 Formal Modeling of the Security-Enhanced OAuth2.0

In this section, a cross-domain access control example of Android APP is given. The example as well as the proposed security-enhanced OAuth 2.0 protocol is modeled in Coq. And we prove that the protocol can avoid redirection attack in cross-domain applications.

The user agent is usually a trusted external browser, which forwards the access token granted by the authorization server to the client through the redirection URL registered by the APP for authorization. This is implemented on Android devices through broadcast intent, and only the App registered with the URL can receive it. In Fig. 3, the function *accept_intent* indicates that the App's intent-filter matches with the user agent's intention. The input parameter *i* is the user agent's broadcast intention, and *f* is the client's intent-filer. The matching is successful only if the three parameters *action*, *category* and *URI* all pass the matching. *Accept_intent_env* is a recursive function, which is the extension of intent function *accept_intent*. Different from *accept_intent* which can only verify one pair of matching result between intent and intent-filter, *Accept_intent_env* can verify whether there is an intent matching with multiple intent-filters. This function is able to complete intent matching of the whole device.

```
(**When the action, category and URI all match, the intent is accepted*)
Definition accept_intent (i: intent) (f: filter) : bool :=
 match i, f with
 | int a cl ul t, filt fal fcl ful ftl =>
    testaction a (filt fal fcl ful ftl) &
    testcategory cl fcl &
    testuri (Some ul) ful.
 end.
Fixpoint accept_intent_env (i: intent) (e: list filter) :   bool :=
 match e with | nil => false | f::tl =>
 orb (accept_intent i f) (accept_intent_env i tl)..
 end.

Definition verify_user_app (user:string) (user_v:string) (app:string) (app_v:string) : bool :=
if (eqb user user_v) then.
 (if (eqb app app_v) then true
  else false)
else false.
```

Fig. 3. The matching between APP intent-filter and user agent's intent modeled in Coq.

The third-party App sends the intent of the URL containing all the request information to the external browser. And the external browser sends a broadcast intent. If there are multiple acceptable filters, the system will give the user multiple options to choose, and the user is easy to make a wrong choice due to negligence, which may easily cause redirection attack. Fig. 4 is the defined ***testuri_strengthen*** function which is used to prevent redirection attacks. This function is also part of the instance of the proposed extended OAuth 2.0 protocol. ***H_user_app_V*** is used to verify the hash value of the string concatenation of user ID and App ID. ***H_user_app_V*** is put in the intent URL as a parameter. ***H_user_App*** provides user authentication for the third-party client by verifying the hash value of the string concatenation of user ID and App ID. ***H_user_App*** is put in the filter URL as a parameter.

```
(***************************Strengthen Url Intent, Filter ********************************)
(*Redefinition of the redirect url, add a parameter H_user_app*)
(*redirect_uri includes scheme,host,port,path and H_user_app*)
Inductive re_uri: Type :=
| redirect_uri: option string -> option string -> option nat -> option string-> string ->re_uri.
(**Implicit intent: action, category, data (re_uri, type)*)
Inductive sintent: Type :=.
    sint: string -> list  string -> re_uri -> string -> sintent.
(**Intent filter: contain specification of actions, categories, URI and MIME types.*)
Inductive sfilter: Type :=
    sfilt: list  string -> list  string -> list re_uri -> list  string -> sfilter.
Fixpoint matchuri_strengthen (filuri iuri: re_uri) : bool :=
    match filuri, iuri with

| redirect_uri (Some scheme)  None H_user_app, redirect_uri (Some scheme') (Some host')  _ _ H_user_app_v =>.
    (eqb scheme scheme') & (eqb host host')& (eqb H_user_app H_user_app_v) (*1*)
| redirect_uri (Some scheme) (Some host)  _ (Some path) H_user_app, redirect_uri (Some scheme') (Some host') _ (Some path') H_user_app_v =>.
    (eqb scheme scheme') & (eqb host host') & (eqb path path')&(eqb H_user_app H_user_app_v) (*2*)
| redirect_uri schemeo hosto porto patho  H_user_app , redirect_uri schemeo' hosto' porto' patho' H_user_app_v  => (*3*)
    cmpoattr schemeo schemeo' & cmpoattr hosto hosto' & beq_nato porto porto' & cmpoattr patho patho' &(eqb H_user_app H_user_app_v)·
(*| redirect ,redirect_ _ _ _ _ => false (*otherwise cases*)*)
end.
Fixpoint testuri_strengthen (iuri:option re_uri)(filuris:list re_uri):bool :=
match iuri, filuris with
| Some u1, cons uh ul  => orb (matchuri_strengthen uh ul)(testuri_strengthen iuri ul)·|
| _, _ => false (*otherwise cases*)
end.
```

Fig. 4. Modeling security-enhanced OAuth2.0 protocol in Coq

Figure 5 gives the security theorem of the proposed extended OAuth2.0 protocol. The theorem ***accept_strengthen*** in Fig. 5 means that for any third-party browser that broadcast intention as well as the receiver APP, only the intent-filter matching the action, category, and URI can receive the intent containing the code. In Fig. 5, ***exampleintent*** and ***examplefilter1*** are examples of the intent broadcasted by the third-party browser and the intent-filter registered by the third-party App.

```
(**The theorem accept_strengthen means that for any third-party browser that broadcast intention
as well as the receiver APP, only the intent-filter matching the action, category,·
and URI can receive the intent containing the code**)
Theorem accept_strengthen: forall a cl ul t  fal fcl ful ftl ,·
    testactions a (sfilt fal fcl ful ftl) = true ->
    testcategory cl fcl = true ->
    testtype ftl t = true ->
    testuri_strengthen (Some ul) ful = true ->
    accept_intent_strengthen (sint a cl ul t) (sfilt fal fcl ful ftl) =true.·
Proof.
intros ???????? TA TC TT TU.·
unfold accept_intent_strengthen.
rewrite TA.
rewrite TC.·
rewrite TT.
rewrite TU.
simpl.·
auto.·
Qed.
```

Fig. 5. The security matching theorem and proof of the proposed extended OAuth2.0 protocol.

Figure 6 gives the redirection security theorem of the proposed extended OAuth2.0 protocol. Theorem ***redirect_security_accept*** means that the App conformed to the enhanced–security matching theorem can receive the intent broadcasted by the third-party browser, and obtain the authorization code, while the illegal redirection will not be accepted.

```
(**exampleintent is the intent broadcasted by the third party browser**)
(**examplefilter1 is the intent_filter registered by the third party APP**)
Theorem  redirect_security_accept:
 accept_intent_strengthen exampleintent examplefilter1 =true.
 Proof.
 unfold accept_intent_strengthen.
 apply accept_strengthen ; simpl.
(**action***).
 rewrite eqb_refl;auto.
(**category***).
 rewrite eqb_refl;auto.
(**type***)
 rewrite eqb_refl;auto.
(**url***)
 do 4 rewrite eqb_refl;auto.
Qed.
```

Fig. 6. The redirection security theorem of the proposed extended OAuth2.0 protocol

5   Conclusion

The security of cross-platform access control in the Internet of Things environment has always been a hot problem. The traditional OAuth2.0 protocol cannot support secure cross-platform access control. This paper proposed a security-enhanced framework SCPAC for mutual authentication and authorization in the Internet of Things environment. By extending the authentication and authorization process of OAuth2.0, secure cross-domain access control is achieved. The proposed protocol is modeled in an Android cross-domain access control example. The effectiveness of the security-enhanced protocol is proved by Coq theorem prover. As future work, we will focus on the transmission security. For example, some third-party applications communicate with the authorization server through HTTPS, but communicate with their own server through HTTP, which allows an attacker to eavesdrop on their information stream easily.

Acknowledgments. This work was supported by the National Natural Science Foundation of China (General Program) under Grant No. 61572253. This work is also supported by Jiangsu Collaborative Innovation Center of Novel Software Technology and Industrialization.

References

1. Gubbi, J., Buyya, R., Marusica, S., Palaniswamia, M.: Internet of Things (IoT): a vision, architectural elements, and future directions. Future Gener. Comput. Syst. **29**(7), 1645–1660 (2013)
2. Da Li, X., Eric, X., Li, L.: Industry 4.0: state of the art and future trends. Int. J. Prod. Res. **56** (8), 2941–2962 (2018)
3. Patton, M., Gross, E., Chinn, R., Forbis, S., Walker, L., Chen, H.: Uninvited connections: a study of vulnerable devices on the Internet of Things (IoT). In: 2014 IEEE Joint Intelligence and Security Informatics Conference (JISIC 2014), Hague, Netherlands, 24–26 September 2014, pp. 232–255 (2014)
4. Fett, D., Küsters, R., Schmitz, G.: A comprehensive formal security analysis of OAuth 2.0. In: Proceedings of the 2016 ACM SIGSAC Conference on Computer and Communications Security (CCS 2016), Vienna, Austria, 24–28 October 2016, pp. 1204–1215 (2016)
5. Bansal, C., Bhargavan, K., Delignat-Lavaud, A., Maffeis, S.: Discovering concrete attacks on website authorization by formal analysis 1. J. Comput. Secur. **22**(4), 601–657 (2014)
6. Sandhu, R., Coyne, E., Feinstein, H., Youman, C.: Role-based access control models. Computer **29**(2), 38–47 (1996)
7. Yuan, E., Tong, J.: Attributed based access control (ABAC) for web services. In: IEEE International Conference on Web Services (ICWS 2005), Florida, USA, 11–15 July 2005, pp. 561–569 (2005)
8. Gusmeroli, S., Piccione, S., Rotondi, D.: A capability-based security approach to manage access control in the Internet of Things. Math. Comput. Model. **58**(5–6), 1189–1205 (2013)
9. Kalam, A., Baida, R., et al.: Organization based access control. In: IEEE 4th International Workshop on Policies for Distributed Systems and Networks (POLICY 2003), Lake Como, Italy, 4–6 June 2003, pp. 120–131 (2003)
10. Chen, H.-C.: Collaboration IoT-based RBAC with trust evaluation algorithm model for massive IoT integrated application. Mobile Netw. Appl. **24**(3), 839–852 (2018). https://doi.org/10.1007/s11036-018-1085-0
11 Kayes, A.S.M., Rahayu, W., Dillon, T.: Critical situation management utilizing IoT-based data resources through dynamic contextual role modeling and activation. Computing **101**(7), 743–772 (2018). https://doi.org/10.1007/s00607-018-0654-1
12. Shengmin, X., Yang, G., Yi, M., Liu, X.: A secure IoT cloud storage system with fine-grained access control and decryption key exposure resistance. Future Gener. Comput. Syst. **97**, 284–294 (2019)
13. Sifou, F., Marwan, M., Hammouch, A.: Applying OM-AM reference to an ABAC model for securing cloud-enabled Internet of Things. In: 2018 3rd International Conference on System Reliability and Safety (ICSRS 2018), Barcelona, Spain, 23–25 November 2018, pp. 86–91 (2018)
14. El Bouanani, S., Kiram, M.A.E., Achbarou, O., Outchakoucht, A.: Pervasive-based access control model for IoT environments. IEEE Access **7**, 54575–54585 (2019)
15. Ouechtati, H., Azzouna, N.B., Said, L.B.: Towards a self-adaptive access control middleware for the Internet of Things. In: 2018 International Conference on Information Networking (ICOIN 2018), Chiang Mai, Thailand, 10–12 January 2018, pp. 545–550 (2018)
16. Buschsieweke, M., Güneş, M.: Access control for medical devices: tweaking LCap for health informatics. In: 2018 IEEE Global Communications Conference Workshops (GLOBECOM 2018), Abu Dhabi, UAE, 9–13 December 2018, pp. 1–7 (2018)
17. Bouij-Pasquier, I., El Kalam, A.A., Ouahman, A.A.: SmartOrBAC enforcing security in the Internet of Things. Int. J. Adv. Comput. Sci. Appl. **6**(11), 17–28 (2015)

18. Rehman, S., Gruhn, V., Shafiq, S., Inayat, I.: A systematic mapping study on security requirements engineering frameworks for cyber-physical systems. In: Wang, Guojun, Chen, Jinjun, Yang, Laurence T. (eds.) SpaCCS 2018. LNCS, vol. 11342, pp. 428–442. Springer, Cham (2018). https://doi.org/10.1007/978-3-030-05345-1_37
19. Ziegler, S., Skarmeta, A., Bernal, J., Kim, E.E., Bianchi, S.: ANASTACIA: advanced networked agents for security and trust assessment in CPS IoT architectures. In: 2017 Global Internet of Things Summit (GIoTS 2017), Geneva, Switzerland, 6–9 June 2017, pp. 1–6 (2017)
20. Truong, N.B., Lee, G.M., Um, T.-W., Mackay, M.: Trust evaluation mechanism for user recruitment in mobile crowd-sensing in the Internet of Things. IEEE Trans. Inf. Forensics Secur. **14**(10), 2705–2719 (2019)

The 6th International Symposium on Sensor-Cloud Systems (SCS 2020)

Adaptive Routing Strategy Based on Improved Q-learning for Satellite Internet of Things

Xiaotian Gong[1,2], Lijuan Sun[1,2(✉)], Jian Zhou[1,2(✉)], Juan Wang[1,2], and Fu Xiao[1,2]

[1] College of Computer, Nanjing University of Posts and Telecommunications, Nanjing 210003, China
sunlijuan_nupt@163.com, zhoujian@njupt.edu.cn
[2] Jiangsu High Technology Research Key Laboratory for Wireless Sensor Networks, Nanjing 210003, China

Abstract. Satellite Internet of Things (S-IoT), which combines satellite networks with IoT, is a ubiquitous IoT system under the integrated satellite-terrestrial information network architecture. It has the advantages of wide coverage, multiple-type services, and strong robustness. However, as a result of the dynamic changes of topology structure and node status in S-IoT, the effective forwarding of data packets is challenging. In view of the above problem, an adaptive routing strategy based on improved Q-learning for S-IoT is proposed in this paper. First, the whole S-IoT is regarded as a reinforcement learning environment. In the meantime, satellite nodes and ground nodes in S-IoT are regarded as intelligent agents, respectively. What is more, the next hop node of data packets is determined according to the Q value. Second, in order to optimize the Q value, this paper improves the discount factor based on the status of satellite nodes. Finally, simulation results show that the proposed strategy can achieve efficient routing in the high dynamic environment. Compared with the state-of-the-art strategies, it improves the performance in terms of delivery rate, average delay, and overhead ratio.

Keywords: Routing strategy · Satellite Internet of Things · Q-learning · Reinforcement learning · Store-carry-forward

1 Introduction

Satellite Internet of Things (S-IoT) is a combination of satellite networks [1, 2] and IoT [3–5]. It is not only using relay satellites to strengthen communication, but a ubiquitous IoT system under the integrated satellite-terrestrial information network architecture and a service platform of multiple information technologies [6]. S-IoT has the advantages of wide coverage, multiple-type services, and strong robustness, so it has attracted wide attention of researchers.

As the core of communication protocol for S-IoT, the routing strategy undertakes the responsibility of data packets forwarding and determines the overall performance of S-IoT. Therefore, the research of routing strategy is of great significance [7, 8]. Compared with terrestrial networks, S-IoT has the following characteristics: (1) The

© Springer Nature Switzerland AG 2021
G. Wang et al. (Eds.): SpaCCS 2020, LNCS 12383, pp. 161–172, 2021.
https://doi.org/10.1007/978-3-030-68884-4_13

high-speed movement of satellite nodes and the frequent failure of sensor nodes cause the dynamic topology structure, so there is no stable end-to-end path in S-IoT. (2) The complex space environment and the uneven amount of terrestrial access data lead to the dynamic node status. (3) Satellite nodes and sensor nodes both have the limited energy, so the energy consumption should be considered in the designed routing strategy to reduce the overhead ratio. (4) The amount of the nodes and the data packets in S-IoT are very large, so the efficiency of data packets forwarding also should be considered in the designed routing strategy. (5) Data services account for a very high proportion in S-IoT and their delay requirements are low, so the store-carry-forward mechanism can be used for data packets forwarding. Considering the above characteristics, the routing strategy for the terrestrial network is not applicable to S-IoT. Therefore, the routing strategy for S-IoT has been researched, especially. Some researchers paid attention to the dynamic topology structure of satellite networks. According to the predictability, periodicity, and regularity of satellite networks, the routing strategies based on virtual topology [9], virtual node [10], and coverage domain partitioning [11] were proposed, respectively. These strategies simplify the complexity of routing, but the additional calculations are large. Some researchers focused on the limited energy of satellite nodes. According to the symmetric constellation structure, the routing strategies based on energy-saving [12] were proposed. These strategies forward data packets on low orbit satellites, and select the path with fewer hop count. These routing strategies can control energy consumption to reduce the overhead ratio, but the requirements for network structure are relatively high. Some other researchers paid attention to the problem of poor Quality of Service (QoS) caused by the large number and the long distances of satellite nodes, the routing strategies based on QoS [13] are proposed. However, most of these strategies focus on improving the QoS of voice and multimedia services, and rarely consider that of data services.

It should be noted that the above routing strategies use the inter-satellite links. However, considering cost and system complexity, in the existing Low Earth Orbit (LEO) or Medium Earth Orbit (MEO) constellation systems, only Iridinm has inter-satellite links, and other constellation systems such as Ocbcomm, Globalstar, O3b, etc. have no inter-satellite links [14]. According to the current state of constellation systems, it is more reasonable to construct the S-IoT based on the constellation systems without inter-satellite links. The store-carry-forward mechanism in Delay Tolerant Networks (DTN) can solve the problems of the dynamic topology structure in S-IoT. Therefore, this paper studies S-IoT as a DTN without considering inter-satellite links. The satellite nodes in S-IoT use the store-carry-forward mechanism to forward data packets.

In recent years, DTN networks have attracted extensive attention of researchers, and many routing strategies for DTN are proposed. These routing strategies usually divided into the flood-based, the utility-based, and the mobility model-based routing strategies. In the flood-based routing strategies, Vahdat et al. [15] proposed the Epidemic routing strategy. One node forwards data packets to every node that it meets. This virus-like propagation mode results in the excessive overhead ratio. In order to improve Epidemic, Spyropoulos et al. [16] proposed the Spray-and-Wait routing strategy. The process of data packets forwarding is divided into two phases: spraying and waiting. The data packets are diffused into some copies in the spraying phase, and these copies are directly forwarded to the destination node in the waiting phase. This strategy has transmission performance close to Epidemic, and can reduce the overhead ratio. In the utility-based routing strategies, Lindgren et al. [17] proposed the Prophet routing strategy. In this strategy, the data packets only make a copy to the node with a large meeting probability, which reduces the amount of replication and overhead ratio. In the mobile model-based routing strategies, Burleigh et al. [18] proposed the Contact Graph Routing (CGR) strategy. The next hop node is selected according to the minimum hop count and the shortest path length, which reduces the average delay.

However, the above routing strategies for DTN cannot quickly adapt to the frequent changes of node status in S-IoT. The reinforcement learning can obtain the optimal result even if the system environment changes frequently. It has been successfully applied in industrial manufacturing, analogue simulation, game competition, scheduling management, and other fields. Existing routing strategies cannot solve the problem of the dynamic changes of topology structure and node status in S-IoT. Q-learning algorithm in reinforcement learning, which can choose the next better hop node by self-learning, provides a way to solve this problem. In this paper, the reinforcement learning is applied in S-IoT and the adaptive routing strategy for S-IoT is studied.

In view of the dynamic topology structure and the dynamic node status in S-IoT, an adaptive routing strategy based on improved Q-learning for S-IoT is proposed. The main contributions of this paper are as follows:

1. The reinforcement learning is applied in S-IoT, so the proposed routing strategy can adapt to the dynamic changes of topology structure and node status in S-IoT.
2. The discount factor is improved based on distance, direction, and buffer occupancy of satellite nodes in S-IoT to improve the forwarding performance.
3. The S-IoT model with ground layer, LEO layer and MEO layer is established for simulation experiments. Simulation results show that the proposed strategy improves the delivery rate, average delay, and overhead ratio, compared with the state-of-the-art strategies.

The rest of this paper is organized as follows: Sect. 2 introduces Q-learning algorithm. The detailed description of the proposed strategy is given in Sect. 3. Simulation analysis is given in Sect. 4. Section 5 concludes this paper.

2   Introduce of Q-learning Algorithm

In recent years, reinforcement learning has attracted widespread attention. As a classic reinforcement learning algorithm, Q-learning algorithm was proposed by Watkins et al. [19]. Q-learning algorithm combines the advantages of dynamic programming algorithm and Monte Carlo algorithm. It does not require a known environment model, and it updates the state-action value function after each step. In addition, Q-learning algorithm obtains the sample data sequence (state, action, reward value) through interaction with the environment, and uses the state-action function value (Q value) to find the best action in the current state. The Q value is a prediction of the reward. More precisely, it is the sum of future reward values.

The core idea of Q-learning algorithm is that the action is selected based on the greedy algorithm in each step and the Q value is updated according to the changes of environment. Tsitsiklis et al. [20] proved that the Q value would converge if the Q value could be infinitely iterated with its update formula and the learning rate satisfies certain conditions.

3 Proposed Strategy

The whole S-IoT is regarded as a reinforcement learning environment in this paper. Satellites in S-IoT are regarded as the satellite nodes, also sensors and data centers are regarded as the ground nodes. For one node, other nodes it can meet constitute its neighbor node set. In particular, the ground nodes can generate and receive data packets, and the satellite nodes use the store-carry-forward mechanism to forward data packets.

The satellite nodes and the ground nodes are considered as intelligent agents. Each node learns the network environment of the whole S-IoT by interaction with the nodes it meets. In particular, all nodes can be seen as the state set of reinforcement learning. In the meantime, the ground node or the satellite node selects one node in its neighbor node set for data packets forwarding, which is considered as an action selection of reinforcement learning. Hence, for one node, the possible action set is its neighbor node set. The state transitions are equivalent to forwarding data packets from one node to its neighbor node.

In the proposed strategy, each node stores a Q table. For one node, its Q table stores the Q value of the action that it selects one of neighbor nodes to forward the data packets with the destination node. Each node only updates its own Q table, and only interacts with its neighbor nodes for local information. The Q value changes as the node status changes, which enables the proposed strategy to adapt to the dynamic node status.

When a new node joins S-IoT, the node has no knowledge of the whole S-IoT environment, thus its Q table is empty. When the new node meets other nodes, it records id of other nodes and initializes the corresponding Q value to 0 in Q table.

The routing process of each node is shown in Fig. 1. If the destination node is in its neighbor nodes, it forwards data packets to the destination node to complete transmission. Otherwise, according to the largest Q value, it selects one node in its neighbor nodes to forward data packets. Afterwards, if the Q value of the selected node is greater than its own Q value, it forwards data packets to the selected node. Otherwise, it stores and carries these data packages until it meets the next node, and then continues to operate as above. The greedy algorithm can ensure the largest cumulative future rewards. Take node c for example, the selected node in its neighbor nodes can be expressed as follows:

$$y^* = \arg\max_{x \in Nc} Q_c(d, x) \tag{1}$$

where N_c is the neighbor node set of node c. $Q_c(d,x)$ is the Q value of the action that node c selects node x to forward the data packets with destination node d. If two nodes both have the largest Q value, one of them is randomly selected.

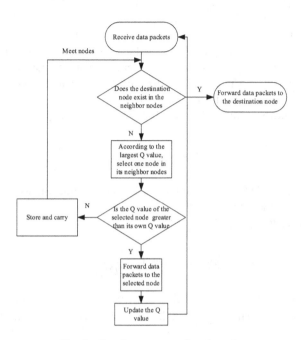

Fig. 1. Routing process of each node.

Because the learning task is assigned to each node, the learning process is the update process of Q table. If the topology of the current node changes or the data packets is forwarded, the Q value in Q table will be updated. Take node c for example, if node c has forwarded the data packets with destination node d to neighbor node x, its Q value is updated as follows:

$$Q_c(d,x) = (1-\alpha)Q_c(d,x) + \alpha(R_c(d,x) + \gamma_c(d,x)\max_{y \in N_x}Q_x(d,y)) \qquad (2)$$

where N_x is the neighbor node set of node x, and α is the learning rate which affects the update speed of Q value. $R_c(d,x)$ and $\gamma_c(d,x)$ are the instant reward value (R value) and the discount factor of the action that node c selects node x to forward the data packets with destination node d, respectively.

As an important component of the update formula of Q value, the discount factor is a weakening of the sum of subsequent reward values. It affects the possibility of forwarding data packets to the same neighbor node next time. In order to adapt the node status, the distance, direction, and buffer occupancy are considered in the calculation of discount factor.

Take node c for example, if node c has forwarded the data packet with destination node d to neighbor node x, the discount factor is calculated as follows:

$$\gamma_c(d, x) = \gamma \times Dir\_F(d, x) \times Dis\_F(d, x) \times Buf\_F(d, x) \tag{3}$$

where γ is the setting value, and $0 < \gamma < 1$. $Dir\_F(d, x)$, $Dis\_F(d, x)$ and $Buf\_F(d, x)$ are the direction factor, the distance factor and the buffer factor, respectively. If these factors are larger, the discount factor will be larger and then the updated Q value will be larger too. As a result, the possibility of forwarding the data packets with the same destination node to node x next time will be larger.

The direction factor is calculated as follows as:

$$Dir\_F(d, x) = 1 - \frac{\theta(d, x)}{180} \tag{4}$$

where $\theta(x, d)$ is the angle between neighbor node x and destination node d. The smaller $\theta(x, d)$ brings about the larger Dir_F_x.

The distance factor is calculated as follows as:

$$Dis\_F(d, x) = 1 - \frac{D(d, x)}{D_{\max}} \tag{5}$$

where $D(x, d)$ is the distance from node x to destination node d, and $D_{\max}$ is the maximum distance between the nodes in the network. The smaller $D(x, d)$ brings about the larger Dis_F_x.

The buffer factor is calculated as follows as:

$$Buf\_F(d, x) = 1 - \frac{S(x)}{B_x} \tag{6}$$

where $S(x)$ is the size of all data packets currently in the buffer of neighbor node x, and B_x is the buffer size of neighbor node x. The smaller $S(x)$ brings about the larger Buf_F_x.

4 Simulation Analysis

4.1 Simulation Environment

The proposed strategy is analyzed in ONE simulator. The S-IoT model in this simulation experiment is shown in Fig. 2. The ground layer is composed of 110 ground nodes, which are uniformly distributed on the Earth's surface. The LEO layer consists of 48 satellite nodes as GlobalStar constellation system. The MEO layer consists of 24 satellite nodes as GPS constellation system. The node parameters in each layer are shown in Table 1. The ground node can generate and receive data packets. The satellite nodes move according to their orbits periodically. Data packets cannot be forwarded between satellite nodes, because there is no inter-satellite links.

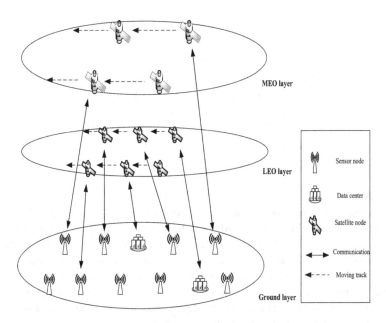

Fig. 2. S-IoT model.

The network environment parameters in this simulation experiment are shown in Table 2. In addition, the learning rate is set to 0.8, and γ in the discount factor is set to 0.9. The delivery rate, average delay, and overhead ratio are used to evaluate the routing strategies at different data packets generation intervals under different failure probabilities.

Table 1. Node parameters.

Layer	LEO layer	MEO layer	Ground layer
Constellation	Global Star	GPS	Distributed evenly
Orbit numbers	8	6	/
Node numbers	48	24	110
Height	189 Km	20200 Km	0

4.2 Simulation Results

The Adaptive Routing Strategy based on Improved Q-learning for S-IoT (ARSIQL) in this paper is compared with the Adaptive Routing Strategy based on original Q-learning (ARSQL), the Spray-and-Wait routing strategy, and the Prophet routing strategy in terms of delivery rate, average delay, and overhead ratio under different failure probabilities.

Table 2. Network environment parameters.

Parameter	Value
Buffer size	35 Mb
Transmission range	100 m
Transmission speed	250 Kb
Data packets generation intervals	10–50 s
Data packet size	500 Kb–1 Mb
Data packet TTL	3600 s

Delivery Rate

Figure 3 shows the comparison of delivery rates of routing strategies at different data packets generation intervals under different failure probabilities. On the whole, the delivery rate of Prophet is the lowest. That is because Prophet calculates the meeting probability of each node, and the data packets are only copied to the node with the larger meeting probability. However, the data packets loss caused by high buffer occupancy of nodes is not taken into account. The delivery rate of Spray-and-Wait is higher than that of Prophet. That is because Spray-and-Wait has the advantage of flood. Specifically, the data packets are diffused into some copies, which increases the probability of data packets arriving at the destination node. The delivery rate of

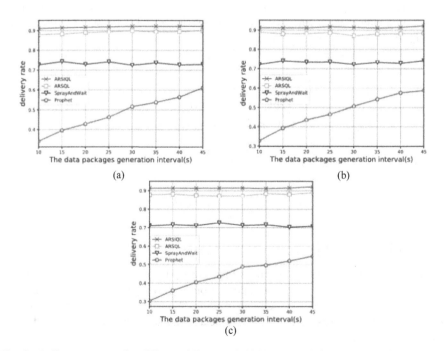

Fig. 3. Delivery rates under different failure probabilities (a. 0% failure probability, b. 10% failure probability, 20% failure probability).

ARSQL is high. That is because the Q-learning algorithm is self-learning and self-adaptive, so it can find a suitable path in a highly dynamic environment. The delivery rate of ARSIQL is very high. On the basis of ARSQL, ARSIQL considers the distance and direction. Hence, the data packets are more likely to arrive at the destination node before the end of their TTL. More importantly, ARSIQL considers the buffer occupancy, which can greatly reduce the data packets loss and then improve the delivery rate.

Average Delay

Figure 4 shows the comparison of average delays of routing strategies at different data packets generation intervals under different failure probabilities. On the whole, the average delay of Spray-and-Wait is the highest. That is because the node can only move and cannot forward data packages before it meets the destination node in the waiting phase. The average delay of Prophet is also high. That is because each node only forwards data packets according to the meeting probability. However, the meeting probability cannot reflect the node status, so Prophet cannot find an appropriate path. ARSQL can adapt to the node status, and it can self-learn to find the next hop node, so its average delay is relatively low. On the basis of ARSQL, ARSIQL considers the distance and direction, so they obtain a lower average delay than ARSQL.

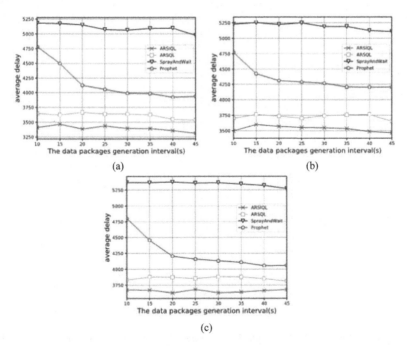

Fig. 4. Average delays under different failure probabilities (a. 0% failure probability, b. 10% failure probability, 20% failure probability).

Overhead Ratio

Figure 5 shows the comparison of overhead ratios of routing strategies at different data packets generation intervals under different failure probabilities. Prophet copies the data packets to the node with a large meeting probability of destination node every time, so the overhead ratio of Prophet is too high and will not be shown in the figure. On the whole, the overhead ratio of Spray-and-Wait is lower than that of Prophet. That is because Spray-and-Wait limits the number of copies, which reduces the forwarding time. ARSQL is not a flood-based routing strategy, so there are fewer data packets in the network, which results in fewer forwarding time and lower overhead ratio. On the basis of ARSQL, ARSIQL considers the distance and direction, so it can reduce the forwarding time and lower the overhead ratio.

In summary, compared with ARSQL, ARSIQL can improve the delivery rate, average delay, and overhead ratio due to the consideration of the distance, direction, and buffer occupancy in S-IoT. Compared with traditional routing strategies, such as the flood-based routing strategy and the utility-based routing strategy, the proposed routing strategy can significantly improve the delivery rate, average delay and overhead ratio due to the application of reinforcement learning.

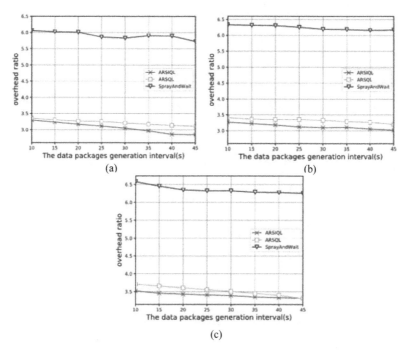

Fig. 5. Overhead ratios under different failure probabilities (a. 0% failure probability, b. 10% failure probability, 20% failure probability).

5   Conclusions

S-IoT is the current research hotspot. Traditional routing strategies cannot adapt to the frequent changes of topology structure and node status in S-IoT. Therefore, this paper proposes an adaptive routing strategy based on improved Q-learning for S-IoT. The proposed strategy selects the next hop node of data packets according to the Q value. Moreover, in order to optimize the Q value, this paper improves the discount factor based on the status of satellite nodes. Simulation experiments show that the proposed strategy can run effectively in complex environments, and increase the delivery rate, and reduce the average delay and the overhead ratio. However, the higher the satellite orbit height, the larger the energy consumption of transmission of the ground node. Next, we will take the satellite orbit height into consideration for the improvement of the reward value.

Acknowledgments. This work is supported by the National Natural Science Foundation of China (No. 61972210, 61873131, 61803212).

References

1. Liu, M., Qu, N., Tang, J.: Signal estimation in cognitive satellite networks for satellite-based industrial internet of things. IEEE Trans. Ind. Inf. **99**, 1 (2020)
2. Li, T., Hao, X., Yue, X.: A power domain multiplexing based co-carrier transmission method in hybrid satellite communication networks. IEEE Access **8**, 120036–120043 (2020)
3. Wang, T., Zhang, G., Liu, A.: A secure IoT service architecture with an efficient balance dynamics based on cloud and edge computing. IEEE Internet Things J. **6**(3), 4831–4843 (2018)
4. Wang, T., Luo, H., Jia, W.: MTES: an intelligent trust evaluation scheme in sensor-cloud-enabled industrial Internet of Things. IEEE Trans. Ind. Inf. **16**(3), 2054–2062 (2019)
5. Huang, M., Liu, A., Wang, T.: Green data gathering under delay differentiated services constraint for internet of things. Wirel. Commun. Mob. Comput. (2018), 1–23 (2018)
6. Geng, X.Z., Xiao, J., Zhi, C.Q.: Development status and challenges of IoT for LEO satellites. J. IoT **1**(3), 6–9 (2017)
7. Jiawei, T., Anfeng, L., Ming, Z.: An aggregate signature based trust routing for data gathering in sensor networks. Secur. Commun. Netw. (2018), 1–30 (2018)
8. Li, Q., Liu, A., Wang, T., Xie, M., Xiong, N.N.: Pipeline slot based fast rerouting scheme for delay optimization in duty cycle based M2M communications. Peer-to-Peer Netw. Appl. **12**(6), 1673–1704 (2019). https://doi.org/10.1007/s12083-019-00753-z
9. Gounder, V.V., Prakash, R., Abu-Amara, H.: Routing in LEO-based satellite networks. In:1999 IEEE Emerging Technologies Symposium. Wireless Communications and Systems, Richardson, TX, USA, pp. 22.1–22.6 (1999)
10. Ekici, E., Akyildiz, I.F., Bender, M.D.: A distributed routing algorithm for datagram traffic in LEO satellite networks. IEEE/ACM Trans. Netw. **9**(2), 137–147 (2001)
11. Hashimoto, Y.: Design of IP-based routing in a LEO satellite network. In: Third International Proceedings of Workshop on Satellite-Based Information Services (WOSBIS), New York, pp.81–88 (1998)
12. Sun, J., Modiano, E.: Routing strategies for maximizing throughput in LEO satellite networks. IEEE J. Sel. Areas Commun. **22**(2), 273–286 (2004)

13. Mao, T., Zhou, B., Xu, Z.: A multi-QoS optimization routing for LEO/MEO satellite IP networks. J. Multimedia **9**(4), 576–582 (2014)
14. Qin, Y.Z., Shu, S.G., Ye, W.: Distributed data storage and transmission technology of the space Internet of things. J. Internet Things **2**(4), 26–34 (2018)
15. Vahdat, A., Becker, D.: Epidemic routing for partially-connected ad hoc networks. In: Handbook of Systemic Autoimmune Diseases (2000)
16. Spyropoulos, T., Psounis, K., Raghavendra, C.S.: Spray and wait: an efficient routing scheme for intermittently connected mobile networks. In: Proceedings of the ACM SIGCOMM Workshop on Delay-Tolerant Networking (WDTN), pp.252–259. ACM (2005)
17. Lindgren, A., Doria, A., Schelén, O.: Probabilistic routing in intermittently connected networks. In: Dini, P., Lorenz, P., de Souza, J.N. (eds.) SAPIR 2004. LNCS, vol. 3126, pp. 239–254. Springer, Heidelberg (2004). https://doi.org/10.1007/978-3-540-27767-5_24
18. Bezirgiannidis, N., Caini, C., Montenero, D.D.P.: Contact graph routing enhancements for delay tolerant space communications. In: Proceedings of 7th Advanced Satellite Multimedia Systems Conference and the 13th Signal Processing for Space Communications Workshop (ASMS/SPSC), pp.17–53. IEEE, Livorno (2014)
19. Watkins, C.J.C.H., Dayan, P.: Q-learning. Mach. Learn. **8**(3–4), 279–292 (1992). https://doi.org/10.1007/BF00992698
20. Tsitsiklis, J.N.: Asynchronous stochastic approximation and Q-learning. Mach. Learn. **16**(3), 185–202 (1994). https://doi.org/10.1023/A:1022689125041

Reliability Evaluation of Sensor Network Based on Information Entropy in Power Grid Planning

Zhe Wang[(⊠)], Mingxia Zhu, and Hongda Zhao

State Grid Jiangsu Electric Power Co., Ltd., Economic Research Institute,
Nanjing 210024, Jiangsu, China
10386057@qq.com, 1242358522@qq.com, 1016744576@qq.com

Abstract. the construction of power sensor network in power grid planning is one of the core tasks to implement the strategic goal of "economical, reliable and flexible". Therefore, the reliability evaluation of power sensor network plays an important role in the long-term development of China's power grid. In this paper, firstly, from four aspects of perception reliability, network reliability, application reliability and cloud edge collaborative reliability, the reliability evaluation index set of power sensor network is established, and the evaluation decision matrix is formed by collecting the data of each index; Then, the expert group of power sensor network reliability index weighting is formed, and the comprehensive weight given by many expert groups is obtained by information entropy method; Finally, Weighted arithmetic average operator is used to gives the reliability evaluation results of power sensor network. At the end of the paper, it is proved that the reliability evaluation index system of power sensor network is comprehensive and the evaluation method is feasible, which is helpful to the planning and construction of distribution network.

Keywords: Power grid planning · Power sensor network · Information entropy · Multi-attribute decision making

1 Introduction

The construction of power supply reliability analysis model has practical significance for defect elimination and power supply risk prevention [1]. Among them, the key power sensor network [2,3] includes the source network load storage, generation transmission distribution use and other links of the power energy network. It closely links the power equipment, network elements and power equipment to achieve ubiquitous (any time, any place, anyone, anything) efficient communication.

© Springer Nature Switzerland AG 2021
G. Wang et al. (Eds.): SpaCCS 2020, LNCS 12383, pp. 173–180, 2021.
https://doi.org/10.1007/978-3-030-68884-4_14

In the construction and operation of sensor network in power planning, one of the core concerns is how to evaluate the reliability based on the factors such as power supply reliability, user behavior, user power failure [4], so as to ensure the reliability of information transmission and data application process and avoid the accidents threatening the reliability of power sensor network system as much as possible. In order to ensure the reliability of power sensor network, it is necessary to comprehensively consider the reliability of sensing layer, network layer, application layer and platform layer [5], and comprehensively evaluate the reliability of power sensor network. Although, many new technologies are emerging from the Internet of Things [6–10], there are few documents and achievements about the reliability evaluation of power sensor network. Therefore, the reliability evaluation of power sensor network is a new research field worthy of discussion no matter from the actual needs or from the perspective of theoretical exploration.

2   Setting of Index System for Reliability Evaluation of Power Sensor Network

How to evaluate the reliability of power sensor network is one of the core problems in the construction and operation of power sensor network. In order to evaluate the reliability of the power sensor network, we must consider the characteristic factors of the reliability of the power sensor network, and establish a complete, scientific and comprehensive comprehensive comprehensive evaluation system based on the actual situation of the power sensor network in China.

The design of the index system should follow the following principles: scientific, integrity and operability, and objectively and accurately reflect the reliability of the power sensor network. In addition, the scale of reasonable control system is also an important aspect,if there are too few indicators, the processing and modeling are relatively simple, but it is difficult to reflect the characteristics of the evaluated object; if there are too many indicators, it is conducive to evaluation, but there are also differences between the objects. According to the above principles, the factors affecting the reliability of power sensor network are systematically analyzed and reasonably integrated to establish the following comprehensive evaluation index system (see Fig. 1)

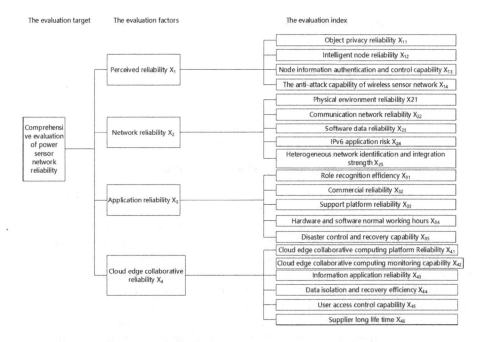

Fig. 1. Evaluation index

3 Reliability Evaluation Model of Power Sensor Network Based on Information Entropy

The factors affecting the reliability evaluation of power sensor network are widely distributed and uncertain. We will establish the reliability evaluation model of power sensor network based on decision-making method to comprehensively evaluate the reliability of power sensor network.

3.1 Evaluation Method of Index Weight – Information Entropy Method

Information entropy method [11] is an objective weighting method, which is based on the information content of decision matrix.Information entropy represents the degree of confusion of an event or variable (also known as the uncertainty of an event), which turns information into quantifiable variables. The larger the amount of information, the smaller the uncertainty and the less the entropy. On the contrary, the smaller the amount of information, the greater the uncertainty and the greater the entropy.In Informatics, entropy is an index of uncertainty, which is represented by probability distribution. It considers that a wide distribution is more uncertain than a distribution with obvious peak value.Therefore, we use the information entropy method to determine the relative weight of the reliability evaluation index of the power sensor network.

The general formula of entropy is:

$$E(P_1, P_2, \ldots, P_n) = -k \sum_{j=1}^{n} P_j \log P_j,$$ (1)

among $\sum_{j=1}^{n} P_j = 1$, k is a positive constant

3.2   Calculation of Membership Function Value

One of the significant characteristics of multi-attribute decision [12] is the incommensurability between objectives, that is, there is no uniform measurement standard between each objective, so it is difficult to compare. Therefore, before the comprehensive evaluation, we should first determine the evaluation value of each index in the index system, that is, calculate the membership function value, and use the information entropy method as the calculation method of the membership function value. Let us assume the decision problem have m schemes and N attributes, the attribute value is X_{ij} (i = 1,2,...,m; j = 1,2,...,n), The decision matrix X = (X_{ij}) (1) For the decision matrix, the linear proportion transformation method (or range transformation method) is used to standardize, and the standardized matrix Y = (Y_{ij}) mxn is obtained, and the normalization is carried out according to the columns

$$P_{ij} = \frac{y_{ij}}{\sum_{i=1}^{m} y_{ij}}, (i = i, 2, \ldots, m; j = 1, 2, \ldots, n)$$ (2)

(2) Calculating the entropy of the jth attribute by column

$$e_j = -k \sum_{i=1}^{m} p_{ij} \log_m p_{ij}$$ (3)

(3) Calculate the difference coefficient of the j-th attribute

$$g_{ij} = 1 - e_j, (j = 1, 2, \ldots, n)$$ (4)

The larger the value is, the greater the difference between indicators, the greater the effect on decision-making, and the greater the weight. (4)Determine the weight. The weight of the j-th attribute is

$$w_j = \frac{g_j}{\sum_{j=1}^{n} g_j}, (j = 1, 2, \ldots, n)$$ (5)

If the decision-maker has no subjective weight in advance, this weight can be used as the actual weight for decision analysis. (5)If the decision-maker already has the subjective right, it can be modified according to the objective right obtained:

$$w_j^0 = \frac{\lambda_j w_j}{\sum\limits_{j=1}^{n} \lambda_j w_j}, (j = 1, 2, \ldots, n) \qquad (6)$$

New rights should be more effective.

3.3 Basic Steps of Integrated Reliability Evaluation Model of Sensor Network Based on Information Entropy

The basic idea of using multi-attribute decision-making method to evaluate the reliability of sensor network with information entropy in power grid planning is as follows:

First, the decision information is obtained, which generally includes attribute weight and attribute value. Then, the decision information is aggregated and the scheme is sorted and optimized in a certain way. The basic steps are:

(1) Build the reliability evaluation index set of power sensor network, collect the reliability evaluation index data, and form the reliability evaluation decision matrix of power sensor network. Suppose that the total number of the power sensor network to be evaluated is m, the number of reliability evaluation indexes is n, and the number of the ith power sensor network is I_i, i = 1,2,..., m, Then the index set of power sensor network is $y_{i1}, y_{i2}, \ldots, y_{ij}, \ldots, y_{in}, j = 1, 2, \ldots, n, y_{ij}$ represents the value of the jth reliability evaluation index of the ith power sensor network,Then the reliability evaluation decision matrix Y of the power sensor network composed of all y_{ij}:

$$Y = (y_{ij})_{m*n} = \begin{bmatrix} y_{11} & y_{12} & \cdots & y_{1j} & \cdots & y_{1n} \\ y_{21} & y_{22} & \cdots & y_{2i} & \cdots & y_{2n} \\ \vdots & \vdots & \ddots & \vdots & \ddots & \vdots \\ y_{m1} & y_{m2} & \cdots & y_{mi} & \cdots & y_{mn} \end{bmatrix} \qquad (7)$$

(2) The expert group of power sensor network reliability evaluation index is formed, and the comprehensive weight $\omega = \omega_1, \omega_2, \ldots, \omega_j, \ldots, \omega_n$ given by the whole expert group is obtained by using information entropy method, among

$$\omega_j = \theta_j / \sum_{j=1}^{n} \theta_j \qquad (8)$$

(3) The multi-attribute decision-making method is used to evaluate the reliability of the power sensor network. Combined with the comprehensive weight given by the expert group, the weighted arithmetic average operator

$$WAA_\omega(a_1, a_2, \ldots, a_n) = \sum_{i=1}^{n} \omega_i a_i \qquad (9)$$

is used for the index value in the reliability evaluation decision matrix, and the evaluation result is given.

4   Application Examples

We use the above methods to evaluate three construction schemes of power sensor network. Here are the specific steps of the evaluation:

(1) Build the reliability evaluation index set of power sensor network, collect the data of each index to form the evaluation decision matrix; the expert group of reliability evaluation of power sensor network will score according to the set standard, and take the average value of each index. The data obtained are shown in Table 1.

Table 1. Reliability evaluation index and evaluation decision matrix element value of power sensor network

Index category	Evaluation indicators	Network 1	Network 2	Network 3
Perceptual reliability	Object privacy reliability	8.47	9.40	5.25
	Intelligent node reliability	5.25	6.97	5.30
	Node information authentication and control capability	5.54	6.90	8.80
	Anti attack ability of wireless sensor network	9.16	8.43	6.83
Network reliability	Physical environment reliability	4.78	8.10	7.41
	Communication network reliability	9.14	6.00	6.65
	Software data reliability	8.25	7.92	4.82
	IPv6 application risk	6.97	6.58	9.24
	Heterogeneous network identification&integration strength	8.30	5.78	8.09
Application reliability	Role recognition efficiency	6.17	5.29	6.31
	Commercial reliability	7.26	5.03	6.67
	Supported platform reliability	7.23	8.75	6.78
	Software and hardware normal working hours	7.92	6.33	7.92
	Disaster control and recovery capability	5.08	4.82	7.22
Cloud edge collaborative reliability	Cloud edge collaborative computing platform reliability	5.91	7.22	5.09
	Cloud edge collaborative computing monitoring capability	5.54	4.54	7.69
	Information application reliability	5.24	7.38	5.34
	Data isolation and recovery efficiency	6.52	5.68	7.74
	User access control capabilities	5.80	4.64	5.76
	Supplier's long life time	6.54	7.88	8.19

(2) The expert group of power sensor network reliability index weighting is formed. The comprehensive weight given by many expert groups is obtained by information entropy method. The expert group of power sensor network reliability index weighting is composed of three experts. The index weight and comprehensive weight given by each expert are obtained by information entropy method. The index weight and comprehensive weight given by each expert are shown in Table 2.

Table 2. Comprehensive weight calculated form index weight given by expert group

Evaluation indicators	Expert 1	Expert 2	Expert 3	Comprehensive weight
Object privacy reliability	0.0500	0.0400	0.0400	0.60920371
Intelligent node reliability	0.0500	0.0500	0.0400	0
Node information authentication and control capability	0.0500	0.0600	0.0500	0.040377269
Anti attack ability of wireless sensor network	0.0500	0.0600	0.0500	0.037241169
Physical environment reliability	0.0500	0.0600	0.0600	0.037241169
Communication network reliability	0.0500	0.0600	0.0500	0.40377269
Software data reliability	0.0500	0.0400	0.0500	0.055186681
IPv6 application risk	0.0500	0.0400	0.0400	0.60920371
Heterogeneous network identification and integration strength	0.0500	0.0500	0.0500	0
Role recognition efficiency	0.0500	0.0400	0.0500	0.55186681
Commercial reliability	0.0500	0.0600	0.0600	0.037241169
Supported platform reliability	0.0500	0.0600	0.0500	0.40377269
Software and hardware normal working hours	0.0500	0.6000	0.4000	0.141441155
Disaster control and recovery capability	0.0500	0.0600	0.0500	0.40377269
Cloud edge collaborative computing platform reliability	0.0500	0.0600	0.0500	0.40377269
Cloud edge collaborative computing monitoring capability	0.0500	0.0400	0.0600	0.141441155
Information application reliability	0.0500	0.0400	0.0500	0.55186681
Data isolation and recovery efficiency	0.0500	0.0500	0.0500	0
User access control capabilities	0.0500	0.0400	0.0400	0.60920371
Supplier's long life time	0.0500	0.0400	0.0500	0.55186681

(3) The multi-attribute decision-making method is used to evaluate the reliability of the power sensor network. Combined with the comprehensive weight given by the expert group, the index values in the reliability evaluation decision matrix are calculated by weighted average, and the evaluation results are given.

$$WAA_1(a_1, a_2, \ldots, a_{20}) = \sum_{j=1}^{2} 0\omega_j a_j = 0.050059692$$

$$WAA_2(a_1, a_2, \ldots, a_{20}) = \sum_{j=1}^{2} 0\omega_j a_j = 0.048847935$$

$$WAA_3(a_1, a_2, \ldots, a_{20}) = \sum_{j=1}^{2} 0\omega_j a_j = 0.050880972$$

According to the weighted arithmetic mean value, the reliability level of the three power sensor networks to be evaluated is $WAA_3 > WAA_1 > WAA_2$. The third construction scheme can make the operation reliability of the power sensor network higher.

5   Conclusion

The comprehensive evaluation of power sensor network reliability plays an important role in the development of power sensor network. Due to the uneven cultural level of the evaluators and the large amount of power sensor network construction plans to be evaluated, the specific evaluation methods are required to be scientific and reliable, simple and practical, and easy to be realized by computers.In this paper, the reliability evaluation of sensor network based on information entropy in power grid planning is studied. Through the multi-attribute decision-making model, the system analysis method which integrates information entropy, expert evaluation and scientific calculation is complementary to each other, it has the characteristics of comprehensive system, scientific reliability, simple and practical, which provides a certain theoretical basis for the comprehensive reliability evaluation of electrical sensor network. The practical application results show that: This method can calculate and give the reliability ranking of the evaluated scheme, so as to help put forward the planning and construction scheme and improve the overall power supply reliability of the power grid.

References

1. Dong, M., Nassif, A.B.: Combining modified weibull distribution models for power system reliability forecast. IEEE Trans. Power Syst. **34**(2), 1610–1619 (2019)
2. Caballero, V., Vernet, D., Zaballos, A., et al.: Prototyping a web-of-energy architecture for smart integration of sensor networks in smart grids domain. Sensors **18**(2), 400–410 (2018)
3. Ma, Y., Huang, C., Sun, Y., et al.: Review of power spatio-temporal big data technologies for mobile computing in smart grid. IEEE Access **99**, 174612–174628 (2019)
4. Yamazaki, T., Jung, J., Kim, Y., et al.: Energy management in home environment using a power sensor network. IEICE Tech. Rep. **107**(430), 71–76 (2008)
5. Hayashikoshi, M., Noda, H., Kawai, H., et al.: Low-power multi-sensor system with power management and nonvolatile memory access control for IoT applications. IEEE Trans. Multi Scale Comput. Syst. **4**, 784–792 (2018)
6. Wang, T., Jia, W., Xing, G., Li, M.: Exploiting statistical mobility models for efficient wi-fi deployment. IEEE Trans. Veh. Technol. **62**(1), 360–373 (2013)
7. Wang, T., Qiu, L., Sangaiah, A.K., et al.: Edge-computing-based trustworthy data collection model in the internet of things. IEEE Internet Things J. **7**(5), 4218–4227 (2020)
8. Wang, T., Wang, P., Cai, S., et al.: A unified trustworthy environment based on edge computing in industrial IoT. IEEE Trans. Ind. Inf. **16**(9), 6083–6091 (2020)
9. Wang, T., Luo, H., Jia, W., et al.: MTES: an intelligent trust evaluation scheme in sensor-cloud enabled industrial internet of things. IEEE Trans. Ind. Inf. **16**(3), 2054–2062 (2020)
10. Ma, Y., Sun, Y., Lei, Y., et al.: A survey of blockchain technology on security, privacy, and trust in crowdsourcing services. World Wide Web **23**(1), 393–419 (2020)
11. Joseph, L., Nils, B., Juergen, J., et al.: Information decomposition of target effects from multi-source interactions: perspectives on previous. Curr. Future Work Entropy **20**(4), 307–315 (2018)
12. Dong, Q., Gou, Y.: Multiperiod multiattribute decision-making method based on trend incentive coefficient. Int. Trans. Oper. Res. **20**(1), 141–152 (2013)

Intelligent Fault Diagnosis and Response Method Based on GIS and IoT in Power Grid Planning

Hongda Zhao[1], Zhe Wang[1(✉)], Mingxia Zhu[1], Zhongmin Shi[2], Zhen Wang[2], and Xianli Wu[2]

[1] State Grid Jiangsu Electric Power Co., Ltd. Economic Research Institute, 210024 Nanjing, Jiangsu, China
`1242358522@qq.com`, `10386057@qq.com`, `1016744576@qq.com`
[2] Xiamen Great Power GEO Information Technology Co., Ltd., 361000 Xiamen, Fujian, China
`bigheadshi@sohu.com`, `ivenwz@163.com`, `28860580@qq.com`

Abstract. The intelligent fault diagnoses and responses of power grid planning are very important parts of the future power grid. This paper proposes an intelligent fault diagnosis and method based on GIS map and IoT. The method mainly includes the stage of automatic fault diagnosis and data analysis based on IoT sensor data, and the process of panoramic display and response optimization based on GIS. The system includes response management and control module, business development monitoring module and power outage analysis module. It can be used for panoramic map display of current response to resource distribution. Besides, it also can support automatic topology tracing and fault analysis to copy with trajectory real-time update and optimal scheduling.

Keywords: IOT · GIS · Fault analysis · Power grid planning

1 Introduction

With the rapid development of economy, people's demands for electricity are also increasing day by day, and the stability of power grid system becomes particularly important. It is necessary to maintain the stability of power transmission system, which is the closest link with users, and it is essential to provide users with reliable and high-quality electricity. However, in recent years, the development of distribution network based on Geographic information system (GIS) [1] and Internet of Things (IOT) [2] has brought new solutions to power system automation. GIS has been favored by most countries for its strong spatial data management ability and topological analysis ability, as well as its unique management advantages for pipeline network. Its technology has also been greatly developed. The distribution network GIS has developed from a simple equipment information management system at the beginning to now add a variety of

© Springer Nature Switzerland AG 2021
G. Wang et al. (Eds.): SpaCCS 2020, LNCS 12383, pp. 181–190, 2021.
https://doi.org/10.1007/978-3-030-68884-4_15

auxiliary decision-makings and analysis functions, and this development trend is bound to gradually replace the traditional manual management mode.

For many years by now, there are big defects in the way of household electricity fault repair. The fault repair process is tedious and long, and the fault cannot be repaired in time. Therefore, the user experience is poor. When the users report for repair, they need to know about some problems of the user's power failure. Due to some professional problems, most of them are not well understood by users and users only know that there is no power at home, which causes the power department not to know how to overhaul. This link reflects factors such as unprofessional and time-consuming handling of problems. Based on this situation and background, it is necessary to study and realize the power supply capability analysis of distribution network based on GIS space service and power Internet of things, so as to grasp the power supply capability of distribution network of the whole province in real time, improve the lean management level of distribution network, and provide decision-making basis for relevant business departments.

On the basis of power grid GIS platform, the professional applications of development planning are deepened. Automatic analysis, efficient design, intelligent decision-making and dynamic tracking are realized on statistical stage diagram, planning stage diagram and construction stage diagram, so as to construct and adapt to the development of different professional visualization work engines. Besides, the whole business processes of distribution network planning, such as simplification of supporting data collection and management, status analysis and diagnosis, load forecasting and checking, intelligent site selection and line selection, comparison and demonstration of planning schemes, and display of planning results, are realized too. Power network analysis and spatial analysis are deepened [3]. Moreover, the three-state management of grid resource information status, plannings and projects in all time and space are also realized; Finally, all-round supporting planning business, intelligent integration of full-space information, intelligent analysis and intelligent interaction are achieved [4–8].

In response to the above requirements, an intelligent autonomous fault diagnosis and method is provided here. The responders can know the fault problems and solve them in the first place based on GIS map and IoT intelligent address location. The method to build the system includes response management and control module, business development monitoring module and power outage analysis module through the construction of the high reliability electricity sensor network, which can realize automatic data collection terminal data, guarantee data integrity, reduce the loss of data, and carry out intelligent research and judgment response. In a word, it plays a supporting role in the distribution network intelligent planning.

2   Related Work

In the traditional power grid planning, the data collection methods were to make the drawing after the field investigation, which resulted in the time-consuming and low-precision situations, and prone to errors when the power grid planners prepare the specific schemes. Rapid changes in geographic graph data and poor real-time performance in traditional planning system make it difficult to draw and calculate survey data accurately, which requires repeated confirmation by planners, greatly increasing the workloads of personnel. The GIS geographic information system [9] contains diversified technical means, which can realize real-time analysis, collection, storage and management of geospatial information, etc. With the support of satellite navigation and positioning technology, the mapping accuracy in GIS application is improved, which is conducive to enhancing the utilization value of corresponding data information.

Using GIS technology based on the spatial location datas and information [10], it has management functions of spatial information with geographic graphics and spatial positioning functions. Moreover, It also integrates computers, geography, urban science, management science and space science, which provides geographical information and space to the management points that are in demand. The advantages of technology are its own information synthesis and evaluation skills. It can obtain important datas on the basis of conventional models, complete the simulation and prediction of geospatial process changes, and at the same time guarantee the scientific nature of the emergency scheduling command by relying on navigation information, so the existence of the GIS technology is very important for power grid planning [11].

The Internet of things [12] is an important part of a new generation of information technology. It means a huge network combined with all kinds of information sensing devices and Internet based on "the concept of Internet", which extends its client to any of the items and items. All in all, it is a network concept for information exchange and communication. The Internet of things (IoT) is a network that enables all ordinary objects with independent functions to connect and achieve artificial intelligence management and control [13,14]. Based on Internet of things intelligent address location on the basis of grid GIS platform, it deepens the development plans for professional applications, covering development figure corresponding, connection mode recognition, vision of the load distribution, visualization of project situation display, site selection and line selection on the map. Besides, it also designs "one picture and three states" (planning state, planning state, current state) in accordance with the principles of "intelligent analysis, visualization of results, and graphical project" to realize automatic analysis on the statistical stage diagram, efficient design on the planning stage diagram, intelligent decision-making on the planning stage diagram, and dynamic tracking on the construction stage diagram. Finally, it constructs and develops visualization work for different specialties.

3   The Proposed Fault Diagnosis and Response Method

3.1   Proposed Fault Diagnosis Method

Combining GIS technology and Internet of Things technology, we propose a new fault diagnosis and method. The steps are as follows:

1. When the users call for fault repair, the user number shall be provided first. According to the user number, the GIS system will automatically inquire the address of the user's power supply fault and confirm with the user;
2. After confirming with the user, the GIS system will automatically report the power failure information (if the user reports a repair call, the account number is known, and the power failure is suspected to be 'multi-family/single-family'), and start the process of research and judgment and order dispatch;
3. If the GIS system automatically determines that it is a planned power failure (known plan/known fault), it will return to inform the customer that it is a known plan/known fault and no repair is required;
   Otherwise, we should continue analysis: In the case of an account number, it conducts a visual copy-through. If the copy-through succeeds, the meter has electricity and no repair is required; If the copy-through fails, it countinues to the next visual dispatch analysis;
   In the case of no account number, it continues to the next visual dispatch analysis without a copy-through;
4. Dispatch analysis is visualized. The nearest coping team is calculated. The map shows the shortest path and the distance of each material point from the closest coping team, and the time of arrival;
5. The response message will be pushed to the response team, and the response team will confirm and repair the message as soon as they see it.
6. GIS system will automatically read data, modify status, simulate bill of lading and dispatch documents; Then it will report repair notices (e.g. "repair calls from users have been recorded, sent to response team, and estimated time of arrival).

Through the panorama display technology of the power failure information based on GIS system, the power failure distribution and areas and users affected by the power outage can be visualized. Besides, the research on big data analysis can be carried out to realize the generation and analysis of the power failure electrothermal force diagram and visually demonstrate the weak links of the power grid. Moreover, The automatic voice warning technology of power failure event is studied to provide visual and rapid response technical support for power supply service command center.

3.2   Response Method

When the power is cut off due to an emergency, the emergency response vehicles and fault tasks should be allocated reasonably, so as to effectively improve the utilization rate of the response vehicles, repair the fault as quickly as possible, shorten the power outage time and reduce economic losses. Besides, the response efficiency can be improved by optimizing the organization of response vehicle teams and optimizing the economic loss of power failure. In the visual dispatch analysis, the optimization model of responding vehicle team includes internal collaborative load and external collaborative load. The internal collaborative load of responding vehicle team G_m is $N(m)$, indicating the cumulative number of responding vehicles assigned to the responding vehicle team

$$N(m) = \sum_{k=1}^{K} R_{G-P}(k, m) \tag{1}$$

$\sum_{k=1}^{K}$ is the sum of k distributions from 1 to k,

$R_{G-P}(k, m)$K for the Kth time, m for the response team id, R_{G-P} represents the algorithm function name of internal collaborative load, and the external collaborative load for vehicle team Gm is $W(m)$,which represents the cumulative load of the responding vehicle team in collaboration with other responding vehicle teams.

$$W(m) = \sum_{n=1, n\neq m}^{M} R(n, m, x_i) \tag{2}$$

$\sum_{n=1, n\neq m}^{M}$ n is the number of accumulations from 1 to M, m represents the id of the response team, and n is not equal to m;

$R(n, m, x_i)$ parameter n represents the nth accumulation, m represents the response team id, x_i represents the id of other response team, R is the name of the algorithm function to calculate the response team external collaborative load;

Therefore, in the case of a given fault, the adaptability measure of vehicle allocation should be

$$\alpha = \sqrt{\frac{1}{M} \sum_{m=1}^{M} [N(m) + W(m)]^2} \tag{3}$$

m is the number of cooperation, M is the total number of cooperation;

α for the team to deal with the vehicle total working load of RMS, while minimizing the response team vehicle mean and variance of total load. The goal is to reduce unnecessary collaboration between the response vehicle teams in troubleshooting (including cooperating with the internal coordination of vehicle teams and cooperating with the external coordination of vehicle teams in troubleshooting), improve the efficiency of troubleshooting. When the value is smaller, it shows the better effect and higher efficiency to deal with the vehicle allocation under current fault conditions.

Its constraints are as follows:

1) Each fault shall be assigned to at least one response vehicle team;

m is for the vehicle team $id.i$ is for the number of collaborations.M is for the total number of collaborations.R_{G-X} means that each fault is assigned to at least one algorithm function for constraints of vehicle team.

$$\sum_{m=1}^{M} R_{G-X}(i,m) \geq 1, \qquad i = 1, 2, ..., N \tag{4}$$

2) Each response vehicle can only be assigned to one response vehicle team;

$$\sum_{m=1}^{M} R_{G-p}(k,m) \geq 1, \qquad k = 1, 2, ..., K \tag{5}$$

k is the number of response vehicle teams.m is the number of coordination.M is the total number of coordination.R_{G-p} represents that each responding vehicle can only be assigned to an algorithm function that responds to the constraints of the vehicle team;

3) Constraints on resource capacity;

$$\sum_{m=1}^{M} R_{G-X}(i,m)r_{ml} \geq r_{il}, i = 1, 2, ..., N; m = 1, 2..., M; l = 1, 2, ..., L \tag{6}$$

i is the number of collaboration.m is the number of response team, l is the number of response vehicle.r_{ml} is for the response team and the response vehicle restraint.r_{il} is for the response vehicle restraint.R_{G-X} is the name of the algorithm function of response resource capacity constraints.

Optimization of economic loss of power failure in the visual dispatching analysis. The optimization objective is to reduce economic loss of power failure caused by power failure of distribution network, and the objective function in this stage is

$$f(x) = \sum_{i=1}^{N} T(x_i) \sum_{l=1}^{3} \omega_l L_l(x_i) - \sum_{j=1}^{N} T_j \omega_l L_j \tag{7}$$

$T(x_i)$ is the power failure time caused by fault point x_i; T_j is the power supply time of the emergency generator when the dual-power user loses power; ω_l for failure is caused by the power failure load rating coefficient; $L_l(x_i)$ is the power value of the load with grade l caused by power failure of fault point Xi; L_j is the load power value supplied by the emergency generator car;

Its constraints are as follows:

After fault response and switch operation, the distribution network should maintain a radial structure, that is, $gk \in GR$, gk is the network structure of the power supply recovery area; GR is to ensure the collection of radial networks; The wait time for collaboration failures should be met $\tau_{(xi)} \leq t^{\varepsilon}$, where t^{ε} is the maximum allowable cooperative wait time.

In the case of household number, we should search and analyze the situation according to the location of access point;

In the case of no household number, we should search and analyze the situation according to the address that can match the GIS address base, locate directly on the map, and then search the corresponding resources nearby. In this way, it is easy to locate, improve response efficiency and save time.

4   System Implementation and Deployment

4.1   System Description

We have deployed this system in Xiamen area, as shown in Fig. 1. The system comprises includes response management and control module, business development monitoring module and power outage analysis module.

The response management and control module is used to display the current response resources (stationary point, response team) and work order distribution in a panoramic way on the map. It can support automatic polling display of work orders in transit, automatic voice reminder of overtime and new work orders, automatic topology tracing and fault analysis, and respond to team trajectory real-time update and optimal scheduling to realize the intelligence of response command and quick response of service.

The business development monitoring module is used for the map integration of the open capacity of medium-voltage lines. According to the coordinates of the user's loading location, it automatically calculates the lines available within the set radius, generates alternative power supply access schemes and recommends the optimal access schemes. The map presents the progress of the on-line industry expansion plan in real time, improves the efficiency of formulating the plan for online acceptance of industry expansion requirements, and realizes efficiency improvement of the business development process management and control;

The power outage analysis module is used to display the power outage information overview, power outage distribution, and areas and users affected by the power outage on the geographic map. It also supports automatic voice reminders for power outage events and provides power outage visual and rapid response technical support for the power supply service command center. At the same time, it supports linkage with the large screen of the power supply service command center.

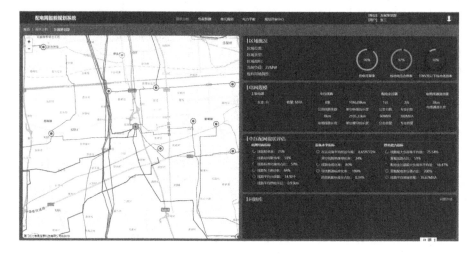

Fig. 1. Evaluation index

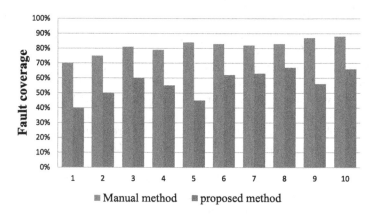

Fig. 2. Evaluation index

4.2 Performance Comparison

The previously undeployed and deployed fault diagnosis results (mainly including: fault location, fault type, elimination plan, etc.) are scored. The final test results are shown in Fig. 2. The index of fault coverage can be expressed as: fault coverage = number of identified faults/actual number of faults × 100%

5 Conclusion

In recent years, the development of distribution network GIS and Internet of Things technology has brought new solutions to power system automation. Geographical Information System (GIS) with its powerful spatial data management and topology analysis ability, as well as its management advantages for pipeline network unique won the favour of most countries. The technology has also got rapid development. The distribution network GIS has developed from a simple equipment information management system at the beginning to now add a variety of auxiliary decision-makings and analysis functions, and this development trend is bound to gradually replace the traditional manual management mode. Based on this situation and background, it is necessary to study and realize the power supply capability analysis of distribution network based on GIS space service, so as to master the power supply capability of distribution network of the whole province in real time, improve the lean management level of distribution network, and provide decision-making basis for relevant business departments.

In this paper, through the panorama display technology based on the power failure information in GIS system, the power failure distribution and the visualization of areas and users affected by the power outage are realized. The researches on big data analysis are carried out to realize the generation and analysis of the power failure electrothermal force diagram and visually demonstrate the weak links of the power grid; The automatic voice warning technology of power failure event is studied to provide visual and rapid response technical support for power supply service command center. Besides, it also provides a reliable and convenient method for intelligent address location and analysis in power grid planning and improves work efficiency.

References

1. Ueta, G., Okabe, S., Utsumi, T., et al.: Electric conductivity characteristics of FRP and epoxy insulators for GIS under DC voltage. IEEE Trans. Dielectr. Electr. Insul. **22**(4), 2320–2328 (2015)
2. Wang, T., Luo, H., Jia, W., et al.: MTES: an intelligent trust evaluation scheme in sensor-cloud enabled industrial internet of things. IEEE Trans. Ind. Inf. **16**(3), 2054–2062 (2020)
3. Marotta, A., Avallone, S., Kassler, A.: A joint power efficient server and network consolidation approach for virtualized data centers. Comput. Netw. **130**(JAN.15), 65–80 (2018)
4. Motepe, S., Hasan, A.N., Stopforth, R.: Improving load forecasting process for a power distribution network using hybrid AI and deep learning algorithms. IEEE Access **7**, 1 (2019)
5. Ma, Y., Sun, Yu., Lei, Y., Qin, N., Lu, J.: A survey of blockchain technology on security, privacy, and trust in crowdsourcing services. World Wide Web **23**(1), 393–419 (2019). https://doi.org/10.1007/s11280-019-00735-4
6. Wang, T., Jia, W., Xing, G., Li, M.: Exploiting statistical mobility models for efficient Wi-Fi deployment. IEEE Trans. Veh. Technol. **62**(1), 360–373 (2013)
7. Xiao, C., Liu, C., Ma, Y., et al.: Time sensitivity-based popularity prediction for online promotion on Twitter. Inf. Sci. **525**, 82–92 (2020)
8. Wu, Y., Huang, H., Wu, Q., et al.: A risk defense method based on microscopic state prediction with partial information observations in social networks. J. Parallel Distrib. Comput. **131**, 189–199 (2019)

9. Lu, G., Batty, M., Strobl, J., et al.: Reflections and speculations on the progress in Geographic Information Systems (GIS): a geographic perspective. Int. J. Geograph. Inf. Sci. **33**(1–2), 346–367 (2019)
10. Leite, J.B., Mantovani, J.R.S., Dokic, T., et al.: Resiliency assessment in distribution networks using GIS based predictive risk analytics. IEEE Trans. Power Syst. (2019)
11. Shu, J., Wu, L., Li, Z., et al.: A new method for spatial power network planning in complicated environments. IEEE Trans. Power Syst. **27**(1), 381–389 (2012)
12. Li, S., Xu, L.D., Zhao, S.: The internet of things: a survey. Inf. Syst. Front. **17**(2), 243–259 (2014). https://doi.org/10.1007/s10796-014-9492-7
13. Wang, T., Qiu, L., Sangaiah, A.K., et al.: Edge-computing-based trustworthy data collection model in the internet of things. IEEE Internet Things J. **7**(5), 4218–4227 (2020)
14. Wang, T., Wang, P., Cai, S., et al.: A unified trustworthy environment based on edge computing in industrial IoT. IEEE Trans. Ind. Inf. **16**(9), 6083–6091 (2020)

Group Authentication for Sensors in Wireless Body Area Network

Yong Ding[1,3], Hui Xu[2], and Yujue Wang[1(✉)]

[1] Guangxi Key Laboratory of Cryptography and Information Security,
School of Computer Science and Information Security,
Guilin University of Electronic Technology, Guilin 541004, China
yjwang@guet.edu.cn
[2] School of Mathematics and Computing Science,
Guilin University of Electronic Technology, Guilin 541004, China
RosieHuiX@163.com
[3] Cyberspace Security Research Center, Peng Cheng Laboratory,
Shenzhen 518055, China

Abstract. Wireless body area network (WBAN) is mainly used in the field of health care, which is composed of sensors for collecting patient data. To ensure the accuracy and reliability of the data obtained by medical staff or patients, the secure data transmission within the body area network becomes particularly important. Both sensors and controllers must have a strict mutual authentication to prevent malicious sensors and controllers from collecting and eavesdropping private data. To address the problem of user identity authentication in WBAN, a group authentication scheme is proposed. It supports the authentication of identity validity before the information interaction between the controller and each sensor node. Also, all signatures from sensor nodes can be aggregately checked by the controller. Security analysis indicates that the proposed scheme is existentially unforgeable against adaptively chosen message attacks, and theoretical analysis shows that it is more efficient than existing schemes.

Keywords: Wireless body area network · Identity authentication · Aggregate verification · Unforgeability

1 Introduction

Wireless body area network is an important branch of the Internet of things (IoT) [1], which has great practical significance in many applications such as remote medicine detection and health care [2]. WBAN is mainly composed of sensors that can sense and collect physiological data of patient as well as around environmental information [3]. The collected data can be sent to the controller with powerful storage and computing capacities. The data are forwarded to the remote medicine data center for processing and analysis. Then, the doctors

© Springer Nature Switzerland AG 2021
G. Wang et al. (Eds.): SpaCCS 2020, LNCS 12383, pp. 191–199, 2021.
https://doi.org/10.1007/978-3-030-68884-4_16

can make the treatment plan according to these data. For example, patients with vascular disease can use wearable pulse oximetry sensors to measure blood oxygen saturation [4]. For emergency case detected by sensors, relevant measures can be taken to relieve the suffering of patients, e.g., implanted blood glucose sensors can be employed to analyze the blood glucose index of the patient in real-time to trigger the insulin pump for insulin injection when necessary [5].

While WBAN brings convenience to patients, some security and privacy issues also arise. For ensuring the authenticity of WBAN communication entities, Li et al. [6] proposed a group device pairing authentication method based on secure sensor association and key management. In [6], the controller and each sensor node in the group need to authenticate all other nodes. The system assigns serial numbers to all nodes in advance, so that the authentication message and group key can be computed by using the parameters of adjacent nodes in the authentication phase. Note that it is difficult to strictly ensure the true identity of each node due to the authentication process mainly depends on the confirmation of the size of the sensor group. Therefore, malicious node may impersonate honest nodes to participate in the authentication process without being tracked.

This paper proposes a group authentication scheme, which supports mutual authentication between sensors and controller. The controller is able to aggregate the signatures of sensor nodes to complete group authentication, which improves the authentication efficiency. The security analysis indicates that the proposed protocol enjoys existentially unforgeability against adaptively chosen message attacks, which can prevent the authentication data from being tampered. Also, the proposed protocol can prevent malicious entities from participating in authentication and ensure the authenticity of sensor nodes. Besides, the theoretical comparison demonstrates that the computational complexity of our scheme is lower than other existing schemes.

2   Related Works

To address the issues in establishing and managing public key in public keys cryptosystems, Yang et al. [7] proposed a certificateless signature scheme, which is unforgeable against adaptive chosen message attack and malicious key generation center attack. Restricted by the computing and storage resources of entities in WBAN, Xu et al. [8] proposed a lightweight anonymous mutual authentication scheme with only hash operations and XOR operations.

In order to achieve efficient and secure data transmission, many schemes have been proposed to support mutual authentication and session key establishment between controller and sensor nodes in the form of groups [9]. Keoh, Lupu and Sloman [10] presented a sensor association scheme based on the synchronous LED flashing mode, where the controller and each sensor need to be authenticated by means of digital signatures, and then the user verifies the flashing result of LEDs. Therefore, multiple associations between sensors and controllers would bring more time costs. The lightweight multi-layer authentication and session key generation scheme proposed by Shen et al. [11] has the advantages of efficient authentication, which allows one-to-many group authentication and group key establishment between the controller and sensor nodes. Liu et al. [12] proposed an improved two-layer authentication scheme based on [11] and proved its security.

WBAN has a small network scale, and there is no need to communicate between sensor nodes. Thus, the star topology structure is often adopted in the distributed acquisition phase [13]. Therefore, in [14], WBAN is divided into two layers, where sensors act as the second layer to send the collected data to the central node through the first layer with powerful storage, calculation and communication capabilities. Li et al.'s scheme [6] also divided WBAN into two layers, and the data collected by sensor nodes in the second layer is transmitted to users through controllers in the first layer. To make the authentication process more efficient and secure, it is needed to simplify the verification process and reduce the number of interactions between sensors and controllers. Therefore, Abro, Deng and Memon [15] proposed an authentication scheme based on ElGamal, which can reduce communication overhead and resist man-in-the-middle attacks.

3 System Model and Security Requirements

3.1 System Model

As shown in Fig. 1, a WBAN system consists of two types of entities, namely, the sensors deployed on and around users and controller for data collection.

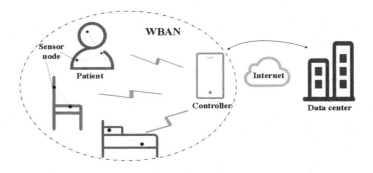

Fig. 1. System model.

The sensors can collect physiological data of users and information of surrounding environment. Limited by the storage space of sensors, the collected data needs to be transmitted to the controller for storing and computing. In WBAN, sensors involved in data collection and the controller need to perform mutual authentication to confirm their respective authenticity. When the controller is legal, the sensor sends the collected data to the controller.

3.2   Security Requirements

In WBAN, it is important to prevent malicious sensors or controllers from impersonating honest entities during data collection and transmission. Therefore, a secure WBAN authentication scheme supporting aggregation verification needs to meet the following security requirements.

Authenticity of Controller: The signature issued by the legal controller can be successfully verified by other sensor nodes in the group. However, a malicious attacker who wants to forge the signature cannot pass the verification conditions.

Authenticity of Sensors: The signatures issued by the legitimate sensors can be successfully verified by the controller by means of aggregation. However, if malicious nodes want to impersonate legitimate sensor nodes to join the group to participate in the authentication, the aggregation authentication conditions would not be satisfied.

Efficiency: As the number of sensor nodes increases, the computations during authentication will increase at both sides of the controller and sensors. Therefore, the WBAN system should support aggregate verification to improve the authentication efficiency.

4   Identity Based Aggregate Authentication Scheme

The security of the proposed scheme depends on the following problem:

Discrete Logarithm (DLog) Problem: Let $\mathbb{G}$ be a cyclic group of order q with generator g. Given an element $g^x \in \mathbb{G}$ where $x \in \mathbb{Z}_q^*$, compute x.

4.1   Scheme Design

The controller and sensor nodes authenticate with each other, where the validity of each entity's identity can be checked through aggregate verification. Figure 2 shows the phases of the authentication process.

Initialization. PKG chooses a cyclic group $\mathbb{G}$ of order q, where q is a large prime and g is a generator of $\mathbb{G}$. PKG randomly chooses $w \in \mathbb{Z}_q^*$, computes $W = g^w$, and picks hash function $H : \{0,1\}^* \to \mathbb{Z}_q^*$. The system public parameter is $param = (\mathbb{G}, q, g, W, H)$ and master key is $msk = w$.

KeyGen. PKG chooses a random integer $r_j \in \mathbb{Z}_q^*$ for each entity u_j ($j = 0, 1, 2, \ldots, n$), where u_0 is the controller and other u_j represents sensor node. PKG computes

$$R_j = g^{r_j}$$
$$s_j = r_j + H(R_j \| u_j)w \mod q$$

and writes the private key (R_j, s_j) to entity u_j.

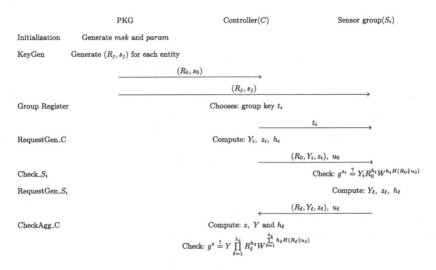

Fig. 2. Mutual authentication between controller and sensors

Group Registration. The controller chooses l group keys $t_1, t_2, \ldots, t_l \in \mathbb{Z}_q^*$. When u_j $(j = 1, 2, \ldots, n)$ performs group registration, the controller allocates it to the corresponding group S_i and writes the group key t_i to u_j.

Controller Sends Out Group Authentication Request. When the controller communicates with group S_i, it needs to mutually authenticate with each node. The controller sets

$$S_i = \bigcup_{\ell=1}^{\lambda_i} u_\ell,$$

chooses randomly $y_i \in \mathbb{Z}_q^*$ for S_i, and computes

$$Y_i = g^{y_i}.$$

The controller computes

$$h_i = H(Y_i \| R_0 \| S_i)$$

$$z_i = y_i + h_i s_0 \mod q$$

and broadcasts signature (R_0, Y_i, z_i) and identity u_0 to group S_i.

Sensor Verification and Response. After receiving the signature and tuple, each sensor node in group S_i computes h_i and verifies the following equation

$$g^{z_i} \stackrel{?}{=} Y_i R_0^{h_i} W^{h_i H(R_0 \| u_0)} \tag{1}$$

If Eq. (1) does not hold, the authentication request from the controller will be rejected. Otherwise, each sensor node u_ℓ chooses a random integer $y_\ell \in \mathbb{Z}_q^*$, computes

$$Y_\ell = g^{y_\ell}, \quad h_\ell = H(Y_\ell \| R_\ell \| H(t_i) \| S_i)$$

and
$$z_\ell = y_\ell + h_\ell s_\ell \mod q$$

and gives the signature (R_ℓ, Y_ℓ, z_ℓ) and identity u_ℓ to the controller.

Controller Aggregate Verification. After the controller receives the signature and the identity of each sensor node, it performs aggregate verification as follows. It first computes

$$z = \sum_{\ell=1}^{\lambda_i} z_\ell$$

$$\prod_{\ell=1}^{\lambda_i} Y_\ell$$

and h_ℓ of each sensor node, and then verifies the following equation

$$g^z \overset{?}{=} Y \prod_{\ell=1}^{\lambda_i} R_\ell^{h_\ell} W^{\sum_{\ell=1}^{\lambda_i} h_\ell H(R_\ell \| u_\ell)} \tag{2}$$

If Eq. (2) holds, the controller accepts the sensor nodes.

4.2 Correctness

To prove the correctness of the proposed scheme, we only need to show both Eqs. (1) and (2) hold.

First, each sensor node in the group verifies the authenticity of the controller by checking Eq. (1). The verification process is as follows.

$$\begin{aligned}
Y_i R_0^{h_i} W^{h_i H(R_0 \| u_0)} &= g^{y_i} g^{r_0 h_i} g^{w h_i H(R_0 \| u_0)} \\
&= g^{y_i + (r_0 + w H(R_0 \| u_0)) h_i} \\
&= g^{y_i + s_0 h_i} \\
&= g^{z_i}
\end{aligned}$$

Second, the controller verifies the authenticity of each sensor node in the group by checking Eq. (2). The verification process is as follows.

$$\begin{aligned}
Y \prod_{\ell=1}^{\lambda_i} R_\ell^{h_\ell} W^{\sum_{\ell=1}^{\lambda_i} h_\ell H(R_\ell \| u_\ell)} &= g^{\sum_{\ell=1}^{\lambda_i} y_\ell} g^{\sum_{\ell=1}^{\lambda_i} r_\ell h_\ell} g^{w \sum_{\ell=1}^{\lambda_i} h_\ell H(R_\ell \| u_\ell)} \\
&= g^{\sum_{\ell=1}^{\lambda_i} (y_\ell + r_\ell h_\ell + w h_\ell H(R_\ell \| u_\ell))} \\
&= g^{\sum_{\ell=1}^{\lambda_i} (y_\ell + s_\ell h_\ell)} \\
&= g^z
\end{aligned}$$

Therefore, the signatures of the controller and each sensor node in the group can be successfully verified. Thus, the proposed authentication scheme for WBAN is correct.

5 Scheme Analysis

5.1 Security Analysis

This section analyzes the security of the proposed scheme.

Theorem 1. *The proposed scheme can ensure that each entity's identity in participating authentication is verifiable. Based on the Schnorr signature scheme, under the DLog assumption, the proposed scheme is existentially unforgeable against adaptively chosen message attacks.*

The authentication request and verification phases of each entity in this scheme are similar to the aggregate signature scheme [16] based on Schnorr signature. The difference lies in that in [16], each entity signs on n messages and then performs aggregate verification. In our scheme, the same message is signed by n entities and then the controller performs aggregate verification. That is, both our scheme and [16] support aggregate verification n signatures. Thus, the proof process of Theorem 1 is similar to that of [16]. Therefore, the proposed scheme has the unforgeability against adaptive selection message attacks under the $DLog$ assumption.

5.2 Functional Comparison

This section compares the proposed scheme with [6] and [12], which are shown in Table 1.

Table 1. Comparison.

	Group authentication	Aggregate validation
GDP [6]	Y	N
SCSLS I [12]	N	N
Our scheme	Y	Y

Y-supported, N-not supported

As shown in Table 1, both our scheme and [6] allow mutual authentication of sensors and controllers in a group way. The difference is that in our scheme, the controller performs aggregate authentication on all sensor nodes in the group, which improves the efficiency of authentication. Whereas the authentication method of [6] requires members in the group are authenticated one by one, and does not support aggregate authentication. Liu, Jin and Li's scheme [12] does not take into account the mutual authentication of sensors and controllers through aggregate verification.

5.3 Efficiency Analysis

This section compares the efficiency of the proposed scheme with the ones of [6] and [12] in terms of computation costs at each stage. In Table 2, the exponentiation operation is represented as E, the hash operation as H, and the number of sensor nodes participating in authentication as n.

Table 2. Theoretical comparison.

	Controller sends out authentication request	Sensor verification	Sensor response	Controller verification	Group key generation
GDP [6]	$3E + 1H$	nH	$3E + 1H$	nH	$1H$
SCSLS I [12]	$(n+1)E + nH$	$2E + 1H$	$1E + 1H$	$1E + nH$	nE
Our scheme	$1E + 1H$	$3E + 2H$	$1E + 2H$	$(n+2)E + 2nH$	—

As shown in Table 2, in the controller sends out group authentication request phase, the computational complexity of our scheme and [6] is independent of the number of sensor nodes in the group, while the complexity of the scheme in [12] is determined by the number n. However, in sensors verification phase, the computational complexity of in [6] is determined by the number of sensors in the group to evaluate hashes. For the controller verification phase, the proposed scheme requires more $(n+2)$ and $(n+1)$ exponentiation operations than [6] and [12], respectively, since our scheme allows strict authentication between the controller and sensor nodes. Note that in the group key generation phase, there is no heavy computations in our scheme, since the group key has been allocated to the sensors in the group registration phase, while [12] has to take n exponentiation operations.

6 Conclusion

To address the authentication issue of WBAN with a large number of sensor nodes, this paper proposed a group authentication scheme supporting aggregate authentication. The controller can verify the authenticity of each sensor node in the way of aggregation, which improves the efficiency of mutual authentication between the controller and each sensor node. Security analysis showed that the proposed authentication scheme can resist impersonate attacks launched by malicious entities, assuming the discrete logarithm problem is hard. Theoretical performance analysis indicated the efficiency of our scheme compared with related solutions.

Acknowledgement. This article is supported in part by the National Natural Science Foundation of China under projects 61772150, 61862012 and 61962012, the Guangxi Key R&D Program under project AB17195025, the Guangxi Natural Science Foundation under grants 2018GXNSFDA281054, 2018GXNSFAA281232, 2019GXNSFFA245015, 2019GXNSFGA245004 and AD19245048, and the Peng Cheng Laboratory Project of Guangdong Province PCL2018KP004.

References

1. Ajey, L.: Internet of Things (IoT). Smart Innov. Syst. Technol. **132**, 187–195 (2019). https://doi.org/10.1007/978-981-13-3384-2_11
2. Malik, M.S.A., Ahmed, M., Abdullah, T., Kousar, N., Awais, M.: Wireless body area network security and privacy issue in e-healthcare. Int. J. Adv. Comput. Sci. Appl. **9**(4), 209–215 (2018)
3. Wang, W.: Data security mix transmission mechanism in body area network. Comput. Sci. **45**(5), 102–107 (2018)
4. Gao, X., Liu, X., Feng, T., Xu, G.: Monitoring system design for rehabilitating training based on wireless body area network. Comput. Technol. Dev. **24**(9), 234–237 (2014)
5. Latré, B., Braem, B., Moerman, I., Blondia, C., Demeester, P.: A survey on wireless body area networks. Wireless Netw. **17**(1), 1–18 (2011)
6. Li, M., Yu, S., Lou, W., Ren, K.: Group device pairing based secure sensor association and key management for body area networks. In: INFOCOM 2010, 29th IEEE International Conference on Computer Communications, Joint Conference of the IEEE Computer and Communications Societies, San Diego, CA, USA, 15–19 March 2010, pp. 2651–2659. IEEE (2010). https://doi.org/10.1109/INFCOM.2010.5462095
7. Yang, X., Wang, M., Pei, X., Li, Y., Chen, C., Tingchun, M.: Security analysis and improvement of a certificateless signature scheme in the standard model. Acta Electronica Sinica **47**(9), 1972–1978 (2019)
8. Xu, Z., Xu, C., Chen, H., Yang, F.: A lightweight anonymous mutual authentication and key agreement scheme for WBAN. Concurrency Comput. Pract. Exp. **31**(14) (2019). https://doi.org/10.1002/cpe.5295
9. Yuan, D., Peng, X., Liu, T., Cui, Z.: A novel approach to authenticated group key transfer protocol based on AG codes. High Technol. Lett. **25**(2), 129–136 (2019)
10. Keoh, S.L., Lupu, E.C., Sloman, M.: Securing body sensor networks: sensor association and key management. In: Seventh Annual IEEE International Conference on Pervasive Computing and Communications, PerCom 2009, Galveston, TX, USA, 9–13 March 2009, pp. 1–6. IEEE Computer Society (2009). https://doi.org/10.1109/PERCOM.2009.4912756
11. Shen, J., Chang, S., Shen, J., Liu, Q., Sun, X.: A lightweight multi-layer authentication protocol for wireless body area networks. Future Gener. Comput. Syst. **78**(3), 956–963 (2018)
12. Liu, X., Jin, C., Li, F.: An improved two-layer authentication scheme for wireless body area networks. J. Med. Syst. **42**(8), 143–157 (2018)
13. Zhang, G., Liu, W.: A compressed sensing based detection for star topology WSNs. J. Taiyuan Univ. Technol. **49**(3), 473–477 (2018)
14. Li, X., Ibrahim, M.H., Kumari, S., Sangaiah, A.K., Gupta, V., Choo, K.K.R.: Anonymous mutual authentication and key agreement scheme for wearable sensors in wireless body area networks. Comput. Netw. **129**(24), 429–443 (2017)
15. Abro, A., Deng, Z., Memon, K.A.: A lightweight elliptic-Elgamal-based authentication scheme for secure device-to-device communication. Future Internet **11**(5), 108 (2019)
16. Liu, J., Baek, J., Zhou, J., Yang, Y., Wong, J.: Efficient online/offline identity-based signature for wireless sensor network. Int. J. Inf. Secur. **9**(4), 287–296 (2010)

Automatic Heart Sound Classification Using One Dimension Deep Neural Network

Qingli Hu[1], Jianqiang Hu[1(✉)], Xiaoyan Yu[2], and Yang Liu[1]

[1] School of Computer and Information Engineering,
Xiamen University of Technology, Xiamen 361024, China
huqingli2014@outlook.com, jqhucn@xmut.edu.cn, shuiwenwuhen@gmail.com
[2] College of Electronic and Electrical Engineering,
Shanghai University of Engineering Science, Shanghai 201620, China
yuxiaoyan126@126.com

Abstract. Cardiovascular disease (CVD) is one of the life-threatening diseases. Many researchers handcrafted features of heart sound to analyze heart sound signals for CVD automatically and achieved great success. But the handcrafted features of heart sound might not fully represent the raw data and it might be useless and redundant. Then the computational resources might be wasted. In this paper, the one dimension deep neural network (1-D DNN) with low parameters is proposed to detect abnormal of Cardiovascular disease. The raw heart sound fragments segmented by sliding window of 3s are fed into the network to extract discriminative features and are classified to normal or abnormal. The 2016 PhysioNet challenge database is used for training and validating the proposed network. Proposed network only has 0.08 Mb parameters and achieves 94.6% classification accuracy. Compared to the related works on heart sound analysis for Cardiovascular disease detection. The proposed 1-D DNN provided comparable performance in heart sound classification without handcrafted feature and precise segmentation.

Keywords: Cardiovascular disease · Heart sound · Deep learning · Low parameters · Handcrafted feature

1 Introduction

Cardiovascular disease (CVD) is one of the life-threatening diseases. Many people suffer from this disease all over the world, especially in low and middle-income countries, they can't get efficient treatment due to the limitations of medical resources and economic level [1]. Early detection can reduce the risk of CVD through exercise and good living habits. Besides, early screening of Cardiovascular disease has important implication for treatment in a timely manner.

Cardiac auscultation is widely used to evaluate heart function in patients. But heart sound is a weak and non-stationary signal which is interfered easily by

© Springer Nature Switzerland AG 2021
G. Wang et al. (Eds.): SpaCCS 2020, LNCS 12383, pp. 200–208, 2021.
https://doi.org/10.1007/978-3-030-68884-4_17

other factors, such as lung sounds, breath sounds, noisy environment and so on. For all this, doctors could still make mistakes because of ear limitation and other subject reasons. Phonocardiogram (PCG) makes the heart sound visualized and it is used to assist physicians in improving the efficiency of diagnosis. Therefore, PCG signal is a key for analysis of Cardiovascular disease.

In recent years, machine learning technique is applied in medical diagnosis and has made great achievements. So there are lots of methods for analysis of PCG signals. Segmentation, feature extraction and classification are the mainly steps of PCG analysis. Segmentation is the first step of heart sound analysis. Potes C et al. [2] used segmentation method proposed by Springer et al. [3] to segment the PCG recordings and extracted the time-domain, frequency-domain and CNN features from segmented heart sound. They won the championship of the 2016 PhysioNet challenge with overall score of 0.8602 by using the ensemble of feature-based and CNN-based classifiers to detect the heart sound. The Springer's method can achieve high accuracy of segmentation for PCG. But it needs the electrocardiogram (ECG) as the reference signals and has high computational cost. In fact, it is difficult to synchronize the acquisition of PCG and ECG. Singh et al. [4] used unsegmented 5s heart sounds from the 2016 PhysioNet challenge database accompanied by continuous wavelet transform (CWT) results to the generation of 2D scalogram images and classified with pre-trained AlexNet. They achieved 90% of classification accuracy. Krishnan [5] achieved overall accuracy of 85.65% by using Feed-forward Neural Network model with unsegmented 6s heart sound. These methods reduce the computational cost by unsegmented heart sound. Moreover, Compared to signals in recording level, signals in patch level are not easy to be corrupted by murmurs, so segmentation usually achieve stronger robustness to deal with the noises in environment, acquisition or transmission [6].

After segmentation, many features are extracted from the segmented PCG fragments. Li et al. [7] extracted time domain, frequency domain and entropy features, and they split three feature sets(time domain, time & frequency domain, time and frequency domain & entropy). The experiments result showed that the back propagation neural network with three different features achieved the high accuracy of 88.56%. Son et al. [8] have used DWT and Mel Frequency Cepstral Coefficients(MFCC) features to classify PCG signals to normal and abnormal. Nogueira et al. [9] combined the time-domain and frequency-domain features of phonocardiogram signals to improve cardiac disease automatic classification. The features extracted above methods might not fully represent the raw PCG signals and might include useless and redundant features that affect the final classification result or waste computational resources.

In this article, we develop a one dimension deep neural network (1-D DNN) for classifying heart sound automatically with low parameters and high accuracy. We try to feed the raw data of PCG signals segmented by 3s sliding window to network we proposed and the network automatically extracts features for final classification. Furthermore, the network mainly consists of stem block, three dense modules and three transition modules. Firstly, stem block is the first layer to extract features with large receptive fields and few parameters. Secondly, dense module contains many blocks and outputs of each block are concatenated as the final outputs of dense module. The point-wise convolution and depth-wise separable convolution are used into each block of dense module in a more efficient way. Finally, channel attention mechanism is applied in transition module to improve the ability of feature extraction. Compared with several related work in heart sound classification methods, the proposed 1-D DNN has lower parameters of 0.08 MB with high accuracy of 94.6%.

2   Proposed Method

The flow-chart of the proposed method showed in Fig. 1, and each step is described as follows.

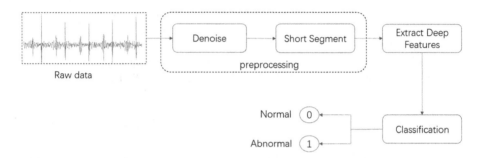

Fig. 1. The flow-chart of classification of PCG signals using the proposed method.

2.1   Preprocessing

The step of preprocessing contains de-noise and short segment. Due to environmental factors, there are a lot of noises in the heart sound signals. These noises seriously affect the accuracy of PCG signals analysis. So the first step we should get rid of the noises from the PCG signals. In this study, we have applied a band-pass filter with lower and upper cut-off frequencies 25 Hz 400 Hz, respectively for the filtering of PCG signals. After that, wavelet threshold method is applied for secondary noise reduction. The PCG signals are decomposed 6 layers with daubechies6 of mother wavelet. Then the high level coefficient of wavelet decomposition becomes zero. And we select 0.06 as the wavelet threshold value. The threshold value is applied to the remaining decomposition coefficients. Finally, the signal is reconstructed by the processed decomposition coefficients. And we use sliding window technique with the window size of 3s and overlap of 1s to segment the heart sounds.

2.2   Extract Features and Classification

After preprocessing, we attained lots of short heart sound fragments. These fragments contain much information of heart status. We need extract useful information about CVD from these fragments. That is very vital to affect the accuracy of classification. In traditional methods, the features are handcrafted by researchers. But the PCG signal is complex and the handcrafted features might not fully represent the PCG signals and it might be useless or redundant. The rapidly growth of deep learning, the researchers start using the deep learning technique to extract features automatically. The mass of experiments demonstrated that Convolutional Neural Network (CNN) has the best performance for extracting features. In our study, we designed a 1-D deep neural network with low parameters to complete extract features and classification automatically.

The proposed 1-D DNN is mainly made up of stem block, three dense modules and three transition modules. Stem block is equivalent to a standard convolution operation with kernel size of 7, but the cost of computation is lower [10]. Feature maps from stem block and max pool layer through three dense modules and transition modules in sequence. After that, the features through average pool layer to obtain squeezed multi-scale representation and then ended with a linear layer with softmax to achieve the classification results.

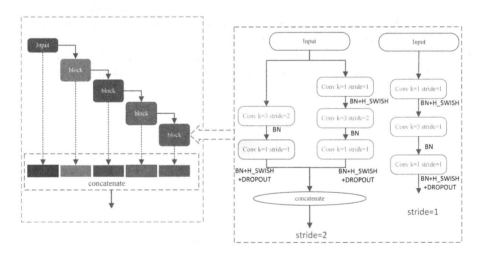

Fig. 2. The structure of each dense module

Dense Module. Dense module is described in Fig. 2. It inspired by the DenseNet and VovNet [11,12]. The density connection is the core of the DenseNet. But it consumes lots of computational resource to training. So the proposed VovNet solved the problem. In our study, we applied part of one-shot aggregation module of VovNet into our DNN to reduce computational cost. As depicted in Fig. 2, while the feature maps are fed into the dense module, the outputs of previous block are fed into next block and the outputs of each block are concatenated in channel dimension as the outputs of dense module. Each block outputs the same channel size. While the stride is 2, the inputs are fed into two branches. One branch reduces the channel of inputs by point-wise convolution, and then depth-wise separable convolution is used to learned potential features. Finally, the point-wise convolution is applied to expanse to output channel size. The other branch don't have the first point-wise convolution. Outputs of two branches, which have abundant features learned by different structure, are concatenated in feature dimension as the final outputs. If the stride is 1, there is no other branch and the inputs through reduction in channel, potential features learned and channel expansion respectively. In this module, h-swish [13], which often used in lightweight neural network is applied to instead of relu.

Transition Module. The outputs of dense module have high channel dimension and it costs lots of computational resources. So point-wise convolution is applied to reduce the dimension in transition module. Besides, the channel attention mechanism is introduced in transition module. The channel attention mechanism can compute the channel's weight of feature maps and if the weight size of channel is greater, the channel can get more attention. In this paper, the feature maps after point-wise convolution operation are fed into global average pooling and global max pooling respectively. Then outputs through the shared Multilayer Perception (MLP) respectively and the results of adding two different feature maps in element-wise through sigmoid. Finally, the outputs of point-wise convolution multiplies by sigmoid's results as the outputs of transition module. The transition module is described in Fig. 3.

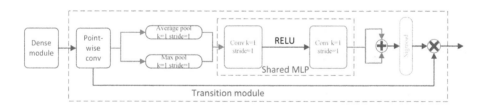

Fig. 3. The structure of each transition module

Classification. Classification is the final step. In this study, the state of heart sounds are classified two categories: normal and abnormal. So it's a binary classification and the result is 0 or 1. So softamx is applied to do it. The representations of raw PCG signal segments are learned from the proposed 1-D DNN, and we use the learned representations to classification by softmax. The implementation details of our proposed 1-D DNN are showed in Table 1.

Table 1. An overview of the implementation details of our proposed DNN architecture.

Layers	Output size	Configurations
Stem block	$1 \times 1500 \times 24$	Conv 3, stride 2 Conv 1, stride 1 Conv 3, stride 2 Max pool 2, stride 2 Conv 1, stride 1
Pool layer	$1 \times 749 \times 24$	Max pool 3 stride 2
Dense module	$[1 \times 749 \times 12] \times 4$	[Conv 1 stride 1 Conv 3 stride 1 Conv 1 stride 1] $\times 4$
Transition module	$1 \times 749 \times 36$	Adaptive max pool Adaptive average pool Conv 1 stride 1 Conv 1 stride 1
Dense module	$[1 \times 749 \times 12] \times 4$	[Conv 1 stride 1 Conv 3 stride 1 Conv 1 stride 1] $\times 4$
Transition module	$1 \times 749 \times 42$	Adaptive max pool Adaptive average pool Conv 1 stride 1 Conv 1 stride 1
Dense module	$[1 \times 749 \times 12] \times 4$	[Conv 1 stride 1 Conv 3 stride 2 Conv 1 stride 1 Conv 3 stride 2 Conv 1 stride 1] $\times 4$
Transition module	$1 \times 749 \times 45$	Adaptive max pool Adaptive average pool Conv 1 stride 1 Conv 1 stride 1
Pool layer	$1 \times 1 \times 45$	Adaptive average pool
Linear & Softmax	2	——

3 Experiments

3.1 DNN Training

In our experiments, the PhysioNet/CinC 2016 Challenge database [14] is applied. There are 5 groups of a-f and 2575 normal and 665 abnormal heart sound recordings in this database. And the distribution of the categories is seriously imbalanced. Firstly, The raw PCG signals are preprocessed. And then 36,360 short fragments were segmented by sliding window of 3s with overlap of 1s. To account for a fair split of training and test samples, 90% of samples are used for training and 10% is used for testing, and 10% of training samples are used for validation. For the training, the cross entropy loss function is selected and the weight ratio of the normal and abnormal is 0.5 for imbalance class. Adam is selected as the optimizer with the learning rate of 0.002 and weight decay of 0.0001. Besides, the dropout technique is applied in dense module to avoid over-fitting with dropout rate of 0.3. The network is built by Pytorch framework [15], and the proposed 1-D DNN with epochs of 150 and batch size of 64 is trained on NVIDIA GTX 1050TI GPU. The curves of loss and accuracy are plot in Fig. 4. From the curves, the trend of training loss is not obvious. We saved the best model in the process of training and tested the test set on best model.

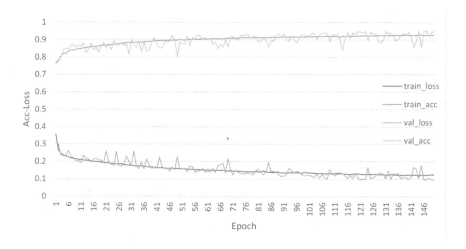

Fig. 4. The curves of loss and accuracy of training and validating

3.2   Experiment Results

In order to evaluate proposed 1-D DNN, many metrics are introduced, such as sensitivity, specificity, F1 score and so on. We compared our study to the state-of-the-art methods for classification of heart sound. As reported in Table 2, 1-D CliqueNet and 1-D DenseNet are proposed by Xiao et al. [6,16], and they also used raw PCG signal fragments as the inputs of the networks. Our proposed 1-D DNN achieved the highest accuracy of 94.6%, the highest sensitivity of 95.7% and the highest F1 score of 96.5%. The specificity of 90.7% is slightly lower than the others and the network still need to be improved. Moreover, our proposed DNN has lower parameters of 0.08 MB than 1-D CliqueNet and 1-D DenseNet. By contrast, our proposed 1-D DNN attained comparable performance with lower parameters and without precise segmentation.

Table 2. Compared to the related works

Related work	Method	Sensitivity	Specificity	F1 score	Accuracy	Params
Xiao et al. [6]	1-D CliqueNet	0.862	0.952	0.907	0.933	0.19M
Xiao et al. [16]	1-D DenseNet	0.852	0.957	0.905	0.936	0.11M
Our study	proposed 1-D DNN	0.957	0.907	0.965	0.946	0.08M

4   Conclusion

In this study, we have demonstrated the application of one dimension deep neural network for detection of Cardiovascular disease with extremely low parameters and without precise segmentation. We apply sliding window for segmentation and the segmented PCG signals are fed into the network to feature extraction and classification directly. The model produced high classification accuracy of 94.6% with only 0.08 Mb parameters. Method we proposed without extra feature extraction technique can use in edge devices (i.e. mobile phone, pad) in real-time. In the future work, we will continue to optimize the network and port to the edge devices to test.

Acknowledgment. This work was supported by Fujian Provincial Natural Science Foundation of China under grant no.2019J01856. The Graduate science and technology innovation project of XMUT no. YKJCX2019041.

References

1. World Health Oragnization. Cardiovascular diseases(CVDs). https://www.who.int/en/news-room/fact-sheets/detail/cardiovascular-diseases-(cvds). Accessed 1 June 2019
2. Potes, C., Parvaneh, S., Rahman, A., Conroy, B.: Ensemble of feature-based and deep learning-based classifiers for detection of abnormal heart sounds. In: 2016 Computing in Cardiology Conference (CinC), pp. 621–624. IEEE (2016)
3. Springer, D.B., Tarassenko, L., Clifford, G.D.: Logistic regression-HSMM-based heart sound segmentation. IEEE Trans. Biomed. Eng. **63**(4), 822–832 (2015)
4. Singh, S.A., Majumder, S., Mishra, M.: Classification of short unsegmented heart sound based on deep learning. In: 2019 IEEE International Instrumentation and Measurement Technology Conference (I2MTC), pp. 1–6. IEEE (2019)
5. Krishnan, P.T., Balasubramanian, P., Umapathy, S.: Automated heart sound classification system from unsegmented phonocardiogram (PCG) using deep neural network. Physical and Engineering Sciences in Medicine, pp. 1–11 (2020)
6. Xiao, B., Xu, Y., Bi, X., Zhang, J., Ma, X.: Heart sounds classification using a novel 1-d convolutional neural network with extremely low parameter consumption. Neurocomputing **392**, 153–159 (2020)
7. Li, L., et al.: Classification of heart sound signals with BP neural network and logistic regression. In: 2017 Chinese Automation Congress (CAC), pp. 7380–7383. IEEE (2017)
8. Son, G.Y., Kwon, S., et al.: Classification of heart sound signal using multiple features. Appl. Sci. **8**(12), 2344 (2018)
9. Nogueira, D.M., Ferreira, C.A., Gomes, E.F., Jorge, A.M.: Classifying heart sounds using images of motifs, MFCC and temporal features. J. Med. Syst. **43**(6), 168 (2019)
10. Wang, R.J., Li, X., Ling, C.X.: Pelee: a real-time object detection system on mobile devices. In: Advances in Neural Information Processing Systems, pp. 1963–1972 (2018)
11. Iandola, F., Moskewicz, M., Karayev, S., Girshick, R., Darrell, T., Keutzer, K.: Densenet: implementing efficient convnet descriptor pyramids. arXiv preprint arXiv:1404.1869 (2014)
12. Lee, Y., Hwang, J.w., Lee, S., Bae, Y., Park, J.: An energy and GPU-computation efficient backbone network for real-time object detection. In: Proceedings of the IEEE Conference on Computer Vision and Pattern Recognition Workshops (2019)
13. Howard, A., et al.: Searching for mobilenetv3. In: Proceedings of the IEEE International Conference on Computer Vision, pp. 1314–1324 (2019)

14. Liu, C., et al.: An open access database for the evaluation of heart sound algorithms. Physiol. Meas. **37**(12), 2181 (2016)
15. Subramanian, V.: Deep Learning with PyTorch: A practical approach to building neural network models using PyTorch. Packt Publishing Ltd (2018)
16. Xiao, B., et al.: Follow the sound of children's heart: A deep-learning-based computer-aided pediatric CHDS diagnosis system. IEEE Internet Things J. **7**(3), 1994–2004 (2019)

Indoor Positioning Technology Based on the Fusion of UWB and BLE

Jingbo Xia[1], Yaoxiang Wu[2], and Xiaofu Du[1(✉)]

[1] School of Information Science and Technology, Xiamen University Tan Kah Kee College, Zhangzhou 363105, China
duxiaofu@xujc.com
[2] School of Electronic Science and Engineering, Xiamen University, Xiamen 361005, China

Abstract. With the development of the Internet of Things, indoor positioning systems based on location services have been widely used in factories, warehouses, hospitals, smart homes, and high-security areas. However, traditional indoor positioning systems are not only expensive but also need to be improved in positioning accuracy. Therefore, this paper proposes an indoor positioning technology based on the fusion of UWB and BLE, which achieves higher positioning accuracy while reducing the cost of the positioning system, and performs the SS-TWR ranging model of UWB and the logarithmic distance path attenuation model of BLE. Analysis, the UWB ranging model based on error correction and the BLE ranging model based on segmentation parameters based on error correction are proposed, and the fusion positioning is performed using the EKF algorithm. Experiments prove that the proposed ranging model has a significant effect on the improvement of positioning performance.

Keywords: Location service · Indoor positioning · Fusion positioning · UWB · BLE · EKF

1 Introduction and Related Work

In recent years, indoor positioning system has become a promising research field due to its great application prospect and practical demand. At present, outdoor positioning technology has been relatively mature. For outdoor environment, the Global Positioning System (GPS), BeiDou (BD), Galileo and Russian GLONASS are widely used in military, industrial and agricultural production, smart city, smart transportation and other fields [1–4]. However, due to multi-path effects, such as attenuation and reflection, etc. of satellite signals caused by shielding large buildings, the feasibility of indoor positioning using satellite positioning system is greatly reduced [5, 6].

With the rapid development of Wireless Sensor Network (WSN) [7], most location-based services in indoor environment are based on WSN. In the past decade, WSN has been widely used to solve indoor positioning problems. In the WSN environment, an observer or user receives a radio frequency signal and can estimate its position based on the signal information. Common indoor positioning wireless sensor networks include WiFi, BLE, UWB, RFID and ZigBee [8–10]. Among them, WiFi is the most common

© Springer Nature Switzerland AG 2021
G. Wang et al. (Eds.): SpaCCS 2020, LNCS 12383, pp. 209–221, 2021.
https://doi.org/10.1007/978-3-030-68884-4_18

positioning technology. Ding et al. [11] proposed a positioning system based on propagation model to collect sparse fingerprints from different access points and then divide the entire positioning space into sub-regions. The proposed propagation model was used to restore the fingerprint, and then the weighted KNN (K Nearest Neighbor) algorithm was used to estimate the user's location with the fingerprint value, achieving a location accuracy of 1.4 m.

BLE has better signal stability than WiFi, and therefore better positioning performance. In addition, BLE is also characterized by its low power consumption. A button battery can be used for more than one year, which facilitates the layout and maintenance of Bluetooth beacons. Zafari et al. [12] provided indoor positioning services by using iBeacons [13], and used user devices to collect RSSI values of different iBeacons, and used Particle Filter (PF), Kalman Filter-Particle Filter (KF-PF) and Particle Filter-Extended Kalman Filter.PF- EKF) new cascade method to improve the positioning accuracy of the system. The experimental results show that the average precision of PF, KF-PF and PF-EKF is 1.44 m, 1.03 m and 0.95 m respectively. Although Bluetooth system has the advantages of low power consumption and high positioning accuracy, it also has the disadvantages of serious delay.

In addition, RFID and ZigBee technologies are similar to WiFi and BLE technologies, with positioning accuracy of meter level. Ni et al. proposed LANDMARC [14] that user devices that need to be tracked should be equipped with positioning tags, and at the same time, the receiving node estimated the location of the devices by measuring the signal strength of positioning tags on the tracking devices. Although LANDMARC has low power consumption and can reach a positioning accuracy of 1 m, its propagation distance is limited and the delay is large. Dong et al. [15] studied the indoor fingerprint identification and location method based on ZigBee, respectively using KNN, WKNN and area-based WKNN algorithm for experiments. Finally, combined with the map matching method and fingerprint identification positioning method, the online tracking process under the simulated indoor environment is completed. However, ZigBee's positioning principle and method are similar to WiFi and BLE, and it is not as good as WiFi and BLE in terms of positioning accuracy and propagation distance.

However, due to the high multipath resolution of UWB signal and the measuring position accuracy reaching centimeter level, indoor positioning technology based on UWB has become very popular. Angelis et al. [16] proposed a technology to model UWB signal propagation in indoor or outdoor environments, which supports the positioning system design based on Round Trip Time (RTT) measurement and particle filter. In the case of noise, the least square method, extended Kalman filter and particle filter are used to detect the slowly moving target and compare the results. Experiments show that particle filtering has the best performance in real indoor environment, but at the cost of computational complexity. In addition, UWB equipment is relatively expensive, difficult to integrate, and has difficulties in data transmission, so it needs high cost if it is installed on a large scale.

Considering the advantages and disadvantages of these wireless sensor network positioning technologies, this paper proposes the fusion positioning technology based on UWB and BLE. Combined with the advantages of high precision of UWB and low cost of BLE, the paper improves the RANGING model of UWB and BLE to reduce the indoor positioning cost and improve the positioning accuracy.

2   UWB Ranging Model Based on Error Correction

2.1   SS-TWR Ranging Model

The most commonly used ranging models for UWB are SS-TWR and DS-TWR. SS-TWR involves a simple measurement of the round-trip delay of a single message from one node to another and the response delay sent back to the original node. DS-TWR, however, is an extension of the basic one-way bidirectional ranging, where two round-trip time measurements are used, combined with a flight time result that reduces the error even with a fairly long response delay. However, compared with SS-TWR, its complexity also increases correspondingly. Therefore, SS-TWR became a more commonly used ranging model for UWB.

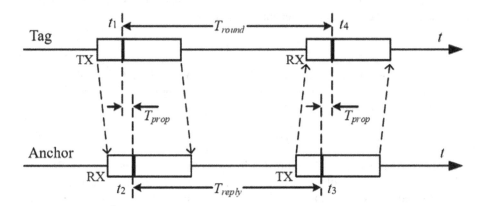

Fig. 1. The ranging principle of SS-TWR.

The ranging principle of SS-TWR is shown in Fig. 1. The exchange is initiated by positioning *Tag* and completed by *Anchor* node response. Each device accurately timestamps the sending and receiving time of message frames, and the *Tprop* of flight time between the Tag and Anchor node of UWB signal can be calculated by simple subtraction.

The specific process is as follows: first, the query data frame is emitted by the positioning tag and the time stamp T1 is recorded at the moment; after the flight time Tprop is received by the anchor node and the time stamp T2 is recorded at the moment; after the delayed Treply, the positioning base station issues the response time stamp T3; finally, the response time stamp is received by the positioning tag and recorded as T4. The calculation of the Tprop for flight time is shown in Eqs. (1).

$$T_{prop} = \frac{(t_4 - t_1) - (t_3 - t_2)}{2} \tag{1}$$

Then the distance between the positioning tag and the anchor node is:

$$d = T_{prop} \cdot c \tag{2}$$

Where, C is the speed of light in a vacuum environment, approximately $3 * 10^8$ m/s.

2.2 Error Correction for SS-TWR Ranging

Although the SS-TWR ranging model can eliminate the errors caused by UWB clock asynchronization to a certain extent, the errors caused by actual environment and system delay of hardware equipment should also be considered. Therefore, it is necessary to correct the error of the SS-TWR ranging results.

In general, the error of ranging presents an increasing trend with the increase of ranging distance. Therefore, we will derive a statistical model based on the average of the distance estimation errors. In general, it can be written as:

$$\hat{r} = r - v(r) \tag{3}$$

Where, r is the true distance, $\hat{r}$ is the ranging distance of UWB, and $v(r)$ is the random variable simulating the ranging error of UWB. Let the ranging error v approximate to the linear increase function of the true distance r:

$$v(r) = a \cdot r + b \tag{4}$$

The coefficients a and b can be estimated by using the least square method. Specifically, given n samples at different locations (v_i, r_i), $i = 1,..., n$. Firstly, linear regression was performed on n samples to obtain the estimated values of scaling factor a and offset b, respectively, as shown in Eqs. (5)-(6).

$$\hat{a} = \frac{\sum_{i=1}^{n} (r_i - \bar{r})(v_i - \bar{v})}{\sum_{i=1}^{n} (r_i - \bar{r})^2} \tag{5}$$

$$\hat{b} = \bar{v} - \hat{a} \cdot \bar{r} \tag{6}$$

Where, $\bar{r}$ and $\bar{v}$ are the average true distance and average ranging error of n measurement points respectively.

3   The BLE Ranging Model Based on Segmental Parameter

3.1 Data Preprocessing

Due to poor anti-jamming capacity of signals, BLE is easy to produce the multipath effect in interior space, so you need to filter the received RSSI value. This paper chose a

Gaussian filter to deal with RSSI, because Gaussian filter has a good effect of dealing with random variable. Using a Gaussian filter can effectively reduce some larger deviation of RSSI values for the whole measurement.

Assume that the m RSSI values received at unknown nodes are p_i, $i = 1, 2, ...,$ m. Then, the mean μ and variance σ^2 of RSSI values measured are shown as:

$$\mu = \frac{1}{m} \sum\nolimits_{i=1}^{m} p_i \tag{7}$$

$$\sigma^2 = \frac{1}{m-1} \sum\nolimits_{i=1}^{m} (p_i - \mu)^2 \tag{8}$$

Then the probability density function of p_i is:

$$f(p) = \frac{1}{\sigma \sqrt{2\pi}} \exp(-\frac{p - \mu}{2\sigma^2}) \tag{9}$$

According to the Gaussian probability density function of RSSI, it can be calculated that the value area in interval $(\mu - \sigma, \mu + \sigma)$ accounts for 68% of the total area [18], that is, most RSSI values are in interval $(\mu - \sigma, \mu + \sigma)$. Therefore, gauss filtering was performed on the m RSSI values received to filter the RSSI values outside this interval, and then the RSSI values within this interval were arithmetically averaged as the optimized RSSI value.

$$\bar{p} = \frac{1}{n} \sum\nolimits_{i=1}^{n} p_i \tag{10}$$

Where, n is the number of RSSI value after Gaussian filtering.

3.2 A Logarithmic Path Attenuation Model Based on Piecewise Parameters

Traditionally, the log-distance path loss model is used to estimate the distance. This model believes that the attenuation signal strength is proportional to the logarithm of the distance traveled, as shown in:

$$RSSI = P_{1m} - 10n \lg d \tag{11}$$

Where, d is the distance between the receiver and the transmitter, P_{1m} is the reference power measured in dBm 1 m away from the transmitter, and n is the path loss index. Then the distance between the two nodes is:

$$d = 10^{\frac{A-RSSI}{10n}} \tag{12}$$

The construction of the ranging model depends on the calculation of constants A and n.

According to literature [19], BLE signal propagation in a small range is relatively stable, and the traditional log-distance path attenuation model can be used to fit well.

However, when the distance increases, the fitting error of the model also presents an increasing trend. Therefore, in the indoor environment of the experiment, a set of data was taken at 0.5 m intervals from 0 to 5 m, and each set of data was 100 continuous measured values, and the optimized RSSI value was obtained after gaussian filtering and weighted average of the measured values, as shown in Table 1.

Table 1. Table of Bluetooth RSSI measurement statistics.

Ranging distance (m)	Optimized RSSI value (dBm)	Ranging distance (m)	Optimized RSSI value (dBm)
0.5	33	3	53
1	39	3.5	47
1.5	43	4	52
2	46	4.5	49
2.5	49	5	52

As shown in the Table 1, the optimized RSSI value is 39dBm at 1 m, so the value of A is 39. Then, 10 optimized RSSI values from 0 to 5 m in the table were fitted to obtain the optimal n value of 2.5. Then the model formula is:

$$d = 10^{\frac{39-RSSI}{25}} \tag{13}$$

According to Eq. (13), the error table of the log-distance path attenuation model can be obtained:

Table 2. Table of logarithmic distance path attenuation model's error.

Real distance (m)	Ranging distance (m)	Distance error (m)	Real distance (m)	Ranging distance (m)	Distance error (m)
0.5	0.57	0.07	3	3.63	0.63
1	1.00	0.00	3.5	2.09	1.41
1.5	1.45	0.05	4	3.31	0.69
2	1.91	0.09	4.5	2.51	1.99
2.5	2.51	0.01	5	3.31	1.69

As can be seen from Table 2, the overall average error of 10 points in the model from 0 to 5 m is 0.67 m, among which the error within 0 to 3 m is small, and the error within 3 to 5 m is large. Among them, the ranging value at 1 m is the estimation point of parameter A, so the error at 1 m is 0. When the ranging distance is more than 3 m, the RSSI has no obvious trend of increasing, and the BLE signal has a large fluctuation due to its propagation characteristics.

Therefore, a logarithmic distance path attenuation model based on piecewise parameters is proposed, and the model is piecewise fitted. The models within 0–5 m are divided into 0–3 m and 3–5 m. The 0–3 m section has a relatively small error, so only the 3–5 m section needs to be fitted. When the test range is greater than 5 m, it can be fitted according to the actual test value, and the number of segments fitted can be multiple. The optimal n value is 1.8 by fitting, and the logarithmic distance path attenuation model based on piecewise parameters can be obtained as follows:

$$\begin{cases} d = 10^{\frac{39-RSSI}{25}}, RSSI \leq 49 \\ d = 10^{\frac{39-RSSI}{18}}, RSSI > 49 \end{cases} \tag{14}$$

4 EKF Location Algorithm

The EKF is customized for tracking mobile nodes. Its main advantage is that it can process multiple measurements at once and provide real-time location estimation. According to the information obtained from motion (such as velocity, acceleration, angular velocity), different forms of EKF modeling can be carried out for human motion. A common pedestrian model USES randomness as a movement model for mobile devices. This simple model has been shown to be more robust than other complex models because human movement is unpredictable. Therefore, better modeling for Gaussian noise. Other optional models include velocity, velocity and acceleration, and direction.

In this paper, a random model is selected to describe the motion of pedestrians. In this model, the change of position is given by gaussian noise. Therefore, the state transition model of the system can be defined as [20]:

$$\mathbf{X}_{k+1} = \mathbf{AX}_k + \mathbf{w}_k \tag{15}$$

Where, X_{k+1} and X_k are the coordinates of the positioning tag, respectively representing the current position state vector and the previous position state vector. w_k is the covariance matrix with the change of location direction. Matrix A represents the state transition matrix:

$$\mathbf{A} = \begin{bmatrix} 1 & Ts \\ 0 & 1 \end{bmatrix} \tag{16}$$

Ts is the sampling time interval of the sensor. Then define the measurement model of the system:

$$\mathbf{Z}_k = \mathbf{h}(\mathbf{X}_k) + \mathbf{v}_x \tag{17}$$

Where, $\mathbf{Z}_k$ is the current measurement vector, and is the ranging distance from the positioning tag to the positioning base station, that is, the ranging distance obtained by the improved UWB and BLE ranging models. $\mathbf{h}(\mathbf{X}_k)$ is the observation matrix, subscript k represents parameters that can change with time, subscript Ai represents the number of locating base stations, and (x_{Ai}, y_{Ai}) is the coordinates of locating base stations. $\mathbf{v}_x$ is the measurement noise.

$$\mathbf{h}(\mathbf{X}_k) = \sqrt{(x_k - x_{Ai})^2 + (y_k - y_{Ai})^2} \tag{18}$$

The Jacobian determinant of $\mathbf{h}(\mathbf{X}_k)$ is its partial derivative. When the number of locating base stations is 3, the Jacobian determinant of $\mathbf{H}_k$ is:

$$\mathbf{H}_k = 2 \begin{bmatrix} \dfrac{x_k - x_{A1}}{\sqrt{(x_k - x_{A1})^2 + (y_k - y_{A1})^2}} & \dfrac{y_k - y_{A1}}{\sqrt{(x_k - x_{A1})^2 + (y_k - y_{A1})^2}} \\ \dfrac{x_k - x_{A2}}{\sqrt{(x_k - x_{A2})^2 + (y_k - y_{A2})^2}} & \dfrac{y_k - y_{A2}}{\sqrt{(x_k - x_{A2})^2 + (y_k - y_{A2})^2}} \\ \dfrac{x_k - x_{A3}}{\sqrt{(x_k - x_{A3})^2 + (y_k - y_{A3})^2}} & \dfrac{y_k - y_{A3}}{\sqrt{(x_k - x_{A3})^2 + (y_k - y_{A3})^2}} \end{bmatrix} \tag{19}$$

Based on the above model, EKF is divided into prediction and update stages to estimate the label position [21].

In the prediction stage, EKF predicts the state vector and covariance matrix, shown as:

$$\mathbf{X}_k^- = \mathbf{A}\mathbf{X}_{k-1} = \mathbf{X}_{k-1} \tag{20}$$

$$\mathbf{P}_k^- = \mathbf{A}\mathbf{P}_{k-1}\mathbf{A}^{\mathrm{T}} + \mathbf{Q}_k \tag{21}$$

As long as there is a new measurement vector $\mathbf{Z}_k$, the update stage can be performed. The goal of this phase is to refine the state vector and covariance matrix estimation. The first step in the update phase is to calculate the Kalman gain. Then, Kalman gain is used to combine the received distance information with the information in the prediction stage to calculate the updated status. Finally, the covariance matrix is updated:

$$\mathbf{K}_k = \mathbf{P}_k^- \mathbf{H}_k^{\mathrm{T}} \mathbf{S}_k^{-1} \tag{22}$$

$$\mathbf{S}_k = \mathbf{H}_k \mathbf{P}_k^- \mathbf{H}_k^{\mathrm{T}} + \mathbf{R}_k \tag{23}$$

$$\mathbf{X}_k = \mathbf{X}_k^- + \mathbf{R}_k \tilde{y}_k \tag{24}$$

$$\tilde{y}_k = \mathbf{Z}_k - \mathbf{h}(\mathbf{X}_k^-) \tag{25}$$

$$\mathbf{P}_k = (\mathbf{I} - \mathbf{K}_k \mathbf{H}_k) \mathbf{P}_k^- \tag{26}$$

5   Experimental Results and Analysis

5.1   Establishment of Experimental Environment

Only three beacons are needed for two-dimensional spatial positioning. The scene of the experiment is shown in Fig. 2. If the coordinates of base station A1 are set as (0, 0), the coordinates of base station A2 are set as (4.8, 0), and the coordinates of base station A3 are set as (2.4, 3.6) in meters. The positioning tag is placed in a rectangular area for positioning experiment. The positioning base station and positioning tag are respectively placed at 1.77 m on the tripod.

Fig. 2.   The Lab scene.

Since each locating base station can be either a UWB or a BLE beacon, there are four ways to configure locating base stations: 1). The three positioning base stations are all UWB base stations; 2). Two positioning base stations are UWB base stations and one positioning base station is BLE beacon; 3). One locating base station is UWB base station and two locating base stations are BLE beacon; 4). All three positioning base stations are BLE beacons.

5.2   Positioning Accuracy

Positioning accuracy is the most commonly used index to evaluate the performance of positioning algorithms. It represents the difference between the actual location and the estimated location. This measurement is usually measured as the Euclidean distance between the estimated position and the real position. Here, the evaluation Euclidean distance of multiple measurements is used to represent the positioning accuracy, which is defined as follows:

$$D_{Accuracy} = \frac{\sum_{i=1}^{i=N} \sqrt{(x_i - x)^2 + (y_i - y)^2}}{N} \tag{27}$$

Where, (x_i, y_i) is the coordinates of the positioning tag estimated by the algorithm, (x, y) is the coordinates of the real position, and N is the number of observations.

In the experimental scene, 10 coordinate points were uniformly selected as measurement points, and their coordinates were (0, 1.2), (0, 2.4), (1.2, 1.2), (2.4, 1.2), (2.4, 2.4), (3.6, 1.2), (3.6, 1.2), (3.6, 2.4), (4.8, 1.2), (4.8, 2.4).

The average positioning accuracy of 10 points in 4 configuration methods is shown in Table 3.

Table 3. The positioning accuracy of EKF algorithm before and after model improvement.

Configuration mode	Average positioning accuracy before improvement (cm)	Average positioning accuracy after improvement (cm)
1	12.2	6.8
2	34.3	29
3	100	71
4	121	83

Table 3 shows that the errors of the four configurations have been reduced by 4.3%, 15.5%, 29% and 31.4% respectively after improvement.

5.3   Locating Coordinate Scatter Diagram

In NO. 1–4 configuration model, the scatter diagrams of EKF algorithm positioning coordinate before and after improvement are shown in Fig. 3.

As can be seen from the locating point scatter diagram, the number of UWB base stations determines the positioning accuracy. The more UWB base stations there are, the closer the positioning coordinates are to the real coordinates, the higher the positioning accuracy will be. The closer the locating point is to the central position, the more concentrated the locating coordinate scatters, the higher the positioning accuracy is, and the more stable the positioning performance is. However, when it is close to the wall, the coordinate scatters diverge, the positioning accuracy is low, and the positioning performance is unstable.

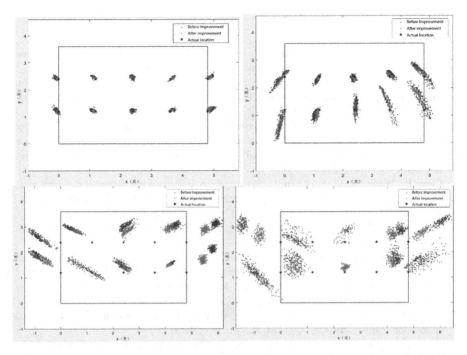

Fig. 3. The coordinate scatter diagrams obtained from configuration 1–4, using EKF algorithm to position.

6   Conclusion

In this paper, the fusion positioning technology based on UWB and BLE is proposed. Combined with the high precision of UWB and the low cost advantage of BLE, the error correction based UWB ranging model and the BLE ranging model based on piecewise parameters are proposed through the improvement of UWB and BLE ranging models. EKF positioning algorithm is used to fuse the ranging results of UWB and BLE. Experiments show that the average positioning accuracy of EKF positioning algorithm of the four combinations before model improvement is 12.2 cm, 34.3 cm, 100 cm and 121 cm respectively, while the average positioning accuracy of EKF positioning algorithm after model improvement is 6.8 cm, 29 cm, 71 cm and 83 cm respectively, which is improved by 44.3%, 34.3%, 15.5% and 29% respectively. At the same time of reducing the indoor positioning cost, the positioning accuracy is improved.

The following research direction is bluetooth 5.1 protocol, which adds the searching function of BLE, that is, the fusion of Angle and UWB.The help of Bluetooth networking function for data transmission of indoor positioning system and the research of positioning in non-line-of-sight environment.

Acknowledgments. This work was supported by the Natural Science Foundation of Fujian, China (Project No. 2018J01101).

References

1. Dayu, Y., Wei, S., Xudan, W., Ziye, H.: Review of development status of indoor location technology in China. J. Navigation Positioning **7**(4), 5–12 (2019)
2. Lemańczyk, M., Demkowicz, J.: Galileo satellite navigation system receiver concept. In: 17th International Conference Radioelektronika, pp. 1–4. Inst. of Elec. and Elec. Eng. Computer Society, Brno (2007)
3. Goncharova, I., Lindenmeier, S.: A compact satellite antenna module for GPS, Galileo, GLONASS, BeiDou and SDARS in automotive application. In: 11th European Conference on Antennas and Propagation, pp. 3639–3643. Institute of Electrical and Electronics Engineers Inc., Paris (2017)
4. Chen, R., Wang, L., Li, D., Chen, L., Wenju, F.: A survey on the fusion of the navigation and the remote sensing techniques. Acta Geodaetica et Cartographica Sinica **48**(12), 1507–1522 (2019)
5. Deng, Z., Yu, Y., Yuan, X., Wan, N., Yang, L.: Situation and development tendency of indoor positioning. China Commun. **10**(3), 42–55 (2013)
6. Lahouli, R., Chaudhary, M.H., Basak, S., Scheers, B.: Tracking of rescue workers in harsh indoor and outdoor environments. In: Palattella, M.R., Scanzio, S., Coleri Ergen, S. (eds.) ADHOC-NOW 2019. LNCS, vol. 11803, pp. 48–61. Springer, Cham (2019). https://doi.org/10.1007/978-3-030-31831-4_4
7. Fekher, K., Abbas, B., Abderrahim, B., et al.: A survey of indoor positioning technology and application. Mob. Networks Appl. **24**(3), 761–785 (2019)
8. Pei, L., Liu, D., Qian, J.: A survey of localization systems in internet of things. Mob. Networks Appl. **14**(3), 1–10 (2018).
9. Hameed, A., Ahmed, H.A.: Survey on indoor positioning applications based on different technologies. In: 12th International Conference on Mathematics, Actuarial Science, Computer Science and Statistics, pp. 1–5. Institute of Electrical and Electronics Engineers Inc., Karachi, Pakistan (2018)
10. Mai, A., Ammar, A., Alhadhrami, S., et al.: Comparative survey of indoor positioning technologies, techniques, and algorithms. In: 2014 International Conference on Cyberworlds, pp. 245–252. Institute of Electrical and Electronics Engineers Inc., Santander (2014)
11. Ding, G., Tan, Z., Zhang, J., et al.: Regional propagation model based fingerprinting localization in indoor environments. In: IEEE 24th Annual International Symposium on Personal, Indoor, and Mobile Radio Communications, pp. 291–295. Institute of Electrical and Electronics Engineers Inc., London (2013)
12. Zafari, F., Papapanagiotou, I., Devetsikiotis, M., et al.: An iBeacon based Proximity and Indoor Localization System. arXiv preprint:1703.07876 (2017)
13. Newman, N.: Apple iBeacon technology briefing. J. Direct Data Digital Mark. Pract. **15**(3), 222–225 (2014)
14. Ni, L.M., Liu, Y., Lau, Y.C., et al.: LANDMARC: indoor location sensing using active RFID. Wireless Netw. **10**(6), 701–710 (2004)
15. Dong, Z., Meng, J.C., Wen, J.L.: Implementation of indoor fingerprint positioning based on ZigBee. In: 29th Chinese Control And Decision Conference, pp. 2654–2659. Institute of Electrical and Electronics Engineers Inc., Chongqing (2017)
16. Angelis, G.D., Moschitta, A., Carbone, P.: Positioning techniques in indoor environments based on stochastic modeling of UWB round-trip-time measurements. IEEE Trans. Intell. Transp. Syst. **17**(8), 2272–2281 (2016)
17. Decawave. DW1000 User Manual. https://www.decawave.com/dw1000/usermanual/. Accessed 21 June 2020

18. Bouchard, K., Ramezani, R., Arjun, et al.: Evaluation of Bluetooth beacons behavior. IEEE 7th Annual Ubiquitous Computing, Electronics & Mobile Communication Conference, pp. 1–3. Institute of Electrical and Electronics Engineers Inc., New York (2016).
19. Li, G., Geng, E., Ye, Z., et al.: An indoor positioning algorithm based on RSSI real-time correction. In: 14th IEEE International Conference on Signal Processing, pp. 129–133. Institute of Electrical and Electronics Engineers Inc., Beijing (2018)
20. Ferreira, A., Duarte, F., Catarino, A., et al.: Performance analysis of ToA-based positioning algorithms for static and dynamic targets with low ranging measurements. Sensors **17**(8), 1915–1943 (2017)
21. Ogle, T.L., Blair, W.D., Slocumb, B.J., et al.: Assessment of hierarchical multi-sensor multi-target track fusion in the presence of large sensor biases. In: 22th International Conference on Information Fusion, pp. 1–7. Institute of Electrical and Electronics Engineers Inc., Ottawa, Canada (2019)

A User Privacy-Preserving Algorithm in Live Streaming Cloud Platforms

Mande Xie[1]([✉]), Xiaowei Sheng[2], Jun Shao[2], Guoping Zhang[3],
and Yingying Ruan[2]

[1] School of Information and Electronic Engineering,
Zhejiang Gongshang University, Hangzhou 310018, China
xiemd@zjgsu.edu.cn
[2] School of Computer Science and Information Engineering,
Zhejiang Gongshang University, Hangzhou 310018, China
jshao@zjgsu.edu.cn
[3] Faculty of Informatics & Electronics, Zhejiang Sci-Tech University,
Hangzhou 310018, China
zgp4508@zstu.edu.cn

Abstract. Due to the variety and rich features of live content, the live
cloud platform has been widely used. However, they also bring the potential threat and huge vulnerability to the users' privacy. At present, the
security mechanism is simple in almost all live streaming cloud platforms. They generally use traditional security method such as Access
Control List (ACL) to prevent unauthorized users from watching live
streaming. In addition, they mainly consider the security of the system
itself. These security measures can only guarantee the correct operation of the platform, and cannot guarantee that the privacy information
of users in the platform is not leaked. Therefore, this paper proposes a
privacy-preserving algorithm to protect private data of all participants in
a live streaming cloud platform, including their follow relationships, live
message, etc. According to semi-trusted live streaming cloud platforms,
the proposed algorithm employs key exchange over elliptic curve and
advanced encryption standard (AES) to preserve user privacy. A blind
matching algorithm based on the encrypted tag is proposed to match the
live message and intended recipients. Finally, the security of our algorithm is analyzed in depth and the results show the proposed algorithm
efficiently preserves user privacy.

Keywords: Live streaming cloud platform · Privacy preserving ·
Advanced encryption standard · Elliptic curve

1 Introduction

In the self-media age, a variety of live streaming cloud platforms spring up.
These live streaming cloud platforms build a bridge between the audiences and

© Springer Nature Switzerland AG 2021
G. Wang et al. (Eds.): SpaCCS 2020, LNCS 12383, pp. 222–232, 2021.
https://doi.org/10.1007/978-3-030-68884-4_19

the content creators. The audiences find the interesting live streaming and the content creators quickly spread their works by the platform. Compared with a traditional social network, a live streaming provides more vivid form and richer content. In addition, live streaming has greater advantages in terms of timeliness and interactivity than traditional television media. However, these platforms mainly consider the security of the system itself and they do not consider the user privacy in the security. Hence, the privacy of users has a great risk of disclosure in these platforms due to the lack of privacy protection mechanism.

The live streaming cloud platforms are generally incentive to safeguard users' content, since doing otherwise might tarnish their reputation or result in legal actions. For example, they do not actively tamper with or destroy data. They also do not actively disclose user privacy. They try to prevent external intrusions through technical means. However, In the case of observing the user agreement, the live streaming cloud platforms collect and mine the user data for their own commercial interest. Then, they may also provide mining results to the third parties including advertising service providers to realize value-added services such as delivering targeted advertising [1], which also results in the leakage of user privacy in reality. Furthermore, content stored at a cloud platform is subject to potential break-ins [2], insider attacks [3]. Therefore, a mechanism is needed in the live streaming cloud platform to effectively protect the privacy information of the users.

In addition, the security research community on user privacy protection has focused on the encryption of individual user data. In fact, privacy applies to potentially sensitive information that users disclose through searches and interests. Specifically, tags used to label and retrieve content might leak personal habits, political views, or even health conditions. Therefore, we can not only focus on the privacy issue of individual data itself, but also the privacy of follow relationship data.

1.1 Motivation

In all existing commercial live streaming cloud platforms, the server is assumed to be fully trusted. Based on this assumption, the server stores all data about individuals and follow relationship. In the situation, it is highly possible that users' private information leaks. In generally, there are two types of users in living streaming cloud platform. One is the broadcaster who is an individual content producer or self-media company. The other is the follower who is an audience. The users' private information leaks in the following three aspects.

- The followers' privacy leaks to the server. After a user registers in the server, all operations such as follow applications, matching, and information distribution need to be completed through the server. As a result, the user's privacy information such as the user's political views, personal habits, and health condition leaks completely to server. For example, if an audience follows a doctor with a tag #cancer, it is easy to infer that there is a cancer patient among the friends or relatives of the audience.
- The followers' privacy leaks to the broadcaster. While submitting a follow request, the broadcaster exactly knows which type of live streaming the

audience is following. The information leakage happens. For example, a financial company (a broadcaster user) knows an audience's investment preference according to the type of stock commentator he is following.
- The broadcasters' privacy leaks to the server. The server provides matching and transmission service between the followers and the broadcasters. After a broadcaster publishes a live message labeled by a tag, the server transfers the message to intended followers. Because information matching and distribution are performed by the server, the live messages published by a broadcaster are available to the server.

At present, the security mechanism is simple in almost all live streaming cloud platforms. They generally use traditional security method such as Access Control List (ACL) to prevent unauthorized users from watching live streaming. However, these security measures can only guarantee the correct operation of the platform, and cannot guarantee that the privacy information of users on the platform is not leaked. Therefore, the paper proposes a privacy-preserving algorithm to protect private data of all participants on a live streaming cloud platform, including their follow relationships, live message, etc.

2   Models and Design Goals

In this section, we formalize our system model and identify our privacy goals.

2.1   System Model

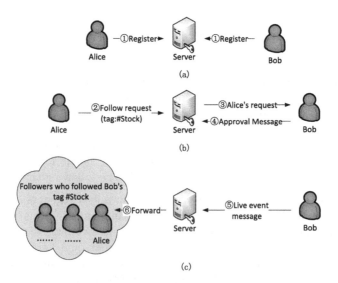

Fig. 1. The workflow of a live streaming cloud platform (a) User registration (b) Establishing follow relationship (c) Transferring live messages

In generally, three parties are involved in live streaming cloud platform. For the convenience of description, we give the following roles and terms definitions.

Broadcasters: the users who are individual content producers or self-media companies. They publish live messages and perform live streaming, such as broadcast news, broadcast financial lectures, and broadcast competitions.

Followers: the users who are audiences. They follow broadcasters' live streaming with some tags.

Server: the live streaming cloud platform who is a centralized entity. It maintains profiles and stores live messages. In addition, it forwards and matches live messages to intended followers.

Tag: a keyword which is use to label a live message. A tag is embedded in a live message and starts with #, such as #recipes, #stocks or #diseases. Followers search and retrieve a live message by a tag.

Live Message: A short message posted by a broadcaster to release a live streaming. It is generally composed of event title and content including live URL, login user name and password. It is labeled by several tags which are embedded in the live message.

Follow Relationship: If a follower (Alice) follows a broadcaster (Bob) on a tag, the relationship between Alice and Bob is the follow relationship. That is, Alice follows Bob on a tag.

Figure 1 briefly shows the workflow of a live streaming cloud platform. In the following part of the paper, we use Bob to represent the broadcaster user and Alice to indicate the follower user. The detailed description is as follows.

1. Bob and Alice register and create accounts on the server.
2. Alice submits a follow request to Bob on a interested tag through the server. For example, Alice asks to follow Bob on the tag #stock.
3. The server forwards the follow request to Bob. In particular, the bob can be offline.
4. After Bob loges in and receives the follow request, he decides whether he accepts the request. If he accepts, he sends an approval message to the server. Then the server stores the follow relationship between Bob and Alice, which likes ¡Bob, Alice, tags¿.
5. According to the follow relationships stored in the server, the server forwards the message to all intended followers who follow Bob on the specific tag (#Stock). If Alice receives the message, she uses the information in the message to watch the live streaming.

2.2   Privacy Goals

According to the user roles of the live streaming cloud platform, we define the privacy goals in the paper as follows.

- **Server Privacy.** The server can only perform blind matching according to the encrypted tags by the follow relationship stored in the server. Plain text of live messages and tags is not available to the server. However, the server can learn whether multiple followers follow the same broadcaster on the same tag, and whether multiple live messages published by a broadcaster contain the same tag.

- **Broadcaster Privacy.** An encrypted live messages published by broadcasters should not be decrypted by unauthorized users. In other word, only followers following the broadcaster on the specific tag can decrypt the message and watch the live streaming. A broadcaster can know who follows him, and how many tags a follower follows. However, he cannot learn which tag the follower is following.

- **Follower Privacy.** A follower can only get the messages which are followed by him on the specific tag. The follower cannot get any information from other broadcasters or other live messages labeled with other tags. In addition, no one except the follower himself can know anything about the followed tags no matter whether a follow request is accepted or not.

3   Our Proposed Privacy-Preserving Algorithm

In the paper, we propose a privacy-preserving algorithm, which bases on elliptic curve key exchange algorithm [4], and Advanced Encryption Standard (AES) algorithm [5]. It protects user privacy in public cloud platforms and public communication channels.

3.1   Overview of the Proposal

There are three phases in this algorithm.

Phase 1: Initialization. Algorithm initialization is divided into system initialization and user initialization. At this phase, broadcasters and followers create their accounts on the server.

Phase 2: Establishing the follow relationship. A follower sends a follow request on a tag to a broadcaster. The broadcaster verifies and approves the request. Key exchange based on elliptic curve is finished in the step.

Phase 3: Publishing and receiving the live message. A broadcaster encrypts a live message by AES and publishes the encrypted live message. The server performs blind matching based on the encrypted tag (without getting the plain text of the tag) and forwards the encrypted live message to the intended followers. The intended followers decrypt the live message.

3.2   Description of the Proposal

Initialization. Algorithm initialization is divided into system initialization and user initialization.

System initialization is performed when the algorithm is deployed. In the progress, the server chooses an elliptic curve as the base of the key exchange algorithm. Generally, an elliptic curve is a curve $E(q) : y^2 = x^3 + ax + b$ over a finite field $GF(q)$, where q is a prime modular and a, b is the coefficients.

Thus, we describe an elliptic curve as a sextuple $T = (q, a, b, G, n, h)$, where G is the base point of $E(q)$, n is the order of G, and $h = \frac{\#E(q)}{n}$. These parameters are published during the system initialization progress. System initialization is performed only once.

While a broadcaster creates his account in the cloud platform, user initialization is performed. During the progress, the broadcaster Bob chooses a 128-bit random number x as his identification code. Only Bob knows it.

Establishing the Follow Relationship. The progress of establishing the follow relationship is shown as Fig. 2, which involves sixe steps. In Fig. 2, Alice indicates a follower and Bob indicates a broadcaster.

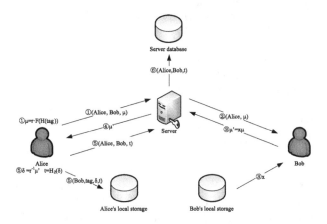

Fig. 2. Establishing the follow relationship

Step 1: Alice sends a request message to the server to follow Bob on an arbitrary tag. In detail, Alice chooses a random integer r, and calculates $\mu = F(H(tag)) \times r$, where $H(*)$ is a hash function and $F(*)$ is the function to encode a big integer as a point of $E(q)$. Finally, Alice sends the message $(Alice, Bob, \mu)$ to the server. In the step, Bob does not need to be online.

Step 2: The server stores message $(Alice, Bob, \mu)$ and forwards it to Bob when Bob is online.

Step 3: Bob verifies Alice's request. If Bob agrees Alice to follow him, he calculates $\mu' = x \times \mu$ and sends the message $(Alice, Bob, \mu')$ to the server.

Step 4: The server stores message $(Alice, Bob, \mu')$ and forwards it to Alice when Alice is online.

Step 5: After receiving the message, Alice calculates $\delta = r^{-1}\mu' \ (mod \ n)$ and $t = H_1(\delta)$, where $H_1(*)$is another hash function different from $H(*)$. Then Alice stores (Bob, tag, δ, t) and sends message $(Alice, Bob, t)$ to the server.

Step 6: The server stores message $(Alice, Bob, t)$ to blind match.

Publishing Live Message. The Algorithm 1 shows the message publishing progress, focusing on the encryption of the message.

Algorithm 1. Message Encryption

Input: $info_p$: plain message
$PLAIN\_TAGS = \{tag_i\}$: tag set
$X = \{x_i\}$:private key set, where x_i corresponds the tag_i
Output: $info_e$: encrypted message
$KEYS = \{encKey_i\}$: encrypted key set where each key
corresponds to a tag
$TAGS = \{t_i\}$:encrypted tag set
1: key $\leftarrow$ 128-bit random number
2: $info_e = AESEnc_{key}(info_p)$
3: for each tag_i in $PLAIN\_TAGS$ do
4:     $\delta_i = x_i F(H(tag_i))$
5:     $t_i = H_1(\delta_i)$
6:     $k_i = H_2(\delta_i)$
7:     $encKey_i = AESEnc_{k_i}(key)$
8:     add $encKey_i$ to $KEYS$
9:     add t_i to $TAGS$
10: end for
11: return($info_e, KEYS, TAGS$)

Step 1: When Bob wants to send a live message $info_p$ labeled with some tags (we use tag_i to represent one of these tags), Bob chooses a random encryption key. Then, the plain message $info_p$ is encrypted using AES as Eq. 1 and the cipher message $info_e$ is gotten.

$$info_e = AESEnc_{key}(info_p) \tag{1}$$

Step 2: Bob calculates the following values.

$$\delta_i = x_i F(H(tag_i))$$
$$t_i = H_1(\delta_i)$$
$$k_i = H_2(\delta_i)$$
$$encKey_i = AESEnc_{k_i}(key)$$

Here, $H_2(*)$ is another hash function different from $H(*)$ and $H_1(*)$ and x_i is a 128-bit random number.

Step 3: Bob sends the message $(info_e, KEYS, TAGS, Bob)$ to the server. The $KEYS$ set and $TAGS$ set are defined as follow.

$KEYS = \{encKey_1, encKey_2, \cdots, encKey_n\}$
$TAGS = \{t_1, t_2, \cdots, t_n\}$

Notice that $encKey_i$ and t_i are one-to-one correspondence.

Step 4: The server stores the message $(info_e, KEYS, TAGS, Bob)$. Later, the server compares it with the records which is stored in the server during establishing follow relationship. The formats of the records like $(Alice, C, t)$. If the record $(Alice, C, t)$ meets the following condition:

$$(C = Bob) \wedge (t \in TAGS)$$

Then the server sends the message $(info_e, encKey, Bob, t)$ to Alice. Here, $encKey$ is the element in $KEYS$ related to t in $TAGS$.

Receiving and Watching Live Streaming. The Algorithm 2 shows the process of message receiving and decryption.

Algorithm 2. Message Decryption

Input: $info_e$: encrypted message
           t: encrypted tag set
           $encKey$: encrypted key on tag t
Output: $info_p$: plain message
1: find δ corresponding to (Bob, t)
2: $k = H_2(\delta)$
3: $key = AESDec_k(encKey)$
4: $info_p = AESDec_{key}(info_e)$
5: return $info_p$

Step 1: After receiving the message $(info_e, encKey, Bob, t)$, Alice finds the value δ related to (Bob, t) in local storage. Then, Alice calculates the AES key as follow:

$$k = H_2(\delta)$$
$$key = AESDec_k(encKey)$$

If an unauthorized user gets the live message, he cannot calculate k and key because he has not the correct δ. Hence, we can ensure any unauthorized user cannot get the message content and watch the live streaming.

Step 2: Alice uses the key to decrypt the message.

$$info_p = AESDec_{key}(info_e)$$

Alice can read the plain live message. Because the live URL and login password are included in the message, Alice can use this information to watch the live streaming.

4   Security Analysis

This section analyzes the security of our algorithm according to the privacy protection goals mentioned above.

4.1   Broadcaster Privacy

The live message and tag published by a broadcaster reveal no information about message content to any party but authorized followers.

For the server, all data stored in it are encrypted. The server cannot obtain these data because the decryption key is not available. Furthermore, the server does not create a spurious user account or collude with other user to obtain data according to the honest-but-curious model.

For unauthorized users, they cannot decrypt the message because they do not know the value δ related to the live message. For example, Alice gets a message that Alice does not follow. Alice cannot decrypt the message because she does not know the value δ related to the message. In addition, Alice tries to calculate x from the broadcaster's other tags to build δ because $\delta = x \times F(H(tag))$. According to the description in Sect. 3.2, δ and $F(H(tag))$ are two points on the elliptic curve. Thus, the mathematic model of this problem is to get value x according to two points $B = x \times A$ on an elliptic curve. It is a representative Elliptic Curve Discrete Logarithm Problem (ECDLP), which is proven to be difficult. Hence, unauthorized users can not obtain the live messages.

4.2   Follower Privacy

The broadcaster, server and any eavesdropper do not learn the content of tags requested by a follower.

Firstly, because all tags are encrypted, the server cannot get the tags information. The broadcaster Bob is curious to get the tag information followed by all followers. However, according to Sect. 3.2, Bob does not get any information about tags from the server when the follow relationship is established. However, he may try to get the tag from μ. We have learnt that $\mu = F(H(tag)) \times r$, and the value r is secret to the server and the broadcaster. In addition, the function $F(*)$ and $H(*)$ are not invertible functions. Hence, Bob cannot get the tag from μ.

Bob may also get Alice's value t by attacking the communication channel. Because $t = H_2(x \times F(H(tag)))$ and x is known by Bob, he seeks to enumerate all t values in a range of tags to get which tag the follower is following. However, Bob still can not get the tag information. Firstly, it is hard to get the value t by attacking method, especially if Bob and attacked user are not in the same network environment. Secondly, different from ABE or some other method, the tags are not limited in a specific range in our algorithm. Hence, it is difficult to enumerate all the tags. As a result, Bob cannot get private information of his followers.

In conclusion, under the semi-trusted model, all the privacy leakage situations under the threaten model does not take place. Hence, the algorithm can protect all users' privacy in live streaming cloud platforms.

5   Related Work

With the rapid development of cloud computing, more Internet applications are deployed on the cloud platform. In this section, we survey some recent researches about privacy protection in untrusted computing environment. The privacy protection in online social networks (OSNs) is a hot research topic. Different from traditional network data, social network data is unstructured, and the graph features are obvious. Therefore, some traditional privacy protection technologies cannot meet the privacy protection requirements of social networks [6,7].

According to the privacy issues faced by the Twitter-like OSNs, Emiliano De Cristofaro et al. proposed a privacy protection framework called Hummingbird. Based on RSA blind signature, Hummingbird matches and transfers encrypted message to prevent privacy leakage caused by insider attack. A method to protect OSNs against neighborhood attacks using k-anonymity model is proposed [8]. The solution does not affect aggregate network queries in the OSN system. According to a decentralized OSN, Cutillo et al. [9] proposed privacy protection solution called SAFEBOOK. The SAFEBOOK provides privacy and trust management, and guarantees end-to-end confidentiality in a decentralized network.

Many studies focus on improving privacy protection on commercial OSNs. The work in [10] proposed an improved privacy protection algorithm on Facebook. The algorithm improves access control model in Facebook, and allows users to have more control over their privacy data. The privacy control policies in many OSNs are too complicated for users to set correctly. The research [11] combined k-nearest neighbor discovery algorithm and decision tree algorithm into privacy policy controlling. The authors in [11] proposed a model called privacy wizard, which lets system automatically set privacy policy according to users' behavior. Semenko et al. [12] propose a distributed privacy preserving platform for ridesharing service.

Nowadays, many social network services are migrating to the smartphone. Some privacy protection methods for traditional OSNs are limited due to the mobile computing performance and power consumption. He et al. [13] proposed an effective privacy-preserving access control method with secure proxy decryption. In the method, the cloud platform transforms a CP-ABE cipher text into an El-Gamal-style cipher text, which is easier and lower-cost for mobile devices to decrypt. For some applications integrated into the sensor-cloud, several security schemes are proposed [14–16], which are mainly to ensure the credibility of data.

The application scene of live streaming platform is similar to OSN. Hence, the research results of privacy protection in social networks have very important reference value for our research. However, due to the differences between the live streaming cloud platform and social networks, these research results can not be directly applied to live streaming platforms.

Acknowledgments. This work was supported by the National Natural Science Foundation of China [grant numbers No. 61972352 and No. 61572435], the Natural Science Foundation of Zhejiang Province [grant number No. LZ16F020001 and No. LY17F020032].

References

1. Jones, H., Soltren, J.: Facebook: Threats to privacy. In: Ethics and the law on the electronic frontier course (2005)
2. Fischetti, M.: Data theft: hackers attack. Sci. Am. **305**(100), (2011)
3. Kincaid, J.: This is the second time a google engineer has been fired for accessing user data. http://techcrunch.com/2010/09/14/google-engineer-fired-security/. Technical report (2010)
4. Miller, V.S.: Use of elliptic curves in cryptography. In: Williams, H.C. (ed.) CRYPTO 1985. LNCS, vol. 218, pp. 417–426. Springer, Heidelberg (1986). https://doi.org/10.1007/3-540-39799-X_31
5. D.R.L. BROWN. Sec 2: Recommended elliptic curve domain parameters. Standards for Efficient Cryptography (SEC) (2010)
6. Wu, Y.K., Huang, H.Y., Wu, Q., et al.: A risk defense method based on microscopic state prediction with partial information observations in social networks. J. Parallel Distrib. Comput. **2019**(131), 189–199 (2019)
7. Schillinger, F., Schindelhauer, C.: End-to-end encryption schemes for online social networks. In: 12th International Conference on Security, Privacy and Anonymity in Computation, Communication and Storage, pp. 133–146, Atlanta, GA, USA, July 14–17 2019 (2019)
8. Zhou, B., Pei, J.: Preserving privacy in social networks against neighborhood attacks. In: IEEE 24th International Conference on Data Engineering, 2008. ICDE 2008, pp. 506–515. IEEE, Cancun, Mexico, 7–12 April 2008
9. Cutillo, L.A., Molva, R., Strufe, T.: Safebook: feasibility of transitive cooperation for privacy on a decentralized social network. In: 10th IEEE International Symposium on a World of Wireless, Mobile and Multimedia Networks-WoWMoM 2009, pp. 1–6, Kos, Greece, 15–19 June 2009 (2009)
10. Pang, J., Zhang, Y.: A new access control scheme for facebook-style social networks. Comput. Secur. **2015**(54), 44–59 (2015)
11. Fang, L., LeFevre, K.: Privacy wizards for social networking sites. In: Proceedings of the 19th international conference on World wide web. ACM, pp. 351–360, Raleigh North Carolina, USA, 6–10 April (2010)
12. Semenko, Y., Saucez, D.: Distributed privacy preserving platform for ridesharing services. In: 12th International Conference on Security, Privacy and Anonymity in Computation, Communication and Storage, pp. 1–14, Atlanta, GA, USA, 14–17 July 2019 (2019)
13. He, Z., Cai, Z., Han, Q., Tong, W., Sun, L., Li, Y.: An energy efficient privacy-preserving content sharing scheme in mobile social networks. Pers. Ubiquit. Comput. **20**(5), 833–846 (2016). https://doi.org/10.1007/s00779-016-0952-6
14. Wang, T., Luo, H., Jia, W.J., Liu, A.F., Xie, M.D.: Mtes: An intelligent trust evaluation scheme in sensor-cloud-enabled industrial internet of things. IEEE Trans. Industr. Inf. **16**(3), 2054–2062 (2019)
15. Wang, T., Ke, H.X., Wang, K., et al.: Big data cleaning based on mobile edge computing in industrial sensor-cloud. IEEE Trans. Industr. Inf. **16**(2), 1321–1329 (2020)
16. Tang, J.W., Liu, A.F., Wang, T.: An aggregate signature based trust routing for data gathering in sensor networks. Secur. Commun. Networks **2018**(5), 1–30 (2018)

Multi-echelon Vehicle Routing Problem in Sensor-Cloud Architecture with Mobile Sinks

Liang Song[1], Haibin Chen[2,3], Hejiao Huang[2,3(✉)], and Hongwei Du[2,3]

[1] School of Informatics, Xiamen University, Xiamen 361005, China
[2] School of Computer Science and Technology,
Harbin Institute of Technology (Shenzhen), Shenzhen 518055, China
huanghejiao@hit.edu.cn
[3] Shenzhen Key Laboratory of Internet Information Collaboration,
Shenzhen 518055, China

Abstract. The sensor-cloud architecture rises the opportunity to overcome intrinsic shortages of wireless sensors, such as computing capacity, storage space and communication range. However, before realizing these complementary effects of cloud computing, there is a challenge of how to plan efficient routes for mobile sinks to gather distributedly sensed data to centralized computing resources on cloud, especially where practical environment limits the travelling range of mobile sinks. This paper models the route planning problem into multi-echelon vehicle routing problem, and formulates it into integer linear programming. To solve this problem, a GPU-based parallel algorithm is proposed. The experimental results verify the accuracy and efficiency of the algorithm.

Keywords: Multi-echelon vehicle routing problem · Parallel algorithm · GPU · Sensor-cloud architecture · Mobile sinks

1 Introduction

The sensor-cloud architecture has arised as a cutting edge direction by integration of the research in wireless sensor networks [1] (WSNs) and cloud computing [2]. The data processing in cloud provides a centralized manner to overcome the intrinsic shortages of sensors [3,4], such as computing capacity, storage space, communication range, etc. However, before the cloud system distinguishes itself, how to gather data from sensors to cloud is not a trivial problem [5,6], which is even worse when the sensing destinations are hard for mobile sinks [7,8] to reach. Glancing at the practical environment in Fig. 1 where the sensor-cloud architecture is deployed, we can unfold the following constraints in data gathering. First of all, the closer to sensing destinations, the worse of travelling conditions. Therefore, the travelling routes of mobile sinks and sensors have to be organized into multi-echelons, so that cumbersome but the most powerful sinks can travel within the 1st-echelon area that around mountain foot, while the relatively small

© Springer Nature Switzerland AG 2021
G. Wang et al. (Eds.): SpaCCS 2020, LNCS 12383, pp. 233–244, 2021.
https://doi.org/10.1007/978-3-030-68884-4_20

sinks travel within the 2nd-echelon area which has higher altitude, thicker forest and more meandered roads, and so on so forth untill the flexible sensors finally reach the sensing destinations around mountain top. Therefore, the distributedly sensed data are gathered from mobile sensors echelon by echelon backwards to the cloud system. In addition, the number of sensing destinations covered by the route of any sensor is limited and depends on its storage space, and the total route length of mobile sinks and sensors needs to be minimized, so that the energy consumption by the WSN is minimum. In a word, our objective is to plan the multi-echelon routes for data gathering by heterogeneous sinks and sensors, which have the shortest total length.

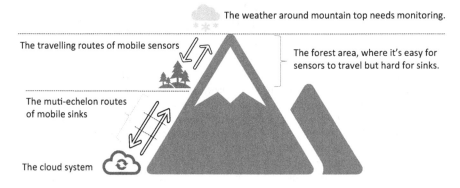

Fig. 1. Practical environment where sensor-cloud architecture is deployed

We model the above problem into the multi-chelon vehicle routing problem, which is variant of the classical vehicle routing problem (VRP) [9] in combinatorial mathematics. In multi-echelon VRP, customers demands are delivered from 1st-echelon depots to 2nd-echelon depots by large vehicle, then from 2nd-echelon depots to 3rd-echelon depots by relatively small vehicle, and so on so forth, finally to customers. Its objective is to find a set of routes for all the vehicles, which successfully deliver all the demands and have the minimum total length in the meanwhile. Given an arbitrary instance of the route planning problem for mobile sinks and sensors, it can be mapped into multi-echelon VRP as follows.

a) The cloud system is corresponding to the 1st-echelon depot.
b) Each data gathering location between mobile sinks (or sensors) is corresponding to some i-th-echelon depot.
c) Each sensing destination is corresponding to a customer.
d) Each mobile sink (or sensor) is corresponding to some i-th-echelon vehicle.
e) Different storage spaces of mobile sinks (or sensors) are corresponding to the maximum loads of different vehicles.

Thus, the mobile sinks play a role of fog layer [10–12] in the sensor-cloud architecture. An illustration of three-echelon VRP is shown in Fig. 2. The rectangles, diamonds, triangles and circles represent the (1st-echelon) depots, 2nd-echelon depots (called entrepots), 3rd-echelon depots (called satellites) and customers, respectively. The thick, thin and dashed lines represent the 1st, 2nd and final-echelon routes, respectively, which together form a feasible solution for gathering data from sensors to the cloud system.

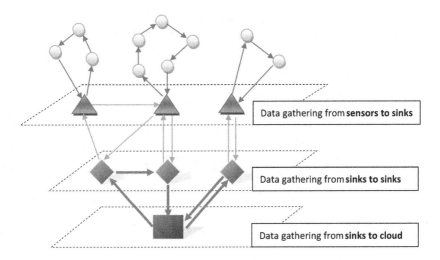

Fig. 2. The dynamic process of three-echelon VRP

Because VRP and its generalized problems are all NP-hard [13], multi-echelon VRP is also NP-hard. To our best knowledge, there was no algorithm with approximation ratio [14] for solving multi-echelon VRP, and most previous works focused on solving two-echelon VRP by the algorithms based on mathematical programming [15–18]. However, in the aspect of parallelization, heuristic algorithms have innate fitness to run on mutli-core platforms, such as GPUs [19,20] which are common computing resources in the cloud system.

In this paper, we firstly propose the integer linear programming formulation of multi-echelon VRP for data gathering from mobile sensors to sinks and then cloud. Secondly, we design a GPU-based parallel algorithm to solve this problem. Thirdly, the correctness of our algorithm is verified by experimental results on small scale instances, and its efficiency is demonstrated by experimental results on large scale instances. Finally, the paper is concluded with summarized future work on further exploiting GPU for parallelization.

2 Problem Formulation

The multi-echelon VRP is modeled as follows. The map is a graph $G(N, E)$. The vertex set $N = N_1 \cup N_2 \cup \cdots \cup N_m \cup N_C$, in which N_i denotes the set of

i-th-echelon depots, N_C denotes the customer set, and each customer $c \in N_C$ has a demand q. The edge set $E = E_{12} \cup E_{23} \cup \cdots \cup E_{m-1,m} \cup E_{m,C}$, in which $E_{i,i+1}$ consists of all the edges connecting i-th-echelon depots and $(i + 1)$-th-echelon depots, and each edge has a *Length*. A route consisting of the edges in $E_{i,i+1}$ is called i-th-echelon route, and the vehicle traveling on this route is called i-th-echelon vehicle, which has the load capacity Q_i. The number of available vehicles at each depot d is denoted as m_d. Then, the integer linear programming formulation of m-echelon VRP is given as below.

$$z(F) = \min \sum_{i \in [1,m]} \sum_{d \in N_i} \sum_{l \in \mathcal{R}_d} x_{dl} \cdot Length_{dl}$$

s.t.

$$\sum_{d \in N_m} \sum_{l \in \mathcal{R}_{dc}} x_{dl} = 1, \quad c \in N_C \tag{1}$$

$$\sum_{l \in \mathcal{R}_d} x_{dl} \leq m_d, \quad i \in [1,m], d \in N_i \tag{2}$$

$$W_{dl} \leq x_{dl} \cdot Q_m, \quad d \in N_m, l \in \mathcal{R}_d \tag{3}$$

$$\sum_{d' \in N_{m-1}} \sum_{l \in \mathcal{R}_{d'd}} q_{d'ld} = \sum_{l \in \mathcal{R}_d} x_{dl} \cdot W_{dl}, \quad d \in N_m \tag{4}$$

$$\sum_{d' \in R_l} q_{dld'} \leq x_{dl} \cdot Q_i, \quad i \in [1, m-1], d \in N_i, l \in \mathcal{R}_d \tag{5}$$

$$\sum_{d' \in N_{i-1}} \sum_{l \in \mathcal{R}_{d'd}} q_{d'ld} = \sum_{l \in \mathcal{R}_d} \sum_{d'' \in R_l} q_{dld''}, \quad i \in [2, m-1], d \in N_i \tag{6}$$

$$x_{dl} \in \{0,1\}, \quad i \in [1,m], d \in N_i, l \in \mathcal{R}_d \tag{7}$$

$$q_{dld'} \in \mathbb{Z}^+, \quad i \in [1, m-1], d \in N_i, l \in \mathcal{R}_d \tag{8}$$

The objective function is to minimize the sum of route lengths within all the echelons. Constraint (1) ensures each customer is visited exactly once, in which $\mathcal{R}_{dc}$ denotes the set of routes starting from $d \in N_m$ and passing through customer $c \in N_C$. Constraint (2) limits the number of vehicles used by depot $d \in N_i$ within m_d, in which $\mathcal{R}_d$ denotes the set of routes starting from d. Constraint (3) and (5) limit the total demands carried by each i-th-echelon vehicle within Q_i, in which W_{dl} denotes the total demands on route l starting from final-echelon depot $d \in N_m$, $q_{dld'}$ denotes the total demands delivered from depot d to d' by route l, and R_l denotes the depots serviced by route l. Constraints (4) and (6) connect each pairs of former and latter echelons, that is to say, the total demands received by a i-th-echelon depot must equal to the total demands it delivers out, in which $\mathcal{R}_{d',d}$ denotes the set of routes starting from the former-echelon depot d' and servicing the latter-echelon depot d. Constraints (7) and (8) indicate the domains of decision variables, in which $x_{dl} = 1$ indicates that route dl is included in the solution, and $x_{dl} = 0$ otherwise.

3   GPU-Based Parallel Algorithm

3.1   Algorithm Framework

Algorithm 1 gives the framework of GPU-Based Parallel Algorithm for multi-echelon VRP. Firstly, each customer is allocated to a final-echelon depot, then each final-echelon depot together with its customers forms a VRP instance. Secondly, each VRP instance is solved by Hybrid SA Algorithm, which runs concurrently on GPU. Thirdly, the routes from depots to depots are computed by solving the integer linear programming $z(F)$. Fourthly, construct a solution S by connecting the routes generated by the second and third steps. Next, repeat updating S for a large number of iterations. The number of depots is limited and hence can be viewed as constant, while the number of customers is large and determines the problem scale of multi-echelon VRP. This is the reason why we only need to parallelize the final-echelon on GPU.

Algorithm 1. GPU-Based Parallel Algorithm

Input: Integer linear programming formulation of multi-echelon VRP
Output: Solution S
1: (CPU) Allocate each customer to a final-echelon depot;
2: (GPU) Run hybrid SA algorithm for each VRP instance concurrently;
3: (CPU) Solve $z(F)$ and compute the routes from depots to depots;
4: (CPU) Connect the routes in all echelons and construct S;
5: Repeat steps 1 to 4 for a large number of iterations;

To allocate each customer to a final-echelon VRP instance $V_d, d \in N_m$, initially, we use the nearest neighbor strategy. Then, two efficiency factors $F_d = W_d/Length_d$ and $F_{c,d} = Length_{c,d}/q_c$ are introduced. In V_d, W_d is the total demands on depot d, and $Length_d$ is the total length of routes starting from d in the current solution S. Therefore, the bigger W_d and smaller $Length_d$, the more efficient of depot d. In $F_{c,d}$, $Length_{c,d}$ is the distance between customer c and depot d, and q_c is customer c's demand. For depot d, the bigger $Length_{c,d}$ and smaller q_c, the more efficient of customer c. In the following interations of Algorithm 1, we select the depot d with the minimum efficiency F_d, remove the customer c with the minimum efficiency $F_{c,d}$ from V_d, and allocate c into another final-echelon VRP instance randomly.

3.2   Hybrid SA Algorithm

We design a hybrid simulated annealing (SA) algorithm (see Algo. 2) to solve each final-echelon VRP instance, which combines Random Swapping Strategy and Load Balance Strategy. Here, array elements $imrd[0]$ and $imrd[1]$ record the numbers of solutions improved by load balancing strategy and random swapping strategy, respectively. The expression $dice < imrd[0]/\sum imrd$ determines which strategy will be used in the next iteration. If this expression holds, it will be load balancing strategy because it is improving solutions better now, otherwise, it will be random swapping strategy. Further, if the generated solution in the next iteration indeed improves current solution, then update array $imrd$. Besides, to enlarge the searching scope, we still replace the current solution with the generated solution on condition that $dice' < \exp(\nabla H/temp)$, where ∇H is the length of current solution minus that of the generated solution.

Algorithm 2. Hybrid SA Algorithm

Input: Final-echelon VRP instance
Output: Solution S'
1: Initialize S', S_{cur}, $temp$, $temp\_0$, $rate$, $imrd$;
2: **if** Random value $dice < imrd[0]/\sum imrd$ **then**
3:　　Use load balancing strategy;
4: **else**
5:　　Use random swapping strategy;
6: **end if**
7: Generate a new solution S_{new} by SA algorithm;
8: **if** $Length(S_{new}) < Length(S_{cur})$ **then**
9:　　Set $S_{cur} = S_{new}$, and update $imrd$;
10:　　 **if** $Length(S_{cur}) < Length(S')$ **then**
11:　　　　Set $S' = S_{cur}$;
12:　　 **end if**
13: **else**
14:　　Compute $\nabla H = Length(S_{cur}) - Length(S_{new})$;
　　　　Set $S_{cur} = S_{new}$ when random value $dice' < \exp(\nabla H/temp)$;
15: **end if**
16: $temp = (1 - rate) * temp$;
17: **if** $temp > temp\_0$ **then**
18:　　go to step 2;
19: **end if**
20: **return** S';

3.3 Load Balancing Strategy

This section describes load balancing strategy (see Algorithm 3) in details. The necessity of balancing loads among routes comes from random swapping strategy in hybrid SA algorithm. Random swapping strategy frequently moves customers among the routes in the current solution, which results in that some routes are overloaded and even violate the vehicle capacity constraint, while some routes carry few and even empty demands. Therefore, we need load balancing strategy to make the load on each route close to the average load.

The idea of load balancing strategy is to remove a customer from a heavily loaded route and insert it into a lightly loaded route. In Algorithm 3, $load(r)$ denotes the total demands in route r, and $load_{max}$ denotes the maximum load

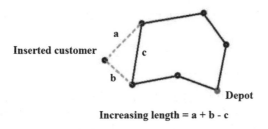

Increasing length = a + b - c

Fig. 3. The insertion of a selected customer

among the routes $r \in S_1$, in which S_1 is the input solution with $vNum$ routes. Then, steps 1–4 of make it more likely to select a route r with a larger load, while steps 5–7 make it more likely to select a route r' with a smaller load. Finally, step 8 remove a random customer c from route r and place it on a position of

---

Algorithm 3. Load Balancing Strategy

Input: Current solution S_1
Output: Balanced solution S_2
1: Compute $load(r)$ and $load_{max}$;
2: Obtain load accumulation array:

$$acc1(r) = \frac{\sum\limits_{k=1}^{r} load(k)}{\sum\limits_{k=1}^{vNum} load(k)}, \ r \in [i, vNum];$$

3: Generate a random value $wheel_1 \in (0, 1)$;
4: Randomly select a customer c from route r_1 s.t.

$$acc1(r_1 - 1) < wheel_1 \leq acc1(r_1)$$

5: Obtain difference accumulation array:

$$acc2(r) = \frac{\sum\limits_{k=1}^{r} (load_{max} - load(k))}{\sum\limits_{k=1}^{vNum} (load_{max} - load(k))}, \ r \in [i, vNum];$$

6: Generate a random value $wheel_2 \in (0, 1)$;
7: Select route r' s.t.

$$acc2(r_2 - 1) < wheel_2 \leq acc2(r_2)$$

8: Place c on the position of r_2 with minimum increasing length;

---

route r', which has the minimum increasing length after c is placed there (as an example shown in Fig. 3).

3.4 Parallelization on GPU

To efficiently parallelize hybrid SA algorithm for solving each final-echelon VRP instance on GPU, the GPU memory hierarchy should be exploited carefully and appropriately for the following reasons. Firstly, register memory whose number is quite limited, has the fastest access velocity. However, the request for unavailable register memory will result in the allocation of local memory instead, which has the lower access velocity. Secondly, shared memory is visible to all the threads in the same block. Therefore, the key to allocate shared memory properly is to make sure that each unit of memory can be accessed by only one thread, otherwise, memory conflict will happen and stop the algorithm. Finally, the global parameters of algorithm should be stored in global memory, which has the lowest access velocity but can be accessed by all the threads.

Our parallelization involves the registers, local memory, global memory and shared memory, and runs multiple kernel function threads in one Block on GPU to solve the final-echelon VRP instances concurrently. The kernel function is the programming model defined in CUDA, by which we implements hybrid SA algorithm with random swapping strategy and load balancing strategy. The thread numbers are correspondingly set to the numbers of final-echelon depots, so that each thread could access its local parameters by using thread number as index. Besides, because kernel function does not provide return values, we use the pointer variables to retrieve the computational results.

4 Experimental Results

The experimental platform consists of Inter Xeon CPU (E5-2603 V2, 1.80 GHz), 64GB RAM Memory, Nvidia GPU (Quadro K2000) and Window 7 OS (x64). The algorithm invokes CPLEX to compute the routes from depots to depots on CPU, and Visual C++ with CUDA to compute the final-echelon routes on GPU.

For the experimental datasets, two-echelon VRP instances are selected from Set 1, Set 2 and Set 3 provided in [17]. Three-echelon VRP instances are obtained by modifying the above instances from two-echelon into three-echelon. In the algorithm parameter setting, temperature is set to $temp = 10000$, and cooling rate is set to $rate = 0.01$. The computational results are given in Tables 1,2 and 3, in which we name the 1st, 2nd and 3rd-echelon depots as depot, entrepot and satellite, respectively.

Table 1 describes the results on instances of Set 1, each of which has a node set consisting of 1 depot, 2 satellites and 13 customers. The *instance* column lists instance numbers and names. The *Satellites* column lists the indices of 2nd-echelon depots in the node set. The *1st-Length*, *2nd-Length* and *Total*

Length columns list the route lengths of 1st-echelon, 2nd-echelon and all echelons, respectively. For comparison, the *OPT* column lists the optimum route length of each instance. The *running time* column lists the time consumed for solving each instance in the second unit. We can see that the route lengths generated by our algorithm are equal to the optimum values.

Table 1. Computational results on set 1

Instance	Satellites	1st-length	2nd-length	Total length	OPT	Running time (s)
1. E-n13-k4-11	1,12	122	154	276	276	40.076
2. E-n13-k4-12	2,3	70	220	290	290	40.294
3. E-n13-k4-23	3,5	86	156	242	242	41.184
4. E-n13-k4-24	3,6	92	150	242	242	41.434
5. E-n13-k4-35	4,9	122	142	264	264	41.028
6. E-n13-k4-36	4,10	130	142	272	272	40.443
7. E-n13-k4-37	4,11	146	150	296	296	41.106
8. E-n13-k4-38	4,12	150	154	304	304	41.121
9.E-n13-k4-39	5,6	94	154	248	248	41.715
10. E-n13-k4-40	5,7	108	146	254	254	41.029

Table 2 describes the results on instances in Set 2 and 3, each of which has 1 depot, 2 satellites and 20 or 30 customers. The *instance* column lists instance numbers and names. The *1st-Length*, *2nd-Length* and *Total Length* columns list the lengths of our generated routes of 1st-echelon, 2nd-echelon and all echelons,

Table 2. Computational results on set 2

Instance	1st-length	2nd-length	Total length	$z1(F)$	Running time (s)
11. E-n22-k4-s10-14	48.7	327.3	376	371.5	58.046
12. E-n22-k4-s6-17	106.2	318.7	424.9	417.07	57.572
13. E-n22-k4-s8-14	62.5	323.8	386.3	384.96	57.89
14. E-n22-k4-s14-18	135.3	363.6	498.9	496.38	57.181
15. E-n22-k4-s15-20	107.4	391.4	498.8	498.8	58.443
16. E-n33-k4-s2-13	360	489	749	742.64	74.094
17. E-n33-k4-s3-17	279	467.4	746.4	744.21	72.611
18. E-n33-k4-s4-5	239.2	611.6	860.8	860.47	73.186
19. E-n33-k4-s7-25	275	491.11	766.11	766.11	76.013
20. E-n33-k4-s14-22	316.7	466	782.7	780.17	71.986

respectively. For comparison, the $z1(F)$ column lists the route lengths generated in [17], which proposed the best algorithm for solving two-echelon VRP till now. The *running time* column lists the time consumed for solving each instance by our algorithm in the second unit. We can see that the route lengths in *Total Length* column are very close to those in $z1(F)$ column. However, the algorithm in [17] can only solve two-echelon VRP, while our algorithm can solve multi-echelon VRP with more than two echelons.

Table 3 describes the results on three-echelon VRP instances, each of which has 1 depot, various numbers of entrepots and satellites, and 100 customers. The *instance* column lists instance numbers and names. The ET, ST column lists the numbers of satellites and entrepots within each instance. The *1st-Length*, *2nd-Length*, *3rd-Length* and *Total Length* columns list the route lengths of 1st-echelon, 2nd-echelon, 3rd-echelon and all the echelons, respectively. The *running time* column lists the time consumed for solving each instance in the second unit.

Table 3. Computational results on set 3

Instance	ET, ST	1st-length	2nd-length	3rd-length	Total length	Running time (s)
21. Z-n101-s93-1	3,9	97.4	184.7	644.7	926.8	107.7
22. Z-n101-s93-2	3,9	83.3	285.5	749.7	1118.5	116.2
23. Z-n135-s93-1	3,9	165	546	1140.1	1851.1	125.5
24. Z-n135-s93-2	3,9	362.5	805	1773.5	2941	160.3
25. Z-n101-s104-1	4,10	200	283.2	451.8	935	104.3
26. Z-n101-s104-2	4,10	131.5	303.9	510.9	946.3	110.3
27. Z-n151-s124-1	4,12	123	347.1	980.7	1450.8	142.8
28. Z-n151-s124-2	4,12	131	378.6	1002.2	1511.8	165.4
29. Z-n121-s125-1	5,12	337	227	649.6	1213.6	119.7
30. Z-n121-s125-2	5,12	415.7	307.5	553.4	1276.6	124.2

Figure 4 the depicts the increasing trends of the total length and running time in above three tables. The X-axis indicates the instance number, while the left and right Y-axes indicate the total length and running time, respectively. The blue line means the growing total length is reasonable because of the increasing number of customers. The green line means the running time of our algorithm is still tolerable when the number of customers in three-echelon instance increases to 100.

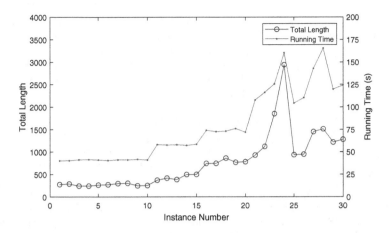

Fig. 4. Comparison of the route lengths $z(F)$ and $z1(F)$

5   Conclusion and Future Work

Facing the challenge of route planning problem for the data gathering by mobile sinks and sensors in the sensor-cloud architecture, the paper modeled it into multi-echelon VRP, and formulated it into integer linear programming. To solve this problem, a GPU-based parallel algorithm was designed, whose accuracy and efficiency can be verified by the experimental results.

The GPU-based parallel algorithm can solve large scale and multi-echelon VRP. However, the GPU potential is still not fully exploited for parallelization. In the aspect of theory, how to switch the feasible routes within GPU memory hierarchy involves the paging problem, whose properties are helpful to enhance the performance of our algorithm. In the aspect of implementation, we only use one block for parallelization. Therefore, in the future work, the algorithm will be developed by considering the above two aspects.

Acknowledgments. This work was supported in part by China Scholarship Council, the Fundamental Research Funds for the Central Universities of China under Grant No. 20720190028, National Key R&D Program of China under Grant No. 2017YFB0803002, National Natural Science Foundation of China under Grants No. 61672195, No. 61732022, No.61772154, and the Shenzhen Basic Research Program (Project No. JCYJ20190806143011274).

References

1. Liu, X., Obaidat, M.S., Lin, C., Wang, T., Liu, A.: Movement-based solutions to energy limitation in wireless sensor networks: State of the art and future trends. IEEE Network (2020). https://doi.org/10.1109/MNET.011.2000445
2. Li, M., Jiang, Y., Sun, Y., Tian, Z.: Answering the min-cost quality-aware query on multi-sources in sensor-cloud systems. In: Wang, G., Chen, J., Yang, L. (eds.) SpaCCS 2018. LNCS, vol. 11342, pp. 156–165. Springer, Cham (2018)

3. Liu, X., Lin, P., Liu, T., Wang, T., Liu, A., XU, W.: Objective-variable tour planning for mobile data collection in partitioned sensor networks. IEEE Trans. Mob. Comput. (2020). https://doi.org/10.1109/TMC.2020.3003004

4. Wang, T., Peng, Z., Liang, J., Wen, S., Bhuiyan, M.Z.A., Cai, Y., Cao, J.: Following targets for mobile tracking in wireless sensor networks. ACM Trans. Sensor Networks 12(4), Article 31 (2016)

5. Fei, C., Zhao, B., Yu, W., Wu, C.: An approximate data collection algorithm in space-based internet of things. In: Wang, G., Feng, J., Bhuiyan, M., Lu, R. (eds.) SpaCCS 2019. LNCS, vol. 11637, pp. 170–184. Springer, Cham (2019)

6. Wang, T., Ke, H., Wang, K., Sangaiah, A.K., Liu, A.: Big data cleaning based on mobile edge computing in industrial sensor-cloud. IEEE Trans. Industr. Inf. 16(2), 1321–1329 (2020)

7. Li, Y., Wang, T., Wang, G., Liang, J., Chen, H.: Efficient data collection in sensor-cloud system with multiple mobile sinks. In: Wang, G., Han, Y., Martínez Pérez, G. (eds.) APSCC 2016. LNCS, vol. 10065, pp. 130–143. Springer, Cham (2016). https://doi.org/10.1007/978-3-319-49178-3_10

8. Huang, M., Liu, A., Wang, T., Huang, C.: Green data gathering under delay differentiated services constraint for internet of things. Wireless Communications and Mobile Computing 2018, Article ID 9715428 (2018)

9. Dantzig, G.B., Ramser, J.H.: The truck dispatching problem. Manage. Sci. 6(1), 80–91 (1959)

10. Zeng, J., Wang, T., Lai, Y.: Data delivery from wsns to cloud based on a fog structure. In: Proceedings of 2016 International Conference on Advanced Cloud and Big Data (CBD), pp. 104–109. IEEE (2016)

11. Deng, X., Li, J., Liu, E., Zhang, H.: Task allocation algorithm and optimization model on edge collaboration. J. Syst. Archit. 110, Article 101778 (2020). https://doi.org/10.1016/j.sysarc.2020.101778

12. Huang, R., Sun, Y., Huang, C., Zhao, G., Ma, Y.: A survey on fog computing. In: Wang, G., Feng, J., Bhuiyan, M., Lu, R. (eds.) SpaCCS 2019. LNCS, vol. 11637, pp. 160–169. Springer, Cham (2019)

13. Toth, P., Vigo, D. (eds.): The vehicle routing problem, chap. 1. An overview of vehicle routing problmes. SIAM, Philadelpia (2000)

14. Du, D.Z., Ko, K.I., Hu, X.: Design and Analysis of Approximation Algorithms, chap. 1. Introduction. Springer, New York (2011)

15. Contardo, C., Hemmelmayr, V., Crainic, T.: Lower and upper bounds for the two-echelon capacitated location-routing problem. Comput. Oper. Res. 39, 3185–3199 (2012)

16. Jepson, M., Spoorendonk, S., Ropke, S.: A branch-and-cut algorithm for the symmetric two-echelon capacitated vehicle routing problem. Transp. Sci. 47, 23–37 (2013)

17. Baldacci, R., Mingozzi, A., Roberti, R., Calvo, R.: An exact algorithm for the two-echelon capacitated vehicle routing problem. Oper. Res. 61, 298–314 (2013)

18. Song, L., Gu, H., Huang, H.: A lower bound for the adaptive two-echelon capacitated vehicle routing problem. J. Comb. Optim. 33(4), 1145–1167 (2016). https://doi.org/10.1007/s10878-016-0028-6

19. Bao, C., Zhang, S.: Algorithm-based fault tolerance for discrete wavelet transform implemented on gpus. J. Syst. Architect. 108, Article 101823 (2020). https://doi.org/10.1016/j.sysarc.2020.101823

20. Chang, Y.M., Liao, W.C., Wang, S.C., Yang, C.C., Hwang, Y.S.: A framework for scheduling dependent programs on GPU architectures. J. Syst. Architect. 106, Article 101712 (2020). https://doi.org/10.1016/j.sysarc.2020.101712

Joint Optimization of Transmission Source Selection and RSU Cache for Vehicular Video Streaming

Jingyao Liu, Guangsheng Feng$^{(\boxtimes)}$, Liying Zheng, and Zihan Gao

College of Computer Science and Technology, Harbin Engineering University, Harbin 150001, China
fengguangsheng@hrbeu.edu.cn

Abstract. Since video data occupies the most majority of total network data, how to solve explosive growth of video data demand has become the main challenge of current network research. In this paper, we propose a transmission architecture that combines roadside base stations and adjacent vehicles as the transmission source to alleviate the transmission pressure of BS and meet the low delay demand for real-time video transmission. In order to satisfy different requirements for video clarity, we apply scalable video coding (SVC) to encode the video. We propose to optimize RSU cache and transmission source selection based on the user's request. To solve the problem, we present a heuristic algorithm which achieves an approximation ratio of $1 - 1/e$. Experimental results show that our scheme is effective in improving quality of experience (QOE) and overall resource utilization.

Keywords: Scalable video coding · Vehicular network · Cooperative transmission · Transmission schedule · RSU cache

1 Introduction

In recent years, development of 5G technology has promoted intelligent transmission systems (ITS) to make people's lives more convenient [1,2], moreover Internet of Vehicles plays an important role in ITS. Internet of Vehicles was originally proposed to enhance road safety, allowing drivers to know road conditions in time, whether there are traffic accidents or congestion [3–5]. However, with user demands increasing, entertainment videos, advertisements, and video conferencing are all needed to enhance driving experience. Therefore, how to improve the quality of vehicular video streaming has become a hot issue for both industry and academic.

At present, two transmission methods, V2I and V2V, are proposed to alleviate pressure of cellular transmission to improve QOE and quality of service (QOS) [6,7]. In order to reduce transmission delay, existing works have selected suitable vehicles as relay points which establish transmission relationship with

© Springer Nature Switzerland AG 2021
G. Wang et al. (Eds.): SpaCCS 2020, LNCS 12383, pp. 245–256, 2021.
https://doi.org/10.1007/978-3-030-68884-4_21

RSU or BS to temporarily cache video data required by target vehicles and then transmit data to target vehicles [8–10]. The disadvantage of this method is that data cached in relay vehicles is worthless to themself, which will cause bandwidth competition and waste of storage resources. Other works attempt to form vehicle clusters by selecting a vehicle as cluster head which is regarded as transmission source to provide service for all vehicles in the cluster [11,12]. However, transmission source in this way is single and transmission pressure is large, which cause transmission congestion and increase transmission delay. Therefore, in this paper we propose RSUs and surrounding vehicles with transmission capabilities cooperate as transmission source to jointly transmit to improve QOE. Our scheme can make full use of resource utilization of entire system and greatly reduce transmission delay to improve driving experience.

Considering the unique challenges caused by the vehicular dynamic characteristics, constantly changing channel quality, time-varying fading, and switching interfaces frequently, SVC technology is proposed to mitigate these negative effects [8,13,14]. Compared with traditional encoding method, SVC is more convenient which can encode all video layers at one time, without special consideration for each layer separately. SVC technology has proved to be relatively less sensitive to packet loss, and is more suitable for circumstance of Internet of Vehicles.

To the best of our knowledge, this is the first study on jointly optimizing RSU cache and selection of transmission source for vehicular SVC video streaming. In this paper, we investigate the joint optimization problem under certain transmission delay conditions. The contribution of our works can be summarized in the following:

– Considering the scenario combined V2I and V2V, we propose a scheme to optimize transmission source selection which cooperate to provide transmission service for target vehicle to satisfy real-time requirement.
– Considering the limited cache capacity of RSUs, we propose to optimize RSU cache, meanwhile RSU caching content changes with user request changing in each slot.
– We present a heuristic algorithm whose time complexity is $O(nlogn)$ to solve the NP-hard optimization problem and it achieves $1 - 1/e$ approximation ratio with the optimal results.
– Simulation results show that the proposed scheme jointly optimizing RSU cache and transmission source selection can improve QOE of vehicular video streaming.

The rest of the paper is organized as follows. In Sect. 2, we introduce the system model and formulate the problem.In Sect. 3, we propose a greedy algorithm to solve integer linear problems. In Sect. 4, simulations are carried out in Section. Sect. 5 concludes this paper.

2   System Model and Problem Formulation

2.1   System Architecture

Considering a collaborative vehicular network scenario, as shown in Fig. 1. Vehicles travel on a straight road where BSs and roadside base stations (RSUs) are on both sides of the road. Vehicle users can request video information (such as real-time broadcast live or movie video) from the BS and RSU. Considering the large number of clients that the BS needs to service, it will seriously affect the data transmission rate. Therefore it is easy to cause broadcast delay and affect the user experience. So RSUs can communicate with the BS to transmit video data, and the BS transmits the corresponding data information to the RSU immediately after receiving the request signal from the vehicle user (the time is negligible and does not affect the transmission to the vehicle user). The amount of video buffered in the RSU is determined in each slot and the coverage is certain. If the video requested by the vehicle is not buffered in advance or the location of the vehicle exceeds the coverage of the RSU, the RSU cannot provide communication to the vehicle. Considering the limitation of relying on RSU transmission uniquely, in order to provide users with a more comfortable viewing experience, information transmission between vehicles can be utilized to accelerate the transmission of video data. Within the transmission range of the vehicle, there is a communication condition for vehicle sources that video data requested by target vehicle must have been cached.

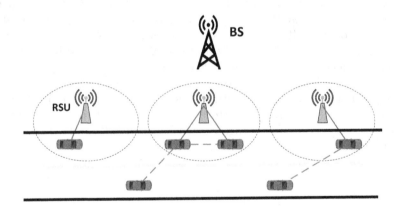

Fig. 1. Architecture of cooperative vehicular networks

Let $\mathcal{K} = \{1,\ldots,K\}$ denote the set of RSUs providing video data to the vehicle users and $\mathcal{A} = \{1,\ldots,A\}$ denote the set of vehicles. The upper limit of the storage video capacity of the kth RSU is C_k and the transmission rate between the kth RSU and the ith car is V_{ki}. The upper limit of the storage video capacity of the ith car is c_i and the upper limit of the transmission bandwidth is B_i. The transmission rate between the vehicles is determined by the distance between the vehicles, and the trajectory of each vehicle is predictable. So the transmission rates between vehicles are available in each time slot.

2.2 Video Layers Model

In order to satisfy the user's different requirements for video clarity, this paper considers to apply SVC-based video transmission, and the video requested by the user consists of N GOPs. Let $\mathcal{N} = \{1, \ldots, N\}$ denotes the set of GOP. Each GOP can be encoded into L video layers (1 base layer, L-1 enhancement layers), where the size of the lth layer of the nth GOP is Z_n^l. In order to improve the time efficiency, this paper proposes that the RSU and the vehicle can simultaneously transmit data for one video layer of one GOP, so it is necessary to divide each layer of each GOP into smaller slices whose size is Z. Due to the high-speed mobility of the vehicle, the position of the vehicle in each time slot changes. Dividing the entire travel process into T time slots, it is supposed that the relative position between the vehicles and the transmission rate maintains invariant in each time slot. At tth time slot the transmission rate from ith vehicle to jth vehicle is $v_{ij}(t)$. At the beginning of each time slot, vehicle request a video block initially. And if the ith vehicle requests the nth GOP at the tth time slot, $r_{in}(t) = 1$, otherwise it is 0. After the vehicle requests the video block, it is determined whether the RSU and the vehicle within the transmission range of the vehicle buffer the video data requested by the vehicle user. And if not, the transmission condition is not available. It is supposed that if the RSU stores one GOP, all layers video data of the GOP are stored. In the tth time slot, if the RSU has already stored the nth GOP, $A_k^n(t) = 1$ otherwise it is 0. The vehicle may store a partial layer of each GOP due to the limitation of the vehicular condition, if the ith vehicle stores the lth layer of the nth GOP, $e_i^{nl}(t) = 1$, otherwise it is 0 (Due to the dependence between the video layers under SVC coding, if the user stores the lth video layer, it must store the $l-1$ layer video, otherwise it cannot be decoded). For the vehicle itself, if the video block transmission is successful in the tth time slot, the vehicle will store the video block at time slots after the tth time slot. Since the total storage capacity of each RSU and vehicle cannot exceed its storage limit, then

$$\sum_{n=1}^{N} \sum_{l=1}^{L} A_k^n(t) Z_k^n \leq C_k \tag{1}$$

$$\sum_{n=1}^{N} \sum_{l=1}^{L} e_i^{nl}(t) Z_k^n \leq c_i \tag{2}$$

$$e_i^{nl_1} \leq e_i^{nl_2} \tag{3}$$

$$e_i^{nl}(t) \leq e_i^{nl}(t+1) \tag{4}$$

2.3   Transmission Model

For all transmission sources (RSU and vehicle) that satisfy the transmission condition, the requested video block is transmitted from a unique transmission source by optimizing the transmission path. If the mth slices of the lth layer of the nth GOP is transmitted to the jth vehicle by the kth RSU, $q_{kj}^{nlm} = 1$, otherwise it is 0. If the mth slices of the lth layer of the nth GOP is transmitted to the jth vehicle by the ith vehicle, $q_{ij}^{nlm} = 1$, otherwise it is 0. In order to improve resource utilization, video slices of each requested video layer are transmitted only by one source under each time slot. There are two conditions for the transmission. First, the vehicle user sends a request signal, and then checking whether the vehicle and the RSU within the communication range have stored the requested video block. The video data blocks stored in RSU within the communication range in each time slot are optimized, and the goal is to cooperate with the surrounding vehicles to provide the highest quality video quality for the requested vehicle. When each vehicle and RSU is used as a transmission source, the sum of the transmission rates of the requested vehicles cannot exceed its own bandwidth limit.

$$\sum_{j=1}^{A} max(q_{kj}^{nlm}, \forall n, l, m)V_{kj}(t) \leq B_k \tag{5}$$

$$\sum_{j=1}^{A} max(q_{ij}^{nlm}, \forall n, l, m)V_{ij}(t) \leq B_i \tag{6}$$

$$\sum_{k=1}^{K} q_{kj}^{nlm}(t) + \sum_{i=1}^{N} q_{ij}^{nlm}(t) \leq 1 \tag{7}$$

$$q_{ij}^{nlm}(t) \leq r_{jn}(t)e_i^{nl}(t) \tag{8}$$

$$q_{kj}^{nlm}(t) \leq r_{jn}(t)A_k^n(t) \tag{9}$$

The transmission time of each requested data block shall be completed within the specified time t_0, otherwise the transmission will fail, and each providing source can only transmit one video slice at the same time. Therefore, the transmission time of all GOPs requested by each vehicle user in the tth time slot should be the maximum time of all providing source.

$$t_1 = max \sum_{n=1}^{N}\sum_{l=1}^{L}\sum_{m=1}^{M_l} \frac{q_{ij}(t)Z}{V_{ij}(t)} \tag{10}$$

$$t_2 = max \sum_{n=1}^{N}\sum_{l=1}^{L}\sum_{m=1}^{M_l} \frac{q_{kj}(t)Z}{V_{kj}(t)} \tag{11}$$

$$t_3 = max(t_1, t_2) \tag{12}$$

$$t_3 < t_0 \tag{13}$$

When the video data layer requested by the vehicle is completely transmitted in the last time slot, the original requesting vehicle can own the data at the next time slot and provide data to other vehicles as a transmission source. Due to the dependence of video layers, the condition for successful video data transmission is to transmit complete video layers orderly. So the transmitted data is more than or equal to the requested data to ensure correct reception for vehicle user.

$$\sum_{i=1}^{A}\sum_{l=1}^{L}\sum_{m=1}^{M_l} q_{ij}^{nlm}(t)Z + \sum_{k=1}^{K}\sum_{l=1}^{L}\sum_{m=1}^{M_l} q_{kj}^{nlm}(t)Z \geq \sum_{l=1}^{L} Z_n^l e_j^{nl}(t+1) \tag{14}$$

2.4   Problem Formulation

Our objective is to maximize the number of GOPs and corresponding layers received by all vehicle users. The primal optimization problem can be formulated as:

$$p0 : Maxmize \sum_{i=1}^{A}\sum_{n=1}^{N}\sum_{l=1}^{L} e_i^{nl}(T) \tag{15}$$

According to the above constraint, it can be seen that there is a mutual relationship between the time slots. The transmission mode in the previous time slot affects the amount of video data buffered in the vehicle in the next time slot. Since the video data buffered in the vehicle at the end of each time slot is equal to the video data at the start of the next time slot. So the above problem can be converted into an optimized form under a single time slot, and the initial state of each time slot turns into determined variable. The objective is to maximize the number of GOP layers transmitted to all requesting vehicles in each time slot. Therefore, problem $p0$ can be converted to the following one:

$$p1 : Maxmize \sum_{j=1}^{A}\sum_{n=1}^{N}\sum_{l=1}^{L} \lfloor \frac{\sum_{i=1}^{A} q_{ij}^{nlm} + \sum_{k=1}^{K} q_{kj}^{nlm}}{M_n^l} \rfloor \tag{16}$$

It is obvious that problem $p1$ is an integer linear programming problem, so the result cannot be obtained in polynomial time. In the existing studies, branch and bound algorithm is widely applied to solve the problem. But when the quantity is large, it will spend a long time to calculate time, which cannot satisfy real-time requirements. So we propose a greedy algorithm to handle the NP-hard problem, which can satisfy returning results in milliseconds.

3   Algorithm Design and Algorithm Analysis

In this section, we introduce the proposed heuristic algorithm, and then analyze time complexity and approximation ratio of the algorithm.

The algorithm is divided into two parts. The first part gets cache result of RSUs and transmission source sequence for each video layer and the second part obtains optimal transmission strategy. Regarding the caching of RSUs, first of all, vehicle requests under coverage of each RSU are counted. Satisfying cache constraint, video blocks are sequentially cached to the RSU according to the number of requests. And then according to position of vehicles, transmission speed between RSUs and vehicles and within vehicles is calculated through Shannon formula. Next transmission speed between transmission sources and target vehicle can be obtained for each requested video layer by judging cache conditions. Finally sorting transmission sources according to speed to get transmission source sequence. Based on the first part, algorithm 1 is designed to optimize the transmission strategy.

It can be seen that we traverse the transmission source according to the speed and firstly transmit video layer whose layer is lower. After satisfying the lower layer transmission, higher layer of each GOP can be transmit. Among the transmission sources that satisfy the transmission conditions, base layer is transmitted by the transmission source with fast speed. If the bandwidth is insufficient, the transmission source with the second-best speed is used to complement. If there is remaining bandwidth, it will provide assistance for the next layer in the order of traversal.

So the original NP problem is transformed into a maximized monotone submodular function using the greedy algorithm. It is proved that algorithm with the characters can achieve a $1 - 1/e$ approximation ratio with the optimal results.

4 Numerical Experiments and Results

In this section, we evaluate the performance of the proposed heuristic algorithm for optimizing RSU cache and transmission source selection through numerical experiments.

4.1 Simulation Scenarios

Similar to [8], we perform the simulation in a highway scenario with one travel direction and a length of 1.2 km. RSUs whose coverage is 400m are located on the road at equal intervals. The simulation settings are set as follows. The entire request and transmission process is divided into 30 time slots and each time slot is set to equal seconds. The video is divided into 20 picture groups (GOPs), each GOP is divided into 4 video layers. Each video layer is further divided into smaller video slices whose size is 1M. If the transmission of the small slices of video layer is incomplete in each time slot, the data reception of the corresponding layer is unsuccessful. The data transmission speed between vehicles varies with the distance between vehicles changing. The threshold of GOP transmission time is determined in each time slot. Our goal is to transmit as more layers of the GOP as possible to vehicle user in each time slot to improve QOE (4 layers is the upper limit for each GOP).

Algorithm 1 : Greedy algorithm for Transmission scheme

1: **Input** : Sequence of vehicles V_{queue}, vehicular storage status e_{mnl}
2: **Output** : total number of video layers transmitted in each time slot M_left
3: List $< V_{queue} > V_{ijl}$=new LinkedList<> ()
4: Rin=new int[M][N]
5: **for** $i = 0$ to $V_{ijl}.size()$ **do do**
6:    **if** $B_{temp}[index\_temp] < V$ **then**
7:       continue
8:    **else**
9:       $B\_temp[index\_temp]- = v$
10:       b_{last}=V*TE
11:    **end if**
12: **end for**
13: lable:
14: **for** $l = 0$ to L **do**
15:    **for** $n = 0$ to $Rin[mt].length$ **do**
16:       **if** $M\_left[t][mt][n] > l$ **then**
17:          continue
18:       **end if**
19:       **if** $VQueue.getMf() >= 0\&\&e[index\_temp][n][l] <= 0$ **then**
20:          continue
21:       **end if**
22:       **if** $Rin[mt][n] > b\_last$ **then**
23:          $Rin[mt][n]- = b\_last$
24:          break label
25:       **else**
26:          $b\_last- = Rin[mt][n]$
27:          $M\_left[t][mt][n] + +$
28:          **if** $M\_left[t][mt][n] == L$ **then**
29:             $Rin[mt][n] = 0$
30:          **else**
31:             $Rin[mt][n] = B[n][M\_left[t][mt][n]]$
32:          **end if**
33:       **end if**
34:    **end for**
35: **end for**
36: return M_left

4.2 Simulation Results

Figure 2 shows the transmission probability of each video layer under the experimental conditions of 20 vehicles. It can be seen that in the same time slot, the lower the number of layers, the greater the probability of successful transmission. The reason is that in the first few time slots, the amount of video accumulated by the vehicle is very small and the video transmission mainly depends on RSUs, so there is almost no transmission for the enhancement layer. And in the case of limited transmission bandwidth, it will preferentially transmit lower layers for each GOP. So there is a very high probability of successful transmission for base layer and the probability is basically stable at 1.

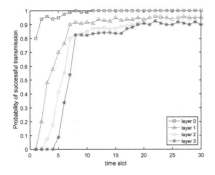

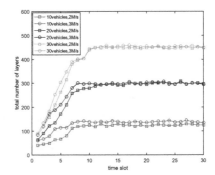

Fig. 2. Successful transmission probability of each video layer

Fig. 3. Conditions under different transmission rates of the RSU and the number of different vehicles

Figure 3 shows the results under different transmission rates of RSUs and the number of different vehicles. It can be seen that video layer successfully transmitted changes obviously with the number of cars in each time slot. With time slot increasing the number of video layers is not significantly affected by the rate of the RSU. The reason is that transmission rate between vehicles is faster than the transmission rate with RSUs, and the number of vehicles is much larger than the number of RSUs within the vehicle transmission range. When the number of cars is 30, the transmission bandwidth of the RSU is basically occupied, so the total number of layers received at the initial moment is basically unchanged. When the number of vehicles is small, the trend of increasing the number of video layers transmitted successfully is not obvious with time slot increasing. And it is greatly affected by the RSU transmission rate compared with the larger number of vehicles. Since the number of vehicles around each vehicle and the storage content on vehicles is varied in each time slot, result of transmission will be affected.

Figure 4 shows the average number of layers of GOPs transmitted in each time slot under the constraints of different time thresholds. Under the same experimental conditions, the smaller the time threshold, the lower video layer transmitted successfully. The reason is that less data can be transmitted in shorter time. In the initial time slots, transmission mainly depends on RSUs with a relatively low transmission rate. So the number of successfully transmitted layers changes significantly with the change of the time threshold. As the time slot increases, transmission mainly depends on V2V and the number of video layers transmitted gradually stabilizes. The transmission speed of V2V is fast and a large amount of data can be transmitted in a short time. Therefore, in the later time slot, when the time threshold is larger than 2s, the size of the time threshold has little effect on the number of layers transmitted and the number of average video layers transmitted tends to be stable.

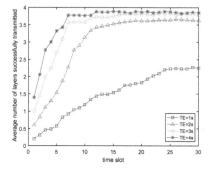

Fig. 4. Average number of layers transmitted under the constraints of different time thresholds

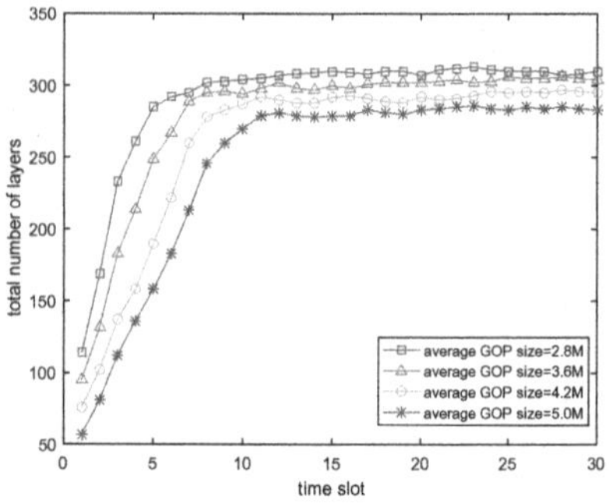

Fig. 5. Successful transmission probability of each video layer

As shown in Figs. 5 and 6, in each time slot, the total number of transmitted video layers and the total time of all video transmission vary with the type of transmitted video. The larger average GOP size, the fewer the number of layers that can be transmitted within a certain threshold time, and transmission time is relatively short. With time slot increasing, more vehicles are capable to be transmission sources contributes to a stable total number of transmission layers

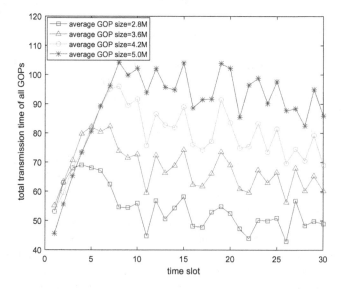

Fig. 6. Total transmission time of all GOPs for different video types

in each slot. Therefore, video type whose average GOP size is large requires long transmission time. Furthermore, transmission speed between target vehicles and transmission source changes with vehicle position, which results in total transmission time changing in each time slot.

5 Conclusion

In this paper, we studied the problem of maximizing of the number of GOP layers under scenario combining RSUs and adjacent vehicles cooperatively to provide transmission service. We proposed to optimize RSU cache and transmission source selection in each time slot. Under constraint of satisfying time threshold, transmission source cooperates to transmit video data to improve user experience. The formulated problem is NP-hard, and we proposed a greedy algorithm whose approximation ratio is $1 - 1/e$ to solve it. We conducted numerous simulations to evaluate performance of the proposed algorithm and extensive simulation have been performed to demonstrate the efficiency of our approach.

Acknowledgments. This work is supported by the System Architecture Project (No. 61400040503), the Natural Science Foundation of China (No. 61872104) the Natural Science Foundation of Heilongjiang Province in China (No. F2016028), the Fundamental Research Fund for the Central Universities in China and Tianjin Key Laboratory of Advanced Networking (TANK) in College of Intelligence and Computing of Tianjin University.

References

1. Wang, T., Ke, H., Zheng, X., Wang, K., Sangaiah, A.K., Liu, A.: Big data cleaning based on mobile edge computing in industrial sensor-cloud. IEEE Trans. Industr. Inf. **16**(2), 1321–1329 (2020)
2. Wang, T., Luo, H., Jia, W., Liu, A., Xie, M.: MTES: an intelligent trust evaluation scheme in sensor-cloud-enabled industrial internet of things. IEEE Trans. Industr. Inf. **16**(3), 2054–2062 (2020)
3. Zhou, H., et al.: Chaincluster: engineering a cooperative content distribution framework for highway vehicular communications. IEEE Trans. Intell. Transp. Syst. **15**(6), 2644–2657 (2014)
4. Xing, M., He, J., Cai, L.: Maximum-utility scheduling for multimedia transmission in drive-thru internet. IEEE Trans. Veh. Technol. **65**(4), 2649–2658 (2016)
5. He, H., Shan, H., Huang, A., Sun, L.: Resource allocation for video streaming in heterogeneous cognitive vehicular networks. IEEE Trans. Veh. Technol. **65**(10), 7917–7930 (2016)
6. Chen, X., Hwang, J., Lee, C., Chen, S.: A near optimal qoe-driven power allocation scheme for scalable video transmissions over mimo systems. IEEE J. Sel. Topics Signal Process. **9**(1), 76–88 (2015)
7. X. Chen, H. Du, J. Hwang, J. A. Ritcey, and C. Lee. A qoe-driven fec rate adaptation scheme for scalable video transmissions over mimo systems. In 2015 IEEE International Conference on Communications (ICC), pages 6953–6958, 2015

8. Zhou, H., Wang, X., Liu, Z., Ji, Y., Yamada, S.: Resource allocation for svc streaming over cooperative vehicular networks. IEEE Trans. Veh. Technol. **67**(9), 7924–7936 (2018)

9. Al-Hilo, A., Ebrahimi, D., Sharafeddine, S., Assi, C.: Revenue-driven video delivery in vehicular networks with optimal resource scheduling. Veh. Commun. **23**, 100215 (2019)

10. Khan, H., Samarakoon, S., Bennis, M.: Enhancing video streaming in vehicular networks via resource slicing. IEEE Trans. Veh. Technol. **69**(4), 3513–3522 (2020)

11. Yaacoub, E., Filali, F., Abu-Dayya, A.: Qoe enhancement of svc video streaming over vehicular networks using cooperative lte/802.11p communications. IEEE J. Sel. Top. Signal Process. **9**(1), 37–49 (2015)

12. Chen, C., et al.: Delay-optimized v2v-based computation offloading in urban vehicular edge computing and networks. IEEE Access **8**, 18863–18873 (2020)

13. Yan, Y., Zhang, B., Li, C.: Network coding aided collaborative real-time scalable video transmission in d2d communications. IEEE Trans. Veh. Technol. **67**(7), 6203–6217 (2018)

14. Sun, Y., Xu, L., Tang, Y., Zhuang, W.: Traffic offloading for online video service in vehicular networks: a cooperative approach. IEEE Trans. Veh. Technol. **67**(8), 7630–7642 (2018)

Who Distributes It? Privacy-Preserving Image Sharing Scheme with Illegal Distribution Detection

Tianpeng Deng[1], Xuan Li[1,2,3(✉)], Biao Jin[1], and Jinbo Xiong[1,2]

[1] College of Mathematics and Informatics, Fujian Normal University,
Fuzhou 350117, China
dengtp97@163.com, jessieli24@163.com, {jinbiao,jbxiong}@fjnu.edu.cn
[2] Fujian Provincial Key Laboratory of Network Security and Cryptology,
Fuzhou 350117, China
[3] Digital Fujian Big Data Security Technology Institute, Fuzhou 350117, China

Abstract. In image sharing schemes, the privacy of shared images can be protected by sending encrypted images to the receiver. However, the decrypted image cannot avoid being illegally distributed by receivers for their own benefits. Some methods have been proposed to solve this problem by embedding query user's identification into the image. However, spatial domain embedding are usually vulnerable to attacks, such as Least Significant Bit (LSB) replacement attacks. We propose a privacy-preserving image sharing scheme for detecting illegal distributors based on edge detection and Arnold transformation. This scheme can adaptively embed the query user's authentication information into 1 to 5 LSBs of each pixel of the image according to the embedded position map. After receiving the scrambled encrypted image and embedded position map, the cloud server will generate the embedded value map and embed in the encrypted domain. The image owner can identify the distributor's identification with the help of cloud server when a suspected illegally distributed image is found. The scheme is robust under different attacks as shown by experiments.

Keywords: Privacy protection · Image sharing · Data hiding · Edge detection · Illegal distribution detection

1 Introduction

With the development of 5G, the rates of data transmission have greatly increased and many tasks have been moved from local to cloud [1]. As a carrier containing a lot of information, image has been widely used in the era of 5G in various fields, such as Internet of Things [2] and social networks [3]. Specially in social networks, image sharing is an important part of people's social activities [4]. However, images usually contain a lot of personal information and thus are privacy-sensitive. When people consider using image outsourcing services for

© Springer Nature Switzerland AG 2021
G. Wang et al. (Eds.): SpaCCS 2020, LNCS 12383, pp. 257–268, 2021.
https://doi.org/10.1007/978-3-030-68884-4_22

storage and sharing, the privacy problem will become one of the most concerned issues [5,6]. As for the scenario when authorized users query an image from the cloud platform, they can illegally distribute the image to other unauthorized persons for their own benefit [7]. This is a great threat to the image owner. The detection of illegal distributor can serve as a deterrent against such illegal behavior.

Embedding user identity in shared images is an effective way to detect illegal distributors [7]. Since the images are stored in the encrypted form, when an authorized user requires to get the shared images from the cloud server, his identity needs to be embedded in encrypted images. Some works has been done on how to perform reversible data hiding in encrypted images [8–10]. A common kind of hiding method is embedding data in the least significant bits. Zhang et al. [11] encrypted the image by stream cipher and then embedded one bit by changing the 3 least significant bitplanes of half pixels in each block. Xia et al. [7] proposed a privacy-preserving image retrieval scheme with copy detection based on Zhang's method. However, these methods are vulnerable to the attacks because the embedding positions are fixed on the least significant bitplanes. Illegal users can change or remove embedded data by modifying or deleting the values of LSB without significantly degrading the visual quality of images. In [12], the image is encrypted by XOR operation and each bit of the message is embedded in the MSB of each available pixel. Since the change of MSB seriously affect the visual quality of the image, a complex process related to prediction error is used for data embedding and recovery. But this scheme increases the computational burden on image owners and image users. In addition, the embedded solution based on XOR encryption cannot support further processing on the encrypted images [13,14].

In this paper, we propose a new image sharing scheme with illegally distribution detection in the cloud environment. The main contributions of the proposed scheme are summarized as follows:

(1) The scheme can reduce the storage and computing burden on the owner's side. Image owners are only responsible for image encryption and transmission, while the embedding and extraction of authentication data are handled by cloud server based on homomorphic properties. Therefore, data owners can delete the local images to greatly reduce the consumption of storage space.
(2) The scheme supports privacy preserving adaptive embedding on the encrypted image, which embeds data in unfixed bitplanes instead of fixed bitplanes. The selection of embedding bitplane positions are adaptively determined by the distance of each pixel to the edge of image, which is consistent with human visual perception to reduce the influence of visual quality of the shared images. Moreover, the experiments show that our scheme is robust under different attacks such as the LSB attack.

The rest of the paper is organized as follows. Section 2 gives the details of system implementation. Section 3 shows experimental results and performance analysis. Section 4 gives the conclusions.

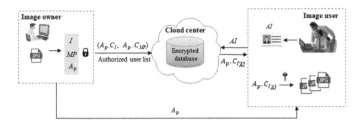

Fig. 1. The framework of privacy-preserving image sharing scheme with illegal distribution detection

2 System Implementation

In this section, we describe in detail the privacy-preserving image sharing scheme with illegal distribution detection.

2.1 System Architecture

The proposed scheme consists of four parts(image sharing, image query, information embedding and illegal distribution detection) with three entities (image owner, cloud server and image users). Image query phase and information embedding phase are always combined because only when the query user requests to the cloud server with his authentication information, the cloud server can embed information into the shared image. For protecting the image content, the image to be shared will be encrypted, so the scheme should support embedding in the encrypted image. Figure 1 shows the framework of the proposed scheme. For the convenience of description, the symbols of the scheme are listed in Table 1. The details of the scheme will be shown in Sect. 2.2.

2.2 Image Sharing

Since the cloud server is set to be semi-trusted in the security model, the image owner will first encrypt the image when sharing the image. Due to the insensitivity of the human vision system to the change of the gray scale of the edge, we proposed an adaptive embedding algorithm based on edge detection. Here are the steps of our scheme:

Step 1: The image owner generates a public key pair (K_{Pa}, K_{Pb}), a symmetric key K_S and Arnold transformation parameter A_p, then assigns A_p and K_{Pb} to the authorized users who can obtain the images and sends K_{Pa}, K_S and the list of authorized users to the cloud server.

Step 2: Generate the embedded position map MP of I to determine which bitplane of each pixel is suitable for embedding data. We use Sobel operator to detect the edge of I, and denote it as I_E. We denote D as the shortest distance of each pixel to I_E, where $D(i, j)$ represents the shortest distance from $I(i, j)$ to I_E. The minimum($= 0$), median and outlier values of D are statistically analyzed

Table 1. Symbols and Descriptions used in the scheme

Symbol	Description
I	Original image
EMP	Edge distance map
MP	Embedding position map
A_p	Arnold parameters
K_{Pa}, K_{Pb}	Homomorphic encryption and decryption key pair
K_S	Symmetric key
C_I	Encrypted image
C_{MP}	Encrypted embedding position map
$A_p.C_I$	Arnold encrypted image
$A_p.C_{MP}$	Arnold encrypted embedding position map
MV	Embedding value map
AI	Authentication information
$\overline{AI}$	Expanded authentication information
$I_{\overline{AI}}$	Image with expanded authentication information

by boxplot. Because different images can generate different D, so the bitplane to be embedded can be adaptively chosen according to different statistical values of D. We denote the bitplanes chosen by D as Edge Distance Map (EMP), and the value k_{ij} of EMP at position (i, j) can be calculated as following:

$$k_{ij} = \begin{cases} 4, & if \ D(i, j) = 0 \\ 3, & if \ 0 < D(i, j) \le 1 \\ 2, & if \ 1 < D(i, j) < Median \\ 1, & if \ Median \le D(i, j) < Outlier \\ 0, & if \ D(i, j) \ge Outlier \end{cases} \tag{1}$$

Because EMP has edge information of I, the content of the image may be leaked to the cloud server, so we improve the randomness of the algorithm in order to increase the ability against attacks. We use k_{ij} as the upper bound of random number, so $r_{ij} = rand(0, k_{ij})$ and r_{ij} is a positive integer. Then the embedded position map (MP) is a matrix with respect to r_{ij}. For example, if $D(i, j) = 0$, then $k_{ij} = 4$. After choosing the integer r_{ij} from $[0, k_{ij}]$ randomly, the value of $MP(i, j)$ will be finally decided as r_{ij}. The map of r_{ij} is denoted as MP.

$$MP(i, j) = GetBit(I(i, j), r_{ij} + 1) \times 2^{r_{ij}}, \ 0 \le i \le M, \ 0 \le j \le N \tag{2}$$

Step 3: After obtaining embedded position map MP, encrypt original image I with homomorphic encryption key K_{PA}.

$$C_I = HE.E_{K_{PA}}(I) \tag{3}$$

In which $HE.E$ is the function of homomorphic encryption.

$$C_I(i) = g^{I(i)} r^n mod\ n^2 \qquad (4)$$

Step 4: To make sure no information will be leaked at the embedding phase, we use Arnold transformation to scramble C_I with A_p in order to better protect the image and MP, as MP contains edge information of original image. Arnold transformation can scramble the position of each pixel of I without changing the gray value.

We denote the encrypted image embedded position map scrambled by A_p as $A_p.C_I$ and $A_p.MP$, respectively. The relative position remains the same by using the same Arnold transformation parameter A_p.

Step 5: Encrypt $A_p.MP$ by symmetric encryption.

$$A_p.C_{MP} = SE.E_{K_S}(A_p.MP) = A_p.(SE.E_{K_S}(MP)) \qquad (5)$$

Step 6: The image owner uploads $A_p.C_I$ and $A_p.C_{MP}$ to the cloud server for secure image sharing and privacy preserving information embedding on the encrypted image

2.3 Information Embedding

When an image user wants to query a shared image on the cloud server, his or her identity information (such as signature) is sent to the cloud server. If the requesting user is not an authorized user, the cloud rejects the request; on the contrary, if the requesting user is an authorized user, the cloud will embed the requested user's authentication information in the encrypted image as follows:

Step 1: The cloud decrypts the information sent by image user when he or she requests the shared image and obtains the authentication information AI in binary form.

Step 2: The algorithm we propose has high embedding rate, because the algorithm is based on image edge feature, and each pixel has a shortest distance to the edge, which means each pixel has theoretically 1 bit room to embed, namely the embedding payload reaches 1 bit/pixel(bpp). The length of the authentication information (l bits) is often smaller than that of the carrier image ($M \times N$ pixels) and the algorithm in this paper has high embedding ratio. Therefore, we propose to expand the authentication information by multiple copies to improve the fault tolerance of authentication information recovery, so as to improve the robustness of the algorithm. The expansion factor can be calculated by the following equation:

$$m = \lfloor MN/l \rfloor \qquad (6)$$

Where l (bits) is the length of authentication information, and M,N are the width and length of carrier image. Generate m copies and connect them in sequence, then the length of expanded authentication information $\overline{AI}$ is ml bits, where $ml \le MN$.

Step 3: $\overline{AI}$ is in binary form with its value $v \in 0, 1$. transform $\overline{AI}$ into the matrix form with size of $M \times N$, which the transformed coordinate (i, j) of the matrix will be calculated by following equation:

$$\begin{cases} i = (\lfloor k/N \rfloor \mod M) + 1 \\ j = (k \mod N) + 1 \end{cases} \tag{7}$$

Where $0 \leq k \leq ml - 1$.

Step 4: Calculate the embedded value map MV by observing $A_p.MP\,(i, j)$ and $\overline{AI}(i, j)$.

$$\begin{cases} MV(i, j) = 0, & A_p.MP\,(i, j) = 0 \,\&\overline{AI}(i, j) = 0 \\ MV(i, j) = 0, & A_p.MP(i, j) \neq 0 \,\&\overline{AI}(i, j) = 1 \\ MV(i, j) = +MP(i, j), & A_p.MP(i, j) \neq 0 \,\&\overline{AI}(i, j) = 0 \\ MV(i, j) = -MP(i, j), & A_p.MP(i, j) = 0 \,\&\overline{AI}(i, j) = 1 \end{cases} \tag{8}$$

In equation above, the embedded value map MV records the change of each pixel value in the original image after embedding the bits of $\overline{AI}$.

Step 5: The cloud encrypt MV by homomorphic encryption and use $HE.E(MV)$ to embed.

Step 6: Embed MV from $A_p.C_{MP} = n$ in orders which n is the highest bitplane to embed. When there is no more room for $A_p.C_{MP} = n$ to embed, then $n-1, n-2, \ldots, 0$. By doing so, the ability to resist attacks can be improved because the higher bitplane to embed, the more visual effects are affected.

The cloud server multiplies $HE.E(MV)$ and $HE.E(I)$ pixel by pixel.

$$HE.E\,(A_p.I\,(i, j)) \times HE.E\,(MV\,(i, j))\,;1 \leq i \leq M, \; 1 \leq j \leq N \tag{9}$$

Based on the properties of homomorphic encryption, we can get:

$$\begin{aligned} &HE.E\,(A_p.I\,(i, j)) \times HE.E\,(MV\,(i, j)) \\ =&HE.E\,(A_p.I\,(i, j) + MV\,(i, j)) \\ =&HE.E\,(A_p.I_{\overline{AI}}) \\ =&A_p.C_{I\overline{AI}} \end{aligned} \tag{10}$$

Step 7: After embedding progress, the cloud sends $A_p.C_{I\overline{AI}}$ to the authenticated user. The user uses A_p to transform $A_p.C_{I\overline{AI}}$ inversely by following formula:

$$A_p^{-1}\,(A_p.C_{I\overline{AI}}) = C_{I\overline{AI}} \tag{11}$$

The authenticated user uses decryption key K_{Pb} to decrypt $C_{I\overline{AI}}$:

$$\begin{aligned} &HE.D\,(C_{I\overline{AI}}) \\ =&HE.D\,(HE.E\,(I\,(i, j) + MV\,(i, j))) \\ =&I\,(i, j) + MV\,(i, j) \\ =&I_{\overline{AI}} \end{aligned} \tag{12}$$

$I_{\overline{AI}}$ is the required image which is embedded with query user's authentication information.

2.4   Illegal Distribution Detecting

When a suspicious image I' is found on the internet, the image owner tries to identify the identification of the illegal distributor. The following procedure are illegal distribution detection phase, which the whole process is shown in Fig. 2(b).

Step 1: The image owner sends a query to the cloud to help identify suspicious images with the Arnold transformed suspicious image using A_p.

Step 2: The cloud extracts the bit values from the corresponding pixel in the suspicious image with Arnold transformation $A_p.I'$ according to $A_p.MP$. The extraction process is the inverse of the embedding process.

Step 3: The identity of the illegal distributor can be identified though checking the authentication information. Denote the extracted authentication information as AI', the cloud server needs to verify whether AI' is equal to AI, then the identification of the illegal distributor will be recognized. Note that AI' is the expansion of the original authentication information. This is to enhance the robustness of the detection algorithm.

3   System Evaluation

3.1   Embedding Performance

In this section, we evaluate the embedding performance of the proposed privacy-preserving illegal distribution detection scheme.

(1) Visual quality of embedded image

In this scheme, the selection of bitplane for each pixel is not fixed but adaptively determined by the distance to the edge detected. If the distance is far from the detected edge, low bitplane is chosen for embedding data; otherwise, high bitplane is chosen for embedding data. This is consistent with human visual perception, so as to reduce the influence of embedded information and maintain high image visual quality. Figure 2(a) shows the cover image 'Lena' sized 512×512 and Fig. 2(d) shows the signature image which is of size 87×325. After the expanding and embedding phase, the image embedded with information is shown in Fig. 2(f). Peak Signal to Noise Ratio (PSNR) is a common way to measure the quality of the image, and our method reaches 39.67, which means the visual quality of the image is barely affected. Also the embedded data is successfully extracted, and the Structural Similarity Index (SSIM) between the original authentication information and the extracted data reaches 1.

(2) Embedding rate

The embedding rate(payload) is expressed by bit/pixel (bpp), representing the maximum amount of data that can be embedded in an image. In the proposed scheme, although the embedding process is performed in the encrypted form, the embedding rate is not actually effected by the homomorphic encryption. For the proposed scheme, each pixel of the encrypted image can be used to embed 1 bit of the authentication information, so the embedding rate is **1 bpp** which is much higher than other schemes [15–17]. The scheme with high payload is able to support the expanding of embedded information as described in Sect. 2.

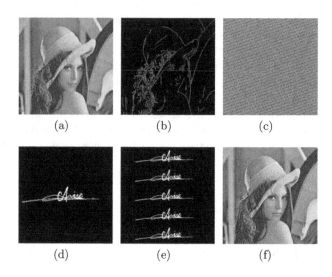

(a)   (b)   (c)

(d)   (e)   (f)

Fig. 2. (a) Original 'Lena' image, (b) Edge of 'Lena', (c) Transformed 'Lena' with Arnold parameter ($a = 7$, $b = 11$, $n = 2$), (d) Authentication information (signature of 'Alice'), (e) Expanded authentication information, (f) Embedded 'Lena' with 'Alice'

3.2   Security Analysis

In this section, we evaluate the proposed scheme from two aspects: privacy protection and robustness. The proposed scheme achieves the following security goals: (a) The content of original images are kept secret against the unauthorized attackers and the semi-trusted cloud server. Because of the encryption of the image, the image data is invisible to the cloud server. The embedding is achieved with the help of MV, which is also perturbed under Arnold transformation. Unauthorized attackers do not have the private key to decrypt the

(a)   (b)   (c)

Fig. 3. (a) Deleting 3 LSB, (b) Deleting 4 LSB, (c) Deleting 5 LSB

image, so the image data is secure to attackers. (b) The embedded image with information is also confidential to the cloud server. All operations of embedding are realized in the encrypted form of the image, so the image data will not be leaked to the semi-trusted cloud server.

In this scheme, the selection of bitplanes for each pixel is not fixed but adaptively determined by the distance to the detected edge. The adaptive design of data embedding can get good trade-off between high visual quality and strong robustness. First, it reduces the influence of embedded information on image quality to maintain high image visual quality. Second, it increases the difficulty for illegal users to remove or change embedded information by slightly processing the image without destroying its visual quality. For example, in many of the existing methods, data is embedded in the least significant bitplane (LSB) or the three least LSB [7,11,12]. These data hiding schemes are not suitable for illegal distribution detection in the cloud environment, because the image user can easily remove the embedded information by directly setting the LSB or the three least LSB easily. This attack is easy to perform and does not affect the visual quality of image. The results of setting the 3 LSB bitplanes to be zero are shown in Fig. 3(a). In order to resist this attack, more significant bitplanes should be also used to embed data to improve the robustness of the algorithm. If the authentication information is randomly embedded in one of the 1st to 5th bitplane, the attacker has to set five LSBs as zero to ensure that the embedded data is deleted. However, this damages the visual quality of the image as shown in Fig. 3(b) and Fig. 3(c). Adopting higher bitplane for embedding can greatly improve the robustness of the algorithm against such attacks, because image users have to consider the impact of image quality degradation on their benefits.

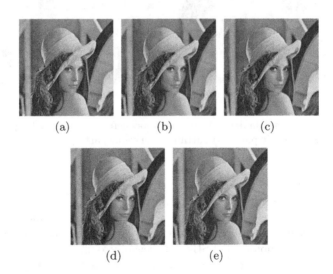

Fig. 4. Embedded 'Lena' under (a) deleting 1 LSB, (b) deleting 2 LSBs, (c) deleting 3 LSBs, (d) deleting 4 LSBs, (e) randomly substitute one of the 1 to 5 LSBs of each pixel.

When an image user 'Alice' requires the shared image 'Lena' from the cloud, the cloud first checks his identification. After verification, the cloud sends back the embedded image which Alice's handwriting signature in it. As deleting 3 LSBs of the image will not severely affect the visual quality of the image, the image user who wants to illegally distribute the shared image may try to set 1 to 3 LSBs as zeros (Fig. 4(a)–4(c)). In our scheme, this kind of attacks will not actually influence the embedded authentication information, because higher bitplanes will also contain information. Moreover, the illegal distributor could delete more biteplanes (Fig. 4(d)) to remove the embedded authentication information, but the visual quality will be severely damaged (An irregular texture appears in the smooth area, such as the shoulder of 'Lena'). Figure 6(a)–6(c) show the extracted signature image which are the same as Fig. 2(d).

Cutting parts of the embedded image is another kind of attack that a scheme must face. Although the image user does not know the exact area of a particular information, he may try to cut different part of the image. Figure 5(a)–5(d) are embedded 'Lena' images under cutting attacks. Figure 6(e)–6(g) show that the extracted authentication information images are different because of the different cutting parts of the image. Figure 2(b) shows the edge of 'Lena', which can be seen that the lower-left part of the image has more edge details of the image. More details of the edge mean the information embedded in this part is are more important. However, because of the adaptive self-replication of the authentication information, other parts of the image will fix the missed message when the information of this part is lost (Fig. 6(g)).

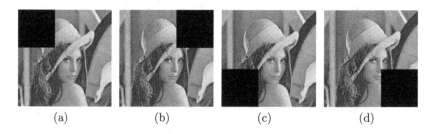

| (a) | (b) | (c) | (d) |

Fig. 5. Embedded 'Lena' under (a) cutting upper-left part, (b) cutting upper-right part, (c) cutting lower-left part, (d) cutting lower-right part

Aiming at our scheme, we randomly choose one bitplane from 1 to 5 LSBs of each pixel and randomly substitute the value of this bitplane. Because our scheme adaptively chooses one bitplane according to the distance to the edge of the shared image, so the attacker does not know the exact position of the embedding value. Removing 5 LSBs will severely damage the visual quality, so the attacker may randomly substitute the 5 LSBs and luckily destroy the embedded authentication information without severely influence the quality of the image (Fig. 4(e)). Figure 6(i) shows the extracted authentication information under the attack of randomly substitute one of the 1 to 5 LSBs of each pixel.

Because of the multi-copy of the authentication information, the quality of the signature image is well protected. Although some extracted signature images have different distortion under different attacks, Alice's handwriting can still be clearly confirmed. Therefore, we can say that the algorithm proposed in this paper has a good robustness against different attacks.

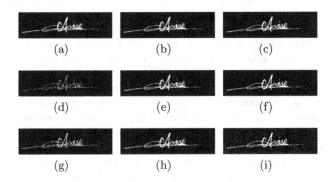

Fig. 6. Extracted authentication information of (a) deleting 1 LSB attack, (b) deleting 2 LSBs attack, (c) deleting 3 LSBs attack, (d) deleting 4 LSBs attack, (e) cutting upper-left part attack, (f) cutting upper-right part attack, (g) cutting lower-left part attack, (h) cutting lower-right part attack, (i) randomly substitute one of the 1 to 5 LSBs of each pixel attack.

4 Conclusion

In this paper, we resolve the problem of illegal distribution detection for privacy-preserving image sharing in the cloud computing. When the image user illegally distributes the private image to unauthorized people for his own benefit, the proposed scheme enables the image owner to detect the identity of illegal distributor through extracting authentication information from the suspicious image. In the scheme, the plaintext is not leaked to the cloud server or the authentication center. Meanwhile, the robustness of detection is greatly improved through the design of privacy-preserving adaptive embedding to achieve high embedding rate and image quality. So the illegal image user cannot easily remove or change the embedded information through traditional attacks. In this way, the proposed scheme can effectively support privacy-preserving image sharing and prevent the illegal distribution behavior.

Acknowledgments. This work is supported by the National Natural Science Foundation of China (61872088, 61872090, 61872086); and the Natural Science Foundation of Fujian Province (2019J01276).

References

1. Wang, T., Ke, H.X., Wang, K., Sangaiah, A.K., Liu, A.F.: Big data cleaning based on mobile edge computing in industrial sensor-cloud. IEEE Trans. Ind. Inform. **16**(2), 1321–1329 (2020)
2. Xiong, J.B., Bi, R.W., Zhao, M.F., Guo, J.D., Yang, Q.: Edge-assisted privacy-preserving raw data sharing framework for connected autonomous vehicles. IEEE Wirel. Commun. **27**(3), 24–30 (2020)
3. Yuan, L., Korshunov, P., Ebrahimi, T.: Secure JPEG scrambling enabling privacy in photo sharing. In: Proceedings of the 11th IEEE International Conference and Workshops on Automatic Face and Gesture Recognition, pp. 1–6. IEEE Computer Society (2015)
4. Amato, F., Moscato, V., Picariello, A.: SOS: a multimedia recommender system for online social networks. Future Gener. Comput. Syst. **93**, 914–923 (2019)
5. Sun, W., Zhou, J., Zhu, S., Tang, Y.Y.: Robust privacy-preserving image sharing over online social networks. ACM Trans. Multimed. Comput. Commun. Appl. **14**(1), 14:1–14:22 (2018)
6. Li, X., Li, J., Yiu, S., Gao, C., Xiong, J.: Privacy-preserving edge-assisted image retrieval and classification in IoT. Front. Comput. Sci. **13**(5), 1136–1147 (2018). https://doi.org/10.1007/s11704-018-8067-z
7. Xia, Z.H., Wang, X.H., Zhang, L.G., Qin, Z., Sun, X.M., Ren, K.: A privacy-preserving and copy-deterrence content-based image retrieval scheme in cloud computing. IEEE Trans. Inf. Forensics Secur. **11**(11), 2594–2608 (2011)
8. Khan, A., Siddiqa, A., Munib, S., Malik, S.A.: A recent survey of reversible watermarking techniques. Inf. Sci. **279**, 251–272 (2014)
9. Wu, H.T., Huang, J., Shi, Y.Q.: A reversible data hiding method with contrast enhancement for medical images. J. Vis. Commun. Image Represent. **31**, 146–153 (2015)
10. Qian, Z., Zhang, X.P.: Reversible data hiding in encrypted images with distributed source encoding. IEEE Trans. Circuits Syst. Video Technol. **26**(4), 636–646 (2016)
11. Zhang, X.P.: Reversible data hiding in encrypted image. IEEE Signal Process. Lett. **18**(4), 255–258 (2011)
12. Puteaux, P., Puech, W.: An efficient MSB prediction-based method for high-capacity reversible data hiding in encrypted images. IEEE Trans. Inf. Forensics Secur. **13**(7), 1670–1681 (2018)
13. Ferreira, B., Rodrigues, J., Leitao, J., Domingos, H.: Privacy-preserving content-based image retrieval in the cloud. IACR Cryptol. ePrint Arch. **2015**, 710 (2015)
14. Zhang, L., et al.: Pic: Enable large-scale privacy preserving content-based image search on cloud[J]. IEEE Trans. Parallel Distrib. Syst. **28**(11), 3258–3271 (2017)
15. Cao, X., Du, L., Wei, X.X., Meng, D., Guo, X.J.: High capacity reversible data hiding in encrypted images by patch-level sparse representation. IEEE Trans. Cybern. **46**(5), 1132–1143 (2016)
16. Ma, K., Zhang, W.M., Zhao, X.F., Yu, N.H., Li, F.H.: Reversible data hiding in encrypted images by reserving room before encryption. IEEE Trans. Inf. Forensics Secur. **8**(3), 553–562 (2013)
17. Wu, X.T., Sun, W.: High-capacity reversible data hiding in encrypted images by prediction error. Signal Process. **104**, 387–400 (2014)

Stepwise-Refined Interval for Deep Learning to Process Sensor-Cloud Data with Noises

Feichou Kou[1][(✉)] and Fan Zhang[2]

[1] Department of Computer Science and Technology, Nanjing Tech University,
Nanjing 211816, China
koufc@njtech.edu.cn
[2] Watson Group, IBM Massachusetts Lab, Littleton, MA 02139, USA
fzhang@us.ibm.com

Abstract. Predicting behaviors of interest in sensor cloud data has been a challenging issue due to the interference of the tremendous background noises. In this paper, a large number of noisy gravitational wave data detected by the sensor array on the laser interferometer gravitational wave observatory (LIGO) measurement arm is taken as a case study, and a model is established to predict the merging time of the two neutron star collision in real-time. After injecting gravitational wave signals with noise data, combined with the current popular deep learning techniques, we first predict the probability value of the merger event within an acceptable interval, then gradually narrow the interval down, and finally make a prediction of a small interval. Our results show that the stepwise-refined interval method has a faster speed without reducing accuracy. The average absolute error of the merge time on the test set is as low as 0.003.

Keywords: Internet of Things · Deep learning · Noise · Merge time · Signal processing

1 Introduction

In recent years, sensor clouds have gained widespread attention while promoting the development of a smart industrial Internet of Things (IoT). Different from the previous sensor data collection network, it has a unique information acquisition and processing technology, through the integration of sensing and networking components, the sensor data collected is transferred in real-time to a cloud. Leveraging the cloud platform the data will be processed and used in real time [1]. However, in reality, the presence of malicious or damaged sensor nodes and environmental factors will cause the data mixed with environmental noises.

In speech recognition tasks, due to the surrounding environment interference, the voice signals collected by the sensor will inevitably be mixed with noises. In gas monitoring alarm tasks, as the sensor accuracy continues to improve, its

© Springer Nature Switzerland AG 2021
G. Wang et al. (Eds.): SpaCCS 2020, LNCS 12383, pp. 269–280, 2021.
https://doi.org/10.1007/978-3-030-68884-4_23

minor changes in the environment will be more sensitive subjective to noises and possibly causing false alarms.

In astrophysics, the process of rotation and merger of compact binary systems, such as white dwarfs, neutron stars, and black holes, will lead to the distortion of space-time and the formation of ripples. This huge energy will spread in the form of gravitational waves. The visualization of the gravitational wave signals monitored by the sensors revealed that the gravitational wave signals are all mixed with a certain degree of background noise, which would lead to a misprediction of the parameters. The noise affecting the laser interferometer sensor can be divided into two main categories: displacement noise and sensing noise. Displacement noise comes from the movement of the experimental apparatus, e.g., low noise, thermal noise. Sensory noise is the noise generated by measuring the slightest movement of the measuring instrument, for example, scattering noise.

The sensor monitoring aspect is the first and foremost aspect of any research, and if the consideration of noise signals is neglected, this may jeopardize the normal operation of the IoT system [2]. How to solve the problem of enhancing the system's performance in extracting core signal data in a large amount of received data containing noisy signals is a key research question.

Although various research efforts have been conducted to meet the challenges in this field, there are still quite a few on-going issues. First, LIGO scientists used matched filtering technology to analyze gravitational waves mixed with noise. It needs to prepare a large number of accurate theoretical waveform templates in advance, which would lead to a complicated calculation process and it was difficult to predict gravitational wave signals outside the theoretical template. In the literature [3–8], the use of a convolutional neural network (CNN) to identify the gravitational wave signal mixed in Gaussian noise, and achieved good results. The accuracy and reliability of the convolutional neural network (CNN) for gravitational wave signal analysis are also verified.

Researchers have been working on the detection of actual gravitational wave signals in the mixed-signal and the prediction of gravitational wave source space parameters, including two star mass, luminosity distance D, right ascension α, and declination δ. Predictive analysis of the merger time of gravitational wave collisions is also of great interest but has been insufficiently studied due to its great difficulty in prediction.

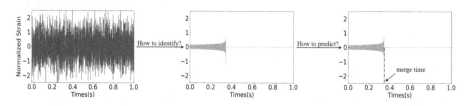

Fig. 1. *Left* : Mixed signal with some degree of noise. *Middle* : Extraction of pure signals. *Right* : Predicting merger time in a pure signal.

In this paper, we propose a deep learning system (DLS) that may predict the time of collision and merger of two neutron stars using gravitational wave signals (see Fig. 1). The experiments show that the neural network model is several orders of magnitude faster than the previous matched filtering technology, and the detection accuracy can also be comparable to the matched filtering technology. In order to determine the merging time step by step to a smaller interval range during detection, we built a total of eight similar CNN models to detect whether collisions and merging occurred in gravitational wave signals of different interval lengths, which also indirectly explains the neural network model can handle signal data streams of any length. At the same time, we also found that the CNN model can be automatically generalized to gravitational wave signal data with different noise types.

The related work is introduced in Sect. 2. The design of network structure is in Sect. 3. The data used in the experiment and the model training and testing process are shown in Sect. 4. Conclusions and future problems to be solved are presented in Sect. 5.

2   Related Work

Nowadays, many sensor cloud related studies use datasets that contain noises. Many methods are used in detection and analysis tasks to improve task performance [9–11].

2.1   Voice Recognition and Gas Monitoring

In [9], the paper by Jin Hong et al. presents a piezoelectric sensor-based speech recognition system to address the noise interference in conventional speech acquisition and recognition tasks. They use an FPGA-controlled ADC to acquire the speech data and transmit it to the computer via UART, then trim the data to get the pronunciation data and perform a short-time Fourier transform to get the time-domain and frequency-domain information of the data, then perform principal component analysis to reduce the dimensionality of the data and get the feature vector, and finally do a linear discriminant analysis to classify the data. In [10], Zhiyu Wang et al. use a hybrid filtering scheme based on median filtering and wavelet threshold filtering to process the noise in the gas monitoring sensor signal and improve the reliability of the monitoring signal.

2.2   Astronomical Wave Signal

In astrophysics, in order to improve the performance of gravitational wave signal monitoring systems, initially researchers used matched filtering techniques on the gravitational wave signals detected by the sensors. To extract useful information from noise-containing signals, the method is continuously matched and compared to more than 300,000 template signals during the detection process [12]. In this process, even though we can use the current advanced computer hardware equipment, it still takes a lot of time. Therefore, it would be impractical to use match filtering for detection in a signal database with a comprehensive wave source parameter space.

In recent years, machine learning techniques have begun to help solve the problem of mining useful information in mixed gravitational wave signals, and a series of research results have been widely presented. As a subset of machine learning, deep learning can solve specific problems by end-to-end learning input data and specific tags using neural networks simulating the human brain [13]. Once trained, the deep learning model can quickly analyze the data and draw inferences using few computational resources, with detection speeds typically in the millisecond time scale. At the same time, deep learning technology has a good generalization ability. The matched filtering technology usually can not detect the gravitational wave signal of wave source parameters outside the template library. However, after the deep learning model trains part of the gravitational wave data of wave source parameters, it can also infer the wave of untrained parameter space well during the detection, which indicates that the generalization learning has learned the waveform outside the distribution feature information. Deep learning is expected to become a popular method to deal with big data and analysis problems.

Daniel George and E. A. Huerta [3] proposed two neural network models, which can detect signals with a peak power that is significantly weaker than background noise and can also predict the quality of two black holes. Experimental results show that this deep filtering technique is significantly better than traditional machine learning techniques, and achieves similar performance while being several orders of magnitude faster than matched filtering.

The neural network classifiers proposed by Xilong Fan and Jin Li et al. [14] can effectively identify gravitational wave signals mixed in noise with different signal-noise ratios (SNRs). The predictor they designed can predict the spatial parameters of the gravitational wave source, including the luminosity distance, right ascension, and declination of the compact binary star mergers, The relative error is less than 23%.

3   Network Structure Design

In this paper, hyper-parameters of the neural network, such as the number of network layers, convolutional kernel size, step size, learning rate, cost function, activation function, etc., are determined after rounds of experiments using the randomized trial method. These optimal parameters ensure that the network learns better in an iterative manner. The Adam optimization algorithm is used in this paper to train the network due to its advantages such as small memory requirement and suitability for solving problems containing very high noise levels [15]. The loss function is the cross entropy loss function of the binary classification task, defined as:

$$L = -\frac{1}{m} \sum_{i=1}^{m} (y_i log a_i + (1 - y_i) log(1 - a_i)) \qquad (1)$$

where y_i and a_i represent real and predicted values for the ith training input data set and m is the size of the training dataset.

In a neural network, each channel of the feature map after convolution and pooling operations can be interpreted as a kind of feature detector, and considering the individual channel features together can help us identify what the input data is. Although each channel represents a portion of the input data, they have different levels of importance. In this paper, the positive sample is intercepted near the merge time, the pure signal wave shows a gradual increase to the peak and then suddenly drops to zero trends, mixed with noise in the signal will still potentially contain such features, will be shown in the network in a layer of a channel feature map, just for the channel feature map to give a high attention weight can do better identification. To effectively assign corresponding attention to each channel of the feature map, a channel attention module is proposed. We added a channel attention module after the convolutional layer in the network, which is leveraged from the network design ideas in the Convolutional Block Attention Module (CBAM) paper [16]. The module structure is shown in the Fig. 2.

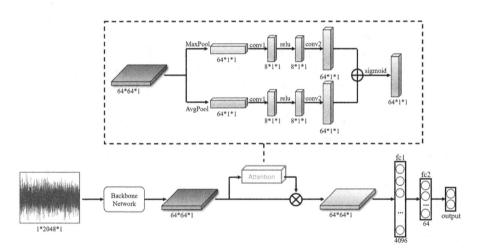

Fig. 2. This is an overview of the channel attention module. The feature maps extracted from the backbone network are automatically assigned different weight coefficients for different channels through the channel attention network, and then multiplied with the original feature map to achieve the purpose of attention distribution.

The convolutional feature map aggregates the spatial information through max-pooling and average-pooling operations, then performs convolution and Relu activation operations on the two aggregated information, and finally uses element-wise summation to generate the corresponding attention coefficients for each channel. The specific formula is as follows:

$$M_c(F) = \sigma(conv2(Relu(conv1(AvgPool(F)))) \\ + conv2(Relu(conv1(MaxPool(F)))))$$
(2)

where σ denotes the sigmoid function. In *conv*1 and *conv*2 operations, the change in the number of channels is C→C/8→C, and the stride is 1.

In the experiment, it was found that after adding the channel attention module, the classification effect of the neural network performs poorly. It is partially caused by the input data being relatively simple. If the model is too complicated, a mismatch will occur. So in the follow-up experiments, we removed the attention module and only used the ordinary neural network structure.

Table 1. The input is one section of waveform 16384 Hz sampling frequency. For classification, we simply added a softmax layer after the 15th layer to obtain the probabilities for two classes. The number of convolution kernels is 16, 32, 64. The convolution kernel sizes of the top seven networks are 17×1, 9×1, 7×1, and the convolution kernel sizes of the last network are 11×1, 7×1, 5×1. In this paper, we choose the maxpool, and the pooling layers kernel size is 4. The stride is 1 for all of the convolution layers and 4 for all of the pooling layers. At the same time, batch normalization is performed before convolution, and a padding operation is added to the convolution.

Input	vector	vector	vector	vector	vector	vector	vector	vector
reshape	1*2048*1	1*1024*1	1*512*1	1*256*1	1*128*1	1*64*1	1*32*1	1*16*1
conv	16*2048*1	16*1024*1	16*512*1	16*256*1	16*128*1	16*64*1	16*32*1	16*16*1
maxpool	16*512*1	16*256*1	16*128*1	16*64*1	16*32*1	16*16*1	16*8*1	16*8*1
relu	16*512*1	16*256*1	16*128*1	16*64*1	16*32*1	16*16*1	16*8*1	16*8*1
conv	32*512*1	32*256*1	32*128*1	32*64*1	32*32*1	32*16*1	32*8*1	32*8*1
maxpool	32*128*1	32*64*1	32*32*1	32*32*1	32*16*1	32*8*1	32*4*1	32*4*1
relu	32*128*1	32*64*1	32*32*1	32*32*1	32*16*1	32*8*1	32*4*1	32*4*1
conv	64*128*1	64*64*1	64*32*1	64*32*1	64*16*1	64*8*1	64*4*1	64*4*1
maxpool	64*64*1	64*32*1	64*16*1	64*16*1	64*8*1	64*4*1	64*2*1	64*2*1
relu	64*64*1	64*32*1	64*16*1	64*16*1	64*8*1	64*4*1	64*2*1	64*2*1
flatten	4096	2048	1024	1024	512	256	128	128
linear layer	64	64	64	64	64	64	64	64
relu	64	64	64	64	64	64	64	64
linear layer	2	2	2	2	2	2	2	2
output	2	2	2	2	2	2	2	2

A total of eight neural networks were built in this experiment, which was used to determine whether a collisional merger of gravitational waves occurred at different sample lengths. The modified version of the model in [3] used for classification. Table 1 shows the optimal network structure used in this paper, with each neural network including three convolutional layers and two fully connected layers. Using the Relu activation function, the derivative is better solved than sigmoid and tanh, which can effectively prevent gradient disappear. The output layer uses the softmax function, which is typically used for classification tasks and map the output to the (0, 1) interval. It corresponds to a probability value belonging to a certain category.

4   Experiments

4.1   Obtaining Training and Test Data

A typical gravitational wave goes through three phases: the inspiral, merge, and ringdown. The purpose of this experiment is to obtain accurate merge time. This paper generates mixed signals of gravitational waves on sensor clouds to be studied with reference to the advanced LIGO-Hanford, advanced LIGO-Livingston, and advanced Virgo detectors, respectively. One sample is shown in Fig. 3.

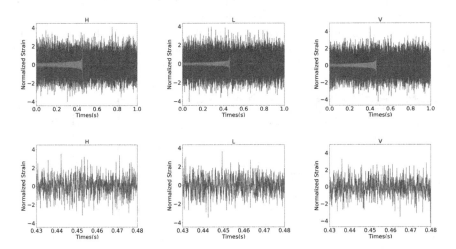

Fig. 3. *Top* : They are data from three different detectors. The blue curve is the simulation time series of LIGO gravitational wave mixed with Gaussian noise, and it is also the input of the neural network model in this paper. The orange curve is the pure gravitational wave signal. *Bottom* : Amplify waves in small areas near merge time. (Color figure online)

The gravitational wave signal monitored on the laser interferometer sensor array is mathematically formulated as:

$$h(t) = F^+(t)h_+(t) + F^\times(t)h_\times(t) \tag{3}$$

where the $h_{+,\times}$ is the two polarization modes of the gravitational wave, and $F^{+,\times}$ is the corresponding response function. There is a detailed description of this equation in [17,18], including information on detector position and detector arm orientation. Assume that the mass $m1$ and $m2$ of two neutron stars are uniformly selected in the range from 1.3 to 1.5 M_{sun}. The luminosity distance D is uniformly selected in the range from 10 to 50 Mpc (Galaxy distance). The simulated waves are randomly placed in the time series. Each wave is continuously sampled 16384 Hz for 1s. The gravitational wave merge time is evenly distributed within the (0.3, 0.5), and each detector has a time delay based on the spatial location of the advanced LIGO and the advanced VIRGO (cf. Table 1 of [19]). To achieve the same effect as the real data on the sensor cloud, we add some degree of Gaussian white noise to the gravitational wave signals.

Supervised learning, as a subset of deep learning, requires train and test datasets to be end-to-end accessible [13]. The train dataset allows the network to iteratively learn weights and biases that satisfy the minimum loss, and the test dataset is used to evaluate the performance of the network [20]. To make the neural network model learn the characteristics of waves in a balanced way, 12,000 training samples are generated by random simulation using MATLAB program. Among them, the positive sample is a fixed interval signal including the merging time, and the negative sample randomly intercepts the same interval signal in the remaining interval, each with 6000. Finally, randomly generate 1800 test waves to verify the experimental effect.

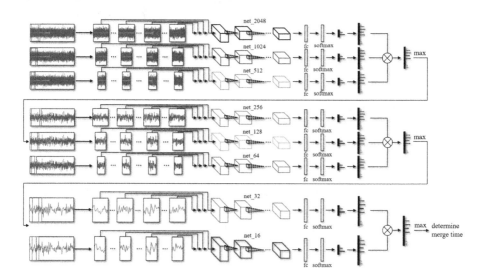

Fig. 4. The whole process of data from input to output. The sliding window strategy is used to gradually intercept different interval lengths in the input signal and send them to the corresponding network for detection and finally determine the merge time.

4.2   Experimental Details

In the first step, we used a sliding window strategy with a step size of 1 in a time series of 1×16384, continuously intercept waves of 2048, 1024, and 512 lengths and send them to the corresponding neural network (net_2048, net_1024, net_512) to detect, determine whether there is gravitational wave merge in this interval length. Then perform a fusion (multiplication operation) of the probability values of the three detection results to find the maximum value in the fusion result, map it to the original waveform and intercept a waveform of 1024 length interval. At this time, the interval segment is most likely to merge with the two neutron stars relative to the total interval segment. In the second step, we use the same sliding window detection strategy as the first step on the 1×1024 sequence intercepted just now, and continuously intercept the 256, 128, and 64 length waves and send them to the corresponding neural network (net_256, net_128, net_64) for detection. The results are fused again, and the maximum value is found in the result and mapped back to the original waveform. At this time, the 128 length waveform is intercepted, and the interval section where the merge occurs is reduced again. Finally, on the 128 length waveform intercepted in the previous step, the 32, 16 length waves are continuously intercepted and sent to the corresponding neural network (net_32, net_16) for detection, the detection results are fused, at which time the maximum probability value of the filtered mapped back to the original waveform is two neutron star merger time. The overall process is shown in Fig. 4.

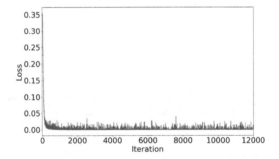

Fig. 5. The loss function of model net_2048 after small batch input data.

In the model version used in this article, the learning rate is set to 0.0001. We use NVIDIA GPU (Gtx 1080ti) to train the model. After 50 epochs of training, the loss of each classification task is close to zero. A model's loss function curve after each input of small-batch data during the training process is shown in Fig. 5, and other models are similar.

After testing 1800 test samples, the absolute error is shown in Fig. 6. The detection results of a sample at different stages are shown in Fig. 7. It can be seen from the figures that the fusion probability curves at different stages can well predict the merge time, and the highest probability value can basically correspond to the gravitational wave merge time. The average absolute error is 0.003.

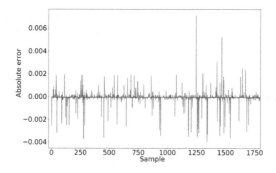

Fig. 6. Absolute error of prediction on test set.

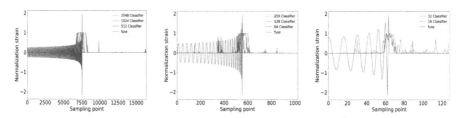

Fig. 7. The detection results at different stages. The blue curve in the left picture shows the initial gravitational wave signal without noise, and the value at each point of the other color curves represents the probability value of the two neutron star merger within a certain length from that point onward. For example, the probability value at each point of the yellow curve in the left figure indicates whether merging occurs in the 2048 length waveform is intercepted forward at this point. The purple curve in the left picture represents the probability value after the fusion of the three detection results, and the blue curve in the middle picture represents the interval where the merger event is most likely to occur in the initial waveform corresponding to the highest probability value in the left picture. In the end, the highest point of fusion probability in the right picture indicates the time when the two neutron stars merged. (Color figure online)

5   Conclusions and Future Works

This paper is dedicated to solving the influence of noise in the cloud sensor big data processing. We take the problem of gravitational wave signal parameter prediction as an example, combined with deep learning technology, innovatively carry out an accurate prediction of merging time in gravitational wave signals mixed with noise. Experimental results show that the model can extract useful information from noise-containing mixed signals, and then infer the accurate combination time. Also, this method greatly reduces the amount of calculation compared with matched filtering technology, so once the model is trained, it takes very little time to make the detection, and the accuracy is very high.

To verify the core strategy, the data set selected in this experiment is relatively simple, resulting in extremely fast loss convergence during model training. After proving the rationality of the experimental method, we will conduct tests on more complex data sets in the future. In the future, the research object will turn to gravitational wave signals that exist in all three stages (inspiral, merge, and ringdown) and mix them with various SNR noises. Analyzing and predicting waveform parameters that are closer to the actual situation is crucial to the development of sensor cloud data.

References

1. Wang, T., et al.: A comprehensive trustworthy data collection approach in sensor-cloud system. IEEE Trans. Big Data, 1 (2018)
2. Wang, T., Luo, H., Jia, W., Liu, A., Xie, M.: MTES: an intelligent trust evaluation scheme in sensor-cloud-enabled industrial internet of things. IEEE Trans. Ind. Inf. **16**(3), 2054–2062 (2019)
3. George, D., Huerta, E.A.: Deep neural networks to enable real-time multimessenger astrophysics. Phys. Rev. D **97**(4), 044039 (2018)
4. George, D., Shen, H., Huerta, E.A.: Deep transfer learning: a new deep learning glitch classification method for advanced LIGO. ArXiv:1706.07446 (2017)
5. George, D., Huerta, E.A.: Deep learning for real-time gravitational wave detection and parameter estimation: results with advanced LIGO data. Phys. Lett. B **778**, 64–70 (2018)
6. Shen, H., George, D., Huerta, E., et al.: Glitch classification and clustering for LIGO with deep transfer learning. APS **L01–027**, 2018 (2018)
7. Shen, H., George, D., Huerta, E.A., Zhao, Z: Denoising gravitational waves using deep learning with recurrent denoising autoencoders. ArXiv:1711.09919 (2017)
8. Li, X., Yu, W., Fan, X.: A method of detecting gravitational wave based on time-frequency analysis and convolutional neural networks. ArXiv:1712.00356 (2017)
9. Hong, J., Chen, X.: Piezoelectric ceramics voice recognition system for vocal cord vibrations. Microcontrollers Embed. Syst. Appl. **20**(7), 56–59,64 (2020)
10. Wang, Z., Xu, B.: Application of a hybrid filter method based on median filter and wavelet transform for propellant monitoring. J. Naval Aviat. Eng. Coll. **35**(2), 211–216 (2020)
11. Wang, T., Ke, H., Zheng, X., Wang, K., Sangaiah, A.K., Liu, A.: Big data cleaning based on mobile edge computing in industrial sensor-cloud. IEEE Trans. Ind. Inf. **16**(2), 1321–1329 (2019)
12. Usman, S.A., et al.: The PyCBC search for gravitational waves from compact binary coalescence. Class. Quantum Gravity **33**(21), 215004 (2016)
13. LeCun, Y., Bengio, Y., Hinton, G.: Deep learning. Nature **521**(7553), 436–444 (2015)
14. Fan, X.L., Li, J., Li, X., Zhong, Y.H., Cao, J.W.: Applying deep neural networks to the detection and space parameter estimation of compact binary coalescence with a network of gravitational wave detectors. Sci. China Phys. Mech. Astron. **62**(6), 1–8 (2019). https://doi.org/10.1007/s11433-018-9321-7
15. Kingma, D.P., Ba, J.: Adam: a method for stochastic optimization. ArXiv:1412.6980 (2014)
16. Woo, S., Park, J., Lee, J.-Y., So Kweon, I.: Cbam: convolutional block attention module. In Proceedings of the European conference on computer vision (ECCV), pp. 3–19 (2018)
17. Cutler, C., Flanagan, E.E.: Gravitational waves from merging compact binaries: how accurately can one extract the binary's parameters from the inspiral waveform? Phys. Rev. D **49**(6), 2658 (1994)

18. Jaranowski, P., Krolak, A.: Data analysis of gravitational-wave signals from spinning neutron stars: the signal and its detection. Phys. Rev. D **58**(6), 063001 (1998)
19. Schutz, B.F.: Networks of gravitational wave detectors and three figures of merit. Class. Quantum Gravity **28**(12), 125023 (2011)
20. Schmidhuber, J.: Deep learning in neural networks: an overview. Neural Networks **61**, 85–117 (2015)

Data Prediction Service Model Based on Sequential Pattern Mining in Sensor-Cloud

Gaocai Wang$^{(\boxtimes)}$, Hengyi Huang$^{(\boxtimes)}$, and Ruijie Pan$^{(\boxtimes)}$

School of Computer and Electronic Information, Guangxi University,
Nanning 530004, China
wanggcgx@163.com, mhx-y@163.com, 457934228@qq.com

Abstract. With the development of cloud computing and Internet of Things, they gradually merged together to form a new system called sensor-cloud. Aiming at the characteristics of Sensing-as-a-Service of sensor-cloud, this paper studies the features of sensing data, a data mining schedule is introduced into data processing and transmission during the service process in sensor-cloud. A sequential pattern mining algorithm is used to predict data sequences that appear more frequently during the service period. By providing prediction data to system user, energy consumption would be saved, and service time would be reduced. We propose a patterns mining and matching scheme that is suitable for sensor-cloud system. By generating predicted data in different tasks to match the existing sensed data with sequential patterns, the prediction model provides a scheme for task migration in sensor-cloud. Simulate result shows that our model is quiet effective in sensor-cloud. It can reduce energy consumption and improve response time under a high accuracy.

Keywords: Sensor-cloud · Sequential patterns mining · Data prediction · Network service

1 Introduction

In recent years, with the connection between the network and the real world, people tend to use Wireless Sensor Network (WSN) to interact network with reality. Although WSN has been widely used in the last decades, its potential has not been fully realized [1]. WSN have many similarities with other distributed systems, they also face various special challenges and constraints that affect the design of WSNs. The biggest constraint is the limited energy budget of the sensor nodes. Usually, a sensor node is powered by a battery. When the energy is exhausted, the battery must be replaced or recharged. For some nodes, neither of these options is appropriate, which means that once the energy is ran out, the node will be discarded [2].

The physical nodes in the WSN are often connected to the manager's IT system. Only applications with IT systems can freely manage the physical nodes of the sensor, that is, existing WSN is basically only work for one or a group of fixed Users, which wastes a lot data collected by these WSNs [3]. These weaknesses limit the application prospects of WSN, and this is why people are trying to combine WSN and cloud computing. Cloud computing has increased the utility of devices. One can make

© Springer Nature Switzerland AG 2021
G. Wang et al. (Eds.): SpaCCS 2020, LNCS 12383, pp. 281–293, 2021.
https://doi.org/10.1007/978-3-030-68884-4_24

decisions and calculations through the cloud, now is sensing services. A sensor network integrated with cloud computing can serve multiple users simultaneously. It also process and utilize data more efficiently than traditional WSN. The location-independent feature of sensor-cloud makes it easy for users to use the sensing cloud system to serve themselves. Since the introduction of the sensor cloud, there have been many branch research fields, including theoretical modeling, service quality, reliability, etc. [4].

In 2010, Yuriyama M. et al. [5] proposed the concept of a sensor-cloud systematically, and gave its basic structure. Since then, it has been formally paid attention to as a research topic. This paper attempts to make use of sensed data collected by sensor-cloud in terms of sequential pattern mining, we can find the data sequences that always appears during services and use these patterns to prediction future data sequences. In some certain scenarios, replacing sensed data with predicted data can prevent the sensor network form uploading a large amount of data. By matching sensed data with sequence pattern set and selecting the best sequential pattern, predicted data can be generated according to the best matched sequential pattern.

2 Related Works

Recently, many researches focus on sensor-cloud, including its infrastructure and servicemodelc [6–8]. The concept of Sensing-as-a-service(S2aaS) infrastructure was formally proposed by Yuriyama M. and Lushida [8]. It aims to provide real-time sensor services to multiple end-users.

Many studies try to optimize its service process to reduce energy consumption. There are three main directions for optimizing the service process in sensor cloud: network infrastructure optimizing, virtual sensor provisioning and data processing. Since 2011, many researchers focus on the first two directions, for example, In [9], the researchers proposed the concept of sensor network sharing based on the multi-user characteristics of the sensor cloud, and introduced the specific framework of multi-application shared sensor networks implemented by middleware; [10] presented a dynamic virtual sensor provisioning scheme for sensor-cloud-based IoT applications, in which the QoS is taken into account for the first time. In [11], a method for measuring valid data and system reliability in the integration model of WSN and MCC is proposed, and a more reliable integration strategy TPSS for acquiring valid data is proposed. It consists of a time and period based data transmission strategy and a sleep strategy algorithm. In [12], the author uses zero-sum game model to study the selection of the gateway in the sensor cloud system and use it for health data monitoring. S. Chatterjee proposed a distributed framework BSCI for sensor-data storage, processing, virtualization, leveraging and efficiently remote management[13]. Recently, some intelligence approach have been introduced into sensor cloud. [14] uses a high-performance approach based on the Max-Min Ant System in sensor cloud to manage its task scheduling. Wang T designed a mobile edge computing-based intelligent trust evaluation scheme is proposed to comprehensively evaluate the trustworthiness of sensor nodes using probabilistic graphical model [15]. These method have taken data size into account, but the historical sensed data has not been fully used In previous studies.

The use of data analysis and processing technology in sensor cloud is a new trend. Some individuals have performed some researches on data processing and prediction in WSN. S. Samarah proposed a prediction model of WSN which is designed for sending a large amount of data and reduces the energy consumption of the sensor's battery, the prediction model is managed to formulate as a line equation through two n-dimensional vectors in n-space [16]. Mou Wu built a novel framework with dedicated combination of data prediction, compression and recovery to simultaneously achieve accuracy and efficiency of the data processing in clustered WSNs [17]. In [18], a data-aware energy conservation technique ARIMA is proposed, and it is constructed by the CH node and is communicated to the cluster nodes.

The most effective method to reduce data transmission in WSN is data prediction. The data prediction scheme is used to generate prediction data, and the prediction data is used to replace actual sensor data to avoid the energy consumption and bandwidth occupied by data transmission [14]. In the process of sensing cloud services, most of the data is not very interesting to users. Many users only care about peak data or abnormal data [17]. In this case, the sequential pattern is used to predict the possible large Part of the usual data is provided to users with predicted data instead of actual sensor data, which can save the energy consumption of the sensor network, improve the responsiveness of the system, and not easily miss the data that users are really interested in. So, it is a very wise choice to design a data prediction model for sensor-cloud, especially using sequential pattern mining technology [19].

In fact, since the sensor cloud is much larger than the scale and scalability of WSN, it is very promising to build a data prediction model in the framework of the sensor cloud. Most of the current researches on sensor cloud only use middle-layer nodes to schedule and manage the WSN, so as to achieve the purpose of system optimization. Few researchers start from the collection, analysis and processing of sensor data. Compared to sensor networks with limited energy and computing capabilities, cloud server is a better choice for data processing.

3   Data Prediction Method in Sensor-Cloud

3.1   Sequential Pattern Mining Scheme

We propose a sequential pattern mining scheme that is suitable for sensor-cloud. It uses the data sequence that collected by WSN in the early stage of service to predict the possible data in current service. The first thing of our method is to get some qualified sequential patterns from the historical data set of sensor-cloud. But it is not necessary to compare and match each bit of data, because two identical data sequences hardly exist, especially when the collected data is non-integer. Therefore, it is necessary to introduce an allowable error range to determine whether the two data series are similar (Table 1).

Table 1. Table of notation

Parameters	Values	Parameters	Values
D_s	Sets of Sensed data	T_s	Service time of current user request
k	Error range in Sequential patterns mining	E_s	Error-tolerant rate in matching sensed data and sequential patterns
l_0	Length of max Sequential pattern	E_m	Error-tolerant rate in mining sequential patterns
N	Numbers of history service requests	**EditDist** (s_1, s_2)	Edit distance between data sequence s_1 and s_2
S_p	Sequential patterns		

In order to facilitate the work of data prediction, we introduce the concept of k-error subsequences in sequence data. The k error subsequence is a sequence whose edit distance from a certain subsequence in the sequence data is less than a threshold k. By using k-error subsequences, data prediction can be performed on a larger scale with less data. The k error subsequences can also be used to accurately extract and describe the more critical and prominent data in the sequence data. Actually, the introduction of the k error subsequence is to add a window length restriction to the sequence pattern, so that the length covered by the sequence pattern in the sequence cannot exceed a certain threshold. If a sequence s_2 is a subsequence of sequence s_1, the two sequences should satisfy the following relationship.

$$\text{EditDist}(s_1, s_2) = l_{s1} - l_{s2} < k * \max(l_{s1}, l_{s2}) \tag{1}$$

The above formula can be equivalent to the following proposition: one sequence contains all elements of the shorter sequence in sequence in order, and the length difference between the two sequences does not exceed k.

When performing sequential pattern mining in a sensor-cloud system, the characteristics of the sensed data collected by the system need to be considered. This paper uses a variable threshold can be calculated by the length of the data sequence of the service record and the length of the sequence used for matching. This threshold reflects the proportion of the sequence used for matching in the entire data set. In order to eliminate unnecessary sequence pattern mining, this paper defines the longest sequence pattern l_0. The support threshold s of the k-error subsequence defined in this paper is as follows.

$$s > knl_0 \frac{1}{l} \tag{2}$$

Here, l is the length of the currently matched sequence.

Besides, it is necessary to specify the maximum sequential pattern length l_0, because the mining of longer sequential patterns is not practical and energy-friendly. The chance of using sequential patterns to predict data is low, as well as its accuracy rate of prediction. So one should avoid mining long sequential patterns when mining patterns in a big dataset. The formula 3 gives the method of calculating the length of the longest sequential pattern in the sensor cloud in this paper,

$$l_0 = \frac{\sum_1^n l(r_i)}{n} * k = \bar{l} * k \tag{3}$$

Theorem 1: According to the standard of (3), if the sequential pattern of $[d_1, d_2, \ldots d_n]$ does not exist in the data set, the threshold of mining in current sequential pattern of $[d_1, d_2, \ldots, d_n, d_{n+1}]$ is $\frac{kn\bar{l}}{l^2+l}$.

Proof: if data sequence s_1 is not a sequential pattern, let $freq(s)$ be the frequency of data sequence s in dataset, then,

$$freq(s_1) < kn\bar{l}\frac{1}{l} \tag{4}$$

Then, for data sequence $[s_1, d_i]$,

$$freq([s_1, d_i]) \leq kn\bar{l}\frac{1}{l} \tag{5}$$

If $[s_1, d_i]$ meet the threshold of a sequential pattern, then we have

$$freq([s_1, d_i]) \in \left[kn\bar{l}\frac{1}{l+1}, kn\bar{l}\frac{1}{l}\right] \tag{6}$$

The length of this interval is $\frac{kn\bar{l}}{l^2+l}$.

for every data d_s in dataset, its range of frequency is

$$freq(d_s) \in \left[0, \frac{n\bar{l}}{l d_s}\right] \tag{7}$$

Assuming that the data d_i obeys the historical distribution $f(d_i)$ with the upper and lower limits of the historical data set $[d_{min}, d_{max}]$, and the error range of E_m is tolerated when comparing the data, the probability distribution of any possible data d_i is

$$F(d_i) = \int_{d_i - E_m}^{d_i + E_m} f(x)dx \tag{8}$$

Then for the sequence $[s_1, d_i]$ the requirements of the sequential pattern can be simplified to solve the probability of $\frac{kn\bar{l}}{l^2+l}d_i$s in freq($s_1$)data, calculated in the form of binomial distribution as follows

$$P\left(freq([s_1, d_i]) > kn\bar{l}\frac{1}{l+1}\right) = \sum_{j=\frac{kn\bar{l}}{l^2+l}}^{freq(s_1)} \binom{freq(s_1)}{j} F(d_i)^j \cdot (1 - F(d_i))^{freq(s_1)-j} \tag{9}$$

In the best situation, that is, when freq(s_1) is very close to the sequential pattern threshold, approximate it to the threshold $knl\frac{1}{l}$, then the ratio required by the above formula is $\frac{1}{l+1}$, which means that In the sequence $[s_1, d_i]$ that satisfies the critical condition of the sequential pattern, if one of the ratio of d_i value reaches $\frac{1}{l+1}$, the sequence can be considered as a sequential pattern. In extreme cases, if the length of the sequential pattern reaches the average length $\bar{l}$ of the historical data set, all sequences prefixed with this sequential pattern will be recognized as sequential patterns. The value of k can be adjusted to control the growth rate of this ratio.

In the worst case, freq(s_1) is too small, so that the requirements of sequential pattern can not be meet even if all d_i take the same value, in these cases we have

$$freq(s_1) < \frac{kn\bar{l}}{l^2 + l} \tag{10}$$

In order to improve the efficiency of sequential pattern mining, when the support of a certain sequence is less than this value, the algorithm will skip this sequence directly and no longer use it as a prefix for mining.

The sequential pattern mining algorithm used in this paper can be used to update the sequential pattern in the service process. Each time a new data sequence is generated, it can be stored in a cloud server and new sequence patterns can be mined in the entire data set. With the continuous progress of the service, all the sequential pattern sets in the cloud server will be continuously updated, so that the data prediction can achieve better results.

Algorithm 1 SP Mining in Sensor-Cloud service

Input: D_t , k, l_0, n

Output: S_p

Begin

  $i = 0$

  While $i < l(D_t)$

    $D_s = \{\}$

    If $l(S) < l_0$

      $D_s = \{D_s, D_t(i)\}$

    Else $D_s = \{\}$

    Calculate S of D_s by Formula (1)

    If $S < knl_0 \frac{1}{l(S)}$

    $S -> S_p$

    $i = i + 1$

  End While

End

Algorithm 1 is an algorithm for sequential pattern mining in the sensor cloud system. By calculating the support of each subsequence in the entire training data, it is determined whether to add the subsequence to the sequence pattern set. The algorithm specifies the allowable error k, the maximum allowable length l_0 of the sequence mode, and the length n of the training set. Mining sequential pattern can be used not only when the system starts a certain stage of service, but also can add the collected sensor data to the database in real time during the service process to update the sequence pattern. Updating the sequential pattern in real time during the service process can improve the timeliness of the sequence pattern set, thereby improving the accuracy of the prediction data. It can also enrich the content of the S_p, so that the prediction rate of the service can be improved as the service progresses.

When using k-error subsequences to mine sequential patterns, it also involves the problem of processing continuous data. Since the time series of two continuous data are almost impossible to be identical, anyone wants to mine sequential patterns needs to specify an allowable error range E_m. This margin of error should be derived from statistical characteristics in historical data.

$$\frac{2\left|S_{1(i)} - S_{2(i)}\right|}{\left(S_{1(i)} + S_{2(i)}\right)} < E_m \tag{11}$$

3.2 Prediction Model

To use sequential pattern to predict sensor data, an initial S_p must be created. Once the S_p met some certain conditions, like its size arrive a certain number, the prediction model will start working. In fact, these conditions can be determined by users and system owners themselves, the prediction model can get to work as long as the initial S_p is created, because S_p can be updated during the service. But a start with a rich S_p will improve the performance of the prediction model.

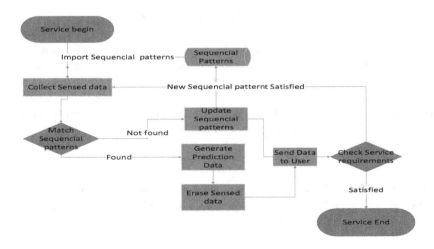

Fig. 1. Prediction process

Figure 1 shows the detailed workflow of the prediction model. Whenever a piece of data is uploaded by WSN, the system will match the existing data sequence with each sequential pattern in S_p. If no matching sequential pattern is found, the system will continue to collect sensed data and calculate the frequency of the current data sequence in the entire historical data set, try to update S_p. If a matching sequential pattern is found, a prediction data sequence will be generated and send to user, and all the data stored in middle node will be uploaded to cloud server, a new period of prediction will be started.

There are two supports need to be calculated. One is the support in common sense, and it indicates how frequently the sequential pattern is in the entire data set. The other is the probability support that the sensed data collected in the service may develop into a certain sequential pattern, called matching support. The calculation of matching support should depend on how often the sensed data appears in the entire data set and the support of the matched sequence pattern in the data set.

When a sequential patterns matching is performed, if a possible matching sequential pattern s_p is found, consider the possibility that current data sequence s will develop into s_p by calculating the frequency of s, then comparing it with $freq(s_p)$. The question is, if there is a sequential pattern that matches s, but the probability of s developing into that sequential pattern is low. In this situation, should the sink node upload s, or wait for the next packet to join the current data sequence and continue matching?

Consider using historical data to calculate the probability of s developing into s_p, then

$$P(s \rightarrow s_p) = \frac{freq(s_p)}{freq(s)} \tag{12}$$

if a new data has been added to s, then

$$P([s, d_i] \rightarrow s_p) = \frac{freq(s_p)}{freq([s, d_i])} = \frac{freq(s_p)}{freq(s) * P(d_i)} \geq P(s \rightarrow s_p) \tag{13}$$

This formula shows that when the newly added data d_i has a lower frequency in the dataset, the probability of data series developing into a sequential pattern is higher.

Assuming that the length of current matching sequential pattern is l_s, the number of sequential patterns in the current index is n_s, the data sequence length is l, the time delay of transmitting 1 bit of data is t_{tr}, and the time it takes to match 1 bit of data is t_m, then the service time reduced by the current match t_s is

$$t_s = l_s * t_{tr} - (n_s * t_m + t_{tr}) * l \tag{14}$$

Once $t_s \leq 0$, continuing to match will affect the speed of delivering data to users and reduce QoS. Therefore, these parameters need to be monitored and managed in real time during the matching process.

Algorithm 2 SP Matching in Sensor-Cloud Service

Input: $D_s(d_1, d_2, \ldots, d_i)$, S_p, E_s
Output: Matched SP
Begin
   Calculate l_0
   While receive new data d_i, do
     If $l(D_s) > l_0$
      $D_s = \{\ \}$
      Continue
     $D_s = \{D_s, d_i\}$
     For each SP in S_p
      Calculate matching score
      If matching score>Max matching score
       S_p ->BestMatch
     End for
     If Max matching score$< E_s$
      Continue
   End While

In the process of matching sequential patterns, each SP will get a matching score, and it helps us to select the best *SP*. The matching score is calculated according to current data sequence's length and edit distance between the *SP* and current data.

Algorithm 2 is an algorithm for sequential pattern matching in sensor cloud services. Once a sensed data is received, it is added to the current sequence to ensure that it is not greater than a length l_0, and then the sequence pattern set is matched. For each matched sequential pattern, a current matching support will be calculated, this support represents the credibility of the current data to develop into this sequence pattern.

4 Experiment Results

The prediction model proposed in this paper uses prediction data instead of sensor data, its purpose is to reduce the working time of the sensor network and avoid the upload of sensed data. In order to assess the proposed prediction model in sensor-cloud, a network with 100 nodes is deployed. The obtained results are depicted in below figures. We use a public database, UCR archive from the internet to test our prediction model. All the algorithms are implemented using MATLAB.

We consider a wireless sensor network consisting of 300 sensors deployed in a 100 m × 100 m rectangle region. This sensor-cloud model has 3 regions, they are managed by a cloud server, and send service request independently. We use different datasets and threshold to test our prediction model. As it can be seen in Fig. 3, our prediction model provides more prediction data when the data trend is flat. This feature can help sensor-cloud to save energy while not missing important data. With the increasing data size, our algorithm will produce more prediction data.

This experiment has three parts. The first part is to examine the impact of the training set on the prediction effect by adjusting the size of the training data set used for sequential pattern mining, and then inputting the same sensing task to the model. The second part is adjusting The matching threshold in the prediction process is used to examine the impact of input parameters on the prediction results; the third part is to insert and perform the same sensing task at different stages of the service process.By adjusting the value of l_0 and E_s, a balance can be achieved between prediction accuracy, energy consumption and prediction rate.

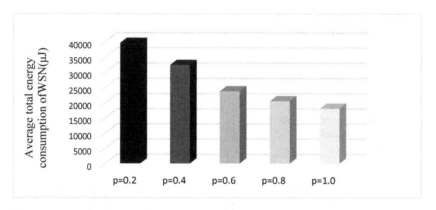

Fig. 2. Average total energy consumption of WSN

Figure 2 shows the average total energy consumption of WSN, including sensing energy consumption, transporting energy consumption and generating prediction data string consumption. P is the usage of our training dataset. It can be seen that energy consumption decrease.

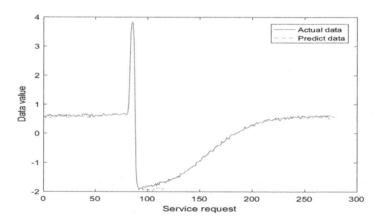

Fig. 3. Prediction result

In Fig. 3 a plot of prediction result is plotted. The graph is plotted for different type of services, the result shows that some regular data can be predicted more accurately, and abnormal data can be sensed and collected for users. As the S_p updated in real time, prediction rate and the actual service time are also change significantly.

Table 2. Prediction result under different matching threshold

SP matching threshold (%)	Prediction rate (%)	PA (%)
15	39.71	48.15
30	37.41	59.94
45	34.12	68.64
60	30.55	74.86
75	26.87	77.34
90	18.20	80.52

As we expected, Using a higher matching threshold to match sequential patterns can significantly increase the prediction accuracy during the service process, but the increasing of accuracy rate will slow down as the threshold increases. In some cases, the change of prediction rate is not very obvious, because as the amount of data increases, there may be some outdated sequential patterns in S_p set, which can no longer reflect the characteristics of the current data. The parameters used in the experiment and the results obtained are presented in Table 2.

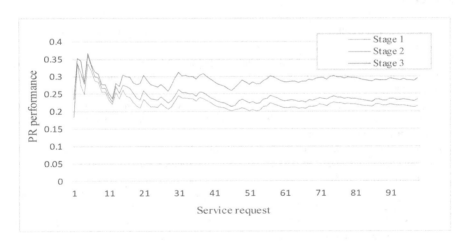

Fig. 4. PR performance in different stages of service

Figure 4 is a comparison chart of the PR results of the predictive model in different service stages, presented in the form of a percentage chart. In each sequential pattern matching threshold shown in Table 2, service process is divided into three stages, and each stage contains 100 service tasks. In order to test the effect of the real-time update of the sequence pattern set by the prediction model, 100 tasks were inserted into the first, second, and third stages of the service after the completion of the service, and the service status was observed. The results of comparison show that when the task is inserted into the later service stage, the PR will be significantly higher than the sensing task performed in the previous stage. This is because as the service progresses, more sequential patterns are added to the database to participate in data comparison, which created more opportunities for our algorithm to generate prediction data.

5   Conclusion and Future Works

We have shown that it is advantageous to use sequential patterns to predict data string in sensor-cloud, which can significantly reduce the total energy consumption maintaining a given level of prediction accuracy requirement. Specifically, we proposed a strategy of mining and matching sequential patterns in sensor-cloud to optimize the efficiency of the system by mining and storing sequential patterns in the cloud server. The proposed scheme can serve as an effective tool to achieve a desirable tradeoff between data accuracy and energy consumption at each node.

In the future work, the following research issues will be considered: 1) Parameters optimization of data processing in sensor cloud networks. 2) Multi-type nodes cooperation. It would be also interesting to consider the multi-type node case where more than one type of sensors can participant in sensor-cloud computing.

References

1. Hanson, M.A., Powell, H.C., Barth, A.T., et al.: Body area sensor networks: challenges and opportunities. Computer **42**(1), 58–65 (2009)
2. Kurschl, W., Beer, W.: Combining cloud computing and wireless sensor networks. In: International Conference on Information Integration & Web-based Applications & Services. ACM (2009)
3. Agrawal, A., Kaushal, S.: A study on integration of wireless sensor network and cloud computing: requirements, challenges and solutions. In: International Conference on Computer & Communication Technology (2015)
4. Parwekar, P.: From Internet of Things towards cloud of things. In: IEEE 2011 2nd International Conference on Computer and Communication Technology (ICCCT) - Allahabad, India, pp. 329–333 (2011)
5. Santos, I.L., Pirmez, L., Delicato, F.C., et al.: Olympus: the cloud of sensors. IEEE Cloud Comput. **2**(2), 48–56 (2015)
6. Misra, S., Chatterjee, S., Obaidat, M.S.: On theoretical modeling of sensor cloud: a paradigm shift from wireless sensor network. IEEE Syst. J. **11**, 1–10 (2014)
7. Madria, S., Kumar, V., Dalvi, R.: Sensor cloud: a cloud of virtual sensors. IEEE Softw. **31**(2), 70–77 (2014)
8. Yuriyama, M., Kushida, T.: Sensor-cloud infrastructure - physical sensor management with virtualized sensors on cloud computing. In: International Conference on Network-based Information Systems (2010)
9. Lim, Y., Park, J.: Sensor resource sharing approaches in sensor-cloud infrastructure. Int. J. Distrib. Sens. Netw. **1**, 1–8 (2014)

10. Ojha, T., Misra, S., Raghuwanshi, N.S., et al.: DVSP: dynamic virtual sensor provisioning in sensor-cloud-based internet of things. IEEE Internet Things J. **6**(3), 5265–5272 (2019)
11. Zhu, C., Sheng, Z., Leung, V.C.M., et al.: Toward offering more useful data reliably to mobile cloud from wireless sensor network. IEEE Trans. Emerg. Topics Comput. **3**(1), 84–94 (2015)
12. Misra, S., Chao, H.C., Tirkey, R., et al.: Optimal gateway selection in sensor–cloud framework for health monitoring. IET Wirel. Sensor Syst. **4**(2), 61–68 (2014)
13. Chatterjee, S., Roy, A., Roy, S.K., et al.: Big-sensor-cloud infrastructure: a holistic prototype for provisioning sensors-as-a-service. IEEE Trans. Cloud Comput. (99), 1–12 (2019)
14. Boveiri, H.R., Khayami, R., Elhoseny, M., et al.: An efficient Swarm-Intelligence approach for task scheduling in cloud- based internet of things applications. J. Ambient Intell. Humanized Comput. **10**(9), 3469–3479 (2019)
15. Wang, T., Luo, H., Jia, W., et al.: MTES: an intelligent trust evaluation scheme in sensor-cloud-enabled industrial internet of things. IEEE Trans. Ind. Inf. **16**(3), 2054–2062 (2020)
16. Samarah, S.: A data predication model for integrating wireless sensor networks and cloud computing. Procedia Comput. Sci. **52**, 1141–1146 (2015)
17. Wu, M., Tan, L., Xiong, N.: Data prediction, compression, and recovery in clustered wireless sensor networks for environmental monitoring applications. Inf. Sci. **329**, 800–818 (2016)
18. Diwakaran, S., Perumal, B., Vimala Devi, K.: A cluster prediction model-based data collection for energy efficient wireless sensor network. J. Supercomput. **75**(6), 3302–3316 (2018). https://doi.org/10.1007/s11227-018-2437-z
19. Lin, J.-W., Li, T., Pirouz, M., Zhang, J., Fournier-Viger, P.: High average-utility sequential pattern mining based on uncertain databases. Knowl. Inf. Syst. **62**(3), 1199–1228 (2019). https://doi.org/10.1007/s10115-019-01385-8

Statistical Method of Space Distribution for Riding Based on R-Tree Under Differential Privacy

Yubing Qiu, Jianping Cai, Lan Sun, Zhenzhen Zhang, and Yingjie Wu[✉]

School of Mathematics and Computer Science, Fuzhou University,
Fuzhou 350108, China
yjwu@fzu.edu.cn

Abstract. This paper outlines a proposal ,which was provided regional riding statistical data query, to address the high vacancy rate in taxis and the low matching rate between taxis and passengers. It proposed a statistical method of space distribution for riding based on R-tree under differential privacy (DBRTree-opt) combined with the information of reference dataset. First, several minimum bounding rectangles (MBRs) were generated through specific spatial distribution rules relating to regional statistic reference dataset as the basic unit of the R-tree index structure. Second, a spatial index structure of optimized R-tree was also designed to solve the problem of overlapping within the R-tree structure. Then, the optimized R-tree for information generation of reference data was applied to unpublished riding space data. Finally, combined with the publishing technology of differential privacy tree structure and consistency processing, the algorithm provided a statistical query related to riding region while ensuring privacy protection standards. The new approach was compared with traditional algorithms in assessing the accuracy of range counting queries in the release data. Experimental results showed that DBRTree-opt is more effective and feasible.

Keywords: Differential privacy · Optimized R-tree · Reference data · Regional statistics of riding · Two-dimensional dataset

1 Introduction

With the development of smart cities, the traffic data information of vehicles is continuously collected and mined for road planning and city construction. As the conventional way of people's daily travel, taxis have become an important part of the comprehensive transportation system of the city. The statistical data of taxis occupy a major position in the intelligent traffic data and taxi management systems. However, the current taxi management has problems, such as random parking of taxis and serious illegal occupation of roads, thus resulting in road congestion. Moreover, the increase in the number of trips of urban residents and the uneven distribution of passenger flow contribute to the difficulty in

© Springer Nature Switzerland AG 2021
G. Wang et al. (Eds.): SpaCCS 2020, LNCS 12383, pp. 294–309, 2021.
https://doi.org/10.1007/978-3-030-68884-4_25

"getting a taxi". At the same time, there is also a high vacancy rate of taxis. In the intelligent management of taxis, the statistical data of taxis play a crucial supporting role, and the regional statistical data of riders account for a significant part.

The statistics of taxi riders in a certain area can intuitively reflect the ride demand in the area. The relevant transportation departments can learn from such statistics and conduct reasonable traffic road planning strategies, such as providing dedicated taxi parking spaces in dense places and performing regular road inspections. Taxi drivers can choose their cruise area, which increases the load factor of taxis by accurately locating the dense space–time relationship of the source of passengers based on statistics. Residents can also directly choose their travel plans and riding areas based on statistics, thus avoiding waiting for a car or the difficulty of getting a taxi.

However, regional riding traffic statistics contain a large amount of personal privacy information. As shown in Fig. 1, once a hacker with relevant background knowledge obtains this data and mines its information, the specific loading and unloading location, time, and even travel trajectory data of the passenger will severely suffer from privacy leaking. Literature [20] proved that the uniqueness and regularity of human movement can be utilized to recover individual trajectories from the aggregated mobility data, with an accuracy between 73% and 91%. Therefore, the relevant departments should be strictly protected before releasing traffic statistics to further ensure the privacy security of people.

At present, many experts and scholars are studying data protection [17–19]. Compared with other [14–16] protection methods, differential privacy [6,7] technology is currently recognized as a model that provides strict privacy protection. The issue of regional passenger statistics is essentially the issue of regional statistics in two-dimensional space. The research on two-dimensional statistical data query based on differences in privacy mainly adopts the spatial segmentation method. In literature [5,23,24], a complete quadtree was used to partition two-dimensional spatial data, and tree nodes were optimized for operation, which effectively improved the query accuracy. However, a relatively high uniform assumption error was observed. In literature [12,13,22], uniform grid was used to divide two-dimensional spatial data. This method is simple and effective but ignored the sparsity of data distribution. The earliest literature [10] on the application of the protection of traffic track data publication with differential privacy used noise prefix tree to protect privacy, which realizes differential privacy trajectory publishing by aggregating trajectory data with a common prefix. In literature [3], the I-trajectory differential privacy protection model is proposed, and the user statistics of different locations on the infinite trajectory stream are released in real time through dynamic budget allocation via exponential decay. The literature [4] used aggregated mobile data publishing to design different differential privacy models to protect mobile data and established a post-processing mechanism to improve the data practicability by analyzing the different mobile characteristics of mobile users in the city during the day and night.

Fig. 1. Attack diagram.

Under the background of big data, a considerable amount of data has a certain regularity in spatial distribution. The published data sets provide an important reference to analyze the spatial distribution of data and will not involve the privacy of users, which can avoid malicious attacks by attackers. However, there is still room for improvement in the utilization of reference data sets in the current research methods of traffic spatial statistics under differential privacy.

Given the differences in taxi demand in various regions, such as large demand in shopping malls, hospitals, and other places, the number of passenger trips is affected by the demand, which shows the similar rules. And these rules can be shown by historical data or a certain scale of taxi data. Therefore, using historical data or taxi data of a certain scale as the reference data for the statistical spatial distribution of the number of riders in the analysis area is reasonable.

Using the reference data information to establish index structures for spatial divisions of unpublished data, the spatial distribution of reference data can be combined to conduct effective spatial division for unpublished data. Therefore, in combination with the reference data information of regional taxi passenger count statistics, this paper designs a statistical method of space distribution for riding based on R-tree under differential privacy (DBRTree-opt). First, the minimum bounding rectangle (MBR) is generated through the specific spatial distribution rules of the regional statistics reference dataset using the clustering algorithm as the basic unit of the R-tree [8] index structure. Second, an optimized spatial index structure of R-tree is proposed in this paper to solve the problem of overlapping spatial regions in traditional R-tree. Then, the optimized R-tree of the information generation of reference data is applied to the unpublished data, and space is divided for the published data. Finally, the differential privacy protection model is combined and the tree structure is adjusted to satisfy the consistent query constraint. The experimental results show that the algorithm proposed in this paper is effective and feasible.

2   Basic Knowledge and Definitions

Two-dimensional spatial data partitioning and publishing are the main forms of differential privacy spatial data publishing. This method mainly divides the data space by index structure and adds a count value attribute to each index region and add noise to it to meet the requirements of differential privacy protection.

2.1   Differential Privacy

Definition 1 ($\mathcal{E}$-Differential Privacy [7]). A privacy mechanism A can provide $\mathcal{E}$-differential privacy if and only if any two databases $D1$ and $D2$ differ on at most one record and for any possible output $O \in Range(A)$:

$$\Pr\left[A\left(D_1\right) = O\right] \le e^{\varepsilon} \times \Pr\left[A\left(D_2 = O\right)\right]. \tag{1}$$

where the possibility is taken over the randomness of A.

2.2   Basic Knowledge of Spatial Index Structure R-Tree

Minimun Bounding Rectangle (MBR). The minimum bounding rectangle refers to the smallest rectangle that can completely cover the space object in two-dimensional coordinates.

Definition 2 (Minimum Bounding Rectangle). A set of two-dimensional spatial points $L = \{l_1, l_2, \dots, l_n\}$, where $l_i = \langle l_i.x, l_i.y \rangle$, $l_i \in L$ is available for a rectangle m. The minimum boundary rectangle of m that meets point set L is presented as follows:

$$m = \{\text{boundx} : [xlow, xup], \text{boundy} : [ylow, yup]\}. \tag{2}$$

where:

$$xlow = \min_{i=1}^{n}(l_i.x), xup = \max_{i=1}^{n}(l_i.x), \\ ylow = \min_{i=1}^{n}(l_i.y), yup = \max_{i=1}^{n}(l_i.y). \tag{3}$$

$Area(m)$ represents the region bounded by the minimum boundary rectangle m.

The set of boundary rectangles is expressed as $\boldsymbol{M} = \{m_1, m_2, \cdots, m_n\}$, where m_i is the minimum boundary rectangle, and $i = 1, 2, ..., n$.

For all rectangles in the set M, the abscissa set and the ordinate sets are respectively represented as $M.X$ and $M.Y$:

$$\boldsymbol{M.X} = \{m_1.\text{boundx}, m_2.\text{boundx}, \cdots, m_n.\text{boundx}\},$$

$$\boldsymbol{M.Y} = \{m_1.\text{boundy}, m_2.\text{boundy}, \cdots, m_n.\text{boundy}\}.$$

Definition 3 (Rectangle Merge). For a rectangle m_k, assume that m_k is generated by merging multiple rectangles m_i ,expressed as $m_k = comb(m_1, m_2, ..., m_n)$ Of which:

$$m_k.\text{boundx} = \left[\min_{i=1}^{n}(m_i.\text{boundx.xlow}), \max_{i=1}^{n}(m_i.\text{boundx.xup})\right], \\ m_k.\text{boundy} = \left[\min_{i=1}^{n}(m_i.\text{boundy.ylow}), \max_{i=1}^{n}(m_i.\text{boundy.yup})\right]. \tag{4}$$

Basic Knowledge of R-Tree. R-tree, a kind of spatial index structure [8], is one of the most widely used algorithms in the spatial database index. All the leaf nodes of R-tree are located in the same layer, which is a highly balanced structure. R-tree uses the MBR of the space object for its approximation, leaves store the MBR of the space object, and intermediate nodes are generated by merging the boundary rectangles corresponding to low-level nodes. This algorithm allows the overlapping of rectangular regions represented by each node of each layer. When the R-tree index structure divides the two-dimensional space, the MBR can be constructed following the data distribution, and the unevenly distributed data can be reasonably divided. Therefore, the gathered spatial objects can be combined as early as possible. The principle of space division can efficiently divide data with uneven spatial distributions.

When $Maxfill$ denoted as the maximum number of records of a node in the R-tree, $Minfill$ is the minimum number of records of a node. Normally, $Minfill = Maxfill/2$ is taken.

R-tree is a dynamic index structure, and query operations can be performed simultaneously with insertion or deletion. Insertion and deletion only require the dynamic adjustment of the tree structure without re-indexing construction, which reflects that the structure has strong flexibility and adjustability.

2.3   Source of Error

The query region is set as Q when performing a region count query. If this query completely includes the divided index region u, then the count value of u is directly added to the query result $\tilde{Q}$. If Q and u partially intersected, assuming that the region data are uniformly distributed, then the count value T_i is estimated by the ratio of the intersecting area of the two and then added to the query result $\tilde{Q}$. The error between the estimated value T_i' and the true value T_i of the corresponding region is denoted as the uniform assumption error. Two kinds of errors affect the results of spatial region query: noise and uniform assumption errors.

Definition 4 (Noise Error [13]). A divided region P, combined with differential privacy technology with additional noise, is considered to obtain P'. The relative error of P' and P is called noise error, which is denoted as $NoiseErr(P)$:

$$\text{Noise Err(P)} =\mid C(P) - C(P') \mid . \tag{5}$$

where $C(P)$ is the initial count value of the region P, and $C(P')$ is the count value of region P after adding noise.

Definition 5 (Uniform Assumption Error [13]). The query region Q, which is used to obtain the divided region $\{P_1, P_2, ..., P_n\}$, satisfies $\bigcup_{i=1}^{n} P_i = Q$ and $P_i \cap P_j = \varnothing (\forall 1 \leq i < j \leq n)$. For each partition region, the true value is T_i, the estimated value obtained under the assumption of uniform distribution is T_i', and the error of the uniformity assumption is as follows:

$$\Delta_{\text{NonErr}} (Q) = \sum_{i=1}^{n} \left| T_i - T_i' \right|. \tag{6}$$

3   Statistical Method of Space Distribution for Riding Based on R-Tree Under Differential Privacy

For the two-dimensional data with a certain regularity in spatial distribution, this paper uses reference data information combined with the optimized R-tree index structure and divides the unpublished two-dimensional data. First, through the specific spatial distribution of the reference dataset of the passenger traffic area statistics, the clustering algorithm is utilized to cluster the scattered points in the set to generate several MBRs, which are used as the index unit to establish an optimized R-tree index structure. Then, the generated optimized R-tree structure is applied to the unpublished data for regional statistics, and the unpublished data are divided into data-independent space. Finally, the differential privacy tree structure publishing technology is combined, and the consistency constraints are adjusted.

3.1   Reference Data

Due to the differences in the demand for taxis in various regions, such as shopping malls, hospitals and other places, the demand is large, while the number of riding is affected by the demand. In terms of regional distribution, there is a similar rules of more passenger trips in shopping malls, hospitals and other places. And these patterns can be shown by a certain scale of taxi data.

Taking the statistical data set of the number of passengers for 4316 taxis in Shanghai on February 20, 2007 as an example, it is randomly divided into two groups of relatively equal size (distribution is shown in Fig. 2). Figure 2(a) represents the regional statistics of 2316 taxis, and Fig. 2(b) shows the regional statistics of another 2000 taxis. From the perspective of the spatial distribution of the data, the two data distributions display certain similarities. Of these two groups, one data set can be selected as the reference data, and combining the specific spatial distribution information of the reference data set, a reasonable spatial division can be obtained.

Therefore, it is feasible to use taxi data of a suitable scale as the reference data when analyzing the spatial distribution of regional statistical passenger data. As far as the spatial distribution of the regional statistical data for riders, an effective spatial distribution towards the statistical unpublished can be conducted on the basis of collecting a sufficient scale of taxi data information and its specific spatial distribution.

When using the information of the reference data to build an index structure to divide the space of the unpublished data, the spatial distribution of the data set can be specifically combined, thus resulting in a reasonable and effective spatial division of the unpublished data. This approach can also prevent the attacker from mining private information through the index structure.

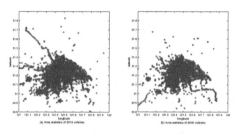

Fig. 2. Taxi area statistics.

For clustering data sets, if current two-dimensional spatial statistical data publishing models under differential privacy, such as Quadtree, UG, and AG algorithms, are directly used in the region of the non-aggregating segmentation, then a large number of empty nodes, that is, the nodes whose true count is 0, will be produced. These empty nodes not only consume the privacy budget but also affect the final release accuracy.

This paper adopts the most widely used spatial index structure R-tree of geographic information system to prevent excessive empty nodes in the spatial division of the regional passenger number statistics. The clustering algorithm is used to cluster the scattered points in the set to generate several MBRs by combining the specific distribution of the reference data of the regional statistics of riders. These MBRs are used as the index unit of the index structure R-tree to combine the data distribution in the spatial region, thus facilitating a reasonable and effective space division.

3.2   Optimized R-Tree Structure

The establishment of R-tree is the process of inserting rectangles continuously. Starting from the root node, we find the leaf node with the smallest "area" expansion of the rectangle after merging with the rectangle to be inserted, insert it into the leaf node and dynamically adjust the tree structure.

However, for R-trees, R*-trees, compressed R-trees, and other R-tree deformed data structures [1,2,11], most of them have the defect that brother node areas overlap each other. If these structures are directly combined with the differential privacy protection mechanism, then the overlapping area will be repeatedly added with privacy budgets. The differential privacy serial combination theorem [9] indicates that the division algorithm does not meet the $\mathcal{E}$-differential privacy, which results in serious privacy disclosure.

Figure 3(a) shows a set of MBR $M = \{a, b, c, e, f\}$. The set M is used to establish an index structure R-tree for region S for spatial segmentation, and $Maxfill$ and $Minfill$ are respectively set as 3 and $Maxfill/2$. The segmentation result and tree structure are shown in Fig. 3(b). The tree height h is 3, and an overlapping region is found in the space covered by rectangles (a and c), (f and g). Combined with the differential privacy tree structure publishing technology, the privacy budget $\frac{\varepsilon}{h}$ is added to the count value of each node of the tree, that is,

$\frac{\varepsilon}{3}$. The shaded part in Fig. 3 is q, and then $q \subset S \wedge q \subset g \wedge q \subset h \wedge q \subset a \wedge q \subset c$. Therefore, the privacy budget added to the region q is $5 \times \frac{\varepsilon}{3} > \varepsilon$. According to the differential privacy serial combination theorem, the partition algorithm does not meet the $\mathcal{E}$-differential privacy.

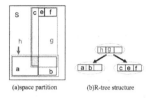

(a)space partition   (b)R-tree structure

Fig. 3. Space partition based of R-tree.

Therefore, before using index structure R-tree to divide the two-dimensional space, this paper optimizes it so that the rectangular frames corresponding to each node in the optimized R-tree structure do not overlap and cover each other, which is called optimized R-tree (RTree-opt).

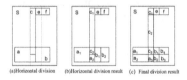

(a)Horizontal division   (b)Horizontal division result   (c) Final division result

Fig. 4. Rectangular division.

Take the spatial region S of Fig. 3 as an example. The set M of horizontal and ordinate coordinates is recorded as $M.X$ and $M.Y$. First, the elements in the collection are horizontally divided into set M. For the rectangle element in M, whether the transverse range of the rectangle intersects the set $M.X$ is determined; if so, then the rectangle is segmented. The segmentation result is shown in Fig. 4(b), and a rectangular set $M1 = \{a_1, a_2, b_1, b_2, c_1, c_2, e, f\}$ is obtained.

Then, the elements of the $M1$ are segmented longitudinally. The longitudinal segmentation method is similar to the transverse segmentation. The result is shown in Fig. 4(c), and then $M2 = \{a_1, a_2, a_3, b_1, b_2, b_3, b_4, c_1, c_2, c_3, e, f\}$. The R-tree structure established by the set $M2$ is used to divide the space of S. $Maxfill$ and $Minfill$ are respectively set as 3 and $Maxfill/2$. As shown in the Fig. 4, the height h of the tree is 4, and the areas of each node in each layer of the tree do not intersect each other. For the convenience of observation, the partially merged rectangle in Fig. 5(a) has not been marked. In this figure, rectangle $g_1 = comb(a_1, a_2)$, $g_2 = comb(a_3, c_3)$ and $k_1 = comb(g_1, g_2)$, and other non-leaf node rectangles are similarly generated. Combined with the differential

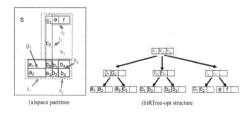

Fig. 5. Space partition based on RTree-opt.

privacy mechanism, a privacy budget $\frac{\varepsilon}{h}$ is added to the count value of each node, that is, $\frac{\varepsilon}{4}$. For the shaded part q, $q \subset S \wedge q \subset k_1 \wedge q \subset g_2 \wedge q \subset c_3$. The spatial areas represented by the nodes in each layer of the tree structure are not intersecting each other. Thus, in the spatial area S, each spatial part only appears once at most in each layer of the tree structure, and the privacy budget of the path from the root node of the tree to each leaf node is $\sum_{i=1}^{h} \frac{\varepsilon}{h} = \varepsilon$. Therefore, the algorithm satisfies ε-differential privacy. The core idea of optimizing R-tree

---

Algorithm 1. RTree-opt (build RTree-opt)

Input: Data set Dt_1 (2d point set), cluster number K, $Maxfill$
Output: The Rtree-opt index structure of each cluster
1: $D \leftarrow KMEANS(Dt_1, K)$
2: **for** each d in D **do**
3:     Generate the set M
4:     **for** each $M_i \in M$ **do**
5:         $idx \leftarrow binarySearch(M.X, Mi.xlow) + 1, (idx \in M.X)$
6:         Use idx as the dividing line to divide M_i and store the result of the division in set $M1$
7:     **end for**
8:     **for** each $M1_i \in M1$ **do**
9:         $idy \leftarrow binarySearch(M.Y, Mi.ylow) + 1, (idy \in M.Y)$
10:     Use idy as the dividing line to divide M_i and store the result of the division in set $M2$
11:     **end for**
12:     RTree-opt= $buildRtree(M2, max)$
13: **end for**

---

establishment is to first divide the initial minimum bounding rectangle set horizontally and vertically. Then, the bounding rectangle set obtained after the division is completed is used. The R-tree establishment algorithm is employed to divide the space area. Finally, the establishment of the optimized R-tree is completed to ensure that the areas represented by the nodes at each level of the tree structure are disjoint.

When dividing the entire space area, to prevent the tree nodes generated by the optimized R-tree from being too many, the tree structure is too large, and the algorithm efficiency is reduced. The k-means clustering algorithm is first used to coarse-grain the entire spatial region Dt_1 into K subspaces when spatially partitioning the reference dataset of the regional statistics of taxi riders and then establish each subspace the index structure optimizes the R-tree for reasonable space division.

The specific algorithm steps of Rtree-opt are as follows algorithm 1.

3.3 Differential Privacy Spatial Data Partitioning Publication Algorithm Based on R-Tree

The generation of the R-tree is optimized to avoid overlapping of the regions represented by the tree nodes of each layer. This optimization not only improves the efficiency of spatial query but also avoids the destruction of differential privacy. Based on the specific distribution of the reference data of the rider traffic statistics, the index structure is used in this paper to optimize the R-tree, and the unpublished data are proposed on statistical method of space distribution for riding based on R-tree under differential privacy (DBRTree-opt). The unpublished data are divided into data-independent space by applying the optimized R-tree structure generated from the information of the reference dataset. Such data are used to calculate the count value of the area corresponding to each node of the optimized R-tree. Laplace noise is then added, and the boost algorithm [9] is finally used to adjust the query consistency constraint of the tree structure.

Algorithm 2. DBRTree-opt (Differential privacy based on the optimized R-tree)

Input: reference dataset Dt_1, unpublished dataset Dt_2, $Maxfill$, cluster number K, privacy budget ε

Output: satisfies the ε difference privacy publishes the data
1: build RTree-opt$(Dt_1, k, Maxfill)$
2: Divide Dt_2 according to the clustering output of 1
3: $\bar{\varepsilon} = \frac{\varepsilon}{h}$
4: **for** each d in D **do**
5:     *space partition*$(d, RTree - opt)$
6:     **for** each node $u_i \in RTree - opt$ **do**
7:       $c(ui) = count(Dt_2, RTree - opt)$
8:       $\widetilde{c}(ui) = c(ui) + \bar{\varepsilon}$
9:     **end for**
10:    boost algorithm consistency processing
11: **end for**

The reference dataset for the regional statistics of riders is assumed to be publicly released data. Given that the optimized R-tree index structure is used for spatial division of the unpublished data, the optimized R-tree is built and generated by referring data of information and does not involve the data information to be released. Therefore, when the differential privacy mechanism is combined, there is no need to add the privacy budget to the tree structure. The specific algorithm steps of DBRTree-opt are as follows algorithm 2.

4   Experimental Result

In order to verify the effect of the space division of the optimizing R-tree and the accuracy of the data released by the algorithm (DBRTree-opt), we compare and analyze the experimental effects with the algorithm DBRTree-opt, the unified meshing method UG [13], the adaptive meshing method AG [13], the complete quadtree partition method Quad-opt [5] and the unbalanced quadtree partition method UBQP [21] in the statistical query accuracy of the area and the efficiency of the algorithm.

4.1   Experimental Data and Environment

In this section, three real data sets were used for experimental testing, which were SanFrancisco Bay Area (SFBA), Shanghai, Chengdu. Among them, the SFBA data set is the travel data of 538 taxis in San Francisco during the last 30 days (From May 17 to June 10, 2008) and the geographical coordinates of getting on and off the taxis. The Shanghai dataset is the 24 h (February 20, 2007) driving data and geographic coordinate data of 4,316 taxis in Shanghai. The Chengdu dataset is the driving data and geographic coordinate data of taxis in a local area of the Second Ring Road in Chengdu from November 1 to 2, 2016. Chengdu data set provided by the website has desensitized the vehicle ID, so the number of vehicles is not provided.

According to the different reference data, the experiment was divided into two groups. In the first group, data of vehicles of a certain size are randomly selected as reference data sets Dt_1 from SFBA data set and Shanghai data set respectively, and the data of the remaining vehicles are used as the data set to be released Dt_2, so as to meet the experimental requirements. For group 2, because the Chengdu data set contains two days' taxi data information, so the vehicle data of the previous day is used as the reference data set, and the vehicle data of the second day is used as the published data set, so as to meet the experimental (Table 1).

Table 1. Characteristics of data

Data sets	Dt_1		Dt_2	
	Number of vehicles	Data volume	Number of vehicles	Data volume
SFBA	338	676,000	200	420,000
Shanghai	2,316	4,168,800	2,000	3,500,000
Chengdu		209,423		214,650

The relative errors in references [4,25] are used to measure the availability of published data. The formula is:

$$RE = \frac{|Q(D) - Q(D')|}{\max(Q(D), \rho)}. \tag{7}$$

where $Q(D)$ is the real query result of the original dataset when executing the query Q, and $Q(D^{'})$ is the query result when publishing the data to execute the query Q after adding differential privacy technology. The parameter $\rho = 0.001|D|$. And $|D|$ is the size of data set.

The experiment in this section tests the relative error of the algorithm when the total privacy budget ε is 0.1, 0.5, 1.0 respectively and Set the range query area Size(Q) in the experiment to 1%, 5%, 25%, and 50% of the total area of the data set, respectively. For each type of query area, 500 spatial range queries are randomly generated to calculate the average of the relative errors.

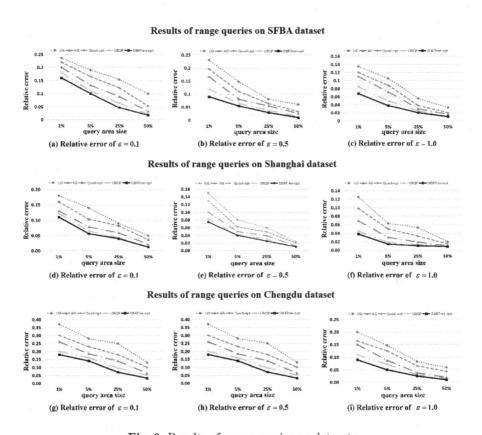

Fig. 6. Results of range queries on datasets.

4.2   Comparative Analysis of Query Accuracy

(1) Comparison of relative error RE value among DBRTree-opt, UG, AG, Quad-opt, UBQP algorithms based on SFBA dataset and Shanghai dataset

It can be seen from Fig. 6(a)–(c) and (d)–(f) that when the privacy budget is fixed and the area query range changes from 1% to 50% of the total area of the data set, the relative errors of the five algorithms are gradually reduced. However, the range query accuracy of DBRTree-opt is better than the other four algorithms, especially when the region query range is 1%. The query relative error of DBRtree-opt algorithm is twice smaller than UG algorithm. At the same time, when the regional range query is 1%, the DBRTree-opt query precision of the algorithm performs better than the other three algorithms, because DBRTree-opt algorithm divide the space considering the time and space distribution law of traffic data, utilizing a certain scale of vehicle data as reference data and combining with the spatial distribution of the reference data to construct indexing structure, which greatly reduce uniform assumption error introduced by sparse area and the noise error introduced by blank nodes, further reducing the relative error, and improving the precision of range queries. Compared with DBRtree-opt algorithm, UG and the Quad-opt algorithm only divide the whole space logically without considering the specific distribution of two-dimensional spatial data and lack adaptive adjustment. Therefore, for data sets with uneven data distribution, more blank grids will be generated, resulting in large relative errors. The AG algorithm performs the second level adaptive division on the basis of UG algorithm, but it is still difficult to offset the errors caused by the unified grid division in the first level.

(2) Comparison of relative error RE values among DBRtree-opt, UG, AG, Quad-opt and UBQP algorithms based on Chengdu data set

It can be seen from Fig. 6(g)–(i) that when the privacy budget is fixed and the area query range changes from 1% to 50% of the total area of the data set, the variation trend of the relative error of the five algorithms decreases gradually with the increase of the query area. However, DBRtree-opt algorithm is still superior to other algorithms in this data set. DBRTree-opt algorithm with UBQP algorithm is relatively close to experimental results, especially when the query in 50% of the region, mainly because when constructing indexing structure, the UBQP algorithm consider the spatial distribution, and according to the data distribution uniformity of adaptive partition prevent the increasing of error noise resulting from sparse region of data distribution or blank area where no data is distributed divided too fine, to a certain extent promoting the balance between noise error and uniform assumption error. However, in the UBQP algorithm, the overall privacy budget is divided into two parts to conducting the data protection for the uniformity judgment and the data protection for the tree node count value. As a result, the added noise in the tree node becomes larger, resulting in the decrease of accuracy. But the DBRtree-opt algorithm which establishes an index structure through historical data information combining with the distribution law of traffic data, is no need to protect the privacy budget allocated to the index structure. Therefore, we only need to allocate the privacy budget to the tree-node count value for data protection.

4.3   Comparative Analysis of Algorithm Operation Efficiency

According to the experimental results shown in Table 2, it can be concluded that in different experimental data sets, The Shanghai data set has the largest data volume, and the running time of different algorithms in this data set is also larger than that of other data sets on the whole. Therefore, it can be seen that the overall running time of the algorithm increases with the increase of experimental data. In different experimental data sets, it can be seen that the running time of the grids algorithms is lower than the index structure algorithms.

Table 2. Algorithm operation efficiency

Algorithm	SFBA			Shanghai			Chengdu		
	$\varepsilon = 0.1$	$\varepsilon = 0.5$	$\varepsilon = 1.0$	$\varepsilon = 0.1$	$\varepsilon = 0.5$	$\varepsilon = 1.0$	$\varepsilon = 0.1$	$\varepsilon = 0.5$	$\varepsilon = 1.0$
UG	1009	1068	1142	3689	3721	4054	652	665	687
AG	1056	1078	1204	3753	3831	4110	674	689	702
Quad-opt	2192	2317	2485	5731	5822	6017	1543	1539	1601
UBQP	3324	3399	3560	6452	6483	6751	1788	1785	1864
RTree-opt	3965	4038	4026	6784	6823	6792	1866	1861	1890

By comparing the running time under the same data set, the different choice of privacy budget parameter has no effect on the query response running time of each algorithm.

Compared to the experimental results, it can be concluded that a long time is consumed by a tree structure algorithm. When establishing a spatial index structure, the DBRTree-opt algorithm use the clustering algorithm to generate the smallest unit of index structure. So the establishment of the index structure in whole space, especially in a large amount of data sets, DBRTree-opt algorithm needed to run for a long time. But it's still very efficient.

5   Conclusion

In this study, DBRTree-opt algorithm is proposed with reference data information. First, the algorithm design and optimize the index structure of R-tree to solve the problem of overlapping spatial regions in R-tree; then, under the requirement of differential privacy, the RTree-opt index structure generated by referring to the spatial distribution information of data is applied to the data to be published. The algorithm provides passengers and drivers with regional riding statistical data query, which is convenient for them to plan their own routes and goals. The algorithm treats the published data reasonably by combining the data distribution rules, reduces uniform assumption error and noise error, and achieves the purpose of improving the query accuracy of two-dimensional data partitioning and publishing. Finally, the feasibility and effectiveness of the DBRTree-opt algorithm are verified by real large-scale data sets.

Acknowledgments. This work is supported by the Natural Science Foundation of Fujian Province of China (2017J01754) and the Natural Science Foundation of Fujian Province of China (2018J01797).

References

1. Beckmann, N., Kriegel, H., Schneider, R., Seeger, B.: The r*-tree: an efficient and robust access method for points and rectangles. In: Proceedings of the 1990 ACM SIGMOD International Conference on Management of Data, (ICMD 1990), pp. 322–331. ACM Press (1990)
2. Berchtold, S., Keim, D.A., Kriegel, H.P.: The X-tree: an index structure for high-dimensional data. In: Proceedings of 22th International Conference on Very Large Data Bases, (ICVLDB 1996), pp. 28–39 (1996)
3. Cao, Y., Yoshikawa, M.: Differentially private real-time data release over infinite trajectory streams. In: 2015 16th IEEE International Conference on Mobile Data Management, (MDM 2015), pp. 68–73. IEEE Computer Society (2015)
4. Chen, Z., Kan, X., Zhang, S., Chen, L., Xu, Y., Zhong, H.: Differentially private aggregated mobility data publication using moving characteristics. arXiv preprint arXiv:1908.03715 (2019)
5. Cormode, G., Procopiuc, C., Srivastava, D., Shen, E., Yu, T.: Differentially private spatial decompositions. In: IEEE 28th International Conference on Data Engineering, (ICDE 2012), pp. 20–31. IEEE Computer Society (2012)
6. Dwork, C.: Differential privacy. In: Bugliesi, M., Preneel, B., Sassone, V., Wegener, I. (eds.) ICALP 2006. LNCS, vol. 4052, pp. 1–12. Springer, Heidelberg (2006). https://doi.org/10.1007/11787006_1
7. Dwork, C., Kenthapadi, K., McSherry, F., Mironov, I., Naor, M.: Our data, ourselves: privacy via distributed noise generation. In: Vaudenay, S. (ed.) EUROCRYPT 2006. LNCS, vol. 4004, pp. 486–503. Springer, Heidelberg (2006). https://doi.org/10.1007/11761679_29
8. Guttman, A.: R-trees: a dynamic index structure for spatial searching. In: Proceedings of the 1984 ACM SIGMOD International Conference on Management of Data, (ICMD 1984), pp. 1805–1817 (2017)
9. Hay, M., Rastogi, V., Miklau, G., Suciu, D.: Boosting the accuracy of differentially private histograms through consistency. Proc. VLDB Endow. **3**(1), 1021–1032 (2010)
10. Hua, J., Gao, Y., Zhong, S.: Differentially private publication of general time-serial trajectory data. In: 2015 IEEE Conference on Computer Communications, (INFOCOM 2015), Kowloon, Hong Kong, 26 April–1 May 2015, pp. 549–557. IEEE (2015)
11. Huang, P., Lin, P., Lin, H.: Optimizing storage utilization in r-tree dynamic index structure for spatial databases. J. Syst. Softw. **3**, 291–299 (2001)
12. Mir, D.J., Isaacman, S., Cáceres, R., Martonosi, M., Wright, R.N.: DP-WHERE: differentially private modeling of human mobility. 2013 IEEE International Conference on Big Data. ICBD 2013, pp. 580–588. IEEE Computer Society, IEEE (2013)
13. Qardaji, W., Yang, W., Li, N.: Differentially private grids for geospatial data. In: 29th IEEE International Conference on Data Engineering, (ICDE 2013), pp. 757–768. IEEE Computer Society (2013)

14. Semenko, Y., Saucez, D.: Distributed privacy preserving platform for ridesharing services. In: Wang, G., Feng, J., Bhuiyan, M.Z.A., Lu, R. (eds.) SpaCCS 2019. LNCS, vol. 11611, pp. 1–14. Springer, Cham (2019). https://doi.org/10.1007/978-3-030-24907-6_1

15. Shahriar, H., et al.: Data protection labware for mobile security. In: Wang, G., Feng, J., Bhuiyan, M.Z.A., Lu, R. (eds.) SpaCCS 2019. LNCS, vol. 11611, pp. 183–195. Springer, Cham (2019). https://doi.org/10.1007/978-3-030-24907-6_15

16. Sweeney, L.: k-anonymity: a model for protecting privacy. Int. J. Uncertainty Fuzziness Knowl. Based Syst. **05**, 557–570 (2012)

17. Wang, T., Luo, H., Jia, W., Liu, A., Xie, M.: MTES: an intelligent trust evaluation scheme in sensor-cloud-enabled industrial Internet of Things. IEEE Trans. Ind. Inf. **3**, 2054–2062 (2020)

18. Wang, T., Ke, H., Zheng, X., Wang, K., Liu, A.: Big data cleaning based on mobile edge computing in industrial sensor-cloud. IEEE Trans. Ind. Inf. **16**, 1321–1329 (2019)

19. Wu, Y.K., Huang, H., Wu, Q., Liu, A., Wang, T.: A risk defense method based on microscopic state prediction with partial information observations in social networks. J. Parallel Distrib. Comput. 131, 189–199 (2019)

20. Xu, F., Tu, Z., Li, Y., Zhang, P., Fu, X., Jin, D.: Trajectory recovery from ash: User privacy is NOT preserved in aggregated mobility data. In: Proceedings of the 26th International Conference on World Wide Web, (WWW 2017), pp. 1241–1250. ACM (2017)

21. Yan, Y., Gao, X., Mahmood, A., Feng, T., Xie, P.: Differential private spatial decomposition and location publishing based on unbalanced quadtree partition algorithm. IEEE Access **8**, 104775–104787 (2020)

22. Yan, Y., Hao, X.: Differential privacy partitioning algorithm based on adaptive density grids. J. Shandong Univ., 15–25 (2018). (SCIENCE EDITION)

23. Zhang, J., Xiao, X., Xie, X.: PrivTree: a differentially private algorithm for hierarchical decompositions. In: Proceedings of the 2016 International Conference on Management of Data, (ICMD 2016), pp. 155–170. ACM (2016)

24. Zhang, X., Fu, N., Meng, X.: Towards spatial range queries under local differential privacy. J. Comput. Res. Dev. **57**, 847 (2020)

25. Zhang, X., Jin, K., Meng, X.: Private spatial decomposition with adaptive grids. J. Comput. Res. Dev. **55**, 1143–1156 (2018)

Multi-target Tracking with EmbedMask and LSTM Model Fusion

Chongben Tao[1,2(✉)], Kangliang Lu[1], and Feng Cao[3]

[1] Suzhou University of Science and Technology, Suzhou 215009, China
tomltao@163.com
[2] Suzhou Automobile Research Institute, Tsinghua University,
Suzhou 215134, China
[3] Shanxi University, Taiyuan 030006, China

Abstract. The problem of occlusion occurs during multi-target tracking may result in loss of characteristics of tracking target and thus lose the tracking targets. This paper proposes a multi-target vehicle tracking algorithm based on fusion of Embedding Coupling for One-stage Instance Segmentation (Embed-Mask) and Long Short-Term Memory (LSTM) model. Firstly, the obtained real-time video data is input into EmbedMask target detection model by frame for target detection. The targets are separated from background, and traditional rectangular box detection is replaced by instance segmentation. Secondly, the maximum feature data of targets is generated by the resent convolution network, which is input into the LSTM model. The continuous data of targets is obtained by calculating and estimating the motion attitude of the tracking target. Finally, the motion and detection data of targets is input into new LSTM model layer, and the fusion calculation is used to reduce the tracking loss caused by over-lapping, which can ensure the accuracy of target tracking. Experimental results on standard MOT data sets show that the proposed algorithm is robust and can be used to accurately track occluded overlapping targets.

Keywords: EmbedMask · Instance segmentation · LSTM · Motion pose · Tracking

1 Introduction

Visual object tracking is an important research field of computer vision and is widely used in video surveillance, unmanned driving, robot and other fields. Among the traditional methods, Li et al. [1] proposed an improved Bayesian tracker with adaptive learning rate (b-tracker), which combined adaptive Bayesian learning with improved incremental subspace learning. Zhong et al. [2] proposed a probabilistic method based on weakly-supervised learning of multiple incomplete predictors for visual tracking. By considering the output of all trackers, the most likely target position was inferred and each tracker was estimated simultaneously. The above methods have achieved good results in different aspects, but they are all based on weakly supervised tracking algorithms, which require manual threshold settings, resulting in the lack of adaptive

© Springer Nature Switzerland AG 2021
G. Wang et al. (Eds.): SpaCCS 2020, LNCS 12383, pp. 310–320, 2021.
https://doi.org/10.1007/978-3-030-68884-4_26

capability for unstable factors. In this paper, the proposed method has good adaptive ability for cases where targets appear to be occluded.

With the continuous development of deep learning, multi-objective tracking methods based on deep learning have been proposed. Li et al. [3] proposed a high-performance visual tracking based on the Siam regional proposal network. The interactive learning for deep focus tracking was investigated in Song et al. [4]. Zhang et al. [5] used interactive learning for deep focus tracking. Wang et al. [6] proposed Limited Memory Eigenvector Recursive Principal Component Analysis in Sensor-cloud Based Adaptive Operational Modal Online Identification. Despite the abovementioned progress, there is still a problem that has not been solved well. First, the tracker makes a limited effort to improve localization accuracy by using only classification confidence to evaluate candidate patches, but candidate patch with the highest classification confidence may not be the most accurate. With the further development of deep learning, many new algorithms appear in the field of multi-target tracking. Such as, Bae et al. [7] applied data association based on confidence degree and discriminant deep appearance learning in robust online multi-target tracking. Zhou et al. [8] considered the multi-person occlusion and motion inference tracking based on deep alignment network. The enhanced detection model of multiple hypothesis tracking by Chen et al. [9]. Choi [10] et al. proposed a near-online multi-target tracking that aggregates local stream descriptors. Chu et al. [11] proposed Online multi-object tracking using cnn-based single object tracker with spatial-temporal attention mechanism. Fang et al. [12] used a recursive autoregressive network for online multi-target tracking. Fu et al. [13] proposed online group structured dictionary learning multiplayer tracking based on particle filters. Above algorithms show good results for multi-target tracking, but most of them use integrated network as total localization parameter, which is not robust due to the loss of targets caused by undetectable. The use of instance segmentation can separate targets from background, which can reduce feature data caused by occlusion and improve robustness of the tracker.

In this paper, a multi-target tracker combined EmbedMask [14] with LSTM model fusion [15] is proposed. A good improvement is made for the loss of features and target tracking IDs caused by target occlusion in traditional trackers. Firstly, video is serialized, and target is separated from background by instance segmentation, then mask data is put into cyclic neural network to calculate motion attitude, and finally target monitoring information is fused to obtain serial multi-target tracking image. Through instance segmentation algorithm, id loss caused by target occlusion is well solved, while the speed of this algorithm is higher than traditional instance segmentation algorithm, which can guarantee real-time performance. Video is first sequenced, and then targets are separated from the background by instance segmentation. A sequence multi-target tracking image is obtained by combining the instance segmentation algorithm with the motion attitude obtained by calculation. By obtaining the mask information of targets, the occlusion problem of targets can be well solved. The overall framework of the algorithm is shown in Fig. 1. In this algorithm, the EmbedMask target detection was used as the front-end treatment to obtain the target, a LSTM model was used to train on the target to get tracking target id, and the multi-feature fusion was used to obtain the accurate multi-target tracking.

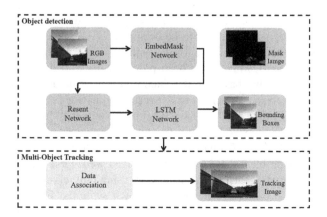

Fig. 1. The overall framework of the algorithm.

2 Target Detection Algorithm Based on EmbedMask

As one of the core problems in machine vision, the task of object detection is to find all the target objects in the image. The traditional target detection is only limited to the first stage, which obtains the boundary box of the target and processes the image directly at the pixel level. This operation is difficult to determine the number of target clusters or the center position, and the performance is poor. However, the new MaskRCNN [16] algorithm still has the problems of feature loss and aspect ratio distortion, and the generated mask cannot retain fine details. Additionally, the recognition speed of MaskRCNN algorithm is very slow, which is difficult to meet the real-time requirements of target recognition.

Target tracking in this paper requires certain real-time requirements for object recognition and there may be a certain occlusion for recognition target. EmbedMask algorithm can detect at high speed and obtain mask data. This feature can quickly recognize and preprocess input image sequence.

The EmbedMask consists of two levels, one is used to find the location of instance suggestions, and the other is used to predict the mask of instance suggestions. Firstly, the most advanced target detection method FCOS [17] is used as the baseline, which is the latest first stage target detection method. At the same time, special module is designed to learn pixel embedding, scheme embedding and scheme margin to extract instance mask, as shown in Fig. 2. Secondly, a 3×3conv layer is added to the maximum feature map from FPN to calculate the embedded variables and share them with the central prediction. Thirdly, variables calculated by box regression output should be guaranteed. Finally, recommended margin provides a clear boundary to determine the final mask.

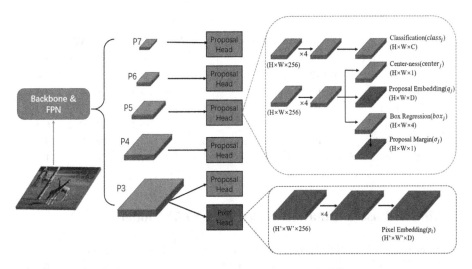

Fig. 2. EmbedMask network framework [14]

Embedding mask is optimized end-to-end using multitasking loss. Their loss function is jointly optimized as:

$$L = L_{cls} + L_{center} + L_{box} + \lambda_1 L_{mask} + \lambda_2 L_{smooth} \tag{1}$$

Among them, in addition to original classification loss L_{cls}, centrality loss L_{center} and box regression loss L_{box} in FCOS, this paper also introduces additional losses L_{mask} and L_{smooth} for mask prediction.

$$L_{mask} = \frac{1}{K} \sum_{k=1}^{k} \frac{1}{N_k} \sum_{pi \in B_k} L(\phi(x_i, S_k), G(x_i, S_k)) \tag{2}$$

$$L_{mask} = \frac{1}{K} \sum_{k=1}^{K} \frac{1}{N_k} \sum_{j \in M_k} \|q_j - Q_k\|^2 + \frac{1}{K} \sum_{k=1}^{K} \frac{1}{N_k} \sum_{j \in M_k} \|\sigma_j - \Sigma_k\|^2 \tag{3}$$

where $\varphi(x_i, S_k)$ is the probability of pixel x_i belonging to example S_k mask.

Therefore, L_{mask} can optimize the loss through binary classification. Since Q_k and Σ_k are different during training and inference, a smooth loss L_{smooth} needs to be added to training to force them to stay close. Meanwhile, mask data is deliberately processed separately and presented independently during the training process. The single color of mask data reduces the cost of subsequent tracking calculation and increases the feasibility of real-time tracking algorithm. A large number of training data sets show that EmbedMask algorithm has been greatly improved in speed compared with other algorithms, and its accuracy is not inferior to MaskRNN algorithm. In addition, it also has the ability of instance segmentation. The data set comparison table of EmbedMask and other algorithms is shown in Table 1.

Table 1. Comparison between EmbedMask and other algorithms.

Method	Backbone	ms	rc	epochs	AP	AP50	AP75	APS	APM	fps
Mask RCNN. [16]	R-50-FPN			24	35	55.5	37.6	14.4	38.1	8.8
Mask RCNN	R-50-FPN	√		36	37.9	62.9	38.9	19.2	39.7	8.4
Mask RCNN	R-101-FPN			24	35.5	59.6	37.5	16.8	37.9	8.2
YOLACT [18]	R-101-FPN	√	√	48	31.3	49.8	33.4	13.1	32.8	23.7
EmbedMask [14]	R-50-FPN			12	32.8	54.6	36.1	14.8	36.2	16.9
EmbedMask	R-101-FPN	√		36	36.9	57.9	41.2	16.9	42.3	14.8
EmbedMask-600	R-101-FPN	√		36	34.5	55.4	37.1	13.1	37.6	21.3

3   Motion Pose Estimation Based on LSTM Model

LSTM is a kind of special Recurrent Neural Network (RNN). The difference between LSTM and RNN is that there is only one state in a single cycle structure. There are four internal states of LSTM. The LSTM loop structure maintains a persistent unit state, which is used to decide which information to forget or continue to pass on. Through the transformation between various state gates, we can judge whether the layer chooses to output or jump to the next layer. By controlling the valve, the LSTM framework can solve the problem of gradient explosion caused by too much data in the training process. This improvement is well applied to the target data association calculation in sequence images.

Traditional LSTM has certain advantages in modeling motion. When looking for the moving posture of the target, building a multi-target tracking appearance model, you can roughly think that c_t represents storage template of appearance of the object, and then out compares previously stored appearance c_{t-1} with new appearance x_t to determine current output h_t. LSTM operates using the following rules:

$$c_t = n_t \circ m_{t-1} + i_t \circ g_t, \quad h_t = n_t \circ \tanh a_t$$

$$i_t = \sigma\left(V_f[m_{t-1}, X_t]\right), \quad n_t = \sigma(V_i[m_{t-1}, X_t]) \tag{4}$$

The LSTM framework model used in this paper as shown in Fig. 3, movement, appearance and sport appearance are combined to form the gating network. For appearance gating, Bilinear LSTM model is the best. Then, two gating layers are trained respectively, and fine-tune is made on the basis of prediction layer to achieve the expected training objectives.

This paper proposed a new LSTM model, which can realize multiplication between memory h_t and input x_t. With the time of Q_t updating, the matrix storage is increasing,

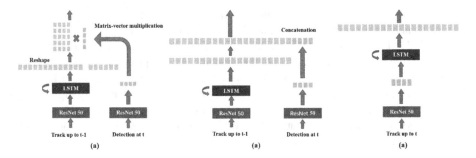

Fig. 3. LSTM feature fusion model [15]

and it is difficult to convert it into memory. Therefore, the reduced rank calculation is chosen to solve the LSTM problem. Therefore, the regression output becomes:

$$W^T x = C_t^T Q_t^{-1} x = \sum C_t^T q_{ti} q_{ti}^T x \tag{5}$$

4   Multi-target Vehicle Tracking Algorithm

In this paper, the LSTM model is combined with the case segmentation module to realize the tracking and recognition of multi-target vehicles. In particular, some improvements are made for the occlusion of the target image. The algorithm framework proposed in this paper will be shown in Fig. 4.

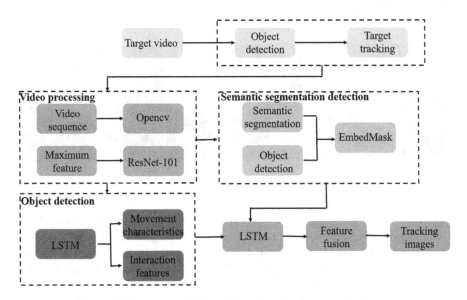

Fig. 4. Multi-target vehicle tracking algorithm framework diagram

In the multi-target tracking, the image information is input into the pre-trained resnet101 network to obtain the simple data processed by CNN network. The pre-trained CNN filter is input into the LSTM model of the first layer, and the target motion attitude is obtained by training, and the tracking target position is preliminarily recorded by using the boundary box. Afterwards, the image sequence is input into the EmbedMask model, and the mask information of the target is obtained by high-speed target recognition, and the specific location details of the target are determined. Finally, these two kind of feature information are fused to obtain the specific sequence target tracking image with mask.

5   Experimental Results and Verification

In this paper, the experimental results and verification are carried out in the Apollo data set of Baidu [19]. In this paper, the continuous road real-time screenshots are extracted from the data set to obtain a set of time series pictures required, so as to detect and track the targets in the images. There are a large number of overlapping vehicles in the selected graph, which can better verify the algorithm. In automatic driving, the overlap between vehicles causes that the tracker has a good effect on the lack of data in the tracking of multiple vehicles.

5.1   Target Detection Experiment Results

For input video sequence images, the resnet101 network is used for rough information recognition of the images, and the simple target position information is input into the first layer LSTM model to calculate the interactive data and displacement data of target position, using bounding box to select target initial position information, so as to obtain simple target tracking effect, as shown in Fig. 5.

Fig. 5. Target detection results

As shown in Fig. 6, the video sequence image is input into the EmbedMask detection model to obtain the mask data information of vehicle targets. The target can be better tracked because of using mask data, which can reduce the amount of tracking network calculations, isolate the target from the background, as well as reduce the loss of object information caused by occlusion.

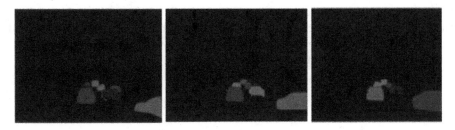

Fig. 6. EmbedMask network obtains mask information for sequence images

In this paper, an EmbedMask network is used to obtain the mask information of the target sequence image. The target acquisition speed is much faster than the initial mask Region Convolutional Neural Network (RCNN), which is about three times of the mask RCNN. And its target capture ability is not inferior to the original network, which can ensure better real-time acquisition of target mask information. In the training of multiple target detection algorithms as shown in Fig. 7, in terms of accuracy, the number of iterations is increased by EmbedMask, and the loss decreases continuously, which is close to 0. And compared with other algorithms, we can see that the final loss is much lower than other three algorithms. Accurate target detection can be performed, and the mask data of the tracked target can be obtained very stably, which improves the robustness of the tracker.

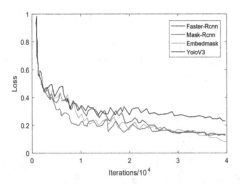

Fig. 7. Comparison of loss iteration curves

5.2   Multi-target Vehicle Recognizer Results

The detection of this algorithm and other algorithms in the MOT [20] dataset is shown in Fig. 8. Based on the LSTM target detection framework, this algorithm optimizes the detection efficiency reduction caused by overlapping problem. It can be seen from the figure that the multiple object tracking accuracy (MOTA) is significantly higher than original LSTM algorithm. In some data sets, algorithm also has the same excellent detection results as other algorithms, especially the performance of automatic driving target data sets such as KITTI [21] is significantly better than LSTM. In order to ensure real-time performance of tracking targets, MOTA is slightly lower than other trackers. This is the direction that needs to be improved: how to balance the unity of speed and accuracy. However, the detection accuracy is slightly lower than other target trackers, which needs to be further improved.

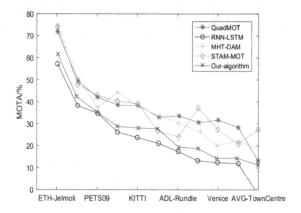

Fig. 8. Performance of multiple target tracking algorithms on MOT

Finally, initial interaction of multiple vehicle targets, motion data and mask data information obtained by EmbedMask are input into the LSTM model at the same time. The fusion of the two data can reduce the overlap of targets, so as to accurately track multiple vehicle targets in sequence video images. The effect is shown in Fig. 9. As can be seen from Fig. 9. For overlapping vehicles, the algorithm can also obtain accurate tracking effect, which is a good solution to the problem of failing to obtain tracking target id due to overlapping target tracking.

Fig. 9. Multi-vehicle target tracking effect

6   Conclusion

In this paper, a multi vehicle target tracking algorithm based on the combination of EmbedMask algorithm and LSTM model solves the problem of target tracking data loss caused by overlapping occlusion of multi-target vehicles in the process of automatic driving. In this paper, based on the target tracking of LSTM model, the mask data information acquired from EmbedMask has been improved, so as to distinguish multiple targets and target from background. The results show that the algorithm can well solve the problem of missing tracking information caused by multiple vehicles overlapping. A vehicle tracking model for real-time road conditions is obtained, which is trained and verified in the Apollo data set of Baidu, and the multi-target vehicle tracking is well realized. The next step is to use real-time camera input tracker to process vehicle decision information based on the detected target data. From the front-end sensor preprocessing information, perform edge calculation to obtain simple decision-making suggestions, and assist the main decision maker to make judgments.

Acknowledgments. This work was supported in part by the National Natural Science Foundation of China (Grants No. 61801323), by the Science and Technology Projects Fund of Suzhou (Grant No. SYG201708, Grant No. SS2019029), by the Construction System Science and Technology Fund of Jiangsu Province (Grant No. 2017ZD066).

References

1. Li, K., He, F., et al.: A parallel and robust object tracking approach synthesizing adaptive bayesian learning and improved incremental subspace learning. Front. Comput. Sci. **13**, 1116–1135 (2019)
2. Zhong, B., Yao, H., Chen, S., et al.: Visual tracking via weakly supervised learning from multiple imperfect oracles. Elsevier Pattern Recogn. **47**(3), 1395–1410 (2014)
3. Li, B., Yan, J., Wu, W., et al.: High performance visual tracking with siamese region proposal network. In: Proceedings of the IEEE Conference on Computer Vision and Pattern Recognition (CVPR), pp. 8971–8980 (2018)
4. Song, Y., Ma, C., et al.: Deep attentive tracking via reciprocative learning. In: Advances in Neural Information Processing Systems (NIPS), pp. 1931–1941 (2018)
5. Zhang, S., Qi, Y., Jiang, F., et al.: Point-to-set distance metric learning on deep representations for visual tracking. IEEE Trans. Intell. Transp. Syst. **19**(1), 187–198 (2017)
6. Wang, C., Huang, H., Zhang, T., Chen, J.: Limited memory eigenvector recursive principal component analysis in sensor-cloud based adaptive operational modal online identification. In: International Conference on Security, Privacy and Anonymity in Computation, Communication and Storage (SCS), pp. 119–129 (2019)
7. Bae, S.H., Yoon, K.J.: Confidence-based data association and discriminative deep appearance learning for robust online multi-object tracking. IEEE Trans. Pattern Anal. Mach. Intell. **40**(3), 595–610 (2018)
8. Zhou, Q., Zhong, B., Zhang, Y., et al.: Deep Alignment network based multi-person tracking with occlusion and motion reasoning. IEEE Trans. Multimedia **21**(5), 1183–1194 (2019)
9. Chen, J., Sheng, H., Zhang, Y., Xiong, Z.: Enhancing detection model for multiple hypothesis tracking. In: Proceedings of the IEEE Conference on Computer Vision and Pattern Recognition Workshops (CVPR), pp. 18–27 (2017)
10. Choi, W.: Near-online multi-target tracking with aggregated local flow descriptor. In: Proceedings of the IEEE International Conference on Computer Vision (ICCV), pp. 3029–3037 (2015)
11. Chu, Q., Ouyang, W., Li, H., Wang, X., Liu, B., Yu, N.: Online multi-object tracking using cnn-based single object tracker with spatial-temporal attention mechanism. In: Proceedings of the IEEE International Conference on Computer Vision (ICCV), pp. 4836–4845 (2017)

12. Fang, K., Xiang, Y., Li, X., Savarese, S.: Recurrent autoregressive networks for online multi-object tracking. In: IEEE Winter Conference on Applications of Computer Vision (WACV), pp. 466–475 (2018)
13. Fu, Z., Feng, P., Angelini, F., Chambers, J.A., Naqvi, S.M.: Particle PHD filter based multiple human tracking using online group-structured dictionary learning. IEEE Access **6**, 14764–14778 (2018)
14. Ying, H., Huang, Z., Liu, S., et al.: EmbedMask: embedding coupling for one-stage instance segmentation. arXiv preprint arXiv:1912.01954 (2019)
15. Kim, C., Li, F., Rehg, J.M.: Multi-object tracking with neural gating using bilinear LSTM. In: Ferrari, V., Hebert, M., Sminchisescu, C., Weiss, Y. (eds.) ECCV 2018. LNCS, vol. 11212, pp. 208–224. Springer, Cham (2018). https://doi.org/10.1007/978-3-030-01237-3_13
16. He, K., Gkioxari, G., Dollar, P., et al.: Mask R-CNN. In: Proceedings of the IEEE International Conference on Computer Vision (ICCV), pp. 2961–2969 (2017)
17. Tian, Z., Shen, C., Chen, H., et al.: FCOS: fully convolutional one-stage object detection. In: Proceedings of the IEEE International Conference on Computer Vision (ICCV), pp. 9627–9636 (2019)
18. Bolya, D., Zhou, C., Xiao, F., et al.: YOLACT: real-time instance segmentation. In: Proceedings of the IEEE International Conference on Computer Vision (ICCV), pp. 9157–9166 (2019)
19. Ma, Y., Zhu, X., Zhang, S., Yang, R., Wang, W., Manocha, D.: TrafficPredict: trajectory prediction for Heterogeneous traffic-agents. In: Proceedings of the AAAI Conference on Artificial Intelligence (AAAI), pp. 6120–6127 (2019)
20. Milan, A., Leal-Taixé, L., Reid, I., Roth, S., Schindler, K.: MOT16: a benchmark for multi-object tracking (2016)
21. Geiger, A., Lenz, P., Urtasun, R.: Are we ready for autonomous driving? The KITTI vision benchmark suite. In: IEEE Conference on Computer Vision and Pattern Recognition (CVPR), pp. 3354–3361 (2012)

Face Detection Using Improved Multi-task Cascaded Convolutional Networks

Xiaolin Jiang$^{(\boxtimes)}$ and Yu Xiang

School of Electronics and Communication, Heilongjiang University of Science
and Technology, Harbin 150022, China
57102526@qq.com

Abstract. Compared with traditional face detection methods, deep learning methods can better deal with face detection in unconstrained environment. In this paper, based on the original Multi-Task Cascaded Convolutional Networks (MTCNN), we make corresponding improvements on it. On the premise of ensuring that the accuracy of the improved algorithm for face detection is similar to the original, we improve the detection speed. First of all, the original network structure is optimized. In order to improve the detection speed, the amount of computation should be reduced as much as possible. Therefore, it is proposed to use Depthwise convolution in MobileNet instead of conventional convolution; in addition, median filter is used before image detection to reduce some noise and improve the performance of the algorithm. After training on the Wider Face and Celeba data set, the test images were tested. Experimental results show that the performance of the improved MTCNN is not significantly reduced, and the detection speed is significantly improved.

Keywords: Deep learning · Multi-task Cascaded Convolutional Networks · Face detection · Face identification · Median filtering

1 Introduction

In recent years, with the continuous popularity of deep learning, artificial intelligence has become a research hotspot, and is widely used in the Internet of Things [1, 2], communicationand other directions [3]. Face detection is one of the most widely studied problems in the direction of target detection, which is the basis of many face applications. It is mainly used in identity authentication, media and entertainment, and image search. In the early face detection used template matching, in which the detected image was matched to various positions of the original image to determine whether there was a face or not. The representative study is the method proposed by Rowley et al. [4, 5]. In the second stage, AdaBoost framework was used, and its main idea was based on the theory of PAC (Probably Approximately Correct) learning. A strong classifier is constructed by several simple weak classifiers. In 2001, Viola and Jones proposed an algorithm [6], which used the haar-like feature and AdaBoost classifier to construct a face detector. Compared with the previous algorithm, the detection effect and speed have made historic progress. With the Convolutional Neural Networks (CNN) making remarkable progress in image classification, it is soon used in face

© Springer Nature Switzerland AG 2021
G. Wang et al. (Eds.): SpaCCS 2020, LNCS 12383, pp. 321–333, 2021.
https://doi.org/10.1007/978-3-030-68884-4_27

detection. Kaipeng Zhan et al. proposed MTCNN [7] in 2016, which cleverly integrated face detection with face key detection. MTCNN is an improvement based on Cascade CNN, with more ingenious and reasonable design ideas and significantly improved performance. In this paper, based on the original MTCNN, by optimizing the network structure and adding the median filter, the detection speed of the improved MTCNN was improved in the early stage to ensure the accuracy of the original algorithm.

2 MTCNN

MTCNN can be divided into P-Net, R-Net and O-Net network structure. Its implementation and training process are as follows.

2.1 MTCNN Implementation Process

Before sending the image to P-Net, the original image is first scaled to different scales to build image pyramid, in order to adapt to different sizes of faces in the original image, as shown in Fig. 1.

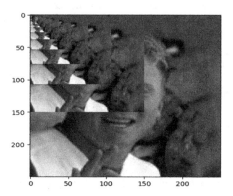

Fig. 1. Image pyramid

P-Net Network Structure. The full name of P-Net is proposal network, which is basically constructed as a full connection network. Initial feature extraction and border calibration were carried out through the fully connected network, the Bounding-Box Regression was used to adjust the window, and then NMS was used to merge the overlapped window. The basic idea of this part is to use the shallow and simple CNN to quickly generate face candidate window. The network structure and results of P-Net are shown in Fig. 2 and Fig. 3 respectively.

R-Net Network Structure. The full name is refine network. Its basic structure is a convolutional neural network. Compared with the first layer of P-Net, a full connection layer is added, making the filtering of input data more rigorous.After the picture passes through P-Met, there will be many prediction windows left. We will send all prediction

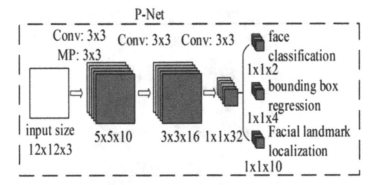

Fig. 2. The network structure of P-Net

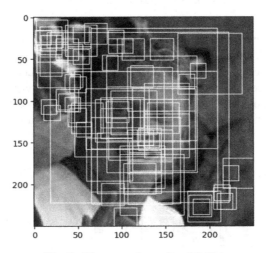

Fig. 3. The network results of P-Net

windows to R-Net. This network will filter out a large number of candidate boxes with poor effect. Finally, we will carry out Bounding-Box Regression and NMS to further optimize the prediction results for the selected candidate boxes. The network structure and results of R-Net are shown in Fig. 4 and Fig. 5 respectively.

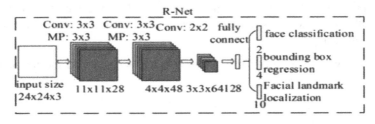

Fig. 4. The network structure of R-Net

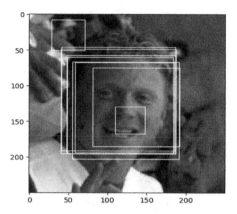

Fig. 5. The network results of R-Net

O-Net Network Structure. The full name is output network. Its basic structure is a more complex convolutional neural network, which has an additional convolution layer compared with R-Net. The difference between the effect of O-Net and R-Net is that this layer structure will recognize the facial area through more supervision, and will regress the facial feature points of people, and finally output five facial feature points. The network structure and results of O-Net are shown in Fig. 6 and Fig. 7 respectively.

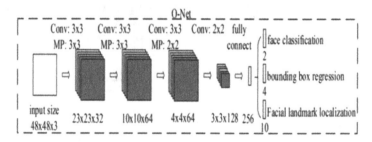

Fig. 6. The network structure of O-Net

2.2 MTCNN Training Process

Training MTCNN requires three tasks to get convergence: (1) Face binary classification: training with positive and negative samples. (2) Bounding-Box regression: training with positive samples and partial samples. (3) Landmark localization: training with key point samples.

(1) Face binary classification: Cross entropy loss is adopted, and the formula is as follows.

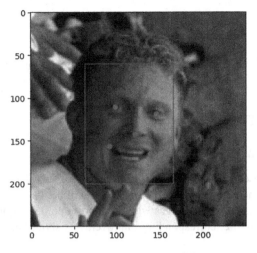

Fig. 7. The network results of O-Net

$$L_i^{det} = -(y_i^{det} log(p_i) + (1 - y_i^{det})(1 - log(p_i)))\tag{1}$$

Where represents the possibility that sample x_i is a face, and $y_i^{det} \in \{0, 1\}$ represents a label.

(2) Bounding-Box regression: For each sample, calculate the Euclidean distance, the formula is as follows.

$$L_i^{box} = \left\| \hat{y}_i^{box} - y_i^{box} \right\|_2^2 \tag{2}$$

Where $\hat{y}_i^{box}$ is the regression box and y_i^{box} is the label box.

(3) Landmark localization: For each sample x_i, calculate the Euclidean distance, the formula is as follows.

$$L_i^{landmark} = \left\| \hat{y}_i^{landmark} - y_i^{landmark} \right\|_2^2 \tag{3}$$

Where $\hat{y}_i^{landmark}$ is the network output and $y_i^{landmark}$ is the location of the annotation point.

There are five coordinates of points in total, which are left eye, right eye, nose, left mouth corner and right mouth corner. Because each CNN network completes different training tasks, it needs different types of training data in the network learning and training stage. Therefore, when calculating the loss, we need to treat the background area differently. The training loss in R-Net and O-Net is 0, because it does not contain the face area, which is represented by the parameter beta = 0. The total training loss can be expressed as follows:

$$min \sum_{i=1}^{N} \sum_{j \in (det,box,landmark)} \alpha_j \beta_i^j L_i^j \qquad (4)$$

Where α_j is task weight, in P-Net and R-Net, $\alpha_{det} = 1.0$, $\alpha_{box} = 0.5$, $\alpha_{landmark} = 0.5$; in O-Net, $\alpha_{det} = 1.0$, $\alpha_{box} = 0.5$, $\alpha_{landmark} = 1.0$.

3 Improved MTCNN

3.1 Algorithm Analysis

According to the research, the original MTCNN has the following problems. (1) The bigger the picture, the more time-consuming P-Net will be. (2) More faces, more time for O-Net and R-Net. (3) Night images with more noise points will lead to more P-Net false detection. Therefore, corresponding improvements should be made to the above three points.

3.2 Improved MTCNN

Depthwise Convolution. In view of the problem that the above 1 and 2 points consume too much time, we can start with optimizing the network structure, and reduce the calculation as much as possible when the accuracy is not too much reduced. Therefore, we think of the Depthwise convolution in MobileNet series [8].

For a conventional convolution, a 6×6 pixel, three channel color input picture (shape is $6 \times 6 \times 3$). After the convolution layer of 3×3 convolution kernel (assuming that the number of output channels is 4, the convolution kernel shape is $3 \times 3 \times 3 \times 4$), four feature maps are finally output. If there is the same padding, then the size is the same as that of the input layer (6×6). If not, the size is changed to 3×3 (Fig. 8).

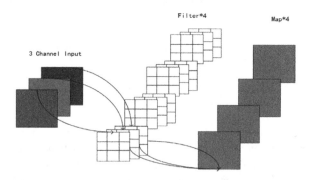

Fig. 8. A conventional convolution

Different from conventional convolution operation, a convolution kernel of Depthwise revolution is responsible for one channel, and only one convolution kernel convolutes one channel. The conventional convolution kernels mentioned above operate on each channel of the input image at the same time.

Similarly, for a 6 × 6 pixel, three-channel color input image (shape is 6 × 6 × 3), the first convolution operation of Depthwise convolution is carried out. Different from the conventional convolution above, DW is completely carried out in a two-dimensional plane. The number of convolutional kernels is the same as the number of channels in the previous layer (channels and convolutional kernels correspond one-to-one). Therefore, a three-channel image is generated into three Feature maps after calculation (if the same padding is used, the size is 6 × 6 as the input layer), as shown in the following figure (Fig. 9).

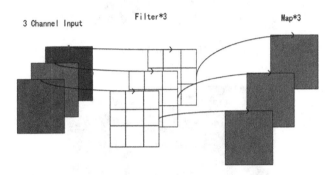

Fig. 9. Depthwise convolution

Depthwise convolution originated from Xception. The idea of this method is more direct. First, each channel of the input graph is convoluted, and then they are combined by 1 × 1 convolution. A large number of experiments prove that this operation can be basically equivalent to the ordinary spatial convolution. And under the condition of constant IO efficiency and performance, the amount of computation is reduced by 9 times. We can use this idea to replace the convolution operation in P-Net, R-Net and O-Net, so that the speed is greatly improved.

Median Filtering. In some cases, for example, the camera's pixel is not high, and in the evening, the pictures taken may have a lot of noise. In addition, due to the instability of CNN, P-Net has produced a large number of false detection constituencies. In order to reduce the noise, we can carry out median filtering and simple denoising before P-Net detection.

Median filter can not only remove noise but also protect the edge of image. It is a non-linear method to remove noise.The realization principle of median filter is to replace the value of a point in a digital image with the median value of each point in a region of that point.We call the neighborhood of a certain length or shape of a point as a window, so for the median filtering of two-dimensional image, we usually use 3 × 3 or 5 × 5 window to filter. Fig. 10 is the original picture. And Fig. 11 is the picture after median filtering.

Fig. 10. Original picture

Fig. 11. Median filtering

4   Experimental Data and Process

4.1   Training Data

The training data was collected from two public databases (https://shuoyang1213.me/ WIDERFACE), Wider and Celeba, which provided face detection data, marked the coordinate information of the ground truth of the face box on the big picture, and Celeba provided data of five landmarks.

Wider data set there were 32203 images in the data set, with a total of 93703 faces marked, as shown below (Fig. 12).

Fig. 12. Wider face

The training data of Celeba face key point detection includes 5590 LFW data sets and 7876 pictures downloaded from the website (Fig. 13).

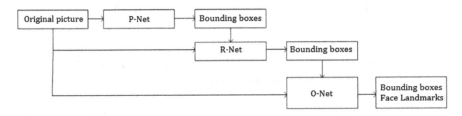

Fig. 13. Celeba

4.2 Training Process

Fig. 14. Training process

Input the original image and P-Net to generate the predicted bounding boxes.Input the original picture and the bounding box generated by P-Net, and generate the corrected bounding box through R-Net.Input the original image and the bounding box generated by R-Net, and generate the corrected bounding box and facial contour key points through O-Net (Fig. 14).

During the training phase, the data are divided into four types. (1) Negative sample: parallel ratio less than 0.3. (2) Positive sample: parallel ratio is greater than 0.65. (3) Partial face: parallel ratio is between 0.4 and 0.65. (4) Landmark face: able to find five landmark positions.

There was no significant difference between the negative samples and some faces. We chose 0.3 and 0.4 as the interval.

The proportion of the whole training number is as follows, Negative sample: positive sample: partial face: landmark face = 3:1:1:2.

4.3   Experimental Results

After retraining MTCNN, put it under the data set FDDB [9], test its performance, and compare it with the original MTCNN. The figure below shows the ROC (receiver operating characteristic curve) curve obtained by different algorithms in the data set FDDB test (Fig. 15).

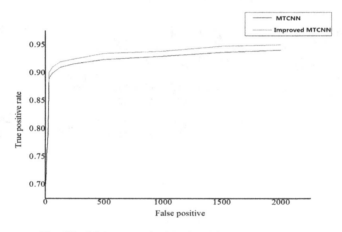

Fig. 15. ROC curve of original and improved MTCNN

With regard to ROC curve, the larger the area under the curve, the higher the diagnostic accuracy. It can be seen that the True positive rate (TPR) of the original MTCNN is higher than that of the improved MTCNN. The specific value of the original MTCNN obtained by testing is about 0.9504, while that of the improved MTCNN is about 0.9369, with a difference of 0.0135. The difference between the two is still within the acceptable range. Meanwhile, compared with other face detection algorithms, the improved MTCNN still has great advantages, as shown in Table 1.

Table 1. Evaluation on FDDB.

Algorithm	Recall	Algorithm	Recall
MTCNN [7]	0.9504	Faceness [11]	0.9098
Improved MTCNN	0.9369	Joint Cascade [12]	0.8667
DP2MFD [10]	0.9173	Cascade CNN	0.8567

As can be seen from Table 1, when the number of false detections in FDDB data set is 2000, compared with other face detection algorithms, the improved MTCNN still has a great advantage. The next step is to verify whether the detection speed has decreased.

Select a picture with a resolution of 400×400. Under the same parameter setting, the results of the two are as follows:

Table 2. Performance comparison between original and improved MTCNN.

Algorithm	Test image size	Test minimum face size	Number of recognition	Recall (%)	Algorithm time (ms)
MTCNN	400×400	20	23	92	68
Improved MTCNN	400×400	20	22	88	53

Fig. 16. Original MTCNN test results

Fig. 17. Improved MTCNN test results

Figure 16 shows the results of the original MTCNN detection. In one picture, 23 faces were successfully detected. Figure 17 shows the results of the improved MTCNN detection. 22 faces were successfully detected. From Table 2, Figs. 16 and Figs. 17, it can be seen that for the same picture size, when the minimum face size is set to 20, the detection accuracy of the improved MTCNN is not much lower than that of the original MTCNN, but detection speed is 15 ms faster, the detection speed of the improved MTCNN is significantly faster than that of the original MTCNN.

5   Conclusion

In this paper, based on the original MTCNN, an improvement was made to the original MTCNN: by replacing the general convolution in the original network with Depthwise convolution, and by adding the median filter before P-Net. It was compared with the original MTCNN, on the premise that the detection accuracy decreases little. The detection speed is improved. And the feasibility of the improved algorithm is proved by experiments.

References

1. Wang, T., Luo, H., Jia, W., Liu, A., Xie, M.: MTES: an intelligent trust evaluation scheme in sensor-cloud-enabled industrial internet of things. IEEE Trans. Ind. Inf. **16**(3), 2054–2062 (2020)
2. Huang, M.F., Liu, A.F., Wang, T., Huang, C.Q.: Green data gathering under delay differentiated services constraint for internet of things. Wirel. Commun. Mobile Comput. **2018**(3), 1–23 (2018)
3. Tang, J., Liu, A., Wang, T.: An aggregate signature based trust routing for data gathering in sensor networks. Secur. Commun. Netw. (S&CN) **2018**, 1–30 (2018)

4. Henry, A.R., Baluja, S., Anade, T.K.: Neural network-based face detection. IEEE Trans. Pattern Anal. Mach. Intell. **20**(1), 23–38 (1998)
5. Henry, A. R., Baluja, S., Anade, T. K.: Rotation Invariant Neural Network-Based Face Detection. In: Proceediongs of Computer Vision and Pattern Recognition (CVPR), pp. 38–44 (1998)
6. Li, S.Z., Zhu, L., Zhang, Z., Blake, A., Zhang, H., Shum, H.: Statistical learning of multiview face detection. In: Heyden, A., Sparr, G., Nielsen, M., Johansen, P. (eds.) ECCV 2002. LNCS, vol. 2353, pp. 67–81. Springer, Heidelberg (2002). https://doi.org/10.1007/3-540-47979-1_5
7. Zhang, K., Zhang, Z., Li, Z., Qiao, Y.: Joint face detection and alignment using multitask cascaded convolutional networks. IEEE Signal Process. Lett. **23**(10), 1499–1503 (2018)
8. Li, H., Lin, Z., Shen, X., Brandt, J., Hua, G.: A convolutional neural network cascade for face detection. In: IEEE Conference on Computer Vision and Pattern Recognition (CVPR), Boston, pp. 5325–5334 (2015)
9. Jain, V., Learned-Miller, E.: FDDB: a benchmark for facedetection in unconstrained settings. University of Massachusetts(Relatório Técnico UM-CS-2010–009), Amherst, pp. 329–337 (2010)
10. Ranjan, R., Patel, V.M., Chellappa, R.: A deep pyramid deformable part model for face detection. In: IEEE 7th International Conference on Biometrics Theory, Applications and Systems (BTAS), Arlington, pp. 1–8 (2015)
11. Yang, S., Luo, P., Loy, C.C., Tang, X.: Faceness-Net: face detection through deep facial part responses. IEEE Trans. Pattern Anal. Mach. Intell. **40**(8), 1845–1859 (2018)
12. Chen, D., Ren, S., Wei, Y., Cao, X., Sun, J.: Joint cascade face detection and alignment. In: Fleet, D., Pajdla, T., Schiele, B., Tuytelaars, T. (eds.) ECCV 2014. LNCS, vol. 8694, pp. 109–122. Springer, Cham (2014). https://doi.org/10.1007/978-3-319-10599-4_8

Access Control Method Based on a Mutual Trust Mechanism in the Edge Computing Environment

Weijin Jiang and Sijian Lv$^{(\boxtimes)}$ ⓘD

College of Computer and Information Engineering,
Hunan University of Technology and Business, Changsha 410205, China
lvsijian8@qq.com

Abstract. The problem of mutual trust between users and edge nodes in an edge computing environment is a sufficient guarantee for the double security of edge computing service users and service providers. How to achieve the user's security and credibility and ensure the trust of the edge service nodes is a serious challenge facing the security of edge computing. In this paper, based on the user behavior trust model and the edge service node trust evaluation model, the concept of mutual trust in edge computing is defined, the mutual trust mechanism and the mutual trust model are designed, and on this basis, the access control model EUSMTM based on mutual trust is proposed. (Edge Users and Edge Servers Mutual Trust Model), the EUSMTM is described in detail in terms of model definition, framework structure, algorithm flow and authorization decision mechanism. The EUSMTM model closely integrates trust management with the RBAC (Role-Based Access Control) model. Aiming at the multi-domain characteristics of the edge computing environment, The EUSMTM model implements intra-domain access control and cross-domain access control strategies based on mutual trust, and it implements the improvement and expansion of the RBAC model in the edge computing environment. By comparing and analyzing the performance of EUSMTM through a simulated environment, the validity of the trust model between the user and the edge server is verified; Through the comparative experiment of two-way trust and one-way trust between the edge user and the edge server, the relative advantages of access control based on two-way trust in the EUSMTM model are analyzed.

Keywords: Edge user · Edge service node · Mutual trust mechanism · Access control · Edge computing

1 Introduction

The dynamic and distributed characteristics of the edge computing environment [1] cause users to face a series of security issues in the process of using the edge computing services and edge platforms [2] in providing services [3], The key to solving these security issues lies in ensuring the security and credibility of the edge computing environment and its users. The security credibility of the edge computing environment is proposed [4], which strengthens the dynamic processing of the edge computing

© Springer Nature Switzerland AG 2021
G. Wang et al. (Eds.): SpaCCS 2020, LNCS 12383, pp. 334–344, 2021.
https://doi.org/10.1007/978-3-030-68884-4_28

network status. It provides a strong policy guarantee for the implementation of more flexible and adaptive edge computing network security and edge service quality [5].

In the edge computing environment, on the one hand, users directly use the software, systems, information resources, programming environment, network infrastructure and other software and hardware devices provided by the edge server [6], which has resulted in the user's impact and destruction on edge computing resources being much more serious than the threat posed by users' use of the Internet, especially the active attacks and sabotage activities initiated by users under cover of their legal identities, which pose a serious threat to the edge computing platform. Therefore, whether the behavior of the edge user is credible and how to predict and evaluate the behavior trust of the edge user is one of the important contents of the edge computing security research. On the other hand, due to the lack of controllability of edge computing resources, devices, and systems, users will psychologically distrust the edge server, including the leakage of user's private information, the security risks of information storage location, data loss, service interruption, and the closure of edge computing operators [7] and other risks. The user's trust in the edge server is the premise to decide whether the user accepts the services provided by edge computing and is willing to store the information in the cloud [8]. Therefore, the user's trust in the edge server is very important. Establishing an effective mutual trust model between the edge server and user behavior is the key to ensuring the security of the edge computing environment. The importance of establishing mutual trust between the user and the edge server is mainly reflected in the following three aspects [9, 10].

(1) Through the problem abstraction to accurately describe the credibility requirements of the edge computing system, it is convenient to achieve a comprehensive understanding of the edge computing security requirements. And through the mathematical method to analyze the loopholes in the credibility of the system and establish a trust model.
(2) The formal description, verification and application of the trust model can improve the credibility of the edge computing system and help the two-way trust choice between users and edge servers.
(3) Establishing a trust assessment theory that includes the risk assessment of the edge computing environment and the description of user's attack behavior is the prerequisite and foundation for the realization of trust monitoring, prediction and assessment of a comprehensive edge computing system.

2 Related Work

Edge computing uses many edge devices to provide users with near-earth real-time computing and storage functions It migrates some or all of the computing tasks in the cloud to edge devices, which can meet the needs of users for low latency and fast response. It has good application effects in scenarios such as smart car networking, virtual reality, medical care, smart home, and smart city [11]. Edge devices take care of consumers and producers of data, and most of the user's privacy information is stored at the edge layer. However, edge computing lacks the same stable infrastructure protection facilities as cloud computing, coupled with the open features of edge computing such as content perception, real-time computing, and parallel processing, resulting in a lack of necessary trust between devices that brings challenges to the security of edge devices.

The trust mechanism can effectively resist internal attacks on the network and is currently one of the key technologies to ensure that the device provides reliable services [12], It is widely used in computing modes such as cloud computing, P2P, and wireless sensor networks [13]. There are many existing trust model research results. In addition to evaluation models based on subjective logic, DS evidence theory, fuzzy evidence theory, Bayesian networks, and neural networks, there are also evaluation models based on other methods such as recommended node similarity, scoring deviation, and reward and punishment measures. However, in the face of a complex and changeable edge computing environment, the old trust model will have certain limitations. Firstly, the edge layer contains a large number of high-frequency interactive devices that form a complex and huge trust network. Storing and querying this trust information will consume a lot of time and space; Secondly, most edge devices are resource-constrained devices, which are difficult to undertake complex storage and query tasks. Therefore, building a lightweight trust evaluation model suitable for edge computing environments has important practical significance.

3 Access Control Method Based on Mutual Trust

3.1 Mutual Trust Model Between the User and Edge Server

Overview of Mutual Trust Mechanism

The mutual trust mechanism between the user and the edge server is divided into two layers: one layer is the trust prediction of the edge server to the user's behavior, and the other layer is the user's trust evaluation of the edge service node [14]. Whether it is the user's trust screening of edge service nodes or the judgment of the edge server's trust in user behavior, the basic trust mechanism follows the general construction process of the trust model.

In the edge computing environment, users interact with edge service nodes to obtain edge computing resources or services. In the interaction process, the user and the edge server are equal, that is, trust is mutual [15]. In order to achieve trusted interaction in the edge computing environment, the edge server must prevent malicious user behavior from damaging the cloud environment. Therefore, the behavior information of the edge user, whether it is the user's legal or malicious behavior, will affect the edge server's judgment on the credibility of the edge user, and then screens users for trust; At the same time, when the edge service node provides resources or services to users, factors such as the timeliness of response, the availability of resources and the effectiveness of the service will affect the user's judgment on the trustworthiness of the edge service node, that is, The trust relationship between the user and the edge service node must include two two-way trust selection processes [16, 17]. As shown in Fig. 1.

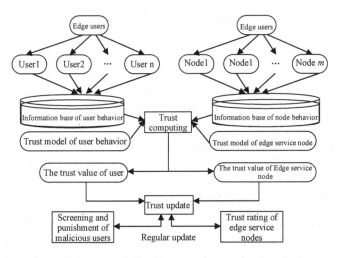

Fig. 1. The process of the trust relationship between edge users and edge service nodes

Through the research of related trust models in distributed systems, grid computing, P2P systems, cloud computing, and edge computing systems, the behavioral trust model between edge users and edge servers in this paper is based on the following basic ideas.

(1) The two-way trust structure of the trust model. During the interaction between users and edge servers, the trust relationship is two-way and equal to each other. Users will screen the trust of each node in the edge server according to the level of trust. At the same time, in order to prevent malicious users from attacking the edge server, the edge server will also screen the user trust and provide selectively users with edge services or resources.

(2) Collection and processing of behavioral trust information. Behavior trust information is divided into two categories, user behavior information and node behavior information, which are stored in the user behavior information database and the node behavior information database respectively.

(3) Calculation and update of trust value. User behavior trust value is obtained through trust evidence and trust attribute matrix, and the update process shows a certain degree of reward and punishment; The calculation of the trust value of the edge server is combined with the ant colony algorithm to introduce trust pheromone, and the trust pheromone is used to determine the degree of user trust in the edge service node. In the process of updating the trust value, the influence of time must be fully considered.

Mutual Trust Model Design

In the edge computing environment, users send resource or service access requests to the edge server according to their needs [18]. In the process of cloud interaction, the user and the edge server are equal, so the trust between the two is mutual [19]. Due to the existence of uncertainty in the edge computing environment, the greater the uncertainty of cloud interaction, the more necessary mutual trust. In addition, due to the vulnerability of edge computing, its potential risks are very large, which also requires mutual trust.

Definition 1. Mutual trust. Due to the different focus, the definition of mutual trust varies. Mutual trust in edge computing is defined as the mutual trust between users and edge servers in uncertain future interaction behavior. At time t, the mutual trust between user u and edge service node c can be formally expressed as MT, $MT = <T_u, T_c(t)>$.

Definition 2. Mutual trust threshold. The mutual trust threshold MTT consists of a two-tuple, $MTT = <TT_{user}, TT_{cloud}>$, that is, the user trust threshold TT_{user}, and the edge server threshold TT_{cloud}, TT_{user} determines whether the edge user is trustworthy. The edge computing environment decides whether to allow the edge service nodes in it to accept and accept user access requests: TT_{cloud} determines whether the edge service node is qualified to provide services to users.

By defining the mutual trust threshold MTT, users with a trust level of less than TT_{user} will not be able to obtain edge computing resources and services, and edge service nodes with a trust level of less than TT_{cloud} will not be able to provide users with cloud resources and services.。

Definition 3 Trust decision. Trust decision is represented by the symbol $Td, Td \in \{0, 1\}$. The trust decision-making process is represented by Eq. (7–1).

$$Td = \{ \begin{array}{l} 1, (T_{user} \geq TT_{user}) \cap (T_c(t) \geq TT_{cloud}) \\ 0, other \end{array} \tag{1}$$

If $Td = 1$, the mutual trust relationship between the user and the edge service node is established, and the edge computing platform allows the two to interact; If $Td = 0$, cloud interaction between the two is not allowed.

4 Simulation Experiment and Performance Analysis

In order to gain a deeper understanding of the mutual trust relationship between the user and the edge server, and analyze the impact of various factors on the mutual trust in the edge computing environment, including the relationship between user behavior trust and edge service node trust, behavior and time, we designed two Group simulation experiment. The first group is the simulation experiment of the trust model between the user and the edge server. Through this group of experiments, on the one hand, the influence of the entity's behavior information and time factors on the degree of trust is studied; on the other hand, the effectiveness of the proposed trust model between users and edge servers in this article is verified by comparison with other trust models. The second group is the EUSMTM model simulation experiment analysis. Through this group of comparative experiments, it is found that trust-based access control is more dynamic than the RBAC model and other untrusted access control systems. Besides, a comparative analysis of cloud interaction success rates based on mutual trust access control and one-way trust access control highlights the superiority of the EUSMTM model proposed in this paper.

4.1 Edge Server Dynamic Trust Evaluation Method

Edge Server Trust Relationship
There are multiple edge service nodes in the edge computing environment to provide users with resources or services, and the network environment and scale of edge computing have been in a dynamic state of change. The interaction and trust relationship between users and edge service nodes are intricate. The historical interaction behavior and time influencing factors, we give the following definition of their trust level.

Definition 4. Direct Trust. Direct trust is the degree of trust established by the user and the edge server through direct interaction experience. The direct trust of the user to the edge server is related to the interaction events and time factors between the two. The more interactions, the higher direct trust of the entity, indicated by the symbol Dt, for two entities that have never interacted, the value of Dt is usually set to zero. At time t, the direct trust of user u in edge service node c is expressed as $Dt_c(t)$.

Definition 5. Trust Pheromone. Trust pheromone is the basic knowledge of the user's direct trust degree of the edge service node behavior. This word is marked as Tp. At time t, the trust pheromone of the user u to the edge service node c can be expressed as $Tp_c(t)$. At the initial moment, $Tp_c(0) = C$ (C is a constant). If the initial trust level is zero, then the trust pheromone must also be zero, $Dt_c(t) = 0 \Rightarrow Tp_c(0) = 0$.

Definition 6. Heuristic Pheromone. Cognitive pheromone is the user's cognitive information about the edge service node, that is, the user's perception of the Euler distance from the node. This word is marked as Hp. At time t, the cognitive pheromone of the user u to the edge service node c can be expressed as $Tp_c(t)$. Cognitive pheromone can be calculated by the following formula:

$$Hp_c(t) = \frac{1}{d_{u,c}} \tag{2}$$

The trust pheromone and cognitive trust element given in Definition 5 and Definition 6 together constitute the direct trust relationship of the user to the entity. In the ACO algorithm, the transfer probability of an ant is used to represent the ant's choice of different paths. In the edge computing environment, the important basis for the user to select an entity that provides resources/services is the entity's direct trust. Therefore, at time t, the direct trust user u in edge service node C can be formalized as:

$$Dt_c(t) = \frac{Tp_c(t)^a Hp_c^\beta}{\sum_{i \in E} Tp_i(t)^a Hp_i^\beta} \tag{3}$$

Among them, a is the weight of the trust pheromone between u and c, which is the weight of the cognitive trust element (the initial value is given according to the actual situation), E represents the set of entities that can be selected by the user u, $E = \{1, 2, ..., m\}$.

4.2   Model Experiment and Performance Analysis of Mutual Trust Between the User and Edge Server

This section verifies the effect of the proposed user and edge server trust evaluation model on the interaction success rate through simulation experiments and verifies the rationality and effectiveness of the improved ant colony optimization algorithm applied in edge server trust management.

Simulation Experiment Environment and Parameter Setting
Hadoop is open-source software that can realize large-scale distributed computing, and is widely used in the field of edge computing. Therefore, the experiment in this paper runs on the MapReduce platform in Hadoop. In order to verify the effectiveness of the mutual trust model between the user and the edge server, and to obtain the relationship of mutual trust with entity behavior and time, the following experimental network environment and entity interaction behavior scenarios were set up with the goal of being close to real random and complex networks.

Experiment 1 is to verify that the amount of data that needs to be processed in the experiments on the influence of entity behavior and time factors on mutual trust is not large, so only a small number of nodes are simulated in this experiment. Experiment 2 is to verify the effectiveness of the trust evaluation algorithm between users and edge servers and requires high network complexity and dynamics. Therefore, a network environment composed of 100–700 nodes is simulated in the laboratory to compare users and the success rate of the interaction between the edge server trust evaluation model and the Apriori model and the ability to resist attacks. The user and edge server trust evaluation model are proposed under the co-inspiration of the analytic hierarchy process AHP and the ant colony optimization algorithm ACO.

In addition, the setting of parameters in the ant colony algorithm has a great influence on the performance of the algorithm. According to the experiment, the best parameter setting of the ant colony model is selected, namely $\alpha = 1$, $\beta = 5$, $\rho = 0.5$.

Experimental Results and Performance Analysis
Experiment 1. The performance comparison between EUSMTM model and APRIORI model.

The APRIORI model is a network trust management model that uses the Apriori algorithm to extract the behavior patterns adopted by users during their network interactions in the literature [20], and uses the naive Bayes classifier for the final decision of the probability of user trust. It can be seen from Fig. 2 that in the initial stage, the interaction success rate of the APRIORI model is lower than that of EUSMTM. The reason is that in the edge computing environment, the number of nodes and the number of users in the network is in a dynamic process, although APRIORI is in The interaction success rate in the static network can reach over 96%, but the interaction success rate in the dynamic network is relatively lower than the EUSMTM model. As the number of interactions increases, both the EUSMTM model and the APRIORI model can continuously learn to select nodes with higher trust to interact with each other through the ant colony algorithm, so as to increase the success rate of their interactions. Malicious implementation problems will inevitably occur in the general trust model. The APRIORI model does not consider malicious recommendation entities, while the EUSMTM model fully considers the trust of intermediate entities and selects entities with relatively high trust as the recommendation entity to reduce the number of attacks.

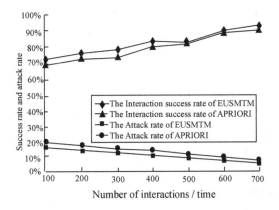

Fig. 2. Performance comparison between EUSMTM model and APRIORI

4.3 EUSMTM Model Simulation Experiment and Performance Analysis

In order to verify the feasibility and effectiveness of the access control model (EUSMTM) based on mutual trust between users and edge servers proposed in this paper, the simulation experiment of EUSMTM algorithm is carried out through the Hadoop edge computing application platform built on the server in the laboratory. Finally, the performance of the algorithm is analyzed and compared according to the experimental results. The experimental evaluation standard adopts Rate of Successful Transaction, which is the ratio of the number of successful interactions between users and edge services to the total number of interactions.

Trust-Based Access Control and Untrusted Access Control Model
Experiment 2. Comparison of trust-based access control and role-based access control.

This experiment compares the trust-based access control model proposed in this paper with the RBAC model. The user entity sends a resource access request to the trust-based access control system and the RBAC system at the same time, and the two systems authorize and access resources according to their respective access control rules. Over time, the number of accessible resources of the user in the two systems is changing. The data obtained from the experiment is shown in Fig. 3. It can be seen that in the RBAC system, the number of resources accessible by the user entity is constant, while in the trust-based access control system, the number of accessible resources of the user entity changes with the change of the trust value, which is sufficient to prove that the model is fine-grained.

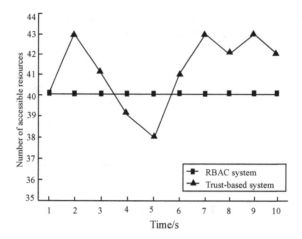

Fig. 3. Number of accessible resources in different access control systems

Experiment 3. Comparison of trust-based access control algorithms with traditional access control methods.

The trust-based evaluation algorithm in this article is compared with other computing methods, the edge service success rate under the edge computing environment is introduced, and the advantages and disadvantages of the two methods are compared. The edge service success rate is defined as the ratio of the number of successful services to the total number of services. It can be seen from Fig. 4 that the success rate of edge computing services based on traditional access control methods shows a decreasing trend over time, while the trust-based evaluation method proposed in this article has a higher success rate and dynamic changes. The accessible resources of trusted entities always have a higher success rate of edge services.

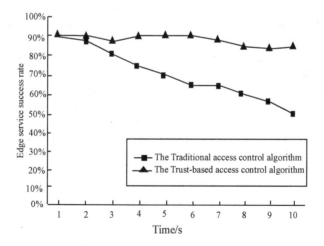

Fig. 4. Comparison of edge service success rate

5 Conclusion

Studying the mutual trust between users and edge servers in the edge computing environment is an effective guarantee for the dual security of edge computing service users and service providers. How to not only achieve user security and credibility but also ensure the trust and reliability of edge service nodes is also a severe challenge facing edge computing security. Based on the user behavior trust model and the edge server trust evaluation model, this paper defines the concept of mutual trust in edge computing designs the mutual trust mechanism and mutual trust model. And on this basis, a mutual trust-based access control model EUSMTM is proposed, and EUSMTM is defined and introduced in detail in terms of model definition, framework structure, algorithm flow and authorization decision mechanism. The EUSMTM model closely combines trust management with the RBAC model, implements intra-domain access control and cross-domain access control strategies based on mutual trust, and realizes the improvement and expansion of the RBAC model in the edge computing environment in view of the multi-domain characteristics of the edge computing environment. The EUSMTM model closely integrates trust management with the RBAC (Role-Based Access Control) model. Aiming at the multi-domain characteristics of the edge computing environment, The EUSMTM model implements intra-domain access control and cross-domain access control strategies based on mutual trust, and it implements the improvement and expansion of the RBAC model in the edge computing environment. By comparing and analyzing the performance of EUSMTM through a simulated environment, the validity of the trust model between the user and the edge server is verified; Through the comparative experiment of two-way trust and one-way trust between the edge user and the edge server, the relative advantages of access control based on two-way trust in the EUSMTM model are analyzed.

Acknowledgments. This work was supported by the National Natural Science Foundation of China (61772196; 61472136), and the Hunan Provincial Focus Natural Science Fund (2020JJ4249), and the Key Social Science Fund of Hunan Provincial (2016ZDB006), and the Key Project of Hunan Provincial Social Science Achievement Review Committee (XSP 19ZD1005), and the Hunan Province Academic Degree and Graduate Education Reform Research Project (2020JGYB234), and the Hunan University of Technology and Business Degree and Graduate Education Teaching Reform Project (YJG2019YB13), and the Hunan University of Technology and Business Teaching Reform Project (School Teaching Word [2020] No. 15).

References

1. Shi, W., Cao, J., Zhang, Q., Li, Y., Xu, L.: Edge computing: vision and challenges. IEEE Internet Things J. **3**(5), 637–646 (2016)
2. Satyanarayanan, M.: The emergence of edge computing. Computer **50**(1), 30–39 (2017)
3. Mäkitalo, N., Ometov, A., Kannisto, J., Andreev, S., Koucheryavy, Y., Mikkonen, T.: Safe, secure executions at the network edge: coordinating cloud, edge, and fog computing. IEEE Softw. **35**(1), 30–37 (2017)

4. Roman, R., Lopez, J., Mambo, M.: Mobile edge computing, fog et al.: a survey and analysis of security threats and challenges. Future Gener. Comput. Syst. **78**, 680–698 (2018).

5. Wang, T., Zhang, G., Liu, A., Bhuiyan, M.Z.A., Jin, Q.: A secure IoT service architecture with an efficient balance dynamics based on cloud and edge computing. IEEE Internet Things J. **6**(3), 4831–4843 (2018)

6. Garcia Lopez, P., et al.: Edge-centric computing: vision and challenges. In: ACM, New York (2015)

7. Alrowaily, M., Lu, Z.: Secure edge computing in IoT systems: review and case studies. In: IEEE/ACM Symposium on Edge Computing (SEC), pp. 440–444. IEEE (2018)

8. Abbas, N., Zhang, Y., Taherkordi, A., Skeie, T.: Mobile edge computing: a survey. IEEE Internet Things J. **5**(1), 450–465 (2017)

9. Xu, X., Xue, Y., Qi, L., Yuan, Y., Zhang, X., Umer, T., Wan, S.: An edge computing-enabled computation offloading method with privacy preservation for internet of connected vehicles. Future Gener. Comput. Syst. **96**, 89–100 (2019)

10. Aggarwal, C., Srivastava, K.: Securing IoT devices using SDN and edge computing. In: 2nd International Conference on Next Generation Computing Technologies (NGCT) 2016, pp. 877–882. IEEE (2016)

11. Shi, W., Dustdar, S.: The promise of edge computing. Computer **49**(5), 78–81 (2016)

12. Guo, J., Ma, J., Li, X., Zhang, T., Liu, Z.: A situational awareness trust evolution model for mobile devices in D2D communication. IEEE Access **6**, 4375–4386 (2017)

13. Ahmed, A., Abu Bakar, K., Channa, M.I., Haseeb, K., Khan, A.W.: A survey on trust based detection and isolation of malicious nodes in ad-hoc and sensor networks. Front. Comput. Sci. **9**(2), 280–296 (2014). https://doi.org/10.1007/s11704-014-4212-5

14. Zhang, P., Zhou, M., Fortino, G.: Security and trust issues in Fog computing: a survey. Future Gener. Comput. Syst. **88**, 16–27 (2018)

15. Zhang, J., Chen, B., Zhao, Y., Cheng, X., Hu, F.: Data security and privacy-preserving in edge computing paradigm: survey and open issues. IEEE Access **6**, 18209–18237 (2018)

16. Chen, L., Xu, J.: Socially trusted collaborative edge computing in ultra dense networks. In: Proceedings of the Second ACM/IEEE Symposium on Edge Computing, p. 11 (2017)

17. Wang, T., Luo, H., Jia, W., Liu, A., Xie, M.: MTES: an intelligent trust evaluation scheme in sensor-cloud enabled industrial Internet of Things. IEEE Trans. Ind. Inf. (2019)

18. He, Y., Yu, F.R., Zhao, N., Yin, H.: Secure social networks in 5G systems with mobile edge computing, caching, and device-to-device communications. IEEE Wirel. Commun. **25**(3), 103–109 (2018)

19. Rathi, S.R., Kolekar, V.K.: Trust Model for Computing Security of Cloud. In: Fourth International Conference on Computing Communication Control and Automation (ICCUBEA), pp. 1–5. IEEE (2018)

20. D'Angelo, G., Rampone, S., Palmieri, F.: Developing a trust model for pervasive computing based on Apriori association rules learning and Bayesian classification. Soft. Comput. **21**(21), 6297–6315 (2016). https://doi.org/10.1007/s00500-016-2183-1

Increasing Crop Yield Using Agriculture Sensing Data in Smart Plant Factory

Zengwei Zheng[1], Pengquan Yan[1,2], Yuanyi Chen[1(✉)], Jianping Cai[1], and Fengle Zhu[1]

[1] School of Computing and Computational Science, Zhejiang University City College, Hangzhou 310015, China
{zhengzw,chenyuanyi,caijp,zhufl}@zucc.edu.cn
[2] School of Computer Science and Technology, Zhejiang University, Hangzhou 310058, China
yanpq@zju.edu.cn

Abstract. With population growth and climate change, traditional agriculture has been unable to meet social needs well. Meanwhile, with the development of sensor hardware equipment and machine learning technology, smart agriculture has become an important transformation direction of traditional agriculture. In this study, we are committed to the analysis and processing of sensor data collected in plant factories and we model crop development as an optimization problem with respect to certain parameters, such as yield and environmental impact, which can be optimized in an automated way. More exactly, we utilize a Markov decision process to characterize crop development, then propose a deep reinforcement learning based optimization algorithm for improved crop productivity. Several simulation experiments were carried out to optimize the yield of sugar beet in plant factories. The experimental results show that this method has a good effect and makes reasonable use of the data obtained by sensors, and provides agricultural experts with a road to more sustainable agriculture.

Keywords: Smart agriculture · Plant factory · Yield optimization · Deep reinforcement learning · Sensor data mining

1 Introduction

As the population continues to expand, the pressure on agricultural cultural systems will increase. Greenhouses, or indoor farming, have sprung up to avoid the loss of produce caused by abrupt weather changes and to help crops plant against the season. In recent years, with the emergence of intelligent machines and lots of sensors on farms, and the increase in the amount and scope of farm data, agricultural processes will become increasingly data-driven and data-enabled [19,20,25]. Computer technology, especially the Internet of Things and cloud computing, have been rapidly applied to production systems such as greenhouses and indoor

G. Wang et al. (Eds.): SpaCCS 2020, LNCS 12383, pp. 345–356, 2021.
https://doi.org/10.1007/978-3-030-68884-4_29

farming [4,12], bringing many changes to the daily production tasks of crops. Various sensors use Wi-Fi signals for information transmission and, ultimately, computing via cloud servers or edge devices [21–23]. At the same time, the researchers also developed advanced greenhouse environment control technology, realized the LED light [8], temperature [5], relative humidity [3,24], CO_2 concentration [9] and other greenhouse environmental variables optimization. However, these researches are not beyond the stage of precision agriculture for the time being. There is still a long way to go to achieve smart agriculture.

Previous studies mainly focused on the optimization of crop growth and crop yield by changing single environmental variable or coupling of two environmental variables [17]. Obviously, since every consideration of environmental factors will lead to the increase of the complexity index of the model, no one has considered all the effects of external environment on the growth of crops at present [6]. The studied control variables have only been restricted to the environmental factors and have been not included any physiological crop responses, the optimization of crop growth has not been realized yet.

In order to realize the optimization of the crop production process and crop production, we're thinking about using deep reinforcement learning. Machine learning approaches are more suitable for dealing with complex systems [2,15], than traditional mathematical methods. Machine learning, especially deep learning [14], has emerged together with big data technologies and high-performance computing to create new opportunities to unravel, quantify, and understand data intensive processes in agricultural operational environments. Deep reinforcement learning methods deliver better-than-human performance in various tasks, such as image analysis, game-playing, control and optimization [16]. Similarly, in agriculture, these methods can be invoked as decision support systems and intelligent controllers to match or even surpass human performance. The power of deep reinforcement learning systems comes with their ability to learn from real world data. Rather than carrying out hardcoded behavior, such algorithms learn by themselves, through large numbers of experiments, to optimize a particular outcome. We established a Markov decision problem to characterize optimal yield for crop management in plant factory. These environmental factors that can be controlled in a plant factory are considered inputs, while the responses of the crops that can be measured are considered outputs. These environmental variables include light intensity, temperature, humidity, CO_2 concentration and the addition of culture medium in the plant factory. These measurable crop responses include plant height, weight, leaf density, calculated respiration rate, photosynthetic rate, and crop yield. In general, however, it is difficult to achieve process optimization because the interactions between the crop responses and the environmental factors are difficult to understand due to the complexity of the physical and physiological processes involved. For such a difficult problem to model, deep reinforcement learning is a good way to learn the interaction model and make corresponding decision optimization. Considering the optimization of crop environmental variables is continuous. We use a deep reinforcement learning algorithm, Deep Deterministic Policy Gradient (DDPG) [18], which can work with high-dimensional continuous state and action space.

Machine learning techniques have not been directly applied to the control of essential agricultural supply channels, such as irrigation, fertilization, and provision of other nutrients. In this paper, we focus on directly applying deep reinforcement learning techniques to control and optimize the crop growth for the yield maximization. Further reducing human intervention in plant factories is a small step towards smart agriculture [7]. The paper is structured as following: in Sect. 2, we introduce previous researchers conducted studies on the optimization of the internal environment of plant factories, In Sect. 3, we describe how to abstract the problem of crop growth into a Markov decision problem and use the deep reinforcement learning to deal with. In Sect. 4, we briey introduce a simulation software, designed by Wageningen University and Research Centre. And we show the simulation results based on the simulation software. In Sect. 5, the conclusion section gives us the overall of the paper and suggests the things to do in the future.

2 Background

Our focus is mainly on smart agriculture, how to use a large number of sensors in plant factories to analyze and obtain environmental regulation strategies conducive to crop growth. We found that most of the current environmental regulation strategies in plant factories are based on the empirical values obtained after the experiment of experts controlling a single environmental variable, which has obvious space for optimization.

2.1 Consider the Control Optimization of Single Variable Within Plant Factory

The growth of crops needs sunshine, and the quality of illumination conditions determines the yield and quality of agricultural organisms. Appropriate control of illumination environment is crucial to the realization and sustainable development of high-quality and high-yield crops in plant factories.

The control of light intensity and light duration is very important during the growth of crops. Within a certain range, the intensity of photosynthesis is positively correlated with the intensity of light. When the crop is at the light compensation point, the accumulation of photosynthetic products is equal to the consumption, so it cannot accumulate dry matter and consumes dry matter in dark period. Therefore, the crop can only grow when the intensity of care is higher than that at the light compensation point [8].

The temperature in the growing environment of crops has great influence on photosynthesis, respiration, accumulation of photosynthetic products and growth of root system. In order for these growth and physiological processes to proceed normally, it is necessary to control the ambient temperature in the plant within a reasonable range. Under the optimum temperature, the growth and physiological activities of crops can be carried out normally, and the accumulation rate of photosynthetic products is higher. The suitable temperature for the growth of crops the type, variety, growth stage and physiological activities of crops change day and night [5]. The suitable temperature for plant factory lettuce obtained by researchers is shown in the Table 1.

Table 1. The temperature at which lettuce grows in a plant factory

Name	Germination	Seedling		Harvest	
		Light period	Dark period	Light period	Dark period
Lettuce	18–20 °C	15–20 °C	12–14 °C	18–20 °C	12–15 °C

The humidity in the air is related to the transpiration of plants and the evaporation of culture medium, thus affecting the intensity of photosynthesis. At the same time, improper humidity control will lead to the occurrence of crop diseases. Too low humidity will lead to too much leaf evaporation, and the root may have insufficient water supply, leading to a decrease in photosynthetic efficiency. When humidity is too high, leaf evaporation is low, water in crops is too much, stems and leaves increase, and crop yield also decreases. At the same time, when the humidity exceeds 90%, the crops are likely to produce serious pests and diseases. When humidity falls below 20%, the chances of a plant contracting powdery mildew greatly increase [3]. Therefore, it is very important for the growth of crops to control the humidity in plant factories.

CO_2 is an important raw material for crop growth. When the CO_2 concentration around leaves increased from the compensation point to the saturation point, the photosynthetic rate increased linearly with the increase of CO_2 concentration. When the CO_2 concentration exceeds the saturation point, the maximum rate of photosynthesis will remain unchanged within a certain range. But as the concentration continues to increase the time cooperation will stop. The concentration of CO_2 in the atmosphere is far less than the saturation point of CO_2 in general crops, so appropriate supplementation of CO_2 has become an important means of efficient production in plant factories. In plant factories, the concentration of CO_2 is generally controlled at 800–1000 ml/L [9].

2.2   Consider Combination of Factors Within Plant Factory

In the past, researchers considered fitting all the external environment of plant growth and crop growth [11], using Q-learning algorithm and Genetic algorithms(GA) to optimize the analysis, hoping to get the most suitable external environment for plant growth. Q-learning is one of the earliest reinforcement learning methods. In the case of a finite-stage process like in a crop management problem, the estimate Q_n of the function Q^* is regularly updated after each trial of the crop simulation, according to the selected actions and to the observed final reward like yield for instance. And in their case, the most promising approach to adapt GA to the sequential decision rule problem we encounter seems to be the one developped in the SAMUEL system. However, the disadvantages are obvious. Like for dynamic programming algorithms, it is difficult to adapt them to more compact strategy representations like decision rules.

3   Sensor Data Analysis and Crop Yield Optimization

The main work flow of smart agriculture is:

- Sensing and monitoring: the environmental attributes and crop attributes of plant factories were measured.
- Analysis and decision making: through analyzing the relationship between environmental data and crop data, appropriate control decisions are made.

3.1   Introduction to Markov Decision Process for Crop

In order to implement a deep reinforcement learning algorithm for solving this optimization problem, we need to model crop management strategies as a Markov decision problem. Crop management can be divided into a series of decision steps about sowing, applying fertilizer, and so on until harvest. In order to optimize crop yields and control the environment in plant factory, we consider each day as a step in crop management. This means that our decision line is as long as the number of days the crop grows. In addition, we took observed crop attributes (including plant height, weight, leaf density, respiration rate, photosynthetic rate, and crop yield) as each state, and defined decisions as environmental variables that could be controlled in the plant factory (including light temperature, humidity, CO_2 concentration, and nutrient solution). The details will be covered in the Sect. 4.

Each step i has an associated state space S_i and decision space D_i, and these spaces S_i and D_i are respectively characterized by a vector composed of a set of state variables and a vector composed of a set of decision variables. A trajectory of this decision process is the result of choosing randomly an initial state s in S_1 and applying a decision d from s to s' in S_2, and so on until S_N. The Markov property requires that the stochastic transition from s in S_i to s' in S_{i+1} given the decision d in D_i is completely determined by the probability $P_i(s'|s,d)$. As for the objective function, we assume maximum crop yield per unit area. The objective function $V = E(r_i + \cdots + r_N)$ where the r_i terms are the rewards from S_i to S_{i+1} along the trajectory. A policy is a function that maps states to decisions. For instance, a policy Π can be represented as a set of sub-policies $(\Pi_1, \cdots, \Pi_N)$. Each sub-policy Π_i is defined as a function which maps state s in S_i to decision d in D_i. Hence, given a policy and an initial state s in S_i we can determine step after step until harvest. What are the decisions to apply to the crop, depending on the current state of the crop and the mapping that we learned. The problem of growing crops in plant factory is now defined as an optimization problem, and generate an optimal policy Π that maximizes $V_n = E(r_i + \cdots + r_N|\Pi)$.

3.2   A Reinforcement Learning Approach

Today reinforcement learning is one the major approach to solving Markov decision problems with unknown transition probabilities and with large state and decision variable domains [10]. One of the main interests of reinforcement learning algorithms stems on their capacity to be adapted to continuous or large-scale state and decision variable domains. Reinforcement learning problems are modeled as a discrete-time Markov decision process with a tuple of $<S, A, P, r, \gamma>$. It includes a state space S; an action space A(in reinforcement learning, we are more used to calling decisions D as actions A.); a transition function $P(s_{t+1}|s_t, a_t)$, that measures the probability of obtaining the next state s_{t+1} given a current state-action pair (s_t, a_t); $r(s_t, a_t)$ defines the immediate reward achieved at each state-action pair, and $\gamma \in (0, 1)$ denotes a discount factor. A sequence of state-action pairs (s_t, a_t) creates a trajectory ε_t (also called an episode) with the discounted cumulative reward given by

$$R(\varepsilon) = \sum_{t=0}^{T} \gamma^t r(s_t, a_t). \tag{1}$$

A RL algorithm tries to find an optimal policy Π in order to maximize the expected total discounted reward as follows:

$$J(\Pi) = \mathbb{E}[\mathbb{R}(\varepsilon)] = \int p(\varepsilon|\Pi) R(\varepsilon) d\varepsilon \tag{2}$$

Policy gradient based methods is one of approach to find the optimal policy [13]. In the policy gradient based methods, the policy is parameterized by parameters vector θ and is updated along the gradient direction of the expected total discounted rewards as

$$\theta_{k+1} = \theta_k + \alpha \nabla_\theta J[\Pi(\theta_k)], \tag{3}$$

where α denotes a learning rate and k is currently update number.

3.3   Using DDPG for Crop Management

DDPG is not a state-of-the-art deep reinforcement learning algorithm. However, its performance in high dimensional space and continuous variable learning is still very excellent [18]. It inherits characteristics of a policy gradient mode and an actor-critic method. One of the big advantages of DDPG is dealing with high dimensional continuous state and action space, which are necessary to apply to control problem. The network parameters in actor's policy are updated based on Deterministic Policy Gradient, which is a recent method in policy gradient.

Overall DDPG procedure is demonstrated in Fig. 1. In this figure, actor network is a deep neural network (DNN) with parameters θ^μ and $\theta^{\mu'}$. Critic Network is another DNN with parameters θ^Q and $\theta^{Q'}$. The procedure of DDPG algorithm is explained as following:

1. The crop observes state s_t and transfers to Actor Network.
2. The Actor Network receives s_t as an input and generates an action a_t as an output.
3. After that, the action is added a small noise and is sent back to the PCSE.
4. Then agent computes a reward r_t, and next state s_{t+1}.
5. The tuple of $<s_t, a_t, r_t, s_{t+1}>$ is stored to an experience pool. In the experience pool, we randomly select a batch of N tuples and use them to learn the policies.
6. Compute loss function (TD error) as follow:
   $L = \frac{1}{N} \sum_i (y_i - Q(s_i, a_i|\theta^Q))^2$ with $y_i = r_i + \gamma Q^{'}(s_{t+1}, \mu^{'}(s_{t+1}|\theta^{\mu^{'}})|\theta^{Q^{'}})$.
7. Then, update critic network by minimizing the loss L and update actor network using deterministic policy gradient theorem.

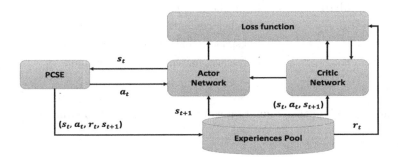

Fig. 1. Procedure of DDPG algorithm in data analysis layer

4 Experiments

The goals of the experiments are (1) to prove that reinforcement learning can better control the growth of crops and (2) to show that this method can achieve yield maximization in plant factory.

4.1 Simulation Environment

Since the real crop growth process is relatively slow, and direct training in plant factories or cause greater economic losses. We need an appropriate simulation software to verify the control and optimization effect of deep reinforcement learning algorithm. In the end we chose crop simulation models developed in Wageningen for the following reasons: first, the Wageningen university that developed it is well-known and trustworthy in agriculture, and second, the simulation software is still under continuous development and maintenance.

PCSE (Python Crop Simulation Environment) is a Python package for building crop simulation models [1]. To implement continuous simulation, the engine uses the same approach as FSE: Euler integration with a fixed time step of one day.

Table 2. All the attribute in each action

Attribute name	Description
TMAX	Daily maximum temperature
TMIN	Daily minimum temperature
VAP	Mean daily vapour pressure
CO_2	Mean daily CO_2 concentration
HUMIDITY	Mean daily environmental humidity
LIGHT	Daily global radiation
N	Nitrogen content in culture medium
P	Phosphorus content in culture medium
K	Potassium content in culture medium

To accommodate the simulation software, we designed the dimension of the action space to be nine dimensions. Table 2 gives a detail of each dimension in action space.

4.2 Analysis of the Reward Function and the Learned Strategies

What kind of reward is designed for a particular problem can be studied. A poorly designed reward will generally result in an non-convergent network, a not ideal result or an agent simply not experiencing what you want it to learn. In general, the reward design follows the principle that the simpler the better. The challenge with designing the reward function is that the consequences of a single action are not fully reflected by the immediate reward feedback, but may have long-term effects. For example, the decision to undergo surgery brings risks and discomfort to the patient (low immediate return) but significantly improves long-term health (high return at a later date). This is also facing the same problem in the agricultural field. We hope to accumulate yield, but only when the crop reaches maturity can yield be accumulated, which means that the agent of reinforcement learning cannot get effective feedback in a long period of time. Therefore, a good reinforcement learning system must optimize the long-term total return, which is challenging because feedback can be severely delayed.

A positive reward function will encourage the agent of reinforcement learning to accumulate rewards and do actions that can obtain higher returns, so as to maximize crop yield accumulation in the process of crop growth. On the contrary, a negative reward can also be called punishment. Training the agent of reinforcement learning to reduce actions that will be punished, so that crops can enter the maturity stage as soon as possible when growing, pass the punishment stage with no yield, and start to accumulate yield.

Our optimization goal is crop yield, and in general crop yield changes over time are shown in Fig. 2(a). We used the real data collected in 2004 to carry out the simulation experiment.

Such optimization goals dictate that rewards will be sparse at certain times during the crop's months-long growth cycle. Sparse reward function leads to slow convergence of the algorithm. Agents need to interact with the environment for many times and learn a large number of samples to converge to the optimal solution, or even fail to converge. The current better solution is to give agents rewards beyond the return function.

$$r'(s_t, a_t, s_{t+1}) = r(s_t, a_t, s_{t+1}) + F(s_{t+1}) \tag{4}$$

where $r'(s_t, a_t, s_{t+1})$ is the reward function after the change, $F(s_{t+1})$ is called the intrinsic reward, and this process is called reward shaping.

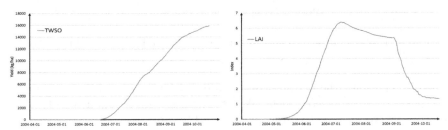

(a) The TWSO(yield) of sugarbeet varies with planting time in real data

(b) The LAI of sugarbeet varies with planting time in real data

Fig. 2. The change of the attribute value of sugarbeet during the real growth process

Observe the change of each attribute of the crop throughout the growth cycle. We consider using leaf area index(LAI) values to calculate the intrinsics reward. LAI changes over the growth cycle of crops are shown in Fig. 2(b). LAI can be reflected in a certain range and the crop yield increases with the increase of leaf area index. So we designed the intrinsic reward $F(s_{t+1})$ as follow:

$$F(s_{t+1}) = (1 - (1 - x)^{0.4}) * 10 \tag{5}$$

Since LAI keeps increasing without yield accumulation, the crop status is always promoted along with LAI, and there is no state cycle. Therefore, it can be theoretically proved that our design of intrinsic reward function is correct.

For positive rewards we mainly consider the increase in current yield accumulation and the increase in yield in the next state. Intuitively, when the crop can live and get more crop yields, it can receive more reward. The positive reward function we designed as following:

$$r(s_t, a_t, s_{t+1}) = \begin{cases} 0 & \text{if crops died} \\ lg(\xi) + lg(\eta^3) & \text{if crops alive} \end{cases} \tag{6}$$

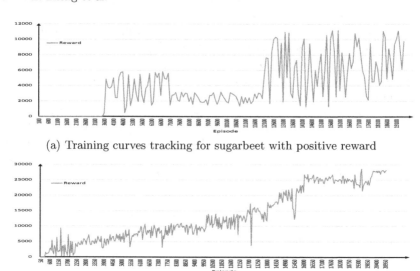

(a) Training curves tracking for sugarbeet with positive reward

(b) Training curves tracking for sugarbeet with positive and intrinsic reward

Fig. 3. Training curves tracking for sugarbeet with different reward functions

Where ξ represents the net increase in crop yield per day and η represents the rate of net increase in crop yield. We use the logarithmic function to keep the positive reward and the intrinsics reward on the same order of magnitude.

For negative rewards we only consider the increase in current yield accumulation and the order of magnitude of the reward.

$$r(s_t, a_t, s_{t+1}) = \begin{cases} 0 & \text{if crops died} \\ 100 - lg(\xi) & \text{if the yield } > 0 \end{cases} \tag{7}$$

We made a comparative analysis of the reward convergence with and without the addition of an intrinsic reward function. Through comparison, as the Fig. 3, we can see that the convergence rate of training with intrinsic reward function is obviously faster than that without intrinsic reward function.

The final yield optimization results using different strategies are shown in the Fig. 4, We used real weather data from 2004 to convert the plant factory interior environment without any optimization decision strategy as a basic control group. And we consulted the Good Agricultural Practices Guidelines, Using expert experience to simulation as a baseline. From the observation results, it can be seen that the final yield of sugar beet optimized with reinforcement learning is better than that without any strategy and using expert's experience strategy, which indicates that our optimization is effective. Secondly, the accumulation amount of the final product using positive rewards is better than negative rewards, indicating that using positive rewards is a better method for the accumulation problem of crop yield. Finally, it can be seen that adding additional reward is helpful for overall optimization. And we also found a very interesting

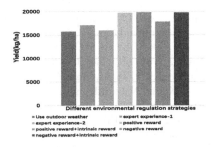

Fig. 4. The yield comparison

coincidence, which is that using positive reward functions and using negative reward functions end up with similar optimization results.

5   Conclusion

We are the first to propose a plant factory sensor data processing model based on deep reinforcement learning. It provides a new idea for sensor data processing and intelligentization in plant factories. Eventually reinforcement learning agents will learn to automatically manage and control the plant environment and maximize crop yields. Using the simulation software to verify our approach can control the crop growth and get a better yield. For future research, we believe that the real application in plant factories is very important and challenging, because the use of simulation is very persuasive and cannot avoid the inherent internal defects of simulation software.

Acknowledgments. This work was supported in part by the Young Scientists Fund of the National Natural Science Foundation of China under Grant 61802343 and 62072402, in part by the Zhejiang Provincial Natural Science Foundation of China under Grant LGF19F020019 and LGN20F020003, and in part by Hangzhou Science and Technology Bureau under Grant 20191203B37 and the Intelligent Plant Factory of Zhejiang Province Engineering Lab.

References

1. Alterra: Simulation environment. https://pcse.readthedocs.io/en/stable/
2. Baltrušaitis, T., Ahuja, C., Morency, L.: Multimodal machine learning: a survey and taxonomy. IEEE Trans. Pattern Anal. Mach. Intell. **41**(2), 423–443 (2019)
3. Barker, J.C.: Effects of day and night humidity on yield and fruit quality of glasshouse tomatoes. J. Hortic. Sci. **65**(3), 323–331 (1990)
4. ChalabiB, Z.S., Bailey, J., Wilkinson, D.: A real-time optimal control algorithm for greenhouse heating. Comput. Electron. Agric. **15**(1), 1–13 (1996)
5. Challinor, A., Wheeler, T., Craufurd, P., Slingo, J.: Simulation of the impact of high temperature stress on annual crop yields. Agric. Forest Meteorol. **135**(1), 180–189 (2005)

6. Chen, Y., Zhang, J., Guo, M., Cao, J.: Learning user preference from heterogeneous information for store-type recommendation. IEEE Trans. Serv. Comput. **13**, 1100–1114 (2017)
7. Chen, Y., Zhang, J., Xu, L., Guo, M., Cao, J.: Modeling latent relation to boost things categorization service. IEEE Trans. Serv. Comput. **13**(5), 915–929 (2020)
8. Choi, H.G., Moon, B.Y., Kang, N.J.: Effects of led light on the production of strawberry during cultivation in a plastic greenhouse and in a growth chamber. Scientia Horticulturae **189**, 22–31 (2015)
9. Culotta, E.: Will plants profit from high CO2? Science **268**(5211), 64–65 (1995)
10. Degris, T., Pilarski, P.M., Sutton, R.S.: Model-free reinforcement learning with continuous action in practice. In: 2012 American Control Conference (ACC), pp. 2177–2182. IEEE (2012)
11. Garcia, F.: Use of reinforcement learning and simulation to optimize wheat crop technical management. In: Proceedings of the International Congress on Modelling and Simulation (MODSIM 1999), Hamilton, New-Zealand, pp. 801–806 (1999)
12. Huang, M., Liu, A., Wang, T., Huang, C.: Green data gathering under delay differentiated services constraint for internet of things. Wirel. Commun. Mobile Comput. **2018** (2018)
13. Kakade, S.M.: A natural policy gradient. In: Proceedings of the 14th International Conference on Neural Information Processing Systems: Natural and Synthetic, pp. 1531–1538 (2002)
14. LeCun, Y., Bengio, Y., Hinton, G.: Deep learning. Nature **521**(7553), 436–444 (2015)
15. Liakos, K.G., Busato, P., Moshou, D., Pearson, S., Bochtis, D.: Machine learning in agriculture: a review. Sensors **18**(8), 2674 (2018)
16. Mnih, V., Kavukcuoglu, K., Silver, D., et al.: Human-level control through deep reinforcement learning. Nature **518**(7540), 529–533 (2015)
17. Morimoto, T., Torii, T., Hashimoto, Y.: Optimal control of physiological processes of plants in a green plant factory. Control Eng. Pract. **3**(4), 505–511 (1995)
18. Silver, D., Lever, G., Heess, N., Degris, T., Wierstra, D., Riedmiller, M.: Deterministic policy gradient algorithms. In: Proceedings of the 31st International Conference on International Conference on Machine Learning, pp. 387–395 (2014)
19. Tang, J., Liu, A., Zhao, M., Wang, T.: An aggregate signature based trust routing for data gathering in sensor networks. Secur. Commun. Netw. **2018** (2018)
20. Vermesan, O., Friess, P.: Digitising the Industry-internet of Things Connecting the Physical, Digital and Virtual Worlds. River Publishers, Denmark (2016)
21. Wang, T., Jia, W., Xing, G., Li, M.: Exploiting statistical mobility models for efficient Wi-Fi deployment. IEEE Trans. Veh. Technol. **62**(1), 360–373 (2012)
22. Wang, T., Ke, H., Zheng, X., Wang, K., Sangaiah, A.K., Liu, A.: Big data cleaning based on mobile edge computing in industrial sensor-cloud. IEEE Trans. Ind. Inf. **16**(2), 1321–1329 (2019)
23. Wang, T., Luo, H., Jia, W., Liu, A., Xie, M.: MTES: an intelligent trust evaluation scheme in sensor-cloud-enabled industrial internet of things. IEEE Trans. Ind. Inf. **16**(3), 2054–2062 (2019)
24. Wang, Y., Shen, J., Zheng, Y.: Push the limit of acoustic gesture recognition. In: IEEE INFOCOM 2020-IEEE Conference on Computer Communications, pp. 566–575. IEEE (2020)
25. Wu, Y., Huang, H., Wu, Q., Liu, A., Wang, T.: A risk defense method based on microscopic state prediction with partial information observations in social networks. J. Parallel Distrib. Comput. **131**, 189–199 (2019)

A Fuzzy Keywords Enabled Ranked Searchable CP-ABE Scheme for a Public Cloud Environment

Gangqi Shu[(✉)], Haibo Hong, Mande Xie, and Jun Shao

School of Computer and Information Engineering, Zhejiang Gongshang University,
Hangzhou 310018, China
shugangqi1997@163.com

Abstract. More and more people and enterprises are willing to store their encrypted data in the cloud. In this context, as an important cryptographic technology, searchable encryption (SE) plays an crucial role in retrieving the data for data owners. Furthermore, the encrypted data are desired to be shared to some data users without destroying the users' privacy. Therefore, in this paper, we proposed a novel fuzzy keywords enabled ranked searchable ciphertext-policy attribute-based encryption (FRSCP-ABE) scheme to address above problems. Firstly, we combined ciphertext-policy attribute-based encryption (CP-ABE) with searchable encryption (SE) to search and utilize the outsourced encrypted data for data owners efficiently. Secondly, we obtain meaningful and accurate searching results by considering the errors in the documents. Furthermore, we took advantage of the probabilistic trapdoor to resist distinguishability attacks. Finally, we improved the accuracy of searching results by employing the weighted zone score to rank the documents. Our theoretical analysis indicated that our proposal realized fuzzy keywords search and more accurate searching result rank, also guaranteed the data security and saved a large amount of storage and computation costs.

Keywords: Searchable encryption · Attribute-based encryption · Fuzzy keyword · Rank · Access control structure

1 Introduction

1.1 Background and Related Works

In view of cloud has the advantages of large storage space and low cost of data management, many users and enterprises prefer to store their data in cloud servers. According to survey data [20], most enterprises will use at least one cloud server. This allows users to manage huge amounts of data by using mobile devices with limited storage via the internet. Apart from those advantage of cloud server, there are certain threats to the privacy of user data.

For example, a medical institution need to store electronic health records (EHR) in the cloud. Because medical institutions need to protect the privacy of

ⓒ Springer Nature Switzerland AG 2021
G. Wang et al. (Eds.): SpaCCS 2020, LNCS 12383, pp. 357–371, 2021.
https://doi.org/10.1007/978-3-030-68884-4_30

patients' data [17], EHRs can not be upload with the plaintext form. Therefore, it is a problem to make search over encrypted data. And searchable encryption (SE) can solve this problem.

According to the encryption key, SE was divided into searchable symmetric encryption (SSE) and public-key encryption with keyword search (PEKS). The notion of SSE was proposed by Song et al. [18] in 2000 and they also gave a SE scheme. But they didn't give the formal security definitions and the scheme in [18] did not need a secure index. It is Curtmola et al. [6] that gave the formal security definitions of SE and a SE scheme which was based on index and can achieve single keyword search in 2011. However, Song et al.'s scheme, Curtmola et al.'s proposal and other constructions [5,12] could not share the searching keywords with others, because they all have a common restriction. For a network with too many users, PEKS is more adaptive than SSE. Boneh et al. [2] introduced the public key settings into SE and came up with the first PEKS scheme. This scheme solve the problem of data sharing.

Other problems in PEKS have also attracted the attention of scholars. Park et al. [16] and Golle et al. [9] proposed the constructions that supposed conjunctive keyword search. In order to rank the results, a new concept that called multi-keyword ranked search was raised [4,7,13]. And SE schemes with multi-users settings were raised by Bao et al. [1], Zhao et al. [24] and [21,23]. In [10,24], attribute-based encryption with keyword search (ABEKS) was proposed to support fine-access control. However, Byun et al. [3] pointed out, under the offline keyword guessing, Boneh et al.'s scheme and other existing scheme are vulnerable. Tahir et al. [19] proposed an scheme which is based on index to rank documents. And above schemes do not support fuzzy SE. Li et al. [14] introduced a SE scheme that enables fuzzy keyword searching at first.

1.2 Our Contribution

In order to enhance the security and practicability of the existing cloud storage schemes, we put forward a FRSCP-ABE scheme. The capability of cloud storage was extended with the SE and CP-ABE. FRSCP-ABE was based on probabilistic trapdoors and can help data owner to control his/her outsourced data. And our scheme realized the goal of fuzzy searching and ranked searching. In FRSCP-ABE, only the data users could pass the access structure that they could get the secret key. FRSCP-ABE scheme realized the following goals.

1. Keyword search by the data owner. Data owner encrypted the documents with his/her secret key and uploaded it to the cloud server. So he/she could make keyword search and decrypt the returned ciphertext.
2. Keyword search by the legal data users. This scheme solved the problems that the ciphertext could't be shared with many data users by introducing the CP-ABE into the SE schemes.
3. Fuzzy keyword search. Our scheme realized the goal of fuzzy searching because of the prevalence of typographical errors. So users could get more meaningful and accurate results.

4. Probabilistic trapdoor. In our scheme, we employed probabilistic trapdoor rather than deterministic trapdoor. So FRSCP-ABE scheme could resist distinguishability attacks.
5. Ranking the returned document. We used the Relevance Frequency formula to calculate the relevancy between keywords and documents so that we could rank the documents. Therefore, data users could get the most needed documents.

1.3 Paper Organization

We would introduce the preliminaries in detail which could help to conceptualize the FRSCP-ABE scheme In the next section. We showed the system model and the concrete structure of the scheme in Sect. 3. In Sect. 4, we proved the security of FRSCP-ABE scheme. We gave the analysis and comparison between this scheme and other schemes in Sect. 5. Finally, we conclude our proposal in the last section.

2   Preliminaries

2.1   Weighted Zone Score

In this paper, we think that even in the same document, the position of keyword is different, their functions are also different. According to the Weighted Zone Score mentioned in [15], a document is divided into three parts, there are title, abstract and the body. Keywords in different domains usually have different weight. Therefor we assume the weight of the title area is g_1, and the weight of the introduction is set to g_2, finally let g_3 be the weight of body. And g_1, g_2, g_3 should satisfy the following conditions:

1. $g_1 + g_2 + g_3 = 1$
2. $g_1, g_2, g_3 \in [0, 1]$.
3. $g_1 \geq g_2 \geq g_3$

And we set score ρ_1, ρ_2, ρ_3 to represent whether a keyword appear in the above areas. For example, if the keyword appear in title, then we set the $\rho_1 = 1$ otherwise we set $\rho_1 = 0$. We use this formula to compute keyword w_j's weighted zone score Z_{ij} in document D_i: $Z_{ij} = \rho_1 g_1 + \rho_2 g_2 + \rho_3 g_3$. If keyword w_j appears in the title and abstract of document D_i, so the weighted zone score Z_{ij} of w_j is $g_1 + g_2$.

2.2   TF-IDF Algorithm

Term frequency-inverse document frequency (TF-IDF) algorithm always be used in situations requiring information retrieval, because it can help to calculate the relevance of a keyword to a document. We use the following formula to compute it:

$$score_{ij} = \frac{D_{i,w_j}}{|D_i|} \cdot ln(\frac{|D|}{|D_{w_j}|} + 1)$$

where D_{i,w_j} denotes the number of keyword w_j in document D_i, and $|D_i|$ means the total amount of keywords in document D_i, and $|D|$ shows the sum of the document in the set of document D, and $|D_{w_j}|$ means the number of documents which contain the keyword w_j.

2.3   Shingled Keywords

Let $W = \{W_1, W_2, ..., W_m\}$ is a set of keywords and l is a constant representing the letters that will appear in the keywords. For example, there is a keyword "keyword", it's shingle set will be { "ke", "ey", "yw", "wo", "or", "rd"}. Then we can transform this keyword to be a vector V according to the shingle set S. In a word, shingled keyword is helping a keyword to be a vector.

2.4   Min Hash and Jaccard Similarity

Assume there are Q number of random hash functions $F : V \rightarrow R$ which can reduce the shingle vector V to a real number R. We random select q number of hash functions to obtain real numbers, and the signature vector will be formed with these. F should be independent, in other word, $F_q(V_1) \neq F_q(V_2)$, where V_1 and V_2 are shingle vectors. According to [11], we can learn that $JS(F_q(V_1), F_q(V_2)) = JS(V_1, V_2)$, where V_1 and V_2 are shingle vectors. And we can calculate $JS(X, Y)$ between set X and Y by the following formula:

$$JS(X, Y) = \frac{|X \cap Y|}{|X \cup Y|}$$

Corollary 1. [11] $JS(X, Y) = 0$ if and only if $X \cap Y = \emptyset$.

2.5   Access Tree

Assuming τ is an access structure tree whose non-leaf nodes denote the threshold gate. And the threshold gate of each non-leaf node is described by a threshold value and its children. We use num_x to represent the number of children of the node x, and use k_x to represent node x's threshold value, and $0 < k_x \leq num_x$. If $k_x = num_x$, the gate is an AND gate and if $k_x = 1$, it is an OR gate. We use an attribute and $k_x = 1$ to describe each leaf node x of τ. Assume there is a set γ of attributes, we say γ satisfy this tree only and only if $\tau_x(\gamma) = 1$.

There are a few functions can help us to work with τ:

1. $parent(x)$: to get the parent node of the node x in τ;
2. $att(x)$: to get the associated attribute with the leaf node x;
3. $index(x)$: to get the number that node x associated with.

2.6   Two Permute Algorithms

The pseudocode of algorithm **PermV** would be showed in Table 1, *PermV* can help randomizing a vector.

Table 1. *PermSpermutation*

$PermV : V \rightarrow V'$, Let $V = [e_1, e_2, ..., e_l]$ denotes a vector that contains l entries. $PermV$ means that vector V will be randomized to vector V'

$V = [e_1, e_2, ..., e_l]$
$V' = []$
$i = random.randint(1, l)$
while $len(v') \leq l$:
    if v[i] not in v':
        v'.append(v[i])
    else:
        i = random.randint(1,l)
print(V')

And because the set and the vector have different properties, we only call **ExtendedVector** algorithm when we no more need the vector properties. We demonstrated its pseudocode in Table 2.

Table 2. *ExtendedVectorpermutation*

$ExtendedVector : V \rightarrow S$, it can help transforming a vector to be a set. Assume there is a vector $V = [e_1, e_2, ..., e_l]$ that contains l entries and an empty set S

$V = [e_1, e_2, ..., e_l]$
$S = []$
$i = 1$
while $i \leq l$:
    add the corresponding string of e_i to S
    i = i + 1
print(S)

---

3   System Model and Our Proposal

3.1   System Model of FKSCP-ABE

Here we demonstrated the system model of our FKSCP-ABE scheme in Fig.1. There were four entities in this system, denoted by data owner, data user, cloud server, trusted authority center, respectively.

1) **data owner** (*DO*): *DO* extracted the keywords $W = \{W_1, W_2, ..., W_m\}$ from the shared documents $D = \{D_1, D_2, ..., D_n\}$. *DO* should generate inverted index table (I) and fuzzy index table (FI). And *DO* also needed to encrypt the documents to obtain ciphertexts $C = \{C_1, C_2, ..., C_n\}$, and then sent I, FI and C to the cloud server in a searchable manner.

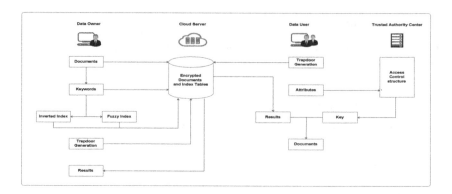

Fig. 1. System model

2) **data user** (*DU*): *DU* generated the trapdoor T_w for himself/herself, and then sent T_w to the cloud server to obtain its required documents associated with special keyword. After *DU* got the documents, he/she needed to send a set of attributes to the trusted authority center to get the decryption key.

3) **cloud server** (*CS*): *CS* provided the storing and computing services for data owner and data user. It would store a massive amount of documents and search on encrypted data according to the trapdoors which were given by *DU*.

4) **trusted authority center** (*TAC*): *TAC* checked whether *DU* had the permission to decrypt the encrypted documents. If the attributes of *DU* could pass the access structure, then it sent the decryption message to *DU*.

3.2   Our Proposal

We provided a detailed algorithm construction of FRSCP-ABE scheme in this section. And then we showed it's workflow in Fig. 2. FRSCP-ABE scheme was consisted of the following algorithms: **Setup, Build_Index, Encryption, Build_Trapdoor, Search_Outcome, Get_Key, Decryption**.

    •*Setup*(G_0, λ) → (*PP, MK, K*): Given a security parameter λ and a bilinear group $\mathbb{G}_0$, and output public parameter *PP*, master key *MK* and secret index key *K*.

– Setting the index key as $K \leftarrow \{0,1\}^\lambda$.
– Choosing two bilinear groups $\mathbb{G}_0$ and $\mathbb{G}_1$ of same prime order p, and g was a generator of group $\mathbb{G}_0$, and $e : \mathbb{G}_0 \times \mathbb{G}_0 \to \mathbb{G}_1$ represented the bilinear pairing.
– We defined the Lagrange coefficient $\Delta_{(i,S)} = \Pi_{j \in S, j \neq i} \frac{x-j}{i-j}$.
– To select a hash function $H^* : \{0,1\}^* \to \mathbb{G}_0$.
– Choosing three random exponents $\alpha, \beta, r \in Z_p$ and setting the master key $MK = (\beta, g^\alpha)$.
– Specify the access control structure τ as mentioned in Sect. 2. And each non-leaf node denoted a threshold gate which was consist of a threshold value and its children.

– Output the public parameters $PP = (\mathbb{G}_0, g, h = g^\beta, e(g,g)^\alpha)$

•**Build_Index**$(W, D, K, PP) \rightarrow (I, FI)$: Taking the public parameters PP, document set D, keyword set W and secret key K as inputs, inverted index table I and fuzzy index table FI were generated.

– Inverted Index table (I) Generation: Actually, I was a matrix whose order was $(n+1) \times (m+1)$, and would be constructed as follows:
  1. DO extracted a keyword set $W = \{W_1, W_2, ..., W_m\}$ from a set of documents $D = \{D_1, D_2, ..., D_n\}$.
  2. Then DO initialized all the elements in the matrix to zero.
  3. Setting $(1, j+1) = Enc_K(W_j); 1 \le j \le m$
  4. Setting $(i+1, 1) = Enc_k(id(D_i)); 1 \le i \le n$
  5. Calculating the $Z_{ij} \cdot score_{ij}$ and masked it by multiply r to obtain $RF(W_j, D_i)$, then we filled $RF(W_j, D_i)$ at $(i+1, j+1)$.
– Fuzzy Index table (FI) Generation: DO constructed a matrix FI whose order was $(q+1) \times (m+1)$ where $1 \le q \le Q$. FI would be built as:
  1. Forming a shingle set for every keywords in W, then we could get $S = \{S_1, S_2, ..., S_m\}$, where S_i was the shingle set of keyword W_t, $1 \le t \le m$.
  2. Constructing the shingle vectors $V = \{V_1, V_2, ..., V_m\}$ corresponding to the shingle sets.
  3. Randomize each vector V_t in V to be $V'_i, 1 \le t \le m$.
  4. For each V'_i compute q number of min hash value to form the corresponding Signature Vectors SV.
  5. Setting $(1, j+1) = Enc_K(W_i); 1 \le j \le m$.
  6. Setting $(i+1, 1) = Enc_k(id(D_i)); 1 \le i \le n$
  7. Setting $(i, j) = SV[q]; 1 \le j \le q$.

•**Encryption**$(D, PP, MK, \tau) \rightarrow (CD)$: Given the public parameters PP, documents set D, access tree τ and master key MK, encrypted data CD was computed.

– Choosing a polynomial q_x for each node x in τ, and setting $d_x = k_x - 1$, where d_x represented the degree of the polynomial q_x, k_x denotes the threshold of node x.
– Assuming node r was τ's root, chose a number $s \in Z_p$ randomly and set $q_r(0) = s$. Then, it selected d_r number of other points of the polynomial q_r at random to define it complexity.
– If x was not the root, then it set $q_x(0) = q_{parent(x)}(index(x))$ and choose d_x other pointed randomly to completely define q_x.
– Assuming Y was the set of leaf nodes in τ. Computing

$$CD = (\tau, CT, C = h^s, \forall y \in Y : C_y = g^{q_y(0)}, C'_y = H(att(y))^{q_y(0)}),$$

where $CT = \{C_1, C_2, ..., C_n\}, C_i = D_i e(g,g)^{\alpha s}, 1 \le i \le n$.
– sent index tables and encrypted data to cloud server CS.

•*Build_Trapdoor(w)* → (*T_w*): When data user *DU* wanted to search documents that he interested in, he run it to generate a probabilistic trapdoor T_w for the searching keyword w he wanted to search as follows:

- Transforming the keyword w to be a shingle set S_w.
- Forming the same random vector V'_m with the help of the shingle set S_w.
- Using the same q number of min hash functions to form a signature vector T.
- DU randomized the vector T to obtain T' according to the algorithm (*PermV*).
- Computing the Euclidean Norm $d(T, T')$.
- Output $T_w = (d, T', num)$ as the trapdoor T_w, num ws the total number of the documents that data user needed.
- DU sent $Enc_{PK_{CS}}(T_w)$ to the Cloud Server.

•*Search_Outcome(I, FI, T_w)* → (*F*): Cloud server got T_w and searched needed documents with help of I and FI. Output the needed documents F.

- CS used his private key to decrypt $Enc_{PK_{CS}}(T_w)$ and obtains (d, T', num).
- Converting T' to a set S' by Using algorithm (*ExtendedVector*).
- Converting each signature vector $SV_t, 1 \le t \le m$ stored in FI to a set S'_t by *ExtendedVector* algorithm.
- Calculating $JS(S', S'_t)$ between set L and set L'_m. If $JS(L, L'_m) = 0$, then compute the $d' = d(T', SV_m)$ and The wanted keyword would meet the condition that $d' = d \pm \epsilon$.
- According to the keywords in FI, to find the eligible documents in the inverted index table, and then returned documents $F = \{F_1, F_2, ..., F_{num}\}$ on the basis of the relevance score in ranked order.
  Note: $F_j \in CT, 1 \le j \le num$.

•*Get_Key(Att)* → (*SK*/ ⊥): Given attributes *Att*, and if *Att* could pass the access structure, then got *SK*. If couldn't, data user would get ⊥. *TAC* would check whether *DU* had the permission to decrypt the encrypted documents.

- After received a set of attributes *Att* of data user, if *Att* could pass the access structure, it chose two random numbers $a, a_k \in Z_p$ for each attribute $k \in Att$.
- Compute the key as:

$$SK = (R = g^{(\alpha+a)/\beta}, \forall k \in Att : R_k = g^a \cdot H(k)^{a_k}, R'_k = g^{a_k})$$

- Compute $DecryptNode(CD, SK, x)$, where x was one of the nodes in τ. If x was a leaf node, let $i = att(x)$ and defined as follows:
  (a) if $i \in Att$, then:

$$DecryptNode(CD, SK, x) = \frac{e(R_i, C_x)}{e(R'_i, C'_x)}$$

$$= \frac{e(g^a \cdot H(i)^{r_i}, h^{q_x(0)})}{e(g_i^a, H(i)^{q_x(0)})} \quad (1)$$

$$= e(g, g)^{a q_x(0)}$$

(b) if $i \notin Att$, then: $DecryptNode(CD, SK, x) = \perp$.

If x was a non-leaf node, then we computed $DecryptNode(CD, SK, x)$ as follows:

$$
\begin{aligned}
F_x &= \Pi_{z \in S_x} F_z^{\Delta_{i,S'_x}(0)} \\
&= \Pi_{z \in S_x} (e(g,g)^{a \cdot q_z(0)})^{\Delta_{i,S'_x}(0)} \\
&= \Pi_{z \in S_x} (e(g,g)^{a \cdot q_{parent(z)}(index(z))})^{\Delta_{i,S'_x}(0)} \\
&= \Pi_{z \in S_x} e(g,g)^{a \cdot q_x(i) \cdot \Delta_{i,S'_x}(0)} \\
&= e(g,g)^{a \cdot q_x(0)}
\end{aligned}
\tag{2}
$$

- Let $DN = DecryptNode(CD, SK, x) = e(g,g)^{a q_R(0)} = e(g,g)^{rs}$. And then TAC sent $Enc_{PK_{DU}}(DN, C, R)$ to the DU.

•$Decryption(SK, CT) \rightarrow (D)$: DU run decryption algorithm to decrypt the ciphertexts. It was decrypted by computing the following formula:

$$
CT/(e(C,T)/DN) = CT/(e(h^s, g^{(\alpha+a)/\beta})/e(g,g)^{\alpha s}) = D
$$

4   Security Analysis

According to the Fig. 2, let's start with the details of the leakages of our FRSCP-ABE scheme, and then prove it was secure by the formal game-based security proofs.

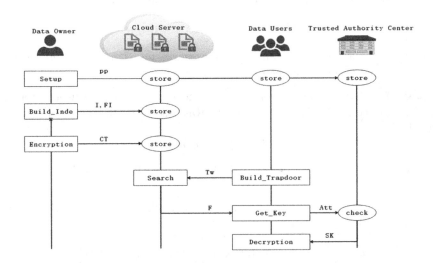

Fig. 2. The workflow of our scheme

4.1   Leakage Profiles

It's impossible to propose a searchable scheme without leaking any information to the adversary. Our scheme could limit the leakage by using probabilistic
trapdoors. Therefore, it was vital to analyze the details of the leakage, even
if the FRSCP-ABE scheme revealed only a small amount of information. The
leaked information came from the artifacts mentioned above, such as I, FI, T_W
which are generated for the particular keyword W, the returned documents after
searching and the information that interact between TAC and DU. FRSCP-ABE
scheme had the following leakages:

Leakage L_1: Leakage L_1 focused the data disclosed by I. Data owner generated
I and outsourced it to the cloud server. We defined the leakage L_1 as:

$$L_1(I) = \{m, n\}$$

where m and n represented the total number of keywords and the documents,
respectively.

Leakage L_2: Leakage L_2 emphasized the message exposed by index FI. DO
created the FI and sent FI to the CS. The definition of leakage L_2 was as
follows:

$$L_2(FI) = \{m, SV_W[Q]\}$$

where $SV_W[Q]$ was the signature vector of W.

Leakage L_3: Leakage L_3 was related to the leak of information in the trapdoor T_W which was generated for the specific keyword W. DU computed the
probabilistic trapdoor T_W and outsourced T_W to the CS. We define L_3 as:

$$L_3(T_W) = \{T_W, d(T, T'), num\}$$

where $d(T, T')$ was the Euclidean Norm between vectors T and T', num was the
total number of needed documents.

Leakage L_4: After cloud server received the trapdoor T_W, it would return
the search outcome (SO). And leakage L_4 was associated to SO. Therefore we
defined L_4 as:

$$L_4 = \{F, num\}$$

where F was a subset of CT, and the documents in F all contained the keyword
W.

Leakage L_5: Leakage L_5 was connected with the interactive information
between the TAC and the DU.

$$L_5 = \{Enc_{PK_{TCA}}(A, PK_{DU}), Enc_{PK_{DU}}(A, C, R)\}$$

Discussion on leakage: By referring to the leakage L_1 related to I, we could
observe that I might only reveal the existence of the keyword in a document,
the total number of the keywords and the documents. FI was bond up to leakage

L_2 which would reveal the total number of keywords, but the keywords themselves would never be known. Because probabilistic trapdoor was used, different trapdoors would be generated for the same keyword. therefore, it didn't leak the pattern prior to the search. And in L_5, adversary could't obtain any valid information except the ciphertext.

4.2 Formal Security Proofs

Lemma 1. *FRSCP-ABE presented in Sect. 4 is "Privacy Preserving" according to Theorem 1 as L_1, L_2, L_3, L_4, L_5 were secure. It was because L_1 only leaked the number of the documents and keywords, L_2 only leaked the total number of the keywords and every keywords' signature vector and L_3 only leaked the information of trapdoor, Euclidean Norm and the number of required documents. None of them would leak keywords and documents itself. And L_4, L_5 are ciphertext, so, adversary could not get any message useful from them.*

We used a game-based method to prove FRSCP-ABE scheme's security and the security proof was divided into three phases, setup, challenge and the guess phase.

Keyword-Trapdoor Indistinguishability in FRSCP-ABE:

Proof. **Setup:** The challenger $\mathcal{C}$ run the setup algorithm to generate the public parameter PP, master key MK, private key K. Then $\mathcal{C}$ run Buid_Index algorithm to create two index tables I and FI. The adversary $\mathcal{A}$ sends each keyword $W_i \in W$ where $W = \{W_1, W_2, ..., W_m\}$ to $\mathcal{C}$. $\mathcal{C}$ run the Build_Trapdoor algorithm to get the corresponding trapdoors. Every time, generating the trapdoor required a randomized shingle vector $\boldsymbol{V'}$. Therefore, signature vector $\boldsymbol{T}$ and random vector $\boldsymbol{T'}$ were also different every time. And then calculating $d(\boldsymbol{T}, \boldsymbol{T'})$. We generated the trapdoors $T_W = (d, T', num)$ for every keyword W_i in W, where $1 \leq i \leq m$, and sent them to $\mathcal{A}$ one-by-one. This result in L_3.

Note: $\mathcal{A}$ random select a number num in $[1, n]$, we could observe that in each instance, random vectors $(\boldsymbol{V'}, \boldsymbol{T}, \boldsymbol{T'})$ were different. Because we used probabilistic trapdoor in our scheme, even for the same keywords, their trapdoors were different. Thus L_3 was harmless.

Challenge: $\mathcal{A}$ adaptively chose two different keywords W_0, W_1 to the challenger $\mathcal{C}$ where $(W_0, W_1) \in W$. $\mathcal{C}$ tossed a fair coin $b \in \{0, 1\}$ and generated a trapdoor T_{W_b}. Then, $\mathcal{C}$ shared it with $\mathcal{A}$. $\mathcal{A}$ keeps sending plentiful keywords to $\mathcal{C}$ again to receive the corresponding trapdoor T_{W_b}. In the challenge phase, $\mathcal{A}$ was allowed to send the same keyword.

Guess: $\mathcal{A}$ guessed whether b was 1 or 0.

Now, we had successfully simulated a game which represented the keyword-trapdoor indistinguishability of FRSCP-ABE scheme. $\mathcal{A}$ was able to distinguish the trapdoors T_{W_0}, T_{W_1} if he could guess b successfully. If we were aware of this, $\mathcal{A}$ could actually distinguish between all n trapdoors generated in the past and those that were likely to be generated in the future. But this was almost impossible because trapdoors were probabilistic, and the trapdoor corresponding to the keyword in each search was unique. So the advantage was:

$$Pr[Key\_Trap] \leq \frac{1}{2} + negl(\lambda)$$

Theorem 1. *The proposed FRSCP-ABE scheme provided Keyword-Trapdoor Indistinguishability and Trapdoor-Index Indistinguishability if I FI were secure and the trapdoors were probabilistic.*

Trapdoor-Index Indistinguishability in FRSCP-ABE:

Proof. **Setup:** C run the setup algorithm to generate PP, MK, K. Then C run Buid_Index algorithm to create I and FI. I stored the information that showed the existence of a keyword within the documents according to the relevance scores. And the scores were hidden thanks to the masking function. FI was generated by the help of a randomly permuted shingle vector V'. And we needed to compute Min hash value of V' to form SV. Share I and FI with A. The adversary A sent each keyword $W_i \in W$ where $W = \{W_1, W_2, ..., W_m\}$ to C. C run the Build_Trapdoor algorithm to get the corresponding trapdoors. Generating the trapdoor required a randomized shingle vector V' each time. Therefore, signature vector T and random vector T' were also different every time. And then calculating $d(T, T')$. C also performed the search over FI by using T_W. The corresponding entries of FI would be shared with A. So, we generated the trapdoors $T_W = (d, T', num)$ for every keyword and sent them as well as FI_W to A one-by-one.

Challenge: A chose two different keywords W_0, W_1 to the challenger where $(W_0, W_1) \in W$. C tossed a fair coin b and generated the trapdoor T_{W_b}. Then, C sent T_{w_b} to A. A kept sending plentiful keywords to C again to receive the corresponding trapdoor T_{W_b}. In the challenge phase, A was allowed to query the same keyword.

Guess: A guessed whether b was 1 or 0.

So far, we had simulated the game which represented the trapdoor-index indistinguishability of the proposed FRSCP-ABE scheme successfully. A was able to distinguish the trapdoors T_{W_0}, TW_1 if he could guess b successfully. If the trapdoors were distinguishable then FI's entries were also distinguishable. Thus, it was impossible to leak the access and search pattern before the search, because trapdoors were unique. Thus, we defined the advantage as:

$$Pr[Trap\_Index] \leq \frac{1}{2} + negl(\lambda)$$

The leakage L_4 was the search outcome of searching keywords. So L_4 was a set of encrypted documents that would leak anything but ciphertext. L_5 was also only leaks information that were encrypted, A could not get any information useful. Therefore, the leakage L_1, L_2, L_3, L_4, L_5 analysis and relevant proofs showed the proposed FRSCP-ABE scheme was privacy preserving.

5   Analysis and Comparison

As shown in Table 3, we compared these schemes [8, 14, 22] with our construction in terms of probabilistic trapdoors, prevent search pattern leakage, ranked search and multi-user. Li et al. [14] proposed scheme could not achieve any goals that mentioned above. Wang's [22] scheme used the probabilistic trapdoors so it could prevent search pattern leakage. And it also supported multi-user but couldn't rank the documents. The scheme of Fu et al. [8] could only meet the need of ranked search, but could not achieve other three goals. However, our construction could achieve the four goals simultaneously.

Table 3. Performance comparisons among different SE schemes

Schemes	Probabilistic trapdoors	Prevent search pattern leakage	Ranked search	Multi-user
[8]	✗	✗	✓	✗
[14]	✗	✗	✗	✗
[22]	✓	✓	✗	✓
Our paper	✓	✓	✓	✓

We showed the comparative analysis in Table 4. And we'd like to compare the computational complexity FRSCP-ABE scheme with other similar existing schemes. The complexity associated to the documents was represented by n and for keywords by m. As most of the schemes comprised of all the 5 phases which were KeyGen, Build_Index, Build_Trapdoor, Search_Outcome and Decryption phase, but our construction also had a Get_Key phase. And we analyzed these phases separately. And because the KeyGen and Decryption phase were similar, so we didn't take their complexities into consideration. We demonstrated the comparative analysis in Table 4, where q was the number of min hashing we selected and H represented the complexity of Get_Key phase.

Table 4. Algorithmic comparative analysis among different SE schemes

Schemes	Build_Index	Build_Trap	Search_OC	Get_Key
[14]	$\Theta(mS)$	$\Theta(mS+1)$	$\Theta(m^2)$	–
[8] and [22]	$\Theta(mn+qm)$	$\Theta(qm+1)$	$\Theta(2m^2)$	–
Our proposal (ranked)	$\Theta(3mn+e(m+n))$	$\Theta(q+1)$	$\Theta(2qm+mn)$	H
Our proposal (unranked)	$\Theta(2mn+e(m+n))$	$\Theta(q+1)$	$\Theta(2qm+n+1)$	H

6   Conclusion

In this paper, we raised a new scheme named fuzzy keywords enabled ranked searchable CP-ABE scheme, which supported a data owner to share encrypted documents with a group of data users securely. The scheme we had proposed was based on probabilistic trapdoors, therefore, our FRSCP-ABE scheme could resist distinguishability attacks. Moreover, our scheme realized fuzzy search by introducing the min hash functions to construct a fuzzy index table. And we made use of the Euclidean norm and Jaccard similarity to achieve the goal of similarity search. And we also improved the accuracy of searching results by employing the weighted zone score to rank the documents.

References

1. Bao, F., Deng, R.H., Ding, X., Yang, Y.: Private query on encrypted data in multi-user settings. In: Chen, L., Mu, Y., Susilo, W. (eds.) ISPEC 2008. LNCS, vol. 4991, pp. 71–85. Springer, Heidelberg (2008). https://doi.org/10.1007/978-3-540-79104-1_6
2. Boneh, D., Di Crescenzo, G., Ostrovsky, R., Persiano, G.: Public key encryption with keyword search. In: Cachin, C., Camenisch, J.L. (eds.) EUROCRYPT 2004. LNCS, vol. 3027, pp. 506–522. Springer, Heidelberg (2004). https://doi.org/10.1007/978-3-540-24676-3_30
3. Byun, J.W., Rhee, H.S., Park, H.-A., Lee, D.H.: Off-line keyword guessing attacks on recent keyword search schemes over encrypted data. In: Jonker, W., Petković, M. (eds.) SDM 2006. LNCS, vol. 4165, pp. 75–83. Springer, Heidelberg (2006). https://doi.org/10.1007/11844662_6
4. Cao, N., Wang, C., Li, M., Ren, K., Lou, W.: Privacy-preserving multi-keyword ranked search over encrypted cloud data. IEEE Trans. Parallel Distrib. Syst. **25**(1), 222–233 (2013)
5. Chang, Y.-C., Mitzenmacher, M.: Privacy preserving keyword searches on remote encrypted data. In: Ioannidis, J., Keromytis, A., Yung, M. (eds.) ACNS 2005. LNCS, vol. 3531, pp. 442–455. Springer, Heidelberg (2005). https://doi.org/10.1007/11496137_30
6. Curtmola, R., Garay, J.A., Kamara, S., Ostrovsky, R.: Searchable symmetric encryption: improved definitions and efficient constructions. J. Comput. Secur. **19**(5), 895–934 (2011)
7. Fu, Z., Sun, X., Xia, Z., Zhou, L., Shu, J.: Multi-keyword ranked search supporting synonym query over encrypted data in cloud computing. In: 2013 IEEE 32nd International Performance Computing and Communications Conference (IPCCC), pp. 1–8. IEEE (2013)
8. Fu, Z., Wu, X., Guan, C., Sun, X., Ren, K.: Toward efficient multi-keyword fuzzy search over encrypted outsourced data with accuracy improvement. IEEE Trans. Inf. Forensics Secur. **11**(12), 2706–2716 (2016)
9. Golle, P., Staddon, J., Waters, B.: Secure conjunctive keyword search over encrypted data. In: Jakobsson, M., Yung, M., Zhou, J. (eds.) ACNS 2004. LNCS, vol. 3089, pp. 31–45. Springer, Heidelberg (2004). https://doi.org/10.1007/978-3-540-24852-1_3
10. Hattori, M., et al.: Ciphertext-policy delegatable hidden vector encryption and its application to searchable encryption in multi-user setting. In: Chen, L. (ed.) IMACC 2011. LNCS, vol. 7089, pp. 190–209. Springer, Heidelberg (2011). https://doi.org/10.1007/978-3-642-25516-8_12
11. Ji, J., Li, J., Yan, S., Tian, Q., Zhang, B.: Min-max hash for Jaccard similarity, pp. 301–309 (2013)

12. Kurosawa, K., Ohtaki, Y.: UC-secure searchable symmetric encryption. In: Keromytis, A.D. (ed.) FC 2012. LNCS, vol. 7397, pp. 285–298. Springer, Heidelberg (2012). https://doi.org/10.1007/978-3-642-32946-3_21
13. Li, H., Liu, D., Dai, Y., Luan, T.H., Shen, X.S.: Enabling efficient multi-keyword ranked search over encrypted mobile cloud data through blind storage. IEEE Trans. Emerg. Top. Comput. 3(1), 127–138 (2014)
14. Li, J., Wang, Q., Wang, C., Cao, N., Ren, K., Lou, W.: Fuzzy keyword search over encrypted data in cloud computing, pp. 441–445 (2010)
15. Manning, C.D., Schütze, H., Raghavan, P.: Introduction to Information Retrieval. Cambridge University Press, Cambridge (2008)
16. Park, D.J., Kim, K., Lee, P.J.: Public key encryption with conjunctive field keyword search. In: Lim, C.H., Yung, M. (eds.) WISA 2004. LNCS, vol. 3325, pp. 73–86. Springer, Heidelberg (2005). https://doi.org/10.1007/978-3-540-31815-6_7
17. Riad, K., Hamza, R., Yan, H.: Sensitive and energetic IoT access control for managing cloud electronic health records. IEEE Access 7, 86384–86393 (2019)
18. Song, D., Wagner, D., Perrig, A.: Practical techniques for searches on encrypted data, pp. 44–55 (2000)
19. Tahir, S., Ruj, S., Rahulamathavan, Y., Rajarajan, M., Glackin, C.: A new secure and lightweight searchable encryption scheme over encrypted cloud data. IEEE Trans. Emerg. Top. Comput. 7(4), 530–544 (2019)
20. Trends, C.C.: State of the cloud survey (2018). https://www.rightscale.com/blog/cloud-industry-insights/cloud-computing-trends-2018-statecloud-survey. Accessed 15 May 2018
21. Van Rompay, C., Molva, R., Önen, M.: Multi-user searchable encryption in the cloud. In: Lopez, J., Mitchell, C.J. (eds.) ISC 2015. LNCS, vol. 9290, pp. 299–316. Springer, Cham (2015). https://doi.org/10.1007/978-3-319-23318-5_17
22. Wang, B., Yu, S., Lou, W., Hou, Y.T.: Privacy-preserving multi-keyword fuzzy search over encrypted data in the cloud, pp. 2112–2120 (2014)
23. Yang, Y., Lu, H., Weng, J.: Multi-user private keyword search for cloud computing. In: 2011 IEEE Third International Conference on Cloud Computing Technology and Science, pp. 264–271. IEEE (2011)
24. Zhao, F., Nishide, T., Sakurai, K.: Multi-user keyword search scheme for secure data sharing with fine-grained access control. In: Kim, H. (ed.) ICISC 2011. LNCS, vol. 7259, pp. 406–418. Springer, Heidelberg (2012). https://doi.org/10.1007/978-3-642-31912-9_27

Identifying Traffic Bottleneck in Urban Road Networks via Causal Inference

Yuanyi Chen[1], Pengquan Yan[1,2], Zengwei Zheng[1(✉)], and Dan Chen[1]

[1] School of Computing and Computational Science, Zhejiang University City College,
Hangzhou 310015, China
{chenyuanyi,zhengzw,chend}@zucc.edu.cn
[2] School of Computer Science and Technology, Zhejiang University,
Hangzhou 310058, China
yanpq@zju.edu.cn

Abstract. Identifying traffic bottlenecks and estimating their impacts on congestion propagation is a critical component of the Intelligent Transportation System (ITS). However, it is very challenging to identify urban traffic bottlenecks since they are caused by many complicated factors that are difficult to be pre-defined in urban road networks. In the paper, the authors propose a novel method to identify urban traffic bottlenecks via causal inference. The method mainly includes two parts: (1) Model causal relationships among traffic flow data from spatially distributed sensors. We firstly extract the uptrend intervals of traffic flow sensors, then calculate the causal strengths among spatially distributed sensors using transfer entropy; (2) Construct causality graphs and perform frequent subgraphs mining to identify traffic bottlenecks. We use a real-life traffic flow dataset from 74 loop detector sensors, which is collected in the urban traffic network of Hangzhou, china over one month. Our experimental results demonstrate significant findings regarding traffic bottlenecks and congestion propagation in Hangzhou, which will be useful for governments to make policy and govern traffic congestions.

Keywords: Bottleneck identification · Traffic congestion · Urban traffic network · Causal inference · Frequent subgraphs mining

1 Introduction

Traffic congestion has seriously caused various problems in almost all modern metropolitan cities, which reduces the efficiency of transportation infrastructure and increases travel time, environment pollution and fuel consumption. According to a recent urban transportation report [21] in 2017, the congestion cost is $179 billion in the U.S. urban areas, the travel delay and wasted fuel due to traffic congestion are 8.8 billion hours and 3.3 billion gallons. As the root cause of traffic congestion, there is a rising demand for identifying traffic bottlenecks and discovering congestion propagation patterns. The reason is that knowing traffic bottlenecks and congestion propagation patterns can help governments

© Springer Nature Switzerland AG 2021
G. Wang et al. (Eds.): SpaCCS 2020, LNCS 12383, pp. 372–383, 2021.
https://doi.org/10.1007/978-3-030-68884-4_31

take timely actions and reasonably allocate transportation resources. Unfortunately, identifying traffic bottlenecks are very challenging as they are caused by many factors and vary with spatio-temporal environment, thus are difficult to be pre-defined and identified.

Recently, wireless sensor network (WSN) applications have been used in several important areas, such as IoT devices recommendation [3–5], road anomaly detection [3], gesture recognition [15,31] and WiFi-based group detection [23,24] and access point deployment [25]. These applications are usually based on sensor-cloud framework [29,30] by connecting sensor networks and clouds, which provides scalable high-performance computing infrastructure for real-time processing and storing of sensor data [11,27,28,32].

Earlier studies [1,6,9,10,13,14,16,26,34] are interested in identifying freeway bottlenecks by evaluating the flow, speed or travel time gap between road upstream and downstream. For example, the study [10] identified freeway bottlenecks by jointly considering intensity and reliability dimensions of traffic congestion via vehicle probe data, the work [13] further utilized spatial and temporal variations of speed profile to identify and classify traffic bottlenecks. However, these methods cannot be applied to identify bottlenecks in urban areas due to extremely complicated travel behavior and road network topology. Dong, S.W. et al. [6] developed a Method of Traffic Network Bottleneck Identification based on Max-flow Min-cut Theorem. And Bai, Y.L. et al. [1] improved the previous speed-based bottleneck recognition methods. In 2013, Elhenawy, M. et al. [9] proposed an algorithm to identify the spatiotemporal activation of bottlenecks by using speed measurements over short temporal and spatial intervals and segments, respectively. Li et al. [16] quantified travel time variability at a single bottleneck based on stochastic capacity and demand distributions, and then evaluated the impact of reducing demand and capacity on travel time. Lee et al. in [14] developed a three-phrase spatio-temporal traffic bottleneck mining model to identify bottlenecks and considered that bottlenecks most likely existed in the spatial cross area of two congestion propagation patterns. A congestion propagation pattern depicts the congestion propagation relationship between two congested areas. Using data collected from a taxi dispatching system, the experimental results showed the effectiveness of the proposed method in congestion prediction and bottleneck identification. In [26], Tao et al. analyzed the congestion relationship between road segments and their simulation results suggested that the congestion of a road segment was affected by the road network structure and congestion of its adjacent road segments.

With the popularization of traffic flow sensing devices, a few studies [15,17, 18,20] proposed data-driven techniques to identify bottleneck by analyzing the traffic flow characteristics and traffic behaviors. The work [32] utilizes the three-phase traffic theory to predict the moving bottleneck with the use of a small share of probe vehicles randomly distributed in traffic flow, the main idea is to recognize phase transition points from synchronized flow to free flow on probe vehicle trajectories. Note that the authors verified their method by using the Kerner–Klenov microscopic stochastic traffic flow model. The study [33] firstly defined traffic bottleneck in urban area based on the congestion propagation costs and the congestion weights of road segments, then identified bottleneck using causal congestion trees and causal congestion graphs. Since the traffic bottleneck may shift due to the demand or supply, the study [19] aims to identify recurrent or non-recurrent bottleneck using traffic state rank distribution, which is fit using Gaussian Mixture Model. The work [17] recognized the bottleneck links using the mean and variance of congestion measurement, while the study [18] identified bottleneck based on the consequences of the road failure from both the traveling cost and the network effectiveness. In [15], they first ranked road links using the weighted sum of specific performance measures, then selected the links that are ranked relatively high as recurrent bottlenecks in urban roadway network. The work [7] further identified traffic bottleneck by calculating both the congestion level cost of a road segment itself and the contagion cost that the congestion may propagate to other road segments. Specifically, the work utilized Markov analysis to determine the probabilities of congestion propagation between road segments. Similarly, the work [22] recognized bottleneck in the urban area based on the congestion propagation costs and the congestion weights of road segments. However, these methods based on congestion cost directly or indirectly to identify congestion have two disadvantages. One is that the definition and calculation of congestion costs were not well-conducted and depended on the pre-designated threshold, which ignored the characteristics of the individual road segment, such as road lengths and the number of lanes. Another is that these methods did not correctly model the congestion causal relationships among road segments caused by traffic bottlenecks.

To the best of our knowledge, our work is the first attempt to identify traffic bottlenecks by modeling causal relationships among spatially distributed traffic flow sensors within urban areas. There are two main technical issues for identifying traffic bottleneck in urban areas, i.e., how to model bottleneck and congestion propagation. As mentioned earlier, the bottleneck location may change significantly and the congestion propagation caused by bottleneck is affected by various factors. To address the challenge, we firstly discover causal relationships by estimating transfer entropy among spatially distributed traffic flow sensors. Then, we construct causality graphs and perform frequent subgraphs mining to identify traffic bottlenecks and discover congestion propagation patterns.

2   Methodology

2.1   Bottleneck Identification Framework

Figure 1 demonstrates the framework of our model, which consists of three steps: 1) Model causality relationship. To select the most likely congestion propagation paths caused by bottlenecks among the monitoring traffic flow sensors, we calculate the causal strengths using transfer entropy [2, 8, 12] among spatially distributed sensors from the collected historical data. Note we are only interested in the uptrend intervals of sensor measurements since the uptrend intervals account for the congestion propagation process and enable us to track the bottlenecks;

2) Construct causality graphs. Based on the calculated causal strengths, we construct the causality graphs to recover the most likely congestion propagation process; 3) Frequent subgraph mining. We regard the source nodes of every distinct frequent subgraph are either potential bottlenecks or locations spatially close to the bottlenecks. For ease of the following presentation, we define the two basic notations used in the proposed method:

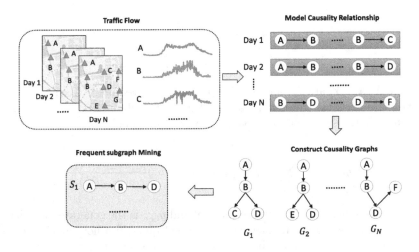

Fig. 1. The framework of our method

2.2   Causality Graphs Construction

Definition 1 (**Uptrend Sequence**). Given a traffic flow sensor s, an uptrend sequence is a consecutive subsequence of measurements $I = (v_i^s, v_{i+1}^s, ..., v_{i+l-1}^s)$ and $\forall j \in [i, i+l-1], v_{j+1}^s > v_j^s$, where l denotes the length of I.

Definition 2 (**Uptrend Event**). An uptrend event e corresponds to an uptrend sequence, and denoted by a triple $e = (s, t, o)$, where s is the identifier of the associated traffic flow sensor, t and o are the timestamp and value of the first measurement in I (i.e., i and v_i).

A straightforward method [15] could be to build causality graphs where each node indicates an uptrend event and each edge denotes the correlation between two uptrend sequences. Specifically, they considered two different uptrend events are causally related only if both the spatial threshold and the congestion propagation speed interval are met. However, such a method is inapplicable for building congestion propagation caused by traffic bottlenecks due to the following reasons. First, the congestion of each road segment may be affected by several bottlenecks and there is no explicit propagation path to track. Second, the congestion propagation caused by bottleneck is not only spatial proximity but also various meteorological factors (e.g., departure time and route choice behavior).

Therefore, we need to address the following problem: How to correctly model the causality relationships between two uptrend events?

Without loss of generality, we assume that uptrend event $e_x = (s_x, t_x, o_x)$ precedes $e_y = (s_y, t_y, o_y)$, and model their causal strength $\pi(e_x \mapsto e_y)$ as follows. Let $x = (v_{t_x}^{s_x}, ..., v_{t_x-N+1}^{s_x})$ and $y = (v_{t_y}^{s_y}, ..., v_{t_y-N+1}^{s_y})$ denote the uptrend sequence of e_x and e_y, we map the time series data x and y to a high dimensional space via delay embedding:

$$
\begin{aligned}
X_i &= <v_i^{s_x}, v_{i-\tau}^{s_x}, v_{i-2\tau}^{s_x}, ..., v_{i-(d_x-1)\tau}^{s_x}> \\
Y_i &= <v_i^{s_y}, v_{i-\tau}^{s_y}, v_{i-2\tau}^{s_y}, ..., v_{i-(d_y-1)\tau}^{s_y}>
\end{aligned}
\tag{1}
$$

where X_i and Y_i are d_x- and d_y-dimensional delay vectors. After reconstructing the state space of the raw data x and y, we calculate the transfer entropy $\theta(y|x)$ from x to y by including a general prediction time u as:

$$
\theta(y|x) = \sum_{y_{i+u}, Y_i, X_i} p(y_{i+u}, Y_i, X_i) \times log \frac{p(y_{i+u}|X_i, Y_i)}{p(y_{i+u}|Y_i)}
\tag{2}
$$

where u is a discrete-valued time-interval and y_{i+u} is the generated prediction for u sample ahead. The transfer entropy $\theta(y|x)$ quantifies how much the past traffic flow data x conditions the transition probabilities of another traffic flow data y.

Using the definition of conditional probabilities, we replace the transition probability by joint probability density functions and rewrite Eq. (3) as:

$$
\theta(y|x) = \sum_{y_{i+u}, Y_i, X_i} p(y_{i+u}, Y_i, X_i) \times log \frac{p(y_{i+u}, Y_i, X_i)p(Y_i)}{p(Y_i, X_i)p(y_{i+u}, Y_i)}
\tag{3}
$$

Before calculating the transfer entropy $\theta(y|x)$ from Eq. (3), we construct the joint probability density functions and transition probabilities with kernel estimation in terms of the high order of the joint probability density functions. Using Gaussian Kernel function, we give a estimate of $p(y)$ as:

$$
\widehat{p}(y) = \frac{1}{N} \sum_{i=1}^{N} \frac{1}{\sqrt{2\pi}w} exp\left(-\frac{(y - y_i)^2)}{2w^2}\right)
\tag{4}
$$

where w is the estimator width and N the number of samples. Similarly, $p(x, y)$ can be estimated as:

$$
\widehat{p}(x, y) = \frac{1}{N} \sum_{i=1}^{N} \frac{1}{2\pi w^2} exp\left(-\frac{(x - x_i)^2 + (y - y_i)^2}{2w^2}\right)
\tag{5}
$$

For the joint probability density functions $p(y_{i+u}, y, x)$, we estimated it according to [22]:

$$\widehat{p}(y_{i+u}, Y_i, X_i) = \frac{1}{N} \sum_{m \neq i}^{N} \Theta \left[\left| \left\{ \begin{array}{c} y_{i+u} - y_{m+u} \\ Y_i - Y_m \\ X_i - X_m \end{array} \right\} \right| - r \right] \tag{6}$$

We use the step kernel $\Theta(x > 0) = 1$ and $\Theta(x \leq 0) = 0$. The norm $|\cdot|$ is the maximum distance and r is the kernel radius that control fall-off rate. Based on Eq. (3)–(6), we define the causal strength $\pi(e_x \mapsto e_y)$ by comparing the influence of time series data x on y with the influence of y on x:

$$\pi(e_x \mapsto e_y) = \theta(y|x) - \theta(x|y) \tag{7}$$

Positive values of $\pi(x \mapsto y)$ means event e_x causes e_y, while negative values mean the reverse case. No causality is detected if both transfer entropy $\theta(y|x)$ and $\theta(x|y)$ have a similar value. From Eq. (1) and (7), we found the causal strength calculation depends on three parameters, i.e., the embedding dimension d_x, d_y and the time delay τ. We learn these parameters by minimizing the prediction error for future samples of the raw time series, and the predicted value is based on parameters of the estimated probability distributions. For d_x and τ (d_y can be estimated with the same way), we calculated the unobserved future value x_{t+u} by meaning the future value $x_{t'+u}$ of its neighbors $X_{t'}$:

$$\widehat{x}_{t+u} = \frac{1}{|U_{t'}|} \sum_{U_{t'}} x_{t'+u} \tag{8}$$

where $U_{t'} = \{X_{t'} : ||X_{t'} - X_t|| \leq \varepsilon\}$ denotes the set of vectors are within a volume with radius ε around $X_{t'}$. Therefore, we learn parameters d_x and τ by minimizing the mean squared prediction error:

$$err = \sum_t (\widehat{x}_{t+u} - x_{t'+u})^2 \tag{9}$$

Definition 3 (**Event Causality**). We define the uptrend event e_x is caused by e_y if and only if the following conditions are satisfied: (1) $0 < t_x - t_y < L$ and L is the maximum time lag we consider, $t_x > t_y$ means a cause necessarily precedes its effect; (2) the causal strength $\pi(e_x \mapsto e_y) > 0$ according to Eq. (3).

Definition 4 (**Causality Graph**). A causality graph $G = <V, E, W>$ is a directed graph that denotes causality relationship among uptrend events, where V is the uptrend event set, $E \subseteq V \times V$ is the set of edges in G. For $e_x, e_y \in V$, an edge from e_x to e_y exists in the graph if and only if the two events satisfy Definition 3.

For an uptrend event, we insert it to the causality graph by searching all its causal parent events and adding an edge from the causal parent event to it based on Definition 4.

Algorithm 1. The algorithm for identifying traffic bottleneck.

Require: 1) Causality graph dataset $D = \{G_1, G_2, ..., G_N\}$; 2) Minimum support threshold:min_sup; 3) The set of frequent subgraphs with one edge F_1.

Ensure: The set of frequent subgraphs.

1: Initialize $F_k = F_1$.
2: **while** $F_k \neq \emptyset$ **do**
3: **for** each frequent subgraph $g_i \in F_k$ **do**
4: **for** each frequent subgraph $g_j \in F_k$ **do**
5:   Generate candidate frequent subgraphs C_{k+1} with $size(k+1)$ by joining g_i and g_j.
6:   Prune C_{k+1} that contain infrequent subgraphs with $size(k)$
7:   **for** each graph $g \in C_{k+1}$ **do**
8:    Count the support of g as $sup(g)$.
9:    **if** $sup(g) \geq$ min_sup
10:    $F_{k+1} = F_{k+1} \cup \{g\}$
11:   **end for**
12: **end for**
13: **end for**
  $k = k + 1$
14: **endwhile**
15: **return** $\cup_{i=1,...,k-1} F_i$.

2.3 Frequent Propagation Patterns Mining

Definition 5 (**Frequent Subgraph**). Given a causality graph dataset $D = \{G_1, G_2, ..., G_n\}$ and a subgraph g, the supporting graph set of g denotes as $D_g = \{G_i | g \subseteq Gi, G_i \in D\}$, we calculate the support of g as $sup(g) = |D_g|/|G|$. Therefore, a frequent subgraph is a graph whose support is larger than a minimum support threshold: min_sup.

Based on Definition 3 and Definition 4, for any path $<e_i, e_{i+1}, ..., e_{i+m}>$ in the causality graph, we have $e_i.t > e_{i+1}.t > ... > e_{i+m}.t$, thus ensure all the constructed causality graphs are directed acyclic graph and their frequent subgraphs will only have one source node. Specifically, we utilize the Apriori-based procedure for identifying traffic bottleneck from causality graph dataset, as shown in Algorithm 1. First, as shown in Line 1, we initialize F_k with F_1 that stores all the subgraphs with single edge. Then, as depicted in Line 2–5, we generate candidate frequent subgraphs with $size(k+1)$ by joining two frequent subgraphs with $size(k)$. Line 6 aims to remove all the infrequent subgraphs in candidate frequent subgraphs with $size(k+1)$. Line 7–11 ensures that the support of all the candidate frequent subgraphs with $size(k+1)$ are no less than the minimum support threshold: min_sup.

Finally, we regard these source nodes in the mined frequent subgraphs as either potential bottlenecks or locations spatially close to the bottlenecks, and further treat each distinct frequent subgraph as a congestion propagation pattern.

3   Experiment Results

Our experiments are conducted on a real-world loop detector dataset, which is collected in the urban traffic network of Hangzhou, china over one month. As shown in Fig. 2, there are 74 detectors are utilized to collect this dataset and we use the traffic flow data to identify bottlenecks in urban areas.

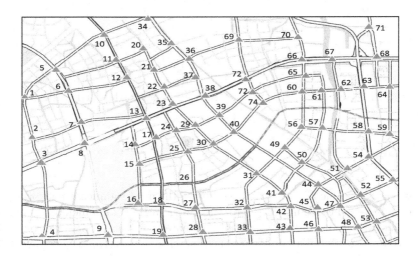

Fig. 2. An illustration of the locations of inductive loop detectors in Hangzhou

Based on the inductive loop detectors dataset, we extract 9,756 uptrend sequences and its corresponding events with the minimum length is 30 min according to the proposed Definition 1 and 2. Then we perform traffic bottlenecks identification with the proposed method. Specifically, we firstly mine the causality relationships among the uptrend events of each day based on Definition 3, and construct a causality graph with these mined events causality according to Definition 4. Then, we generate 30 causality graphs from this dataset and identify bottlenecks using Algorithm 1. We count the number of times that these road segments were identified as traffic bottlenecks, as illustrated in Fig. 3. We can see that in Fig. 3, road segments 3, 13, 38 and 54 are four road segments with the most frequent times in the urban road network of Hangzhou, which can be considered as bottlenecks in the road network. However, road segments 7, 8, 38 and 67 will be regarded as bottlenecks if we consider congestion levels on road segments only to identify bottlenecks. The results suggest that identifying bottlenecks only based on road segments' congestion levels may lead to inaccuracy and ineffectiveness.

It is very challenging to directly verify the effectiveness of the proposed method as we lack the ground truth data (i.e., the actual traffic bottlenecks). To tackle this problem, we use a traffic simulator PTV-VISSIM to analyze traffic operations by increasing the number of lanes on each road segment. The rationale

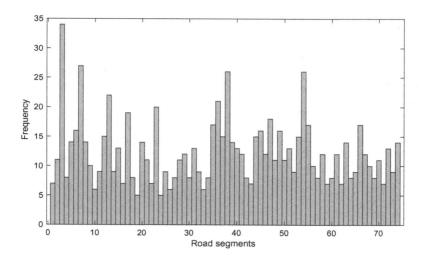

Fig. 3. The frequency that a road segment is identified as a bottleneck

is that the true traffic bottlenecks should bring the most significant network-wide traffic improvement. We utilize the road network in Hangzhou mentioned in Fig. 2 for this simulation and compare the percentage of travel time improvement in the road network before and after each increase, respectively. Note the travel time indicates the required average time interval when vehicles pass away the detection area. Figure 4 reports the simulation results, we observe: 1) the travel efficiency of road network will be improved for all road segments after increasing

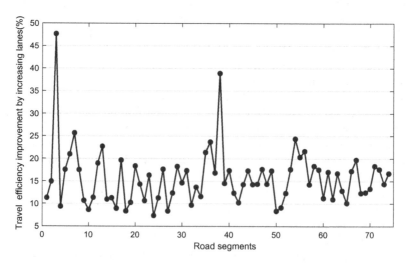

Fig. 4. Percentage of travel efficiency in road network after increasing the number of lanes on each road segment

the number of lanes; 2) the most significant improvements of the travel time is to increase the number of lanes on road segments 3 and 38, which are 47.6% and 38.9% respectively. The result suggests that the proposed bottleneck identification method via causal inference can better capture the features of urban traffic bottlenecks.

4 Conclusion

Traffic congestion reduces the efficiency of transportation infrastructure and increases travel time, air pollution and fuel consumption. As the source of traffic congestion, identifying traffic bottleneck is the function prerequisite for ITS navigation, which has great contribution to alleviating congestion and improving the performance of traffic network. In this paper, we propose a novel method to identify potential traffic bottlenecks based on urban traffic flow sensors. The proposed method models causal relationships among spatially distributed traffic flow sensors with transfer entropy, based on which we construct a few causality graphs to illustrate the congestion propagations caused by potential bottlenecks. Finally, we utilize an apriori-based procedure to identify traffic bottleneck by mining frequent subgraphs. To the best of our knowledge, this is the first work to identify traffic bottleneck in urban road networks via causal inference. The simulation and experiment results with a real-world traffic flow dataset demonstrate the proposed method can effectively identify urban traffic bottlenecks.

Acknowledgments. This work was supported in part by the Young Scientists Fund of the National Natural Science Foundation of China under Grant 61802343 and 62072402, in part by the Zhejiang Provincial Natural Science Foundation of China under Grant LGF19F020019 and LGN20F020003, and in part by Hangzhou Science and Technology Bureau under Grant 20191203B37 and the Intelligent Plant Factory of Zhejiang Province Engineering Lab.

References

1. Bai, Y., Wu, Z., Sun, S., Wang, C.: Automatic identification algorithm for freeway bottleneck. In: Proceedings 2011 International Conference on Transportation, Mechanical, and Electrical Engineering (TMEE), pp. 1857–1860 (2011)
2. Chen, H., Rakha, H.A.: Automatic freeway bottleneck identification and visualization using image processing techniques. arXiv preprint arXiv:1911.07395 (2019)
3. Chen, Y., Zhang, J., Guo, M., Cao, J.: Learning user preference from heterogeneous information for store-type recommendation. IEEE Trans. Serv. Comput. **13**, 1100–1114 (2017)
4. Chen, Y., Zhang, J., Xu, L., Guo, M., Cao, J.: Modeling latent relation to boost things categorization service. IEEE Trans. Serv. Comput. **13**(5), 915–929 (2020)
5. Chen, Y., Zhou, M., Zheng, Z., Chen, D.: Time-aware smart object recommendation in social internet of things. IEEE Internet Things J. **7**(3), 2014–2027 (2020)

6. Dong, S., Zhang, Y.: Research on method of traffic network bottleneck identification based on max-flow min-cut theorem. In: Proceedings 2011 International Conference on Transportation, Mechanical, and Electrical Engineering (TMEE), pp. 1905–1908 (2011)

7. Duan, P., Yang, F., Chen, T., Shah, S.L.: Direct causality detection via the transfer entropy approach. IEEE Trans. Control Syst. Technol. **21**(6), 2052–2066 (2013)

8. Ehlert, A., Schneck, A., Chanchareon, N.: Junction parameter calibration for mesoscopic simulation in Vissim. Transp. Res. Procedia **21**, 216–226 (2017)

9. Elhenawy, M., Rakha, H.A., Chen, H.: An automated statistically-principled bottleneck identification algorithm (ASBIA). In: 16th International IEEE Conference on Intelligent Transportation Systems (ITSC 2013), pp. 1846–1851 (2013)

10. Gong, L., Fan, W.: Developing a systematic method for identifying and ranking freeway bottlenecks using vehicle probe data. J. Transp. Eng. Part A Syst. **144**(3), 04017083 (2018)

11. Huang, M., Liu, A., Wang, T., Huang, C.: Green data gathering under delay differentiated services constraint for internet of things. Wirel. Commun. Mobile Comput. **2018** (2018)

12. Inokuchi, A., Washio, T., Motoda, H.: An Apriori-based algorithm for mining frequent substructures from graph data. In: Zighed, D.A., Komorowski, J., Żytkow, J. (eds.) PKDD 2000. LNCS (LNAI), vol. 1910, pp. 13–23. Springer, Heidelberg (2000). https://doi.org/10.1007/3-540-45372-5_2

13. Jose, R., Mitra, S.: Identifying and classifying highway bottlenecks based on spatial and temporal variation of speed. J. Transp. Eng. Part A Syst. **144**(12), 04018075 (2018)

14. Lee, W., Tseng, S., Shieh, J., Chen, H.: Discovering traffic bottlenecks in an urban network by spatiotemporal data mining on location-based services. IEEE Trans. Intell. Transp. Syst. **12**(4), 1047–1056 (2011)

15. Li, C., Yue, W., Mao, G., Xu, Z.: Congestion propagation based bottleneck identification in urban road networks. IEEE Trans. Veh. Technol. **69**(5), 4827–4841 (2020)

16. Li, M., Zhou, X., Rouphail, N.M.: Quantifying travel time variability at a single bottleneck based on stochastic capacity and demand distributions. J. Intell. Transp. Syst. **21**(2), 79–93 (2017)

17. Lu, W., Wang, F., Liu, L., Hu, G.: Identifying bottlenecks in roadway networks in hurricane evacuation. J. Transp. Eng. Part A Syst. **144**(9), 04018047 (2018)

18. Ma, J., Li, C., Liu, Z., Duan, Y., Lei, Y., Xiong, L.: On traffic bottleneck in green its navigation: an identification method. In: IEEE 83rd Vehicular Technology Conference (VTC Spring), pp. 1–5 (2016)

19. Qi, H., Chen, M., Wang, D.: Recurrent and non-recurrent bottleneck analysis based on traffic state rank distribution. Transportmetrica B Transp. Dyn. **7**(1), 275–294 (2019)

20. Qi, H., Liu, M., Zhang, L., Wang, D.: Tracing road network bottleneck by data driven approach. PloS One **11**(5), e0156089 (2016)

21. Schrank, D., Lomax, T., Turner, S.: Urban mobility report Texas transportation institute. Texas Transportation Institute, Texas (2009)

22. Schreiber, T.: Measuring information transfer. Phys. Rev. Lett. **85**(2), 461 (2000)

23. Shen, J., Cao, J., Liu, X.: BaG: behavior-aware group detection in crowded urban spaces using wifi probes. IEEE Trans. Mobile Comput. 1 (2020)

24. Shen, J., Cao, J., Liu, X., Tang, S.: Snow: detecting shopping groups using WiFi. IEEE Internet Things J. **5**(5), 3908–3917 (2018)

25. Shen, J., Cao, J., Liu, X., Zhang, C.: DMAD: data-driven measuring of Wi-Fi access point deployment in urban spaces. ACM Trans. Intell. Syst. Technol. **9**(1), 2157–6904 (2017)

26. Tao, R., Xi, Y., Li, D.: Simulation analysis on urban traffic congestion propagation based on complex network. In: IEEE International Conference on Service Operations and Logistics, and Informatics (SOLI), pp. 217–222 (2016)

27. Wang, T., Jia, W., Xing, G., Li, M.: Exploiting statistical mobility models for efficient Wi-Fi deployment. IEEE Trans. Veh. Technol. **62**(1), 360–373 (2012)

28. Wang, T., Ke, H., Zheng, X., Wang, K., Sangaiah, A.K., Liu, A.: Big data cleaning based on mobile edge computing in industrial sensor-cloud. IEEE Trans. Ind. Inf. **16**(2), 1321–1329 (2019)

29. Wang, T., et al.: When sensor-cloud meets mobile edge computing. Sensors **19**(23), 5324 (2019)

30. Wang, T., Luo, H., Jia, W., Liu, A., Xie, M.: MTES: an intelligent trust evaluation scheme in sensor-cloud-enabled industrial internet of things. IEEE Trans. Ind. Inf. **16**(3), 2054–2062 (2019)

31. Wang, Y., Shen, J., Zheng, Y.: Push the limit of acoustic gesture recognition. In: IEEE INFOCOM 2020 - IEEE Conference on Computer Communications, pp. 566–575 (2020)

32. Wegerle, D., Kerner, B.S., Schreckenberg, M., Klenov, S.L.: Prediction of moving bottleneck through the use of probe vehicles: a simulation approach in the framework of three-phase traffic theory. J. Intell. Transp. Syst. **24**(6), 598–616 (2020)

33. Yue, W., Li, C., Mao, G.: Urban traffic bottleneck identification based on congestion propagation. In: IEEE International Conference on Communications (ICC), pp. 1–6 (2018)

34. Zheng, Z., et al.: A fused method of machine learning and dynamic time warping for road anomalies detection. IEEE Trans. Intell. Transp. Syst. 1–13 (2020)

NAS-WFPN: Neural Architecture Search Weighted Feature Pyramid Networks for Object Detection

Xiaohan Li[1], Ziyan Xie[1], Taotao Lai[2], Fusheng Zhao[3], Haiyin Xu[4], and Riqing Chen[1(✉)]

[1] School of Computer Science, Fujian Agriculture and Forestry University, Fuzhou 350002, China
Riqing.chen@fafu.edu.cn
[2] School of Computer and Control Engineering, Minjiang University, Fuzhou 350108, China
[3] School of Mathematics and Computer Science, Quanzhou Normal University, Quanzhou 362000, China
[4] Department of Information Engineering, Hebei Vocational and Technical College of Building Materials, Qinhuangdao 066000, China

Abstract. As we known, most of convolution neural architectures are manually designed. However, they cannot obtain the optimal structures. To address this problem, based on Weighted Feature Pyramid Networks (WFPN), in this paper, we use gaussian kernel to calculate the weight to design a novel method called the Neural Architecture Search Weighted Feature Pyramid Networks (i.e., NAS-WFPN). NAS-WFPN mainly consists of three parts (i.e., top-down pathway, bottom-up pathway and lateral connections) to fuse features across different scales. Experimental results show that NAS-WFPN achieves higher accuracy compared with the existing object detection methods. Specifically, NAS-WFPN increases accuracy by 2.3 AP compared to SSDLite with MobileNetV2 model and gets 49.1 AP, which exceeds NAS-FPN and Mask R-CNN.

Keywords: Convolution neural architectures · Weighted Feature Pyramid Networks · Neural Architecture Search · Gaussian kernel · Object detection

1 Introduction

1.1 A Subsection Sample

Object detection and image classification are fundamental problems in computer vision. In the last couple of years, with the rapid development of deep convolution networks, it has been made on designing the model architecture for object detection [1, 2] and image classification [3, 4], which achieved a great progress. However, object detection is different from image classification, and object detection always has severe problems when it wants to locate and detect multiple objects in a wide range of scales and locations. Many modern object detectors [5–7] commonly use the pyramid feature architecture to generate multiscale feature layers for dealing with the above problems.

© Springer Nature Switzerland AG 2021
G. Wang et al. (Eds.): SpaCCS 2020, LNCS 12383, pp. 384–394, 2021.
https://doi.org/10.1007/978-3-030-68884-4_32

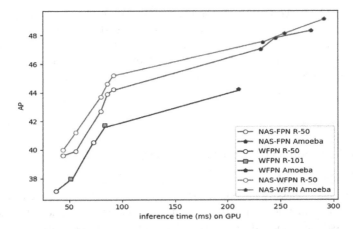

Fig. 1. Average precision vs. Inference time per image across accurate model. The gray curve highlights result of NAS-WFPN combined with RetinaNet.

Weighted Feature Pyramid Network (WFPN) generates multiscale feature layers base on the Feature Pyramid Network (FPN) [2]. WFPN builds feature pyramid by combining two layers via a top-down pathway and lateral connections. One layer is semantically strong but lower resolution, and thus WFPN up-samples this layer, and then combines with the other layer with higher resolution. WFPN uses Gaussian kernel function to compute weights and sets these different weight values at the lateral connections layer when WFPN creates a feature pyramid. Thus, the features produced by WFPN are both higher resolution and semantically strong. Compared with FPN, WFPN has better accuracy and effective. However, WFPN lacks flexibility and does not cover all possible cross-scale connections. In addition, more and more recent work [9–17] propose different methods to generate feature pyramid.

As we known, designing feature pyramid always needs a big design space, which makes searching pyramidal architectures unmanageable and can't early exit. In recent years, image classification using Neural Architecture Search algorithm [18] can efficiently discover an architecture in a big design space, and this architecture is manageable. Recently, by using Neural Architecture Search Feature Pyramid Networks (NAS-FPN) [8] designs the search space and covers multi-scale feature representations and all possible cross-scale connections. However, NAS-FPN does not pay attention to the amount of information contained in different feature layers that has been considered in WFPN.

Based on the above analyses, to effectively use the advantages of both Neural Architecture Search (i.e., NAS) and Weighted Feature Pyramid Networks, we propose a new method by combining NAS and WFPN (i.e., NAS-WFPN). NAS-WFPA considers the amount of information contained in different feature layers and discovers manageable architecture that covers all possible scales to generate multiscale feature pyramid.

NAS-WFPN can work with all kinds of backbone models, such as ResNet [3], MobileNet [19] and AmoebaNet [20]. It has the characteristics of fast speed and high accuracy. At the same inference time, NAS-WFPN combining with MobileNetV2 [19] backbone surpasses SSDLite by 2.3AP. NAS-WFPN achieves 49.1AP accuracy, and exceeds Mask R-CNN [5]. Figure 1 shows a summary of our results.

2   Relate Work

2.1   Deep Convolutional Neural Network for Object Detection

Object detection is a basic problem of computer vision in artificial intelligence field. Its goal is to accurately classify the objects in various categories and find the location with bounding box information. Object detection methods based on deep learning have been widely discussed and applied in industry. This type of method widely uses massive data and labels in data sets such as ImageNet, PASCALVOC, COCO to train the convolutional neural network (CNN).

In 2014, Girshick et al. proposed a pioneering architecture named RCNN for object detection based on convolutional neural network. RCNN has achieved a better result than traditional methods. However, some drawbacks in this framework still exist, such as cumbersome training steps, multiple calculations, and slow detection speed.

In 2015, Girshick continued to propose an improved architecture of RCNN called Fast RCNN [21] with a faster detection speed and higher accuracy. Although Fast RCNN achieves an average accuracy of 70% on the PASCALVOL2007 dataset, its speed is still slow because of the region proposed algorithm SelectiveSearch.

Later in 2015, a Faster RCNN [22] architecture designed by Ren et al. became the first end-to-end detector which can be run at a quasi-real-time speed. Instead of using regions proposed algorithm SelectiveSearch, Region Proposal Network (RPN) is applied in Faster RCNN. Faster RCNN breaks the speed bottleneck of Fast RCNN, but it still cannot achieve a real-time object detection. Meanwhile, a large amount of computations have to be needed for finding candidate regions.

He et al. proposed the Mask RCNN [5] in 2017 which was a further improvement of Faster RCNN. The ResNet101-FPN is applied as a backbone. Compared with other methods, Mask RCNN achieved the best performance. In 2019, Li et al. proposed the TridentNet using ResNet101 as the basic backbone network. It achieves the accuracy of 48.4% on the COCO dataset, which is the optimal result of the single model at present. These object detection methods are manually designed and have a good performance, but they have little flexibility and cannot automatically design different architectures for different tasks.

2.2   Neural Architectures Search

Deep learning can automatically learn useful features and get rid of the dependence on feature engineering. Thanks to more and more new neural network structures such as ResNet, Inceptin and DenseNet etc., Deep learning has shown a better performance than other traditional algorithms in image, voice processing etc. However, designing a high-performance neural network requires a lot of professional experience and high cost, which limits its application in industry. Neural Architecture Search (NAS) is a kind of automatic neural network design technology. According to the sample set of high-performance network structure, a suitable neural network can be designed automatically by NAS. Some tasks can even match the level of human experts, and even find never proposed network structure, which can effectively reduce the use of neural network and implementation costs.

The principle of NAS is that given a set of candidate neural network structures called search space, using a certain strategy searches out the optimal network structures. Some indexes such as precision and speed are used to evaluate the performance of a neural network which is called performance evaluation and returned to search strategy.

In each iteration of the search process, one neural network structure called `subnetwork' can be obtained when a "sample" is generated from search space. The subnetwork is applied to train with the sample set and evaluated on validation set. The network continues to be optimized until the optima subnetwork is found.

Search space, search strategy and performance evaluation strategy are the core elements of NAS. The search space defines the set of searchable neural network structures, which is the solution set. The search strategy defines how to find the optimal network structure in the search space. The performance evaluation strategy defines how to evaluate the performance of the searched network structure.

NAS-FPN [8] uses Neural Architecture Search [18] cover all possible cross-scale connections for achieving better accuracy and latency compared with state-of-the-art object detection models. However, they did not take into account the impact of different information contained in different feature layer on object detection.

2.3 RetinaNet

First of all, RetinaNet is a unified object detection method with a backbone and two subnets. The backbone is mainly used to obtain a feature map of input image by a series of convolution operations. The two subnets respectively perform object classification and location regression according to the feature map of backbone output. As a one-stage network, RetinaNet is a durable detection because of high detecting speed and accuracy. Currently, many one-stage detections apply RetinaNet as the baseline for various improvements. The strategies used in RetinaNet are extremely simple, RetinaNet modifies original focal loss and adds the weights, which reduces the weights of the easily classified samples, and increases the weights of the difficult classified samples. Meanwhile, RetinaNet remains unchanged the regression loss.

3   Method

Because the RetinaNet framework is efficient and simple, our method is based on it. NAS-WFPN's goal is to build a better WFPN architecture with RetinaNet. Figure 2 shows the RetinaNet architecture.

NAS-WFPN

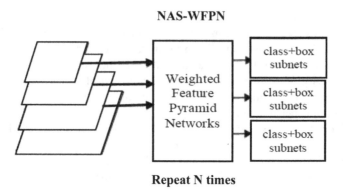

Repeat N times

Fig. 2. In NAS-WFPN, we use Neural Architecture Search to generate weighted feature pyramid architecture. Class and box predictions are regular design in RetinaNet. We repeat N times to achieve better performance.

3.1   Architecture Search Space

In our search space, a number of "merging cells" form a weighted feature pyramid network of NAS-WFPN. We introduce the WFPN's input and how each merging cell is constructed as follows.

Weighted Feature Pyramid Network. WFPN is built according to FPN. Compare with FPN, WFPN takes into account the influence of different information contained in different feature layer on object detection. Multiscale feature layers are WFPN's inputs and output feature layers are in the same scales. We use the last layer in each group of feature layers as the inputs to the first pyramid network. The next pyramid network input is the output of the current pyramid network. We called input features as {C2, C3, C4, C5}. At first, we attach a 1×1 convolutional layer on C5. Then we use a 3×3 convolution to get P5. In order to adapt RPN, we append a down-sampling process on P5, and the result is called P6. We append an up-sampling process on P5, and the result is called D4. We use gaussian kernel function to calculate the different between C4 and D4, and use weights to show the difference. We fuse C4 and D4 with weight to get P4. By repeating same operation, we can get P3 and P2. So WFPN's output feature called as {P6, P5, P4, P3, P2}. The architecture of the WFPN can be stacked repeatedly to get a better accuracy because both inputs and outputs of pyr-amid network have same scales.

Merging Cell. We use a merging cell, which combines high-level features with strong semantics and low-level feature with high resolution. It's different from WFPN in our method, where every merging cell takes two inputs that have different scales. Then, after applying process operation, combining two inputs generate a different scales output feature layer. N different merging cells make up NAS-WFPN, and before search, N has been given. We use RNN to decide how to make up the merging cell. RNN selects any two input layers and combines them to generate a output feature layer. The steps of NAS-WFPN are as follows:

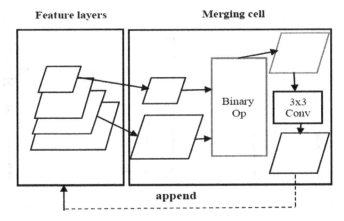

Fig. 3. Seven steps required in a merging cell. The merge feature layer is always followed by a RELU, a 3×3 convolution, and a batch normalization layer. The final feature layer will push back to candidates.

Step 1. Select a feature layer k_i from candidates (Fig. 3).

Step 2. Select another feature layer kj from candidates.

Step 3. Use gaussian kernel function to calculate the different between k_i and k_j, and use the weight to show the difference.

Step 4. Choose output feature layer resolution.

Step 5. Use binary operation to combine ki and kj with weighted to generate a feature layer with the resolution that you want.

Step 6. Put this generated feature layer in the candidates.

Step 7. Repeat the above step N times.

Weight Calculation. The weight calculation includes four steps. First, we do the normalization of data to reduce the amount of calculation. Second, we use the improved gaussian kernel to create gaussian matrix. The improved gaussian kernel is Eq. (1), where H and W are width and height of the feature layer. Third, we convolved the ki layer and kj layer with the gaussian matrix. The value of the ki layer convolved with the gaussian matrix is x, and the value of the kj layer convolved with the gaussian matrix is y. The absolute value of x subtracts y is used to show the difference between the ki layer and kj layer. The result is denoted as a. Finally, we use Eq. (2) to calculate b, because the larger the difference between ki and kj is, the larger the value of weight between them is. The weights $\omega 1 = a / (a + b)$ and $\omega 2 = b / (a + b)$ are used for binary operations as shown in Fig. 4.

$$gauss(\sigma, r, c) = e^{-\frac{\left(r - \frac{H-1}{2}\right)^2 + \left(c - \frac{W-1}{2}\right)^2}{2\sigma^2}} \tag{1}$$

$$b = e^{(a-\omega)} \tag{2}$$

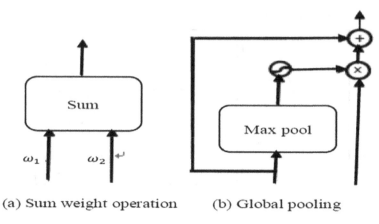

(a) Sum weight operation   (b) Global pooling

Fig. 4. Binary operations.

Binary Op. Binary Op includes two parts: sum weight operation and global pooling, which were selected because the two operations have no additional parameters and they are efficiency and simplicity. As we known, the sum operation is always used for combining features. In order to handle the different information contained in different feature layer on object detection, sum weight operation adds weights to the traditional addition as shown in Fig. 4(a). Before putting feature layer into Binary Op, global pooling uses up-sampling or max pooling to let output resolution become same resolution.

3.2   Deeply Supervised Anytime Object Detection

One advantage of our method is that it can be stopped at any time. This property allows detection at any time using feature pyramid generating with early exit. Then we can use it to connect with classifier and box regression to train networks. This makes the management of resources and time more manageable, and this provides a solution for dynamically allocating resources.

4   Results and Discussion

In this section, we first describe the implementation details of the proposed method. Then, we show concrete steps of how to build an accurate architecture. Finally, the results of experimental will be explained and use test-dev accuracy to show the NAS-WFPN's performance.

4.1   Implementation Details

NAS-WFPN uses the open-source RetinaNet. When we calculate the weight, in order to effectively consider the influence of edges on the image, is set to a relatively large value. According to the properties of gaussian kernel function, the value of is actually adjusting the effect of the surrounding pixels on the current pixel. The value of is set to bigger, it is the more dispersed and the difference of each part is little. So, the resulting template has little difference in the value of each element, and is similar to the average template. The model is trained on COCO train2017 and evaluated on COCO val2017. COCO is a large and rich dataset, which is used for object detection and labels. By far, the dataset takes scene understanding as the goal and is the mainly largest dataset with semantic segmentation, providing 80 categories, more than 330000 image segmentation. This intercepts from complex daily scenes. Objects in the images are calibrated by precise segmentation. Images include 91 class objects, 328000 images and 2500000 labels, where 200000 images are annotated, and the number of individuals in the whole dataset is more than 1.5 million.

4.2 Discovering Feature Pyramid Architectures

We use visualizing to discover architectures. To show the generation of the architecture of the experiment is a good feature pyramid architecture. In Fig. 5, we plot NAS-WFPN architectures with progressively higher reward during training. As the controller converges, the controller discovers architectures different from the traditional WFPN. We also find that, instead of randomly picking any two input layers from the candidate, the controller learns to build connections on the new generated layers. In Fig. 6, we show how our model works.

4.3 Discussions

We combine Neural Architecture Search with Weighted Feature Pyramid Networks for object detection to improve the accuracy. According to the result that our experiments on the COCO dataset, our model is flexible. We use our model to compare with WFPN, NAS-FPN and other traditional models. By the results, the performance of NAS-WFPN is better than those of traditional models. In Table 1, we report test-dev accuracy compared with existing methods. NAS-WFPN gets 49.1 test-dev AP to exceeds NAS-FPN and WFPN.

Table 1. The results obtained by our model and other state-of-the-art models on test-dev set of COCO.

Model	Image size	Inference time (ms)	Test-dev AP
WFPN R-50	640 × 640	37.5(GPU)	37.1
WFPN R-101	640 × 640	51.1(GPU)	38.0
WFPN R-50	1024 × 1024	73.0(GPU)	40.5
WFPN R-101	1024 × 1024	83.7(GPU)	41.7
WFPN AmoebaNet	1280 × 1280	210.4(GPU)	44.2
NAS-FPN R-50	640 × 640	56.1(GPU)	39.9
NAS-FPN R-50	1024 × 1024	92.1(GPU)	44.2
NAS-FPN R-50	1280 × 1280	131.9(GPU)	44.8
NAS-FPN R-50 + DropBlock	1280 × 1280	192.3(GPU)	46.6
NAS-FPN AmoebaNet + DropBlock	1280 × 1280	278.9(GPU)	48.3
NAS-WFPN AmoebaNet + DropBlock	1280 × 1280	291.2(GPU)	49.1

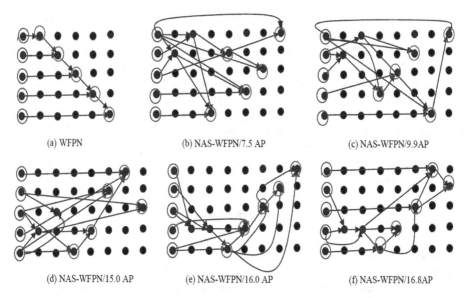

Fig. 5. Architecture search of NAS-WFPN. Each point represents a feature layer. Feature layers in the same row have the same resolutions. The bottom ones have high resolutions and the top ones have low resolution. Input layers are on the left side. The inputs to a pyramid network are marked with green circles and outputs are marked with red circles. (a) Traditional WFPN architecture. (b–f) The NAS-WFPN architectures discovered by NAS via training the RNN controller. (f) The final architecture in our experiments. As we can see that as the AP increases, the final architecture becomes more and more convergent. (Color figure online)

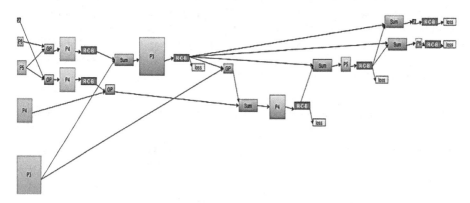

Fig. 6. This is the concrete realization process of the Fig. 5(e). Architecture of the discovery pyramid network in NAS-WFPN with five input layers (marked with yellow) and five output layers (marked with blue). GP stands for Global Pooling and R-C-B stands for ReLU-Conv-BatchNorm, respectively. (Color figure online)

5 Conclusion

Compared with manual designed methods and the state-of-art method NAS-FPN for object detection on the COCO dataset, under the same input resolution and the same number of model parameters, NAS-WFPN achieves better results than traditional methods. If we apply AmoebaNet as the backbone, the detection accuracy is further improved as shown in Table 1.

Acknowledgements. This work was supported in part by the National Natural Science Foundation of China under Grant 61972093, and Grant 61702101, and in part by the Young and Middle-aged Teachers Education and Research Project in Fujian Province under Grant JAT170477.

References

1. Li, Z., Peng, C., Yu, G., et al.: Detnet: a backbone network for object detection. arXiv preprint arXiv:1804.06215 (2018)
2. Lin, T.Y., Dollár, P., Girshick, R., et al.: Feature pyramid networks for object detection. In: Proceedings of the IEEE Conference on Computer Vision and Pattern Recognition (CVPR 2017), pp. 2117–2125 (2017)
3. He, K., Zhang, X., Ren, S., et al.: Deep residual learning for image recognition. In: Proceedings of the IEEE Conference on Computer Vision and Pattern Recognition (CVPR 2016), pp. 770–778 (2016)
4. Huang, G., Liu, Z., Van Der Maaten, L., et al.: Densely connected convolutional networks. In: Proceedings of the IEEE Conference on Computer Vision and Pattern Recognition (CVPR 2017), pp. 4700–4708 (2017)
5. He, K., Gkioxari, G., Dollár, P., et al.: Mask R-CNN. In: Proceedings of the IEEE International Conference on Computer Vision (ICCV 2017), pp. 2961–2969 (2017)
6. Lin, T.Y., Goyal, P., Girshick, R., et al.: Focal loss for dense object detection. In: Proceedings of the IEEE International Conference on Computer Vision (ICCV 2017), pp. 2980–2988 (2017)
7. Liu, W., et al.: SSD: single shot MultiBox detector. In: Leibe, B., Matas, J., Sebe, N., Welling, M. (eds.) ECCV 2016. LNCS, vol. 9905, pp. 21–37. Springer, Cham (2016). https://doi.org/10.1007/978-3-319-46448-0_2
8. Ghiasi, G., Lin, T.Y., Le, Q.V.: NAS-FPN: learning scalable feature pyramid architecture for object detection. In: Proceedings of the IEEE Conference on Computer Vision and Pattern Recognition (CVPR 2019), pp. 7036–7045 (2019)
9. Fu, C.Y., Liu, W., Ranga, A., et al.: DSSD: deconvolutional single shot detector. arXiv preprint arXiv:1701.06659 (2017)
10. Kong, T., Sun, F., Huang, W., Liu, H.: Deep feature pyramid reconfiguration for object detection. In: Ferrari, V., Hebert, M., Sminchisescu, C., Weiss, Y. (eds.) ECCV 2018. LNCS, vol. 11209, pp. 172–188. Springer, Cham (2018). https://doi.org/10.1007/978-3-030-01228-1_11
11. Kong, T., Sun, F., Yao, A., et al.: Ron: reverse connection with objectness prior networks for object detection. In: Proceedings of the IEEE Conference on Computer Vision and Pattern Recognition (CVPR 2017), pp. 5936–5944 (2017)

12. Kim, S.-W., Kook, H.-K., Sun, J.-Y., Kang, M.-C., Ko, S.-J.: Parallel feature pyramid network for object detection. In: Ferrari, V., Hebert, M., Sminchisescu, C., Weiss, Y. (eds.) ECCV 2018. LNCS, vol. 11209, pp. 239–256. Springer, Cham (2018). https://doi.org/10.1007/978-3-030-01228-1_15

13. Woo, S., Hwang, S., Kweon, I.S.: Stairnet: Top-down semantic aggregation for accurate one shot detection. In: IEEE Winter Conference on Applications of Computer Vision (WACV 2018), pp. 1093–1102 (2018)

14. Kim, Y., Kang, B.-N., Kim, D.: SAN: learning relationship between convolutional features for multi-scale object detection. In: Ferrari, V., Hebert, M., Sminchisescu, C., Weiss, Y. (eds.) ECCV 2018. LNCS, vol. 11209, pp. 328–343. Springer, Cham (2018). https://doi.org/10.1007/978-3-030-01228-1_20

15. Yu, F., Wang, D., Shelhamer, E., et al.: Deep layer aggregation. In: Proceedings of the IEEE Conference on Computer Vision and Pattern Recognition (CVPR 2018), pp. 2403–2412 (2018)

16. Zhang, S., Wen, L., Bian, X., et al.: Single-shot refinement neural network for object detection. In: Proceedings of the IEEE Conference on Computer Vision and Pattern Recognition (CVPR 2018), pp. 4203–4212 (2018)

17. Zhou, P., Ni, B., Geng, C., et al.: Scale-transferrable object detection. In: Proceedings of the IEEE Conference on Computer Vision and Pattern Recognition (CVPR 2018), pp. 528–537 (2018)

18. Zoph, B., Le, Q.V.: Neural architecture search with reinforcement learning. arXiv preprint arXiv:1611.01578, 2016.

19. Sandler, M., Howard, A., Zhu, M., et al.: Mobilenetv2: inverted residuals and linear bottlenecks. In: Proceedings of the IEEE Conference on Computer Vision and Pattern Recognition (CVPR 2018), pp. 4510–4520 (2018)

20. Real, E., Aggarwal, A., Huang, Y., et al.: Regularized evolution for image classifier architecture search. In: Proceedings of the AAAI Conference on Artificial Intelligence (AAAI 2019), pp. 4780–4789 (2019)

21. Girshick, R.: Fast R-CNN. In: Proceedings of the IEEE International Conference on Computer Vision (ICCV 2015), pp. 1440–1448 (2015)

22. Ren, S., He, K., Girshick, R., et al.: Faster R-CNN: towards real-time object detection with region proposal networks. In: Advances in Neural Information Processing Systems, pp. 91–99 (2015)

Performance Benchmarking and Optimization for IIoT-oriented Blockchain

Kai Qian[1], Yinqiu Liu[1], Yamin Han[1], and Kun Wang[2(✉)]

[1] Nanjing University of Posts and Telecommunications, Nanjing 210023, China
[2] University of California, Los Angeles 90024, USA
wangk@ucla.edu

Abstract. The Industrial Internet of Things (IIoT) is profoundly chang-ing the production mode, *e.g.*, rail freight industry and medical industry, with the widespread applications of sensor technology and wireless net-work in the industrial field. However, traditional techniques can no longer meet the demand of future IIoT due to rapid data explosion and low data privacy. In this paper, we present a comprehensive benchmarking method with accurate metrics to quantize the blockchain performance. The results of our benchmarking indicate the low resource efficiency of the IIoT-oriented blockchain system. Moreover, the Proof-of-Work (PoW) mechanism is proved to be the reason for the poor performance. To address the shortcomings of blockchain, we optimized the original PoW mechanism, making it better support IIoT-oriented blockchain. Specifically, we introduce energy and confidence to reward nodes based on their behaviors, thereby improving the efficiency of the PoW. More-over, we attend to the slow ledger synchronization and present a fast synchronization strategy, which is suitable for IIoT scenarios. Extensive performance evaluations demonstrate that our optimization proposals are effective in IIoT scenarios. This study serves as a guideline for deploy-ing and improving the performance of blockchain in IIoT under various operating conditions.

Keywords: Industrial Internet of Things (IIoT) · Blockchain · Performance analysis · Optimization · Stability

1 Introduction

With the rapid development of information technology, the Industrial Internet of Things (IIoT) has exhibited incredible potential. For instance, in a supply chain system, suppliers, manufacturers, and retailers adopt IIoT to improve resource efficiency and reduce the management costs [1,2]. However, as the applications of IIoT become ever-increasing, some security [3] and scalability [4] issues also expose. For example, leaving feedbacks may reveal much sensitive consumer information, which can be used to track and profile consumers [5]. Meanwhile, the consumers may be reluctant while leaving a negative review to a specific retailer in fear of related consequences.

© Springer Nature Switzerland AG 2021
G. Wang et al. (Eds.): SpaCCS 2020, LNCS 12383, pp. 395–406, 2021.
https://doi.org/10.1007/978-3-030-68884-4_33

Fortunately, the blockchain technology in IIoT is committed to helping solve these issues. In blockchain, all transactions content will be packaged by blocks distributed throughout the Peer-to-Peer (P2P) network [6]. Each node has a complete copy of the encrypted ledger [7]. Multiple nodes on the network cooperate in confirming every legitimate transaction on blockchain [8]. In this way, the IIoT network reaches the fault-tolerance and the IIoT data is saved through a traceable and tamper-proof approach. Nevertheless, due to the distributed operating methods, blockchain will consume huge resources, which in turn causes low performance. Taking Bitcoin as an example, it can only process seven transactions per second, while the confirmation costs 60 min and the energy consumption is awful [9]. A sharp contradiction has arisen due to the lack of IIoT devices' computing power and hardware performance requirements for blockchain systems. In general, deploying the blockchain system in IIoT still faces multiple challenges, which are listed as follows:

First, as the IIoT devices mainly focus on ensuring low-power connectivity, most of IIoT devices can hardly support the high-cost blockchain running due to insufficient processing power [10]. Second, the IIoT device's characteristics of heterogeneity and dynamic the low-power feature makes blockchain deployment in IIoT have serious problems. Hence, we need to benchmark and evaluate various aspects before formally deploying blockchain.

Motivated by such observations, we propose an innovative method for benchmarking blockchain in IIoT. Specifically, we conduct an in-depth requirements modeling for blockchain-assisted IIoT, which considers most potential entities and factors that might affect the blockchain performance in typical IIoT scenarios [11]. Using this method, we conduct a detailed benchmarking of IOTA blockchain in a practical IIoT environment [12]. Observing several defects of blockchain when running in IIoT, we propose the corresponding optimization strategies, including the Power-confidence Proof of Work (Power-confidence PoW) mechanism and the optimized strategy for ledger synchronization. Our main contributions are summarized as follows:

- We propose a comprehensive method to benchmark the blockchain performance in IIoT. The performance is evaluated objectively from three dimensions. Using the proposed method, we conduct a detailed benchmarking for IOTA, the most famous IIoT-oriented blockchain. Note that, our benchmarking also covers Fabric v1.4 and Ethereum, which are used for comparison.
- Through the comparison of Ethereum and Fabric v1.4, the benchmarking results of IOTA reveal its two significant drawbacks, *i.e.* low resource utilization caused by PoW and slow ledger synchronization time. We analyze the cause of the problems through experimental results.
- To optimize blockchain in IIoT, we first optimize traditional PoW by introducing energy and confidence to reward nodes based on their behaviors, called the Power-Confidence PoW mechanism. Furthermore, we change the synchronization strategy and data database configuration to speed up the ledger synchronization. Extensive evaluations demonstrate that our optimization proposals are effective in IIoT scenarios.

2   Benchmarking Model

In this part, we implement the IOTA blockchain in IIoT, as shown in Fig. 1. IOTA is designed to adapt to the Internet of Things. IOTA's distributed ledger structure called *Tangle*. In *Tangle*, each node represents a transaction.

2.1   Incorporating Blockchain of IIoT

As shown in Fig. 1, we illustrate a smart factory scenario assisted by IOTA. A great proportion of IIoT devices are complicated, *e.g.*, mechanical devices and sensors. In general, nodes in blockchain system play the role in both transaction relay and network information provider called full nodes. On the contrary, nodes without full transaction validation are called lightweight nodes. The factory in Fig. 1 primarily has massive edge devices *i.e.*, battery-powered devices. In addition, the network of factory is complex. Due to this condition, deploying blockchain projects faces enormous challenges. Blockchain's functions include monitoring, security, tracking, and logistics [14]. These functions should be taken into consideration, even regular communication with the outside world. To this end, we need a proper benchmarking and reasonable quantized metrics to measure the performance of blockchain in IIoT.

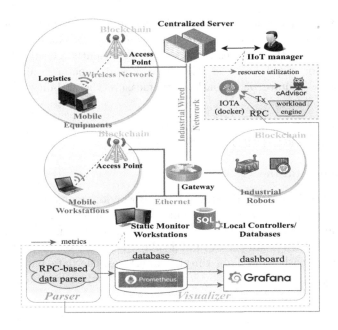

Fig. 1. Context of blockchain-assisted IIoT.

2.2   Problem Statement

Based on Sect. 2.1, we summarize the problems which are yet to be addressed as follows:

Availability Analysis. As shown in Fig. 1, numerous IIoT devices in the production line record massive manufacturing data and rapidly submit transactions to blockchain nodes, resulting in an extremely high concurrency. However, the speed of transaction processing by blockchain is low due to the complex consensus mechanism and encryption algorithm. Therefore, our benchmarking is required to measure the capacity of the given blockchain system, thereby judging its availability in the targeted IIoT scenarios.

Resource Efficiency. Recall that most IIoT devices are resource-constrained. For example, as shown in Fig. 1, the watch and the infrared sensors are battery-powered wireless devices whose power and physical resource are limited. Even for laptops or personal computers, running blockchain system nodes might seriously consumes their resource, thereby affecting the normal executions of the IIoT tasks. Hence, the second requirement for benchmarking is to analyze the resource efficiency of the given blockchain.

Stability Analysis. Aside from resource constraints, a part of IIoT devices also exhibit excellent dynamics. On the one hand, some wireless communication modules need to switch their modes to save energy frequently. During the dormant state, the sensor might quit the P2P network and re-enter it after resuming. Thus, it should require benchmarking to measure the stability of peers in a changing environment.

3   Benchmarking in IIoT Scenario

3.1   Implementation

As shown in Fig. 1, our benchmarking framework adopts a modular architecture to support multiple types of blockchain systems. Specifically, the whole system is divided into three connected modules, *i.e.*, blockchain, data parser, and metric visualizer. The data parser module plays a critical role in our benchmarking. Interacting with blockchain through interfaces, the data parser can grasp the latest ledger states. We deploy some workload engines to simulate different workloads.

3.2   Evaluation

Based on the benchmarking framework, we explain the detailed benchmarking process using self-proposed metrics in this part. Note that, these metrics apply to not only IOTA, but also the future IIoT-oriented blockchain.

Availability. First of all, we analyze the availability of IIoT-oriented blockchain system. In order to benchmark blockchain's availability, we design the following two indicators:

Throughput. *Throughput* is a common metric for benchmarking blockchain systems. The *throughput* refers to the average number of transactions that can be confirmed by blockchain system node within one second. The unit of *throughput* is transactions per second (TPS).

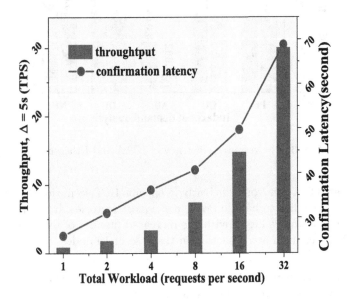

Fig. 2. The throughtout and confirm latency of IOTA.

Confirmation Latency. In blockchain, the processing of transaction Tx is accomplished when Tx is appended to the ledger. Nonetheless, the current state of Tx is still not confirmed. The interval of sending a transaction and confirming by blockchain is $T_{confirm}$, the *confirmation latency* can be calculated as:

$$confirmation\ latency = \frac{\sum_{i=1}^{n}(T_{confirm}^{i} - T_{submit}^{i})}{\mathsf{Count}\,(Tx, \Delta_t)}\ s \qquad (1)$$

where $n = \mathsf{Count}\,(Tx, \Delta_t)$. Most IIoT scenarios put forward strict demands on *confirmation latency*.

Figure 2 shows the *throughtout* and *confirmation latency* of IOTA. Note that every transaction submission in IOTA requests a PoW-styled proof, which means that the workload engines need to solve a hash puzzle before sending one transaction to full nodes. Hence, each workload engine at most reaches 3.2 TPS. In this way, the maximum workload for IOTA is 32 TPS in our experiments. We

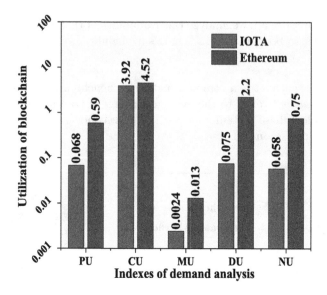

Fig. 3. The resource efficiency of IOTA and Ethereum

conclude that IOTA can work efficiently in specific IIoT scenarios, whose devices own enough capability to handle PoW, *e.g.*, smart factories. In addition, *confirmation latency* becomes larger with the increased number of total workloads. It takes 67.32 s to confirm a transaction in the case of 10 nodes.

Resource Utilization. In this part, we mainly consider five types of resources, namely power, CPU, memory, disk, and network. Additionally, we deploy Fabric v1.4 and Ethereum as a comparison.

Power Utilization. Considering the power limitation in IIoT, we design a metric for measuring the power efficiency of each peer, named *Power Utilization* (PU). PU is defined by the following equation:

$$PU = \frac{\text{Count}\,(Tx, \Delta_t) + \text{Count}\,(Ops, \Delta_t)}{\int_{t_i}^{t_j} P(t)\,dt}, \tag{2}$$

where Tx indicates the transactions in Δ_t, $P(t)$ indicates the instantaneous power of peer at time t, and Ops indicates other operations.

CPU Utilization. CPU supports almost every task of blockchain. In the consensus phase, it helps execute hash operations (for PoW), digital signatures, *etc.* We design a metric for measuring the CPU utilization of blockchain, named *CPU Utilization* (CU). The CU of peer can be calculated by the following equation:

$$CU = \frac{\text{Count}\,(Tx, \Delta_t) + \text{Count}\,(Ops, \Delta_t)}{\int_{t_i}^{t_j} \varphi \cdot C(t)\,dt}, \tag{3}$$

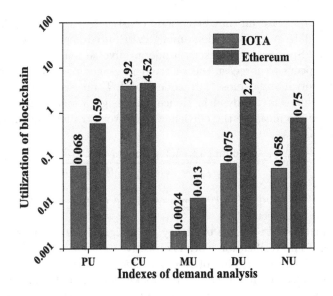

Fig. 4. The SUE of IOTA under different bandwidth.

where φ means the CPU frequency of peer. $C(t)$ indicates the CPU usage of peer at time t.

Memory Utilization. During the running of blockchain, various types of data will be preserved in memory, including the world states, the parameters and arrays within smart contracts, and the temporary ledger objects. Hence, we propose MU to analyze the memory utilization of blockchain, which is calculated by:

$$MU = \frac{\mathsf{Count}\,(Tx, \Delta_t) + \mathsf{Count}\,(Ops, \Delta_t)}{\int_{t_i}^{t_j} M(t)\,dt},\tag{4}$$

where $M(t)$ represents the total memory occupation (both virtual and physical) of peer at time t.

Disk Utilization. Apart from memory, blockchain also occupies considerable disk space for saving smart contracts and historical ledger data. Inspired by this, we present a metric named Disk Utilization (DU) to measure the disk space utilization of blockchain. DU can be calculated by the following equation:

$$DU = \frac{\mathsf{Count}\,(Tx, \Delta_t) + \mathsf{Count}\,(Ops, \Delta_t)}{\int_{t_i}^{t_j} (D(t)^{Read} + D(t)^{Write})\,dt}.\tag{5}$$

For peer at time t, $D(t)^{Read}$ and $D(t)^{Write}$ represent the data volume read from and written into disk, respectively.

Network Utilization. Recall that blockchain constructs a P2P network, message exchanges and data synchronization among distributed peers will consume huge network traffic. Specifically, blockchain adopts diverse multi-casting protocols, which require peers to forecast the received messages to a part of connected neighbors. Unfortunately, most full nodes in IIoT are wireless IIoT devices, resulting in insufficient bandwidth. Hence, we design a metric named *Network Utilization* (NU) to measure the efficiency of network traffic consumed by peer. NU is defined as:

$$NU = \frac{\text{Count}\,(Tx, \Delta_t) + \text{Count}\,(Ops, \Delta_t)}{\int_{t_i}^{t_j} (N(t)^{Download} + N(t)^{Upload})\, dt}, \tag{6}$$

where $N(t)^{Download}$ and $N(t)^{Upload}$ represent the download and upload traffic of peer at time t, respectively.

The five metrics of resource efficiency we designed are to measure the cost of transactions. The verification work is objective and reasonable. Figure 3 illustrates the 30-min average value of resource efficiency of metrics of IOTA and Ethereum. We observe that IOTA is not as efficient as Ethereum in terms of resource efficiency in general. The system will consume a large part of resources to verify at first, which will increase the difficulty of PoW over time. From these results, it is easy to see the drawbacks of the PoW mechanism in terms of resource efficiency.

Stability. For IIoT-oriented blockchain systems, not only availability and resource utilization, but also stability need to be considered. Thus, we also design a metric to measure the stability of blockchain.

SUE. We consider blockchain's stability in a dynamic environment. Stability can be analyzed from one perspectives, *i.e.*, the single peer. We refer to two nodes in same blockchain system called **Peer 1** and **Peer 2**. When **Peer 1** attempts to re-enter blockchain after the crash, mode switching, or movement, it should first restart connections with **Peer 2** and then update its state, mainly synchronizing the historical transactions. We design a novel metric named *State Updating Efficiency* (SUE), which is defined as:

$$SUE = \frac{\text{Count}\,(Tx, \Delta_{t1}) + \text{Count}\,(Tx, \Delta_{t2})}{\Delta_{t2}}, \tag{7}$$

where $\text{Count}\,(Tx, \Delta_{t1})$ and $\text{Count}\,(Tx, \Delta_{t2})$ represent the current and historical transactions that **Peer 2** transfers to **Peer 1**, respectively. Note that $\text{Count}\,(Tx, \Delta_{t2})$ cannot be ignored, especially in IIoT scenarios with high concurrency.

Figure 4 shows that the values of IOTA's SUE in different bandwidths are 9.65, 16.64, 17.32, and 18.17, respectively. Meanwhile, the values of Fabric's SUE in different bandwidths are 161.7, 616.19, 623.27, and 645.23, respectively. It is obvious that IOTA is far below the performance of Fabric in SUE. This is due to the fact that RocksDB (adopted by IOTA) has low concurrency than golevelDB (adopted by Fabric v1.4 and Ethereum).

4   Optimization Strategies Implementation and Evaluation

In this section, we put forward the optimization strategies according to the drawbacks of IOTA, especially in IIoT. Figure 3, 4 show that resource efficiency and stability of IOTA is poor, especially PU, MU, and SUE. This can be explained that the transaction processing occupies great power and hard disk. By observing and analyzing the experimental results, we make some improvements and optimizations.

4.1   Optimization of Resource Efficiency

Power-Confidence PoW Mechanism. Observing the deficiency of PoW mechanism in IOTA, we design Power-confidence PoW mechanism to solve the low resource utilization in consensus mechanism. We define that node has a property of computation capacity as H and the MU value will change in real time based on node's computation. One of the significant points of the PoW mechanism is pre-adaptation according to the computation value of each node. The lower the computation capacity is, the longer the time will be taken to run the PoW algorithm. Thus, we change the difficulty of trading and mining by controlling H. Nodes have deliberately behavior to destroy network called malicious modes, according to the behavior and power of node. For node b, its H_b can be denoted as:

$$H_b = (\beta_1 \cdot \frac{\sum_{k=1}^{I_b} w_k}{\Delta T} - \beta_2 \sum_{k=1}^{M_b} \cdot \frac{\Delta T}{t - t_k}) * \gamma, \tag{8}$$

where I_b denotes the number of valid transactions processed by node b during the latest unit of time, ΔT denotes a unit of time, and w_k denotes the weight of the kth Tx, β_1 and β_2 present the weight coefficient of each part, respectively, and γ can be calculated by $(e^{PU})^{-1}$. The weight of a Tx means the number of validations to this Tx. M_b represents the total number of malicious nodes conducted by node b, t represents current time, t_k represents the time point of the kth malicious behavior conducted by node b.

4.2   Fast Synchronization and Database Storage

From the results of our benchmarking, IOTA has poor performance in SUE. Therefore, it is necessary to improve the rate of ledger synchronization. In original IOTA, all the ledger information is synchronized, which results in a significant time consumption [15]. All data from the genesis transaction by the coordinator and occurred transactions is spread by *Tangle*. Thus, we can take a fast synchronization (Fast-sync) approach considering the limited resource in IIoT. We only need to synchronize the snapshot when synchronization.

In addition to synchronization strategies to reduce the synchronization of data, we also adopt the strategy of changing storage. The database storage of

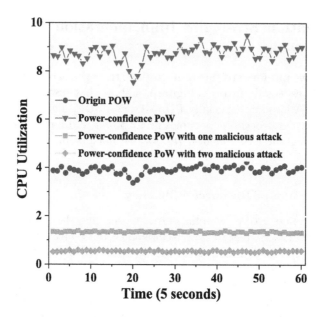

Fig. 5. The real-time CU monitoring of IOTA.

IOTA is RocksDB, a C++ library for storing Key-Value (KV) data, which supports atomic read and write. The basic concepts of RockDB is *ColumnFamily*. Thus, we need to traverse from new data to old data or from layer by layer to find data, until the data found in the reading process to improve resource utilization. It leads to more frequent I/O reading and writing. In particular, the impact is pretty obvious in the case of Range Query. Furthermore, because all writes are written sequentially (append-only), expired data is not cleaned up immediately. Finally, written data is more than written by the upper program. Because the blockchain system will constantly generate KV value to store the transaction data, RocksDB creates a short-board obviously under this mechanism.

4.3   Validation of Optimization

Up till now, we optimize blockchain system by PoW mechanism algorithm of IOTA, synchronization, and database. We verify the effectiveness of our algorithm and work through the experimental results. In our experiment, the minimum difficulty of PoW is 1, and the maximum difficulty is 14. For malicious nodes, sending a transaction consumes a mass of resource. We simulate the situation of malicious nodes, the system actively considers the nodes to be a malicious node. Figure 5 shows the real-time CU. Note that our power-confidence PoW mechanism increases on the CPU resource utilization about 2.34 × higher than before. We simulate the situation of malicious nodes, the system actively considers the nodes to be a malicious node.

5   Conclusion

In this paper, we discuss the problems of benchmarking and optimization in the blockchain-assisted IIoT scenario. Firstly, we conduct a model of blockchain-assisted IIoT to design metrics. We are the first to present a comprehensive method for benchmarking IIoT-oriented blockchain, which focuses on the features of IIoT. Then, we conduct a blockchain benchmarking from three dimensions. By analyzing the experimental results, we focus on IOTA's resource efficiency and propose the power-confidence PoW mechanism. Moreover, we modify the implementation of IOTA in terms of synchronization strategies in order to get faster synchronization speeds. Our optimization scheme makes the blockchain system better support IIoT.

This work will be of importance to blockchain research in IIoT. Our benchmarking and metrics are suitable for blockchain projects, as mentioned in this paper, and other projects. Likewise, the optimization is also effective for other PoW-based blockchain systems.

Acknowledgments. This work is supported by National Natural Science Foundation of China under Grant No. 61872195.

References

1. Xu, L.D., He, W., Li, S.: Internet of things in industries: a survey. IEEE Trans. Ind. Inf. **10**(4), 2233–2243 (2014)
2. Zhang, K., Zhu, Y., Maharjan, S., Zhang, Y.: Edge intelligence and blockchain empowered 5G beyond for the industrial internet of things. IEEE Netw. **33**(5), 12–19 (2019)
3. Li, Z., Kang, J., Yu, R., Ye, D., Deng, Q., Zhang, Y.: Consortium blockchain for secure energy trading in industrial internet of things. IEEE Trans. Ind. Inf. **14**(8), 3690–3700 (2018)
4. Huang, J., Kong, L., Chen, G., Wu, M.Y., Liu, X., Zeng, P.: Towards secure industrial IoT: blockchain system with credit-based consensus mechanism. IEEE Trans. Ind. Inf. **15**(6), 3680–3689 (2019)
5. Ra, G.J., Seo, D., Bhuiyan, M.Z.A., Lee, I.Y.: An anonymous protocol for member privacy in a consortium blockchain. In: 12th International Conference Security, Privacy, and Anonymity in Computation, Communication, and Storage (SpaCCS), pp. 456–464 (2019)
6. Alvaro-Hermana, R., Fraile-Ardanuy, J., Zufiria, P.J., Knapen, L., Janssens, D.: Peer to peer energy trading with electric vehicles. IEEE Intell. Transp. Syst. Mag. **8**(3), 33–44 (2016)
7. Lu, Y., Huang, X., Dai, Y., Maharjan, S., Zhang, Y.: Blockchain and federated learning for privacy-preserved data sharing in industrial IoT. IEEE Trans. Ind. Inf. **16**(6), 4177–4186 (2020)
8. Li, H.N., Wang, K., Miyazaki, T., Xu, C.H., Guo, S., Sun, Y.F.: Trust-enhanced content delivery in blockchain-based information-centric networking. IEEE Netw. **33**(5), 183–189 (2019)

9. Wu, M.L., Wang, K., Cai, X.Q., Guo, S., Guo, M., Rong, C.M.: A comprehensive survey of blockchain: from theory to IoT applications and beyond. IEEE Internet Things J. **6**(5), 8114–8154 (2019)

10. Liu, Y.Q., Wang, K., Qian, K., Du, M., Guo, S.: Tornado: enabling blockchain in heterogeneous internet of things through a space-structured approach. IEEE Internet Things J. **7**(2), 1273–1286 (2020)

11. Liu, Y.Q., Wang, K., Lin, Y., Xu, W.Y.: LightChain: a lightweight blockchain system for industrial internet of things. IEEE Trans. Ind. Inf. **15**(6), 3571–3581 (2019)

12. Xu, C.H., Wang, K., Li, P., Guo, S., Luo, J.T., Ye, B.L., Guo, M.Y.: Making big data open in edges: a resource-efficient blockchain-based approach. IEEE Trans. Parallel Distrib. Syst. **30**(4), 870–882 (2019)

13. Lee, H., Ma, M.D.: Blockchain-based mobility management for LTE and beyond. In: 12th International Conference Security, Privacy, and Anonymity in Computation, Communication, and Storage (SpaCCS), pp. 36–49 (2019)

14. Xu, C.H., Wang, K., Guo, M.Y.: Intelligent resource management in blockchain-based cloud datacenters. IEEE Cloud Comput. **4**(6), 50–59 (2017)

15. Du, M., et al.: Spacechain: a three-dimensional blockchain architecture for IoT security. IEEE Wirel Commun. **27**(3), 38–45 (2020)

The 2nd International Workshop on Communication, Computing, Informatics and Security (CCIS 2020)

A Multi-patch Deep Learning System for Text-Independent Writer Identification

Dawei Liang[1,2] and Meng Wu[2(✉)]

[1] Department of Computer Information and Cyber Security,
Jiangsu Police Institute, Nanjing 210031, China
`liangdawei@jspi.cn`
[2] College of Computer, Nanjing University of Posts and Telecommunications,
Nanjing 210023, China

Abstract. Offline handwriting identification is widely used in many fields of modern society, such as judicial authentication, identity verification, ancient manuscripts, etc. Compared with traditional methods, methods based on deep learning have been proven to extract more distinctive handwriting features from large amounts of data and show better performance. For deep learning methods, data preprocessing and global feature coding determine its performance. To solve this problem, this paper proposes an offline writer identification method, which combines multi-patch data preprocessing and transfer learning. First, multi-patching and data enhancement techniques are used to process handwritten images. Subsequently, the pretrained residual network of the image dataset is used for local feature extraction, and finally, the mean feature method is used for global feature encoding. The proposed system is tested on ICDAR2013 and CVL standard datasets. Experimental results show that this novel method has a relatively stable and good recognition effect

Keywords: Writer identification · Convolutional neural network · Data augmentation · Feature extraction · Transfer learning

1 Introduction

Handwriting is an important part of a natural pattern of behavior, reflecting a person's bio-metric attributes. Writer identification is a similar technique to face recognition, fingerprint recognition, and iris recognition, which belongs to the category of automatic identification, and in recent decades has been widely used in the field of bio-metrics and forensic identification. Writer identification system extracts the features of an unknown writer document, compared with the documents of known writers in the database to identify the writer of the document.

According to the data processed, the writer identification system can be classified into online [2] and offline [15]. The former analyzes the spatial coordinates

© Springer Nature Switzerland AG 2021
G. Wang et al. (Eds.): SpaCCS 2020, LNCS 12383, pp. 409–419, 2021.
https://doi.org/10.1007/978-3-030-68884-4_34

information such as the speed of writing text, stroke order, and strength to identify the writer, while the latter processes the temporal handwriting information in the form of images. Besides, according to whether there is a requirement for the textual content of the handwriting material during the identification, offline writer identification can be classified into text content-independent and text content-independent. The former requires the handwritten data images to be the specified as text content, while the latter does not.

Due to the versatility and usability of offline handwritten data images, offline writer identification research is more extensive, simultaneously, it is more tricky to apply owing to the scarcity of character attributes. Additionally, offline writer identification is also affected by various objective factors: (1) As the writer's age changes, writing features may change; (2) The external environment may affect the writer's writing habits; (3) The performance of different pen influences on handwriting particulars. Therefore, researchers are committed to extract discriminative features from handwritten text. And two types of approaches were employed, one based on global features [1,3,22] and another one based on local features [12,24,25]. The former processes the entire document, obtains global features directly, while the latter extracts features from local parts of the document, obtains global features through encoding.

Extracting features requires human expertise and domain knowledge. To extract discriminative features, early researchers applied scale-invariant feature transform(SFIT) [4,6], speed up robust features(SURF) and other methods [17,20,26] to extract manual features, fisher vectors, the vector of locally aggregated descriptors(VLAD) [6], Gaussian mixture model (GMM) [4], etc. to encode the feature vector. And now the current state-of-the-art methods [21] utilize deep Convolutional Neural Networks (CNN) to extract features independent of domain knowledge and expertise in language or patterns [8]. The Model extracts automatic features from raw images directly.

A convolutional neural network is a kind of deep learning model, utilizing a large amount of data to update the parameters in the nonlinear network. In this process, the backpropagation algorithm achieves the purpose of fitting representation. Different CNN architectures, such as AlexNet, GoogleNet, ResNet, VGG, etc. have been widely used in artificial intelligence, computer vision, machine translation, pattern recognition, speech recognition, natural language processing, etc.

This paper presents an approach that uses Convolutional Neural Networks for offline writer identification. We use transfer learning to solve the problem of insufficient handwriting data. Transfer learning pretrains the neural network on a large, then applies the learned parameters and features to the target. For image data, the basic features learned are universal, and then fine-tuning to learn advanced features can achieve better performance. To further improve the generalization ability of the model, data augmentation techniques are used to generate a large amount of images before fine-tuning, and then local feature vectors are obtained. Subsequently, the local feature vector is encoded by PCA whitening, etc. to form the global feature vector, which is used to do classification.

The rest of the paper is organized as follows: Sect. 2 brief reports the closely related work for writer identification. Section 3 describes the proposed pipeline. The experiments and results are presented in Sect. 4. Finally, a short conclusion is given in Sect. 5.

2   Related Work

In the past few decades, researchers have used traditional techniques to do a lot of work in this domain, and learning methods have appeared for several years, which have achieved better outcomes. In 2015, Fiel and Sablatnig [12] first used image processing technology to obtain more data in the, subsequently extracted features through CaffeNet, and calculated the Euclidean distance between the features to identify the writer. They conducted experiments on IAM, ICDAR2011 [19], ICDAR2013 [18] and CVL [16] datasets. The processing of handwriting pictures includes binarization, text line segmentation, and sliding window, which artificially enlarge the original training set, and a large number of image patches are generated. Subsequently, the patches were fed to the eight-layer CNN, and the features generated from the fully connected layer were regarded as local features. The mean of the local features were calculated as the global feature to measure the distance between the samples. On the ICDAR2011 and CVL datasets, using hard criterion evaluation methods, they achieved the highest recognition rates of 98.6% and 97.6%, respectively. At the same time, the recognition rate on the ICDAR2013 dataset was 40.5%. The problem was that when applying data augmentation, the line segmentation method proposed by Deim et al. [11] was not intensive. At the same time, Greek data was not considered when training neural network parameters.

V. Christlein et al. [5] used six-layer CNN to extract local descriptions from image patches. They aggregated all local descriptions in a document through ZCA whitening and GMM. The estimated hard criterion TOP-1 was 0.989 and 0.994 on ICDAR2013 and CVL datasets, respectively. Researchers have also adopted new models to improve the recognition effect. In [7], LeNET and ResNet were used to extract local features, Vlad and exemplar SVM to encode global features. The accuracy of the scheme on the CVL, icdar2013, and KHATT datasets was 99.5%, 99.6%, and 99.6%, respectively. Rehman et al. [21] discussed the application of transfer learning in the field of handwriting identification and obtained an accuracy rate of 88.11% on the QUWI dataset through AlexNet. Simultaneously, they studied the problem of fine-tuning the number of layers in the network architecture by transfer learning. Cilia et al. [9] conducted experiments on Avila Bible with 870 two-column pages from scribal hands. They used row detection to generate image data, testing five kinds of CNNs(VGG19, ResNet50, InceptionV3, InceptionResNetV2, and NASNetLarge) for the best classification effect.

3 Writer Identification Pipeline

The proposed Writer Identification pipeline (see Fig. 1) consists of three main steps: preprocessing and data augmentation; feature extraction from image patches using a pretrained ResNet50; classification and identification using exemplar SVM.

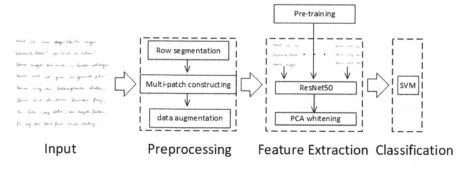

Fig. 1. The structure of the Writer Identification pipeline.

3.1 Dataset

We mainly conduct experiments and evaluations on CVL [16] and ICDAR2013 [18] datasets. There are a total of 310 writers in the CVL dataset, each of which has contributed at least 5 pages in English and German. All page information has been labeled. Because CVL provides row-segmented images directly for training and evaluation. The ICDAR2013 standard dataset also contains a divided training set and test set, with handwriting materials contributed by 100 and 250 writers, respectively. Each writer writes four pages, two of which are in English and two in Greek. Because the dataset provides page scan documents, it needs to be a row segmentation to obtain a suitable patch.

3.2 Pre-processing

In the proposed pipeline, the first step is preprocessing. In this process, the images are processed into an appropriate format and fed into subsequent processing for parameter training or feature vector generation.

Row Segmentation. For a full-page handwriting document, row segmentation needs to be applied to obtain suitable data. The CVL dataset directly provides row images without processing, while the ICDAR2013 dataset requires row segmentation according to the method of Diem et al. [11]. At the same time, because of the skew between words during writing, the method of Ahmad et al. [10] is used to detect and correct the skew.

Multi-patch Constructing. For the processed rows, we use the sliding window technique to intercept the appropriate patch. Since the handwriting language to be processed is in English, German, and Greek, to reduce the loss of features during the preprocessing process, the height of the segmented rows are resized to 128 pixels while maintaining its aspect ratio. Subsequently, we use the sliding window technique to process the segmented rows. Row images are slid from left to right in a 128 × 128 size sliding window, without overlapping processing. In the process of row segmentation, data such as letters g and f will be split up and down, and there is also a feature correlation between the front and back patches. We use a multi-patch method to combine adjacent patches to ensure handwriting features are not lost as much as possible (Fig. 2).

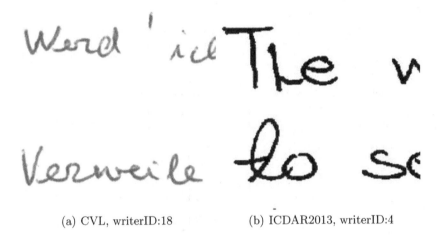

(a) CVL, writerID:18   (b) ICDAR2013, writerID:4

Fig. 2. Sample images pre-processed

In the multi-patch method, to reduce the noise generated by the feature extraction, we first delete the blank pixel patches and the patches with fewer handwriting features, and then combine the adjacent upper, lower, left and right patches to form a new size of 256 × 256 patches as training and testing data. For the ICDAR2013 and CVL, the number of training sets obtained after processing is 39200 and 16230, respectively. Since the input of the following feature extraction neural network is 224 × 224, the processed patch also needs to be resized.

Data Augmentation. To improve the performance of the neural network, we further expand the number of training sets and pay attention to the problem of overfitting at the same time. After the multi-patch method is applied, data enhancement techniques are used. General image data enhancement techniques include rotation, inversion, local magnification, etc. To reduce image feature loss and overfitting, we use contour, sharp and negative methods.

3.3 Generation of the Feature Vector

ResNet. The ResNet was proposed by He et al. [14]. The addition of residual units solves the degradation problem, therefore the accuracy is improved by increasing the depth. The ResNet method has achieved first place in the ILSVRC and COCO2015 comparisons, which proves that it has a strong feature learning ability. In this paper, we use resnet50 to extract handwriting features. In response to the needs of handwriting identification and two different training sets, certain changes are made to the original network structure (see Table 1), such as changing the original average pooling to global pooling, adding a fully connected layer after global pooling, doing Relu activation and using dropout technology to prevent overfitting. During training, we use the multi-result classification method of 100 and 50 for the ICDAR2013 dataset and the CVL dataset, respectively.

Table 1. The proposed ResNet50.

Layer name	Output size	50-layer
conv1	112×112	7×7, 64, stride 2
conv2-x1	56×56	3×3 max pool, stride 2
conv2-x2	56×56	$\begin{bmatrix} 1 \times 1, 64 \\ 3 \times 3, 64 \\ 1 \times 1, 256 \end{bmatrix} \times 3$
conv3-x	28×28	$\begin{bmatrix} 1 \times 1, 128 \\ 3 \times 3, 128 \\ 1 \times 1, 512 \end{bmatrix} \times 4$
conv4-x	14×14	$\begin{bmatrix} 1 \times 1, 256 \\ 3 \times 3, 256 \\ 1 \times 1, 1024 \end{bmatrix} \times 6$
conv5-x	7×7	$\begin{bmatrix} 1 \times 1, 512 \\ 3 \times 3, 512 \\ 1 \times 1, 2048 \end{bmatrix} \times 3$
	1×1	Global pooling, FC, dropout, softmax

Transfer Learning. Transfer learning is a system that recognizes and applies knowledge and skills learned in previous tasks to novel tasks [13]. The features learned on the base will be fine-tuned training on the target. Due to the similarity of the data characteristics, the target extracts advanced features utilizing the common features learned from the base. In this paper, we use the parameters trained on the Image dataset through the ResNet50 general architecture, then feed the multi-patches obtained above into the system, continue to use the backpropagation algorithm for fine-tuning.

Feature Vector. When the training converges, the parameters of ResNet50 for handwriting identification are obtained. We use the parameters optimized by the cost function to calculate the output of the fully connected layer, which are the local features of the input handwriting material. To improve the generalization ability, the local features will be processed by PCA whitening [6], subsequently encoded by the mean method to obtain the global features of handwriting. Therefore, the global feature of the jth original handwriting data F_j is:

$$F_j = \frac{1}{N_m} \sum_{i=1}^{N_m} m_i^{(j)} \tag{1}$$

where N_m represents the number of multi-patches obtained from the jth original handwriting sample after preprocessing, and $m_i^{(j)}$ represents the ith multi-patch local feature vector in the jth sample extracted by NesNet50.

3.4 Writer Identification

In the process of writer identification, the system architecture is slightly different. In the process of training, the last layer is softmax. During training, the number of feature extractions of the fully connected layer is set to 1024, and the parameter of dropout is set to 0.5 to enhance the regularization of recognition and prevent overfitting. The initial learning rate of training is 0.001, the momentum parameter is 0.9. The input size of the system is 224×224, and the number of classifications is different according to the dataset. It is set to 50 for CVL and 100 for ICDAR2013. In the writer identification process, we remove the last layer of ResNet50, preprocess the sample into multi-patches and then feed them to the system, subsequently use Eq. (1) method to process the local features extracted from the fully connected layer, obtain the global features of the sample, which are compared to the feature library.

4 Experiments and Results

According to the pipeline described above, we conduct experiments on ICDAR2013 and CVL data. In the following sections, we describe the evaluation metrics and evaluation results based on our proposed method. Furthermore, we compare and analyze our method with other methods for writer identification.

4.1 Evaluation Metrics

In the task of image information retrieval, to evaluate the generalization ability and recognition ability of the model, the commonly used evaluation standard is the TOP-N index. Measuring the distance from a global feature vector to the others in the library, you can get an array of vectors for the test example. At this time, there are two criteria. For the soft criteria, as long as one of the first N samples and the test sample are from the same writer, the identification is correct. For hard criteria, only when the first N samples and the test sample are all from the same writer, the identification is correct. The index percentage of all test samples is the value of TOP-N. In this paper, we use soft TOP-1, TOP-5 and TOP-10 to measure the performance of the system. At the same time, due to the different numbers of pages provided by each writer in the test, we use the hard TOP-2 and TOP-3 criteria.

4.2   Results and Analysis

CVL Dataset. The test results of the criteria and the comparison with other methods are presented in Table 2. It can be seen from the experimental results that the model proposed by Tang et al. has better performance, while the model we proposed only differs by 0.4%, 0.3% and 0.4% respectively on the soft TOP-1, TOP-5 and TOP-10 criteria. The main reasons may be in two aspects. First, there is a problem in the data preprocessing stage. When the multi-patch processing is performed after the line segmentation, there are more gaps between the patches, and they contain less handwriting features. Second, the average method used in the process of obtaining global features is less efficient.

Table 2. Evaluation of the soft and hard criteria on the CVL dataset (in%).

Models	S-TOP1	S-TOP5	S-TOP10	H-TOP2	H-TOP3
CS-UMD [16]	97.9	99.1	99.4	90.9	71.0
TEBESSA C [16]	97.6	98.3	98.5	94.3	88.2
TSINGHUA [16]	97.7	99.0	99.1	95.3	94.5
Tang [23]	**99.7**	**99.8**	**100**	**99.0**	**97.9**
Proposed method	99.3	99.5	99.6	98.3	95.1

ICDAR2013 Dataset. The test results of the criteria and the comparison with other methods are presented in Table 3. The ICDAR2013 is a mixture of English and Greek data, which is a challenge for the generalization ability of the model. From the performance of the model, the data of the soft criteria is relatively good, and the performance of the hard criteria is not good. The performance of our model is relatively stable compared to other models, and the gap with the best performing models is not very large. The discrepancy between best on soft TOP-1, TOP-5 and TOP-10 criteria is 1.9%, 0.5% and 0.1%, respectively. And the reason for the more stable performance is that the preprocessing method using multi-patch makes the convolutional neural network obtain more high-discrimination features on a patch, while suitable data enhancement methods do not affect the generalization ability of the model.

Table 3. Evaluation of the soft and hard criteria on the ICDAR 2013 dataset (in%).

Models	S-TOP1	S-TOP5	S-TOP10	H-TOP2	H-TOP3
CS-UMD-a [18]	95.1	98.6	99.1	19.6	7.1
CS-UMD-b [18]	95.0	98.6	**99.2**	20.2	8.4
HIT-ICG [18]	94.8	98.0	98.3	**63.2**	36.5
Fie [12]	88.5	96.0	98.3	40.5	15.8
Christlein [4]	**97.1**	**98.8**	99.1	42.8	23.8
Proposed method	95.2	98.3	99.1	45.5	**36.8**

5   Conclusion

This paper proposes a text-independent handwriting identification method based on multi-patch line segmentation. For better patch preprocessing and appropriate data enhancement, we use ResNet50 which has been pretrained and finetuned on the Image dataset. The model has good stability and robustness. Good experimental results have been obtained on ICDAR2013 and CVL standard datasets.

In future work, the multi-patch model has further room. Through experiments, we plan to determine more effective stitching methods of multiple patches, reduce the invalid gaps between patches, and make the model obtain more handwriting features. Besides, local features are more efficiently encoded to obtain global features, thereby improving the standard of discrimination.

Acknowledgments. This work was supported in part by the Postgraduate Research & Practice Innovation Program of Jiangsu Province under Grant KYCX20_0758, and in part by Scientific Research Innovation Team of Jiangsu Police Institute under Grant 2018SJYTD15.

References

1. Al-Maadeed, S., Hassaine, A., Bouridane, A., Tahir, M.A.: Novel geometric features for off-line writer identification. Pattern Anal. Appl. **19**(3), 699–708 (2014). https://doi.org/10.1007/s10044-014-0438-y
2. Aliakbarzadeh, M., Razzazi, F.: Online Persian/Arabic writer identification using gated recurrent unit neural networks. Majlesi J. Electr. Eng. **14**(3), 73–79 (2020). https://doi.org/10.29252/mjee.14.3.9. http://www.mjee.org/index/index.php/ee/article/view/mjee.14.3.9
3. Bertolini, D., Oliveira, L.S., Justino, E.J.R., Sabourin, R.: Texture-based descriptors for writer identification and verification. Expert Syst. Appl. **40**(6), 2069–2080 (2013). https://doi.org/10.1016/j.eswa.2012.10.016
4. Christlein, V., Bernecker, D., Hönig, F., Maier, A.K., Angelopoulou, E.: Writer identification using GMM supervectors and exemplar-SVMs. Pattern Recognit. **63**, 258–267 (2017). https://doi.org/10.1016/j.patcog.2016.10.005

5. Christlein, V., Bernecker, D., Maier, A., Angelopoulou, E.: Offline writer identification using convolutional neural network activation features. In: Gall, J., Gehler, P., Leibe, B. (eds.) GCPR 2015. LNCS, vol. 9358, pp. 540–552. Springer, Cham (2015). https://doi.org/10.1007/978-3-319-24947-6_45

6. Christlein, V., Gropp, M., Fiel, S., Maier, A.K.: Unsupervised feature learning for writer identification and writer retrieval. In: 14th IAPR International Conference on Document Analysis and Recognition, ICDAR 2017, Kyoto, Japan, 9–15 November 2017, pp. 991–997. IEEE (2017). https://doi.org/10.1109/ICDAR.2017.165

7. Christlein, V., Maier, A.K.: Encoding CNN activations for writer recognition. In: 13th IAPR International Workshop on Document Analysis Systems, DAS 2018, Vienna, Austria, 24–27 April 2018, pp. 169–174. IEEE (2018). https://doi.org/10.1109/DAS.2018.9

8. Cilia, N.D., De Stefano, C., Fontanella, F., Marrocco, C., Molinara, M., Freca, A.S.d.: An experimental comparison between deep learning and classical machine learning approaches for writer identification in medieval documents. J. Imaging 6(9), 89 (2020)

9. Cilia, N.D., De Stefano, C., Fontanella, F., Marrocco, C., Molinara, M., Scotto di Freca, A.: A page-based reject option for writer identification in medieval books. In: Cristani, M., Prati, A., Lanz, O., Messelodi, S., Sebe, N. (eds.) ICIAP 2019. LNCS, vol. 11808, pp. 187–197. Springer, Cham (2019). https://doi.org/10.1007/978-3-030-30754-7_19

10. Dengel, A., Ahmad, R.: A novel skew detection and correction approach for scanned documents. In: 12th International IAPR Workshop on Document Analysis Systems, DAS 2016, April 2016

11. Diem, M., Kleber, F., Sablatnig, R.: Text line detection for heterogeneous documents. In: 12th International Conference on Document Analysis and Recognition, ICDAR 2013, Washington, DC, USA, 25–28 August 2013, pp. 743–747. IEEE (2013). https://doi.org/10.1109/ICDAR.2013.152

12. Fiel, S., Sablatnig, R.: Writer identification and retrieval using a convolutional neural network. In: Azzopardi, G., Petkov, N. (eds.) CAIP 2015. LNCS, vol. 9257, pp. 26–37. Springer, Cham (2015). https://doi.org/10.1007/978-3-319-23117-4_3

13. Glorot, X., Bordes, A., Bengio, Y.: Domain adaptation for large-scale sentiment classification: a deep learning approach. In: Getoor, L., Scheffer, T. (eds.) Proceedings of the 28th International Conference on Machine Learning, ICML 2011, Bellevue, Washington, USA, 28 June - 2 July 2011, pp. 513–520. Omnipress (2011). https://icml.cc/2011/papers/342_icmlpaper.pdf

14. He, K., Zhang, X., Ren, S., Sun, J.: Deep residual learning for image recognition. In: IEEE Conference on Computer Vision and Pattern Recognition, CVPR 2016, Las Vegas, NV, USA, 27–30 June 2016, pp. 770–778. IEEE (2016). https://doi.org/10.1109/CVPR.2016.90

15. Javidi, M., Jampour, M.: A deep learning framework for text-independent writer identification. Eng. Appl. Artif. Intell. 95, 103912 (2020). https://doi.org/10.1016/j.engappai.2020.103912. http://www.sciencedirect.com/science/article/pii/S0952197620302463

16. Kleber, F., Fiel, S., Diem, M., Sablatnig, R.: CVL -database: an off-line database for writer retrieval, writer identification and word spotting. In: 12th International Conference on Document Analysis and Recognition, ICDAR 2013, Washington, DC, USA, 25–28 August 2013, pp. 560–564. IEEE (2013). https://doi.org/10.1109/ICDAR.2013.117

17. Li, Z., Jiang, X., Pang, Y.: Evaluation of face recognition techniques based on Symlet 2 wavelet and support vector machine. In: Wang, G., Feng, J., Bhuiyan, M.Z.A., Lu, R. (eds.) SpaCCS 2019. LNCS, vol. 11637, pp. 228–239. Springer, Cham (2019). https://doi.org/10.1007/978-3-030-24900-7_19

18. Louloudis, G., Gatos, B., Stamatopoulos, N., Papandreou, A.: ICDAR 2013 competition on writer identification. In: 12th International Conference on Document Analysis and Recognition, ICDAR 2013, Washington, DC, USA, 25–28 August 2013, pp. 1397–1401. IEEE (2013). https://doi.org/10.1109/ICDAR.2013.282

19. Louloudis, G., Stamatopoulos, N., Gatos, B.: ICDAR 2011 writer identification contest. In: 2011 International Conference on Document Analysis and Recognition, ICDAR 2011, Beijing, China, 18–21 September 2011, pp. 1475–1479. IEEE (2011). https://doi.org/10.1109/ICDAR.2011.293

20. Oser, P., Kargl, F., Lüders, S.: Identifying devices of the internet of things using machine learning on clock characteristics. In: Wang, G., Chen, J., Yang, L.T. (eds.) SpaCCS 2018. LNCS, vol. 11342, pp. 417–427. Springer, Cham (2018). https://doi.org/10.1007/978-3-030-05345-1_36

21. Rehman, A., Naz, S., Razzak, M.I., Hameed, I.A.: Automatic visual features for writer identification: a deep learning approach. IEEE Access **7**, 17149–17157 (2019). https://doi.org/10.1109/ACCESS.2018.2890810

22. Shaus, A., Turkel, E.: Writer identification in modern and historical documents via binary pixel patterns, Kolmogorov-Smirnov test and Fisher's method. In: Rogowitz, B.E., Pappas, T.N., de Ridder, H. (eds.) Human Vision and Electronic Imaging 2017, Burlingame, CA, USA, 29 January 2017–2 February 2017, pp. 203–211. Ingenta (2017). https://doi.org/10.2352/ISSN.2470-1173.2017.14.HVEI-144

23. Tang, Y., Wu, X.: Text-independent writer identification via CNN features and joint Bayesian. In: 15th International Conference on Frontiers in Handwriting Recognition, ICFHR 2016, Shenzhen, China, 23–26 October 2016, pp. 566–571. IEEE (2016). https://doi.org/10.1109/ICFHR.2016.0109

24. Wu, X., Tang, Y., Bu, W.: Offline text-independent writer identification based on scale invariant feature transform. IEEE Trans. Inf. Foren. Secur. **9**(3), 526–536 (2014). https://doi.org/10.1109/TIFS.2014.2301274

25. Xing, L., Qiao, Y.: Deepwriter: a multi-stream deep CNN for text-independent writer identification. In: 15th International Conference on Frontiers in Handwriting Recognition, ICFHR 2016, Shenzhen, China, 23–26 October 2016, pp. 584–589. IEEE (2016). https://doi.org/10.1109/ICFHR.2016.0112

26. Yan, X., Cui, B., Li, J.: Malicious domain name recognition based on deep neural networks. In: Wang, G., Chen, J., Yang, L.T. (eds.) SpaCCS 2018. LNCS, vol. 11342, pp. 497–505. Springer, Cham (2018). https://doi.org/10.1007/978-3-030-05345-1_43

Classification of Abnormal Traces in a Collaborative Fog Computing Architecture

Qingmin Meng[1,2](✉), Hao Zheng[1,2], and Haiyan Guo[1,2]

[1] School of Communication and Information Engineering, Nanjing University of Posts and Telecommunications, Nanjing 210003, China
{mengqm, guohy}@njupt.edu.cn, 1037385693@qq.com
[2] Key Laboratory of Dynamic Cognitive System of Electromagnetic Spectrum Space, Nanjing University of Aeronautics and Astronautics, Ministry of Industry and Information Technology, Nanjing 210003, China

Abstract. A large number of fog nodes located at a network edge not only have the characteristics of resource limitation and clustered location distribution, but also are susceptible to variable intrusion from illegal intruders from outside. For the above fog computing environment, a collaborative fog computing architecture is proposed where a lightweight fog node in each cluster is used to collect data from multiple low-power IoT devices around. This miniature fog computing architecture facilitates integration with the next-generation WiFi communication method, thereby effectively realizing communication and edge perception. Although a single lightweight fog node is difficult to complete the overall perception, the fog computing center can effectively integrate features from multiple lightweight fog nodes, such as radio frequency fingerprinting (RF fingerprinting) features and MAC address information features. After feature extraction, the feedforward neural network is trained and tested, thus effectively detecting the intruder traces.

Keywords: Fog computing · Intrusion detection · Communication · Probe · Machine learning

1 Introduction

The integration of the Internet of Things (IoT) with emerging technologies such as fog computing and edge computing, and the next generation of wireless technologies has driven the development of the Internet of Everything technology. This integration can facilitate the processing of large-scale geographically distributed sensor data, thereby improving the real-time processing and security capabilities of the Internet of Things. For example, the newly emerging ubiquitous power Internet of Things (UPIoT), which refers to the application of ubiquitous Internet of Things technology in power systems [1]. The essence of UPIoT is to achieve overall perception and ubiquitous energy connection. This perception can enhance rapid response performance and network security performance. At the same time, the edge-fog cloud computing architectures for different cyber-physiscal systems are constantly being upgraded to efficiently complete

© Springer Nature Switzerland AG 2021
G. Wang et al. (Eds.): SpaCCS 2020, LNCS 12383, pp. 420–429, 2021.
https://doi.org/10.1007/978-3-030-68884-4_35

distributed intelligence and intelligent perception based on low power & bandwidth IoT nodes [2]. For the application scenarios of clustered IoT devices, this paper mainly considers a collaborative fog computing architecture and its machine learning enhanced intruder behavior detection.

1.1 Research Background

Intrusion detection has been a hot spot in network security research in recent years. The concept of intrusion in the network intrusion detection system (IDS) mainly refers to the unauthorized use of system resources, which can cause system data loss and destruction, system denial of service and other hazards [3]. The intrusion detection system will respond in a timely manner after discovering an intrusion, including cutting off the network connection, recording events and alarms. Intrusion detection is generally divided into three steps, followed by information collection, data analysis and response. Among them, the content of information collection includes the status and behavior of the system, network, data, and user activities. Its source is composed of system logs, abnormal behavior during program execution, and intrusion information of the physical environment et al. Therefore, most of these data are network traffic data. However, this paper mainly considers the data from the physical layer and MAC layer, such as the received signal strength (RSS) and its MAC address information, rather than directly using network traffic data.

Data analysis is the core of intrusion detection and probe. Traditional data analysis is generally carried out by means of pattern matching, statistical analysis and completeness analysis. The first two methods are used for real-time intrusion detection, while the integrity analysis is used for post-mortem analysis. In the last five years, machine learning has become a research hotspot in the direction of network security, such as malware software detection, abnormal protocol detection, network intrusion detection, etc. [4]. For this hot spot, we introduce a definition of abnormal network behavior under machine learning. First establish a model of normal behavior based on normal packets in the network. Second, match the established model with new data packets. If this type of packet does not conform to the model, the network activity is called abnormal network behavior.

Abnormal network behaviors based on machine learning can be divided into supervised learning, semi-supervised learning, and unsupervised learning [5]. For example, Principal Component Analysis (PCA) of unsupervised learning can be used to detect the existence of intrusive behavior; Classification of normal behavior and abnormal behavior can be accomplished by supervised learning. The fog computing detection task studied in this paper is not to find anomalies in intrusion detection, but to perceive and classify the network behavior of intruders.

1.2 Contribution of This Paper

We have proposed a collaborative fog computing architecture and relay communication method. In this architecture, multiple lightweight fog nodes that are geographically close to each other can coordinate and perform distributed sensing. Through access point (AP) belonging to the next-generation WiFi, data packets are transmitted to the fog data center. Secondly, the intrusion detection system only needs to use limited physical layer information and MAC layer information for feature extraction, so as to complete the training of machine learning and realize the classification of abnormal trajectories.

2 Related Work

In the past three years, there have been many documents that have studied the application of communication, network security and machine learning in fog computing. Compared with cloud platforms, fog nodes have limited resources and are more vulnerable to attacks or interference. This is because the fog nodes at the edge of the network need to communicate wirelessly with a large number of IoT devices. The literature [6] pointed out that fog computing boosts real-time processing of data from IoT devices. If the data of the IoT device is transmitted to the remote cloud, this will waste a lot of delay and communication energy overhead. The literature [7, 8] introduces a neural network-based abnormal behavior analysis method to implement an adaptive intrusion detection system. By detecting when the fog node is attacked and making corresponding treatment after detecting anomalies, the detection system will ensure that the subsequent communication link is not interrupted. Literature [9] uses online sequential extreme learning machine (OSELM) to distribute the detection information to the local fog nodes in order to respond to interference faster and achieve high-speed intrusion detection. Fog wireless access networks have been proposed in recent years. It can avoid the large-scale and high real-time requirements of wireless signal processing in the baseband unit pool of the traditional cloud wireless access network, and it can also make full use of the computing and storage capabilities of edge network devices. Under the architecture of the fog radio access network, the literature [10] has studied an intrusion detection scheme based on skyline query, which can analyze the IDS log statistics of fog nodes and provide a complete data processing process to achieve the purpose of reducing communication overhead and calculation complexity. The literature [11] proposed an IoT device recognition scheme based on RF fingerprint recognition. It uses convolutional neural networks to extract features from the RF signals of the physical layer, and performs dimensionality reduction and decorrelation on the extracted features. For indoor location traces recognition, the early literature [12] proposes a random model for context-aware anomaly detection. This method can predict lost events and Indoor Location Traces that may be caused by theft of IoT devices. In the end, the literature [13] provided a brief survey of machine learning and their sensor and IoT applications, and discussed applications of machine learning algorithms in various fields including pattern recognition, sensor networks, anomaly detection, Internet of Things (IoT).

3   System Model

This paper proposes a collaborative fog computing architecture. This hierarchical architecture is integrated into a collaborative system with multiple access points (Access Points, APs) in next-generation WiFi and a fog computing center to complete network security monitoring functions. Since multiple fog nodes can collect data of the physical environment at the same time, the overall perception of network behavior can be achieved. The system model is shown in Fig. 1.

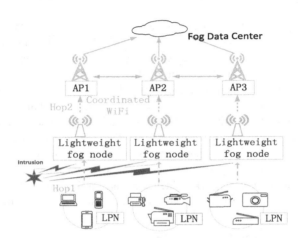

Fig. 1. A collaborative fog computing architecture with coordinated multiple APs

The micro fog architecture under study contains a large number of IoT devices or low power consumption nodes (LPNs) and communication links. Here, the lightweight node similar to LPNs has limited communication, control, calculation and wireless relay functions, so this architecture is also known as a miniature fog computing architecture. Multiple (three here) geographically adjacent wireless APs are arranged in a triangle and connected to the fog data center. Each access point (AP) is wirelessly connected to the nearest fog node, and each fog node is connected to (N-1) LPNs in each cluster. Consider that each of LPNs uses an uplink channel to transmit data packets to the fog node in each cluster. The fog node is responsible for receiving and forwarding data packets to the corresponding AP. The fog data center merges data packets from multiple APs and stacks them into a data matrix and performs data analysis based on machine learning. In addition, intruders will walk near multiple fog nodes in the studied scenario. Therefore, intruders generate variable power interference to multiple fog nodes. Consider that the intruder will use a fixed interference channel j. Therefore, on the j-th channel, the interference signal from the intruder will interfere with the reception of the fog node.

4 Problem Formation and Methods

4.1 Problems and Methods

Figure 1 can be seen as a specific IoT perception scenario. There are many types of network data related to fog nodes, such as RSS received signal strength in physical layer, MAC address, IP address, and so on. The goal here is to use the distributed architecture to identify intruder traces. So how to perform feature extraction to implement machine learning based intrusion detection and intruder trajectory classification?

Under normal circumstances, using the RSS data collected by a single fog node, an intrusion detection system can detect the presence or absence of an intruder. But when the intruder walks through the scene according to different trajectories, the features from a single fog node obviously cannot identify the intruder's trajectory. Because the number of RSS features from a single fog node is too small. In response to this problem, we propose a data collection and feature extraction scheme as follows. After the distributed fog nodes simultaneously collect the intruder's interference signals, the fog computing center needs to perform data fusion on the network data from these fog nodes to obtain more features. The data fusion utilizes the characteristics of distributed architecture and AP coordination, and the data analysis method used is a low complexity feedforward neural network, which facilitates a fast anomaly detection at the edge of the network. The basic knowledge related to this method is introduced below.

4.2 Basic of Feedforward Neural Networks

In feed-forward neural networks, neurons are organized into different layers: an input layer, multiple hidden processing layers, and an output layer [14]. The network is the simplest neural network, and the neurons are arranged in layers. Each neuron is only connected to the neuron in the previous layer. It is one of the most widely used and fastest-growing artificial neural networks. The main goal of the feedforward network is to approximate some function $f(.)$. For example, the regression function $y = f(x)$ maps the input x to the value y. The feedforward network defines the $y = f(x; \theta)$ map and learns the value of the parameter θ to bring the result closer to the optimal function. In feedforward networks, information flows forward. Because the feature x is used to calculate some intermediate functions in the hidden layer, and the hidden layer is used to calculate y. The layer between the input layer and the output layer is called the hidden layer.

Deep learning models, here meaning Deep Feedforward Network, the goal is to fit a function $f(.)$. Common deep feedforward networks include: multi-layer perceptions, autoencoders, restricted Boltzmann machines, convolutional neural networks, and so on. A feedforward neural network with a single hidden layer usually requires fewer training samples, but its accuracy performance is not as good as a deep feedforward network with multiple hidden layers. Considering the constraints of complexity and delay, the fog computing center in this paper considers a single hidden layer feedforward neural network.

5   Experiment and Simulation

The scope of the scene is a square area with a length and width of 50 m, and the three APs are at the three vertices of the square. The total number of uplink channels of the three clusters is $(3N + 2)$. There are N LPNs in each cluster, each fog node contains $(N - 1)$ uplink channels, and each uplink channel bandwidth is 0.3125 MHz. The total transmit power of each AP is 23 dBm, the transmit power of each LPN is -10 dBm, and the data rate threshold is 0.2 Mbps. Without loss of generality, it is defined that the first cluster contains $N = 10$ LPNs, and one of the N LPNs is selected as fog node such as fog1 in cluster 1. The channel index used by the first cluster is $[1, 2, ..., N]$, and the channel index used by the intruder is j. Therefore, on the channel with index j, the LPN and an intruder may simultaneously transmit signals to the fog node. The wireless channel between the LPNs in cluster 1 and fog 1 follows Rayleigh-like model.

This experiment considers the trace 1 and trace 2 of the intrusion node, and the velocity of the intruder moving at a uniform speed is 0.05 m/s.

5.1   Trace 1 in Fig. 2

Suppose the intruder's starting position is $[x, y] = [0, 15]$ in unit of meter, it first moves straight to the right at a constant speed, and when $x_{turn} = 25$ m, it changes direction and moves upward. As shown in Fig. 3, when the intruder is near the first cluster, it produces strong interference to the first fog node on the channel with index j, and the degree of the interference changes from small to large first, and then from large to small. When the three fog nodes receive the signal from the intruder, the RSS sequence through the link between the fog node and the AP is transmitted to the AP and the fog computing center. The fog computing center uses Gaussian filtering to preprocess RSS sequences to obtain feature vectors. To show the maximum delay of the one-hop uplink (links between LPNs to fog 1, i.e., hop 1), Fig. 4 plots the delay each channel when there is no interference (no intruders are present) in cluster 1. The fluctuation of the delay is due to the uncertainty caused by the wireless channel. Note that when the intruder approaches a fog node, the value of signal-to-interference ratio (SIR) becomes smaller, and the LPN's delay on channel j will increase significantly.

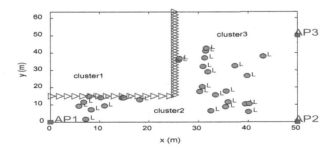

Fig. 2. Trace of the intruder 1

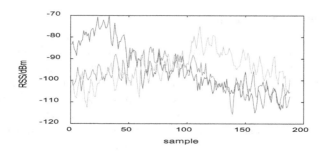

Fig. 3. The RSS sequences of the three fog nodes at trace 1

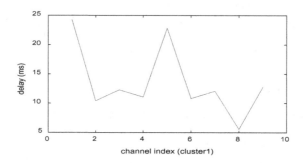

Fig. 4. Time delay without interference in cluster 1

5.2   Trace 2 in Fig. 5

Suppose that the starting position of the intrusion point is [x, y] = [0, 20] in unit of meter, it first moves straight to the right at a constant speed, and when x_{turn} = 40 m, it changes direction and moves upward. The RSS values are shown in Fig. 6.

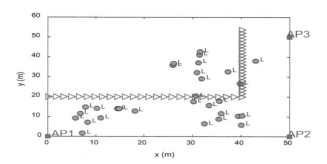

Fig. 5. Trace of the intruder 2

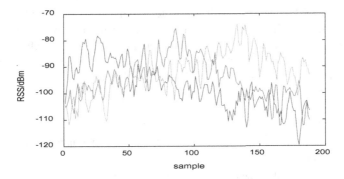

Fig. 6. The RSS sequences of the three fog nodes at trace 2

As mentioned in Sect. 4, trace 1 and trace 2 cannot be distinguished only by considering the intruder's interference with the first fog node. Therefore, we need other RSS sequences, which come from distributed fog nodes. At this time, we also consider the intruder's interference to the second fog node and the third fog node. The first data array $V_j = [RSS_1 \, RSS_2 \, RSS_3]$ is formed. Different machine learning algorithms can be used to train the feature array from V_j. Due to the small number of samples, a feedforward neural network with a low network size is considered here. Under this machine learning model, the prediction accuracy is only 61%, and the classification performance is shown in Fig. 7.

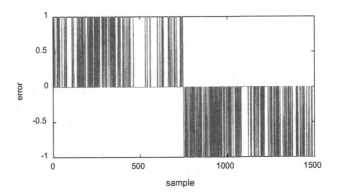

Fig. 7. Error of the predictor

One of the ways to improve classification accuracy is to provide more features or better samples. After taking the MAC addresses of the three fog nodes (or numerical representation of the addresses) as the fourth feature, we train the feedforward neural network again. Here we need to further explain the network structure and parameter optimization. For a fully connected neural network, when the number of features increases from 3 to 4, adjusting the network structure is the key. The number of hidden layer neurons in Table 1 was chosen to be 20 and 40, respectively. Therefore, the increasing size of the network will facilitate the handling of complex real-world problems. At the same time, the increase in network size also requires an increase in the number of samples. The accuracy of the four features reached 71%. After considering the uncertainty caused by the wireless channel (also the uncertainty of the MAC address), the accuracy rate is 67% (not shown in Table 1).

Table 1. Influence of network structure and parameter optimization on accuracy

	Before improvement	After improvement
Number of features	3	4
Number of hidden neurons	20	40
Epoch	294	300
Performance (MSE)	0.233	0.191
Gradient	0.0170	0.0374
Validation checks	0	6
Feature array dimension	1500	3000
Accuracy	0.61	0.706

6   Conclusion

We have proposed a collaborative fog architecture that is easy to integrate into the next-generation WiFi system. This hierarchical micro-architecture is a supplement to the existing fog architecture, because it facilitates the communication and perception of a large number of low-power IoT devices. In the proposed architecture, a low-power node in a cluster is selected as a lightweight fog node. The fog node is responsible for collecting network data in this cluster and transmitting it to the AP through the uplink channel. Second, multiple geographically adjacent access points also coordinate with each other to effectively collect and fuse network data. The fog computing system implements an anomaly detection paradigm embedded in machine learning. It can not only distinguish whether an invasion has occurred, but also classify the intruder's abnormal trace earlier, so as to efficiently detect abnormal network behavior and achieve active interference avoidance. Feature extraction for the network layer, transport layer, and application layer will be a next step. This feature engineering work will help achieve better edge perception.

Acknowledgements. The Open Research Foundation of Key Laboratory of Dynamic Cognitive System of Electromagnetic Spectrum Space (Nanjing Univ. Aeronaut. Astronaut.), Ministry of Industry and Information Technology under Grant KF20181910.

References

1. Yin, D., Mei, F., He, W.: Ubiquitous power Internet of Things technology for equipment monitoring. In: 45th Annual Conference of the IEEE Industrial Electronics Society, Lisbon, pp. 5456–5460 (2019)
2. Ficco, M., Esposito, C., Xiang, Y., et al.: Pseudo-dynamic testing of realistic edge-fog cloud ecosystems. IEEE Commun. Mag. **55**(11), 98–104 (2017)
3. Buczak, A.L., Guven, E.: A survey of data mining and machine learning methods for cyber security intrusion detection. IEEE Commun. Surv. Tutorials **18**(2), 1153–1176 (2016)
4. Kolias, C., Kambourakis, G., Stavrou, A., et al.: Intrusion detection in 802.11 networks: empirical evaluation of threats and a public dataset. IEEE Commun. Surv. Tutorials **18**(1), 184–208 (2016)
5. Xu, S., Qian, Y., Hu, R.Q.: A semi-supervised learning approach for network anomaly detection in fog computing. In: 2019 IEEE International Conference on Communications (ICC), Shanghai, pp. 1–6 (2019)
6. Yang, S.: IoT stream processing and analytics in the fog. IEEE Commun. Mag. **55**(8), 21–27 (2017)
7. Pacheco, J., Benitez, V.H., Félix-Herrán, L.C., et al.: Artificial neural networks-based intrusion detection system for internet of things fog nodes. IEEE Access **8**, 73907–73918 (2020)
8. Pacheco, J., Benitez, V.H., Tunc, C., et al.: Anomaly behavior analysis for fog nodes availability assurance in IoT applications. In: 16th International Conference on Computer Systems and Applications (AICCSA), Abu Dhabi, pp. 1–6 (2019)
9. Prabavathy, S., Sundarakantham, K., Shalinie, S.M.: Design of cognitive fog computing for intrusion detection in Internet of Things. J. Commun. Netw. **20**(3), 291–298 (2018)
10. An, X., Lü, X., Yang, L., et al.: Node state monitoring scheme in fog radio access networks for intrusion detection. IEEE Access **7**, 21879–21888 (2019)
11. Bassey, J., Adesina, D., Li, X., et al.: Intrusion detection for IoT devices based on RF fingerprinting using deep learning. In: 2019 Fourth International Conference on Fog and Mobile Edge Computing (FMEC), Rome, pp. 98–104 (2019)
12. Liu, C., Xiong, H., Ge, Y., et al.: A stochastic model for context-aware anomaly detection in indoor location traces. In: 12th International Conference on Data Mining, Brussels, pp. 449–458 (2012)
13. Shanthamallu, U.S., Spanias, A., Tepedelenlioglu, C., et al.: A brief survey of machine learning methods and their sensor and IoT applications. In: 2017 8th International Conference on Information, Intelligence, Systems & Applications (IISA), pp. 1–8, Larnaca (2017)
14. Bishop, C.M.: Pattern Recognition and Machine Learning (Information Science and Statistics), 1st edn. Springer-Verlag, New York, New York (2008)

A Muti-detection Method of Covert Timing Channel Based on Perceptual Hashing

Quan Sun, Yonghong Chen[(✉)], and Tian Wang

Fujian Key Laboratory of Big Data Intelligence and Security,
Huaqiao University, Xiamen 361021, China
djandcyh@163.com

Abstract. Covert Timing Channel (CTC) is a process of covert information transmission using existing network resources for information hiding and distribution of secret and sensitive date. By exploiting Inter-packet delays (IPDs) of legitimate network traffic, which is a network resources that were not designed for the purpose of communication, they have the ability that traditional security strategies, such as firewalls and intrusion detection systems, cannot effectively distinguish and disrupt them. In this paper, we propose a novel approach, CTC Multi-Threshold Detection (CTCMTD) to detect different CTCs and legitimate traffic. We extract four features of traffic samples for muti-classification by analysis its perceptual discrimination and robustness. We have shown that the method based on perceptual hashing has great potential to muti-classificate CTCs blindly.

Keywords: Network security · Network traffic · Inter-packet delays · Covert timing channels · Perceptual hash

1 Introduction

CTCs are a kind of information hiding approach, which provides a method to transmit information by manipulating timing or ordering of network events which is a network resources that were not designed to carry data, likes IPDs. This makes them invisible to common network security mechanisms like firewalls. Because of their ability to evade detection, they create a grave cyber security threat. On the one hand, the information leakage caused by the CTCs poses a serious threat to the network users. The user's private information, such as passwords and personal information, may be easily stolen by the CTCs. On the other hand, the detection of covert time channel is a challenging task in the field of network security, especially in how to introduce a general and effective method target at a broad range of CTC algorithms.

Generally speaking, the detection method of CTCs distinguishes covert channel and normal channel by statistical method. However, due to the large variation of network traffic in the normal channel, the statistical method lacks the accuracy and robustness in detecting the covert channel. At present, many researches are devoted to the detection of CTCs, some of them [1–3] are only for a specific covert timing channel, and cannot detect other types of CTCs. There are also detection methods for multiple types of CTCs, but these methods [4–6] are very sensitive to the high-speed change of network

© Springer Nature Switzerland AG 2021
G. Wang et al. (Eds.): SpaCCS 2020, LNCS 12383, pp. 430–443, 2021.
https://doi.org/10.1007/978-3-030-68884-4_36

traffic. In the face of the real high-speed change network, it is difficult to ensure a high detection rate. All in all, previous methods cannot effectively detect multiple types of covert time channels. And almost all of the past methods didn't concern how to distinguish different type of CTCs.

In this paper, we propose a detection framework based on perceptual hashing, and analyze various features through the theory of perceptual hashing. The features are extracted from the existing methods and analyze its discrimination and robustness for muti-classification. Perceptual hash function [7, 8] is a kind of one-way mapping from content to perceptual hash set. Perceptual set is the unique representation of the content. The same content is mapped to a similar or the same perceptual hash set, which refers to the properties of perceptual robustness. Different content is mapped to a different perceptual set, which refers to the properties of perceptual discrimination. And the difference of content will be reflected in the distance of perception hash set, the greater the difference, the greater the distance.

More specifically, we study the application of perceptual hashing theory used in muti-classification of network traffic. We definite the perceptual robustness and perceptual discrimination of network traffic. In this paper, we have derived four types of features-Kolmorov-Smirnov (K-S) score, Regularity score, entropy and corrected conditional entropy (CCE)-from the IPDs. The experimental results show that the perceptual robustness and perceptual discrimination of the features above, to some extend, can used in muti-classification of CTCs and normal channel.

The remainder of this paper is structured as follows: Sect. 2 covers the background and related work of CTCs and detection method. Section 3 describes the theory of perceptual hashing. Section 4, we present the detection results. We conclude the paper and discusses the direction for our future work in Sect. 5.

2   Background and Related Work

There are three countermeasure approaches to covert communications: detect, destroy and eliminate. The way to destroy the covert communication is to add random delay to CTCs, so as to reduce the capacity of CTCs and the performance of the system. The detection of covert channel mainly distinguishes covert channel from normal channel by statistical test. Although the previous work mainly focused on the destruction of covert channel, or the elimination of covert channel in the system design, at present, more research focuses on the design of covert channel and the detection of CTCs. In the following chapters, we will give an overview of the recent research and detection methods in CTCs.

2.1   Covert Timing Channels

Cabuk et al. [16] proposed a CTC based on IP protocol called IPCTC, in which the covert sender and covert receiver both use an agreed-upon covert time interval to decide packets' sending time. The covert sender changes the delays of two consecutive packets to send covert bit '1' of '0'. The covert sender sends a packet within the covet time interval represents transmitting the covert bit '1', while remains silent and do not transmit any packets within the covert time interval represents transmitting covert bit '0'. The number of covert bits '0' between two covert bits '1' determines the distribution of the IPD of IPCTC. On the receiver side, receiving a network traffic packet within the covert time interval is interpreted as covert bit '1'. If no packet is received during this time, the covert receiver interprets that as a covert bit '0'. Cabuk et al. later designed a more advanced CTC based on replay attack in [2], which we refer to as TRCTC. IPDs that from legitimate traffic are sorted and divided into two different IPD bins based on a given threshold which are shared between covert sender and cover receiver. Covert sender transmits covert bit '1' by randomly selecting an IPD from the first bin, and transmits covert bit '0' by randomly selecting an IPD from the second bin. On the receiver side, IPDs are measured and the covert bits '0' or '1' are decoded simply by comparing the incoming IPDs with the median. In [17] the author introduced a CTC algorithm, which embeds L bits covert data into different sequences of N IPDs. The way that map L-bits covert data into N IPDs in a one-to-one way enhance the channels' capacity and decrease the bit error rate of covert data. In [18], Shah et al. invented a keyboard device called Jitterbug which can slowly leak typing information through the network by embedding covert bits into legitimate traffic by adding additional delay to the current IPDs. Jitterbug is a passive CTC. The covert sender increases the IPD to satisfy modulo $W/2$ equals to 0 for sending covert bit '0'. For sending covert bit '1', the IPD is added to a value that modulo W equals to 0.

2.2 Detection Tests

The Kolmogorov-Smirnov test [4] is a non-parametric test which is distribution free, i.e. the traffic is not strictly defined by parameters. The Kolmogorov-Smirnov test can be used to determine whether a sample come from a known distribution or determines whether two samples differ. The Kolmogorov-Smirnov test compares the empirical cumulative probability distribution of the IPDs of two traffic samples to get the test score. Cabuk et al. [2] has developed a detection based on regularity. The author assumes that the variance of the IPDs will change over time for legitimate traffic, however, for covert time channel, if the coding method of covert channel remains unchanged, the variance of the IPDs remain relatively stable over time. The test calculates the variance change of the data. The normal traffic is tended to get higher regularity scores than covert traffic. Gianvecchio et al. [5] proposed an entropy-based detection method. Gianvecchio believes that in the process of constructing CTCs, the entropy of IPDs will be affected. Based on the assumption, the entropy detection method can detect part of the common covert time channels and works well in detecting JitterBug. In the same paper, the author proposed another method based on corrected conditional entropy. Gianvecchio believes that in the process of constructing the covert channel, the construction will increase the correlation between the nth data and the data before it. Based on this, Gianvecchio used the modified conditional entropy to calculate the entropy rate of finite data. It is proved that this method can detect mutiple CTCs effectively except for JitterBug.

3   Perceptual Hashing

Perceptual hashing [7, 8] is a kind of information processing theory based on cognitive psychology. It is a class of one-way mapping from perceptual content to a perceptual hash value in term of their perceptual content. Perceptual hash has been used in the recognition, authentication [9–12] and retrieval of multimedia content [13–15] in the past. In this paper, we combine the theory of perceptual hashing to analyze whether the four characteristics of CTCs features robustness and discrimination. In this chapter, we describe the use of perceptual hashing in detection of CTCs. First, we describe the perceptual hashing theory and the framework of perceptual hashing in network field. Second, we show the detection framework of CTCs using perceptual hashing theory and describe the detection algorithm flow.

3.1   Perceptual Hash Theory

Figure 1 shows the detection framework of perceptual hash theory used in network traffic, which is divided into three parts. The first part is traffic filter. The input data of traffic filter is network traffic. The preprocessing of traffic filter helps us accurately extracting features. The second part is perceptual feature extractor. By signal processing method, perceptual feature extractor selects characteristics with perceptual significance. The third part is perceptual hash Matching. The extracted features are then transformed into perceptual hash sequences in order to facilitate hardware implementation and reduce storage requirements then use perceptual hash matching strategy for detection. In the framework, accurate perceptual feature extraction is the premise of good perceptual robustness and perceptual discrimination of perceptual hash value. In the detection of CTCs, the perceptual discrimination and perceptual robustness are the primary performance indicators of perceptual hash value.

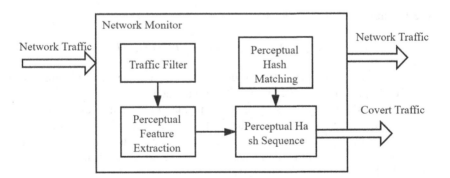

Fig. 1. Detection framework based on perceptual Hash theory

3.2   Detection Model Based on Perceptual Hashing

In this section, it describes the design of each part of the detection framework above. The specific content is as follow.

Step 1 Perceptual Features Extraction. First, generating IPDs series $S(i) = (s_i, \ldots, s_n), i \in C$. C is the set of channels types. s_i represents the time interval between the current packet and the previous packet.

$$C = (Normal, IPCTC, TRCTC, JitterBug, L - N) \tag{1}$$

$$M = (Regularity, KS, EN, CCE) \tag{2}$$

M is the set of feature extraction methods. When we extract features, we need to segment the time series according to a certain length to form different time series. $F(i,j)$ is feature vector, calculated by the first parameter-type of traffic and the second parameter-type of features. Empirical distribution functions of samples are represented as W. The KS feature vector are calculated by (3).

$$F(i, KS) = \max|W(i) - W(Normal)| \tag{3}$$

The Regularity feature vector are calculated by (6). τ_i represent the standard deviation of non-overlapping packets samples data separated by windows of sizes w.

$$F(i, Regularity) = STDEV(\frac{|\tau_i - \tau_j|}{\tau_j}, i < j, \forall i, j) \tag{4}$$

The entropy provides a measure of uncertainty in a random process. Traffic samples can be considered as a random variable sequence $X = \{X_i\}$. The estimates of the entropy or conditional entropy, based on the empirical probability density functions, are represented as $EN(X)$ and $CE(X)$, respectively.

$$F(i, EN) = EN(X) \tag{5}$$

The features of CCE is define as:

$$F(i, CCE) = CE(X_m|X_1, \ldots, X_{m-1}) + perc(X_m) \cdot EN(X_1) \tag{6}$$

Where $perc(X_m)$ is the percentage of unique pattern, a sequence of bin number, of length m. $EN(X_1)$ is first-order entropy with m fixed at 1.

Step 2 Hash Modeling. PH is generation function of perceptual hash value, which generates perceptual hash value for selected features. Hash construction further reduces the dimension of perceptual features. $H(i, m)$ represents perceptual hash value. Because we only analyze the single dimension feature, we use the perceptual feature value as the perceptual hash value directly in our tests.

$$PH : C \rightarrow H_p \tag{7}$$

$$H(i, m) = PH(F(i, m)) \tag{8}$$

Step 3 Result Analysis and Matching. We analysis results from two aspects, one is robustness analysis, the other is discrimination analysis. The perceptual discrimination value, represented as *DValue*. *D* is distance vector.

$$D(i,j,m) = (d_1, \ldots, d_n), i,j \in C, m \in M \tag{9}$$

Then the distance vector is defined as (10).

$$D(i,j,m) = |H(i,m) - mean(H(j,m))| \tag{10}$$

The robustness means perceptual distance between same type of channel. The value is defined as (11).

$$RValue(i,m) = \log D(i,i,m) \tag{11}$$

The discrimination means perceptual distance between different type of channels. The value is defined as (12).

$$DValue(i,m) = \frac{1}{4} \sum\nolimits_{j \in C-i} \log D(i,j,m) \tag{12}$$

After getting the *DValue* and *RValue* of test data as the database of perceptual hash, we set the detection threshold according to detection strategy. During detection, judge the interval of hash value of sample data to determine the category of sample data. The meaning of *DValue* and *RValue* is described in more detailed in the next part. The use of detection strategy is described in more detailed in Sect. 4.1.

4 Experiment Evaluation

In this section, we test the perceptual hash values derived from four perceptual features mentioned in Sect. 3. The focus of these experiments is to measure the ability whether the four kinds of perceptual hash values are able to blind detect different kinds of channels. We use false-positive and true-positive rate to measure the experiments' performance. The experiment result with high true-positive rates and low false-positive rate is desirable.

4.1 Experiment Setup

We collect IPDs of outgoing HTTP traffic as the training set and test set of normal channels due to the wide acceptance of HTTP for passing through network perimeter. According to the construction method and coding method of CTCs mentioned in Sect. 2, the normal channels' IPDs are manipulated to achieve the purpose of simulating IPCTC, TRCTC, JitterBug and L-N. We have prepared 200000 HTTP packets for both training set and test set of five types of channel. The normal data set is the out of office traffic of the network, which is transmitted from the host to a specific port. Covert samples are generated from normal data set and from the encoding methods for

IPCTC, TRCTC, L-N and JitterBug. The setting used in CTCs' construction are as follows: For IPCTC, we rotate the timing interval t among 40, 60 and 80ms. For TRCTC, we use the BMC type. For JitterBug, we subtract the random sequence before the modulo operation. For L-N, we use 2-bits to 1-packets way. The input messages transmitted in our tests are random bits generated by a pseudorandom number generator, which avoids creating patterns in the output due to repeated bit sequences.

Detection Methodology. We run our tests on training samples, then get the range of *DValue* and *RValue*, which represent the perceptual distance with other type channels and the same type channel respectively. Then we use threshold strategy to get the range of *DValue* and *RValue* for detection. Under the same perceptual feature, like KS feature, the rules of threshold strategy are as follows. For any type of channels, we set the target false positive rate at 0.1 for both *DValue* and *RValue*. When there is no overlapping value range between the two intervals, we use the original interval which means false positive rate equals 0. To achieve this false positive rate, the cutoff of *DValue*, which decides whether a sample belong to the chosen type of channels or not and *RValue*, which are used for further decision if can't decide by *DValue*, are set at 5th and 95th of the sample score. Then, sample's *DValue* within the range are identified as the chosen type of channel. If it falls into the interval that overlapped with others type of channels, the sample can be identified as any type of channel involved. Then we use *RValue* for further judgment. If it's *RValue* falls into the range one of the involved type of channels, then we can decide it's type according to its *RValue*, else the samples' type is unrecognizable.

The *DValue* and *RValue* are interpreted as follows: the *DValue* measures the average distance of the distance the assumed type of channel with other types. Thus, if the *DValue* is small compared in the same method, it implies that the sample is close to other types, else it implies the discrimination of the perceptual hash value is not well and vice versa. The *RValue* measures the average distance of the distance the same type of channel. Thus, if the *RValue* is small compared in the same method, it implies that the sample is not close to itself, else it implies that the robustness of the perceptual hash value is not good and vice versa.

4.2   Experimental Results

The analysis of experimental results is divided into two parts. The first part, we analysis perceptual discrimination between different methods for a certain covert channel. By doing so we can see the advantages and disadvantages of different methods in perceptual discrimination. The higher the detection sensitivity is, the better the method can distinguish this kind of channel from other types of channels. The second part, we analysis perceptual robustness between different channels for a certain detection method. The higher the detection robustness is, the better the method can distinguish the same kind of covert channel. The third part, we show the result of detection.

Discrimination. We run each detection test 100 times for 2,000 covert samples. our first set of experiments investigates how perceptual discrimination of different type of perceptual hash value works in IPCTC and L-N. The result shows in Fig. 2 means that perceptual hash value of regularity has a good performance in sensing the discrimination about IPCTC and L-N. For IPCTC, discrimination of regularity is significantly higher than that of other detection methods and the discrimination of others deceases from KS test, EN to CCE. The reason why regularity is more sensitive than other methods is of high variation of legitimate traffic. IPCTC is obviously lower regularity scores than other channels in variance changes of data especially channels like JitterBug, Normal, TRCTC. Caused by its coding rules of covert data, the variance of IPCTC is stable over time, so it gets the relatively low scores in regularity and the same reason for L-N. The discrimination of regularity is higher than that of other detection methods, and the sensitivity of EN, KS and CCE decreases in turn.

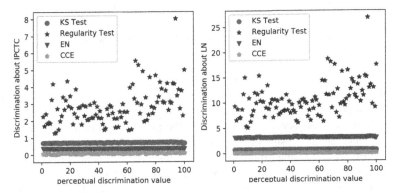

Fig. 2. Discrimination score of IPCTC and L-N

Our second set of experiments investigates how perceptual discrimination of different type of perceptual hash value works in in TRCTC and JitterBug. The result shows in Fig. 3 means that perceptual hash value of KS has a good performance in sensing the discrimination about TRCTC and JitterBug. TRCTC is a more advanced covert timing channel that makes use of a replay attack. TRCTC replays a set of legitimate IPDs to simulate the behavior of legitimate traffic. Thus, TRCTC has approximately the same shape as legitimate traffic. The result shows in Fig. 3, the discrimination of KS is significantly higher than that of the others, and the sensitivity decreases from Regularity, EN to CCE. The reason why KS is more sensitive in discrimination than other feature extract methods is that its IPDs are randomly selected from legitimate traffic. The KS score of TRCTC is low than other type of channel, which makes the difference between TRCTC with other type of channel is great. JitterBug manipulates the IPDs of existing legitimate traffic. The timing window determines the maximum delay that JitterBug adds. By slightly increasing the IPDs, JitterBug has similar shape with legitimate traffic. In addition, although the perceptual hash value of KS achieves the highest scores in both JitterBug and TRCTC, the discrimination of TRCTC is around 5 which is bigger than JitterBug about twice. The reason is that JitterBug do has difference in distribution between with Normal traffic thought slightly.

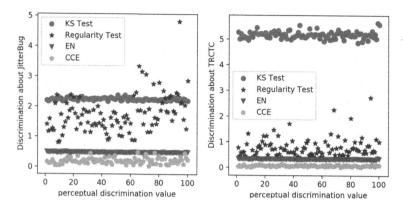

Fig. 3. Discrimination score of JitterBug and TRCTC

Robustness. Our first set of experiments investigates how perceptual hash value of KS and Regularity test perform in robustness. From Fig. 4, we can see that IPCTC achieve the maximum perceptual robustness value for KS. The robustness of TRCTC, L-N, JitterBug decrease in sequence. And normal traffic gets the minimum robustness in all the type of channels. the result shows that in KS test the distance between perceptual hash value of IPCTC is the smallest, which value ranges around [2.50, 2.75]. The reason is that the relatively fixed IPDs makes it get stables test score in KS. From the test we can see that all covert channels' test scores are more stable than normal.

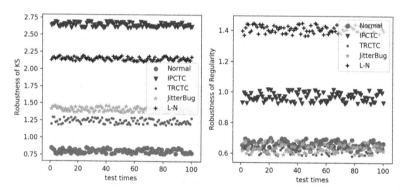

Fig. 4. Robustness score of KS and regularity

For perceptual hash value of Regularity test. In the robustness test of Regularity. L-N achieve the maximum perceptual robustness value. The robustness of IPCTC, Normal, TRCTC, JitterBug decrease in sequence. Regularity scores use change of standard deviation of IPDs to characterize covert channels. The construction method of L-N makes the number size of L-N's IPD relatively fixed. The result means that the standard deviation change of L-N is well described by the perceptual hash value of regularity. For the number size of normal channel data is highly variable, as well as

TRCTC and JitterBug, the standard deviation is changing by the time, regularity get low perceptual robustness value for IPCTC, TRCTC and JitterBug.

Our second set of robustness experiments investigates how perceptual hash value of EN and CCE test perform in robustness. The result shows in Fig. 5. In the robustness test of EN, L-N achieve the maximum perceptual robustness value, the robustness of TRCTC, IPCTC, Normal, JitterBug decrease in sequence. The construction method of L-N makes the number size of L-N's IPD relatively fixed. The result means that the loss of information of L-N is the least. The reason why Jitterbug has the worst robustness in entropy detection is that in the construction of jitterbug, we divide the data into many intervals according to the distribution of normal channel data. Information entropy is used to detect the consistency of packet interval data in different time intervals. Little changes caused by jitterbug to IPD data are common in normal channels. Therefore, jitterbug can't be detected by detecting the maximum distance of IPD cumulative distribution, such as KS test, but entropy is very sensitive to these changes in IPD. The data modification of jitterbug will change according to the different hidden bytes, and the proportion of data in different intervals will change. Therefore, the entropy robustness of the same jitterbug is the lowest, that is, the perception robustness of different jitterbug channels is poor.

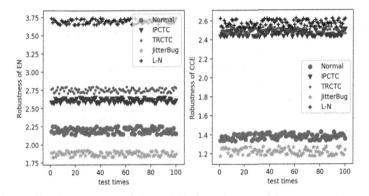

Fig. 5. Robustness score of EN and CCE

For perceptual hash value of CCE. CCE is the modified conditional entropy. In the robustness test of CCE, L-N achieve the maximum perceptual robustness value, the robustness of TRCTC, IPCTC, Normal, JitterBug decrease in sequence. Compared with the results of EN, CCE has the same pattern of decline, but they have difference, we can see that in the robustness detection of CCE, the robustness of TRCTC and IPCTC is almost unchanged, slightly reduced, while the robustness of L-N is much reduced in CCE. The robustness of normal and jitterbug is reduced to some extent. From all robustness to see, CCE have a good average robustness. The disadvantage of CCE is that the robustness value range of L-N, IPCTC, TRCTC are close, it may cause some difficulty in detection.

Detection. The detection step is divided into two parts. The first part is to obtain the threshold interval of all type of channels. In the second part, calculate its detection rates with *DValue* and *RValue*. The detection algorithm is described above. We call the four detections as PHV-KS, PHV-Regularity, PHV-CE and PHV-CCE for short. PHV is the abbreviation for perceptual hash value. We run detection of each test 100 time for 2000 packet samples of all type of channel.

First, the test of PHV-KS can detect the five channels effectively. Table 1 shows threshold and detection rate of PHV-KS for various channels. The *DValue* of JitterBug are separated with no overlap with others, which means that the samples' *DValue* falls into range of [2.156, 2.376] has a high probability of being JitterBug. The *DValue* of Normal and TRCTC are overlapped in the range of [4.863, 5.212], and the *DValue* of L-N and IPCTC are overlapped in the range of [0.666,0.736]. From the *DValue*, the test has good detection rate for JitterBug. When the *DValue* falls into the overlapped ranges above, the test can't detect the channels' type, such as L-N and IPCTC. But the *RValue* can help the further detection. The *RValue* of L-N and IPCTC are separated with non-overlapped ranges, which is the same for Normal and TRCTC. By calculating *RValue*, the test can detect the channels with overlapped *DValue*. For example, if the *RValue* of test sample falls into [2.114, 2.195], then type of tested sample is L-N rather than IPCTC.

Table 1. Threshold and detection rates of PHV-KS

	DValue	*RValue*	FPR	TPR
Normal	[3.803, 5.212]	[0.759, 0.855]	0.00	0.90
IPCTC	[0.666, 0.736]	[2.599, 2.697]	0.00	0.95
TRCTC	[4.863, 5.640]	[1.187, 1.295]	0.00	0.93
JitterBug	[2.156, 2.376]	[1.370, 1.464]	0.00	0.94
L-N	[0.642, 0.732]	[2.114, 2.195]	0.00	1.00

Second, the test of PHV-Regualrity can detect L-N and IPCTC effectively. Table 2 shows threshold and detection rate of PHV-Regularity. IPCTC has a wide range of *DValue*, which overlapped with the range of Normal, JitterBug, TRCTC. L-N also has a wide range of *DValue*, from 5.130 to 26.896. From Table 2, we can see that IPCTC and L-N have a separated range of *RValue* with others ranges, so IPCTC and L-N have a high detection rate. However, the *DValue* and *RValue* of Normal, JitterBug, TRCTC are all overlapped with the others two ranges. The detection of PHV-Regularity cannot detection the three type channels with other channels.

Third, the test of PHV-EN can detect JitterBug and L-N effectively. The detection of Normal, JitterBug and TRCTC, as shown in Table 3, are relatively low. Table 3 shows threshold and detection rate of PHV-EN. JitterBug and L-N both has a non-overlapping range of *DValue*, but Normal, IPCTC and TRCTC are all overlapped with the others two ranges. It's worth mentioning that the *DValue* of IPCTC is covered by the other two ranges. It means that the detection cannot detect IPCTC with Normal and

Table 2. Threshold and detection rates of PHV-Regularity

	DValue	RValue	FPR	TPR
Normal	[0.275, 1.782]	[0.615, 0.701]	0.05	0.04
IPCTC	[1.296, 8.007]	[0.925, 1.017]	0.1	1.00
TRCTC	[0.330, 2.732]	[0.585, 0.667]	0.1	0.03
JitterBug	[0.807, 4.827]	[0.594, 0.686]	0.1	0.02
L-N	[5.130, 26.896]	[1.365, 1.449]	0.1	1.00

TRCTC by *DValue*. From Table 3, we can see that all types channels have a separated range of *RValue* with others ranges. Thought Normal, IPCTC and TRCTC can't detected by *DValue*, the non-overlapping *RValue* improve their detection.

Table 3. Threshold and detection rates of PHV-EN

	DValue	RValue	FPR	TPR
Normal	[0.311, 0.356]	[2.137, 2.251]	0.05	0.53
IPCTC	[0.335, 0.353]	[2.563, 2.643]	0.1	0.72
TRCTC	[0.319, 0.368]	[2.704, 2.794]	0.05	0.50
JitterBug	[0.435, 0.508]	[1.822, 1.920]	0.00	1.00
L-N	[3.004, 3.286]	[3.646, 3.737]	0.00	1.00

Finally, the test of PHV-CCE can detect JitterBug and Normal effectively. The detection of Normal, JitterBug and TRCTC, as shown in Table 4, are relatively low. Table 4 shows threshold and detection rate of PHV-EN. All type of channels has overlapped range of *DValue*, especially for TRCTC. The *DValue* of TRCTC is covered by L-N. From Table 8, we can see that JitterBug and Normal have a separated range of *RValue* with others ranges, TRCTC has an overlapped range of *RValue* with others ranges. The *RValue* of IPCTC and L-N aren't overlapped. We can see the detection has a high detection in Normal and JitterBug.

Table 4. Threshold and detection rates of PHV-CCE

	DValue	RValue	FPR	TPR
Normal	[0.029, 0.280]	[1.333, 1.424]	0.00	0.90
IPCTC	[0.012, 0.133]	[2.425, 2.511]	0.05	0.56
TRCTC	[0.017, 0.141]	[2.456, 2.540]	0.1	0.57
JitterBug	[0.030, 0.475]	[1.169, 1.273]	0.00	1.00
L-N	[0.019, 0.141]	[2.523, 2.624]	0.05	0.50

5 Conclusion and Future Work

In this paper, we introduce the perceptual hash method and analyze the discrimination and robustness of four features of normal traffic and covert traffic with the perceptual hash theory. Among the four detection methods, the PHV-KS have good discrimination for JitterBug and good robustness for all five types channels. The discrimination of detection PHV-Regularity works good for L-N, and its robustness works good for IPCTC and L-N. The discrimination of detection PHV-EN works good for L-N and JitterBug, and its robustness works good for all five types channels. The PHV-CCE have good robustness for JitterBug and Normal, but it works not good in its discrimination. From the detection result, we know that different perceptual hash value works different in discrimination and robustness. In the future works, we hope to focus on extracting better features, which is in accordance with the perceptual hash property and can better used in Muti-Detection of channels based on this paper.

References

1. Cabuk, S.: Network covert channels: design, analysis, detection, and elimination. ETD Collection for Purdue University (2006)
2. Girling, C.G.: Covert channels in LAN's. IEEE Trans. Softw. Eng. **13**(2), 292–296 (1987)
3. Cabuk, S., Brodley, C.E., Shields, C.: IP covert channel detection. ACM Trans. Inf. Syst. Secur. **12**(4), 1–29 (2009)
4. Peng, P., Ning, P., Reeves, D.S.: On the secrecy of timing-based active watermarking trace-back techniques. In: IEEE Symposium on Security and Privacy (S&P), vol. 15 (2006)
5. Gianvecchio, S., Wang, H.: An entropy-based approach to detecting covert timing channels. IEEE Trans. Dependable Secure Comput. **8**(6), 785–797 (2011)
6. Shrestha, P.L., Hempel, M., Rezaei, F., Sharif, H.: A support vector machine-based framework for detection of covert timing channels. IEEE Trans. Dependable Secure Comput. **13**(2), 274–283 (2016). https://doi.org/10.1109/TDSC.2015.2423680
7. Chen, L., Li, Z., Yang, J.F.: Compressive perceptual hashing tracking. Neurocomputing **239**, 69–80 (2017)
8. Neelima, A., Singh, K.M., et al.: Perceptual hash function based on scale-invariant feature transform and singular value decomposition. Comput. J. **59**(9), 1275–1281 (2016)
9. Wang, X., Pang, K., Zhou, X., et al.: A visual model-based perceptual image hash for content authentication. IEEE Trans. Inf. Forensics Secur. **10**(7), 1336–1349 (2015)
10. Ji, J., Yao, Y., Wei, J., Han, L., et al.: Perceptual hashing for SAR segmentation. Int. J. Remote Sens. **40**(9–10), 3672–3688 (2019)
11. Qin, C., Sun, M., Chang, C.: Perceptual hashing for color images based on hybrid extraction of structural features. Signal Processing **142**, 194–205 (2018)
12. Fang, W., Hu, H.M., Hu, Z.H.: Perceptual hash-based feature description for person re-identification. Neurocomputing **272**, 520–531 (2018)
13. Saikia, N., Bora, P.K.: Perceptual hash function for scalable video. Int. J. Inf. Secur. **13**(1), 81–93 (2013). https://doi.org/10.1007/s10207-013-0211-z
14. Major, R.D.: Pre-distribution identification of broadcast television content using audio fingerprints (2014)

15. Yang, G., Chen, X., Yang, D.: Efficient music identification by utilizing space-saving audio fingerprinting system. In: IEEE International Conference on Multimedia and Expo (ICME), pp. 1–6 (2014)
16. Cabuk, S., Brodley, C.E., Shields, C.: IP covert timing channels: design and detection. In: Proceedings of the 11th ACM Conference on Computer and Communications Security (CCS), pp. 178–187 (2004)
17. Sellke, S.H., Wang, C.-C., Bagchi, S., Shroff, N.: TCP/IP timing channels: theory to implementation. IEEE INFOCOM, 2204–2212 (2009)
18. Shah, G., Molina, A., Blaze, M.: Keyboards and covert channels. In: Proceedings of the 15th USENIX Security Symposium. 59–75 (2006)

Deep Learning-Based Dew Computing with Novel Offloading Strategy

Md Noman Bin Khalid(✉)

College of Computer Science and Technology, Nanjing University
of Aeronautics and Astronautics, Nanjing 210016, Jiangsu, China
noman01930@gmail.com

Abstract. Deep learning applications are prevalent. Its popularity is increasing day by day. But the deep learning model cannot be efficiently run with any device. If we want to take advantage of this up to low-level devices, we have to find a unique way. Dew Computing (DC) has arisen as a modern computational paradigm, Wide Cloud Storage acceptability. This paper has shown how to use an offloading strategy and use the dew computing layer to efficiently run a deep learning application without the internet at low latency. Moreover, we also showed how a deep learning model could have an online impact when it comes to training and how long it takes to train.

Keywords: Dew computing · Fog computing · Cloud computing · Offloading strategy · Deep learning

1 Introduction

With the advancement of the next decade's mobile wireless network infrastructure, many data are generating day by day. In this modern era, we need data for a better business process and a reduction in wasted time and resources. For that, we need to store all of our data and have to access any time when we want. For that purpose, Cloud computing is first invented for data storage and is making a significant shift in the technological world with that idea. Professor Ramnath Chellappa first coined the term cloud computing in 1997 and explained it as a novel computing model. And after that, cloud computing became popular with Amazon.com launches the first Elastic Disk Cloud in 2006 [1]. But it's can't possible to transfer data without the Internet.

After that, several cloud computing jobs were done, and Edge computing, fog computing, was invented, and now the latest concept is Dew computing. All of these are working like clouds. Fog is considered as a layer between the user and the Cloud. The Edge is very close to the users [1, 2]. Most researchers have been working on Edge, fog, and Cloud computing and developing new models or structures to make the data transfer method simpler. Dew computing is a new area in this modern world, and it works as a Highly distributed computing for the user [3]. We can make a novel offloading system model that can show a new area using a deep model to make the data transfer system more versatile. It is imperative to make it easy to transmit data, and for this, it is crucial to create a good network infrastructure that can function efficiently. Our work's most significant plus point is that the Dew server can access data using a

© Springer Nature Switzerland AG 2021
G. Wang et al. (Eds.): SpaCCS 2020, LNCS 12383, pp. 444–453, 2021.
https://doi.org/10.1007/978-3-030-68884-4_37

deep model with an offloading strategy for low-level devices. This article presents a system model that will explain how easily data can be transmitted from the end-user to the Dew server and use a deep neural network that makes the optimum route more fixable to data transmission.

2   Research Background

Cloud computing is an on-demand computer system resource availability without direct user management, particularly data storage (cloud storage) and computer power. The term is usually used to describe data centers for many Internet users [4]. In short, cloud storage requires the storage of data over the Internet rather than a hard drive. Cloud computing provides various model services, but the standard models are Infrastructure as a Service, Platform as a Service (PaS), and Software as a Service [5]. Cloud computing creates new problems and has significantly transformed the whole IT industry. However, the low latency and time-consuming crisis cannot be addressed in cloud storage.

A lot of people are working on this to find the right solution to this problem. For this purpose, Cisco has first launched Fog Computing, which is closer to users and will minimize the time it takes to transmit data. Fog Computing is a horizontal system architecture that provides the Cloud-to-Thing continuum with computing, storage, control, and networking functions closer to users [6]. In the IOx platform at CISCO, the idea of fog computing took shape. Fog is the name that CISCO invented. It's a layer in both devices and the cloud. Fog reduces the time needed for data in the cloud to be transferred or received. As a means of driving cloud computing technologies to the edge of the network, Cisco launched the fog technology concept in January 2014. The primary purpose of Fog Computing was to improve performance through the transmission of data directly to a network such as an IoT device or a network router. Fog computing is an advanced technological approach that addresses many Internet devices' demands, often called the Internet of Things (IoT) [5]. In this current environment, Fog computing will also play a significant role in the growth of 5G mobile networks and utilities and enhanced website efficiency. The Open Fog Consortium is essential for further development, research, and fog computing [7].

Dew Computing is an on-premises, program equipment association worldview in the distributed computing condition where the on-premises PC gives usefulness autonomous cloud benefits and is collaborating with cloud services. The objective of Dew Computing is to realize the potential of computers and cloud services on-site fully [3]. Dew Computing relies on Dew-Cloud architecture, which combines the power of cloud computing with Dew computing. Using the dew server, users can transfer data without an internet connection. Dew Computing was also proposed as a Post-Cloud Paradigm for Computing. Some researchers have already suggested different Dew-Cloud architecture types to share data information to end-users when there is no internet connection [8]. The Dew server is located on a local computer and serves a single client with the services offered by the cloud server. The database of the dew server must be synchronized with the database of the cloud server. Dew applications are not entirely online and must use cloud computing services and exchange information automatically with them while performing. The Dropbox, OneDrive, and Google Drive Offline are an example of dew applications. Users can use their services regardless of connection to the Internet and synchronize with cloud services [7]. The difference between fog computing and dew computing is fog computing involving automation devices with on-site computers and dew computing involved. As an example, fog computing involves routers and sensors in the Internet of Things (IoT), while dew computing is primarily engaged with computers (Fig. 1).

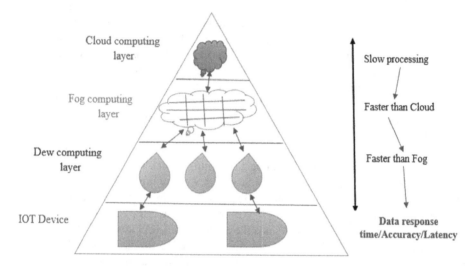

Fig. 1. Distributed computing hierarchy

Computation offloading is the transfer of resource-intensive computing errands to a different processor, such as a hardware accelerator or an outer stage, such as a cluster, grid, or cloud [9]. To quicken applications, including image rendering and numerical estimations, offloading to a co-processor can be used. Offloading computation to an outdoor stage over a network can deliver computing power and overcome device hardware constraints, such as limited computing power, storage, and energy [10]. We will show a novel offloading process on Dew computer networking based on Deep neural networks.

3   Methodology

3.1   Overview

In this chapter, we will explain how everything is done. It contains the design of our project, which has been depicted using a block diagram. Besides, it broadly discusses the theories of the dew, cloud, edge, and offloading strategies and how it is implemented. Moreover, this chapter not only shows the approaches but also shows the relationship of every component. Finally, this chapter explains in detail the proposed system model.

3.2   Problem Statement

As we know, the popularity and usability of deep learning models are increasing day by day. Like mobile devices and IoT devices, many end-users cannot use deep learning models [10]. And if there is no internet, it's challenging to use everything together. We show the optimal solution to use deep learning applications using the dew cloud paradigm with an offloading strategy. We are looking to reduce memory space, less latency to transfer data, and minimize computational time.

3.3   System Model

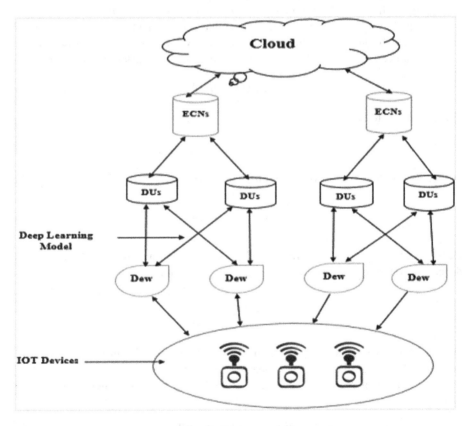

Fig. 2. System model

Mainly, three different sections integrated the system model. These are offloading framework, dew-cloud architecture, and computational time of a deep learning model (Fig. 2).

HOM (Heuristic Offloading Method) is an offloading framework for deep learning edge services for fast internet [10]. It shows the optimal computation offloading by heuristically placing the deep learning tasks to the appropriate computing infrastructure [10]. Tasks are transmitted to the local ECN and then the best ECN and the cloud offloading method. HOM confirms shortest way of offloading from every initial and destination ECNs, depending on the distribution of ECNs. HOM stops spending time waiting for ECNs' services and considers the perfect destination to maximize download speed VM from ECNs and cloud.

The offloading framework is divided into five parts: Cloud, Edge computing nodes (ECNs), Distributed unit (DUs), Dew, and IoT Devices. As we know, Cloud, furnished with adaptable figuring computing assets, is impressive to execute the deep learning models by utilizing Virtual Machines (VMs) that are being used for facilitating the profound learning model [11]. ECNs, co-located with a centralized unit (CU), which have similar functions with cloud, are edge computing nodes, where a certain number of Virtual Machines (VMs) with deep learning models are installed.

Here the Dew is working as a third-party offline server. The ECNs receive a mass of data produced by the surrounding Mobile devices (MDs) through the dew server.

When a deep learning task (p_n) is connected with a DU instance, the relation is:

$$f_n^m = \{1, \text{where true } 0, \text{otherwise} \tag{1}$$

Thus, for ECN to DUs

$$I_m^k = \{1, \text{where true } 0, \text{otherwise} \tag{2}$$

In this case, ECN instants connect with DUs instances.

$$\text{So now, MT}(z_n) = \frac{da_n}{\lambda_n^m} \tag{3}$$

Here is the size of all deep learning tasks and λ_n^m is the transmission rate. $MT(z_n)$ is depended on the transmission rate among MDs, DUs and da_n.

$$\text{Thus, } DT(z_n) = \frac{da_n}{\lambda_m^k} \tag{4}$$

Where, λ_m^k is transmission rate between ECN instance and DUs instance. The calculation of $MT(z_n)$ and $DT(z_n)$ has similar mathematical formula.

Finally, the paper showed a summation of all delay time as latency, and that is:

$$T_n = \sum_{m=1}^{m} \sum_{k=1}^{k} f_n^m I_m^k (MT(z_n) + WT(z_n) + DT(z_n) + CT(z_n)) \tag{5}$$

Here, T_n is the offloading time, the calculation of $WT(z_n)$ is decided by the time of the other tasks that are transmitted before p_n taking up DU and the calculation of $CT(z_n)$ is divided into two cases in terms of the location of the destination VM of p_n [10].

And,

$$T_{all} = \sum_1^m T_n \tag{6}$$

Where, T_{all} is the total offloading time and m is for all deep learning tasks [10].

In their case, they showed a relation between MDs and DUs. In our case, we have added a new layer, which is a dew layer. We are assuming the Dew layer as the same number of a component as MDs was, and the rate of transmission of data is the same because Dew exists in a local server or local PC [14]. To address cloud computing systems' data usability issue, the Dew cloud architecture has been introduced, and we want to be more transparent as these servers are delivering cloud services. Yingwei Wang's concept for Dew-cloud architecture is the primary design pursued by investigators. The dew cloud infrastructure is a customer-server software extension. It presents a structured scheme for the organization, combining the use of such local information/programs with web browsing operations smoothly and optimizing the synchronization between local information/program and the cloud, the main contribution to the dew-cloud architecture [8].

4 Dataset and Deep Learning Model

The CIFAR-10 data set consists of six hundred thousand 32×32 color images in 10 classes with six hundred images per category. We have 50000 training images and 10000 test images. The dataset consists of five training batches and one batch, each of which contains 10,000 images. Exactly 1000 random images from every class are in the test batch. There are random pictures in the training batches, but some training batches may contain several more photos from one type than from another. There are precisely 5000 images of each class in the training batches.

We used a prevalent vgg16 model as our reference model for a deep learning application (Table 1).

The input for layer conv1, as can be seen, is the fixed-sized picture 224×224 RGB. The image passes through a stack of convolution layers (Conv.) with filters using a tiny field of reception: 33 (the smallest size to capture the idea of left/right, right/down, central). It also uses a 1×1 convolution filter in one of the configurations that can be considered a linear transformation channel (followed by non-linearity). The convolution step is set to 1 pixel; space padding is arranged. The layer's input is such that the spatial resolution is preserved after convolution, i.e., the padding is 1-pixel for 3×3 Conv. Layers. Five layers of max pooling, following some invaders, perform spatial pooling—the layers (all Conv layers do not follow the max-pool). Max pooling is performed over a 2-pixel window, step 2 [13].

Table 1. Architecture of VGG-16

Layer	Patch size	Input size
conv×2	3×3/1	3×224×224
pool	2×2	64×224×224
conv×2	3×3/1	64×112×112
pool	2×2	128×112×112
conv×3	3×3/1	128×56×56
pool	2×2	256×56×56
conv×3	3×3/1	256×28×28
pool	2×2	512×28×28
conv×3	3×3/1	512×14×14
pool	2×2	512×14×14
fc	25088×4096	25088
fc	4096×4096	4096
fc	4096×2	4096
softmax	classifier	2

Finally, we performed a softmax for image classification in our case with the cifr_10 dataset in VGG16's final layer [13]. Our interest in time computing per epoch occurred in the cloud. We try to see under which batch sizes of data, the time it usually takes to complete to train.

5   Result and Discussion

Since we divided our system model into three parts, we counted the result in three-parts as well. Firstly, we refer to the HOM strategy that we refer to in the methodology section. We found that the system Compares the total computation offloading transmission delay, the number of employed VMs in ECNs, the range of running time, and the content of data volume [10]. Where all the parameters were significantly better than other offloading strategies, the result shows, by following this offloading strategy, the data can quickly transfer from cloud to Dew and vice-versa.

According to HOM's paper, the total latency of HOM for 500 deep learning tasks is about less than 500 ms, where Computation offloading (CO) and local offloading (LO) strategy surpasses 500 ms. Besides, the total number of employed VMs is also greater than LO. Which means, by this offloading strategy, we can transfer the data faster, and since the VMs and ECN capacity is more generous than other offloading schemes, we can run more deep learning tasks at a time [10].

We have developed a classification model. Our interest is in the computation time while training a batch of data. We have passed the different sizes of batches of data as a parameter in our model, and we saw the changes in time concerning the size of batches per epoch (Fig. 3).

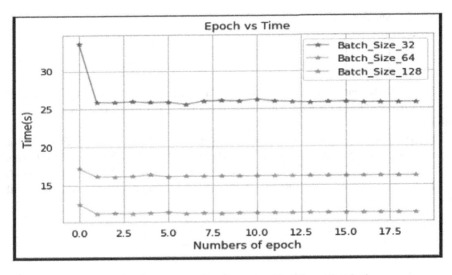

Fig. 3. Training time vs. Epoch graph with different batch size

As we can see, the size of 64 batches is significantly smaller than 32. And the accuracy tradeoff is okay as well. However, for batch size 128, computation time is less than any other model. But for accuracy trade-off, we may use 64 batch sizes in deep learning models in a time of training or more than that (Table 2).

Table 2. Low processor device

Device name	RAM	Storage	Speed
Samsung Galaxy J2	1GB	8GB	1.3GHz quad-core
Xiaomi Amazfit Bip	1MB SDRAM	4MB, Flash (EEPROM)	208Mhz Single-Core ARM Cortex-M4
Arduino Uno SMD R3	SRAM	Flash, EEPROM	Atmel AVR (8-bit), ARM Cortex-M0+ (32-bit), ARM Cortex-M3 (32-bit), Intel Quark (x86) (32-bit)

On the other hand, Google Colab's cloud computer has a memory of up to 12 GB and Tesla NVIDIA K80 GPU which is continuously up to 12 h.

If we equate the lower device to the high configuration cloud device, we can see that, because of lower RAM, fewer clock speeds and less computational speed, it's difficult to train deep learning tasks. But we can train the deep learning algorithms in the lower device through our aim model.

The online impact is an index that measures the Internet's effect on a node on the Internet [12].

So, the equation is:

$$I = \log_2 \frac{U}{V} \tag{7}$$

Here, I is the online impact of a node on the Internet; U indicates the amount of information available to a node if this node is online; V is similar to U except that it is offline [12].

In our model, we have 60000 images with 32×32 sizes and 3 channels for training the model. So, the size of the data $60000 \times 32 \times 32 \times 3 = 184320000$ bytes or 184 MB. And in the Cloud, we can assume more or less 10 GB data stored though it's higher than that on a specific cloud. So, U = 10 GB and V = 512 MB, the local device's available storage.

$$\text{So, } I = \log_2 \frac{10}{0.5} = 4.32 \tag{8}$$

So, the more the value of U, the more the online impact and vice-versa.

When the Internet becomes not available, it could significantly impact one user, but have a less severe impact on another user. There are different stages of internet development. These are the mainframe stage, the cloud computing stage, and the dew computing stage. In the mainframe stage, major computing tasks were done by each node. In the cloud computing stage, major computing tasks are done at the server-side [12]. In the dew computing stage, the dew server and related databases on a node provide useful information to the user. The whole dew mechanism increased the V value, and thus decreased the online impact.

Another subjective index is the redundancy rate that measures how much information on a node has a copy on the Internet [12].

$$\text{Which denotes, } R = \frac{w}{v} \tag{9}$$

Where R is the redundancy rate, V is the node's free data sum, and W is the measure of data inside V that has a duplicate on the Internet [12].

In the dew computing stage, the dew server and related databases on a node provide useful information to the user. These dew components are supported by the cloud servers and synchronized with the cloud servers; these dew components all have redundant copies [14]. If the node has completely adopted dew computing, all the available information in this node would be dew component information. Since all the dew components have redundant copies on the Internet, the redundancy rate would be 100%. If the node also contains information other than that related to dew computing, the redundancy rate could be less than 100% [12]. We can conclude that dew computing significantly increases the redundancy rate. If dew computing components dominate the node, the redundancy rate could be close to 100% [12].

Using a subjective index, we can conclude that dew computing is a solution to minimize internet dependency. The offloading strategy is used for transferring the into the node in low latency. With this system model, we can easily use any deep learning application using any low-level devices such as Mobile devices (MDs) or IoT.

6 Conclusion and Future Work

For dynamic and deep computation, we have found a successful approach. We will reach the new age of digital technology quickly with its introduction. We can run complicated things, like deep learning models, on our phones or IoT devices, less dependent on the cloud, and the Internet. As the dew computing system is a possible technology and researchers are working on it, we will look at this technology more closely to enable the whole system to be applied without harm. Thus, we want to improve and use this system model in the future. We want a new age for the human race.

References

1. Kukreja, P., Sharma, D.: A detail review on cloud, fog and dew computing. Int. J. Sci. Eng. Technol. Res. (IJSETR) 5(5), 1412–1420 (2016)
2. Pan, Y., Thulasiraman, P., Wang, Y.: Overview of cloudlet, fog computing, edge computing, and dew computing. In: Proceedings of the 3rd International Workshop on Dew Computing, pp. 20–23 (2018)
3. Wang, Y.: Definition and categorization of dew computing. Open J. Cloud Comput. (OJCC) 3(1), 1–7 (2016)
4. Mell, P., Grance, T.: The NIST Definition of Cloud Computing. NIST Special Publication 800-145 (2011)
5. Skala, K., Davidovic, D., Afgan, E., Sovic, I., Sojat, Z.: Scalable distributed computing hierarchy: cloud, fog and dew computing. Open J. Cloud Comput. 2(1), 16–24 (2015)
6. Mahmood, Z., Ramachandran, M.: Fog computing: concepts, principles and related paradigms. In: Mahmood, Z. (ed.) Fog Computing, pp. 3–21. Springer, Cham (2018). https://doi.org/10.1007/978-3-319-94890-4_1
7. Loncar, P.: Data-intensive computing paradigms for big data. In: Annals of DAAAM and Proceedings of the International DAAAM Symposium, vol. 29, no. 1, pp. 1010–1018 (2018)
8. Wang, Y.: Cloud-dew architecture. Int. J. Cloud Comput. 4(3), 199 (2015)
9. Kang, J., Eom, D.S.: Offloading and transmission strategies for IoT edge devices and networks. Sensors (Switzerland) 19(4), 835 (2019)
10. Xu, X., Li, D., Dai, Z., Li, S., Chen, X.: A heuristic offloading method for deep learning edge services in 5G networks. IEEE Access 7, 67734–67744 (2019)
11. Huang, Y., Ma, X., Fan, X., Liu, J., Gong, W.: When deep learning meets edge computing. In: IEEE 25th International Conference on Network Protocols (ICNP), vol. 1, pp. 1–2 (2017)
12. Wang, Y., Skala, K., Rindos, A., Gusev, M., Yang, S., Pan, Y.: Dew computing and transition of internet computing paradigms. ZTE Commun. 15(4), 30–37 (2017)
13. Simonyan, K., Zisserman, A.: Very deep convolutional networks for large-scale image recognition. In: 3rd International Conference on Learning Representations (ICLR), p. 14 (2015)
14. Pan, Y., Luo, G.: ZTE communications special issue on cloud computing, fog computing, and dew computing. ZTE Commun. 14(4), 14–15 (2017)

Detecting Credential Stuffing
Between Servers

Qi Zhang[✉]

College of Computer Science and Technology, Nanjing University
of Aeronautics and Astronautics, Nanjing 211106, China
15807194710@163.com

Abstract. The goal of Detecting Credential Stuffing is to detect the
Credential Stuffing attack in time and effectively. Based on OT and
Cuckoo Filter, an effective credential stuffing detection protocol is proposed in this paper. The protocol involves two servers holding a collection
of suspect credentials, get the result by private set intersection. By executing this protocol, the inquirer gets the same elements of both sets
without knowing anything about the other elements in the other set,
and the responder does not get any additional information. The validity,
correctness and safety of the scheme under the semi-honesty model are
verified by theoretical analysis.

Keywords: Credential stuffing · Detection compromised credentials ·
Private set intersection

1 Introduction

With the widespread use of social networks, financial records and data stored
in the cloud by Internet users, there is often only one account that supports
the security of the entire identity. The root of this trust can be undermined by
the exposure or recovery of the victim's email password. Once compromised, the
hijacker can reset the victim's password to another service and use it as a spring-
board for attack. Downloading personal information of all victims; Removals of
victim data and backups; Or impersonate a victim and send spam or worse.

In recent years, a large number of user account credentials have been leaked
through various means (password database leaks, phishing and so on). As many
as 2.3 billion leaked credentials were reported in 2017, and hundreds of millions
of credential padding attacks were observed every day in 2018, targeting various industries such as social media, entertainment, gaming and retail. Because
people tend to reuse their passwords on different sites, such a breach puts other
accounts at risk. Attackers use one or more leaked passwords from other sites
to try to break into accounts. This type of attack is called a credential padding
attack. Credential padding has become one of the main ways attackers take over
accounts, allowing them to steal stored data, credit information and other personal information. It costs 3.85 million dollers a year to fill in corporate defense

© Springer Nature Switzerland AG 2021
G. Wang et al. (Eds.): SpaCCS 2020, LNCS 12383, pp. 454–464, 2021.
https://doi.org/10.1007/978-3-030-68884-4_38

credentials. Estimates of actual losses are 1.7 billion dollers, 400 million dollers, 300 million dollers, and 6 billion dollers a year in consumer finance, hotels, airlines, and retail.

Password reuse is an important reason why credential stuffing attacks work, and many users are reluctant to stop password reuse even with explicit warnings [1]. Because of the strict password requirements, users will reuse the same password on the site in order to cope with the cognitive burden of creating and remembering a strong password [2]. According to the report, it took an average of 15 months to detect and report certificate leaks in 2017 [1]. The longer the time interval between the voucher being leaked to the report, the greater the damage caused by the leak. Therefore, it is necessary to find a timely means to detect the credentials stuffing attack.

For this purpose, we propose a framework through this framework, the website can get the compromised credential set used by the credential stuffing attacker by interacting with other members in the protocol by detecting the suspicious set itself. At present, a number of efforts have been made to enable websites to take advantage of features other than the input password to distinguish between legitimate users and attackers' login attempts with better accuracy [3,4]. Therefore, our framework is based on the application scenario in which the website obtains a collection of detected suspicious credentials, and we want to judge whether there is a credential stuffing attack based on this.

Our Main Contributions: we proposed a new private set intersection protocol to ensure that the servers in the protocol don;t get any information except the intersection when they interact.

To sum up, our contributions are as follows:

1) We have developed a new framework that enables websites to detect credential stuffing attacks by obtaining suspicious collection intersections. The detection rate of the algorithm is estimated by probability model.
2) We instantiate the framework with a new PSI protocol that ensures security under the semi-trust model and reduces computational complexity.

2   Related Work

OT and PSI: At present, some OT Based Private Set Intersection protocols have been proposed, such as [5–7] etc. This paper refers to the application ideas of OT and PSI in [7] and [8], and proposes a new PSI protocol according to the requirements of the framework.

Other Credential Stuffing Methods: Methods to detect credential stuffing have been proposed, such as PMT (private Membership test) queries, essential to the proper functioning of a C3 server [9], and PMT queries based on account identifier [4], etc. This paper refers to some of the ideas mentioned above and propose a new framework to detect credential stuffing attacks between servers.

2.1 Cuckoo Filter

According to the research of [10], Cuckoo Filter is a kind of filter with better efficiency than bloom filter, is a kind of filter with high space utilization, which meets the requirements of our protocol. Therefore, we propose a new PSI protocol based on Cuckoo Filter [10] and ROT [7], which controls the communication complexity within the acceptable range while having lower computational complexity and storage space.

Cuckoo Filter stores element e in buckets $hash(e)$ or $hash(e) \oplus hash$ $(fingerprint(e))$. Therefore, the Reverse operation is set for the Cuckoo Filter as: insert each $fingerprint(e)$ in the Filter bucket $index$ into $index \oplus hash(fingerprint(e))$ bucket of a new Filter table. In this paper, ROT and Cuckoo Filter are applied to THE PSI protocol by using the Cuckoo Filter and the reverse of Filter, so as to obtain higher efficiency and space utilization.

3 Detecting Credential Stuffing

In this section, we provide a framework for detecting credential stuffing attacks between servers. By intersecting the list of accounts held by the server with questionable behavior, the accounts that may be subject to attack can be inferred.

3.1 Problem Description

Credential Stuffing: Credential stuffing is a kind of network attack in which a stolen account Credential, typically composed of a user name/email address and corresponding password, usually from a data breach, is used to gain unauthorized access to a user account through a massive automated login request to a Web application. Unlike credential cracking, credential stuffing attack does not attempt to brute force or guess any passwords – an attacker simply gets a collection of leaked credentials and tries to log in using standard Web automation tools. The validity of credential stuffing attacks depends on the behavior of users using the same password on different sites. We can summarize the characteristics of such attacks: the number of credentials filling attacks is extremely large, totaling 30 billion malicious logins from November 2017 to June 2018, averaging 3.75 billion per month [2].

Moreover, the success rate of credential stuffing is not linearly dependent on the size of the set held by the attacker, but rather on the source of the leaked credentials. From the perspective of users' usage of strong passwords and password reuse habits [11], attackers should use a leak set containing users' strong passwords to attack high-value servers if they want to improve the attack success rate. Therefore, a protocol proposed in this paper could be reached between servers holding high-value information to identify possible Credential stuffing attacks for the purpose of speeding up the reporting time of leaking credentials and reducing risk.

With the increasing occurrence of credential leakage events and the increasing number of attacks, it is difficult for the server to judge the Credential stuffing attack from a large number of abnormal login behaviors simply through its own security measures. But failure to promptly determine a Credential stuffing attack and mount a counter-measure could result in a loss of account value.

This attack is characterized by attacks on accounts through compromised credentials. Therefore, it is very important to detect and report compromised credentials in time in order to achieve the goal of defensive credential stuffing attack. An important idea for detecting credential stuffing attacks between servers is that if a credential is detected on two or more servers for abnormal login attempt, then it can be considered as a compromised credential that attackers use to attack multiple servers.

Report Compromised Credentials: Once the compromised credentials are publicly reported, servers can take security measures through the reported credentials, and achieve the effect of defence credentials stuffing attack. However, in the current statistics, the cycle from the leak to the detection report is very long. For attackers, the long life cycle of leak voucher can be used to do more damage. Therefore, to limit the credential stuffing attack, it is essential to shorten the detection and reporting time of leaked credentials.

In summary, to achieve the purpose of detecting credential stuffing attacks between servers and defending against such attacks, we need a technical method to help calculate the intersection of the credentials used for abnormal logins recorded by the servers, and the obtained intersection will be reported as the leaked credentials. In this way, all servers can take corresponding measures against the leaked credentials to achieve the effect of defending the credentials stuffing attack.

3.2 Our Protocol

To solve this problem, we proposed a new protocol to obtain a collection of highly dubious credentials by using PSI to obtain the intersection between servers. With the proliferation of leaked credentials, the number of attackers who holding leaked credentials increases, and the successful detection rate of the protocol will be higher. The attack description for compromised credentials is shown in Fig. 1.

Therefore, we proposed a protocol to detect credentials stuffing between servers, as shown in Fig. 2. After the server obtains a set of suspicious credentials, it issues PSI request to other servers that also participate in the protocol, and calculates the intersection of suspicious sets, with the proliferation of compromise credentials, the success rate of protocol detection will increase.

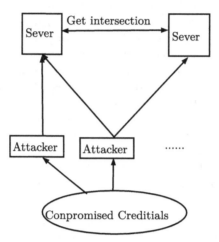

Fig. 1. Attacks based on compromised credentials

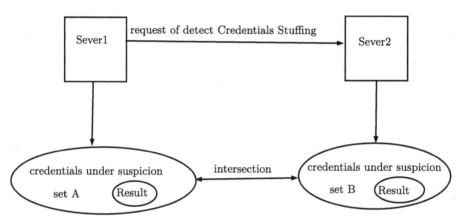

Fig. 2. Executes the protocol between servers

System Model: Our protocol involves multiple servers, each holding suspicious credentials for unusual logins that they detect, and they want to know which of these are the leaked credentials used in the credential stuffing attack. For a server holding a suspicious collection, it periodically issue queries to other servers in the protocol. The data in the intersection obtained by PSI means that these credentials appear in the suspicious collection of more than one server, indicating that these credentials belong to the leaked credentials, on which the server takes security measures and reports those leaked credentials. As leaked credentials spread, the likelihood that servers in the protocol will be attacked by the same credentials will increase, so the detection of leaked credentials will become more accurate.

According to the four life cycles of leaked credentials proposed in the [1], with the expansion of the group holding leaked credentials, it is more likely that multiple servers participating in the protocol will be attacked by the leaked credentials. Through the interactive system of this protocol, these servers can get the account attacked by credential stuffing and leaked credentials from the result of the intersection of suspicious collections of each other. This protocol is more timely than C3 queries [9] because it detects leaked credentials without depending on whether the C3 server has it, and this protocol has lower storage pressure than detecting leaked credentials [4] based on account identifiers.

Security Model: The security of the protocol depends on the characteristics of PSI, and the server issuing the request cannot obtain any information other than the intersection information, so there is no security threat to the data other than the intersection of the responders.

Design Goal: The protocol in this paper is designed to help the server to interact with one or more other servers in the protocol based on the detected suspicious credential set, determine whether it has suffered from the credential filling attack, and detect the leaked credentials to report these credentials in time.

3.3 Server

There are some existing technologies to distinguish user login attempts from malicious login attempts [4,12]. Therefore, our protocol is based on the premise that the server has obtained a suspicious set through its own security measures, and we hope to determine which accounts in the suspicious set are subject to the credentials stuffing attack. The server should have added a protocol for the purpose of detecting credential stuffing, and interact with other servers in the protocol holding suspicious collections to obtain an intersection that is highly likely to be attacked by credential stuffing.

3.4 ROT

In previous works, the core idea of ROT based PSI was to transform the PSI problem into PMT sub-problems [5,7,8]. Our PSI protocol has the similar idea as those except that we use Cuckoo Filter instead. We will use 1-out-of-N-ROT on L bit string, Let C be a public linear error correcting code that has at least κ Hamming distance [8].

3.5 Private Set Intersection

Our PSI algorithm is described in Algorithm 1:

Algorithm 1. PSI based on OT and cuckoo filter

Input:

  Input of P1:X={x1...xn1};
  Input of P2:Y={y1...yn2};
  $b \leftarrow$ bucket size;
  $m \leftarrow$ bucket number;
  $Hash() \leftarrow$ a hash function for Cuckoo filter;
  $F \leftarrow$ Fingerprint length;
  $\kappa \leftarrow$ symmetric security parameter;
  $\lambda \leftarrow$ statistical security parameter;
  $L \leftarrow$ mask length $L = \lambda + 1 + 2\log_2 b + log_2 m$;
  $H() \leftarrow$ hash function $H() : \{0,1\}^F \rightarrow \{0,1\}^L$.
  Oracles and cryptographic primitives:
  Both parties have access to a $\binom{1}{N} - ROT_L^1$ functionality.

Output:

  Filter:

1: P1 inserts X into a Cuckoo Filter CF1 using Hash(), and reverses the CF1 to obtain CF0;
2: P2 inserts Y into a Cuckoo Filter CF2 using Hash();
  ROT evaluation:
3: $f_1[i][j]$ represents the jth fingerprint in $bucket[i]$ on $CF1(1 \le j \le b)$,$f_0[i][p]$ and $f_2[i][q]$ represents fingerprints on $CF0$ and $CF2$, respectively.
4: For each $w_q = f_2[i][q]$, each $u_j = f_0[i][p]/f_1[i][j]$,use w_q and u_j as the selection vector for ROT,with each ROT interaction, P1 gets a random key t_k,P2 gets $q_k = t_k \oplus (C_{uj} \odot s)$
5: P1 computes $H(t_k)$,P2 computes $H(t'_k) = (q_k \oplus (C_{uj} \odot s))$
6: P2 saves the $H(t'_k)$,and send $S = ...H(t'_k)...$ it to P1.
7: P1 calculates the intersection $I = X \bigcap Y$.
8: **return** I

Both the requester and the responder insert their own suspect collection into a cuckoo filter that USES the same hash function, get the filters CFS and CFR, and execute ROT [7] in pairs for each element in the filter's bucket in the same location. Responders hash the resulting values and store them in Cuckoo Filter CFE. The requestor then performs a Reverse operation on the CFS to obtain a new Filter table CFS2, ROT each element in the same position bucket in CFS2 and CFR, and hashes the values obtained and inserts the CFE. The CFE is sent to the requester, who can determine whether the corresponding element also exists in the set of responders by determining whether the ROT random key is in the CFE.

4   Analysis

4.1   Correctness

For each $x_i \in X$,$y_j \in Y$,x_i store in $Hash(x_i)$ bucket of $CF1$ and $Hash(x_i) \oplus Hash(fingerprint(x_i))$ bucket of $CF0$ or store in $Hash(x_i) \oplus Hash$

$(fingerprint(x_i))$ bucket of $CF1$ and $Hash(x_i)$ bucket of $CF0$; y_j store in $Hash(y_j)$ bucket or $Hash(y_j) \oplus Hash(fingerprint(y_j))$ bucket. If $x_i = y_j$,x_i and y_j will participate in a same ROT as choice vectors in the protocol(in $CF1$ and $CF2$ interaction or $CF0$ and $CF2$ interaction). Let **index** be the bucket number corresponding to y_j,$x' \in X'$,X' is the collection of elements in $CF0$ and $CF1$ bucket $index$. In the interaction of bucket $index$, P1 get $H(t_{x'})$, p2 get $H(q_{x'} \oplus (C(y_j) \odot s))$. According to the ROT protocol, s is the random number generated by P2,$q_{x'} = t_{x'} \oplus (C(x') \odot s)$, therefor we have:

$$H(q_{x'} \oplus (C(y_j) \odot s)) = H(t_{x'} \oplus (C(x') \odot s) \oplus (C(y_j) \odot s)) \tag{1}$$

If $x_i = y_j$, According to the properties of Cuckoo Filter we can know that $x_i \in X'$, so that:

$$H(t_{xi} \oplus (C(x') \odot s) \oplus (C(y_j) \odot s)) = H(t_{xi}) \tag{2}$$

In other words, if $x_i = y_j$, then P1 and P2 must can get the same mask value $H(t_{xi})$ corresponding to x_i and y_j, P1 only needs to query in the set of Mask values sent by P2 to obtain the intersection from the clear text corresponding to the Mask values. If $x_i \neq y_j$, he probability that $H(q_{x'} \oplus (C(y_j) \odot s)) = H(t_{xi})$isP $= 2^{-L}$ due to Hash collision. Also, because elements in the same bucket are required to interact differently, So the probability of a collision is $2 * m * b^2 * 2^{-L}$, m is bucket number. So in order to get the accuracy rate $1 - 2^{-\lambda}$, let $L = \lambda + 1 + 2\log_2 b + \log_2 m$.

4.2   Security

In security analysis we assume that the $\binom{N}{1} - ROT$ protocol implements an ideal $\binom{N}{1} - ROT$ functionality, its security in a semi-honest model is like [5]. In our protocol, P1 should gets no information except a Random key, while P2 should gets no information. The probability of P1 reverses the mask value in the non-intersection through S is 2^{-L}, and the probability of guessing the random value s is 2^{-F}, so for each mask value, the probability for P1 to guess the element of Y is $2^{-L-F} = 2^{-F-1} * b^{-2} * m^{-1}$. As the number of elements increases and the m value increases, the guessing becomes more and more difficult.

4.3   Computation Complexity and Communication Overheads

The number of ROT that protocol executes depends on the distribution of elements in the Filter Table, ROT times num satisfy $m \leq num \leq m * 2 * b^2$, value of m and max number num of elements in $X\&Y$ and the maximum space utilization α corresponds to b satisfy $(num \div b \div \alpha) \leq m \leq num$.

The Computation Complexity for every element is two times Hash for Cuckoo Filter and $1 \leq t \leq b$ times ROT.

5   Experiment Results

In the case that $b = 4$ and false positive rate of the Cuckoo Filter is 0.0001, the Filter run time and OT run times of the protocol are shown in the Table 1. We can find that the false positive rate decreases with the increase of data volume. If we want to get a lower false positive rate at a lower data volume, the computation time may increase, Table 2 is the result when false positive rate of the Cuckoo Filter is 0.000001. As we can see, decreasing the false-positive rate of Cuckoo Filter can effectively increase the accuracy of the protocol, but decreasing the false-positive rate means increasing the length of the fingerprint, which leads to an increase in computing time.

Table 1. Run result on Cuckoo Filter false positive rate 0.0001

$b = 4$	2^8	2^{12}	2^{16}
Cuckoo runtime (ms)	257	327	732
OT times	8192	131072	4194304
False positive rate (%)	1.92	0.55	0.15

Table 2. Run result on Cuckoo Filter false positive rate 0.000001

$b = 4$	2^8	2^{12}	2^{16}
Runtime (ms)	293	447	22885
OT times	8192	131072	2097152
False positive rate (%)	0.6	0.02	0.007

6   Conclusion

6.1   Protocol Summary

A new framework to Detecting Credential stuffing between servers is proposed. This framework can run among servers to help them to detect the suspected collection with safe and private intersection, and to obtain the collection suspected to be attacked by voucher stuffing, so as to reduce risks and detect voucher stuffing as soon as possible. We analyze the credential filling attack pattern to show the practicability and effectiveness of this framework.

In order to implement this framework, we proposed a new PSI protocol based on Cuckoo filter and ROT, which allows the initiator of THE PSI to obtain the intersection of two parties without disclosing other contents in his own set, and at the same time cannot understand other non-intersection contents in the other party's set, while the corresponding responder does not get any valid information. We have proved its safety and correctness through theoretical analysis and experiment

6.2 Possible Improvements

Framework Combined with Honeyword: This protocol is combined with Honeyword and other technical means to further accelerate detection efficiency and shorten attack escalation time. We assume that the server where the certificate leak occurred USES Honeyword to store the credentials. Then, after the server in the protocol collects the suspicious collection, it can use the detected Honeyword to issue a query request to other servers, so as to quickly locate the server where the leak occurred and the scope of the leaked credentials.

Directory: Selecting a trusted third party as the directory server can greatly improve the working efficiency of the protocol. The server that collects a certain suspicious collection can issue PSI request to the directory, and the directory will schedule the server to improve the efficiency. Furthermore, the catalog can help the framework integrated with Honeyword locate the source of Honeyword more efficiently and schedule relevant servers to participate in PSI, thus further improving the efficiency of detecting Credential stuffing attacks and leak reports.

References

1. Shape: Shape credential spill report (2018). https://info.shapesecurity.com/rs/935-ZAM-778/images/ShapeCredentialSpillReport2018.pdf
2. P. Institute: 2018 the cost of credential stuffing: Asia-pacific (2018). https://www.akamai.com/us/en/multimedia/documents/white-paper/the-cost-of-credential-stuffing-asia-pacific.pdf
3. Freeman, D.M., Jain, S., Duermuth, M., Biggio, B., Giacinto., G.: Who are you? a statistical approach to measuring user authenticity. In: Proceedings of Network & Distributed System Security Symposium (2016)
4. Wang, K.C., Reiter, M.K.: Detecting stuffing of a user's credentials at her own accounts. In: 29th USENIX Security Symposium (USENIX Security 20) (2020)
5. Kolesnikov, V., Kumaresan, R., Rosulek, M., Trieu, N.: Efficient batched oblivious PRF with applications to private set intersection. In: ACM SIGSAC Conference on Computer & Communications Security (2016)
6. Pinkas, B., Schneider, T., Zohner, M.: Faster private set intersection based on OT extension. In: Proceedings of the 23rd USENIX Conference on Security Symposium, SEC'14, pp. 797–812, USA, 2014. USENIX Association
7. Kolesnikov, V., Kumaresan, R.: Improved OT extension for transferring short secrets. In: Canetti, R., Garay, J.A. (eds.) CRYPTO 2013, Part II. LNCS, vol. 8043, pp. 54–70. Springer, Heidelberg (2013). https://doi.org/10.1007/978-3-642-40084-1_4
8. Pinkas, B., Schneider, T., Zohner, M.: Scalable private set intersection based on OT extension. ACM Trans. Priv. Secur. **21**, 1–35 (2018)
9. Li, L., Pal, B., Ali, J., Sullivan, N., Chatterjee, R., Ristenpart, T.: Protocols for checking compromised credentials. In: Proceedings of the 2019 ACM SIGSAC Conference on Computer and Communications Security, pp. 1387–1403 (2019)

10. Fan, B., Andersen, D.G., Kaminsky, M., Mitzenmacher, M.D.: Cuckoo filter: practically better than bloom. In: Proceedings of the 10th ACM International on Conference on Emerging Networking Experiments and Technologies, pp. 75–88 (2014)
11. Wang, K.C., Reiter, M.K.: How to end password reuse on the web (2018)
12. Freeman, D., Jain, S., Dürmuth, M., Biggio, B., Giacinto, G.: Who are you? a statistical approach to measuring user authenticity. In: NDSS, pp. 1–15 (2016)

The 1st International Workshop on Intelligence and Security in Next Generation Networks (ISNGN 2020)

A Critical Node Detection Algorithm Based Node Interplay Model

Lingxiao Zhang[1,2] and Xuefeng Yan[1,2(⊠)]

[1] College of Computer Sciences and Technology, Nanjing University
of Aeronautics and Astronautics, Nanjing 211106, China
{zlx914,yxf}@nuaa.edu.cn
[2] Collaborative Innovation Center of Novel Software Technology
and Industrialization, Nanjing University of Aeronautics and Astronautics,
Nanjing 211106, China

Abstract. Identifying critical nodes helps people to protect these nodes from attacks and prevent these critical nodes from rapidly infecting other nodes in the network with viruses. Gateway Local Rank (GLR) algorithm cannot distinguish the difference between the importance of nodes near the geometric center of the network and ignores the critical nodes located at the edge of the network, because it only considers the distance between the node and communities. Gateway Local Rank Extension (GLREX) was proposed to improve GLR by adopting the node interplay model, which not only considers the distance between nodes but also the degree of nodes. The node interplay model supposes the interaction force between nodes is inversely proportional to the exponential power of the distance but not the square of the distance. The influence of nodes cannot be spread out uniformly in a circular manner to affect surrounding nodes, so it is different from the gravitational force between objects in the real world, which obeys the inverse-square law. Because of the node interplay model, GLREX not only considers the interplay between nodes and communities but also the interplay between communities and communities. The experiments showed that compared to GLR, GLREX can effectively identify the critical nodes at different positions of the network.

Keywords: Critical node detection · Node interplay · Node importance · Community · Gateway local rank

1 Introduction

In complex networks, there are some nodes that are more important than other nodes. They can more easily control the propagation and structural characteristics of the network. For example, in local area network, once the core switch as the critical node is infected with viruses [1], other switches will also be infected quickly. As a result, identifying these critical nodes and protecting them from attacks help people to maintain the security [2] of the entire network.

Communities [3] can also help us understand the structural and spreading characteristics of complex networks. Nodes within one community often have many similarities and strong connections between them. Information like virus can spread

G. Wang et al. (Eds.): SpaCCS 2020, LNCS 12383, pp. 467–479, 2021.
https://doi.org/10.1007/978-3-030-68884-4_39

quickly within communities, and through these communities, it can quickly spread throughout the whole network. BridgeRank [4] first made use of one community detection algorithm like Louvain method [5] to divide the entire network into a communities set, and then apply the Betweeness centrality [6] to identify the core nodes in each community. At last, BridgeRank calculates the importance ranking of nodes by considering the sum of the shortest paths from the node to these local community core nodes. Similarly, Gateway Local Rank (GLR) [7] also relied on the community core nodes to identify critical nodes. Compared to BridgeRank, GLR believed that there is more than one core node in a community. Not only the central core node is needed to be considered, but also the node at the edge of the community that connects with many other communities is necessary to be included in the core node set. These edge nodes are like gateways that serve as bridges for information to flow between different communities.

However, the number of communities grows up with the increase of the size of the network. It means that calculating the shortest path from each node to these core nodes will be very difficult because of the huge number of the core nodes in communities. In addition, noises may be included every time the information flows through one node, so it is difficult for two distant nodes to have a substantial and meaningful interaction between them. In fact, the intrinsic nature of GLR is Closeness centrality [8], but the time complexity is reduced. Similar with Closeness centrality, GLR prefers the nodes located at the geometric center of the network, but ignores the important nodes near the edge of the network. So the Gateway Local Rank Extension (GLREX) algorithm was proposed by adopting the node interplay model to solve these defects. The node interplay model not only considers the distance between nodes but also the degree of nodes. It suppose the interaction force between nodes is inversely proportional to the exponential power of the distance but not the square of the distance unlike the gravitational force between objects in the real world.

The remainder of this paper is organized as follows. Section 2 is the related work. The node interplay model is described in Sect. 3. Section 4 illustrates the entire framework of GLREX algorithm. Section 5 shows the experiment results. The final part is the conclusion.

2   Related Work

A complex network can be represented $G = \{V, E\}$, where V is the nodes set and E is the edges set. The goal of the critical node detection can be formalized as follows [9]:

Given an integer k, the goal is to find k critical nodes as seed nodes, and then spread information like virus from these seed nodes to maximize the final number of expected affected nodes.

Many algorithms have proposed various node centrality measures to identify key nodes in complex networks. These centrality measures are often based on the network structure and make use of the local properties of the nodes to calculate the importance of the nodes. For example, Degree centrality [10] supposed that the more neighbors one node has, the more important this node is. Although the importance of a node can be quickly obtained by only calculating the degree of the node, the result is often poor performance because it only simply consider the first-order neighbors of the node. K-Shell centrality [11] mainly considers the degree of the node at the different location of the network. The closer to the center of the network and the larger the degree, the higher the node ranking is. Therefore, the outer nodes can be stripped layer by layer, and the nodes in the inner layer will be considered to have higher influence. Eigenvector centrality [12] not only considers the number of neighbors one node has, but also the importance of the neighbors themselves. It is defined as:

$$EC(i) = c \sum_{j=1}^{n} a_{ij} EC(j) \tag{1}$$

where c is a constant, a_{ij} indicates the weight of the edge between node i and j.

Most of the above methods rely on the local structure of the network and cannot grasp the overall structure of the network. Closeness centrality [8] considers the average distance from one node to the other remaining nodes. The shorter the average distance, the more important the node is. The spreading ability of each node is determined by the sum of the length of the shortest path from the node to all other nodes. The formula is as follows:

$$CC(v) = \frac{1}{\sum_{u \neq v} d(u,v)} \tag{2}$$

where $d(u, v)$ is the length of the shortest path between node u and node v.

Betweenness centrality [6] evaluates the number of shortest paths from one node to another node that pass through the node, measuring the ability of one node to control the shortest paths between the other two nodes. It means that Betweenness centrality values more the role of nodes acting as bridges that connect different parts of the network. Therefore, it considers the global structure of the network. The detail is as follows:

$$BC(v) = \sum_{v \neq s, v \neq t, s \neq t} \frac{g_{st}^{v}}{g_{st}} \tag{3}$$

where g_{st} represents the number of shortest paths between node s and t and g_{st}^{v} is the shortest path that passes through the node v.

The GLR [7] algorithm is based on the community. The network is first divided into a collection of communities, and then the core nodes are selected in each community. Finally, the importance of each node is measured by the sum of the shortest paths from the node to these core nodes.. The specific process is as follows:

1. GLR uses the community detection algorithm like the Louvain method to discover the community structure in the network.
2. It ignores the edges between each community and assumes that each community is isolated from each other. Calculate the Betweenness centrality for each community and select the node with the largest Betweenness centrality value as the community center core node.

3. The goal is to find the gateway node as the core node. The gateway node is the node with the most connections to other communities in each community. Obviously, the gateway node can serve as a bridge between this community and other communities, and spreads the information like virus to other communities.
4. Similar to the Closeness centrality, the sum of the shortest paths from the node to the previous two types of core nodes is used as an index to measure the spreading ability of the nodes. The formula is described as follows:

$$GLR(v) = \frac{1}{\alpha_1 \sum_{u \in \Gamma_k} d(u,v) + \alpha_2 \sum_{p \in \Gamma_g} d(p,v)} \tag{4}$$

where Γ_k are the local center core nodes and Γ_g are the local gateway core nodes.

3   The Node Interplay Model

3.1   The Defects of Closeness Centrality and GLR

The GLR algorithm is essentially close to the Closeness centrality, taking only the distance from the node to the other nodes into consideration, regardless of the other properties of the node. So there will be the situation shown in the following figure.

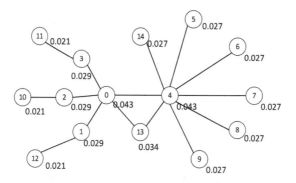

Fig. 1. The example network with Closeness centrality.

The network in the Fig. 1 can be regarded as a small community, and we can see that there are three core nodes in it, namely, node 0, node 4 and node 13. The importance of node 0 and node 4 is obviously different, because the nodes of the entire community are divided into two parts respectively around node 0 and node 4. From the perspective of information dissemination, node 4 is more important, because node 4 can directly deliver the information to the rightmost 6 nodes; while node 0 needs to distribute the message through the nodes 1, 2, and 3, so that all left nodes can receive the message. It adds a more layer of propagation process compared to node 4, which increases the possibility of inclusion noise. However, the Closeness centrality of node 0 and 4 is the same.

As it can be seen, there is no way for Closeness centrality to clearly distinguish the importance differences between the nodes at the central location of the network. Because the distance from the network center to other nodes should be relatively short, and there are often multiple nodes at the center of the network. Therefore, the Closeness centrality differences between them will be small. In order to solve this problem, it's necessary to consider other attributes of the node like the degree of the node. Generally, the degree of the node can be considered as the inherent attribute of the node in the network. The degree of node 0 is much lower than the degree of node 4, so we can consider the distance between nodes and degree of nodes at the same time, and get the Node Interplay Model.

3.2 The Relationship Between Distance, Degree and Interplay

The nodes in the network are often the abstractions of the entities in the real system, and the edges are the representatives of the relationship between these entities. As described by the law of universal gravitation, there is a mutual attraction between any two mass points in the real world, and we can reasonably think that there is also a kind of interaction force between the nodes in the network [13]. Generally speaking, a node with larger degree is easy to have a great impact on other nodes, and often the influence is mutual. Therefore, the degree of the node can be used to analogize the mass of the object, and the length of shortest path between nodes can be analogized to the distance between objects. Then, the interaction force between the two nodes propagates along the shortest path between them. Obviously, the closer the nodes are, the stronger the interaction force is, and the farther the nodes are, the weaker the interaction force is. Therefore, the form of interaction force between the two nodes u, v is as follows:

$$F(u,v) = \frac{k(u)*k(v)}{d(u,v)^{\alpha}} \tag{5}$$

where $k(u)$, $k(v)$ is the degree of node u, v. $d(u,v)$ is the length of the shortest path between node u, v. α is the parameter that regulates the influence of distance.

Different from the force of gravity, coulomb force that obey the inverse-square law, the interplay between nodes here is not necessarily inversely proportional to the square of the distance. Taking the gravitational force of the earth on the surrounding objects as an example, the "force line" is used to indicate the unit gravitational strength of the earth, and the earth uniformly distributes the `force line' from the center of the sphere to the periphery. Then the higher the density of "force line" at some place, the greater the gravitational force of the object at this place. As shown in Fig. 2, for a unit square object, when the distance between it and the earth is r, the density of the "force line" is assumed to be 1; then when the distance from the earth is 2r, the density of "force line" will be 1/4. Because the surface area of the sphere is $4\pi r^2$, the total number of force lines cannot change, the distance is twice as far as the original, the area is 4 times the original area, and the gravity force becomes 1/4 of the original force.

As a result, as the distance increases, the strength of gravity force decreases at a speed inversely proportional to the square of the distance. By the same token, in two-dimensional space, the interaction force between objects is inversely proportional to the first order of distance. However, the interaction force between nodes in the network is transmitted through the shortest path between nodes. It doesn't emit uniformly in all directions along a straight line like in 3D or 2D space. The influence emitted from the source node does not spread outward in a circular manner, so the α is not necessarily 2 or 1.

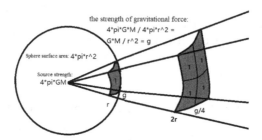

Fig. 2. The gravitational force of the earth

3.3   The Importance of Node Based Node Interplay

Assuming that the node v is interacted by all other nodes in the network, then the importance of this node should be the sum of its interaction force with all other nodes in the network, that is:

$$I_{global}(v) = \sum_{u \neq v} \frac{k(u) * k(v)}{d(u,v)^{\alpha}} \tag{6}$$

It means that the more neighbors one node has and the closer it is to other nodes, the greater the influence of this node, which is consistent with common sense. Figure 3 shows a comparison of Closeness centrality and $I_{global}(v)$ for each node.

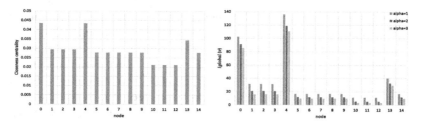

Fig. 3. The comparison of Closeness centrality and $I_{global}(v)$

It can be seen that the Closeness centrality of each node is relatively close, and the discrimination is not obvious enough, especially the difference between node 0 and node 4 cannot be distinguished. The $I_{global}(v)$ based on the interaction force between nodes is clearly distinguishable, which clearly reflects the importance of each node. At the same time, it can be found that as α increases, $I_{global}(v)$ decreases, and the importance difference between each node becomes smaller, but the relative ordering among the nodes does not change.

However, computing the interaction force between node u and all other nodes in the network will bring about two problems. Firstly, for large networks, it is very time-consuming and impractical to calculate the shortest path between each node pairs. Secondly, in the real propagation process, it is difficult for a node to affect nodes that are far away from it. Every time the information passes through an intermediate node, it may be distorted and added with noise, leading to the decay of strength of node interplay.

In addition, the six-degree separation theory [14] also shows that the length of the real path of influence dissemination between nodes is unlikely to be too long, and tends to be as short as possible. In order to solve these two problems, a node can only consider the interaction force between the surrounding nodes in a certain range, and these surrounding nodes are preferably representative and influential nodes. The core nodes in each community often meet these requirements, because these core nodes are representatives of each community, they have similar properties with the community and can replace the community to some extent. It means considering the interaction force between nodes at the node and community level, rather than considering it directly at the node level. Therefore, the final importance of a node is the sum of the interaction force between it and the core nodes in surrounding communities. The specific formula is as follows:

$$I(v) = \sum_{u \in \Gamma_v} \frac{\alpha_{v,u} * k(u) * k(v)}{(d(u,v) + 1)^x} \tag{7}$$

where $\alpha_{v,u}$ is the weight coefficient of different surrounding communities to the current community which node v belongs to. Γ_v is the core nodes in communities around the node v. Since node v and node u may be the same node, $d(u, v)$ may be equal to 0. For convenience, all distances are incremented by 1 so that the denominator is not 0 and the minimum value is 1. Different communities obviously have different impacts on node v. Generally speaking, the community $C(v)$ where node v is located has the greatest influence on node v. Secondly, the impact of the surrounding communities that are more similar to $C(v)$ will be greater, because things of a kind come together, people of a kind fall into the same group. Information like virus is easier to spread between two similar groups, and it is easier for two similar groups to share information with each other. Therefore, $\alpha_{v,u}$ mainly reflects the similarity between $C(v)$ and the community $C(u)$ where node u is located. The specific form is as follows:

$$\alpha_{v,u} = \frac{\sum_{i \in c_v, j \in c_u} \left| A_{ij} - \frac{k(i) * k(j)}{2 * m} \right|}{\sum_{i \in c_v} k_i} \tag{8}$$

where A_{ij} is the adjacency matrix of network G, $k(i)$, $k(j)$ is the degree of node i, j, and m is the number of edges in the network. In the Configuration model [15], the edges between node i and j are $\frac{k_i * k_j}{2m}$ if connections are made at random, so $\sum_{i \in c_v, j \in c_u} \frac{k_i * k_j}{2m}$ represents the number of the expected connections between c_v and c_u. And then, $\sum_{i \in c_v, j \in c_u} A_{ij}$ equals the number of the real edges between c_v and c_u. It can be reasonably assumed that if the two communities are dissimilar and irrelevant, the number of edges connected between them should be subject to the distribution of the corresponding edges in the random network. And then, if these two communities are similar, there will be a large difference between the number of expected edges and real edges. It means the larger the value of $\alpha_{v,u}$ is, the more similar these two communities are.

In this way, $I(v)$ actually considers the interaction force between nodes from the level of the node and the community, as well as from the level of the community and the community, so it can get more accurate node importance.

4   The GLREX Method Based Node Interplay Model

The detail steps of the GLREX algorithm are as follows:

1. Input the graph G (V, E) and the number of critical nodes k to be obtained at the end
2. The entire network is divided into a set of multiple communities using the community detection algorithm.
3. Find the community central core node and gateway node in each community, and each community has two core nodes.
4. Calculate the similarity coefficient for each community with its surrounding communities. And then calculate the interaction force between the node and the core nodes of the surrounding community to get the importance of the node.
5. Sort by node importance, output the first k top nodes.

The entire process of GLREX is similar with GLR, but they are different in nature. GLREX solves the defects of Closeness centrality, considering not only the distance between nodes but also the degree, so it can effectively distinguish the importance differences of nodes located in the center of the network. Finally, the Pseudo-code of our algorithm is as follows.

Algorithm 1 GLREX

Input: $G(V,E)$, the number of critical nodes k
Output: k top rank nodes
Process:
1. Use the community detection algorithm to find the communities C in the network.
2. **for** each community C_i in C **do**
3.   Find the community central core node and gateway node in C_i
4. **end for**
5. **for** each community C_i in C **do**
6.   Calculate the similarity coefficient $\alpha_{i,j}$ between C_i and the neighbor community C_j according to formula 8.
7.   **for** each node v in C_i **do**
8.   Calculate the interaction force between the node v and the core nodes of the surrounding community to get the importance of the node $I(v)$ according to formula 7.
9.   **end for**
10. **end for**
11. Sort by node importance, output the first k top nodes
---

5 Experiments

SIR [16] is widely used to theoretically analyze the propagation characteristics of the network, such as the spread viruses of and diseases. So it is used by us to evaluate the performance of the algorithms. In this model, each node has three states:

1. The susceptible state, representing that the node can be infected but not yet infected.
2. The infected state, it means that the node has been infected, and is to infect the other nodes in the next step.
3. The recovered state, representing that the node has been recovered and will not be infected again.

At first, all nodes are susceptible to be infected except some source infected nodes. Then, at each time step, the infected node infects the surrounding susceptible nodes with the probability of β, and then transforms to the recovered state with the probability of γ, which means that it is immune to the infection and will not become an infected node again. At the t moment, the number of nodes in the infected state and the recovered state is counted as $F(t)$, which can effectively assess the infectious ability of the source infected nodes. It is clear that $F(t)$ will begin to rise rapidly with time and eventually stabilize. The spreading probability β is set to 0.05 and γ is set to 1. A too high β value will cause the selection of the initial infected nodes without affecting the final infection result, that is, most nodes in the final network will be infected.

5.1 Real World Networks

The details of four real networks are listed in Table 1.

Table 1. Description of real networks

Networks	Nodes	Edges	Average degree	Brief description
Yeast	1870	2277	2.44	A protein network [17]
Hamsterster	1858	12534	13.49	A hamster website user network [18]
Ca-HepTh	8638	24827	5.26	A communication network [19]
PGP	10680	24316	4.55	A high-energy physicists cooperation network YY [20]

Figure 4 shows the SIR model propagation results of GLREX, GLR, EC, KS on four real networks, where EC, KS are abbreviated to Eigenvector centrality and K-Shell centrality respectively. It can be seen that GLREX has the best performance, not only the infection speed is the fastest, but also the total number of infected nodes is the most, followed by GLR, and the effects of KS and EC are not satisfactory. Specifically, the critical nodes discovered by GLREX have strong explosive power in the early stage and have a strong infectious capacity. On Yeast and Ca-HepTh networks, GLREX outperforms other algorithms greatly, which is 16% and 20% higher than GLR respectively. On Hamsterster network, GLREX increased by 5% compared to GLR. Only on PGP network, GLREX overlaps slightly with GLR, and the difference is small. And then both GLR and GLREX work better than the KS, EC algorithm. This shows that considering the importance of nodes from the community and node level is indeed more comprehensive and reliable than considering the importance of nodes from the node and node level alone. Because the community can bring some global network information, it makes up for the shortcomings of only considering the local characteristics of nodes.

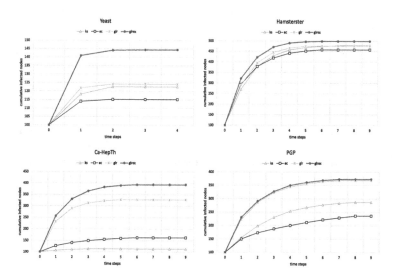

Fig. 4. The SIR results on 4 real networks

5.2 Artificial Networks

The artificial networks is generated by the LFR network benchmark [20]. The node degree and community size in the LFR network obey the power law distribution, which is different from the simple uniform distribution, so the constructed network is closer to the real network. Here are the information of 4 LFR networks (Table 2):

Table 2. Parameter of LFR networks

ID	N	$<k>$	k_{max}	μ	γ	β	$|C|_{min}$	$|C|_{max}$
1	1000	5	50	0.1	2	1	10	100
2	1000	10	50	0.1	2	1	10	100
3	1000	5	50	0.3	2	1	10	100
4	5000	5	50	0.1	2	1	10	100

Among them, N represents the number of network nodes, <k> represents the average degree of the nodes, μ represents whether the community structure of the network is obvious, and the other four parameters of the network are the same. The higher <k>, the denser the network edges, the closer the nodes are. The higher μ the less obvious the community structure in the network.

Figure 5 shows the SIR model propagation results of GLREX, GLR, EC, KS on four LFR networks. The result of GLREX is still ahead of other algorithms. By comparing the results of the network 1 and 2, it can be found that the number of nodes infected by all algorithms has increased. Because the average degree of the network has increased, indicating that the connections between nodes have increased, so the infection becomes easier. The comparison of network 1 and 3 shows that whether the community structure is obvious does not have much impact on GLR and GLREX. Similarly, the comparison of network 1 and 4 shows that the network size does not have a significant impact on GLREX to identify critical nodes.

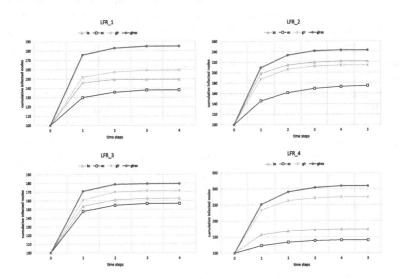

Fig. 5. The SIR results on 4 LFR networks

5.3   Complexity Analysis

Suppose the number of nodes is n, the number of edges is m, s is the number of the communities, the average community size is $|c|$ and the average number of neighbor community is h.

The communities are detected by the Louvain algorithm with the time complexity of $O(n \log n)$. The process of finding core nodes costs $O\left(s\left(|c|^2 \log|c| + |c|\right)\right)$ [7]. The time complexity of calculating similarity coefficient is $O(m + s*h)$. Calculating the importance of each node needs $O(n(h+1)|c|)$. The selection of k top rank nodes cost

$O(nlogk)$ time. $s*|c| = n$, $h < s$, $h < |c|$, $|c|^2log|c| < n^2logn$, so the total time complexity is as follows:

$$O\left(nlogn + s\left(|c|^2log|c| + |c|\right) + m + s*h + n(h+1)|c| + nlogk\right)$$
$$< O(nlogn + n|c|log|c| + n + m + s*|c| + n(s*|c| + |c|) + nlogn)$$
$$< O(2nlogn + n^2 \log n + 2n + m + n^2 + n*|c|)$$
$$< O(n^2 + m)$$

(9)

6 Conclusion

The node interplay model effectively described the interaction force between nodes. It supposes the interaction force between nodes is inversely proportional to the exponential power of the distance but not the square of the distance. Because the influence of nodes cannot be spread out uniformly in a circular manner to affect surrounding nodes, so it is different from the gravitational force between objects in the real world, which obeys the inverse-square law. Based on the node interplay model, GLREX considers the node importance not only at the level of nodes and community but also at the community and community level, because the similarity coefficient can evaluate the different effects of surrounding communities to the current community. Compared to GLR, GLREX can distinguish the importance differences of central nodes and identify the critical nodes at the edge of the network. By protecting these critical nodes from attacks, the security of the network can be effectively maintained. Future work will focus on optimizing the calculation of similarity coefficients between communities.

Acknowledgments. The research in this paper was supported by the 13th Five-Year Plan Foundation of Equipment Development Department Founding No. (41401020401, 41401010201).

References

1. Peters, M., Goltz, J., Wiedenmann, S., Mundt, T.: Using machine learning to find anomalies in field bus network traffic. In: Wang, G., Feng, J., Bhuiyan, M.Z.A., Lu, R. (eds.) SpaCCS 2019. LNCS, vol. 11611, pp. 336–353. Springer, Cham (2019). https://doi.org/10.1007/978-3-030-24907-6_26
2. Schillinger, F., Schindelhauer, C.: End-to-end encryption schemes for online social networks. In: Wang, G., Feng, J., Bhuiyan, M.Z.A., Lu, R. (eds.) SpaCCS 2019. LNCS, vol. 11611, pp. 133–146. Springer, Cham (2019). https://doi.org/10.1007/978-3-030-24907-6_11
3. Majbouri Yazdi, K., Yazdi, A.M., Khodayi, S., Hou, J., Zhou, W., Saedy, S.: Integrating ant colony algorithm and node centrality to improve prediction of information diffusion in social networks. In: Wang, G., Chen, J., Yang, L.T. (eds.) SpaCCS 2018. LNCS, vol. 11342, pp. 381–391. Springer, Cham (2018). https://doi.org/10.1007/978-3-030-05345-1_33
4. Salavati, C., Abdollahpouri, A., Manbari, Z.: BridgeRank: a novel fast centrality measure based on local structure of the network. Phys. A **496**, 635–653 (2018)

5. Fazlali, M., Moradi, E., Malazi, T.: Adaptive parallel Louvain community detection on a multicore platform. Microprocess. Microsyst. **54**, 26–34 (2017)
6. Riondato, M., Kornaropoulos, E.M.: Fast approximation of betweenness centrality through sampling. Data Min. Knowl. Disc. **30**(2), 438–475 (2015). https://doi.org/10.1007/s10618-015-0423-0
7. Salavati, C., Abdollahpouri, A., Manbari, Z.: Ranking nodes in complex networks based on local structure and improving closeness centrality. Neurocomputing. **336**, 36–45 (2019)
8. Liu, L., Ma, C., Xiang, B., et al.: Identifying multiple influential spreaders based on generalized closeness centrality. Phys. A **492**, 2237–2248 (2018)
9. Kempe, D., Kleinberg, J., Tardos, É.: Maximizing the spread of influence through a social network. In: Proceedings of the ninth ACM SIGKDD International Conference on Knowledge Discovery and Data Mining, pp. 137–146. ACM (2003)
10. Zhong, F., Liu, H., Wang, W., et al.: Comprehensive influence of local and global characteristics on identifying the influential nodes. Phys. A **511**, 78–84 (2018)
11. Das, K., Samanta, S., Pal, M.: Study on centrality measures in social networks: a survey. Soc. Netw. Anal. Min. **8**(1), 1–11 (2018). https://doi.org/10.1007/s13278-018-0493-2
12. Li, X., Liu, Y., Jiang, Y., et al.: Identifying social influence in complex networks: a novel conductance eigenvector centrality model. Neurocomputing. **210**, 141–154 (2016)
13. Fei, L., Zhang, Q., Deng, Y.: Identifying influential nodes in complex networks based on the inverse-square law. Phys. A **512**, 1044–1059 (2018)
14. Dave, H., Keller, D., Golmer, K., et al.: Six degrees of separation: connecting research with users and cost analysis. Joule. **1**(3), 410–415 (2017)
15. Molloy, M., Reed, B.: A critical point for random graphs with a given degree sequence. Random Struct. Algorithms **6**(2–3), 161–180 (1995)
16. Satsuma, J., Willox, R., Ramani, A., et al.: Extending the SIR epidemic model. Phys. A **336**(3–4), 369–375 (2004)
17. Jeong, H., Mason, P., Barabási, L., et al.: Lethality and centrality in protein networks. Nature **411**(6833), 41 (2001)
18. Leskovec, J., Kleinberg, J., Faloutsos, C.: Graph evolution: densification and shrinking diameters. ACM Trans. Knowl. Discov. Data. **1**(1), 2 (2007)
19. Boguná, M., Pastor-Satorras, R., Díaz-Guilera, A., et al.: Models of social networks based on social distance attachment. Phys. Rev. E. **70**(5), 056122 (2004)
20. Lancichinetti, A., Fortunato, S.: Benchmarks for testing community detection algorithms on directed and weighted graphs with overlapping communities. Phys. Rev. E. **80**(1), 016118 (2009)

A Posteriori Preference Multi-objective Optimization Using Machine Learning

Zheren Sun[1(✉)], Yuhua Huang[1], Wanlin Sun[2], and Zhiyuan Chen[1]

[1] College of Computer Science and Technology, Nanjing University of Aeronautics
and Astronautics, Nanjing 211106, China
szheren2k@163.com
[2] Department of Physics, Changji College, Changji 831100, China

Abstract. As a widely accepted way to solve multi-objective optimization problems (MOPs), evolutionary algorithms (EAs) can produce a
well converged and well diverse Pareto Front (PF). However, only the
partial PF around the decision maker (DM) preference is crucial in making decisions. The paper proposed an a posteriori method to help DMs
to find solutions of interest (SOIs), i.e. solutions DMs interested in and
to make well decisions. The proposed method is divided into three parts:
the optimization part, learning part and operation part. With an EA,
the optimization part works out optimal nondominated solutions. Then,
the learning part trains an inverse mapping model according to the solutions. In the operation part, a set of probable preference vectors (PPVs)
are generated to predict more SOIs. Finally, the feasibility of the proposed method is verified with the experiments on 2- and 3-objective test
problems.

Keywords: A posteriori · Multi-objective optimization · Evolutionary
computation · Random forest · Decision maker · Preference

1 Introduction

The multi-objective optimization refers to optimizing of two or more objectives
simultaneously. It often appears in many different fields, such as the network [23],
economics [19] and engineering [2]. The hardest part of MOPs is the trade-off
among multiple conflicting objectives.

Due to well dealing with the conflict and efficiently obtaining a entire PF,
the EA is widely accepted as a main way to solve MOPs at present. In the past
three decades, the EA having been extensively studied and many advanced EAs
have emerged [18,26]. However, providing DMs with hundreds even thousands
selective solutions is meaningless, because no one knows which ones are good.
Therefore, getting a PF is not the ultimate goal, but finding DM's SOIs and
making final decisions is.

In order to help DMs successfully find SOIs, researchers have made a lot
of efforts and proposed many preference optimization methods [20], including

© Springer Nature Switzerland AG 2021
G. Wang et al. (Eds.): SpaCCS 2020, LNCS 12383, pp. 480–491, 2021.
https://doi.org/10.1007/978-3-030-68884-4_40

the a priori, interactive and a posteriori method. The a priori method mainly adopts the weight [10,14], indicator [22], aspired level vector [17,24] and trade-off information [4,13] to represent DM preferences. Its effectiveness is based on DMs being able to write down preference smoothly before the algorithm running. However, without any hint,, even experienced DMs almost impossibly give accurate preferences at very beginning. The interactive method periodically collects [11,12] and progressively learns [16] DM preferences. During optimization, DMs are gradually guided to express preferences. Because of participating in optimization, DMs can learn together with the whole system and be easier to get satisfying solutions. Admittedly, if the participation time was enough, the interactive method could guide DMs to accurately express preferences. However, everyone's energy is limited in the real life. It is difficult to require someone to participate continuously in entire optimization. In addition, it also is a problem to determine the appropriate participation time and ensure good results simultaneously.

Compared with the a priori and interactive method, the a posteriori method asks DMs to express preferences after obtaining a PF and can tolerate DM's lack of knowledge on the problem to some extent. On the one hand, DMs are more likely to express accurate preferences after more intuitive understanding of variable ranges and objective relationships. On the other hand, the DM can participate in the process for many times and progressively learn his or her preferences like the interactive method. Moreover, due to the independence of each part, the a posteriori method can provide faster reaction. In addition, the EA can be used just like an interface to provide a PF without any modification. Applying different EAs become very easy. Based on the above, the paper proposed an a posteriori method to help DMs in making decision. The proposed method is divided into three parts: the optimization part, learning part and operation part. In the optimization part, a well-converged and well-diverse PF is obtained by an advanced EA. In the learning part, an inverse mapping model is built with the PF. In the operation part, some PPVs are generated around the DM preference. Then SOIs are predicted with the PPVs by the model. In the experimental section, we carried out experiments on ZDT1 [27] and DTLZ1-2 [9] test problems which were used in the 2- and 3-objective experiments respectively. The experimental results have verified the feasibility of the proposed method.

The rests of the paper are organized as follows. The Sect. 2 introduces some current related works about preference optimization and provides some preliminaries. The Sect. 3 describes the proposed method in detail. The Sect. 4 shows and explains the experimental results. The Sect. 5 concludes the paper and put forward possible future work directions.

2 Background

2.1 Related Work

Lots of interesting preference optimization researches have been done and here is the introduction.

In the a priori method, DMs are requested to provide preferences at very beginning and the DM preference is incorporated into the whole process. In each generation, solutions close to the preference are of higher probability to survive. Thus, final solutions are of certain tendency which the DM may want. Past studies proposed many ways for expressing DM preferences to guide the optimization. In [10,14], each objective is assigned a weight according to the importance given by the DM. In [4,13], hierarchies or priorities are assigned based on the difference of solutions. The paper [22] guide the optimization of indicator-based EAs by combining the DM preference into the indicators. The papers [17,24] use the aspired level vector, also called the preference vector, to represent the DM preference.

To some extent, the interactive method where DMs are required to participate is the generalization of the a priori method. In the interactive method, final solutions are gradually obtained through multiple participation of DMs, which is like do the a priori method many times. However, the DM can learn with the algorithm and progressively knows what he or she wants, which decreases the cognitive pressure. The paper [11,12] models the DM preference with periodically participation of the DM. The paper [16] progressively learns the DM preference by machine learning methods.

In the a posteriori method, a few SOIs are produced by some method after getting the PF, which greatly reduces the selection load and cognitive pressure of DMs in making decisions. The paper [1] predicts SOIs by learning the DM preference. The paper [21] uses a clustering method to divide solutions into several clusters, one of which represents a kind of solutions.

2.2 Basic Definitions

The general form of a multi-objective optimization problem is as follows.

$$\begin{aligned}
\text{minimize } F(x) &= (f_1(x), ..., f_m(x))^{\mathrm{T}}, \\
\text{subject to } x &\in \Omega
\end{aligned} \tag{1}$$

where $F(x)$ is the m-dimension objective vector and $x = \{x_1, ..., x_d\}^{\mathrm{T}}$ is the d-dimension variable vector. Ω is the variable space, described as $\Omega = \{x \in R^d\}$. $F : \Omega \rightarrow R^m$ is a map from the variable space to the objective space R^m. We say that x^k dominates x^l, if and only if $\forall i = \{1, ..., m\}, f_i(x^k) \leq f_i(x^l)$ and $\exists j = \{1, ..., m\}, f_j(x^k) < f_j(x^l)$. If a solution has no other solutions that dominate it, we call it a nondominated solution. The set of points of all the nondominated solutions on the variable space is called the Pareto Set (PS) and the set of points on the corresponding objective space is called the Pareto Front (PF).

2.3 MOEA/D

MOEA/D[25] is a decomposition-based EA, which decomposes a multi-objective problem into many scalar subproblems and optimizes the original problem by optimizing all subproblems. Many methods can achieve the goal of decomposition. The tchebycheff approach (TCH) [26] is a classic one of them.

In the TCH, the form of the i_{th} subproblem is as (2).

$$\text{minimize } g^{te}(\boldsymbol{x}|\boldsymbol{w}^i, \boldsymbol{z}^*) = \max_{1 \leq j \leq m} \left\{ w_j^i |f_j(\boldsymbol{x}) - z_j^*| \right\}, \tag{2}$$

where $\boldsymbol{z}^* = \{z_1^*, ..., z_m^*\}$ is the ideal point, i.e. $z_i^* = \min \{f_i(\boldsymbol{x})\}, i = 1, ..., m$ and $\boldsymbol{w}^i = \{w_1^i, ..., w_m^i\}$ is the i_{th} reference point.

The implementation of the TCH requires uniform distribution of the reference points, which the Das and Dennis method [7] can produce. In the method, an important parameter H controls the generation of reference points, including the number and interval. More precisely, every reference point $\boldsymbol{w}^i = \{w_1^i, ..., w_m^i\}, i = 1, 2, ..., N$ is from $\{\frac{0}{H}, \frac{1}{H}, \frac{2}{H}, ..., \frac{H}{H}\}$ and the sum of $w_1^i, ..., w_m^i$ is one, i.e. each reference point is in the plane $\sum_{i=1}^m y_i = 1$. The number of reference points N is calculated according to the formula $N = C_{H+m-1}^{m-1}$.

Here are MOEA/D steps.

Step1: Initialization.
Generate the initial population P of size N. Update the ideal point $\boldsymbol{z}^*$. Obtain the T nearest neighbor references set $B(i)$ of the i_{th} solution, $i = 1, 2, ..., N$.
Step2: Updating.
For each $i = 1, ..., N$,
Step2.1: Randomly select two parents from the T neighbor solutions of the i_{th} solution.
Step2.2: Generate the child $\boldsymbol{x}^c$ with crossover and mutation operators.
Step2.3: For each neighbor reference $\boldsymbol{w}^j \in B(i), j = 1, ..., T$, if and only if $g^{te}(\boldsymbol{x}^c|\boldsymbol{w}^j, \boldsymbol{z}^*) < g^{te}(\boldsymbol{x}^j|\boldsymbol{w}^j, \boldsymbol{z}^*)$, update $\boldsymbol{x}^j$.
Step3: Stopping criteria. If the stopping criteria is reached, then stop. Otherwise go to Step2.

2.4 Random Forest

The ensemble learning integrates many independent base learners into a single one which has significantly superior generalization performance. Bagging [5] is a classic algorithm. It obtains multiple sample sets through the bootstrap method. Then, each base learner is trained with one sample set, and all these base learners are combined. Extending Bagging, RF [6] is a kind of integrated learning based on the decision tree. Compared to Bagging, random attribute selection is added into RF to further improve of the randomness of the sample sets. RF have many advantages of good performance, fast learning and easy implementation.

RF is shown in the Fig. 1. When partitioning attributes, the decision tree in RF firstly selects a subset containing k attributes from the attribute set of the current node, and then selects an optimal attribute from the subset. The parameter k essentially controls the degree of randomness and [6] suggests that $k = \log_2 n_a$, where n_a is the number of attributes. From a sample set containing m_{train} samples, we can obtain n_t training sets through the bootstrap method and

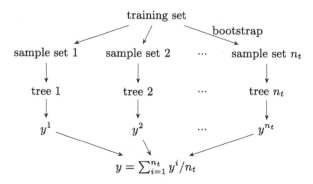

Fig. 1. Illustration of RF

each of the training sets contains k attributes and m_{train} samples. Therefore, we can get n_t base learners and combine into an integrated learner. The output of the integrated learner is $y = \sum_{i=1}^{n_t} y^i / n_t$, which is the most common combination strategy in the regression task.

3   Proposed Method

The proposed method includes three parts: the optimization part, learning part and operation part, shown in the Fig. 2. In the optimization part, it runs an EA for several times to get many enough nondominated solutions. In the learning part, it trains an inverse mapping model with a training set D made from the last part. In the operation part, when the DM gives the preference, it produces some PPVs used to predict SOIs with the model. We will go through each of these parts in more detail next.

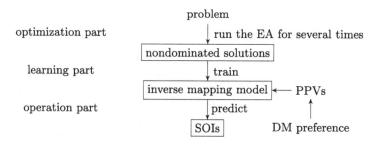

Fig. 2. The flowchart of the proposed method

3.1   Optimization Part

In principle, as long as the EA can provide a well converged and diverse PF, it can be used here. If the PF is not converged the model cannot be built correctly, and if the PF is not diverse the vacancy which actually has solutions can not be considered by the model. As a classic EA, MOEA/D is the representative algorithm used in the paper. In addition, running the EA for several times to get better and more nondominated solutions is necessary.

3.2   Learning Part

Similarly, almost all machine learning algorithms can be used in this part. Here, we build the model with the regression RF.

Define $D = \{(\boldsymbol{y}^1, \boldsymbol{x}^1), (\boldsymbol{y}^2, \boldsymbol{x}^2), ...)\}$ as the training set, where $\boldsymbol{x}^i = \{x_1^i, ..., x_d^i\}$, as the output, is the i_{th} variable vector and $\boldsymbol{y}^i = \{y_1^i, ..., y_m^i\}$, as the input, is the i_{th} objective vector corresponding to $\boldsymbol{x}^i$. The inverse mapping model can be trained with the training set and SOIs can be predicted directly without running the EA again.

3.3   Operation Part

Due to RF characteristics, the closer to the PF the PPV is, the more accurate the predicted SOI is, but the DM can not usually give the entirely right preference vector, which may be far away from the PF. So, the preference vector needs to be amended. Besides, the DM is hard to know whether the SOI is good if only one SOI is provided. So, it is necessary to extend the preference vector and give the DM more options.

In order to amend and extend the preference vector and considering that the partial PF can be approximated as a plane when η is small, the modified Das and Dennis method is used to generate PPVs, where three parameters are defined: the preference vector $\boldsymbol{z}^r = \{z_1^r, ..., z_m^r\}$, the expectation number of PPVs μ, whose value is related to H and m and calculated as described in the Sect. 2.3, and the expectation range η, which is a small real determining the proximity degree of SOIs to $\boldsymbol{z}^r$.

First, the closest vector $\boldsymbol{z}^c$ to the preference vector $\boldsymbol{z}^r$ on the PF is computed according to Euclidean distance and evenly distributed PPVs are produced with the original Das and Dennis method. Then, we move all PPVs onto the plane the same as $\boldsymbol{z}^c$, like (3).

$$\boldsymbol{v}_m^i = \frac{\boldsymbol{v}^i}{\sum_{j=1}^m z_j^c}, \tag{3}$$

where $i = 1, ..., \mu$, $\boldsymbol{v}_m^i$ is the i_{th} PPV after move, $\boldsymbol{v}^i$ is the i_{th} PPV generated by the original Das and Dennis method.

Next, we gather $\boldsymbol{v}_m$ around $\boldsymbol{z}^c$, like (4).

$$\boldsymbol{v}_g^i = \boldsymbol{z}^c + \left(\boldsymbol{v}_m^i - \boldsymbol{z}^c\right) \cdot \eta, \tag{4}$$

where $\boldsymbol{v}_g^i$ is the i_{th} PPV after gathering.

Later, the PPVs are used to predict SOIs with the model trained in the learning part. Hence, a few SOIs can be predicted and provided for the DM, which reduces the selection load and cognitive pressure of DMs in making decisions.

4 Experiments

The experimental section mainly includes two parts. First, we tried different η to observe effects on the distribution of SOIs. Then, the feasibility of the proposed method was verified on the 2- and 3-objective test problems. The Table 1 is details of the test problems.

Table 1. Test problems

Problem	m	d	Variable bounds	Objective functions
ZDT1 [27]	2	30	[0, 1]	$f_1(x) = x_1$ $f_2(x) = g(x)\left[1 - \sqrt{\frac{f_1(x)}{g(x)}}\right]$ $g(x) = 1 + \frac{9\left(\sum_{i=2}^{n} x_i\right)}{(n-1)}$
DTLZ1 [9]	3	12	[0, 1]	$f_1(x) = \frac{1}{2} x_1 x_2 \ldots x_{M-1}(1 + g(x_M))$ $f_2(x) = \frac{1}{2} x_1 x_2 \ldots (1 - x_{M-1})(1 + g(x_M))$ $\ldots$ $f_{M-1}(x) = \frac{1}{2} x_1 (1 - x_2)(1 + g(x_M))$ $f_M(x) = \frac{1}{2}(1 - x_1)(1 + g(x_M))$ $g(x_M) = 100\left(|x_M| + \sum_{x_i \in x_M}(x_i - 0.5)^2 - \cos(20\pi(x_i - 0.5))\right)$
DTLZ2 [9]	3	12	[0, 1]	$f_1(x) = (1 + g(x_M))\cos\left(\frac{\pi}{2} x_1\right) \ldots \cos\left(\frac{\pi}{2} x_{M-1}\right)$ $f_2(x) = (1 + g(x_M))\cos\left(\frac{\pi}{2} x_1\right) \ldots \sin\left(\frac{\pi}{2} x_{M-1}\right)$ $\ldots$ $f_M(x) = (1 + g(x_M))\sin\left(\frac{\pi}{2} x_1\right)$ $g(x_M) = \sum_{x_i \in x_M}(x_i - 0.5)^2$

4.1 Experiment About η

Here, we studied the distribution of SOIs with different η and set η to 0.05, 0.5, 1 and 1.5 respectively and z^r to $[0.3, 0.5]$. The mean experimental results of several times running are shown in the Fig. 3, where we can observe that the smaller η is, the denser the distribution of the SOIs are, and vice versa. Moreover, the SOIs are close to z^r when $\eta < 1$. The wide distribution of SOIs results in some SOIs being far away from z^r. So, a small η is suggested.

4.2 2- and 3-Objective Experiments

A. Experimental Settings

1) MOEA/D settings:
   - The crossover operator used simulated binary crossover [3], where the probability was set to 1.0 and distribution index was set to 20;
   - The mutation operator used polynomial mutation [8], where the probability was set to $1/d$ and distribution index was set to 20;
   - T was set to 20, as suggested in [15];

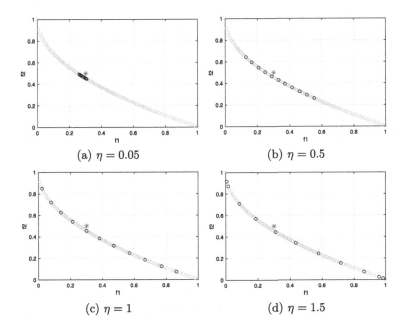

Fig. 3. The distribution of SOIs with different η, where the asterisk is z^r, the gray circles are solutions on the PF, and the black circles are SOIs

- The population was set to 100 in the 2-objective experiment and 500 in the 3-objective experiment;
- The number of iteration was set to 200 in the 2-objective experiment and 300 in the 3-objective experiment.

2) RF settings:
  - $k = \log_2 d$;
  - The number of decision trees was set to 10;
  - The program was from *scikit-learn* package.

3) Other settings:
  - $\eta = 0.05$;
  - $\mu = 11(H = 10)$ in the 2-objective experiment and $\mu = 55(H = 9)$ in the 3-objective experiment.

The settings not mentioned here are the same as the original paper.

B. Experimental Results

In the 2-objective experiment, z^r was set to $[0.5, 0.3]$, $[0.3, 0.5]$ and $[0.2, 0.5]$ respectively, where $[0.5, 0.3]$ is on the PF, $[0.3, 0.5]$ is above the PF, and $[0.2, 0.5]$ is below the PF. The experimental results are as Fig. 4. Whether z^r is on the PF, the SOIs are close to z^r and on the PF.

In the 3-objective experiment, z^r was set to $[0.25, 0.12, 0.14]$ for DTLZ1 whose PF shape is a plane and $[0.25, 0.12, 0.14]$ for DTLZ2 whose PF shape is a spherical surface, and z^r was not on the PF. The experimental results are as Fig. 5, the SOIs are around z^r and on the PF.

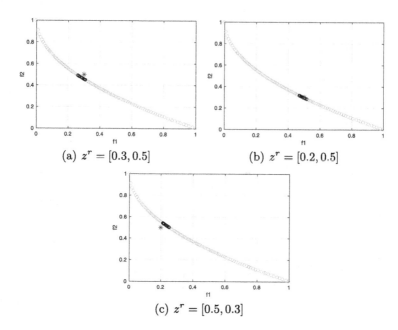

Fig. 4. The distribution of SOIs on ZDT1, where the asterisk is z^r, the gray circles are solutions on the PF, and the black circles are SOIs

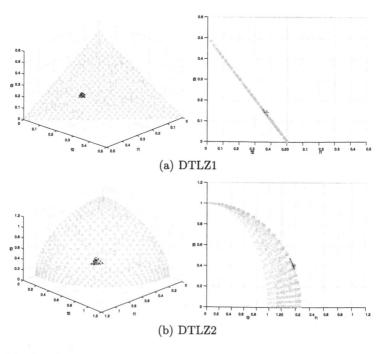

Fig. 5. The distribution of SOIs on DTLZ1-2, where the asterisk is z^r, the gray circles are solutions on the PF, and the black circles are SOIs

Obviously, compared to solutions on a PF, SOIs the proposed method producing is easier for DMs in making decision. Admittedly, widly distributing and large number solutions are cognitively barriers for DMs. For a DM, precisely understanding his or her preferences at only one time is very difficult. The DM can try many different z^r and progressively knows which SOIs he or she wants. It is similar with the interactive method in some aspects. But each part of the proposed method can be run independently. So the reaction to DMs changing preferences can be very quick.

The experimental results show the proposed method is valid on some 2- and 3-objective problems and is not only intuitive, but also easy to apply.

5 Conclusions

The paper proposed a simple and general a posteriori method to help DMs in making decision. In the optimization part, an EA is used to get the PF. In the learning part, a machine learning algorithm is adopted to train an inverse mapping model. In the operation part, PPVs are generated based on the DM preference and used to predict SOIs. Finally, SOIs are shown to the DM for the final decisions. The experimental results show the influence of different η on SOIs distribution and have verified the feasibility of the proposed method.

The proposed method still has some shortcomings. First, the DM preference is a form of digital, not language. Secondly, PPVs cannot self-adapt with the PF shape. Thirdly, it is hard to overcome the situation that the PF is discontinuous.

In future, we will continue to study the direction and try to solve the problems above. In addition, how to make decisions on the high dimension problem and how to make decisions when the DM preference is partially defaulted also are challenges.

Acknowledgments. The work was supported by the Science and Technology Support Plan of Jiangsu Province of China (BE2013879).

References

1. Aggarwal, M.: Learning of a decision-maker's preference zone with an evolutionary approach. IEEE Trans. Neural Netw. Learn. Syst. **30**(3), 670–682 (2019)
2. Arias-Montano, A., Coello, C.A.C., Mezura-Montes, E.: Multiobjective evolutionary algorithms in aeronautical and aerospace engineering. IEEE Trans. Evol. Comput. **16**(5), 662–694 (2012)
3. Deb, K., Agrawal, R.B.: Simulated binary crossover for continuous search space. Complex Syst. **9**(2), 115–148 (1995)
4. Branke, J., Kaussler, T., Schmeck, H.: Guidance in evolutionary multi-objective optimization. Adv. Eng. Softw. **32**, 499–507 (2001)
5. Breiman, L.: Bagging predictors. Mach. Learn. **24**, 123–140 (1996). https://doi.org/10.1007/BF00058655
6. Breiman, L.: Random forests. Mach. Learn. **45**(1), 5–32 (2001). https://doi.org/10.1023/A:1010933404324

7. Das, I., Dennis, J.E.: Normal-boundary intersection: a new method for generating the pareto surface in nonlinear multicriteria optimization problems. SIAM J. Optim. **8**(3), 631–657 (1998)
8. Deb, K., Goyal, M.: A combined genetic adaptive search (GeneAS) for engineering design. Comput. Sci. Inform. **26**(4), 30–45 (1999)
9. Deb, K., Thiele, L., Laumanns, M., Zitzler, E.: Scalable test problems for evolutionary multi-objective optimization. 2001 TIK-Technical report, 112 (2001)
10. Deb, K.: Multi-objective evolutionary algorithms: introducing bias among pareto-optimal solutions. In: Ghosh, A., Tsutsui, S. (eds.) Advances in Evolutionary Computing. NCS, pp. 263–292. Springer, Heidelberg (2003). https://doi.org/10.1007/978-3-642-18965-4_10
11. Deb, K., Sinha, A., Korhonen, P.J., Wallenius, J.: An interactive evolutionary multiobjective optimization method based on progressively approximated value functions. IEEE Trans. Evol. Comput. **14**(5), 723–739 (2010)
12. Fowler, J.W., Gel, E.S., Köksalan, M.M., Korhonen, P., Marquis, J.L., Wallenius, J.: Interactive evolutionary multi-objective optimization for quasi-concave preference functions. Eur. J. Oper. Res. **206**(2), 417–425 (2010)
13. Hu, J., Yu, G., Zheng, J., Zou, J.: A preference-based multi-objective evolutionary algorithm using preference selection radius. Soft. Comput. **21**(17), 5025–5051 (2016). https://doi.org/10.1007/s00500-016-2099-9
14. Zitzler, E., Thiele, L., Deb, K., Coello Coello, C.A., Corne, D. (eds.): EMO 2001. LNCS, vol. 1993. Springer, Heidelberg (2001). https://doi.org/10.1007/3-540-44719-9
15. Li, H., Zhang, Q.: Multiobjective optimization problems with complicated pareto sets, MOEA/D and NSGA-II. IEEE Trans. Evol. Comput. **13**(2), 284–302 (2009)
16. Li, K., Chen, R., Savic, D., Yao, X.: Interactive decomposition multiobjective optimization via progressively learned value functions. IEEE Trans. Fuzzy Syst. **27**(5), 849–860 (2019)
17. Li, K., Chen, R., Min, G., Yao, X.: Integration of preferences in decomposition multiobjective optimization. IEEE Trans. Cybern. **48**(12), 3359–3370 (2018)
18. Liu, Z., Li, J., Song, Q.: Optimized analysis based on improved mutation and crossover operator for differential evolution algorithm. In: Wang, G., Atiquzzaman, M., Yan, Z., Choo, K.-K.R. (eds.) SpaCCS 2017. LNCS, vol. 10656, pp. 1–16. Springer, Cham (2017). https://doi.org/10.1007/978-3-319-72389-1_1
19. Ponsich, A., Jaimes, A.L., Coell, C.A.C.: A survey on multiobjective evolutionary algorithms for the solution of the portfolio optimization problem and other finance and economics applications. IEEE Trans. Evol. Comput. **17**(3), 321–344 (2013)
20. Rachmawati, L., Srinivasan, D.: Preference incorporation in multi-objective evolutionary algorithms: a survey. In: 2006 IEEE International Conference on Evolutionary Computation, Vancouver, BC, pp. 962–968 (2006)
21. Taboada, H.A., Baheranwala, F., Coit, D.W., Wattanapongsakorn, N.: Practical solutions for multi-objective optimization: an application to system reliability design problems. Reliab. Eng. Syst. Saf. **92**(3), 314–322 (2007)
22. Purshouse, R.C., Fleming, P.J., Fonseca, C.M., Greco, S., Shaw, J. (eds.): EMO 2013. LNCS, vol. 7811. Springer, Heidelberg (2013). https://doi.org/10.1007/978-3-642-37140-0
23. Wu, H., Wang, N., Wang, G.: CCN hotspot cache placement strategy based on genetic algorithm. In: Wang, G., Atiquzzaman, M., Yan, Z., Choo, K.-K.R. (eds.) SpaCCS 2017. LNCS, vol. 10658, pp. 350–360. Springer, Cham (2017). https://doi.org/10.1007/978-3-319-72395-2_32

24. Yu, G., Zheng, J., Shen, R., Li, M.: Decomposing the user-preference in multiob-jective optimization. Soft. Comput. **20**(10), 4005–4021 (2015). https://doi.org/10.1007/s00500-015-1736-z
25. Zhang, Q., Li, H.: MOEA/D: a multiobjective evolutionary algorithm based on decomposition. IEEE Trans. Evol. Comput. **11**(6), 712–731 (2007)
26. Zhang, J., Xing, L.: A survey of multiobjective evolutionary algorithms. In: 2017 IEEE International Conference on Computational Science and Engineering (CSE) and IEEE International Conference on Embedded and Ubiquitous Computing (EUC), Guangzhou, pp. 93–100 (2017)
27. Zitzler, E., Deb, K., Thiele, L.: Comparison of multiobjective evolutionary algo-rithms: empirical results. Evol. Comput. **8**(2), 173–195 (2000)

HVH: A Lightweight Hash Function Based on Dual Pseudo-Random Transformation

Yuhua Huang[1(✉)], Shen Li[1], Wanlin Sun[2], Xuejun Dai[1], and Wei Zhu[1]

[1] College of Computer Science and Technology, Nanjing University of Aeronautics and Astronautics, Nanjing 210016, China
hyuhua2k@163.com, li_shen163@163.com, daixuemai@163.com, zhu_wei2019@163.com
[2] Department of Physics, Changji College, Changji 831100, China
sunwanlin815@163.com

Abstract. Along with the popularization of RFID technology and wireless sensor network, it has been more and more difficult for common hash-functions to meet the application demands in the Internet of Things. Furthermore, the design and analysis of lightweight hash function have gradually become a research focus at current days. This paper presents the HVH family of lightweight hash functions based on the sponge iterative structure and the lightweight block cipher algorithm VH. HVH offers five different lengths of message digest for different constrained environments and security levels. Moreover, HVH can operate efficiently not only in hardware environments but also on software platforms, such as 8-bit microcontroller. Hardware implementation of HVH-88 is around 1129GE with a throughput of 44.44 Kbps at 100 kHz, which is comparable with the 1237 GE hardware implementation of SPONGENT-88. The software implementation of HVH-88 on 8-bit microcontroller is about 1.47 Mb/s, and its efficiency is 10 times as much as that of SPONGENT-88 in RFID environment. Security evaluation shows that HVH can achieve sufficient security margin against known attacks, such as linear cryptanalysis, differential cryptanalysis, impossible differential cryptanalysis, (second) pre-image and collision resistance.

Keywords: Hash function · Lightweight cryptograph · Sponge construction · VH · HVH

1 Introduction

Hash function has been widely used in the fields of digital signature, authentication, message integrity detection, digital certificate, pseudo-random number generation and security protocol design. Hash function as one of the important branches of cryptography, is a significant technical means of information security. With the popularization of RFID technology and wireless sensor network, it has been increasingly difficult for common hash-functions to meet the application demands of the Internet of Things. Moreover, the design and analysis of

ⓒ Springer Nature Switzerland AG 2021
G. Wang et al. (Eds.): SpaCCS 2020, LNCS 12383, pp. 492–505, 2021.
https://doi.org/10.1007/978-3-030-68884-4_41

lightweight hash function have become a research focus at present. At the same time, the research and progress of lightweight Hash functions will also push the development of security mechanism in the terminal system of the Internet of Things. The Hash function [1] is a mapping from an input or message with arbitrary length to an output with fixed length through the Hash algorithm.

At present, the studies of lightweight Hash function have become very popular and many of the lightweight Hash functions have been designed, such as SQUASH [2], DM-PRESENT [3], H-PRESENT [3], L-CAHASH [4], QUARK [5], PHOTON [6], SONGENT [7], Neeva [8], GLUON [9], and LNHASH [10]. SPONGENT is a light-weight Hash function proposed by A. Bogdanov et al. based on CHES 2011. Its designed iterative structure is a sponge construction [11] based on a wide PRESENT-type [12] permutation. Such algorithm can provide different lengths of abstract, including 88-bit, 128-bit, 160-bit, 224-bit and 256-bit. The GE number of their hardware implementation is 1237, 1831, 2406, 3220 and 3639 respectively. PHOTON is a lightweight Hash function proposed by J. Guo et al. based on CRYPTO 2011. Its design adopts the sponge construction based on a wideAES-type [13] permutation. Actually, AES is not suitable for resource constrained environment. However, designer utilizes a serialization method to reduce the demand of GE number. In the case of providing 264 security intensity, PHOTON can be implemented with the least 1120GE.

This paper proposes a new lightweight Hash function, namely Hash Vertical Horizontal (HVH). The Hash function should be applied to the resource constrained mobile terminal. Therefore, the design of HVH needs to consider two aspects, including low implementation of hardware and appropriate requirement of security level. In a lightweight environment, the length of input M is expected to be less than or equal to 256 bit. The length of output $H(M)$ message abstract should between 64 bit and 256 bit. Therefore, five different lengths of output message, including 88-bit, 128-bit, 160-bit, 224-bit and 256-bit are provided for different application scenarios. Such algorithm can at least use 869GE to achieve the standard of ultra-lightweight RFID environment and compare favorably with the hardware implementation of SPONGENT-88. SPONGENT selects the PRESENT-type permutation and has low speed due to the great amount of bit manipulation. Nonetheless HVH uses the VH with higher software implementation efficiency. The software efficiency of HVH-88 is 10 times of SPONGENT-88. The hardware implementation of HVH demonstrates excellent performance as it reduces the security level of the second pre-image. The VH can achieve sufficient security margin against known attacks and is highly efficient in both hardware implementation and software implementation. It can be considered that the HVH family of Hash functions has achieved a superior balance between security and performance to meet the hardware usage needs of extreme environments with limited resources, such as RFID and to meet some software implementation needs in the environment such as embedded mode and MCU.

2   Experimental Section

The design of the lightweight Hash function includes an iterative construction and a permutation function. The design and security analysis of Hash function have always been emphasizing on researches on the security of the iterative construction in the hash function. People have put forward many different kinds of iterative construction of hash function, and have conducted security proof. With the development of research, some new iterative constructions have emerged. At present, the common iterative constructions are MD [14–16], Rabin [14], DM [14], HAIFA [17], Sponge, etc. Due to the lack of forward feedback in sponge construction, less GE numbers are required in practical hardware implement to meet the design requirements of the lightweight Hash function. Thus, the HVH family adopts the sponge construction. From the construction mode of the permutation function, the design methods of lightweight Hash function can be divided into two categories. One category particularly focuses on designing permutation function while another utilizes existing block cipher design permutation function. The HVH family of permutation function uses the existing lightweight block cipher, namely Vertical Horizontal (VH). VH uses the SP structure, using the pseudo-random transformation to construct 256 bytes encryption and decryption tables to simplify the design of S-box and meet the design requirements of the small occupying space of permutation function.

2.1   Permutation-Based Sponge Construction

As shown in Fig. 1, sponge construction relies on a simple iterated design that compress an input M of variable length into an output message abstract of arbitrary length through an internal status, B with fixed b-bit length and a permutation function, F. The length of its internal state is $b = r + c \geqslant n$, where n refers to the length of message abstract, r is the throughput rate and c is capacity. It mainly consists of the following three steps.

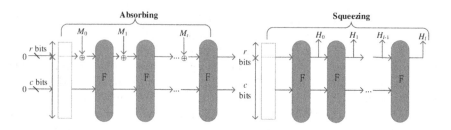

Fig. 1. Permutation-based sponge construction.

Initialization Phase. If the length of M is not the multiple of r-bit length, we need to fill. The message is padded with a string line to make the message become multiple of r-bit length. Such string line is a 1 followed by a necessary number of 0. Subsequently, the message is divided into sub-groups of r-bit length. Furthermore, the initial value of internal state B is set as 0.

Absorbing Phase. Conduct exclusive-or operation in message sub-groups of r-bit and internal state of pre-r bits; then upgrade internal state with the applications of permutation function, F till all the message sub-groups are absorbed completely.

Squeezing Phase. The internal state of pre-r bits as output return upgrades the internal status through the application of permutation function F until n-bit returns. Meanwhile, the return of n-bit is the final message digest.

2.2 VH-Type Permutation

In the design of the permutation function (F function), we use the lightweight block cipher VH. VH adopts the SP structure, has a block length of 64 bits, and supports the keys of 64, 80, 96, 112 and 128 bits. The number of rounds is d = 10, 11, 12, 13 and 14, respectively. The simple description of the VH is as follows.

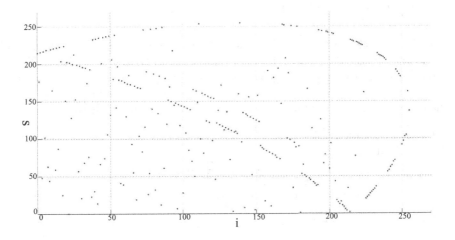

Fig. 2. Pseudorandom transformation.

Encryption Transformation Table and Decryption Transformation Table. The encryption and decryption S-box is generated via pseudorandom transformation. We first compute $T(i) = \lfloor |256\sin(i)| \rfloor$, where $\lfloor \rfloor$ denote the round-down operation; to generate 256 non-repetitious bytes, i ranges from 1 to 30000, eliminating repetitions that occur. The encryption transformation table $S[256]$ and decryption transformation table $S^{-1}[256]$ are a pseudorandom combination of 256 bytes, which is obtained by alternating bytes in T:

$$S[T(j)] = T(j+1) \quad S[T(255)] = T(0)$$
$$S^{-1}[T(j+1)] = T(j) \quad S^{-1}[T(0)] = T(255) \tag{1}$$

where $0 \le j \le 254$. The 256 bytes of the pseudo random transformation is shown in Fig 2. The distribution of the S-box can be seen by the distribution of the points.

Key Schedule. Key scheduling is achieved via iterations, so the L-byte key K is expanded to $8(d+1)$ bytes: the expanded key:

$$Key = K_0 \mid K_1 \mid ... \mid K_i \mid ... \mid K_r = K_0 \mid K_1 \mid ... \mid K_i \mid ... \mid K_{8d+7} \tag{2}$$

where each K_i has 8 bytes, $0 \le i \le d$, each K_i has a unit byte, $0 \le i \le 8d+7$. For the key K with 8, 10, 12, 14 and 16 bytes, the number of rounds is $d = 10$, 11, 12, 13, and 14. The first L bytes of the expanded key is the key $K : K = k_0 \mid k_1 \mid ... \mid k_{L-1}$. In the case of $L \le i \le 8d+7$, k_i in the expanded key is obtained via recursion of k_{i-L} and k_{i-1}, i.e. $k_i = S[k_{i-1}] \oplus k_{i-L}$.

Data Encryption Process. The encryption process of VH is shown in Fig 3. At the first, we get the results of the initial key K_0 and plaintext by XOR. Then, through further d-round to encrypt the result of the previous step, each round of encryption including S-box transformation, P permutation and round key XOR. The output is the next round of input. Finally we get final ciphertext C.

- Initial Encryption
  The initial cipher text:
  $$C_0 = P \oplus K_0 \tag{3}$$
  where P is the 64-bit initial plain text, K_0 is the first 8 bytes of the key K.
- d-round Encryption

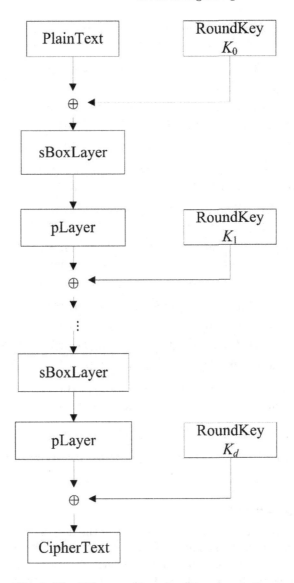

Fig. 3. The VH encryption algorithm description.

For i within $[1, d]$, each round of iteration has the following three steps. Firstly, perform pseudorandom transformation on each byte of the data using the encryption S-box:

$$M_i(j) = S[C_{i-1}(j)] \tag{4}$$

where i range from 1 to d, $X_i(j)$ denotes the j byte of X_i, $0 \le j \le 7$.

Secondly, arrange the 64-bit data X_i into a 8*8 matrix, perform pseudorandom transformation on each diagonal line of X_i using the encryption S-box:

$$P_i(0) = S\{[M_i(0)\&128]||[M_i(1)\&64]||[M_i(2)\&32]||[M_i(3)\&16]$$
$$||[M_i(4)\&8]||[M_i(5)\&4]||[M_i(6)\&2]||[M_i(7)\&1]\}$$
$$P_i(1) = S\{[M_i(1)\&128]||[M_i(2)\&64]||[M_i(3)\&32]||[M_i(4)\&16]$$
$$||[M_i(5)\&8]||[M_i(6)\&4]||[M_i(7)\&2]||[M_i(0)\&1]\}$$
$$P_i(2) = S\{[M_i(2)\&128]||[M_i(3)\&64]||[M_i(4)\&32]||[M_i(5)\&16]$$
$$||[M_i(6)\&8]||[M_i(7)\&4]||[M_i(0)\&2]||[M_i(1)\&1]\}$$
$$P_i(3) = S\{[M_i(3)\&128]||[M_i(4)\&64]||[M_i(5)\&32]||[M_i(6)\&16]$$
$$||[M_i(7)\&8]||[M_i(0)\&4]||[M_i(1)\&2]||[M_i(2)\&1]\}$$
$$P_i(4) = S\{[M_i(4)\&128]||[M_i(5)\&64]||[M_i(6)\&32]||[M_i(7)\&16]$$
$$||[M_i(0)\&8]||[M_i(1)\&4]||[M_i(2)\&2]||[M_i(3)\&1]\}$$
$$P_i(5) = S\{[M_i(5)\&128]||[M_i(6)\&64]||[M_i(7)\&32]||[M_i(0)\&16]$$
$$||[M_i(1)\&8]||[M_i(2)\&4]||[M_i(3)\&2]||[M_i(4)\&1]\}$$
$$P_i(6) = S\{[M_i(6)\&128]||[M_i(7)\&64]||[M_i(0)\&32]||[M_i(1)\&16]$$
$$||[M_i(2)\&8]||[M_i(3)\&4]||[M_i(4)\&2]||[M_i(5)\&1]\}$$
$$P_i(7) = S\{[M_i(7)\&128]||[M_i(0)\&64]||[M_i(1)\&32]||[M_i(2)\&16]$$
$$||[M_i(3)\&8]||[M_i(4)\&4]||[M_i(5)\&2]||[M_i(6)\&1]\}$$

$$(5)$$

Finally, obtain the ciphertext of the current iteration by performing XOR operation on the output P_i above and the sub-key K_i of the current iteration:

$$C_i = P_i \bigoplus K_i \qquad (6)$$

where r range from 1 to d. The result output in the last round is the final cipher text C.

2.3 *VH*-Type Permutation

This paper aims to address the gap by exploring the design space of lightweight hash function based on the sponge construction instantiated with VH-type permutation function. As a result, a lightweight hash function, called HVH is generated. According to different sizes of hash n-bit, its various parameters are referred to as HVH-$n/c/r$, where r is throughput rate and c is capacity. According to the application of the HVH family into different constrained environment requirements, five different sizes are put forward, including 88-bit, 128-bit, 160-bit, 224-bit and 256-bit. As for the HVH family 18 rounds of iteration are used. The HVH family is composed of the following three parts.

Initialization Function. The internal state of B and message abstract of Mare divided into a number of r-bit sub-groups. Through $B = r + c \geq n$, the length of internal state can be calculated as 88-bit, 136-bit, 176-bit, 240-bit and 280-bit respectively. Subsequently, the internal state of B is set as 0.

Absorbing Phase. The process of the HVH absorption phase is shown in Algorithm 1. Algorithm 1 defines several u-bit long packet messages M and an initialized internal state B. Each u-bit-length message packet is XOR with the first u-bits of the internal state, and then the internal state is updated with a compression function until all message packets have been absorbed.

Algorithm 1. Absorbing algorithm in HVH function absorption phase.

Input: Message M, internal state B;
Output: Updated internal status B;
1:   **For** i = 1 to R **do**;
2:       $B \leftarrow M[\text{i}] \oplus B[0]$;
3:       $B \leftarrow \text{SBoxLayer}(B)$;
4:       $B \leftarrow \text{PLayer}^*(B)$;
5:   **End for**;

The SBoxLayer(B) function: the internal state of B carries out a pseudo-random transformation, that is, each byte of data encryption S-box for pseudo-random transformation:

$$M_i(j) = S[B_{i-1}(j)] \tag{7}$$

where i ranges from 1 to R, M_i(j) denotes the j byte of M_i, $0 \leq \text{j} \leq 15$.

The PLayer*(B) function: The data of S-box is replaced by P. The B data of 88-bit, 136-bit, 176-bit, 240-bit and 280-bit are arranged into the matrix of 11*8, 17*8, 22*8, 30*8 and 35*8 bits respectively through using a deformation of permutation functions in the VH. Figure 4 shows the schematic diagram of the HVH-128/128/8 permutation. The bit data in internal status B with the same shape and color are permuted to the corresponding location of the B*. The K line data of P output is the m byte data in the (k+m) mod μ bits of input, $0 \leq$ k $\leq$ 15, $0 \leq$ m $\leq$ 7, $\mu \in \{11, 17, 22, 30, 35\}$.

Squeezing Phase. The process of the squeeze phase of HVH is shown in Algorithm 2. Algorithm 2 defines the absorbed internal state B. The first u-bit long packet of the internal state is returned as the output, and then the internal state is updated by the compression function until n-bit return is obtained. At this time, the n-bit return is the final message digest.

The SBoxLayer and the PLayer as the S and P layer functions of the VH block cipher, are used to update the internal state B of HVH. The SBoxLayer(B) conducts pseudo-random transform to state, and the PLayer*(B) conducts permutation to state. Both of them constitute the compression functions of HVH.

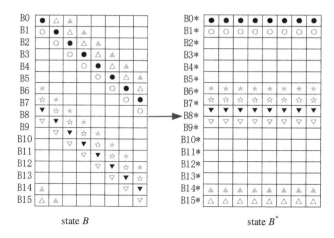

Fig. 4. The PLayer*(B) function of HVH-128/128/8.

Algorithm 2. Absorbing algorithm in HVH function absorption phase.

Input: Internal state B;
Output: Message digest H, updated internal status B;
1:    **For** i = 1 to R **do**;
2:        $H[i] \leftarrow B[0]$;
3:        $B \leftarrow$ SBoxLayer(B);
4:        $B \leftarrow$ PLayer*(B);
5:    **End for**;

---

3   Results and Discussion

3.1   Implementation Results

Results and Comparison of Hardware Comparison. Efficiency of hardware implementation is usually measured by the equivalent number of GE. The number of GE needed to achieve hardware implementation of CLEFIA-128 was estimated in reference [18]. The authors reported that 5979 GE were required to implement CLEFIA-128, neglecting the effect of different ASIC libraries. The authors in reference stated that 6 GE were needed to store 1 bit, and 2.67 GE were required for a XOR operation [19].

In evaluating hardware implementation of the HVH family, a rough estimation can be made for reference [18]. To provide compact implementations, we first focus on serialized designs. Two different data path sizes for each HVH variant is explored to focus on DataPath $\in \{4, n\}$. Hardware implementation of the HVH family is shown in Table 1. It can be seen that the throughput rate of HVH-88/80/8 is 2.02 kb/s and the area is 857GE, which is obviously better than the same parameters of SPONGENT-88/80/8. With the increase of n, the corresponding rate increases with the increase of n. It can be seen that the throughput rate of HVH-128/128/8 is higher than that of HVH-160/160/16.

FOM as an index evaluates the comprehensive performance of hardware implementation. The greater FOM is, the better the performance of hardware will have. According to Table 1, the hardware implementation of HVH family is better than that of SPOGENT.

Table 1. Hardware performance of the HVH family.

Hash function	DataPath	Cycles	Throughout (kb/s)	Area (GE)	FOM (10^{-6})
HVH-88/80/8	4	396	2.02	857	2.75
HVH-88/80/8	88	18	44.44	1129	3.49
HVH-128/128/8	4	612	1.31	1145	1.00
HVH-128/128/8	136	18	44.44	1537	18.82
HVH-160/160/16	4	792	2.02	1385	1.05
HVH-160/160/16	176	18	88.89	1876	25.25
HVH-224/224/16	4	1080	1.48	1769	0.47
HVH-224/224/16	240	18	88.89	2420	15.18
HVH-256/256/32	4	1260	2.54	2009	0.63
HVH-256/256/32	280	18	177.78	2680	24.76
Spongent-88/80/8	4	990	0.81	869	1.07
Spongent-88/80/8	88	45	17.78	1237	11.62

Software Implementation. In Table 2, the efficiency of software implementation of the HVH and SPONGENT-88/80/8 is compared. According to the comparison, the time of SPONGENT-88/80/8 consumption is ten times as much as that of HVH-88/80/8. Thus, it can be concluded that the software implementation of HVH-88/80/8 is better than that of SPONGENT-88/80/8. SPONGENT-88/80/8 has good hardware implementation. However, it adopts the PRESENT type of compression function design and performs low software implementation efficiency due to the massive use of bit manipulation. On the other hand, the HVH family of Hash permutation function adopts the VH type of algorithm to perform higher software implementation efficiency. It can be considered that the HVH family has achieved a good balance between the hardware implementation and software implementation to meet the hardware usage needs of extreme environments with limited resources, such as RFID and to meet some software implementation needs in the environment such as embedded mode and MCU.

3.2 Security Evaluation

Differential and Linear Attacks on Block Ciphers. Differential cryptanalysis [20] and linear cryptanalysis [21] have been the most effective attack against block cipher. The authors in reference detailed the method for evaluating a cipher's resistance against differential and linear cryptanalysis, and proposed to compute the maximum differential and linear probability by counting the number of dynamic S-boxes [20,21]. This method was used by reference to evaluate CLEFIA [18].

Table 2. Software performance of the HVH family.

HVH-$n/c/r$	Time (ms)	Efficiency (Mb/s)	c/B
HVH-88/80/8	5712	1.4703	4399
HVH-128/128/8	9091	1.4350	7023
HVH-160/160/16	6092	2.7552	4708
HVH-224/224/16	8872	2.5848	6869
HVH-256/256/32	6537	4.0849	4939
Spongent-88/80/8	58673	0.1444	45302

The maximum differential probability of VH's S-box is computed to be $2^{-4.415}$. The number DS of dynamic S-boxes for the first ten rounds of VH with a key of 80-bit long, is computed by using the program, which is shown in Table 3. It can be observed that the 4-round maximum differential probability of VH is $DCP_{max}^{4r} \leq 2^{21*(-4.415)} = 2^{-92.715} \leq 2^{-88}$. When the round number is larger than 4, no effective differential characteristic is found for cryptanalysis. So the full-round VH can resist differential cryptanalysis.

The maximum linear probability of VH's S-box is computed to be $2^{-2.83}$. The number LS of dynamic S-boxes for the first ten rounds of VH with a key of 80-bit long, is computed by using the program, which is shown in Table 3. It can be observed that the 4-round maximum linear probability of VH is $LCP_{max}^{4r} \leq 2^{24*(-2.82)} = 2^{-67.92} \leq 2^{-64}$. When the number of rounds is larger than 4, no effective linear characteristic is found for cryptanalysis. So the full-round VH can resist linear cryptanalysis.

Table 3. Guaranteed number of active S-boxes of VH.

Rounds	DS	LS	Rounds	DS	LS
1	0	0	6	35	40
2	7	8	7	42	48
3	14	16	8	49	56
4	21	24	9	56	64
5	28	32	10	63	72

Impossible Differential Cryptanalysis. Impossible differential cryptanalysis [22] is a very effective attack against VH. J. Kim [23] proposed a moment algorithm μ-method to perform impossible differential cryptanalysis of the structure of the block cipher. Their method can find different impossible differential paths.

Impossible differential cryptanalysis of VH is carried out by using this method, determining the maximum number of rounds is 6, finding 8 non-differential paths:

$$
\begin{aligned}
(0,0,0,\alpha,0,\alpha,\alpha,\alpha) &\xrightarrow{6r} (0,0,0,0,\alpha,\alpha,\alpha,\alpha) & p &= 1 \\
(0,0,\alpha,0,\alpha,\alpha,\alpha,0) &\xrightarrow{6r} (0,0,0,0,\alpha,\alpha,\alpha,\alpha) & p &= 1 \\
(0,\alpha,0,\alpha,\alpha,\alpha,0,0) &\xrightarrow{6r} (0,0,0,\alpha,\alpha,\alpha,\alpha,0) & p &= 1 \\
(0,\alpha,\alpha,\alpha,0,0,0,\alpha) &\xrightarrow{6r} (0,\alpha,\alpha,\alpha,\alpha,0,0,0) & p &= 1 \\
(\alpha,0,0,0,\alpha,0,\alpha,\alpha) &\xrightarrow{6r} (\alpha,\alpha,0,0,0,0,\alpha,\alpha) & p &= 1 \\
(\alpha,0,\alpha,\alpha,\alpha,0,0,0) &\xrightarrow{6r} (0,0,\alpha,\alpha,\alpha,\alpha,0,0) & p &= 1 \\
(\alpha,\alpha,0,0,0,\alpha,0,\alpha) &\xrightarrow{6r} (\alpha,\alpha,\alpha,0,0,0,0,\alpha) & p &= 1 \\
(\alpha,\alpha,\alpha,0,0,0,\alpha,0) &\xrightarrow{6r} (\alpha,\alpha,\alpha,\alpha,0,0,0,0) & p &= 1
\end{aligned}
\tag{8}
$$

Where $\alpha \in GF(2^8)$ denotes the non-zero differential. Therefore, impossible differential cryptanalysis is invalid for VH.

Preimage, Second Preimage and Collision Resistance. G. Bertoni [24] demonstrates the sponge structure. The random oracle is indistinguishable. It shows the ability of preimage attack, second preimage attack and collision resistance attack.

- Preimage attack: $\min\{2^n, 2^c, \max\{2^{n-r}, 2^{c/2}\}\}$
- Second preimage attack: $\min\{2^n, 2^{c/2}\}$
- Collision attack: $\min\{2^{n/2}, 2^{c/2}\}$

As for the HVH family of Hash functions, the advantages of hardware implementation stem from the reduction of the safety level of the second preimage, and meanwhile maintain the standard level of collision. Therefore, according to the above conclusion, the preimage attack, second preimage attack and collision attack can be shown in Table 4.

Table 4. Preimage, second preimage and collision resistance of HVH.

HVH-$n/c/r$	Pre 2^{n-r}	2nd Pre $2^{c/2}$	Coll $2^{c/2}$	Applicable environment
HVH-88/80/8	72	40	40	Extremely constrained
HVH-128/128/8	120	64	64	Highly constrained
HVH-160/160/16	144	80	80	Highly constrained
HVH-224/224/16	208	112	112	Extremely constrained
HVH-256/256/32	224	128	128	Lightweight embedded

4   Conclusions

This paper proposes HVH. Our proposal is established on the well-known sponge function and the VH that perfectly fit small area scenarios. The software efficiency test shows that software implementation of the HVH family is superior to that of the SPONGENT. Through hardware implementation, the overall performance of HVH hardware implementation is slightly better than SPONGENT which adopts the same sponge structure. Through comparing hardware implementation with SPONGENT, it can be concluded that the comprehensive hardware implementation of HVH family is better than that of SPONGENT. In general, the HVH Family integrates the implementation of hardware and software to meet the hardware usage needs of extreme environments with limited resources, such as RFID and to meet some software implementation needs in the environment such as embedded mode and MCU.

Acknowledgments. The subject has been supported by the Science & Technology Support Plan of Jiangsu Province under Grant No. BE2013879.

References

1. Peyravian, M., Roginsky, A., Zunic, N.: Hash-based encryption system. Comput. Secur. **18**(4), 345–350 (1999)
2. Shamir, A.: SQUASH – a new MAC with provable security properties for highly constrained devices such as RFID tags. In: Nyberg, K. (ed.) FSE 2008. LNCS, vol. 5086, pp. 144–157. Springer, Heidelberg (2008). https://doi.org/10.1007/978-3-540-71039-4_9
3. Bogdanov, A., Leander, G., Paar, C., Poschmann, A., Robshaw, M.J.B., Seurin, Y.: Hash functions and RFID tags: mind the gap. In: Oswald, E., Rohatgi, P. (eds.) CHES 2008. LNCS, vol. 5154, pp. 283–299. Springer, Heidelberg (2008). https://doi.org/10.1007/978-3-540-85053-3_18
4. Hanin, C., Echandouri, B., Omary, F., El Bernoussi, S.: L-CAHASH: a novel lightweight hash function based on cellular automata for rfid. In: Sabir, E., García Armada, A., Ghogho, M., Debbah, M. (eds.) Ubiquitous Networking. LNCS, vol. 10542, pp. 287–298. Springer, Cham (2017). https://doi.org/10.1007/978-3-319-68179-5_25
5. Aumasson, J.P., Henzen, L., Meier, W., Naya-Plasencia, M.: Quark: a lightweight hash. J. Cryptol. **26**(2), 313–339 (2013). https://doi.org/10.1007/s00145-012-9125-6
6. Guo, J., Peyrin, T., Poschmann, A.: The PHOTON family of lightweight hash functions. In: Rogaway, P. (ed.) CRYPTO 2011. LNCS, vol. 6841, pp. 222–239. Springer, Heidelberg (2011). https://doi.org/10.1007/978-3-642-22792-9_13
7. Bogdanov, A., Knežević, M., Leander, G., Toz, D., Varıcı, K., Verbauwhede, I.: SPONGENT: a lightweight hash function. In: Preneel, B., Takagi, T. (eds.) CHES 2011. LNCS, vol. 6917, pp. 312–325. Springer, Heidelberg (2011). https://doi.org/10.1007/978-3-642-23951-9_21
8. Bussi, K., Dey, D., Biswas, M.K., Dass, B.: Neeva: a lightweight hash function. IACR Cryptol. ePrint Arch. **2016**, 42 (2016)

9. Berger, T.P., D'Hayer, J., Marquet, K., Minier, M., Thomas, G.: The GLUON family: a lightweight hash function family based on FCSRs. In: Mitrokotsa, A., Vaudenay, S. (eds.) AFRICACRYPT 2012. LNCS, vol. 7374, pp. 306–323. Springer, Heidelberg (2012). https://doi.org/10.1007/978-3-642-31410-0_19

10. Zhang, X., Xu, Q., Li, X., Wang, C.: A lightweight hash function based on cellular automata for mobile network. In: 15th International Conference on Mobile Ad-Hoc and Sensor Networks, MSN 2019, pp. 247–252. IEEE (2019). https://doi.org/10.1109/MSN48538.2019.00055

11. Bertoni, G., Daemen, J., Peeters, M., Van Assche, G.: Sponge functions. In: ECRYPT Hash Workshop, vol. 2007. Citeseer (2007)

12. Bogdanov, A., et al.: PRESENT: an ultra-lightweight block cipher. In: Paillier, P., Verbauwhede, I. (eds.) CHES 2007. LNCS, vol. 4727, pp. 450–466. Springer, Heidelberg (2007). https://doi.org/10.1007/978-3-540-74735-2_31

13. Daemen, J., Rijmen, V.: The block cipher Rijndael. In: Quisquater, J.-J., Schneier, B. (eds.) CARDIS 1998. LNCS, vol. 1820, pp. 277–284. Springer, Heidelberg (2000). https://doi.org/10.1007/10721064_26

14. Forouzan, B.A.: Cryptography & Network Security. McGraw-Hill Inc., New York (2007)

15. Merkle, R.C.: One way hash functions and DES. In: Brassard, G. (ed.) CRYPTO 1989. LNCS, vol. 435, pp. 428–446. Springer, New York (1990). https://doi.org/10.1007/0-387-34805-0_40

16. Damgård, I.B.: A design principle for hash functions. In: Brassard, G. (ed.) CRYPTO 1989. LNCS, vol. 435, pp. 416–427. Springer, New York (1990). https://doi.org/10.1007/0-387-34805-0_39

17. Biham, E., Dunkelman, O.: A framework for iterative hash functions - HAIFA. IACR Cryptol. ePrint Arch. **2007**, 278 (2007)

18. Shirai, T., Shibutani, K., Akishita, T., Moriai, S., Iwata, T.: The 128-bit blockcipher CLEFIA (extended abstract). In: Biryukov, A. (ed.) FSE 2007. LNCS, vol. 4593, pp. 181–195. Springer, Heidelberg (2007). https://doi.org/10.1007/978-3-540-74619-5_12

19. Juels, A., Weis, S.A.: Authenticating pervasive devices with human protocols. In: Shoup, V. (ed.) CRYPTO 2005. LNCS, vol. 3621, pp. 293–308. Springer, Heidelberg (2005). https://doi.org/10.1007/11535218_18

20. Biham, E., Shamir, A.: Differential Cryptanalysis of the Data Encryption Standard. Springer, New York (1993). https://doi.org/10.1007/978-1-4613-9314-6

21. Matsui, M.: Linear cryptanalysis method for DES cipher. In: Helleseth, T. (ed.) EUROCRYPT 1993. LNCS, vol. 765, pp. 386–397. Springer, Heidelberg (1994). https://doi.org/10.1007/3-540-48285-7_33

22. Biham, E., Biryukov, A., Shamir, A.: Cryptanalysis of skipjack reduced to 31 rounds using impossible differentials. In: Stern, J. (ed.) EUROCRYPT 1999. LNCS, vol. 1592, pp. 12–23. Springer, Heidelberg (1999). https://doi.org/10.1007/3-540-48910-X_2

23. Kim, J., Hong, S., Sung, J., Lee, S., Lim, J., Sung, S.: Impossible differential cryptanalysis for block cipher structures. In: Johansson, T., Maitra, S. (eds.) INDOCRYPT 2003. LNCS, vol. 2904, pp. 82–96. Springer, Heidelberg (2003). https://doi.org/10.1007/978-3-540-24582-7_6

24. Bertoni, G., Daemen, J., Peeters, M., Van Assche, G.: On the indifferentiability of the sponge construction. In: Smart, N. (ed.) EUROCRYPT 2008. LNCS, vol. 4965, pp. 181–197. Springer, Heidelberg (2008). https://doi.org/10.1007/978-3-540-78967-3_11

SVHF: A Lightweight Stream Cipher Based on Feistel and OFB

Yuhua Huang[1($\boxtimes$)], Wei Zhu[1], Wanlin Sun[2], Xuejun Dai[1],
and Shen Li[1]

[1] College of Computer Science and Technology, Nanjing University
of Aeronautics and Astronautics, Nanjing 210016, China
hyuhua2k@163.com, zhu_wei2019@163.com,
daixuemai@163.com, li_shen163@163.com
[2] Department of Physics, Changji College, Changji 831100, China
sunwanlin815@163.com

Abstract. For the demand of the resource constrained mobile terminal to the lightweight cipher, this paper presents a new lightweight stream cipher, which is based on the Feistel and OFB mode called SVHF. Similar to many other lightweight stream ciphers, the key-stream size of SVHF is 128-bit while the IV is specified to be 128 bits. Our security evaluation shows that SVHF can achieve enough security margin against known attacks, such as differential cryptanalysis, linear cryptanalysis and impossible differential cryptanalysis. Furthermore, SVHF can be implemented efficiently not only in hardware environments but also in software plat-forms. Hardware implementation of SVHF requires about 1632GE, which is comparable with the 2194 GE hardware implementation of WG-7. The software implementation of SVHF on 8-bit microcontroller is about 50.82 Mb/s, and its efficiency is 4 times as much as that of WG-7 in RFID environment.

Keywords: Lightweight · Stream Cipher · OFB · Cryptanalysis · VHF

1 Introduction

The Internet of things is a new kind of computing and communication technology, which is applied to many intelligent devices such as RFID tags. Although it provides a lot of new experience, but intelligent device needs to use low-cost, low-power solutions to meet the needs of applications and terminal users. Mobile terminals with constrained resource on computing and storage capacity have brought great challenge to the traditional cryptography, so we need to use lightweight cipher to solve this problem. CLEFIA, PRESENT and MIBS as an outstanding representative of the lightweight block cipher, provide us with a good opportunity based on the most advanced technologies designed for mobile terminals with constrained resources. However, except eSTREAM candidates Grain [1] and WG-7 [2], lightweight stream cipher does not receive much attention to date. Therefore, it is very important to research and design a lightweight stream cipher. Stream cipher is such a mathematical transformation, as shown in Fig. 1, it is divided into an encryption unit, such as a character (e.g., a single letter), or the basic unit of encoding (0/1), or other unit which is easily encrypted (typically a 8,32,64 bits binary number); and

© Springer Nature Switzerland AG 2021
G. Wang et al. (Eds.): SpaCCS 2020, LNCS 12383, pp. 506–518, 2021.
https://doi.org/10.1007/978-3-030-68884-4_42

the length of key stream is used to synchronize in decryption, where KG is the key stream generator, and KI is the initial key. The design of traditional stream cipher focuses on the security intensity, while ignoring its application in restricted resources and equipment. Lightweight stream cipher focuses on the application of mobile terminal, which is restricted by resource, not only to consider the safety performance, but also to achieve the performance of the stream cipher. The number of GE [3] hardware implementation is required to evaluate whether the stream cipher is the main index of lightweight. To ensure that the hardware implementation of the 3500 GE number that is a lightweight stream cipher, stream cipher requires two important parameters, the initial vector and the key stream, a lightweight stream cipher requires each encryption and decryption key length at 56 bits to 256 bits.

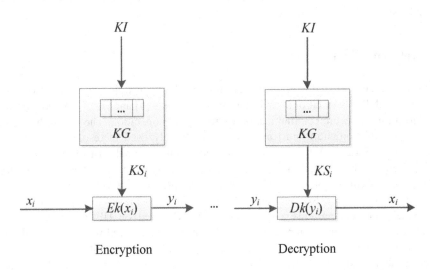

Fig. 1. The mathematical model of stream cipher.

The difficulty in the design of lightweight stream cipher is the key stream generator. Grain and WG-7 are based on Nonlinear Feedback Shift Register (NFSR) and Linear Feedback Shift Register (LSFR) to construct key stream generator. In order to improve the software efficiency of lightweight stream cipher, this paper proposes a key stream generator based on Output Feedback mode (OFB) of block cipher, named Stream Vertical Horizontal Feistel (SVHF). The key stream generator is based on the lightweight block cipher VHF, where the block length of each encryption key stream is 128 bit, and the length of initial vector is also 128-bit; the initial vector acts as KS_0, the 1st input of key stream generator KG, while KS_i, the output of KG is regarded as the next input of KG. The cipher text $Y_i = X_i \oplus KS_i$, where Xi is the plaintext. The KG adopts Feistel structure, and the round function F is based on the pseudo random transformation and diagonal pseudo random transformation. Initial vector of KG is divided into 64 bits length of about two branches, supporting the encryption key lengths of 80 and

128 bits. One novel design method of round function F is the use of SP structure, with a pseudo-random transformation to construct 256-byte encryption transformation table, where the simplified S-box design fully reflects the realization of lightweight stream cipher to achieve small space occupation. In addition, KG after P permutation, have been purged diagonal pseudo-random data transformation, and improve its security. SVHF on currently known attack methods to achieve adequate immunity and exhibits efficiency in hardware and software on consumption. SVHF's hardware implementation requires 1632GE. The software efficiency of SVHF is computed to be 50.82 Mb/s. However, the hardware implementation of WG-7 reaches 2194 GE and the software efficiency is computed to be 13.43 Mb/s. We believe that the software and hardware efficiency of SVHF is higher than WG-7. SVHF in the safety and performance achieves excellent balance, which, on the basis of meeting the security, improves the efficiency of the software, at the same time takes into account hardware efficiency. So the thus is more feasible.

2   Related Work

With the demand for lightweight ciphers for resource constrained devices, more and more research has been carried out in this area. In papers [4] and [5], the authors design an algorithm for secure communication by using PUF operation. The design has good performance in computing cost and can be effectively used in resource constrained devices. ABKS-LD-MA [6] greatly reduces the computational cost of users by combining lightweight decryption with searchable ABE scheme. In paper [7], a hybrid encryption system combining ECC and XXTEA is proposed, which is effectively used in resource-constrained IoT intelligent devices, and has achieved high performance.In the same paper [8] presents a proposal for MAC based on HECC, which is also effectively used in small computing devices. However, compared with ours SVHF, we show that not only perform well on resource-constrained devices, but also perform well in cross device communication. Lightweight algorithm is mainly reflected by lightweight block ciphers, lightweight Hash functions and lightweight stream ciphers. In the symmetric cryptosystem, the block cipher appears early, the design technology is mature, and it has typical security structures, such as Feistel and SP (Substitution permutation) structures, which makes the design of lightweight block ciphers relatively easy. An Enhanced Key Management Scheme for LoRaWAN [9] has been designed with a lightweight block cipher, which greatly reduces the requirements for computing resources.

The Hash function is an one-way cryptosystem, which can provide an irreversible mapping from plaintext to ciphertext, and can transform an input of any length to a fixed length output. In paper [10], based on Hash function and the randomization of the tag's identifier, a lightweight authentication protocol is proposed. It works well in resource constrained RFID system. In recent years, there is a new trend of using Sponge structure to design Hash functions. Some new Hash functions designed with Sponge structure are GLUON [11], QUARK [12] and SPONGENT [13].

3   Design of SVHF

This paper proposes a lightweight stream cipher based on Output Feedback mode (OFB) of block cipher. Key stream generator is based on the lightweight block cipher VHF, each encryption key stream block length for 128-bit, the initial vector length for 128 bits. OFB mode is shown in Fig. 2, the initial vector after key stream generator KG with the plaintext XOR the corresponding ciphertext $y_1 y_2 \ldots y_m$, and as a group of key stream generator input. The core of SVHF is the design of the key stream generator KG. KG's randomness and unpredictability allow us to generate new ideas for the use of a double pseudo-random transformation of the lightweight block cipher VHF as a key stream generator.

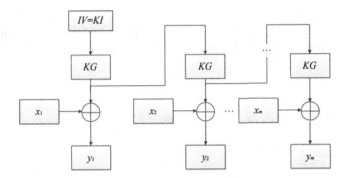

Fig. 2. OFB mode of block cipher.

3.1   Key Stream Generator KG

The key stream generator KG is based on the double pseudo-random transformation and Feistel structure. The initial vector KI is divided into two branches, L_0 and R_0. SVHF uses the Feistel structure to encrypt them. As shown in Fig. 3, the F is a round function and K_i is a sub key of VHF. The length of K_i is 80 and 128 bits. The number of iterations is 14 and 16, respectively, VHF encryption process includes 4 steps:

Step 1. The KI is divided into two the same length branches, L_0 and R_0;
Step 2. $L_i = R_{i-1}$, $0 \leq i \leq r - 1$;
Step 3. After SBoxLayer, PLayer and SBoxLayer, R_i XOR sub-key K_i. Finally get R_i: $R_i = L_{i-1} \oplus F(R_{i-1}, K_{i-1})$;
Step 4. After r rounds iteration, we get the 128-bit key stream bit string $L_r \parallel R_r$ and as the input of the next set of key stream generator.

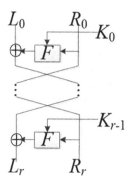

Fig. 3. Key stream generator KG.

Round function *F* including pseudo random transform and pseudo-random diagonal transform, as shown in Fig. 4, followed by SBoxLayer(), PLayer() and SBoxLayer() for R_i.

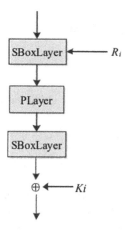

Fig. 4. Round function *F*.

SBoxLayer(): it is a nonlinear transformation of the byte, which transforms each byte in the encryption process to another byte. The *S*-box is generated via pseudo-random transformation. We first compute $T(i) = \lfloor 256 \sin(i) \rfloor$, where $\lfloor \rfloor$ denote the round-down operation; to generate 256 non-repetitious bytes, *i* ranges from 1 to 30000, eliminating repetitions that occur. The S-box is a pseudorandom combination of 256 bytes, which is obtained by alternating bytes in T:

$$S[T(j)] = T(j + 1), S[T(255)] = T(0) \tag{1}$$

Where $0 \leq j \leq 254$. The 256 byte of the pseudo random transformation is shown in Fig. 5. The distribution of the S-box can be seen by the distribution of the points.

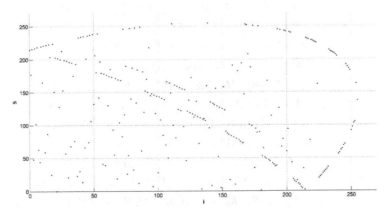

Fig. 5. Pseudorandom transformation.

PLayer(): it is a diagonal permutation of each byte into another byte. The 64-bit data M_i is denoted as 8 * 8 square matrix, as shown in Fig. 6, where each diagonal data of M_i is regarded as one byte to achieve the P permutation.

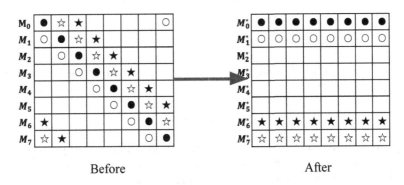

Fig. 6. Permutation function Player().

For each byte permutation for pseudo-random transform, finally obtained P_i:

$$P_i(0) = S\{[M_i(0)\&128]||[M_i(1)\&64]||[M_i(2)\&32]||[M_i(3)\&16]$$
$$||[M_i(4)\&8]||[M_i(5)\&4]||[M_i(6)\&2]||[M_i(7)\&1]|\};$$
$$P_i(1) = S\{[M_i(1)\&128]||[M_i(2)\&64]||[M_i(3)\&32]||[M_i(4)\&16]$$
$$||[M_i(5)\&8]||[M_i(6)\&4]||[M_i(7)\&2]||[M_i(0)\&1]|\};$$
$$P_i(2) = S\{[M_i(2)\&128]||[M_i(3)\&64]||[M_i(4)\&32]||[M_i(5)\&16]$$
$$||[M_i(6)\&8]||[M_i(7)\&4]||[M_i(0)\&2]||[M_i(1)\&1]|\};$$
$$P_i(3) = S\{[M_i(3)\&128]||[M_i(4)\&64]||[M_i(5)\&32]||[M_i(6)\&16]$$
$$||[M_i(7)\&8]||[M_i(0)\&4]||[M_i(1)\&2]||[M_i(2)\&1]|\};$$
$$P_i(4) = S\{[M_i(4)\&128]||[M_i(5)\&64]||[M_i(6)\&32]||[M_i(7)\&16] \qquad (2)$$
$$||[M_i(0)\&8]||[M_i(1)\&4]||[M_i(2)\&2]||[M_i(3)\&1]|\};$$
$$P_i(5) = S\{[M_i(5)\&128]||[M_i(6)\&64]||[M_i(7)\&32]||[M_i(0)\&16]$$
$$||[M_i(1)\&8]||[M_i(2)\&4]||[M_i(3)\&2]||[M_i(4)\&1]|\};$$
$$P_i(6) = S\{[M_i(6)\&128]||[M_i(7)\&64]||[M_i(0)\&32]||[M_i(1)\&16]$$
$$||[M_i(2)\&8]||[M_i(3)\&4]||[M_i(4)\&2]||[M_i(5)\&1]|\};$$
$$P_i(7) = S\{[M_i(7)\&128]||[M_i(0)\&64]||[M_i(1)\&32]||[M_i(2)\&16]$$
$$||[M_i(3)\&8]||[M_i(4)\&4]||[M_i(5)\&2]||[M_i(6)\&1]|\};$$

Key scheduling is achieved via iterations, so the L-byte key K is expanded to $L *$ $(r + 1)$ bytes: the expanded key.

$$\text{Key} = K_0|K_1|\ldots|K_i|\ldots|K_r = K_0|K_1|\ldots|K_i|\ldots|k_{l*r+7} \qquad (3)$$

where each K_i has L bytes, $0 \leqslant i \leqslant r$, each k_i has a unit byte, $0 \leqslant i \leqslant L * r - 1$. For the key K with 10 and 16 bytes, the number of rounds is $r = 14$ and 16. The first L bytes of the expanded key is the key K:

$$K = k_0|k_1|\ldots|k_{L-1} \qquad (4)$$

In the case of $L \leqslant i \leqslant L * r - 1$, k_i in the expanded key is obtained via recursion of k_{i-L} and k_{i-1}, i.e.

$$k_i = S[k_{i-1}] \oplus k_{i-L} \qquad (5)$$

Finally, the F_i of the current iteration is obtained by performing XOR operation on the previous output P_i and the sub-key K_i of the current iteration to get $R_{i+1} = L_i \oplus F_i$. After r-round, the key stream is obtained by cascading (L_r, R_r).

3.2   SVHF

SVHF is based on Output Feedback mode (OFB) of block cipher. VHF is used to produce key stream of SVHF. SVHF encryption process is shown in Fig. 7. SVHF has 3 parameters: the plaintext $x = x_1 x_2 \dots x_m$, the ciphertext $y = y_1 y_2 \dots y_m$ and the IV. The length of the x_i and the y_i is 128-bit and the length of the initial vector is 128 bits.

Step 1. The initial vector by VHF, the results obtained for KS_1 to save and update the key stream;

Step 2. The results of step 1 obtained with the plaintext XOR to get y_1;

Step 3. Repeat step 1and 2 to get the ciphertext stream $y = y_1 y_2 \dots y_m$;

Step 4. $x_i = y_i \oplus KS_i$, $i \in \{1, 2, \dots m\}$, we can decrypt the plaintext stream $x = x_1 x_2 \dots x_m$.

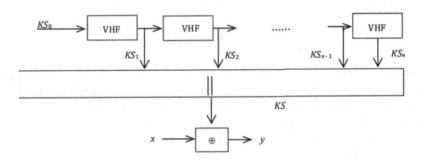

Fig. 7.   The SVHF encryption description.

4   Performance Evaluation

4.1   Software Implementation

The implementation performance of SVHF is tested by using the C language in the environment of Intel(R) Core(TM) i7-3610QM 2.3 GHz CPU and 8 GB memory. From the comparison with existing lightweight symmetric cipher Grain, WG-7, A2U2, PRESENT and MIBS, it can be seen that the software implementation of SVHF consumes much less time than other symmetric cipher. The software efficiency of Grain, WG-7, A2U2, PRESENT and MIBS is 53.31 Mb/s, 0.61 Mb/s, 13.43 Mb/s, 0.31 Mb/s, 0.98 Mb/s and 33.26 Mb/s respectively, which are shown in Fig. 8. It can be observed that SVHF outperforms other symmetric cipher in terms of software efficiency.

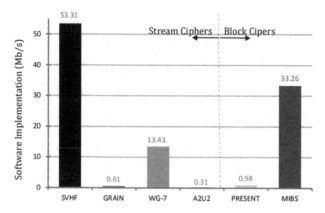

Fig. 8. Comparison of lightweight symmetric cipher software implementation. Software Implementation (MB/S): the operating efficiency of software implementation, where the operating throughput speed is MB/S.

4.2 Hardware Performance

Efficiency of hardware implementation is usually measured by the equivalent number of GE. The number of GE needed to achieve hardware implementation of CLEFIA-128 was estimated in reference [14]. The authors reported that 5979 GE were required to implement CLEFIA-128, neglecting the effect of different ASIC libraries. The authors in reference stated that 6 GE were needed to store 1 bit, and 2.67 GE were required for a XOR operation.

SVHF includes two parts. The key stream generator KG requires 1 XOR gates for storage of key expansion; a 80-bit sub-key needs total 480GE to be stored during each round; the S-box demands 200 GE; the encryption process requires 64 AND gates, totaling 85.12GE and 56 OR gates, totaling 74.48GE; the XOR operation needs to be performed on the cipher text and the sub-key during each round, demanding 8 XOR gates, totaling 21.36GE. The other one is to update the key stream. A 128-bit result needs to be stored during each round, totaling 768GE.

The number of gate circuits needed by SVHF and other lightweight symmetric ciphers are given in Fig. 9. Compared with WG-7 which needs 2194GE for hardware implementation, SVHF only demands 1632GE. It demonstrates that hardware efficiency of SVHF is higher than WG-7. It can be considered that the SVHF in the hardware implementation and software implementation has achieved a good balance to meet the hardware usage needs of extreme environments with limited resources, such as RFID and to meet some software implementation needs from environment, such as embedded mode and MCU.

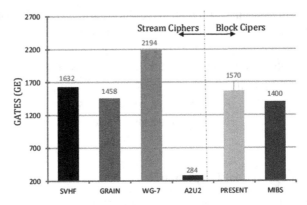

Fig. 9. Comparison of lightweight symmetric cipher hardware performance. Ge: the number of gates required for hardware implementation.

4.3 Different Devices

According to the above description, we also evaluate the SVHF among different power consumption devices. The evaluation shows that SVHF still performs well on low-power devices. And in fact, we need to use the same lightweight cipher when communicating with low-power devices using lightweight ciphers. Therefore, the above comparison is comparable.

5 Security Evaluation

5.1 Differential Cryptanalysis and Linear Cryptanalysis

Differential cryptanalysis [15] and linear cryptanalysis [16] have been the most effective attack against stream cipher. The authors in reference detailed the method for evaluating a cipher's resistance against differential and linear cryptanalysis, and proposed to compute the maximum differential and linear probability by counting the number of dynamic S-boxes [15, 16]. This method was used by reference to evaluate CLEFIA [14].

The maximum differential probability of SVHF's S-box is computed to be $2^{-4.415}$. The number DS of dynamic S-boxes for the first ten rounds of SVHF, is computed by using the program, which is shown in Table 1. It can be observed that the 4-round maximum differential probability of SVHF is $DCP_{max}^{4d} \leq 2^{21*(-4.415)} = 2^{-67.92} \leq 2^{-64}$. When the number round is larger than 4, no effective differential characteristic is found for cryptanalysis. So the full-round SVHF can resist differential cryptanalysis.

The maximum linear probability of SVHF's S-box is computed to be $2^{-2.83}$. The number LS of dynamic S-boxes for the first ten rounds of SVHF is computed by using the program, which is shown in Table 1. It can be observed that the 4-round maximum linear probability of SVHF is $LCP_{max}^{4d} \leq 2^{24*(-2.83)} = 2^{-67.62} \leq 2^{-64}$. When the number of round is larger than 4, no effective linear characteristic is found for cryptanalysis. So the full-round SVHF can resist linear cryptanalysis.

Table1. Guaranteed number of active S-boxes of SVHF.

Round	1	2	3	4	5	6	7	8	9	10
DS	0	7	14	21	28	35	42	49	56	63
LS	0	8	16	24	32	40	48	56	64	72

5.2   Impossible Differential Cryptanalysis

Impossible differential cryptanalysis is a very effective attack against SVHF. J. Kim [17] proposed a moment algorithm μ − method to perform impossible differential cryptanalysis of the stream cipher structure. Their method can find different impossible differential paths. Impossible differential cryptanalysis of SVHF is carried out by using this method, determining the maximum number of rounds is 6, finding 8 non-differential paths.

$$
\begin{aligned}
(0,0,0,\alpha,0,\alpha,\alpha,\alpha) &\overset{6r}{\nrightarrow} (0,0,0,0,\alpha,\alpha,\alpha,\alpha) \quad && p=1 \\
(0,0,\alpha,0,\alpha,\alpha,\alpha,0) &\overset{6r}{\nrightarrow} (0,0,0,0,\alpha,\alpha,\alpha,\alpha) \quad && p=1 \\
(0,\alpha,0,\alpha,\alpha,\alpha,0,0) &\overset{6r}{\nrightarrow} (0,0,0,\alpha,\alpha,\alpha,\alpha,0) \quad && p=1 \\
(0,\alpha,\alpha,\alpha,0,0,0,\alpha) &\overset{6r}{\nrightarrow} (0,\alpha,\alpha,\alpha,\alpha,0,0,0) \quad && p=1 \\
(\alpha,0,0,0,\alpha,0,\alpha,\alpha) &\overset{6r}{\nrightarrow} (\alpha,\alpha,0,0,0,0,\alpha,\alpha) \quad && p=1 \\
(\alpha,0,\alpha,\alpha,\alpha,0,0,0) &\overset{6r}{\nrightarrow} (0,0,\alpha,\alpha,0,0,0,0) \quad && p=1 \\
(\alpha,\alpha,0,0,0,\alpha,0,\alpha) &\overset{6r}{\nrightarrow} (\alpha,\alpha,\alpha,0,0,0,0,\alpha) \quad && p=1 \\
(\alpha,\alpha,\alpha,0,0,0,\alpha,0) &\overset{6r}{\nrightarrow} (\alpha,\alpha,\alpha,\alpha,0,0,0,0) \quad && p=1
\end{aligned}
\tag{6}
$$

Where $\alpha \in \mathrm{GF}(2^8)$ denotes the non-zero differential. Therefore, impossible differential cryptanalysis is invalid for SVHF.

6   Conclusion

A new lightweight stream cipher, SVHF, has been introduced. It is designed with small hardware and software implementation in mind. A complete description of the algorithm as well as a security analysis based on known attacks have been given. The construction is based on Feistel and OFB. The block of key stream size is 128 bits and SVHF can achieve sufficient security margin against known attacks, such as linear cryptanalysis, differential cryptanalysis, impossible differential cryptanalysis. Comparison with other lightweight stream cipher in hardware implementation indicates that SVHF needs 1632 GE, less than 2194GE of the international standard WG-7. It can be considered that the SVHF has achieved a superior balance in security and performance to meet the hardware usage needs of extreme environments with limited resources, such as RFID and to meet some software implementation needs from environment, such as embedded mode and MCU.

Acknowledgement. In this paper, the research was sponsored by the Science & Technology Support Plan of Jiangsu Province under Grant No. BE2013879 and the NUAA Research Funding under Grant No. NS2010097.

References

1. Hell, M., Johansson, T., Meier, W.: Grain: a stream cipher for constrained environments. Int. J. Wireless Mobile Comput. **2**(1), 86–93 (2007)
2. Luo, Y., Chai, Q., Gong, G.: A lightweight stream cipher WG-7 for RFID encryption and authentication. In: IEEE Global Telecommunications Conference, pp. 1–6. IEEE (2010)
3. Özen, O., Varici, K., Tezcan, C., Kocair, Ç.: Lightweight block ciphers revisited: cryptanalysis of reduced round PRESENT and HIGHT. In: Boyd, C., González Nieto, J. (eds.) ACISP 2009. LNCS, vol. 5594, pp. 90–107. Springer, Heidelberg (2009). https://doi.org/10.1007/978-3-642-02620-1_7
4. Mall, P., Bhuiyan, M.Z.A., Amin, R.: A lightweight secure communication protocol for IoT devices using physically unclonable function. In: Wang, G., Feng, J., Bhuiyan, M.Z.A., Lu, R. (eds.) SpaCCS 2019. LNCS, vol. 11611, pp. 26–35. Springer, Cham (2019). https://doi.org/10.1007/978-3-030-24907-6_3
5. Babaei, A., Schiele, G.: Spatial reconfigurable physical unclonable functions for the Internet of Things. In: Wang, G., Atiquzzaman, M., Yan, Z., Choo, K.-K. (eds.) SpaCCS 2017. LNCS, vol. 10658, pp. 312–321. Springer, Cham (2017). https://doi.org/10.1007/978-3-319-72395-2_29
6. Long, J., Zhang, K., Wang, X., Dai, H.-N.: Lightweight distributed attribute based keyword search system for Internet of Things. In: Wang, G., Feng, J., Bhuiyan, M.Z.A., Lu, R. (eds.) SpaCCS 2019. LNCS, vol. 11637, pp. 253–264. Springer, Cham (2019). https://doi.org/10.1007/978-3-030-24900-7_21
7. Ragab, A., Selim, G., Wahdan, A., Madani, A.: Robust hybrid lightweight cryptosystem for protecting IoT smart devices. In: Wang, G., Feng, J., Bhuiyan, M.Z.A., Lu, R. (eds.) SpaCCS 2019. LNCS, vol. 11637, pp. 5–19. Springer, Cham (2019). https://doi.org/10.1007/978-3-030-24900-7_1
8. John, A.L., Thampi, S.M.: Encryption scheme based on hyperelliptic curve cryptography. In: Wang, G., Ray, I., Alcaraz Calero, J.M., Thampi, S.M. (eds.) SpaCCS 2016. LNCS, vol. 10066, pp. 491–506. Springer, Cham (2016). https://doi.org/10.1007/978-3-319-49148-6_40
9. Han, J., Wang, J.: an enhanced key management scheme for LoRaWAN. In: Wang, G., Chen, J., Yang, L.T. (eds.) SpaCCS 2018. LNCS, vol. 11342, pp. 407–416. Springer, Cham (2018). https://doi.org/10.1007/978-3-030-05345-1_35

10. Shi, Z., Wu, F., Wang, C., Ren, S.: A lightweight RFID authentication protocol with forward security and randomized identifier. In: Wang, G., Ray, I., Alcaraz Calero, J.M., Thampi, S. M. (eds.) SpaCCS 2016. LNCS, vol. 10066, pp. 1–13. Springer, Cham (2016). https://doi.org/10.1007/978-3-319-49148-6_1

11. Berger, T.P., D'Hayer, J., Marquet, K., Minier, M., Thomas, G.: The GLUON family: a lightweight hash function family based on FCSRs. In: Mitrokotsa, A., Vaudenay, S. (eds.) AFRICACRYPT 2012. LNCS, vol. 7374, pp. 306–323. Springer, Heidelberg (2012). https://doi.org/10.1007/978-3-642-31410-0_19

12. Aumasson, J.-P., Henzen, L., Meier, W., et al.: Quark: a lightweight hash. J. Cryptol. **26**(2), 313–339 (2013)

13. Bogdanov, A., Knežević, M., Leander, G., Toz, D., Varıcı, K., Verbauwhede, I.: spongent: a lightweight hash function. In: Preneel, B., Takagi, T. (eds.) CHES 2011. LNCS, vol. 6917, pp. 312–325. Springer, Heidelberg (2011). https://doi.org/10.1007/978-3-642-23951-9_21

14. Shirai, T., Shibutani, K., Akishita, T.: The 128-bit Block cipher CLEFIA. Fast Softw. Encryption **4593**, 181–195 (2007)

15. Su, B., Wu, W., Zhang, W.: Differential Cryptanalysis of SMS4 Block Cipher. IACR. Cryptology Eprint Archive (2010)

16. Matsui, M.: Linear cryptanalysis method for DES cipher. In: Helleseth, T. (ed.) EUROCRYPT 1993. LNCS, vol. 765, pp. 386–397. Springer, Heidelberg (1994). https://doi.org/10.1007/3-540-48285-7_33

17. Kim, J., Hong, S., Sung, J., Lee, S., Lim, J., Sung, S.: Impossible differential cryptanalysis for block cipher structures. In: Johansson, T., Maitra, S. (eds.) INDOCRYPT 2003. LNCS, vol. 2904, pp. 82–96. Springer, Heidelberg (2003). https://doi.org/10.1007/978-3-540-24582-7_6

A Novel Quantum Color Image Encryption Scheme Based on Controlled Alternate Quantum Walks

Ting Yan$^{(\boxtimes)}$ and Dan Li

College of Computer Science and Technology, Nanjing University
of Aeronautics and Astronautics, Nanjing 211106, China
17768119694@163.com

Abstract. With the development of network era, how to ensure the security of important information has become increasingly prominent. However, modern data security tools based on computational complexity may be cracked by quantum computing. Quantum walk (QW), which is a universal computing model, plays an important role in designing quantum algorithms. In this paper, we use controlled alternate quantum walk (CAQW) as a pseudorandom number generator (PRNG) to control the encryption of quantum color images, and provide a quantum circuit for the quantum color image encryption scheme. Simulation and analysis results show that our scheme can resist attacks such as differential attack, statistical analysis attack, etc., and the processing efficiency can be improved exponentially compared with the classical image encryption scheme, which has good encryption effect and high security.

Keywords: Information security · Quantum color image encryption · Quantum walks · Pseudo-random number generator · Quantum circuit

1 Introduction

With the rapid development of computer and network technology, information globalization has become an important feature of today's world, and how to ensure the security of important information has become increasingly prominent. Image encryption technologies are widely used in military classified images, medical images and other privacy digital image information that needs to be transmitted safely. Therefore, image encryption technology is crucial. The encryption of these confidential images can be achieved by cryptography. However, with the development of quantum computing, modern data security tools based on mathematical calculations may be cracked. In the meantime, because of the characteristics of parallelism and entanglement of quantum state, the efficiency of quantum image processing algorithm is improved exponentially compared with that of classical image processing algorithm in theory, it is essential to design the quantum image processing algorithm on quantum computer.

© Springer Nature Switzerland AG 2021
G. Wang et al. (Eds.): SpaCCS 2020, LNCS 12383, pp. 519–530, 2021.
https://doi.org/10.1007/978-3-030-68884-4_43

Quantum walk is a quantum counterpart of classical random walk, and an advanced tool for constructing quantum algorithms, which is a general model of quantum computing. The basic principle if quantum walk is as follows: after a series of unitary transformations, the calculation of the position probability distribution of the final state requires the quantum amplitude, which can be regarded as a nonlinear mapping from Hilbert space to probability distribution [8,13,14]. According to the properties of discrete quantum walk, many researchers have proposed different pseudo-random number generation (PRNG) schemes based on quantum walk and given their applications [6,8,9].

Quantum image representation (QIMP) is devoted to utilizing quantum computing technologies to capture, manipulate, and recover quantum images in different formats for various purposes [1,3]. There are many representations of quantum images [4], among which a novel enhanced quantum representation (NEQR) [11] is widely used. Each qudit in the NEQR image can be processed independently of any other qudit in the quantum image, and the classical gray value can be reliably retrieved by measuring along the center direction using projection operator. Novel quantum representation for color digital images (NCQI) model extends the NEQR to encode color image pixel information in three channels of R, G and B [12]. Therefore, NEQR and NCQI are models suitable for quantum grayscale image processing tasks and quantum color image processing tasks respectively.

A new CAQW-based quantum color image encryption scheme is proposed in this paper. In this scheme, the classical color image is first represented by the quantum NCQI model, and then the control quantum qubit $|K1\rangle$ and intermediate participating qubit $|K2\rangle$ are generated by CAQW-based PRNG. For each single channel in R, G and B channels, the pixel values are cyclic shift transformed controlled through $|K1\rangle$ and the then are encrypted by adding $|K2\rangle$ in parallel. The security of this scheme is based on CAQW. The paper is structured as follows. In Sect. 2, we introduce the CAQW and NEQR model and dedicated quantum circuit modules as the preliminaries. In Sect. 3, the quantum image encryption and decryption scheme is described. Simulation and analysis results on a classical computer are given in Sect. 4. Finally, a short conclusion is given in Sect. 5.

2   Preliminaries

2.1   A Novel Enhanced Quantum Representation (NEQR)

Based on the properties of quantum entanglement and parallelism, NEQR model [11] contains the color information and corresponding position information of each pixel in the image. Suppose that we have an image I of size $2^n \times 2^n$. Then, the NEQR representation of $|I\rangle$ can be expressed

$$|I\rangle = \frac{1}{2^n} \sum_{i=0}^{2^n-1} \sum_{j=0}^{2^n-1} |c_{i,j}\rangle \otimes |i\rangle|j\rangle, |c_{i,j}\rangle = |c_{i,j}^{q-1} \ldots c_{i,j}^1 c_{i,j}^0\rangle, c_{i,j}^k \in \{0,1\}$$

where $i, j = 0, 1, \ldots, 2^n - 1, k = 0, 1, \ldots, q-1$. The two parts in the NEQR: $|c_{i,j}\rangle$ and $|i\rangle|j\rangle$ respectively encodes information about the colors and their related positions in the image. The grey value $|c_{i,j}\rangle$ with grey range 2^q is encoded by the sequence $|c_i^{q-1} \ldots c_i^1 c_i^0\rangle$.

For a binary digital image, NEQR model only needs one qubit encoding the pixel information, where the computational basis state $|0\rangle$ denotes black, while $|1\rangle$ denotes white. Based on NEQR model, NCQI model was proposed in [12], which encode the color information in corresponding position (i, j) into three channels (R, G, B) described as follows:

$$|I\rangle = \frac{1}{2^n} \sum_{i=0}^{2^n-1} \sum_{j=0}^{2^n-1} |I_{i,j}\rangle \otimes |i\rangle|j\rangle = \frac{1}{2^n} \sum_{i=0}^{2^n-1} \sum_{j=0}^{2^n-1} |R_{i,j}\rangle|G_{i,j}\rangle|B_{i,j}\rangle \otimes |i\rangle|j\rangle$$

where binary sequences $|I\rangle = |R_{i,j}\rangle|G_{i,j}\rangle|B_{i,j}\rangle$, $|R_{i,j}\rangle$, $|G_{i,j}\rangle$, $|B_{i,j}\rangle$ encode the gray scale value in three channels R, G and B respectively.

2.2 Controlled Alternate Quantum Walks (CAQW)-Based Pseudo-random Number Generator

Controlled alternate quantum walk is introduced in [14]. CAQW-based PRNG is the core of this scheme, the paremeters for CAQW-based PRNG are as follows.

1) N, M are the node number of a cycle, notice that, N, M are all odd numbers;
2) θ_1, θ_2 are selected to determine the coin operation C_0, C_1 respectively, θ_1, $\theta_2 \in (0, \pi/2)$;
3) α and β are parameters of the initial coin state, $|\alpha|^2 + |\beta|^2 = 1$, the initial state is $|\psi_0\rangle = |00\rangle(\alpha|0\rangle + \beta|1\rangle)$);
4) $message$ is selected to control every step of the CAQW;
5) k is used to transform the probability distribution obtained by the CAQW into a binary string of length $N_1 \times N_2 \times k$;
6) h is the number of iterations of the CAQW;

So the key format is $(N, M, (\theta_1, \theta_2), (\alpha, \beta), message, k, h)$.

Notice that, its basic principle is as follows: after a series of unitary transformations, the calculation of the position probability distribution of the final state requires the quantum amplitude, which can be regarded as a nonlinear mapping from Hilbert space to probability distribution.

2.3 Dedicated Quantum Circuit Modules for Proposed Scheme

Reverse Rarallel Adder. Based on quantum circuit design for the reverse half adder (RHA) and reverse full adder (RFA) in [15], the quantum circuit for reverse parallel adder(RPA) [16] module calculates the sum of two n-qubit states $|A\rangle$ and —$B\rangle$, where $|A\rangle = |a_{n-1}a_{n-2} \ldots a_1 a_0\rangle$ and $|B\rangle = |b_{n-1}b_{n-2} \ldots b_1 b_0\rangle$, the qubits $|S\rangle = |s_n s_{n-1} \ldots s_1 s_0\rangle$ represent the sum of $|A + B\rangle$.

Reverse Parallel Subtractor. Reverse Parallel Subtractor (RPS) [17] can calculate two n-qubit sequences differences based on quantum circuits of reverse half subtracter (RHS) and reverse full subtracter (RFS).

Comparator. Reference [18] gives the quantum comparator (C) for two n-qubit quantum states $|a\rangle$ and $|b\rangle$ based on quantum bit string comparator U_C, which is described as follows:

$$|a\rangle|b\rangle|0\rangle^m|0\rangle|0\rangle \rightarrow U_C|a\rangle|b\rangle|\psi\rangle|x\rangle|y\rangle$$

where ψ is a m-qubit output state that has no important information and the last two qubits carry the comparison information. In another words, if $a = b$, then $x = y = 0$; if $a > b$, then $x = 1$ and $y = 0$; if $a < b$, then $x = 0$ and $y = 1$.

Cyclic Shift Transformation. Based on the cyclic shift transformation (CST) designed in [19], two different cyclic shift transformations: $CST(+1)$ and $CST(-1)$, where n-qubit sequence $|Y\rangle = |y_{n-1}y_{n-2}\cdots y_1y_0\rangle$. The function of $CST(+1)$ and $CST(-1)$ can be expressed as: $CST(+1)|Y\rangle = |(Y+1)\ mod\ 2^n\rangle$, $CST(-1)|Y\rangle = |(Y-1)\ mod\ 2^n\rangle$

3 The Quantum Color Image Encryption and Decryption Scheme

In this section, we present our encryption/decryption scheme for quantum color images.

Encryption
The frame circuit diagram of the quantum image encryption process is shown in the upper part of Fig. 1. As described in the picture, the steps of quantum color image encryption scheme are as follows:

Initial The original color image with the size of $N * M * 3$ can be converted into NCQI representation model $|P\rangle$, and the NCQI representation is equivalent to the NEQR representation of each channel in the R, G and B channels.

$$|P\rangle = \frac{1}{2^n} \sum_{i=0}^{2^n-1} \sum_{j=0}^{2^n-1} |I_{i,j}\rangle \otimes |i\rangle|j\rangle = \frac{1}{2^n} \sum_{i=0}^{2^n-1} \sum_{j=0}^{2^n-1} |R_{i,j}\rangle|G_{i,j}\rangle|B_{i,j}\rangle \otimes |i\rangle|j\rangle$$

Step 1 Input the initial key parameters (N, M, θ_1, θ_2, (α, β), k, h) and generate a pseudorandom number sequence L with length of $N \times M \times k \times h$ by using CAQW-based PRNG.

Step 2 Select the first $M * N * 3$ bits of L as the $k1$ sequence and the first $M * N * 8 * 3$ bits of L as the $k2$ sequence. Store $k1$ in the qubit sequence $|K1\rangle$ and Store $k2$ in the NCQI representation model $|K2\rangle$.

Step 3 According to $|K1\rangle$, the cyclic shift transformation(CST) is carried out to the pixel value in $|P\rangle$. The comparator is used to control the $CST(+1)$ of each element of $|P\rangle$ according to the value of $|K1\rangle$. If the pixel value of position (i, j) of $|K1\rangle$ is equal to $|0\rangle$, then the pixel value of the same position in $|P\rangle$ will be conducted $CST(+1)$ operation. Then $|CP\rangle$ is obtained.

$$|CP(i,j)\rangle = \begin{cases} CST(+1)|P(i,j)\rangle, \ if \ |K1(i,j)\rangle = 0 \\ |P(i,j)\rangle, \qquad\quad if \ |K1(i,j)\rangle \neq 0 \end{cases}$$

Step 4 Add the result obtained in step 3 to $|K2\rangle$ through a reverse parallel adder(PRA) to get $|EP\rangle$, that is: $|EP\rangle = |P + K2\rangle$.

After the above operation, the encrypted color image EP is obtained after measurement.

Decryption

The frame circuit diagram of the quantum image encryption process is shown in the lower part of Fig. 1. As described in the picture, the steps of quantum color image decryption process are as follows:

Step 1' Input the initial key parameters $(N, M, \theta_1, \theta_2, (\ \alpha, \beta), k, h\ )$ and generate a pseudorandom number sequence L' with length of $N \times M \times k \times h$ by using CAQW-based PRNG.

Step 2' Select the first $M * N * 3$ bits of L' as the $k1$ sequence and the first $M * N * 8 * 3$ bits of L' as the $k2$ sequence. Store $k1$ in the qubit sequence $|K1\rangle$ and Store $k2$ in the NCQI representation model $|K2\rangle$.

Step 3' From the $|EP\rangle$ obtained in step 4 minus $|K2\rangle$, $|P'\rangle$ is obtained through reverse parallel subtractor (PRS), that is: $|P'\rangle = |EP - K2\rangle$.

Step 4' According to $K1\rangle$, the cyclic shift transformation is carried out to the pixel value in $|P'\rangle$. The comparator is used to control the $CST(-1)$ of each element of $|P'\rangle$ according to the value of $|K1\rangle$. If the pixel value of position (i, j) of $|K1\rangle$ is equal to $|0\rangle$, then the pixel value of the same position in $|P'\rangle$ will be conducted $CST(-1)$ operation. Then, $|DP\rangle$ is obtained.

$$|DP(i,j)\rangle = \begin{cases} CST(-1)|P'(i,j)\rangle, \ if \ |K1(i,j)\rangle = 0 \\ |P'(i,j)\rangle, \qquad\quad if \ |K1(i,j)\rangle \neq 0 \end{cases}$$

After the above operation, the encrypted color image DP is obtained after measurement.

4 Analysis Results

Since the quantum computer has not been realized yet, the simulation is carried out on the classical computer. Simulation is carried out on MATLAB 2016Ra, and the results are shown in Fig. 2. The color Lena image is used as the plaintext as shown in Fig. 2(a) with the size of $256 \times 256 \times 3$. The key is set as $N_1 = N_2 = 51$, $\theta_1 = \pi/3$, $\theta_2 = \pi/5$, $\alpha = \sqrt{1/2}$, $\beta = \sqrt{1/2}$, $h = 41$, $k = 16$, *message* is the binary string converted from 'HELLOWORLDHELLOWORLD-HELLOWORLD' to binary numbers. The encrypted Lena image is shown in Fig. 2(b) and the corresponding decrypted image is shown in Fig. 2(c).

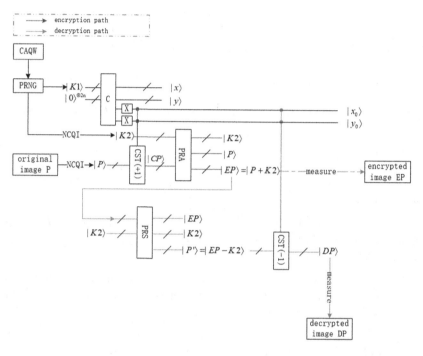

Fig. 1. Frame circuit diagram of the quantum image encryption and decryption process.

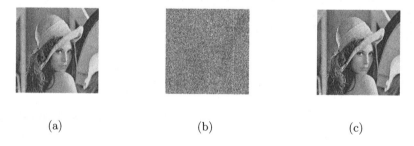

(a)   (b)   (c)

Fig. 2. (color on line) Encryption and decryption results (a) original Lena image; (b) encrypted Lena image; (c) decrypted Lena image.

4.1 Key Space

The key space is one of the most important measures for image encryption. A good encryption algorithm should have enough key space. The 2 dimensional position space of CAQW can be extended to high-dimensional position space, which shows that the key space of our proposed scheme can be large enough to resist brute force attack.

4.2   Statistical Analysis

Diffusion and confusion in cryptosystems are often used to destroy powerful statistical analysis. The histogram and correlation coefficients of two adjacent pixels are used to evaluate the ability of resistance to statistical attacks.

Histogram Analysis. Image histogram is widely used in image processing, which reflects the pixel gray distribution of image. A good encryption scheme should not display any relationship information between the original image and its encrypted version in the histogram. Histograms of the original Lena image and its encrypted image are shown in Fig. 3. Original image in R, G, B channel are shown in 3(a), 3(b), 3(c) respectively; encrypted image in R ,G, B channel are shown in 3(d), 3(e), 3(f) respectively. From these configurations, it is clear that the histogram of the encrypted image is the uniform and significantly different from those of the original image.

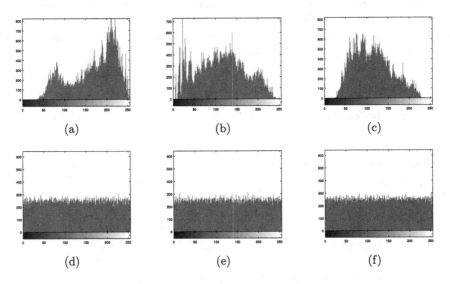

Fig. 3. (color on line) Histograms of the original Lena image and its encrypted image. (a) Original image in R channel; (c) original image in G channel; (e) original image in B channel; (b) encrypted image in R channel; (d) encrypted image in G channel; (f) encrypted image in B channel.

Correlation Coefficient Analysis. Correlation Coefficient reflects the degree of similarity of two variables. An effective image encryption algorithm should produce an encrypted image with sufficiently low correlation in the horizontal, vertical, and diagonal directions. We use covariance(cov) to measure correlation coefficients between two adjacent pixels x and y, which is defined by the following expressions

$$\begin{cases} r_{xy} & = \frac{cov(x,y)}{\sqrt{D(x)D(y)}}, \\ cov(x,y) & = E\{[x - E(x)][y - E(y)]\}, \\ E(x) & = \frac{1}{N}\sum_{i=1}^{N} x_i, \\ D(x) & = \frac{1}{N}\sum_{i=1}^{N}[x_i - E(x)]^2, \end{cases}$$

where N is the total number of pixels, and $E(x)$ and $E(y)$ are the means of x_i and y_i respectively. The correlation coefficients of the horizontal, vertical and diagonal adjacent pixels of the original Lena image and its encrypted image in R, G and B channels are listed in Table 1.

The diagonal correlation distribution of adjacent pixels in lena image are shown in the Fig. 4. As shown in Fig. 4(a), 4(b) and 4(c), there is a strong correlation between adjacent pixels of the original image, because all points are clustered along a diagonal line. Instead, these points of the encrypted image are scattered throughout the plane, as shown in the Fig. 4(d), 4(e) and 4(f). The pictures show that the correlation of the encrypted image is greatly reduced. In summary, the results indicate that the correlations of the original images are high, while the correlations of the encrypted images are very low, which shows that the encryption effect is satisfactory.

4.3   Differential Attack

For an encryption algorithm, the ability to resist differential attacks is related to the sensitivity of the original image. By comparing and analyzing plaintext with specific differences, differential attacks attack the cryptographic algorithm by changing the propagation after encryption. It is evaluated by the number of pixels change rate (NPCR) and unified average changing intensity (UACI). The formulas of calculating NPCR and UACI are defined as

$$\begin{cases} NPCR_{R,G,B} = \frac{\sum_{i,j} D_{R,G,B}(i,j)}{L} \times 100\%, \\ UACI_{R,G,B} = \frac{1}{L}\sum_{i,j} \frac{|C_{R,G,B}(i,j) - C'_{R,G,B}|}{255} \times 100\%, \end{cases}$$

where L is the number of pixels in the image. $C_{R,G,B}$ and $C'_{R,G,B}$ are respectively encrypted images before and after one pixel of the original image is changed, and $D_{R,G,B}(i,j)$ is defined by

$$D_{R,G,B}(i,j) = \begin{cases} 1, & if C_{R,G,B}(i,j) \neq C_{R,G,B}(i,j), \\ 0, & if C_{R,G,B}(i,j) = C_{R,G,B}(i,j). \end{cases}$$

In the simulation we tried, we only change the lowest bit of one pixel of the plain image randomly. After 100 trials, the results show that the mean NPCRs

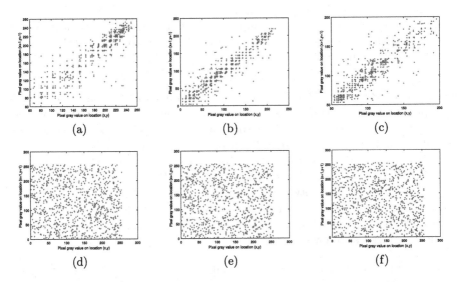

Fig. 4. (color online) Correlation distributions between two diagonal adjacent pixels: (a) original image in R channel; (b) encrypted image in R channel; (c) original image in G channel; (d) encrypted image in G channel; (e) original image in B channel; (f) encrypted image in B channel.

Table 1. Correlation coefficients of the original and encrypted images in R, G, B channels

Channels	Directions	Original image	Our algorithm
R channel	Horizontal	0.9447	0.0477
	Vertical	0.9680	0.0170
	Diagonal	0.9240	0.0155
G channel	Horizontal	0.9318	0.0698
	Vertical	0.9622	0.0241
	Diagonal	0.9081	0.0242
B channel	Horizontal	0.8906	0.0470
	Vertical	0.9251	0.0197
	Diagonal	0.8703	0.0177

and UACIs of the proposed algorithm are over 99.6 and 32.7 respectively. In other words, the proposed algorithm could resist plaintext attack and differential attack effectively.

4.4   Circuit Complexity

The quantum circuit's complexity depends very much on what is considered to be elementary gates. For all complex unitary operations on arbitrarily many qubits n, it can be expressed as compositions of the one-qubit quantum gates and the two-qubit quantum exclusive-or gate [21]. In this paper, we take 1-qubit and 2-qubit quantum gates as a basic unit.

Encryption Process. The effective quantum circuit for quantum color image encryption scheme is composed by a series of controlled quantum modules. Among these modules, it contains one q-qubit Controlled RPA module, one $2n$-qubit C module, and one q-qubit controlled-$CST(+1)$ modules.

As illustrated in [16], we can get: the complexity for single $2n$-qubit C module is deduced as: $68n - 18$; The complexity of one RPA modules is calculated as: $45q - 20$; The complexity for q-qubit Controlled-$CST(+1)$ modules can be deduced as: $12q^2 + 73$. Thus, the quantum circuit complexity for quantum color image decryption scheme is equal to the sum of all quantum modules complexity, which is deduced as follows:

$$(68n - 18) + (45q - 20) + (12q^2 + 73) = 68n + 12q^2 + 45q + 35 = O(q^2 + n)$$

Decryption Process. The quantum circuit for quantum color image decryption scheme contains the following modules: one $2n$-qubit C module, one q-qubit Controlled RPS module. Thus, the complexity of secret images extraction process is deduced as $O(q^2 + n)$.

Generally, quantum image preparation and measurement operations are always not considered as a part of quantum image processing algorithm. Therefore, we omit the circuitcomplexity in these two stages. The circuit complexity of our proposed quantum color images encryption and decryption processes are square complexity. Compared to classical computers that can only process the image pixel-by-pixel, the complexity for any classical image processing algorithm will be no less than $O(2^{2n})$ for a $2^n \times 2^n$ digit image. This is because quantum image processing algorithm can process pixel information in parallel due to the unique properties of quantum mechanics, such as superposition storage and entanglement. Therefore, it can be concluded that our proposed quantum image encryption scheme can achieve an exponential speed higher than all the classical encryption scheme.

5   Conclusion

In this paper, a new quantum color image encryption algorithm based on controlled alternate quantum walks is proposed. In this scheme, the color image is first represented by the quantum NCQI model, and then the control quantum qubit $|K1\rangle$ and intermediate participating qubit $|K2\rangle$ are generated by CAQW-based PRNG. For each single channel in R, G and B channels, the pixel values are cyclic shift transformed controlled through $|K1\rangle$ and the then are encrypted by adding $|K2\rangle$ in parallel. The core of this scheme is CAQW-based PRNG, and its security depends on the infinite possibilities of the initial state, not on the algorithmic complexity of a complex problem. According to the results of circuit complexity, the circuit complexity of encryption and decryption in this scheme is $O(q^2 + n)$. Compared with the complexity of the classical image encryption algorithm $O(2^{2n})$, Our proposed quantum color image encryption scheme can achieve higher exponential speed. Simulation and Analysis results show that the scheme can resist statistical analysis, differential attack and other attacks, and the key space can be expanded to resist the brute force attack. Therefore, our scheme can guarantee the image security, which has good encryption effect and high security.

Acknowledgments. This work is Supported by NSFC (Grant Nos. 61701229, 61702367, 61901218), Natural Science Foundation of Jiangsu Province, China (Grant Nos. BK20170802, BK20190407), China Postdoctoral Science Foundation funded Project (Grant Nos. 2018M630557, 2018T110499), Jiangsu Planned Projects for Postdoctoral Research Funds (Grant No. 1701139B), the Open Fund of the State Key Laboratory of Cryptology (Grant No. MMKFKT201914).

References

1. Venegas-Andraca, S., Bose, S.: Storing, processing, and retrieving an image using quantum mechanics. In: Proceedings of SPIE Conference of Quantum Information and Computation, vol. 5105, pp. 137–147 (2003)
2. Mastriani, M.: Quantum image processing? Quantum Inf. Process. **16**(1), 1–42 (2016). https://doi.org/10.1007/s11128-016-1457-y
3. Yan, F., Venegas-Andraca, S.E.: Quantum image processing, Quantum Information Processing (2020)
4. Yan, F., Iliyasu, A.M., Venegas-Andraca, S.E.: A survey of quantum image representations. Quantum Inf. Process. **15**(1), 1–35 (2015). https://doi.org/10.1007/s11128-015-1195-6
5. Abd-El-Atty, B., Abd El-Latif, A.A., Venegas-Andraca, S.E.: An encryption protocol for NEQR images based on one-particle quantum walks on a circle. Quantum Inf. Process. **18**(9), 1–26 (2019). https://doi.org/10.1007/s11128-019-2386-3
6. Abd EL-Latif, A.A., Abd-El-Atty, B., Venegas-Andraca, S.E.: Controlled alternate quantum walk-based pseudo-random number generator and its application to quantum color image encryption. Physica A **547**, 123869 (2019)
7. Abd EL-Latif, A.A., et al.: Controlled alternate quantum walks based privacy preserving healthcare images in internet of things. Opt. Laser Technol. **124**, 105942 (2020)
8. Yang, Y.G., Zhao, Q.Q.: Novel pseudo-random number generator based on quantum random walks. Sci. Rep. **6**, 1–11 (2016)
9. Yang, Y.G., Xu, P., Yang, R., Zhou, Y.H., Shi, W.M.: Quantum Hash function and its application to privacy amplification in quantum key distribution, pseudorandom number generation and image encryption. Sci. Rep. **6**, 19788 (2016)
10. Yang, Y.-G., Bi, J.-L., Chen, X.-B., Yuan, Z., Zhou, Y.-H., Shi, W.-M.: Simple hash function using discrete-time quantum walks. Quantum Inf. Process. **17**(8), 1–19 (2018). https://doi.org/10.1007/s11128-018-1954-2
11. Zhang, Y., Lu, K., Gao, Y., Wang, M.: NEQR: a novel enhanced quantum representation of digital images. Quantum Inf. Process. **12**(8), 2833–2860 (2013)

12. Sang, J., Wang, S., Li, Q.: A novel quantum representation of color digital images. Quantum Inf. Process. **16**(2), 1–14 (2016). https://doi.org/10.1007/s11128-016-1463-0

13. Li, D., et al.: Discrete-time interacting quantum walks and quantum hash schemes. Quant. Inf. Process. **12**, 1501–1513 (2012). https://doi.org/10.1007/s11128-012-0421-8

14. Li, D., et al.: Controlled alternate quantum walks based quantum hash function. Sci. Rep. **8**, 1–7 (2017). https://doi.org/10.1038/s41598-017-18566-6

15. Zhou, R.-G., Hu, W., Fan, P.: Quantum watermarking scheme through Arnold scrambling and LSB steganography. Quantum Inf. Process. **16**(9), 1–21 (2017). https://doi.org/10.1007/s11128-017-1640-9

16. Hu, W.W., Zhou, R.G., Liu, X.A., et al.: Quantum image steganography algorithm based on modified exploiting modification direction embedding. Quantum Inf. Process. **19**(5), 1–28 (2020)

17. Zhou, R.G., Hu, W.W., Luo, G.F., Liu, X.A., Fan, P.: Quantum realization of the nearest neighbor value interpolation method for INEQR. Quantum Inf. Process. **17**(7), 1–37 (2018). https://doi.org/10.1007/s11128-018-1921-y

18. David, S.O., Ramos, R.: Quantum bit string comparator: circuits and applications quantum bit string comparator: circuits and applications. Quantum Comput. Comput. **7**, 26 (2007)

19. Le, P.Q., Iliyasu, A.M., Dong, F., Hirota, K.: Strategies for designing geometric transformations on quantum images. Theor. Comput. Sci. **412**(15), 1406–1418 (2011)

20. Zhang, L.M., Sun, K.H., Liu, W.H., et al.: A novel color image encryption scheme using fractional-order hyperchaotic system and DNA sequence operations. Chin. Phys. B **26**(10), 100504 (2017)

21. Barenco, A., et al.: Elementary gates for quantum computation. Phys. Rev. A **52**, 3457–3488 (1995)

The 1st International Symposium on Emerging Information Security and Applications (EISA 2020)

Security Analysis of a Multi-secret Sharing Scheme with Unconditional Security

Min Xiao[1] and Zhe Xia[1,2(✉)]

[1] School of Computer Science, Wuhan University of Technology,
Wuhan 430070, China
xiazhe@whut.edu.cn
[2] Guizhou Key Laboratory of Public Big Data,
Guizhou University, Guiyang 550025, China

Abstract. Harn has introduced a (t, n) threshold secret sharing scheme recently, in which shareholders' shares are not disclosed in the secret reconstruction phase. The benefit is that the outside adversary cannot learn the secret even if it is recovered by more than t shareholders. Moreover, Harn has further extended this scheme into a multi-secret sharing scheme so that multiple secrets can be recovered individually at different stagies. Both schemes are claimed to achieve the perfectness property using heuristic arguments. However, in this paper, we show that the above claim is false and these schemes are not perfect. In the first scheme, the coalition of $t-1$ shareholders can conclude that the secret is not uniformly distributed. And in the multi-secret sharing scheme, when the public parameters satisfy some special conditions, the coalition of $t-1$ shareholders can even use the recovered secrets to preclude some possible values for the unrecovered secrets.

Keywords: Threat analysis · Multi-secret sharing · Unconditional security

1 Introduction

Secret sharing is an fundamental building block in information security and cryptography. Over the last few decades, great efforts have devoted to designing various secret sharing schemes [1,3,14].

In traditional (t, n) threshold secret sharing schemes [4,5,11–13], the dealer first generates the shares and sends each share to a shareholder. Afterwards, the secret can be recovered if t or more than t of these shareholders reveal their shares. However, one drawback of these schemes is that when there are more than t shareholders in the secret reconstruction, the outside adversary may impersonate to be a shareholder, contribute an invalid share or even do not contribute any share, and learn the secret after the other shareholders have

© Springer Nature Switzerland AG 2021
G. Wang et al. (Eds.): SpaCCS 2020, LNCS 12383, pp. 533–544, 2021.
https://doi.org/10.1007/978-3-030-68884-4_44

revealed their shares. Obviously, this is not ideal for many applications where the secret should only be recovered among the legitimate shareholders. The problem can be solved if some proper authentication mechanism is added on top of the secret sharing scheme, but this will introduce additional complexity, because most of the user authentication schemes authenticate one user at a time.

In order to solve the above problem, Harn has proposed an interesting solution in [10]. To recover the secret in Harn's scheme, each shareholder uses her share as well as a value u (where $t \leq u \leq n$) to compute a shadow, where u is the expected number of shareholders participated in the secret reconstruction. Afterwards, each shareholder reveals this shadow instead of her share. The secret can be reconstructed if and only if there are exactly u shadows and all these shadows are correctly computed. Therefore, the outside adversary cannot use the same strategy to learn the secret, because she cannot compute a shadow without the knowledge of a valid share. Another appealing feature of this scheme is that the shadow will not disclose the corresponding share. And Harn has used this property to further extend the scheme into a multi-secret sharing scheme, in which the shareholders can reuse their shares to recover multiple secrets individually at different stages. Note that both these schemes are not relying on any computational assumption, and the shareholders or the outside adversary are allowed to have unlimited computational power.

It was claimed in [10] that these two schemes both satisfy the perfectness property. Informally, this means that in the single secret sharing scheme, the coalition of $t-1$ shareholders cannot learn any information of the secret, and in the multi-secret sharing scheme, $t-1$ colluded shareholders cannot learn any information of the unrecovered secret even if some secrets have already been recovered. The above claims are argued based on the following reasons. Because the number of equations obtained by the $t-1$ shareholders and the outside adversary is less than the number of unknown values, the system of equations cannot be solved and the unkonwn values cannot be retrieved. Therefore, no information about the secret can be learned either by the colluding shareholders or by the outside adversary[1].

Our Contributions. In this paper, we demonstrate that Harn's schemes in [10] are not perfect. Firstly, we extend Ghodosi's results [8] to prove that Harn's single secret sharing scheme is not perfect. Although $t-1$ colluded shareholders can neither recover the secret nor preclude some possible values for the secret, they are able to conclude that the secret is not uniformly distributed. Secondly, we introduce a new method to analyse secret sharing schemes based on hyperplane geometry, and we use it to illustrate that in Harn's multi-secret sharing scheme, the coalition of $t-1$ shareholders can conclude that the secret is not uniformly distributed as well. Our method is more versatile than Ghodosi's one [8] and it may have some independent interests. Moreover, we show that when the public parameters satisfy some special conditions, these colluding shareholders also can

---

[1] Note that similar technique has been used in [9] and this scheme was attacked by a novel cryptanalysis, called linear subspace attack [2]. But our work is different from the existing attack and it illustrates some other weaknesses of Harn's work.

use the recovered secrets to preclude some possible values for the unrecovered secrets. Because both Harn's schemes have been claimed to achieve the perfectness property using heuristic arguments, our results provide some evidences that heuristic arguments may not be adequate to analyse the perfectness properties of secret sharing schemes. In order to carry out proper security analysis, formal methods should be used instead.

Outline of the Paper. The rest of this paper is organised as follows: some prelimilaries are outlined in Sect. 2. Harn's proposed secret sharing schemes are reviewed in Sect. 3. And in Sect. 4, we describe why both Harn's schemes fail to achieve the perfectness property, and how to make them perfect. Finally, we conclude in Sect. 5.

2 Prelimilaries

In this section, we describe some prelimilaries relate to the perfectness property of secret sharing schemes, including its definitions, the necessary conditions for lower bounds on the length of each share, and Ghodosi's results on perfectness.

2.1 Perfectness in Single Secret Sharing Schemes

Let $\mathcal{P} = \{P_1, P_2, \ldots, P_n\}$ be the set of n shareholders, and let $\mathcal{K}, \mathcal{S}$ be the secret set and the share set respectively. Let Γ be a collection of authorised subsets of $2^{\mathcal{P}}$, called the access structure. In the share distribution phase, to share a secret $s \in \mathcal{K}$, each shareholder $P_i \in \mathcal{P}$ receives a share $\mathsf{sh}_i \in \mathcal{S}$ from the dealer. In the secret reconstruction phase, any authorised subset $\mathcal{A} \in \Gamma$ of shareholders can use their shares to recover the secret. But any non-authorised subset $\mathcal{B} \notin \Gamma$ of shareholders can learn no information about the secret.

The above two requirements can be formalised using the entropy $\mathsf{H}(\cdot)$ of random variables in information theory. Denote S as the random variable associated to the secret, SH_i as the random variable associated to P_i's share, and $\mathsf{SH}_{\mathcal{A}}$ as the vector of random variables associated to the shares belonging to the shareholders in the subset $\mathcal{A} \subset \mathcal{P}$. The perfect secret sharing scheme should satisfy the following two requirements:

- *Correctness:* Given the subset of shares $\{\mathsf{sh}_i\}_{P_i \in \mathcal{A}}$, we have $\mathsf{H}(\mathsf{S}|\mathsf{SH}_{\mathcal{A}}) = 0$ for any subset $\mathcal{A} \in \Gamma$.
- *Secrecy:* Given the subset of shares $\{\mathsf{sh}_i\}_{P_i \in \mathcal{B}}$, we have $\mathsf{H}(\mathsf{S}|\mathsf{SH}_{\mathcal{B}}) = \mathsf{H}(\mathsf{S})$ for any subset $\mathcal{B} \notin \Gamma$.

For any threshold secret sharing scheme that achieves the perfectness property, Brickell [7] has given the lower bounds on the length of each share: the equation $\mathsf{H}(\mathsf{SH}_i) \geq \mathsf{H}(\mathsf{S})$ needs to be hold for every shareholder $P_i \in \mathcal{P}$. In other words, the length of each share has to be equal or larger than the length of the secret.

2.2   Perfectness in Multi-secret Sharing Schemes

Let $s_1, s_2, \ldots, s_h \in \mathcal{K}$ be h secrets shared at the same time, and $\Gamma_1, \Gamma_2, \ldots, \Gamma_h \subset 2^{\mathcal{P}}$ be the corresponding access structures. In the share distribution phase, the dealer distributes the secrets according to their access structures. Each shareholder $P_i \in \mathcal{P}$ receives a share $\mathsf{sh}_i \in \mathcal{S}$. In the secret reconstruction phase, given a subset of shares and an index $j \in \{1, 2, \ldots, h\}$, the expected output is the j-th secret s_j. Denote S_j as the random variable associated to the secret s_j. The perfect multi-secret sharing scheme should satisfy the following two requirements:

- *Correctness:* Given the subset of shares $\{\mathsf{sh}_i\}_{P_i \in \mathcal{A}}$ and an index j, we have $\mathsf{H}(\mathsf{S}_j | \mathsf{SH}_\mathcal{A}) = 0$ for any subset $\mathcal{A} \in \Gamma_j$.
- *Secrecy:* Denote $\mathsf{T} \subset \{s_1, s_2, \ldots s_h\} \backslash \{s_j\}$ as the set of recovered secrets in the previous stagies. Given the subset of shares $\{\mathsf{sh}_i\}_{P_i \in \mathcal{B}}$ and an index j, we have $\mathsf{H}(\mathsf{S}_j | \mathsf{SH}_\mathcal{B}, \mathsf{T}) = \mathsf{H}(\mathsf{S}_j | \mathsf{T})$ for any subset $\mathcal{B} \notin \Gamma_j$.

For any threshold multi-secret sharing scheme that satisfies the perfectness property, Blundo et al. [6] have given the lower bounds on the length of each share: the equation $\mathsf{H}(\mathsf{SH}_i) \geq \sum_{j=1}^{h} \mathsf{H}(\mathsf{S}_j)$ needs to be hold for every shareholder $P_i \in \mathcal{P}$. In other words, the length of each share has to be equal or larger than the total length of the secrets.

2.3   Ghodosi's Results on Perfectness

In [13], Shamir has proposed a perfect (t, n) threshold secret sharing schemes, in which at least t shareholders can recover the secret. In other words, the access structure is $\Gamma = \{\mathcal{A} \subset \mathcal{P} : |\mathcal{A}| \geq t\}$. The secret set $\mathcal{K}$ is a finite field. To share a secret $s \in \mathcal{K}$, a random polynomial $f(x) \in \mathcal{K}[x]$ with degree *at most* $t - 1$ is generated by the dealer, such that $f(0) = s$. Then every shareholder $P_i \in \mathcal{P}$ receives the share $\mathsf{sh}_i = f(x_i)$, where $x_i \in \mathcal{K} \backslash \{0\}$ are publicly known and pairwise different values. In the secret reconstruction phase, any subset of t or more shares can recover the secret through polynomial interpolation, but less than t shares can derive no information of the secret.

Note that many papers in the literature have misused Shamir's secret sharing by requiring the dealer to randomly select the polynomial $f(x)$ of degree $t - 1$. In this case, although the length of each shareholder's share still satisfies the lower bounds given by Brickell, Ghodosi et al. [8] have pointed out that if the degree of $f(x)$ was known to be $t - 1$, then Shamir's secret sharing scheme is not perfect. The consequence is that any coalition of $t - 1$ shareholders can preclude a possible value for the secret using the following strategy.

Denote $f(x) = a_0 + a_1 x + \cdots + a_{t-1} x^{t-1}$ with $a_{t-1} \neq 0$. Then, $t - 1$ colluded shareholders can interpolate a $t - 2$ degree polynomial $g(x) = b_0 + b_1 x + \cdots + b_{t-2} x^{t-2}$, such that $f(x_i) = g(x_i)$ for $1 \leq i \leq t - 1$. This leads the system of equations:

$$\begin{cases} (a_0 - b_0) + (a_1 - b_1)x_1 + \cdots + (a_{t-2} - b_{t-2}){x_1}^{t-2} + a_{t-1}{x_1}^{t-1} & = 0 \\ (a_0 - b_0) + (a_1 - b_1)x_2 + \cdots + (a_{t-2} - b_{t-2}){x_2}^{t-2} + a_{t-1}{x_2}^{t-1} & = 0 \\ \qquad\qquad\qquad\qquad\qquad\qquad\qquad\qquad\qquad\qquad \vdots \\ (a_0 - b_0) + (a_1 - b_1)x_{t-1} + \cdots + (a_{t-2} - b_{t-2}){x_{t-1}}^{t-2} + a_{t-1}{x_{t-1}}^{t-1} = 0 \end{cases}$$

By contradiction, if we assume that $a_0 = b_0$, then the above system of equations with $t - 1$ equations and $t - 1$ unknown values $\{a_1, a_2, \ldots, a_{t-1}\}$ will have a unique solution. This is because the determinant of a Vandermonde matrix is not 0. Hence, the solution must be $a_1 = b_1, a_2 = b_2, \ldots, a_{t-2} = b_{t-2}$, and $a_{t-1} = 0$. This contradicts the assumption that $a_{t-1} \neq 0$. Therefore, any $t - 1$ shareholders can preclude b_0 as a possible value of the secret.

3 Review of Harn's Schemes

In this section, we review Harn's secret sharing schemes [10] and briefly explain why it is claimed that they can satisfy the perfectness property.

3.1 Models

The system model, communication model and adversary model used in Harn's schemes are as follows:

System Model. The players include a trusted dealer $\mathcal{D}$, n shareholders $\mathcal{P} = \{P_1, P_2, \ldots, P_n\}$ and some insider or outsider adversaries. It is assumed that all these players have unlimited computational resources. Among these shareholders, it is assumed that at least t of them are honest, where $t > n/2$. Note that this setting prevents the dishonest shareholders from learning the secret even if they all collude. Here, the word "dishonest" means honest-but-curious. That is, these dishonest shareholders will follow the protocol, but they may try to learn information that should remain private.

Communication Model. It is assumed that there exists a secure channel between the dealer and every shareholder, so that the shares can be securely distributed to the shareholders. Moreover, it is assumed that every player is connected to a common authenticated broadcast channel $\mathcal{C}$. Any message sent through $\mathcal{C}$ can be heard by the other players. The adversary can neither modify messages sent by an honest player through $\mathcal{C}$, nor she can prevent honest players from receiving messages from $\mathcal{C}$. Note that these are standard assumptions widely used in existing secret sharing schemes.

Adversary Model. Two types of adversaries are considered in Harn's secret sharing schemes:

- *Inside adversary* is a legitimate shareholder who owns a valid share generated by the dealer. An insider adversary may work alone or collude with some other inside adversaries in order to learn the secrets before they are reconstructed. The restriction is that the maximum number of colluded inside adversaries is $t - 1$.

- *Outside adversary* is an attacker who does not own any valid share. But she may participate in the secret reconstruction phase, impersonate to be a shareholder, and learn the secret after the other shareholders have revealed their shares.

3.2 The Single Secret Sharing Scheme

- **Share distribution phase.**
    1. The dealer $\mathcal{D}$ selects k random polynomials $f_l(x)$ over $\mathbb{F}_p$ for $l = 1, 2, \ldots, k$, having degree $t - 1$ each. Here, p is a prime that satisfies $p > n$.
    2. Then, $\mathcal{D}$ generates the shares $\mathsf{sh}_i = f_l(x_i) \pmod{p}$ for $i = 1, 2, \ldots, n$, and sends each share to the corresponding shareholder through the secure channel. The values $x_i \in \mathbb{F}_p \backslash \{0\}$ are publicly known and pairwise different. In the rest of this paper, we assume that all equations are modulo p unless otherwise stated.
    3. To share the secret $s \in \mathbb{F}_p$, the dealer finds integers $w_l, d_l \in \mathbb{F}_p$ for $l = 1, 2, \ldots, k$, such that $s = \sum_{l=1}^{k} d_l f_l(w_l)$. The values w_l need to be pairwise different, and the intersection of the two sets $\{x_1, x_2, \ldots, x_n\}$ and $\{w_1, w_2, \ldots, w_k\}$ needs to be empty. The dealer $\mathcal{D}$ makes these integers w_l, d_l publicly known for $l = 1, 2, \ldots, k$.
- **Secret reconstruction phase.**
    1. Suppose u shareholders participate in the secret reconstruction phase, where $t \leq u \leq n$. Each shareholder P_i uses her share sh_i and the value u to compute the shadow c_i as:

    $$c_i = \sum_{l=1}^{k} d_l f_l(x_i) \prod_{v=1, v \neq i}^{u} \frac{w_l - x_v}{x_i - x_v}$$

    And then, P_i sends the shadow c_i to the authenticated broadcast channel.
    2. After receiving all the shadows c_i for $i = 1, 2, \ldots, u$, every shareholder can compute the secret as $s = \sum_{i=1}^{u} c_i$.

To prove that the above scheme is perfect, it needs to show that both the correctness and secrecy requirements (introduced in Sect. 2) are satisfied. It is easy to see that the correctness requirement holds, because we have

$$
\begin{aligned}
s = \sum_{i=1}^{u} c_i &= \sum_{i=1}^{u} \sum_{l=1}^{k} (d_l f_l(x_i) \prod_{v=1, v \neq i}^{u} \frac{w_l - x_v}{x_i - x_v}) \\
&= \sum_{l=1}^{k} (d_l \sum_{i=1}^{u} (f_l(x_i) \prod_{v=1, v \neq i}^{u} \frac{w_l - x_v}{x_i - x_v})) \\
&= \sum_{l=1}^{k} d_l f_l(w_l)
\end{aligned}
$$

Harn has claimed that if $kt > n-1$, then the secrecy requirement also holds. Considering the worst case that n players are involved to recover the secret and the outside adversary is the last one to reveal her shadow. Then, the outside adversary can obtain at most $n - 1$ equations. But because the number of unkonwn values kt is larger than the number of equations, the outside adversary cannot learn any information of the secret. Moreover, the coalition of $t - 1$ shareholders can obtain at most $k(t - 1)$ equations, which is smaller than the number kt of unkonwn values. Hence, the inside adversaries cannot learn any information of the secret neither. Therefore, it is concluded that the secrecy requirement holds, and this scheme is perfect with unconditional security.

3.3 The Multi-secret Sharing Scheme

- **Share distribution phase.**
  1. To share h secrets $\{s_1, s_2, \ldots, s_h\}$, the dealer $\mathcal{D}$ first selects k random polynomials $f_l(x)$ over $\mathbb{F}_p$ for $l = 1, 2, \ldots, k$, having degree $t - 1$ each.
  2. Then, $\mathcal{D}$ generates the shares $\mathsf{sh}_i = f_l(x_i)$ for $i = 1, 2, \ldots, n$, and distributes them to the corresponding shareholders through the secure channel. Similarly, the values $x_i \in \mathbb{F}_p \backslash \{0\}$ need to be publicly known and pairwise different.
  3. The dealer $\mathcal{D}$ finds some integers $w_l \in \mathbb{F}_p$ for $l = 1, 2, \ldots, k$, such that they are pairwise different and $w_l \notin \{x_1, x_2, \ldots, x_n\}$. For every secret s_j, where $j \in \{1, 2, \ldots, h\}$, the dealer $\mathcal{D}$ also finds some integers $d_{j,l} \in \mathbb{F}_p$ for $l = 1, 2, \ldots, k$, such that $s_j = \sum_{l=1}^{k} d_{j,l} f_l(w_l)$. Moreover, it is required that all the vectors $< d_{j,1}, d_{j,2}, \ldots, d_{j,k} >$ are linearly independent. The dealer $\mathcal{D}$ makes these integers $w_l, d_{j,l}$ publicly known.
- **Secret reconstruction phase.**
  1. Suppose u shareholders participate to recover the secret s_j, where $t \le u \le n$ and $j \in \{1, 2, \ldots, h\}$. Each shareholder P_i uses her share sh_i as well as the values u and j to compute the shadow $c_{j,i}$ as:

$$c_{j,i} = \sum_{l=1}^{k} d_{j,l} f_l(x_i) \prod_{v=1, v \ne i}^{u} \frac{w_l - x_v}{x_i - x_v}$$

Then, P_i sends this shadow $c_{j,i}$ to the authenticated broadcast channel.
  2. After receiving all the shadows $c_{j,i}$ for $i = 1, 2, \ldots, u$, every shareholder can calculate the secret as $s_j = \sum_{i=1}^{u} c_{j,i}$.

Similar as in the above secret sharing scheme, the multi-secret sharing scheme also satisfies the correctness requirement. In order to achieve the secrecy requirement, Harn has imposed the restriction that all the vectors $< d_{j,1}, d_{j,2}, \ldots, d_{j,k} >$ are linearly independent. Because these vectors are public parameters, and they satisfy the following condition:

$$\begin{bmatrix} d_{1,1} & d_{1,2} & \cdots & d_{1,k} \\ d_{2,1} & d_{2,2} & \cdots & d_{2,k} \\ \vdots & \vdots & & \vdots \\ d_{h,1} & d_{h,2} & \cdots & d_{h,k} \end{bmatrix} \cdot \begin{bmatrix} f_1(w_1) \\ f_2(w_2) \\ \vdots \\ f_k(w_k) \end{bmatrix} = \begin{bmatrix} s_1 \\ s_2 \\ \vdots \\ s_h \end{bmatrix}$$

If there exists some linear relationship among these vectors, anyone may learn some uncovered secret using the linear combination of previously recovered secrets. Moreover, the parameters need to satisfy $kt > h(n + 1) - 2$ and $k > (h - 1)(n - t + 2)$ as well. This ensures that even in the worst case, neither the outside adversary nor the coalition of $t - 1$ shareholders can obtain enough equations to learn the polynomials' coefficients. Therefore, Harn has also claimed that this multi-secret sharing scheme is perfect with unconditional security.

4   Threat Analysis of Harn's Schemes

In this section, we revisit Harn's schemes in [10], demonstrating that both his schemes fail to achieve the perfectness property. Because we have already shown in Sect. 3 that the correctness requirement holds, our focus is only to prove that Harn's schemes fail to satisfy the secrecy requirement. Then, we explain how to modify Harn's schemes to be perfect.

4.1   Analysis of the Single Secret Sharing Scheme

We first analyse whether Brickell's lower bounds on the length of each share are satisfied in Harn's single secret sharing scheme. If not, it can be simply concluded that this scheme is not perfect. Recall that in the threshold secret sharing scheme, the threshold value t has to be in the range $n/2 < t \leq n$. Then, $kt > n-1$ implies that $k \geq 1$. Hence, each shareholder's share is at least one value $f_l(x_i)$ in $\mathbb{F}_p$. Moreover, since the dealer $\mathcal{D}$ is assumed to be trusted, she will randomly generate the polynomial $f_l(x)$ over $\mathbb{F}_p$. The value $f_l(x_i)$ is randomly distributed in $\mathbb{F}_p$. Therefore, we have $\mathsf{H}(\mathsf{SH}_i) \geq \mathsf{H}(\mathsf{S})$ for every shareholder $P_i \in \mathcal{P}$, and Brickell's lower bounds on the length of each share are satisfied.

Now, we extend Ghodosi's results [8] to prove that Harn's single secret sharing scheme fails to satisfy the secrecy requirement. Without loss of generality, suppose the first $t - 1$ shareholders $\{P_1, P_2, \ldots, P_{t-1}\}$ are colluding.

1. Firstly, based on Harn's description that "the dealer $\mathcal{D}$ selects k random polynomials $f_l(x) = a_{l,0} + a_{l,1}x + \ldots + a_{l,t-1}x^{t-1}$ over $\mathbb{F}_p$ for $l = 1, 2, \ldots, k$, having degree $t - 1$ each", these colluded shareholders can apply Ghodosi's results (introduced in Sect. 2.3) to preclude one possible value for every $a_{l,0}$.
2. Secondly, we show that these shareholders also can preclude one possible value for every $f_l(w_l)$:

$$f_l(w_l) = a_{l,0}\lambda_{l,0} + \sum_{i=1}^{t-1} f_l(x_i)\lambda_{l,i}$$

where

$$\lambda_{l,0} = \prod_{j=1}^{t-1} \frac{x_j - w_l}{x_j}, \quad \text{and} \quad \lambda_{l,i} = \prod_{j=0, j \neq i}^{t-1} \frac{w_l - x_j}{x_i - x_j}$$

Because the values $x_i \in \mathbb{F}_p \backslash \{0\}$ and $w_l \notin \{x_1, x_2, \ldots, x_n\}$ for $l = 1, 2, \ldots, k$, we have $\gcd(\lambda_{l,0}, p) = 1$. The function $f_l(w_l)$ is bijective when treating $a_{l,0}$

as the unknown value. Hence, every different value of $a_{l,0}$ will result a unique value of $f_l(w_l)$.

3. Finally, recall that the secret is $s = \sum_{l=1}^{k} d_l f_l(w_l)$. Since one possible value for every $f_l(w_l)$ have been precluded, every $d_l f_l(w_l) \in \mathbb{F}_p$ can have only $p-1$ possible values if $d_l \neq 0$, and $d_l f_l(w_l) = 0$ if $d_l = 0$. Denote k' as the number of d_l values that equal to 0. Obviously, $k' = k$ is meaningless, because the secret s will be fixed as 0 in this case. Before the modulo p operation, the secret s will have $(p-1)^{k-k'}$ possible values. Since p does not divide $(p-1)^{k-k'}$, after the modulo p operation, the secret s cannot be uniformly distributed within $\mathbb{F}_p$. Therefore, for the subset of shares $\{sh_i\}_{P_i \in \mathcal{B}}$, we have $H(S|SH_{\mathcal{B}}) < H(S)$ for any set $|\mathcal{B}| = t-1$. In other words, the secrecy requirement does not hold, and this secret sharing scheme is not perfect.

4.2 Analysis of the Multi-secret Sharing Scheme

We first analyse whether Blundo's lower bounds on the length of each share are satisfied in Harn's multi-secret sharing scheme. When they are not satisfied, we can easily conclude that the scheme is not perfect. Since $n/2 < t \leq n$, and Harn has required that $kt > h(n+1) - 2$ and $k > (h-1)(n-t+2)$, we have $k \geq h$. Each shareholder's share is k values of $f_l(x_i)$ for $l = 1, 2, \ldots, k$ that are randomly distributed in $\mathbb{F}_p$. Therefore, we have $H(SH_i) \geq \sum_{j=1}^{h} H(S_j)$ for every shareholder $P_i \in \mathcal{P}$, and Blundo's lower bounds on the length of each share are satisfied.

Now, we introduce a new method to analyse secret sharing schemes based on hyperplane geometry, and we use it to illustrate that Harn's multi-secret sharing scheme fails to satisfy the secrecy requirement. For each polynomial $f_l(x) = a_{l,0} + a_{l,1}x + \cdots + a_{l,t-1}x^{t-1}$ randomly selected by the dealer $\mathcal{D}$, we have

$$
\begin{bmatrix} 1 & x_1 & \ldots & x_1^{t-1} \\ 1 & x_2 & \ldots & x_2^{t-1} \\ \vdots & \vdots & & \vdots \\ 1 & x_n & \ldots & x_n^{t-1} \end{bmatrix} \cdot \begin{bmatrix} a_{l,0} \\ a_{l,1} \\ \vdots \\ a_{l,t-1} \end{bmatrix} = \begin{bmatrix} f_l(x_1) \\ f_l(x_2) \\ \vdots \\ f_l(x_n) \end{bmatrix}
$$

Hence, the vector $< a_{l,0}, a_{l,1}, \ldots, a_{l,t-1} >$ can be considered as the coordinates of some point $\mathbb{P}$ in the t dimensional space $\mathbb{S}$. Each shareholder's share $f_l(x_i)$ can be considered as a t dimensional plane in $\mathbb{S}$ that passes through the point $\mathbb{P}$. The Vandermonde matrix ensures that all these n planes intersect uniquely at the point $\mathbb{P}$. The coalition of $t-1$ shareholders can use their planes to derive a line $\mathbb{L}$ in the space $\mathbb{S}$. Based on Harn's description, the polynomial $f_l(x)$ is konwn to have degree $t-1$, so that $a_{l,t-1} \neq 0$. Now, all the points with the coordinate $a_{l,t-1} = 0$ will form another plane in the space $\mathbb{S}$, and this plane will intersect the line $\mathbb{L}$ by a point $\mathbb{P}'$. Then, we can conclude that $\mathbb{P}$ and $\mathbb{P}'$ are not the same point. Note that this method is very versatile. For example, in one hand, if we know that the coordinates satisfy some linear relationship, we can use this relationship to form a plane to derive the point $\mathbb{P}$. In the other hand, if we can exclude some linear relationship for these coordinates, we can also use this relationship to form a plane to derive a point $\mathbb{P}'$ and conclude that $\mathbb{P}$ and $\mathbb{P}'$ are not the same point.

Using this new method, the $t-1$ colluded shareholders can also preclude one possible value for every $a_{l,0}$ in the polynomials $f_l(x)$ for $l = 1, 2, \ldots, k$. Then, they can adapt the same strategy in Sect. 4.1 to preclude one possible value for every $f_l(w_l)$. Hence, they can conclude that the secret are not uniformly distributed within $\mathbb{F}_p$. This proves that the multi-secret sharing scheme fails to be perfect.

Moreover, we further show that compared with the single version of secret sharing, its multiple version may leak more information about the secret. In some special circumstances, when the public parameters satisfy some conditions, the colluded shareholders can even use the recovered secrets to preclude some possible values for the unrecovered secrets. Assume that two secrets s_i and s_j are recovered in different stagies. Without loss of generality, we assume s_i is already recovered but s_j is yet to be recovered. The vectors $< d_{i,1}, d_{i,2}, \ldots, d_{i,k} >$ and $< d_{j,1}, d_{j,2}, \ldots, d_{j,k} >$ are their corresponding public vectors, respectively. Moreover, we assume that the colluding shareholders already know that $f_v(w_v) \neq 0$ for some $v \in \{1, 2, \ldots, k\}$, and these two vectors happen to satisfy the following conditions:

- For all $u \in \{1, 2, \ldots, k\} \backslash \{v\}$, we have $d_{j,u} = \alpha \cdot d_{j,u}$.
- But for v, we have $d_{j,v} = \alpha d_{i,v} + \beta$.

where $\alpha, \beta \in \mathbb{F}_p \backslash \{0\}$. Note that in this case, the two vectors are linearly independent, and all the h vectors could still be linearly independent. However, if the secret s_i is recovered, the value of the unrecovered secret s_j cannot be $\alpha \cdot s_i$, and this is because $\beta \neq 0$. Therefore, the colluding shareholders can preclude one possible values for s_j.

4.3 Making Harn's Schemes Perfect

Harn's two secret sharing schemes can be easily modified to be perfect. The only required change is that the dealer $\mathcal{D}$ selects k random polynomials $f_l(x) = a_{l,0} + a_{l,1}x + \ldots + a_{l,t-1}x^{t-1}$ over $\mathbb{F}_q$ with degree at most $t-1$. Here, we only describe why such change can make the single secret sharing scheme to be perfect. And similar reasons also can be applied to the multi-secret sharing scheme.

If the polynomial is randomly generated with degree at most $t-1$, for every polynomial $f_l(x)$, the colluded shareholders only have $t-1$ points $(x_i, f_l(x_i))$ for $i = 1, 2, \ldots, t-1$. Because the colluded shareholders' view of $a_{l,0}$ is uniformly distributed in $\mathbb{F}_p$, every additional point $(0, a_{l,0})$ can interpolate $f_l(x)$ into a different polynomial with equal probability. Hence, every value $f_l(w_l)$ will be uniformly distributed in $\mathbb{F}_p$. This also implies that these shareholders' view of the secret $s = \sum_{l=1}^{k} d_l f_l(w_l)$ will be uniformly distributed in $\mathbb{F}_p$. Therefore, the secrecy requirement will hold, since for any subset of shares $\{sh_i\}_{P_i \in \mathcal{B}}$, we have $H(S|SH_{\mathcal{B}}) = H(S)$ for any set $|\mathcal{B}| \leq t-1$.

5 Conclusion

In this paper, we have revisited Harn's secret sharing schemes introduced in [10]. We have demonstrated that both Harn's schemes fail to achieve the perfectness property. In the single secret sharing scheme, if it was known that all the random polynomials are with degree $t-1$, the coalition of $t-1$ shareholders can conclude that the secret is not uniformly distributed. In the multi-secret sharing scheme, when the public parameters satisfy some special conditions, the colluding $t-1$ shareholders may use the recovered secrets to preclude some possible values for the unrecovered secrets. We have also introduced a new method to analyse secret shairng schemes. Compared with Ghodosi's method in the literature, this new method is more versatile and it could be used in more circumstances. Moreover, this paper is another demonstration that formal security analyses [15,16] are crucial for secret sharing schemes.

Acknowledgement. This work was partially supported by the Guizhou Key Laboratory of Public Big Data (Grant No. 2019BDKFJJ005).

References

1. Aggarwal, D., et al.: Stronger leakage-resilient and non-malleable secret sharing schemes for general access structures. In: Boldyreva, A., Micciancio, D. (eds.) CRYPTO 2019, Part II. LNCS, vol. 11693, pp. 510–539. Springer, Cham (2019). https://doi.org/10.1007/978-3-030-26951-7_18
2. Ahmadian, Z., Jamshidpour, S.: Linear subspace cryptanalysis of Harn's secret sharing-based group authentication scheme. IEEE Trans. Inf. Forensics Secur. **13**(2), 502–510 (2017)
3. Applebaum, B., Beimel, A., Farràs, O., Nir, O., Peter, N.: Secret-sharing schemes for general and uniform access structures. In: Ishai, Y., Rijmen, V. (eds.) EUROCRYPT 2019, Part III. LNCS, vol. 11478, pp. 441–471. Springer, Cham (2019). https://doi.org/10.1007/978-3-030-17659-4_15
4. Asmuth, C., Bloom, J.: A modular approach to key safeguarding. IEEE Trans. Inf. Theory **29**(2), 208–210 (1983)
5. Blakley, R.: Safeguarding cryptographic keys. In: Proceedings of American Federation of Information Processing Societies (AFIPS'79), vol. 48, pp. 313–317 (1979)
6. Blundo, C., De Santis, A., Di Crescenzo, G., Gaggia, A.G., Vaccaro, U.: Multi-secret sharing schemes. In: Desmedt, Y.G. (ed.) CRYPTO 1994. LNCS, vol. 839, pp. 150–163. Springer, Heidelberg (1994). https://doi.org/10.1007/3-540-48658-5_17
7. Brickell, E.F.: Some ideal secret sharing schemes. In: Quisquater, J.-J., Vandewalle, J. (eds.) EUROCRYPT 1989. LNCS, vol. 434, pp. 468–475. Springer, Heidelberg (1990). https://doi.org/10.1007/3-540-46885-4_45
8. Ghodosi, H., Pieprzyk, J., Safavi-Naini, R.: Remarks on the multiple assignment secret sharing scheme. In: Han, Y., Okamoto, T., Qing, S. (eds.) ICICS 1997. LNCS, vol. 1334, pp. 72–80. Springer, Heidelberg (1997). https://doi.org/10.1007/BFb0028463
9. Harn, L.: Group authentication. IEEE Trans. Comput. **62**(9), 1893–1898 (2012)

10. Harn, L.: Secure secret reconstruction and multi-secret sharing schemes with unconditional security. Secur. Commun. Netw. **7**(3), 567–573 (2014)
11. Harn, L., Xia, Z., Hsu, C., Liu, Y.: Secret sharing with secure secret reconstruction. Inf. Sci. **519**, 1–8 (2020)
12. Mignotte, M.: How to share a secret. In: Beth, T. (ed.) EUROCRYPT 1982. LNCS, vol. 149, pp. 371–375. Springer, Heidelberg (1983). https://doi.org/10.1007/3-540-39466-4_27
13. Shamir, A.: How to share a secret. In: Proceedings of 22nd Communication of ACM, pp. 612–613 (1979)
14. Srinivasan, A., Vasudevan, P.N.: Leakage resilient secret sharing and applications. In: Boldyreva, A., Micciancio, D. (eds.) CRYPTO 2019, Part II. LNCS, vol. 11693, pp. 480–509. Springer, Cham (2019). https://doi.org/10.1007/978-3-030-26951-7_17
15. Xia, Z., Yang, B., Zhou, Y., Zhang, M., Shen, H., Mu, Y.: Provably secure proactive secret sharing without the adjacent assumption. In: Steinfeld, R., Yuen, T.H. (eds.) ProvSec 2019. LNCS, vol. 11821, pp. 247–264. Springer, Cham (2019). https://doi.org/10.1007/978-3-030-31919-9_14
16. Xia, Z., Yang, Z., Xiong, S., Hsu, C.-F.: Game-based security proofs for secret sharing schemes. In: Yang, C.-N., Peng, S.-L., Jain, L.C. (eds.) SICBS 2018. AISC, vol. 895, pp. 650–660. Springer, Cham (2020). https://doi.org/10.1007/978-3-030-16946-6_53

Simultaneous Deauthentication of Equals Attack

Stephan Marais$^{(\boxtimes)}$, Marijke Coetzee⬥, and Franz Blauw⬥

University of Johannesburg, Johannesburg, Gauteng, South Africa
stefmarais@outlook.com, {marijkec, fblauw}@uj.ac.za

Abstract. Wi-Fi Protected Access 3 (WPA3) is a certification program that seeks to improve the security of its predecessor Wi-Fi Protected Access 2 (WPA2) by introducing the Simultaneous Authentication of Equals authentication process and mandating the use of Protected Management Frames. This paper details the development of a fuzzing strategy called WPA3Fuzz that seeks to identify vulnerabilities or implementation errors in the Simultaneous Authentication of Equals process and the Protected Management Frames mechanism. Using WPA3Fuzz three vulnerabilities are discovered that are exploited into Denial of Service attacks. Specifically, the *Simultaneous Deauthentication of Equals* attack is described. The fuzzing strategy successfully identified vulnerabilities in Linux virtualization utilities as well as well as commercially available WPA3 devices.

Keywords: WPA3 · Simultaneous authentication of equals · Protected management frames · Fuzzing Strategy

1 Introduction

Wi-Fi Protected Access (WPA) is a set of certification programs managed by the Wi-Fi Alliance that seeks to provide secure solutions for Wi-Fi networks. A certified Wi-Fi device adheres to the minimum requirements of the applicable 802.11 standard. Wi-Fi Protected Access 3 (WPA3) was introduced in 2017 [1] to address security vulnerabilities discovered in its predecessor, WPA2. The WPA2 authentication process is susceptible to offline dictionary attacks when using weak passwords [2]. Obtaining a WPA2 password allows prior traffic to be decrypted since WPA2 does not provide forward secrecy. WPA2 is also susceptible to Denial of Service (DoS) attacks when Protected Management Frames (PMF) is not enabled. PMF was introduced to prevent certain spoofed management frames from being accepted by a target that would cause the target to disconnect from the network. However, PMF was added as an optional feature of WPA2 to ensure backward compatibility [3] and is often disabled by default on the AP.

WPA3 provides a more secure method of connecting to wireless networks by mandating the use of PMF and introducing the Simultaneous Authentication of Equals (SAE) authentication mechanism [4]. Even though WPA3 was recently released, researchers have discovered vulnerabilities and weaknesses in the new SAE

© Springer Nature Switzerland AG 2021
G. Wang et al. (Eds.): SpaCCS 2020, LNCS 12383, pp. 545–556, 2021.
https://doi.org/10.1007/978-3-030-68884-4_45

authentication mechanism [4–6]. This research continues the investigation of the security of WPA3 by making use of a fuzzing strategy.

In the next section two significant changes to WPA3 namely SAE and the mandating of the PMF are described. Section 3 investigates WPA3 attacks that have been reported, highlighting that the focus of attacks is mostly on the authentication process. Section 4 identifies fuzzing to be the most appropriate technique for investigating WPA3. The contribution made by this research is twofold. First, WPA3Fuzz is described in Sects. 5 and 6. WPA3Fuzz fuzzes the authentication process of WPA3 and the implementation of PMF in both virtualized and physical environments. In Sect. 7, vulnerabilities are described that were identified, as well as the Simultaneous Deauthentication of Equals attack. Finally, the paper is concluded in Sect. 8.

2   Wi-Fi Protected Access

The susceptibility to offline dictionary attacks, deauthentication attacks and lack of forward-secrecy are considered to be the most prominent security flaws of WPA2. To address these flaws, WPA3 introduced two significant changes. Protected Management Frames is mandated and a more secure method of authentication namely Simultaneous Authentication of Equals, described next.

Protected Management Frames. The Protected Management Frames (PMF) mechanism was introduced in the 802.11w amendment in 2009 to provide integrity and non-repudiation of certain management frames exchanged in WLANs [7]. Management frames are exchanged to facilitate stations joining and leaving networks, and to exchange information required to establish a connection. Management frames are categorized into three frame classes that correspond with the authentication and association states of a Wi-Fi device. The three states are: State 1, not authenticated and not associated; State 2, authenticated but not yet associated; State 3, authenticated and associated. PMF protects management frames of class 2 or higher, i.e. management frames exchanged after authentication, by appending a Message Integrity Check (MIC) value to the frame which is validated by the recipient before it is accepted. If the MIC value cannot be verified, the frame is discarded.

WPA3 networks are expected to provide improved availability by mandating the use of PMF since Denial of Service in the form of deauthentication attacks are effectively prevented.

Simultaneous Authentication of Equals. The Simultaneous Authentication of Equals authentication process was introduced as part of the Wi-Fi Protected Access 3 (WPA3) certification program to provide robust security, including forward secrecy and offline dictionary attack prevention, even when users choose weak passwords. SAE implements an Elliptic Curve Cryptography mechanism that negotiates new encryption keys for each new session. Since every client in a WPA3 network derives a distinct encryption key at every new session, it is unfeasible, if not impossible, to perform dictionary attacks on the SAE-derived keys.

The mandatory Protected Management Frames (PMF) is strengthened by SAE since PMF uses keys derived from SAE and are therefore harder to forge. Figure 1 illustrates the process that a WPA3 Wi-Fi client follows in order to connect to an

Access Point (AP). The SAE process, shown in the shaded area of Fig. 1(a–c), is completed in three phases. The first phase of SAE, deriving the PassWord Element, is completed before exchanging SAE frames [4].

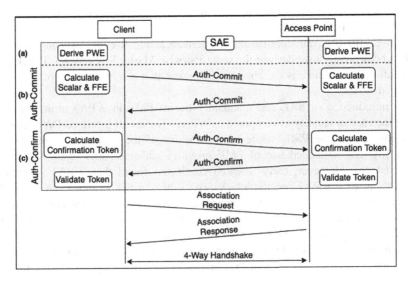

Fig. 1. WPA3 authentication model

Derive PassWord Element (PWE) - The PWE shown in Fig. 1(a) is derived by both the client and the AP using a hunting-and-pecking technique that repeatedly hashes the network password, client and AP MAC addresses, and a counter value.

Auth-Commit - The auth-commit frame shown at Fig. 1(b) is the first SAE management frame exchanged between a WPA3 client and Access Point (AP) in the SAE process. The PWE is used to derive values contained in the auth-commit frame. Figure 2(a) illustrates a generic 802.11 management frame divided in two parts: the MAC header and the MAC data payload, often referred to as the frame body. Figure 2 (b) illustrates the individual frame fields contained in the frame body of an auth-commit frame.

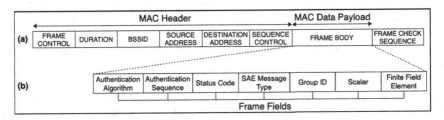

Fig. 2. Generic 802.11 management frame & auth-commit payload

Upon receipt of the auth-commit frame, each party confirms that the received FFE is a valid point on the elliptic curve and that the received scalar and FFE are not identical to its own, as identical values would constitute a reflection attack [4]. Should any of these checks fail, the handshake is aborted.

If not aborted, both parties use the exchanged information to derive a mutual secret key known as a Pairwise Master Key (PMK).

Auth-Confirm - Auth-confirm frames derived at Fig. 1(c) are exchanged to confirm that both parties have derived the same Pairwise Master Key (PMK). The payload of the auth-confirm frame is the confirmation token that is a hash digest of previously exchanged values.

The introduction of SAE and mandatory use of PMF in WPA3 promised a significant increase in security as compared to WPA2. The use of a derived PWE results in a high entropy of the PMK while the mechanics of the exchange ensure forward secrecy [8]. The mandated use of PMF provides added security against Denial of Service attacks. However, early research conducted found that WPA3 is not only susceptible to new WPA3-specific attacks, but is also at risk of inheriting vulnerabilities that exist in WPA2. A further concern is the correct implementation of security features by vendors as faults may lead to unintentional vulnerabilities that can bypass unrelated security features. The *Simultaneous Deauthentication of Equals* attack contributed by this paper highlights a faulty implementation of the auth-commit frame, that leads to the Protected Management Frames mechanism being bypassed, resulting in a Denial of Service attack.

3   WPA3 Attacks

Existing research into the security vulnerabilities of WPA3 is largely focused on the implementation of the SAE process. Shortly after the announcement and release of early implementations of WPA3, Vanhoef et al. [4] identified several flaws in, and attacks against WPA3.

Kohlios et al. [5] found that while WPA3addresses some flaws in WPA2, WPA3 is still susceptible to Evil Twin, SSL Stripping and DNS Spoofing attacks [5].

Lounis et al. [6] identified a vulnerability in the WPA3 authentication mechanism, which they exploited by the Bad-Token attack. The Bad-Token attack prevents legitimate clients from authenticating by sending concurrent auth-confirm frames that contain an incorrect authentication confirmation value. Lounis et. al also describe a ghost attack that is effective against WPA2 and was inherited by certain implementations of WPA3. The ghost attack is one in which the association response frame is spoofed to contain a rejection message from the AP and sent to a client that is in the process of associating to the AP.

Attacks described here interact directly or indirectly with the authentication process, emphasizing the importance of investigating the security of the SAE process. Notably, research into the security of WPA3 largely ignores the implementation of Protected Management Frames (PMF). The omission of PMF is motivated by the fact that PMF is not a new security feature, instead it is mandated in WPA3 rather than being optional as in WPA2. However, this research shows that mandating PMF does not ensure its correct implementation.

4 Investigating WPA3

There are several established strategies for investigating the security of an application in order to identify vulnerabilities. Common techniques used for vulnerability discovery include static analysis, dynamic analysis, taint analysis, symbolic execution and fuzzing [9–11]. This research identifies fuzzing to be the most appropriate technique for investigating WPA3. Static and dynamic analysis are considered unfeasible due to the complexity and lack of access to the underlying Wi-Fi standard.

Fuzzing is a form of testing where a system is provided with unexpected, random or faulty inputs, to expose implementation faults or bugs in an automated way [12]. The difference between fuzzing and classic software testing is that fuzzing specifically identifies bugs through software implementation faults that result in security flaws as compared to software testing that is focused on interoperability and reliable operation of implemented features [12]. As fuzzing injects inputs through user interfaces, all flaws found through fuzzing are guaranteed to correspond to some bug [12].

4.1 Fuzzing WPA3

Fuzzing WPA3 requires the construction of SAE and PMF frames such that they can be iteratively altered and transmitted to the AP to cause unexpected behavior of the AP. Frames exchanged during SAE and those protected by PMF are 802.11 management type frames. Since it is not known what causes unexpected behavior, the constructed frames are only slightly altered in an iterative manner until a certain input causes unexpected behavior. The response from the AP is monitored by a callback function that analyzes the response to determine whether the altered input caused the AP to behave in an unexpected manner. Callback functions are constructed to not only determine the type and validity of response frames, but also to determine the aliveness of an AP. To determine the aliveness of an AP, the callback function transmits beacon frames to the AP. Under normal operation, the AP always responds to a beacon frame with its own beacon response frame. By transmitting a beacon frame at fixed intervals and monitoring the beacon response from the AP ensures that the AP is still operating normally.

The primary requirements of a WPA3 fuzzer as determined by this research are to construct a frame, alter the frame, and monitor the response through a callback function.

The Dragonfuzz script developed by Tschacher [8] largely influenced the work presented by this research. The Dragonfuzz script fuzzes the authentication frames exchanged during the Simultaneous Authentication of Equals (SAE) of WPA3.

The authors of this research observed areas for development as Dragonfuzz specifically excludes the PMF and only alters a limited number of frame fields within the auth-commit frame. Most notably, the callback function used in Dragonfuzz only confirms the aliveness of the AP by listening for any authentication frame received, without considering the source or destination addresses of the received authentication frame. In a real-world environment, any exchange of authentication frames within range of the fuzzer would therefore interpret that the target AP is alive. Furthermore, the callback function does not consider the receipt of unexpected frames such as deauthentication or disassociation frames. By only monitoring the aliveness of the target AP, Dragonfuzz is limited to discovering vulnerabilities that cause total failure of the AP.

The fuzzer proposed by the authors of this research is named WPA3Fuzz. It extends Dragonfuzz to include all frames exchanged during the SAE process as well as those protected by PMF. WPA3Fuzz includes callback functions that analyze various management frames sent by the target AP. The expanded functionality of WPA3Fuzz allows it to be deployed in real-world environments to investigate the implementation of SAE and PMF of commercial WPA3 devices.

5 WPA3Fuzz

WPA3Fuzz provides functionality for fuzzing the SAE process and to validate the implementation of PMF in both virtualized and physical environments. The operation of WPA3Fuzz is illustrated by the flow chart shown in Fig. 3 with the core functionality highlighted in Fig. 3(a)–(c) that construct frames, alter fields, and a callback function that analyzes response frames. The source code of WPA3Fuzz is available on Github [13].

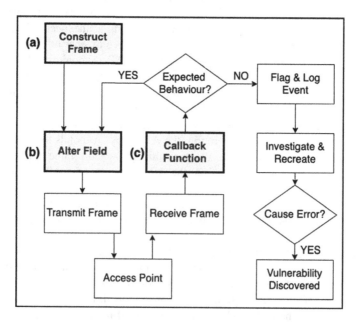

Fig. 3. WPA3Fuzz functionality

Construct Frames: The first step in the fuzzing process is to construct a frame, as shown in Fig. 3(a). In contrast to DragonFuzz, separate frame bodies are constructed for the auth-commit, auth-confirm, association request and association response frames, i.e. each of the management frames exchanged during the SAE and association process. In addition to authentication frames, separate frame bodies are constructed for the deauthentication and disassociation frames to validate the implementation of PMF.

Alter Field: WPA3Fuzz constructs all frames in a modular manner with addressable frame fields. Altering only one field at a time simplifies the process of further investigating and recreating any unexpected behavior that may be caused by the fuzzer. WPA3Fuzz can alter a single field in a frame, inject the frame and when a valid response is received, alter the same field again. The process is repeated until all possible permutations of the field is exhausted.

Callback Functions: Expanding the types of frames that WPA3Fuzz constructs as compared to Dragonfuzz increases the probability of discovering vulnerabilities or implementation errors in WPA3. Implementing callback functions that are capable of detecting unexpected response frames and ignoring frames not sent by the target AP greatly improves the accuracy and efficacy of WPA3Fuzz and allows the fuzzing strategy to be implemented more accurately in physical wireless network environments.

The callback functions implemented in WPA3Fuzz interpret response frames and confirm that the response contains only the addresses of devices included in the test, i.e. that of the target AP. A response is considered to be unexpected when the response frame type does not correspond to the frame being fuzzed or when an unsolicited frame is received from the fuzzing target. As an example, consider authentication frames being fuzzed for an unauthenticated client. The expected behavior from the AP is to respond with similar authentication frames. If, however, the AP responds with a deauthentication frame, the response is considered unexpected. The callback function would recognize the unsolicited deauthentication frame as an unexpected behavior and flag the event for further investigation.

In certain cases, the AP is expected to ignore or discard frames. For example, management frames that are protected by PMF and contain an incorrect Message Integrity Check (MIC) value would be ignored. Ignored frames illustrate the difficulty of fuzzing wireless networks.

6   Fuzzing Environment

WPA3Fuzz is developed to be deployed in both physical and virtualized environments. The virtualized environment allows for detailed investigation in the event of any unexpected behavior caused by the fuzzing strategy since detailed debugging interfaces are available. Fuzzing physical Wi-Fi hardware is a more complex and time-consuming exercise compared to fuzzing in a virtualized environment. Physical APs generally provide limited debugging information that adds complexity to the investigation of unexpected behavior caused by the fuzzing process. Fuzzing in a physical environment also requires dealing with noise caused by Wi-Fi devices operating within range of the fuzzing environment.

Virtualized Environment. Virtualization of a WPA3 network is achieved by creating three virtualized Wi-Fi radios, one configured as an AP, one configured as a client and one used as the fuzzing interface through which WPA3Fuzz transmits its altered frames. The virtualized radios are created with Hwsim, a wireless simulation utility that allows an arbitrary number of virtual 802.11 radio stations to be created [14]. Hostapd, a user-space Wi-Fi router daemon [15], and wpa_supplicant, a user-space Wi-Fi client daemon [16], are bound to the simulated radios in order to create a virtualized AP and client.

Physical Environment. The physical environment tested in the current research consisted of Apple macOS device connecting to a Netgear RAX200 AP. A Raspberry Pi with a Wi-Fi dongle was used to fuzz and monitor the network. The physical WPA3 network was established by configuring the Netgear AP to operate in WPA3-only mode and having the macOS device connect to the AP.

7   Results

The expanded fuzzing strategy of WPA3Fuzz resulted in the identification three vulnerabilities, all of which could be exploited into Denial of Service attacks. The fuzzer detected unexpected behavior in the AP caused by fuzzed frames.

- The AP transmits an unsolicited deauthentication frame after receiving a single SAE frame – this unexpected behavior is exploited into the Simultaneous Deauthentication of Equals attack.
- During the exchange of association and reassociation frames, sent after completion of SAE, the AP transmits an unsolicited deauthentication frame. This behavior is exploited as a ghost attack.
- Commercially available devices incorrectly implement the PMF and are susceptible to basic deauthentication attacks.

Next, more detail is provided for each case. For all attacks described below, detailed packet captures and steps taken to reproduce results are available in the WPA3Fuzz repository on Github [13].

7.1   Simultaneous Deauthentication of Equals Attack

WPA3Fuzz flags the receipt of an unsolicited deauthentication frame sent from the Hostapd AP to a client while fuzzing the SAE process of a Hostapd AP. After further investigation of the unsolicited frame, the authors discovered that Hostapd deauthenticates a client if it is inactive for 300 s, even if the client did not complete the authentication process. More importantly, the Hostapd AP accepts authentication type frames from the broadcast address. As such, injecting a spoofed auth-commit frame (the first frame sent during SAE), that contains the broadcast address as its source address, results in the AP sending a deauthentication frame to the broadcast address. Since the deauthentication frame is sent to the broadcast address, all legitimate clients accept the deauthentication frame and disconnect from the network, thereby interrupting normal operations. Injecting a single, specially crafted auth-commit frame results in the simultaneous deauthentication of all legitimate, associated clients. Based on this result, the authors named the attack the Simultaneous Deauthentication of Equals attack. Next, more details are provided about this attack.

Prior to the attack, a carefully crafted auth-commit frame is constructed to contain the broadcast address as the source address of a client and the AP's MAC address, 02:00:00:00:00:00, as the destination address. As shown in the first line of Fig. 4, the constructed auth-commit frame is sent to the AP. The second line of Fig. 4 shows the AP's auth-commit response frame sent to the broadcast address, as expected in the SAE process. Since only the auth-commit frame is injected, the auth-confirm frames are not exchanged and the authentication process is not completed. The third line of Fig. 4 shows the deauthentication frame sent to the broadcast address 300 s after the spoofed auth-commit frame is first transmitted to the AP.

Time	Source	Destination	Info
2.91...	Broadcast	02:00:00:00:00:00	Authentication,
2.91...	02:00:00:00:00:00	Broadcast	Authentication,
302....	02:00:00:00:00:00	Broadcast	Deauthentication

Fig. 4. Packet capture of simultaneous deauthentication of equals attack

When the spoofed auth-commit frame is sent to the AP, the AP interprets the received frame as a legitimate client attempting to authenticate to it, and begins the inactivity countdown timer of 300 s. Since the AP receives no more frames from the broadcast address, the AP's countdown timer for the broadcast address runs out after which the AP deauthenticates the inactive client, i.e. the broadcast address. The result of the deauthentication of the broadcast address is that all legitimate clients that are authenticated at the time of transmission are deauthenticated from the AP and need to reauthenticate.

The deauthentication frame sent by the Hostapd AP is a Protected Management Frame (PMF) and therefore contains a valid Message Integrity Check (MIC) value that will be accepted by all legitimate clients. This vulnerability indicates that an incorrect implementation of SAE can impact unrelated security mechanisms, in this case PMF.

7.2 Ghost Attack

WPA3Fuzz detected unexpected behavior of the Hostapd AP while fuzzing the association frames, after the completion of SAE. Exploiting this unexpected behavior leads to an attack that was previously described by Lounis et al. [6] as the ghost attack.

The ghost attack spoofs association frames to contain the source address of a nonexisting or ghost client. Association frames are exchanged after the authentication process and are therefore classified as class 3 frames that are protected by the Protected Management Frames (PMF) mechanism. An AP deauthenticates a client that sends an association frame when it is not yet authenticated. As such, spoofing an association frame to contain the source address of a client in the process of associating to an AP results in the AP sending a deauthentication frame to that client. The client then deauthenticates itself from the AP before fully authenticating and associating with the AP. When the ghost attack is targeted against a single client, the attacker requires prior knowledge of the target's MAC address and needs to time the attack to coincide with the target's authentication.

However, the Hostapd AP accepts authentication type frames from the broadcast address. Since the broadcast address will never be an authenticated client, an association frame that contains the broadcast address as the source address results in the deauthentication of all legitimate, associated clients. Spoofing the association frame to contain the broadcast address results in the AP sending a Protected Management Frame (PMF) with a valid Message Integrity Check (MIC) value and effectively deauthenticating all authenticated clients. The ghost attack is another example of an implementation error having an unintended effect on unrelated security mechanisms.

7.3   Deauthentication Attack

WPA3Fuzz was developed with the purpose of investigating the Simultaneous Authentication of Equals (SAE) and the implementation of Protected Management Frames (PMF). The implementation of PMF is investigated by fuzzing various fields in frames protected by PMF including the Message Integrity Check (MIC) value appended to PMF frames. The expected behavior of the AP while fuzzing the MIC value is for the AP to discard the PMF frame with an altered MIC value.

However, while fuzzing a Netgear RAX200 AP, WPA3Fuzz detected that the AP accepted fuzzed deauthentication frames. Upon further investigation, the authors discovered that the Netgear RAX200 AP, operating in WPA3 only mode, accepted unprotected deauthentication frames despite advertising PMF as a mandated requirement. Spoofing and repeatedly injecting a deauthentication frame with a source address of a legitimate client and destination address of the AP results the AP deauthenticating the legitimate client. The client would then need to reauthenticate and since the deauthentication frames are repeatedly injected, would repeatedly get disconnected.

7.4   Attack Mitigations

All attacks that were discovered can be effectively mitigated by existing security mechanisms. Deauthentication attacks have been mitigated since the introduction of Protected Management Frames (PMF) in 2009 [7]. The Netgear RAX200 AP that was tested incorrectly implemented PMF and was therefore susceptible to a deauthentication attack. This discovery was unexpected since PMF is not only mandated by WPA3 but is also advertised as a requirement by the Netgear AP.

The discovery of the deauthentication attack emphasizes the importance of validating even the most basic security mechanisms. The discoveries made justify the decision to expand the fuzzing strategy to include deauthentication and association frames in addition to authentication frames.

A mitigation against the Simultaneous Deauthentication of Equals and Ghost attacks also exists. The mitigation comes in the form of a recently released patch for Hostapd that discards management frames addressed to the broadcast address [17].

However, the mitigation requires manually patching and rebuilding the Hostapd package, it is unlikely to be implemented and Hostapd applications will likely remain vulnerable.

In addition to existing mitigations, Bhuiyan et al. [18] proposed systems hardening techniques, including a multi-factor authentication scheme, to further improve the security of Wi-Fi devices. The proposed multi-factor authentication scheme would effectively mitigate the Simultaneous Deauthentication of Equals attack by preventing the AP from accepting the spoofed frames.

Despite the availability of effective attack mitigations, vendors are susceptible to incorrect implementations thereof. The distribution of patches or firmware updates often require manual intervention resulting in devices not necessarily being updated and remaining vulnerable. The vulnerabilities presented in this paper illustrate the importance of investigating the security of implementations and not limiting the research only to newly introduced features.

8 Conclusion and Future Work

The vulnerabilities discovered in the current research are proof of the efficacy of the fuzzing strategy contained in WPA3Fuzz. While effective mitigations exist for all discovered vulnerabilities, the mitigations require either manual intervention by the end-user or firmware changes by the vendors.

Suggested improvements to WPA3Fuzz include expanding the code coverage. In its current form WPA3Fuzz, only fuzzes frames exchanged during the authentication and deauthentication processes of WPA3. Fuzzing frames exchanged outside of these processes could potentially lead to the discovery of more implementation errors and vulnerabilities.

WPA3Fuzz would also benefit from improved logging functionality. The information provided when an unexpected event is logged can be overwhelming. In the case of the vulnerability that led to the Simultaneous Deauthentication of Equals attack, WPA3Fuzz detected an unexpected deauthentication frame received from the AP at some point throughout the fuzzing process. The information provided in the WPA3-Fuzz logs flagged the receipt of the deauthentication frame as well as the frames sent previously including unrelated frames and the information contained in those frames. The overwhelming logs led the authors to initially attributing the unsolicited deauthentication frame to a misconfigured auth-commit frame. Only upon further detailed investigation was the true cause determined. WPA3Fuzz would benefit from simplified, time-based logging that can be expanded when required.

The current paper has shown that, despite the enhanced security features introduced in WPA3 and the existence of effective mitigations, certain vendor-specific implementations of WPA3 contain errors that can be exploited into attacks.

References

1. WiFi-Alliance: "WPA3 Specification," *Wi-Fi Alliance* (2018). https://www.wi-fi.org/download.php?file=/sites/default/files/private/WPA3_Specification_v1.0.pdf, Accessed 20 June 2018
2. Kammerstetter, M., Muellner, M., Burian, D., Kudera, C., Kastner, W.: Efficient high-speed WPA2 brute force attacks using scalable low-cost FPGA clustering. In: Gierlichs, B., Poschmann, A.Y. (eds.) CHES 2016. LNCS, vol. 9813, pp. 559–577. Springer, Heidelberg (2016). https://doi.org/10.1007/978-3-662-53140-2_27
3. Wi-Fi Alliance: "Wi-Fi Protected Access: Strong, standards-based, interoperable security for today's Wi-Fi networks [White Paper]" (2003). https://www.cs.kau.se/cs/education/courses/dvad02/p1/PapersWireless/Wi-FiProtectedAccess-Whitepaper.pdf, Accessed 08 Aug 2020
4. Vanhoef, M., Ronen, E.: "Dragonblood: analyzing the dragonfly handshake of WPA3 and EAP-pwd. In: IEEE Symposium on Security and Privacy-S&P, pp. 517–533 (2020)
5. Kohlios, C.P., Hayajneh, T.: A comprehensive attack flow model and security analysis for Wi-Fi and WPA3. Electronics 7(11), 284 (2018). https://doi.org/10.3390/electronics7110284
6. Lounis, K., Zulkernine, M.: Bad-token: denial of service attacks on WPA3. In: ACM International Conference Proceeding Series, pp. 1–8 (2019). https://doi.org/10.1145/3357613.3357629.
7. Ahmad, M.S., Tadakamadla, S.:Short paper: security evaluation of IEEE 802.11w specification. In: WiSec 2011 - Proceedings of the 4th ACM Conference on Wireless Network Security, pp. 53–58 (2011). https://doi.org/10.1145/1998412.1998424.
8. Tschacher, N.P.: Model based fuzzing of the WPA3 Dragonfly handshake (2019). https://sar.informatik.hu-berlin.de/research/publications/SAR-PR-2020-01/SAR-PR-2020-01_.pdf, Accessed 15 Jan 2020
9. Chess, B., Mcgraw, G.: Static analysis for security. IEEE Secur. Priv. 2(6), 76–79 (2004)
10. Li, J., Zhao, B., Zhang, C.: Fuzzing: a survey. Cybersecurity 1(1), 1–3 (2018). https://doi.org/10.1186/s42400-018-0002-y
11. Butti, L., Tinnés, J.: Discovering and exploiting 802.11 wireless driver vulnerabilities. J. Comput. Virol. 4(1), 25–37 (2008). https://doi.org/10.1007/s11416-007-0065-x
12. Banks, G., Cova, M., Felmetsger, V., Almeroth, K., Kemmerer, R., Vigna, G.: SNOOZE: toward a stateful network protocol fuzzer. In: Katsikas, S.K., López, J., Backes, M., Gritzalis, S., Preneel, B. (eds.) ISC 2006. LNCS, vol. 4176, pp. 343–358. Springer, Heidelberg (2006). https://doi.org/10.1007/11836810_25
13. Marais, S.: WPA3Fuzz (2020). https://github.com/stephan-marais/WPA3Fuzz, Accessed 10 Aug 2020
14. Holtmann, M.: hwsim (2019). https://www.mankier.com/1/hwsim, Accessed 01 June 2019
15. Malinen, J.: hostapd: IEEE 802.11 AP, IEEE 802.1X/WPA/WPA2/EAP/RADIUS Authenticator (2013). https://w1.fi/hostapd/, Accessed 01 June 2019
16. Malinen, J.: Linux WPA/WPA2/IEEE 802.1X Supplicant (2013). https://w1.fi/wpa_supplicant/, Accessed 01 June 2019
17. Malinen, J.: AP mode PMF disconnection protection bypass (2019). https://w1.fi/security/2019-7/ap-mode-pmf-disconnection-protection-bypass.txt, Accessed 01 Mar 2020
18. Bhuiyan, M.Z.A., Islam, M.M., Wang, G., Wang, T.: Investigation on unauthorized human activity watching through leveraging wi-fi signals. In: Wang, G., Chen, J., Yang, L.T. (eds.) SpaCCS 2018. LNCS, vol. 11342, pp. 511–521. Springer, Cham (2018). https://doi.org/10.1007/978-3-030-05345-1_44

Impact of Active Scanning Tools for Device Discovery in Industrial Networks

Thomas Hanka$^{(\boxtimes)}$, Matthias Niedermaier, Florian Fischer, Susanne Kießling,
Peter Knauer, and Dominik Merli

Hochschule Augsburg, An der Hochschule 1, 86161 Augsburg, Germany
{thomas.hanka,matthias.niedermaier,florian.fischer,susanne.kiessling,
peter.knauer,dominik.merli}@hs-augsburg.de
https://www.hsainnos.de/

Abstract. The number of networked devices for automation in industrial environments is growing constantly. Therefore, network operators face the task of managing and securing these networks, as attacks and failures in these systems tend to have serious consequences. The decentralized nature of Operational Technology (OT) networks and the usage of legacy network equipment make passive scanning not feasible for device identification. To manage these networks properly, active network scans would be a suitable tool. However, these may influence or damage the fragile industrial devices and the physical processes they control. Nevertheless, device identification and asset management is increasingly important in industrial networks. An understanding of the impact of active scans on those devices is necessary to minimize the risk of negative effects. In this paper, we analyze the impact of five active scanning tools, capable of identifying Industrial Control System (ICS) components, on seven Programmable Logic Controllers (PLCs). Most devices show measurable influences during the scans, these range from few milliseconds to several hundred milliseconds. However, we are also able to show that it is possible to scan PLCs without influences at all, while gathering the required information. The results of the experiments can be used to evaluate the potential risks of these tools and whether or how they should be used in industrial environments.

Keywords: Industrial control systems · Network scanning · Device discovery · Asset management · Denial of service

1 Introduction

As a central part of modern infrastructures, Industrial Control Systems (ICSs) are used in many different systems, like factories or power plants to control automation processes. These processes require a high amount of reliability to guarantee an optimal execution flow. To achieve this, industrial networks consist of various interconnected devices, such as Programmable Logic Controllers (PLCs), Human Machine Interfaces (HMIs), sensors and actuators.

© Springer Nature Switzerland AG 2021
G. Wang et al. (Eds.): SpaCCS 2020, LNCS 12383, pp. 557–572, 2021.
https://doi.org/10.1007/978-3-030-68884-4_46

Especially PLCs are a vital part of these networks, as they are able to offer hard real-time capabilities, which are essential for controlling fast physical processes. These devices repeatedly execute a control program at a specified rate. The program and the specified cycle time are responsible that physical inputs are processed within a certain time. Deviations from the cycle time may disturb the controlled process and could cause physical consequences.

When PLCs were first introduced, they were normally not connected to networks and usually only communicated within their controlled process. Thus, security measures were not as relevant as today. Nowadays, most PLCs offer Ethernet interfaces and network capabilities, and are integrated in larger TCP/IP networks. Through the process of digitalization, it is not uncommon that these networks have grown over the years and administrators and operators have lost track of currently active devices. As a consequence, many devices have been running untouched for years, using outdated software and firmware. Due to the missing security strategies for those industrial environments and the uncontrolled growth of networks, PLCs are often vulnerable to network-based attacks.

A first step to increase the security level of an OT environment is device identification. Vulnerabilities and risks can only be properly assessed when each active device of a network is known. A common method to detect and identify network devices in traditional Information Technology (IT) networks is network scanning.

Many ICS devices were not intended to be part of large networks, and therefore lack sufficient robustness against network traffic [16]. As a result, especially legacy ICS devices are often fragile and prone to errors due to uncommon communication. However, network scanning tools often use modified packets or unusual communication processes to increase the efficiency of the scanning process [17]. This leads to a potential risk of an unexpected behavior of PLCs, if network scans are performed.

Especially for internet-facing devices, active scans are unavoidable. Since external services like Shodan [8] and Censys [4] or attacker scan devices regardless of fragility or deployment in critical environments, it is necessary to analyze the impact of current state-of-the-art active scanners on PLCs, to identify risks and possible mitigation measures.

The contribution of this paper is the assessment, how active network scans could influence industrial devices. Therefore, we conducted experiments with five different state-of-the-art scanning tools on seven PLCs. We measure the direct impact of the network scan, using a minimal control program, that switches an output of a Programmable Logic Controller (PLC) as fast as possible. The results show that, except for one device, all PLCs are influenced by active scans. While some tools only cause insignificant jitter, other could cause disturbances of the controlled process through major increases in the duration of a program cycle.

The rest of the paper is organized as follows. First we provide a summary of related work in Sect. 2 followed by the presentation of technical background about PLCs and network scanning in Sect. 3. In Sect. 4 we explain our experimental methods and test setup. The results of our experiments are presented in Sect. 5 and conclusions are drawn in Sect. 6.

2   Related Work

Influences of network communication on ICS components have been an urgent topic in research. However, measurements of the direct influence of active scanning tools are rarely conducted.

Coffey et al. discuss experiments of active scanning methods against PLCs [3]. For their setup, they connected the PLCs to a physical process and monitored the communication and behavior of the devices during the scans. However, this approach is process dependent and deviations from the expected behavior are only visible, if the physical process is influenced significantly. We want to observe even slight deviations from the expected cycle time. Therefore, we measure the influences directly on the electrical side of the device.

Similar to Coffey et al., Ljøsne present experiments of the impact of various network tools on Siemens and ABB devices [6]. The focus in this work was the identification of parameters, with which scanning tools could negatively affect the PLCs. To measure the influences, the network communication was monitored. While this indicates connectivity issues, caused by the tools, the direct impact on the PLCs may not be observed.

In [5], Kalluri et al. conducted flooding attacks on a Remote Telemetry Unit (RTU). They measured the response time of the targeted device during different packet rates. Niedermaier et al. provide measurements of the influences of network-based flooding attacks on PLCs [11]. The measurement setup used in this work monitors the deviations of the cycle time of the PLCs during the attacks. However, flooding represents a worst case scenario, usually as part of an attack. While active scanning may utilizes high communication load, these processes are often part of the security strategies of operators. Thus, the influence of active scanning tools should be considered specifically.

Teixeira et al. [15] describes various attacks on control systems. The focus of this work was the disruption of communication between a targeted PLC and connected devices. While several attack scenarios are discussed, they overlook the effect of these attacks on the electrical side of the targeted PLC Even if a device is able to communicate, changes in the cycle time may disrupt controlled processes. Additionally, the negative effect of active scanning is not considered.

3   Technical Background

PLCs are devices specifically designed to manage and control industrial processes. Most of them are dedicated industrial grade embedded devices and computers, electrically connected to sensors and actuators. The priority of a PLC is to control industrial processes, not their computing power or security measures. Therefore, many lack even minimal security functions and are fragile to unexpected requests and therefore, untypical network traffic.

3.1   PLC Cycle Time

Cycle-based PLCs process their control task in a loop of four phases. These four phases are shown in Fig. 1. In phase 1, *read inputs*, all digital and analog inputs are read in. During phase 2, *program execution*, the program is executed, using the input values from phase 1. After the control programs execution, phase 3, the *housekeeping*, handles communication requests, internal checks or diagnostics. At the end in phase 4, *write outputs*, the logic values resulted from the control program are written back to the electric analog or digital output. After completion of phase 4, the process starts again with phase 1. This loop is executed periodically within the configured cycle time. If a controlled process requires exact timings, even slight deviations from the configured cycle time can disturb the expected control behavior.

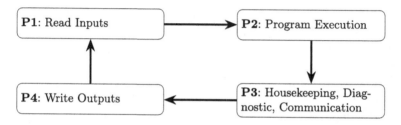

Fig. 1. Program execution of a PLC cycle.

3.2   Network Scanning in Industrial Networks

Most OT infrastructures have changed drastically in the last years. Many devices were added and connected to a network, in parts without proper documentation. These devices often run without knowledge of the operators and partially even without a known purpose.

For proper asset management several information have to be documented, e.g. the type of device, where they are deployed, how they are used and what they cost [9]. Newly purchased devices can be added to the inventory with all required information, by documenting the data before deploying the device. For legacy devices some of the asset management core questions cannot be answered easily, without a high amount of manual work.

Network scanning is essential for device identification and asset management processes and allows an operator to maintain overview of currently deployed devices in the network infrastructure. While in traditional IT environments defined processes and tools for asset management exist, most ICS environments have no specialized solutions. Hence, manual documentation or network reconnaissance has to be utilized. Network scanning tools should offer at least answers to two essential questions:

- Is a device present? (Device Discovery)
- What kind of device is there? (Device Identification)

Network scanning can be implemented either by active or passive methods [1]. While both techniques are used for the same goals, they have different benefits and constrains.

Active Scanning. Active scanning sends additional packets, so called probes, into a network, and analyzes the resulting answers and behavior of the target. Thus, services and devices hosted in the network can be identified. In OT environments, where network conditions are not always optimal and the devices are fragile, this could lead to unexpected behaviors of connected devices. Therefore, many operators try to avoid active scanning methods generally or only use it with caution [16]. While there may be a significant risk, active probes allow focusing the queries on device specific information, like type of device or firmware version. The duration to gather information through active scans depends on the amount of required data and the configured packet rate of the used scanning tool. Hence, the scanning process can be reliably scheduled.

Port scanning is the first step of most active tools, whereby a connection is initiated by the scanner. Depending on whether this port is open and the device listens on it, the target answers to the scanner and reveals its status. Subsequently, a connection may be established. Additional probes may reveal information about the service listening on the open port or indicate what type of Operating System (OS) is running on the device.

Passive Scanning. Passive scanning identifies services and devices only by observing network traffic. Monitoring nodes need to be placed at multiple locations in the network to capture the traffic. The information gathered by this approach depends on the communication of each device in a network. The monitoring node can be configured to limit the captured traffic to certain packets of interest. Nevertheless, longer periods of time are usually required for specific communication events to happen. Hence, the required amount of data and effort to extract relevant information increases. Especially for asset management purposes, passive scanning is often not sufficient, as necessary information, like device type and firmware version, might not be communicated by the device.

4   Methodology

We want to provide measurements and a comparison of influences on the regular execution of a control program during network scans. To assess the impact of network communication on PLCs, changes to the signals are captured on the electrical outputs of the Devices under Test (DuTs). We used a selection of commonly used scanning tools to create realistic communication loads and analyze the behavior of ICS devices under an active scan.

This includes port scanning, service scanning/identification and OS detection.

The following describes our test setup and gives an overview of our methods. The control program for measurements of all PLCs inverts a selected output from 0 to 1 and vice versa, every cycle, resulting in a periodic square wave signal. With such an implementation, minimal resources are used to process the control program and influences of the program are minimized. To identify the direct impact of network communication, all tested PLCs are configured to run as fast as possible to take up the maximum performance. With this, the devices use the shortest possible cycle time for the given control program. Depending on the devices, the configured cycle time is between 0.2 ms and 10 ms.

With this configuration of our setup, each device switches an output at the maximum rate. The result is a device specific periodic reference signal, while no external influence occurs. If a device is influenced by the network communication load during an attack or network scan, this signal should differ from the reference. Figure 2 depicts a reference signal (blue, solid) and shows the deviation from the excepted cycle time (blue, dotted) and the cycle time delayed by network traffic (red, dashed).

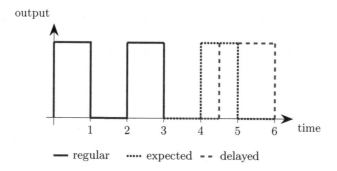

Fig. 2. Impact on output signal by delayed cycle time. (Color figure online)

4.1   Setup of the Test Framework

In our experiments, we run different network scanning tools against our DuTs and measure the cycle time of the device. Figure 3 shows the architecture of our test setup. It consists of three main components: a capture device, a controller machine, and the DuTs.

To monitor and capture the changing edges of a selected PLC output over a specified time, a Saleae Logic Pro 16 logic analyzer [14] was used as capture device. It is directly wired to the selected output of the Device under Test (DuT). To interact with the logic analyzer, the Saleae Logic application is used. This application serves for configuration of the logic analyzer and allows to start and stop the measurements. In our experiments, the sample rate is configured to 100

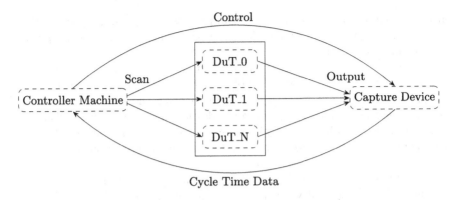

Fig. 3. Test setup for the measurements.

Megasamples per second (Ms/s). The device supports up to 16 channels and communicates over Universal Serial Bus (USB) with the controller machine.

The controller machine is a PC, running Linux. This device is connected to the logic analyzer via USB and uses a Gigabit Ethernet connection to the DuTs. The controller machine is used to control the logic analyzer and runs the different network scanning tools. An automated process was implemented to configure the capture device, start and stop the measurements, store the data captured by the logic analyzer, and start the network scanning tools. This scripted process was required to match the measurement period to the varying duration of the active network scans.

The DuTs are PLCs from different vendors. We selected a variety of devices in order to get a representative sample of the current market. Table 1 shows the devices in our testbed [10] used within our experiments.

Table 1. Currently deployed devices in our test setup.

No.	Vendor	Manufacturer number	Name	Firmware	Mean cycle time
1	Schneider	TM221CE16T	Modicon M221	1.5.1.0	2.000 ms
2	Siemens	6ES7211-1AE40-0XB0	Simatic S7-1211C	V4.2.0	0.222 ms
3	Phoenix	2700974	ILC 151 ETH	V.4.42.04	1.000 ms
4	ABB	1SAP120600R0071	PM554-TP-ETH	2.5.4.15626	1.000 ms
5	Crouzet	88981133	em4 Ethernet	1.2.75/1.0.27	9.984 ms
6	Wago	750–889	Controller KNX IP	01.07.13	2.000 ms
7	Wago	750–880	Controller ETH	01.07.03	2.000 ms

4.2 Measurement Process

One experiment consists of three measurement parts. The first and third measurement has a duration of one minute each. During these periods, no external communication occurs, hence the DuT can process the control program without additional load. In the following, these measurements are referred as *pre idle* and *post idle* measurement.

The second measurement is taken while an active network scan is run from the controller machine. The duration of this phase depends on the specific tool, used parameters and the network conditions. During the scan phase, the DuT has to process the control program and additionally process the packets sent by the network scanning tool. This measurement gives information about the consequences of increased work load by network communication and shows, if any unexpected behaviors are triggered.

In combination, the experiment allows a comparison of the direct impact of communication loads relative to the idle behavior of each PLC. Additionally, the *pre idle* measurement shows if something unexpected happens, even without external influences. The *post idle* measurement, after the scan, reveals if the scanning process caused errors or unexpected behaviors, that are persistent even after the scan. If any persistent anomaly is detected, e.g. a system crashed under the communication load, the affected DuT has to be power cycled and the expected behavior has to be verified.

After each measurement has been executed, the captured data is stored as a raw waveform file and as a Comma-Separated Values (CSV) file, containing only transitions of the digital signal. For further monitoring, a Packet Capture (PCAP) file is generated during each measurement, to verify expected network behaviors. At the end of the process, the files are analyzed.

This automated process was implemented in Python. The process starts the first idle measurement (*pre idle*), saves the captured data and sleeps for five seconds. Thereafter, the network scan starts at the same time as the capture of the digital signal (*scan phase*). The capture as well as the PCAP generation are canceled after the scan process has finished. The captured files are saved. After another five seconds sleep, the second idle measurement is executed (*post idle*). This automation serves not only convenience, but allows exact observation periods, too.

4.3   Network Scanner

To create a realistic scenario, we used five different active network scanning tools. To analyze the impact of these tools, we chose state-of-the-art tools commonly used in IT environments capable of identifying PLCs, or tools specifically designed to scan industrial devices.

If not specifically designed to interact with particular protocols and services, these tools are able to execute a scan on all 65535 ports. However, not only the port scanning process is analyzed in our experiments, but also communication to identify a systems OS and service versions. Without any packet rate limitation, some of these tools are able to generate massive network load for the DuTs.

These tools are not intended to disturb the target device or influence its processes, but since a large number of packets can be sent, the communication may be similar to a flooding attack. Under these network loads, influences on the cycle time are possible. Additionally, modified or unsupported network traffic may also cause malfunctions on the devices.

The duration of active scans depends on the scope of the executed tool and scan type, the implemented process, and the packet rate utilized by the tool or specified by configuration. The tools used in our experiments are: Nmap, Modscan, PLCScan, ZGrab, and OpenVAS.

Nmap. *Nmap* is a open source network scanning tool used for device discovery, service detection and security auditing [7]. In addition to various scanning features and service detection capabilities, the main advantage of *Nmap* is the extensibility through the Nmap Scripting Engine (NSE). With NSE scripts, compatibility with new protocols or new features could be added.

In our experiments, we scan all ports without rate limitation, to analyze the impact of port scanning.

Modscan. ModScan is a python utility written by Mark Bristow [2]. It was designed specifically to scan Modbus-based devices. The script uses the information a Modbus device discloses and tries to get additional information about the device, vendor and firmware. This information can be used to identify a Modbus/TCP device and allows asset management.

The ModScan script was adapted by Nmap as an NSE script (*modbus-discover*). We chose to use the Nmap version of ModScan, because the NSE script is still maintained.

PLCScan. PLCScan was developed by Positive Research and Scadastrangelove [13]. Like ModScan, PLCScan is a python utility, that is able to collect information from Modbus/TCP devices. Additionally, it is capable of collecting information from the Siemens S7comm protocol. For this purpose, it sends S7comm packets and parses the content answered by the targeted device. This information allows the identification of the device and firmware version.

The S7comm identification capabilities were adapted by Nmap as an NSE script (*s7-info*). We chose for our experiments the Nmap version of the S7comm identification, because the current version of the PLCScan script is no longer compatible with current S7comm versions.

ZGrab. *ZGrab* is an open source application scanner developed by Durumeric et al. [4]. As part of the ZMap Project it is also used in the search engine Censys. It supports several application handshakes for protocols like Siemens S7comm, Modbus, Niagara Fox, DNP3, BACnet, HTTP, HTTPS, SMTP, IMAP, POP3, FTP and SSH. Each protocol is written as a Go module. Thus, new protocols could be implemented and added to *ZGrab*.

We configured *ZGrab* to scan all available protocols on their default port.

OpenVAS. *OpenVAS* [12] is a vulnerability assessment tools capable of identifying active services, open ports and running applications. The scan engine is updated regularly with new and updated modules. Vulnerability scanning is important to identify vulnerable systems and to fix security issues. However, vulnerability probes may pose additional risk to ICS devices.

We use *OpenVAS* without vulnerability scanning modules for better comparison with the other tools.

5   Results and Discussion

In our experiments, we measured the impact of different active scanning tools. Each tool was used in a minimal setup with the necessary flags and without further configuration. This allows us to assess the influence of the default behavior of each tool in the absence of user optimizations.

The results of the measurements are shown in a boxplot with calculated arithmetic mean (▼) and median (−). The quantiles are respectively 25 % and 75 %, with whiskers up to factor 1.5 of the box.

5.1   Port Scanning with Nmap

In the first experiment, we used a port scan, to test whether a port is open or not. Therefore, we scan all ports from 0–65535 with *Nmap*. In known environments, the number of scanned ports could be reduced to only include the required. However, in an unknown network, it may be necessary to use such a generic approach as a first step, to discover and identify all devices.

Our experiments showed influences by the *Nmap* port scan on most PLCs in our testbed. The only exception is the Crouzet em4 (5), which was not influenced by any network scanning tool during the experiments in this work. However, this device also has the longest cycle time with 10 ms and potentially compensates the communication load with available resources.

Additionally, the Schneider M221 (1) and the ABB PM554 (4) showed no continuous deviation from their idle behavior. However, there are significant outliers observed as shown in Fig. 4. These appear only in small amounts and mostly at the beginning of the scan process. Figure 5 depicts the cycle time over the scan duration. The reason for this behavior may be the self optimization of *Nmap*. Without additional parameters for packet rate limitation, *Nmap* adjusts the number of sent packets freely, depending on network and target conditions.

On the other hand, a significant impact was observed on the Wago 750–889 (6) and Wago 750–880 (7) as shown in Figs. 6 and 7. In spite of the outlier around 95 ms, the Wago 750–889 (6) keeps a lower mean cycle time compared to the Wago 750–880 (7). Nevertheless, both PLCs are not able to keep their mean cycle time of 2 ms during the *Nmap* scan. Considering the significant deviation of the cycle time, the influences of *Nmap* on these devices may be enough to disturb the control process or communication with other devices.

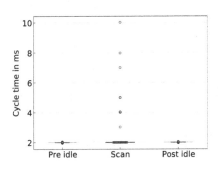

Fig. 4. Impact of *Nmap* on a Schneider M221 (1).

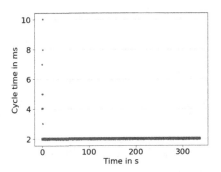

Fig. 5. Cycle time during a *Nmap* scan on a Schneider M221 (1).

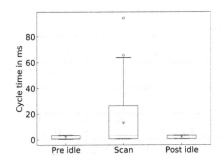

Fig. 6. Impact of *Nmap* on a Wago 750–889 (6).

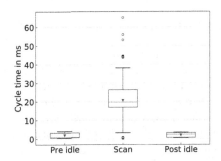

Fig. 7. Impact of *Nmap* on a Wago 750–880 (7).

5.2 Modbus Discovery Scan with NSE modbus-discover

In this experiment, the NSE script *modbus-discover* is used against each PLC. The scan tries to communicate with the DuT using the Modbus protocol. If the DuT supports the protocol, the script tries to get as much information as possible using the protocol's mechanics.

The analysis of these scans showed no measurable impact on most of the DuTs. Exceptions are the Wago 750–889 (6) and Wago 750–880 (7).

Both devices show minor influences as seen in Fig. 8 and 9. While the mean cycle time only increases slightly, the worst case cycle time increases up to 9 ms from 3.5 ms. These two PLCs use the Modbus protocol and, therefore, the script queries all information from the devices. A scan runs between 18 and 20 s on the Wago PLCs and sends around 2800 network packets. The increased communication load and probably the processing of the queries influence the PLC and slows down the process handling.

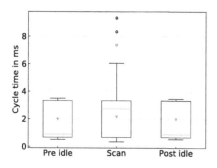

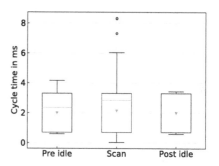

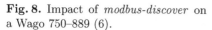

Fig. 8. Impact of *modbus-discover* on a Wago 750–889 (6).

Fig. 9. Impact of *modbus-discover* on a Wago 750–880 (7).

5.3   S7 Discovery Scan with NSE s7-info

Similar to the *modbus-discover* script, the *s7-info* script from the NSE is used to scan a device with the proprietary Siemens S7comm protocol. The scan tries to initiate a S7comm connection with the devices. If the connection is successful and the target is a S7comm host, the information to identify the device is gathered.

Each PLC with closed S7 port (default port 102) was not measurable affected by the scan. Since the communication is finished after the initiated TCP handshake, no communication load is generated. However, the Siemens Simatic S7-1211C (2), which has an open port 102 and uses the protocol, was not measurable affected by this experiment, too (see Fig. 10). In contrast to the communication load generated by *modbus-discover* in the previous experiment, only 27 packets are sent over a period of 0.1 s by *s7-info*, to gather the required information.

Even if the boxplot looks like the Siemens Simatic S7-1211C (2) was slightly affected by the scan, there was no measurable impact. The reason for the lower outliers is the short process time. During the scan, the same range of outliers occur as in the idle measurements.

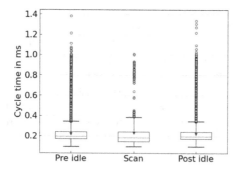

Fig. 10. Impact of *s7-info* on a Siemens Simatic S7-1211C (2).

5.4 Application Scanning with ZGrab

Equally to the mentioned NSE scans, the goal of *ZGrab* is to gather information of devices by using protocol functions. However, *ZGrab* supports various protocols. Therefore, connections for each supported protocol are initiated.

The experiments showed no noteworthy influences on the DuTs. Despite the influences *modbus-discover* had on the Wago 750–889 (6) and Wago 750–880 (7), only insignificant deviations are caused by *Zgrab*, as depicted in Fig. 11. Similarly, the Siemens Simatic S7-1211C (2) was not measurable influenced by this scan at all (see Fig. 12). This indicates, that different implementations and process sequences affect the influences on the DuTs, too.

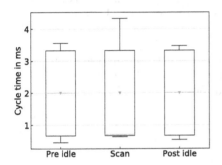

Fig. 11. Impact of *ZGrab* on a Wago 750–889 (6).

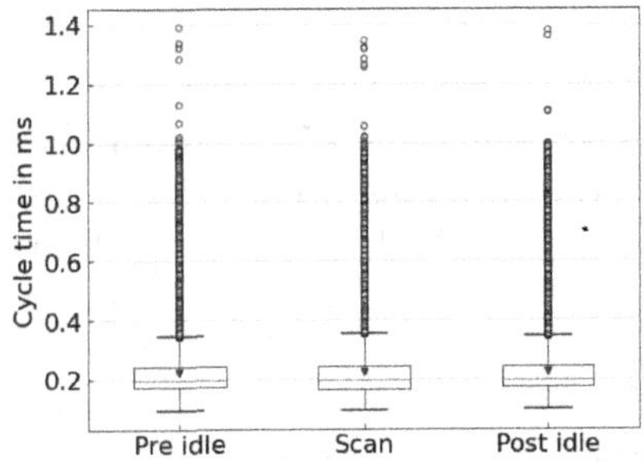

Fig. 12. Impact of *ZGrab* on a Siemens Simatic S7-1211C (2).

5.5 Application Scanning with OpenVAS

OpenVAS was configured to use the pre-defined scan configuration *"System Discovery"*. All available modules designed to discover and identify devices are part of this scan task. These modules use a variety of techniques and protocols on the targeted device. This includes several tests, to avoid the execution of dangerous modules on known fragile devices or services.

Overall, in these experiments most DuTs were at least slightly influenced. The DuTs were able to keep their mean cycle time and only had some outlier.

For the Phoenix ILC 151 (3), the *OpenVAS* scan had the highest impact in our experiments, with a maximum cycle time of 2.1 ms, as seen in Fig. 13. However, the device was able to compensate the increased cycle duration, through shorter cycles, following after. Thus, the duration of a cycle came closer to the configured cycle time of 1 ms. Figure 14 illustrates this compensating behavior.

While most PLCs were able to keep their mean cycle time without influences, the Wago 750–889 (6) and Wago 750–880 (7) are exceptions. The impact of the *OpenVAS* scan on these devices caused single cycles to last several hundred milliseconds as depicted in Fig. 15 and 16. Even if the PLC is able to keep the mean cycle time, such a significant deviation could cause disturbances in the control

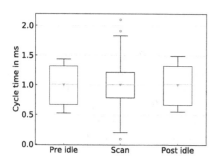

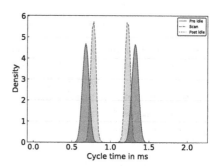

Fig. 13. Impact of *OpenVAS* on a Phoenix ILC 151 (3).

Fig. 14. Probability Density Function of the cycle time of an Phoenix ILC 151 (3), during an *OpenVAS* scan.

process. While the PLCs are not measurable influenced during the majority of the scan, it seems like specific modules, processes or spikes in communication load are responsible for the significant deviations.

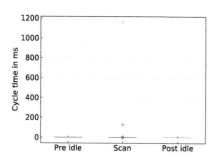

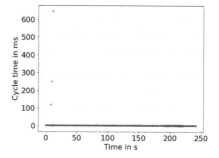

Fig. 15. Impact of *OpenVAS* on a Wago 750–889 (6).

Fig. 16. Cycle time during a *OpenVAS* scan on a Wago 750–880 (7).

6 Conclusion

In this paper, we evaluated the impact of five different active scanning tools used for device identification in industrial networks. Each tool, used for our experiments, is capable of identifying industrial components and could possibly be used in such environments. Our results show that active scanning remains a potential risk in industrial environments and is able to influence PLCs significantly. These influences range from high deviations of the cycle time, to disturbances in the communication with connected devices. Most PLCs in our testbed were affected to some degree by at least one of the used tools.

While some tools influenced the devices significantly, we could show that targeted and restricted scans can yield the required information for identification, without negative influences. Especially scans targeting only few ports and querying only essential information from the PLC, like *modbus-discover*, *s7-info* or *ZGrab*, showed only minor impact. However, as the small communication load of these tools reduces the risk of disturbances, it also reduces the amount of information possibly gathered by a scan.

Depending on the knowledge about deployed devices and required information for a successful device identification, generic approaches may be necessary. Because generic approaches, like *Nmap* or *OpenVAS*, use a large number of network packets to gather as much information as possible, these tools showed the highest impact in our experiments. The main influence was generated by network communication load and not the protocol specific communication. Even with build-in features like *Nmaps* self optimization, some PLCs were not able to process the network communication load uninfluenced. Therefore, further research on how risks of such scans can be reduced is required.

We were not able to identify device specific vulnerabilities to active scans. During our experiments, no device was malfunctioning or entered an error state. However, in early experiments, a PLC entered a fatal error state after an Open-VAS vulnerability scan. The reason behind this malfunction is currently unclear and further research has to be done.

An active scan in industrial networks should be planned carefully, requiring more effort than for IT networks. There are cases where network scans are necessary to organize the uncontrolled growth of OT networks in the past. Nevertheless, operators and administrators need to adapt active as well as passive network scanning as part of their security concept, to gain an overview of their network and to identify possible security problems.

References

1. Bou-Harb, E., Debbabi, M., Assi, C.: Cyber scanning: a comprehensive survey. IEEE Commun. Surv. Tutorials **16**(3), 1496–1519 (2013)
2. Bristow, M.: ModScan. https://code.google.com/archive/p/modscan/, Accessed 31 July 2020
3. Coffey, K., Smith, R., Maglaras, L., Janicke, H.: Vulnerability analysis of network scanning on scada systems. Secur. Commun. Netw. **2018**, 1–21 (2018). https://www.hindawi.com/journals/scn/2018/3794603/
4. Durumeric, Z., Adrian, D., Mirian, A., Bailey, M., Halderman, J.A.: A search engine backed by internet-wide scanning. In: Proceedings of the 22nd ACM SIGSAC Conference on Computer and Communications Security, pp. 542–553 (2015)
5. Kalluri, R., Mahendra, L., Kumar, R.S., Prasad, G.G.: Simulation and impact analysis of denial-of-service attacks on power SCADA. In: 2016 National Power Systems Conference (NPSC), pp. 1–5. IEEE (2016)
6. Ljøsne, M.J.: Network scanning industrial control systems: A vulnerability analysis. Master's thesis, University of Oslo (2019)

7. Lyon, G.F.: Nmap network scanning: The official Nmap project guide to network discovery and security scanning. Insecure (2009)

8. Matherly, J.: The complete guide to shodan: Collect. analyze. visualize. In: Make Internet Intelligence Work for You. Leanpub (2016)

9. Mohan, V.: IT asset management benefits & best practices. SolarWinds Worldwide LLC White Paper (2013)

10. Niedermaier, M., von Bodisco, A., Merli, D.: CoRT: a communication robustness testbed for industrial control system components. In: 4th International Conference on Event-Based Control, Communication, and Signal Processing EBCCSP 2018 (2018)

11. Niedermaier, M., et al.: You snooze, you lose: measuring PLC cycle times under attacks. In: 12th USENIX Workshop on Offensive Technologies (WOOT 18) (2018)

12. OpenVAS: Open vulnerability assessment system. http://www.openvas.org/, Accessed31 July 2020

13. PLCScan: PLCScan the internet. http://www.scada.sl/2012/11/plcscan.html, Accessed 31 July 2020

14. Saleae Inc.: Saleae logic analyzer. https://www.saleae.com/about/, Accessed 31 July 2020

15. Teixeira, A., Pérez, D., Sandberg, H., Johansson, K.H.: Attack models and scenarios for networked control systems. In: Proceedings of the 1st International Conference on High Confidence Networked Systems, pp. 55–64 (2012)

16. Wedgbury, A., Jones, K.: Automated asset discovery in industrial control systems - exploring the problem. In: 3rd International Symposium for ICS & SCADA Cyber Security Research 2015 (ICS-CSR 2015), vol. 3, pp. 73–83 (2015)

17. Wiberg, K.C.: Identifying supervisory control and data acquisition (SCADA) systems on a network via remote reconnaissance. Technical report, Naval Postgraduate School Monterey CA (2006)

Designing Double-Click-Based Unlocking Mechanism on Smartphones

Wenjuan Li[1,2], Jiao Tan[3], Nan Zhu[3], and Yu Wang[1(✉)]

[1] Institute of Artificial Intelligence and Blockchain, Guangzhou University,
Guangzhou, China
yuwang@gzhu.edu.cn
[2] Department of Applied Mathematics and Computer Science, Technical University
of Denmark, Kongens Lyngby, Denmark
[3] KOTO Research Center, Macao, China

Abstract. Smartphones have gained huge popularity and rapidly changed the way of people's living habits and communication style. Despite the widespread adoption, there is a big challenge to protect data security on smartphones. This is because phone users often store their personal data (e.g., images) and proceed sensitive tasks (e.g., financial operations) on the device. To secure the device from unauthorized access, designing an appropriate unlocking mechanism is an expected solution. To complement existing schemes, we advocate that combining behavioral biometrics can enhance the security of unlocking mechanisms. In this work, we develop a double-click-based unlocking scheme (DCUS), which allows users to unlock the phone by double clicking on the pre-selected location on an image. For verification, DCUS has to check selected images, image location and behavioral features of double-click action. In the user study, we involve 40 participants and explore some common supervised algorithms. The results demonstrate that participants can achieve a good success rate (over 96%) with positive feedback.

Keywords: User authentication · Double click · Smartphone security · Behavioral authentication · Touch dynamics

1 Introduction

A recent survey from Deloitte indicated that around 1.4 billion smartphones have been shipped in 2019, which have become the world's most ubiquitous and most-used consumer electronic device [5]. Due to the popularity, smartphones are often used to store lots of private and personal data such as photos, contacts, banking information, commercial applications and more. With data security becoming more important (e.g., GDPR [12]), there is an increasing requirement to enforce access control and authenticate users on smart devices.

One of the most widely used authentication methods is password-based authentication (e.g., textual passwords, unlock patterns), but it has some flaws

© Springer Nature Switzerland AG 2021
G. Wang et al. (Eds.): SpaCCS 2020, LNCS 12383, pp. 573–585, 2021.
https://doi.org/10.1007/978-3-030-68884-4_47

regarding security and usability. For example, people are usually difficult to remember complex passwords for a long time due to the memory limitation and multiple password inference [25, 26], and thus they might choose a weak password instead [3, 41]. Also, smartphone passwords may be suffered from various attacks like recording attacks [28] and charging attack [23, 24], in which attackers can record the phone screen and extract sensitive information.

To verify users, graphical password (GP) is an option like Android unlock patterns, which allows users to create a pattern and unlock their devices, within a grid of 3×3 [21, 22]. The motivation behind is that users can remember images better than texts [29]. However, graphical password may suffer many similar issues as traditional passwords, like recording attacks and charging attacks. For example, the password space of Android unlock patterns may be vulnerable to brute-force attack, and attackers can reduce password space by identifying the left touch trails [1]. In addition, usability is still a concern with GP, i.e., *PassPoints* [40] allows users to click on some locations on an image as credentials, while some users may still suffer a high error rate.

Now research is moving to investigate how to enhance the security of authentication by involving behavioral biometrics, which aims to verify users based on their behavioral features. For instance, De Luca et al. [4] presented an idea of combining unlock patterns with behavioral features (e.g., touch coordinates) using dynamic time warping (DTW). Users are not only verified by the shape they input but also by the way how users input. Li et al. [15, 16] introduced SwipeVLock, a supervised unlocking mechanism with swipe action. The scheme can verify a user according to both unlock patterns and swipe features.

Motivated by the literature, in this work, we advocate the advantage of applying behavioral biometric into unlock patterns. We particularly design a double-click-based unlocking scheme (shortly DCUS), which allows users to unlock their devices by double clicking on the pre-selected location on a selected image. The choice of double clicking is due to its common usage when users play their phones. The contributions can be summarized as below.

- We design DCUS, a double-click-based unlocking scheme on smartphones for authenticating users based on their double-click action. For registration, users have to select a background image and perform a double-click action on a selected location. A successful login requires to check these two aspects. The merits of this mechanism are the transparency and easy-to-use property.
- To build a normal model of users' double-click behavior, we extract some behavioral features like pressure, finger size and time difference, and evaluate some supervised learning algorithms.
- We involve 40 common phone users to evaluate the performance of DCUS. By collecting data and users' feedback, our scheme is found to be usable and secure (i.e., similar to 8-digit PIN code) in practice.

The remaining parts are structured as follows. Section 2 introduces related work on unlock mechanisms and behavioral authentication schemes. Section 3 introduces DCUS in detail, and Sect. 4 presents a user study with 40 participants. We conclude our work in Sect. 5.

2 Related Work

2.1 Unlocking Mechanism

To protect mobile devices from unauthorized access, the design of unlocking mechanisms is an effective solution. Amongst the current unlocking mechanisms, Android unlock patterns [4, 22] are one widely used scheme on smartphones, allowing people to draw a pattern within a 3×3 grid. This Android unlocking application is actually an extension from *Pass-Go* [36], which requires users to create a pattern on an image.

In the literature, there are many unlocking schemes proposed on mobile devices. Findling and Mayrhofer [7] introduced a Face Unlock system by using both frontal and profile face information during a pan shot around the user's head, based on camera and movement sensor. They showed a success rate of around 90.5%, but face recognition also suffers some issues [13]. Guo et al. [10] introduced OpenSesame, which verifies users based on their shaking patterns for locking/unlocking. By using a support vector machine (SVM) classifier, they could reach an FNR of 11%, with a standard deviation of 2.0%, and an FPR of around 15% with a standard deviation of 2.5%. Izuta et al. [11] presented a screen unlocking system on phones based on an accelerometer and pressure sensor arrays. They considered users' behavioral features when taking a mobile phone from the pocket and the pressure distribution when gripping the mobile phone, i.e., a taking-out action. In the evaluation, an FAR of around 0.43 was achieved at 30th trial with 18 training data. Meng et al. [22] introduced TMGuard, a touch movement-based security mechanism aiming to improve the security of Android unlock patterns.

Yi et al. [42] introduced WearLock, which uses acoustic tones as tokens to automate the phone unlocking. The design includes signal detection using preamble identification, time synchronization using preamble and cyclic prefix, channel estimation, etc. They finally showed an average success rate of 90% among five participants. Wang et al. [38] introduced an unlocking scheme based on the built-in accelerometer to capture the heartbeat vibration. To unlock the device, users only need to press the device on their chest to collect heartbeat signals, and the system can identify the user within a few heartbeats. Their evaluation collected more than 110, 000 heartbeat samples from 35 participants, and reached an Equal Error Rate (EER) of 3.51% for user authentication when using five heartbeat cycles. Li et al. [15, 16] introduced SwipeVLock, an unlocking mechanism that verifies users based on swiping action. Their results showed that participants could perform well with a success rate of 98% in the best case.

Basically, unlock mechanism can be considered as pure graphical password schemes or hybrid schemes with other elements [27, 34]. For example, in order to enlarge the password space, recent schemes may consider involving world map so that users can create a password by selecting one or more locations on the map [31]. Meng [20] introduced *RouteMap*, which requires users to make a route on a world map. Sun *et al.* [35] presented *PassMap* in which two locations should be selected by users, while Thorpe *et al.* [37] showed *GeoPass* in which only one location should be selected by users. The number of locations may affect the scheme performance, while there is no significant difference by selecting one or two locations [27].

2.2   Behavioral Authentication

With the rapid development of Internet-of-Things (IoT), there is a trend to design behavioral authentication schemes to provide implicit user verification on smart devices. As most current phones are touch-enabled, many behavioral schemes have been studies. For instance, Fen et al. [6] introduced a user authentication scheme based on their finger gesture, and provided an FAR of 4.66% and an FRR of 0.13% using a random forest classifier. An early behavioral authentication scheme was proposed by Meng et al. [17]. They employed a total of 21 features and provided an average error rate of 3% using a hybrid algorithm called PSO-RBFN. Then *Touchalytics* was introduced by Frank et al. [8], with a number of 30 features. Their scheme could achieve a median equal error rate of around 4%.

To design a suitable behavioral authentication scheme, it is important to understand users' habits. The scheme of CD-GPS was introduced by [18], which explored the effect of multi-touch on creating graphical passwords in the aspect of security and usability. They found that by integrating the action of multi-touch, graphical passwords can be generally enhanced. Zheng et al. [43] investigated users' tapping habits on phones with passcode input. With a one-class algorithm, they could reach an averaged equal error rate of nearly 3.65%. Smith-Creasey and Rajarajan [30] believed that a stacked classifier could help address some prevalent issues, and introduced a set of meta-level classifiers. They showed an equal error rate of 3.77% for a single sample. Sharma and Enbody [33] explored users' habits when they play with the application interface, and studied an SVM-based ensemble classifier. Their results showed a mean equal error rate of 7% during the authentication. Shahzad et al. [32] focused on how participants input a gesture on phones and introduced a scheme with features like velocity, device acceleration, and stroke time. Li et al. [14] introduced three practical anti-eavesdropping password entry schemes on stand-alone smart glasses, named gTapper, gRotator and gTalker. This aims to break the correlation between the underlying password and the interaction observable to attackers. Some more schemes can refer to research surveys like [9,19].

3   Our Proposed Scheme

As discussed above, many unlocking schemes have been studied in combination with behavioral features. Motivated by this, in this work, we advocate this trend and introduce a double-click-based unlocking scheme (named DCUS), which requires users to double click on a location on a selected image. Figure 1 shows the scheme design with two major steps: choosing one background image and double-clicking on one location.

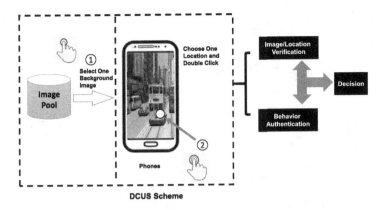

DCUS Scheme

Fig. 1. DCUS scheme: (1) Step 1: select one background image; and (2) Step 2: choose one location on the image and double click.

- **DCUS registration.** Phone users should choose one image from the image pool as the background, and then select one location on the image to double click. The number and the themes of images can be adjusted according to the concrete application scenario. There is a balance should be made between usability and security.
- **DCUS authentication.** To unlock the phone, users have to choose the same image from the image pool, and double click on the same (pre-selected) location. A successful unlock requires verifying background image, location and behavioral features extracted from the double-clicking action.

Scheme Implementation. Figure 2 shows an implementation case of DCUS. There are a total of six images in the image pool (including buildings, ferris wheel, playground and public transportation), and users need to select one and double click to unlock the phone. To decide whether current user is legitimate, our scheme should compare image & location selection and double-click behavior with the pre-stored information. For image and location matching, we can compare the input with the stored pattern. For behavioral verification, our scheme can use machine learning algorithms (e.g., SVM, decision tree) to help build a normal profile and make a decision.

To make the scheme usable in practice, we set the error tolerance to a 21×21 pixel box around the selected location. The setting is selected based on the previous work [15,27], i.e., Meng et al. [27] had demonstrated that it is usable to adopt an error tolerance of 21×21 pixel in geographical password design and implementation.

Double-Click Features. As a study, this work considers some typical and popular behavioral features such as time difference between two touches, touch pressure, touch duration and acceleration. The coordinates of touches would be examined by location matching process.

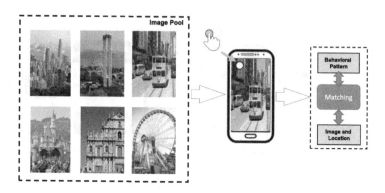

Fig. 2. A case implementation of DCUS in our user study.

- *Time difference between two touches.* Our scheme records the time difference between the first touch and the second touch. Intuitively, phone users should perform the double-click action differently.
- *Touch pressure.* Most smartphones are able to record touch pressure values, which can be utilized to model a user's touch behavior.
- *Touch duration.* This feature is used to measure the time difference between a touch press and a touch release, which can be used to distinguish users. For our scheme, this feature contains two vectors: the touch duration for the first click, and the touch duration for the second click.
- *Touch acceleration.* Similar to the previous work [43], this work considers touch acceleration with three vectors, such as the magnitude of acceleration when the touch is pressed down; the magnitude of acceleration when the touch is released; and the average value of magnitude of acceleration during touch-press to touch-release.

4   User Study

To evaluate the scheme performance, we conduct a user study with 40 common phone users, among which 80% Android phone users and 20% iPhone& Android phone users (currently using both types of phones). Table 1 shows the information of participants like occupation and gender. In particular, we have 22 males and 18 females who aged from 20 to 50, including students, business people, university staff and faculty members. Each participant would get a $20 gift voucher after the study.

The Consideration of Machine Learning. Similar to previous work [15], this work considers some typical learning algorithms such as Decision tree (J48), Naive Bayes, Support Vector Machine (SVM), K-nearest neighbours (IBK) and Back Propagation Neural Network (BPNN). These classifiers are easy to run on smart devices.

Table 1. Participants' information in the user study.

Information	Male	Female	Occupation	Male	Female
Age < 25	13	7	Students	16	11
Age 25–35	6	9	University Faculty & Staff	4	5
Age 35–50	3	2	Business People	2	2

To avoid implementation bias, we extract the above classifiers from the WEKA platform [39], which provides a set of open-source machine learning collection in Java. In the evaluation, we adopt the default settings for all classifiers as a study. To judge the performance, we use two common metrics as follows.

- False Acceptance Rate (FAR): shows the rate of how many intruders are classified as legitimate users.
- False Rejection Rate (FRR): shows the rate of how many legitimate users are classified as intruders.

Study Steps. Before the study, we began by illustrating our objectives to all participants and explained what kind of data would be collected. We also provide a note with the same guidelines for all participants. Before the formal start, each participant could have three trials to get familiar with the scheme, when they got the Android phone (Samsung Galaxy Note). All participants performed the study in our lab environment. The detailed steps are shown as below.

- Step 1. Creation phase: participants need to register their credentials according to DCUS steps.
- Step 2. Confirmation phase: participants have to confirm the DCUS credentials by verifying both the image, location and double-click behavior for 5 times. Participants can change their credentials if they fail or want to create a new one.
- Step 3. Distributed memory: participants are given one paper-based finding tasks to distract them for 15 min.
- Step 4. Login phase: participants should unlock the phone with their credentials for 5 trials.
- Step 5. Feedback form: participants are provided with a set of questions (*feedback from*) regarding the scheme usage.
- Step 6. Retention. After three days, participants are invited to unlock the phone for 5 times in our lab.
- Step 7. Participants are provided with another *feedback from* regarding the scheme usage.

Study Results. After the study, we could collect 200 trials in the confirmation phase and 200 trials in the login phase. Similar to previous work [15], we used 60% of trials as training data and the rest as testing data. Table 2 shows the performance of different classifiers with a 10-fold cross-validation mode, such as J48, NBayes, SVM, IBK (k = 3), and BPNN.

Table 2 indicates that SVM could achieve better performance than other classifiers, i.e., it could achieve an average error rate (AER) of 3.8%, as compared with J48 8.9%, NBayes 12.05%, IBK 7.95%, and BPNN 8.15%. Therefore, our scheme used SVM for user authentication and Table 3 shows the successful rate for confirmation, login and retention phase.

Table 2. The performance of different classifiers under different groups.

Metric	J48	NBayes	SVM	IBK (k = 3)	BPNN
FAR (%)	8.3	11.8	3.5	8.4	7.6
FRR (%)	9.5	12.3	4.1	7.5	8.7
AER (%)	8.9	12.05	3.8	7.95	8.15

Table 3. Success rate in the confirmation, login and retention phase.

Phase	Success rate
Confirmation	184/200 (92.0%)
Login	193/200 (96.5%)
Retention	153/165 (92.7%)

- *Confirmation phase.* In this phase, participants could reach a success rate of 92%. The errors were mainly caused by behavioral matching, and there are two main error types: 1) a double-click action is too fast or slow than the registered one, and 2) the touch acceleration is not matched.
- *Login phase.* Participants could perform well in this phase with a success rate of 96.5%. The reasons for those errors were similar to the confirmation phase (double click and touch acceleration). Hence there is a need to enhance users' double-click action in these two aspects.
- *Retention phase.* Participants were invited to return after three days, and 35 of them successfully came back. It is found that a success rate of 92.7% could be achieved, which is still higher than the rate achieved in the confirmation phase. After analyzing the collected data, only two participants made an error due to the input of a wrong location. This indicates that our scheme is usable in practice.

Overall, after analyzing the data among these three phases, it is observed that few errors were caused regarding image and location selection. This implies two points: 1) the selected error tolerance is usable, and 2) users can remember the image and location well. For the errors occurred in the behavioral matching process, more practice should be an option to improve the authentication performance, according to the observation from previous studies like [22].

User Feedback. In the user study, two feedback forms were provided to each participant in relating to the scheme usage, in the aspects of both security and usability. Ten-point Likert scales are used for each question, where 1-score indicates strong disagreement and 10-score indicates strong agreement. The major questions and scores are shown in Table 4.

Table 4. Major questions and average scores from the participants.

Questions (Login phase)	Average scores
1. I could easily create a credential under DCUS	9.2
2. The time consumption for confirmation is acceptable	8.8
3. The time consumption for login is acceptable	9.0
4. I could easily login to the system	8.4
5. I prefer textual passwords than DCUS	4.1
6. 4-digit PIN code is more secure than DCUS	2.2
7. 8-digit PIN code is more secure than DCUS	6.7
Questions (Retention phase)	Average scores
1. I could easily login to the system	8.8
2. I can remember my selected image	8.6
3. I can remember my selected location on the image	8.9
4. I prefer textual passwords than DCUS	3.5
5. 4-digit PIN code is more secure than DCUS	2.4
6. 8-digit PIN code is more secure than DCUS	5.6
7. The time consumption is acceptable	8.4

- *The first feedback form.* For the first three questions, it is found that most participants felt positive on the scheme usage, i.e., they believe it is easy to create the password, and the time consumption is acceptable. Also, a majority of participants believed they could easily login to the system, with a score of 8.4. As compared with textual password schemes, it is found more than half participants were likely to vote for our scheme. We further compared DCUS with PIN-code, it is found that most participants believed DCUS is more secure than 4-digit PIN codes, but may be less secure than 8-digit PIN codes. After an informal interview, they considered DCUS seemed simpler than 8-digit PIN codes, with only one double-click action.
- *The second feedback form.* This form is a bit different from the first one, while most participants still considered our scheme is very usable with a score of

8.8. They also believed that it is easy to remember the selected image and location, with a score of 8.6 and 8.9 respectively. Then as compared with the first form, it is found that more participants preferred our scheme than textual passwords, i.e., they reflected that DCUS is easy to remember and use. For the security, the score is still similar to the first form, but nearly half participants believed that DCUS might have a similar security level as 8-digit PIN codes (i.e., they realized that behavioral authentication could provide additional protection). At last, most participants accepted the time consumption required by DCUS with a score of 8.4.

Based on the collected feedback, most participants are positive on the usage of DCUS. They believed that DCUS is easy to use without causing much time consumption in the login phase. They also considered the security of DCUS is similar to a 8-digit PIN code and much better than a 4-digit PIN code. Most of them also considered using DCUS in practice. This motivates us to resolve some challenges and further develop a more secure DCUS in practice, i.e., we can further deploy an additional authentication layer based on RFID and thermal image for better security [2].

5   Conclusion

With smartphones being popular, there is an increasing need to design proper unlocking mechanisms to enforce access control and examine the legitimacy of current phone users. As current unlocking schemes like Android unlock patterns are vulnerable to many attacks, this work advocates the merit of combining unlocking mechanisms with behavioral biometrics. Motivated by this, we introduce DCUS, a double-click-based unlocking scheme, which allows users to unlock the phone by double clicking on the preselected location on an image. A successful login requires to check the selected image, image location and double-click action. In the study, we involved 40 participants and examined the scheme performance according to success rate and users' feedback. Among several typical supervised learning algorithms, it is found that SVM could outperform other algorithms such as J48, NBayes, IBK and BPNN. In the study, we found that most participants could provide positive feedback and work well with DCUS, with a success rate of 96.5% and 92.7% in the login phase and retention phase.

Acknowledgments. We would like to thank the participants for their hard work in the user study. This work was partially supported by National Natural Science Foundation of China (No. 61802080 and 61802077).

References

1. Aviv, A.J., Gibson, K., Mossop, E., Blaze, M., Smith, J.M.: Smudge attacks on smartphone touch screens. In: Proceedings of the 4th USENIX Conference on Offensive Technologies, pp. 1–7. USENIX Association (2010)

2. Al-Sudani, A.R., Gao, S., Wen, S., Al-Khiza'ay, M.: Checking an authentication of person depends on RFID with thermal image. SpaCCS **2018**, 371–380 (2018)
3. Bonneau, J.: The science of guessing: analyzing an anonymized corpus of 70 million passwords. In: Proceedings of the 2012 IEEE Symposium on Security and Privacy, pp. 538–552 (2012)
4. De Luca, A., Hang, A., Brudy, F., Lindner, C., Hussmann, H.: Touch me once and i know it's you!: implicit authentication based on touch screen patterns. In: Proceedings of CHI, pp. 987–996. ACM (2012)
5. Deloitte's 2019 global mobile consumer survey. https://www2.deloitte.com/content/dam/insights/us/articles/glob43115_2019-global-mobile-survey/DI_2019-global-mobile-survey.pdf
6. Feng, T., et al.: Continuous mobile authentication using touchscreen gestures. In: Proceedings of the 2012 IEEE Conference on Technologies for Homeland Security (HST), pp. 451–456. IEEE, USA (2012)
7. Findling, R.D., Mayrhofer, R.: Towards face unlock: on the difficulty of reliably detecting faces on mobile phones. In: MoMM, pp. 275–280 (2012)
8. Frank, M., Biedert, R., Ma, E., Martinovic, I., Song, D.: Touchalytics: on the applicability of touchscreen input as a behavioral biometric for continuous authentication. IEEE Trans. Inf. Forensics Secur. **8**(1), 136–148 (2013)
9. Gomez-Barrero, M., Galbally, J.: Reversing the irreversible: a survey on inverse biometrics. Comput. Secur. **90**, 101700 (2020)
10. Guo, Y., Yang, L., Ding, X., Han, J., Liu, Y.: OpenSesame: unlocking smart phone through handshaking biometrics. In: INFOCOM, pp. 365–369 (2013)
11. Izuta, R., Murao, K., Terada, T., Iso, T., Inamura, H., Tsukamoto, M.: Screen unlocking method using behavioral characteristics when taking mobile phone from pocket. In: MoMM, pp. 110–114 (2016)
12. Larrucea, X., Moffie, M., Asaf, I.S.: Santamaria: towards a GDPR compliant way to secure European cross border healthcare industry 4.0. Comput. Stand. Interfaces **69**, 103408 (2020)
13. Li, Y., et al.: A closer look tells more: a facial distortion based liveness detection for face authentication. In: AsiaCCS, pp. 241–246 (2019)
14. Li, Y., Cheng, Y., Meng, W., Li, Y., Deng, R.H.: Designing leakage-resilient password entry on head-mounted smart wearable glass devices. IEEE Trans. Inf. Forensics Secur. **16**, 307–321 (2021)
15. Li, W., Tan, J., Meng, W., Wang, Yu., Li, J.: SwipeVLock: a supervised unlocking mechanism based on swipe behavior on smartphones. In: Chen, X., Huang, X., Zhang, J. (eds.) ML4CS 2019. LNCS, vol. 11806, pp. 140–153. Springer, Cham (2019). https://doi.org/10.1007/978-3-030-30619-9_11
16. Li, W., Tan, J., Meng, W., Wang, Y.: A swipe-based unlocking mechanism with supervised learning on smartphones: design and evaluation. J. Netw. Comput. Appl **165**, 102687 (2020)
17. Meng, Y.: Designing click-draw based graphical password scheme for better authentication. In: Proceedings of the 7th IEEE International Conference on Networking, Architecture, and Storage (NAS), pp. 39–48 (2012)
18. Meng, Y., Li, W., Kwok, L.-F.: Enhancing click-draw based graphical passwords using multi-touch on mobile phones. In: Proceedings of the 28th IFIP TC 11 International Information Security and Privacy Conference (IFIP SEC), IFIP Advances in Information and Communication Technology, vol. 405, pp. 55–68 (2013)
19. Meng, W., Wong, D.S., Furnell, S., Zhou, J.: Surveying the development of biometric user authentication on mobile phones. IEEE Commun. Surv. Tutorials **17**(3), 1268–1293 (2015)

20. Meng, W.: RouteMap: a route and map based graphical password scheme for better multiple password memory. In: Proceedings of the 9th International Conference on Network and System Security (NSS), pp. 147–161 (2015)

21. Meng, W.: Evaluating the effect of multi-touch behaviours on android unlock patterns. Inf. Comput. Secur. **24**(3), 277–287 (2016)

22. Meng, W., Li, W., Wong, D.S., Zhou, J.: TMGuard: a touch movement-based security mechanism for screen unlock patterns on smartphones. In: Proceedings of the 14th International Conference on Applied Cryptography and Network Security (ACNS), pp. 629–647 (2016)

23. Meng, W., Lee, W.H., Liu, Z., Su, C., Li, Y.: Evaluating the impact of juice filming charging attack in practical environments. In: Kim, H., Kim, D.-C. (eds.) ICISC 2017. LNCS, vol. 10779, pp. 327–338. Springer, Cham (2018). https://doi.org/10.1007/978-3-319-78556-1_18

24. Meng, W., Fei, F., Li, W., Au, M.H.: Harvesting smartphone privacy through enhanced juice filming charging attacks. In: Proceedings of ISC, pp. 291–308 (2017)

25. Meng, W., Li, W., Kwok, L.-F., Choo, K.-K.R.: Towards enhancing click-draw based graphical passwords using multi-touch behaviours on smartphones. Comput. Secur. **65**, 213–229 (2017)

26. Meng, W., Li, W., Lee, W., Jiang, L., Zhou, J.: A Pilot Study of Multiple Password Interference between Text and Map-based Passwords. In: Proceedings of the 15th International Conference on Applied Cryptography and Network Security (ACNS), pp. 145–162 (2017)

27. Meng, W., Lee, W.H., Au, M.H., Liu, Z.: Exploring effect of location number on map-based graphical password authentication. In: Pieprzyk, J., Suriadi, S. (eds.) ACISP 2017. LNCS, vol. 10343, pp. 301–313. Springer, Cham (2017). https://doi.org/10.1007/978-3-319-59870-3_17

28. Nyang, D., Kim, H., Lee, W., Kang, S., Cho, G., Lee, M.K., Mohaisen, A.: Two-thumbs-up: physical protection for PIN entry secure against recording attacks. Comput. Secur. **78**, 1–15 (2018)

29. Shepard, R.N.: Recognition memory for words, sentences, and pictures. J. Verbal Learn. Verbal Behav. **6**(1), 156–163 (1967)

30. Smith-Creasey, M., Rajarajan, M.: A continuous user authentication scheme for mobile devices. In: Proceedings of the 14th Annual Conference on Privacy, Security and Trust (PST), pp. 104–113 (2016)

31. Spitzer, J., Singh, C., Schweitzer, D.: A security class project in graphical passwords. J. Comput. Sci. Coll. **26**(2), 7–13 (2010)

32. Shahzad, M., Liu, A.X., Samuel, A.: Behavior based human authentication on touch screen devices using gestures and signatures. IEEE Trans. Mob. Comput. **16**(10), 2726–2741 (2017)

33. Sharma, V., Enbody, R.: User authentication and identification from user interface interactions on touch-enabled devices. In: Proceedings of the 10th ACM Conference on Security and Privacy in Wireless and Mobile Networks (WiSec), pp. 1–11 (2017)

34. Suo, X., Zhu, Y., Owen, G.S.: Graphical passwords: a survey. In: Proceedings of the 21st Annual Computer Security Applications Conference (ACSAC), pp. 463–472. IEEE Computer Society, USA (2005)

35. Sun, H., Chen, Y., Fang, C., Chang, S.: PassMap: a map based graphical-password authentication system. In: Proceedings of AsiaCCS, pp. 99–100 (2012)

36. Tao, H., Adams, C.: Pass-Go: a proposal to improve the usability of graphical passwords. Int. J. Netw. Secur. **2**(7), 273–292 (2008)

37. Thorpe, J., MacRae, B., Salehi-Abari, A.: Usability and security evaluation of geopass: a geographic location-password scheme. In: Proceedings of the 9th Symposium on Usable Privacy and Security (SOUPS), pp. 1–14 (2013)
38. Wang, L., et al.: Unlock with your heart: heartbeat-based authentication on commercial mobile phones. In: Proceedings of ACM Interactive, Mobile, Wearable Ubiquitous Technologies, vol. 2, no. 3, pp. 140:1–140:22 (2018)
39. Weka: Machine Learning Software in Java. https://www.cs.waikato.ac.nz/ml/weka/
40. Wiedenbeck, S., Waters, J., Birget, J.-C., Brodskiy, A., Memon, N.: Passpoints: design and longitudinal evaluation of a graphical password system. Int. J. Hum.-Comput. Stud. **63**(1–2), 102–127 (2005)
41. Weir, M., Aggarwal, S., Collins, M., Stern, H.: Testing metrics for password creation policies by attacking large sets of revealed passwords. In: Proceedings of CCS, pp. 162–175 (2010)
42. Yi, S., Qin, Z., Carter, N., Li, Q.: WearLock: unlocking your phone via acoustics using smartwatch. In: ICDCS, pp. 469–479 (2017)
43. Zheng, N., Bai, K., Huang, H., Wang, H.: You are how you touch: user verification on smartphones via tapping behaviors. In: Proceedings of the 2014 International Conference on Network Protocols (ICNP), pp. 221–232 (2014)

An Efficient Blind Signature Scheme with Untraceability for Data Privacy in Smart Grid

Weijian Zhang[1], Chao Lin[2(✉)], Zhuo Lyu[3], Chen Cen[3], and Min Luo[4(✉)]

[1] State Grid Henan Electric Power Company, Zhengzhou 450052, China
[2] College of Mathematics and Informatics, Fujian Normal University,
Fuzhou 350007, China
linchao91@qq.com
[3] State Grid Henan Electric Power Research Institute, Zhengzhou 450052, China
[4] School of Cyber Science and Engineering, Wuhan University, Wuhan 430072, China
mluo@whu.edu.cn

Abstract. Smart grid has been expected to provide exquisite consumption monitoring or energy trading for its equipped abundant facilities together with two-way communication, but it inevitably leads to privacy leakage of consumption data during data retransmission. Although blind signature schemes can reduce the risk of privacy leakage due to the properties of unforgeability and blindness, most of them are traceable meaning that some malicious signers can still obtain the real information of blinded signatures. In this paper, we propose an improved blind signature scheme with untraceability to further enhance privacy protection of consumption data in smart grid. We also provide security analysis and comparative performance analysis to demonstrate its feasibility.

Keywords: Smart grid · Data privacy · Blind signature · Untraceability · Provable security

1 Introduction

Smart grid is a modern electricity transmission system that greatly optimizes control and achieves advanced grid functionalities via combining two-way communication, information and software [1–3]. Especially the concept of industry 4.0 facilitates the optimization of operating and managing smart grid for all kinds of equipments and facilities can be conveniently connected. A typical system model of smart grid mainly consists of three entities, namely, control center, smart substation and smart meter (as shown in Fig. 1). Here, control center is responsible for initializing system parameters, member management and data verification. Smart substation can directly communicate with the smart meter to obtain and retransmit consumption data, and smart meter is in charge of recording data regularly and reporting them to smart substation.

© Springer Nature Switzerland AG 2021
G. Wang et al. (Eds.): SpaCCS 2020, LNCS 12383, pp. 586–597, 2021.
https://doi.org/10.1007/978-3-030-68884-4_48

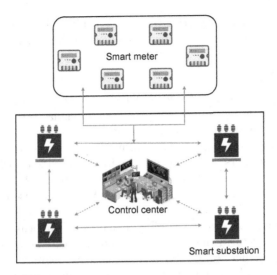

Fig. 1. A typical system model of smart grid.

There are some security concerns have been arisen in such a system model of smart grid among the two-way communication, which is easy to be eavesdropped by adversary especially at the user side. This may lead to the leakage of users' power consumption information and causes the users' lifestyles being maliciously analyzed [4–6]. In this paper, we are concerned about protecting the consumption data privacy when smart substation retransmits smart meter's consumption data to control center. That is, smart meter can obtain the signature of smart substation without revealing the detail of consumption data to smart substation.

Blind signature [7], as one of popular cryptographic primitives, ensures that a user can ask a signer to sign a message without revealing its content. This property enables severing the relationship between the user identity and data during the data retransmission efficiently [8,9]. Hence, it can be applied into the smart grid to protect the privacy of consumption data. Unfortunately, most of the existing blind signature schemes are faced with a problem of traceability. That is, once the requester makes its signature public, the malicious signer can trace the concrete blinded signature to the public one via its keeping list of all the blinded signatures. This will pose a threat to participants' privacy in the incentive mechanisms. Hence, we focus on proposing an untraceable blind signature scheme to enhance the data privacy protection in smart grid or other similar scenarios.

Specifically, we first find an efficient but traceable blind signature scheme (i.e. Popescu's [10]). On basis of analyzing its security, namely, demonstrating that it cannot hold the untraceability, we provide an improved method to achieve this property. This method can also inspire other traceable blind signature schemes for achieving untraceability. After describing our solution, we also prove its correctness and security properties (i.e. unforgeability, blindness and untraceability) with a comparative performance analysis to show its advantage.

2   Related Work

Blind signature was first introduced by Chaum [7] in 1982 for constructing an electronic cash (e-cash) system. This special digital signature allows a requester to ask signatures from a signer on any document, but without revealing anything about the document to the signer. Thus, blind signature has been widely applied into protecting customers' right and privacy in untraceable e-cash systems [11]. In addition, other services such as anonymous credentials [12], electronic voting over Internet [13], or incentive mechanisms in IoV [14], also use blind signatures to protect the privacy of users.

For guaranteeing the security of blind signature in applications, Pointcheval and Stern [15] first defined the security of blind signature and proposed a provably secure design. Juels et al. [16] also focused on defining the security and blindness, and showed both of them can be satisfied simultaneously. While many blind signature schemes have been proven secure in the standard model, but most of them are extremely inefficient.

To improve the efficiency of blind signature schemes, both Camenisch et al. [17] and Hazay et al. [18] proposed more efficient blind signatures without random oracles. The latter was the first design that can be proven secure in a concurrent setting. Fischlin [19] constructed executable blind signature schemes for reducing the communication cost between the user and signer, and defined the universally composable (UC) blind signature. In the UC blind signature setting, a user is required committing on the candidate signed message. To remove the requirement of commitment, Abe and Ohkubo [20] designed a non-committing UC blind signature scheme.

In recent years, lattice-based blind signature schemes [21,22], and some derivative schemes from blind signature such as proxy blind signature [23,32] and group blind signature [24–26] have also been proposed. However, most of them paid less attention to untraceability, or only achieved "claimed" untraceability [27]. That is, in most of the existing blind signature schemes, once the malicious signer is given a public signature, he/she can trace it to the corresponding blinded signature via its keeping list of all the blinded signatures. Obviously, this problem of traceability is detrimental to the aforementioned services emphasizing privacy of users.

3   Preliminaries

3.1   Notations

The involved notations are denoted as follows. Let $x \in \mathbb{S}$ denote that randomly choosing x from the set $\mathbb{S}$. Define $f : \mathbb{N} \to \mathbb{R}$ as a negligible function if, for any polynomial function $p(\cdot)$, there is an integer $n_0 \in \mathbb{N}$ satisfying $\forall n > n_0 : f(n) < 1/p(n)$. We regard a algorithm as $\mathcal{PPT}$ algorithm if it is probabilistic and run in polynomial-time.

3.2 Mathematical Hard Problems

Discrete Logarithm Problem. Given a cyclic group $\mathbb{G}$ of prime order p and two random elements $G, H = aG \in \mathbb{G}$ (where $a \in \mathbb{Z}_p$), the adversary's goal is to compute a such that $H = aG$. This problem refers to that no $\mathcal{PPT}$ adversary can achieve the above goal with a non-negligible probability.

One-more Discrete Logarithm Problem. This problem is an extension of discrete logarithm problem, which focuses on finding the discrete logarithm of l group elements via strictly querying less than l oracles. Here, the oracle can return the discrete logarithm of a given group element. Specifically, given a cyclic group $\mathbb{G}$ of prime order p and a generator G, the adversary can also query the following oracles.

1. $\mathcal{O}_{chal}()$: this oracle randomly chooses $x \leftarrow \mathbb{Z}_p$ to compute $X = xG$, it returns X.
2. $\mathcal{O}_{DLog}(X)$: after receiving a group element X, this oracle will return its discrete logarithm $x = log_G(X)$ and sets the number of query as $l = l+1$. Here, $log_G(X)$ is the oracle returning the discrete logarithm in base G of its input X.

After querying enough times of $\mathcal{O}_{chal}$ and $\mathcal{O}_{DLog}$, the adversary contributes to computing the discrete logarithm of more than l group elements. The one-more discrete logarithm problem refers to that no $\mathcal{PPT}$ adversary can achieve this goal with a non-negligible probability.

3.3 Blind Signatures

A blind signature scheme consists of four algorithms, namely, BSetup, BKGen, BSign and BVerf.

1. $sp \leftarrow$ BSetup(λ). This setup algorithm takes as input a security parameter λ, and outputs system parameters sp.
2. $(sk, pk) \leftarrow$ BKGen(sp). This key generation algorithm takes as input system parameters sp, and outputs a secret/public key pair (sk, pk).
3. $(b, \sigma) \leftarrow$ BSign(Signer(sk), User(pk, msg)). This interactive protocol is executed between a signer and a user, where the signer takes as input a secret key sk and the user takes inputs a public key pk and a message msg. The signer outputs $b = 1$ if this interaction executes successfully and $b = 0$ otherwise. Correspondingly, the user outputs a signature σ if it terminates normally and $\perp$ otherwise. The interaction between signer and user can be denoted as follows.

$$(msg_{u,0}, state_{u,0}) \leftarrow \mathsf{User}_0(pk, m)$$
$$(msg_{s,1}, state_{s,1}) \leftarrow \mathsf{Signer}_1(sk, msg_{u,0})$$
$$(msg_{u,1}, state_{u,1}) \leftarrow \mathsf{User}_1(state_{u,0}, msg_{s,1})$$
$$(msg_{s,2}, b) \leftarrow \mathsf{Signer}_2(state_{s,1}, msg_{u,1})$$
$$\sigma \leftarrow \mathsf{User}_2(state_{u,1}, msg_{s,2}),$$

where User_0 represents the beginning of the session, and hence $msg_{u,0} = ()$ and $state_{u,0} = (pk, m)$.

4. $b \leftarrow \mathsf{BVerf}(pk, msg, \sigma)$. This verification algorithm takes as inputs a public key pk, a message msg and a signature σ, and it outputs $b = 1$ if σ is a valid signature of msg under pk and $b = 0$ otherwise.

The blind signature scheme is mainly concerned about privacy and authentication, and it should satisfies these three properties.

Correctness. This property requires that the signature generated by BSign must be accepted by BVerf. That is,

$$\Pr \left[\begin{array}{c} sp \leftarrow \mathsf{BSetup}(\lambda), (sk, pk) \leftarrow \mathsf{BKGen}(sp), \\ (b, \sigma) \leftarrow \mathsf{BSign}(\mathsf{Signer}(sk), \mathsf{User}(pk, msg)), \\ b' \leftarrow \mathsf{BVerf}(pk, msg, \sigma) : b = 1 = b' \end{array} \right] = 1.$$

Unforgeability. This property ensures that no adversary, after interacting any number of times with a signer and n of these interactions were considered successful by the signer, is able to generate more than n signatures. It should be noted that the adversary can schedule and interleave the interaction in any arbitrary way. To formally define the unforgeability, we simulate a game executed between a challenger $\mathcal{C}$ and adversary $\mathcal{A}$.

In the game, two counters n_1 and n_2 (which are initially set as 0) are used to present session identifier and a set $\mathcal{S}$ of "open" sessions. Concretely, $\mathcal{C}$ first invokes BSetup and BKGen to obtain sp and (sk, pk) respectively. Then, $\mathcal{C}$ sends pk to $\mathcal{A}$. In addition, $\mathcal{A}$ can also query the following oracles.

1. $\mathcal{O}_{sign1}(msg)$. After receiving the adversary's query (i.e. the user's first message msg), $\mathcal{C}$ increments n_1, adds n_1 into $\mathcal{S}$, and uses sk to run the first round on the signer's side. Formally, $n_1 = n_1 + 1, (msg', state_{n_1} \leftarrow \mathsf{Signer}_1(sk, msg)), \mathcal{S} = \mathcal{S} \cup \{n_1\}$. This oracle finally returns (n_1, msg'), and $\mathcal{C}$ stores its state $state_{n_1}$.

2. $\mathcal{O}_{sign2}(j, msg)$. After receiving the adversary's query (i.e. a session identifier j and a user's message msg), $\mathcal{C}$ runs the second round on the signer's side if $j \in \mathcal{S}$, namely, $(msg', b) \leftarrow \mathsf{Signer}_2(state_j, msg)$. Then, $\mathcal{C}$ removes j from $\mathcal{S}$ and increments n_2 if $b = 1$, that is, $\mathcal{S} = \mathcal{S}/\{j\}, n_2 = n_2 + 1$. This oracle finally returns msg'.

After querying enough times of $\mathcal{O}_{sign1}$ and $\mathcal{O}_{sign2}$, $\mathcal{A}$ will outputs n message/signature pairs $(msg_i^*, \sigma_i^*)_{i=1}^n$. The $\mathcal{A}$ attacks successfully if and only if the following conditions are satisfied.

1. The number of "open" sessions is less than that of generated message/signature pairs, that is, $k_2 < n$.
2. $\forall i \neq j \in \{1, 2 \ldots, n\} : (msg_i^*, \sigma_i^*) \neq (msg_j^*, \sigma_j^*)$.
3. $\forall i \in \{1, 2, \ldots, n\} : \mathsf{BVerf}(pk, msg_i^*, \sigma_i^*) = 1$.

We denote $Adv_{BS,\mathcal{A}}^{unf}(sp)$ as the advantage of $\mathcal{A}$ succeeding in the above game. A blind signature satisfies the unforgeability if $Adv_{BS,\mathcal{A}}^{unf}(sp)$ is negligible for all $\mathcal{PPT}$ adversaries $\mathcal{A}$.

Blindness. This property requires that a signer is unable to link a message/signature pair to a specific execution of the BSign. Formally, the adversary $\mathcal{A}$ prepares two message msg_0 and msg_1 and the challenger $\mathcal{C}$ invokes the interaction protocol BSign acting as the user with $\mathcal{A}$. After executing the BSign, two message/signature pairs (msg_b^*, σ_b) and $(msg_{1-b}^*, \sigma_{1-b})$ will be generated, where b is a random bit (i.e. 0 or 1). $\mathcal{A}$ is given (σ_0, σ_1) if both message/signature pairs are valid, and $\mathcal{A}$ must provide his/her guess b'. We call that $\mathcal{A}$ wins the game if $b' = b$ and denote $Adv_{BS,\mathcal{A}}^{bld}$ as $\mathcal{A}$'s advantage of winning the game.

Untraceability. This property refers to an enhanced *Blindness*, that is, a signer cannot link a message/signature pair to a particular execution of BSign even when the signature has been disclosed publicly.

4   Review of Popescu's Scheme

In this section, we briefly review Popescu's blind signature scheme [10].

1. BSetup. This setup algorithm initializes system parameters $\{E, \mathbb{G}, P, p, q, a, b, \mathcal{H}\}$, where p, q are two large prime numbers, E is a non-singular elliptic curve defined by $y^2 = x^3 + ax + b \mod p$ (where $a, b \in \mathbb{F}_p$), $\mathbb{G}$ is a additive cyclic group which consists of all points on E and an infinity point O, P is the generator of $\mathbb{G}$ with order q, and $\mathcal{H} : \{0,1\}^* \times \mathbb{Z}_p^* \to \{0,1\}^{|q|/2}$ is a collision-resistant hash function.
2. BKGen. This key generation algorithm randomly chooses $x \in \mathbb{Z}_q^*$ as a private key. It also computes $Q = xP$ as the corresponding public key.
3. BSign. In the blind signature generation algorithm, the user asks the signer to initiate the following communication.
   - The signer randomly chooses $k \in [2, q-1]$ to compute $R' = kP$, then he/she sends R' to the user.
   - The user randomly chooses two blinding factors $\alpha, \beta \in [2, q-1]$ to compute $R = \alpha P + \beta R' = (x_R, y_R)$ and $h = \mathcal{H}(m, x_R)$. Also, the user computes $m' = h\beta^{-1} \mod q$ and sends m' to the signer.
   - The signer computes $s' = k - m'x \pmod{q}$ and sends s' to the user.
   - The user computes $s = s'\beta + \alpha \pmod{q}$ and obtains the final message-signature pair $(m, \sigma = (h, s))$.
4. BVerf. This verification algorithm computes $R'' = hQ + sP = (x_{R''}, y_{R''})$ and $h' = \mathcal{H}(m, x_{R''})$. The $\sigma = (h, s)$ is a valid signature of m if $h = h'$, otherwise, it is invalid.

5   Cryptanalysis of Popescu's Scheme

Let the signer store all the transcripts (R', m', s') of his signatures, where $m' = h\beta^{-1} \mod q$ and $s = s'\beta + \alpha \pmod{q}$. After the user makes the generated signature $\sigma = (m, h, s)$ public, the signer can solve the blind factors α and β. With these blind factors, the signer can link his/her signed signature (R', m', s') to the message m. Specifically, the signer executes the following operations.

1. The signer stores all the transcripts (R', m', s') in a list $\mathcal{L}$.
2. Given (m, h, s), the signer computes $\beta = hm'^{-1} \pmod{q}$ and $\alpha = s - s'\beta \pmod{q}$.
3. The signer computes $R'' = \alpha P + \beta R'$ and he/she checks if the equation $R'' = hQ + sP$ holds on.
4. The signer finds the message m' he/she have signed if the above equation holds on, otherwise he/she traverses the next transact in the $\mathcal{L}$.

6   Proposed Blind Signature Scheme

1. BSetup. System parameters in our proposal are the same as that in Popescu's scheme, that is, $\{E, \mathbb{G}, P, p, q, a, b, \mathcal{H}\}$.
2. BKGen. This algorithm randomly chooses $x \in \mathbb{Z}_q^*$ and computes $Q = xP$. It returns x as a private key and Q as the corresponding public key.
3. BSign. The user asks the signer to initiate the following communication.
   - The signer randomly chooses $k \in [2, q-1]$ to compute $R' = kP$, then he/she sends R' to the user.
   - The user randomly chooses two blinding factors $\alpha, \beta \in [2, q-1]$ to compute $R = \alpha P + \beta R' - \alpha\beta Q = (x_R, y_R)$ and $h = \mathcal{H}(m, x_R)$. Also, the user computes $m' = h\beta^{-1} + \alpha \bmod q$ and sends m' to the signer.
   - The signer computes $s' = k - m'x \pmod{q}$ and sends s' to the user.
   - The user computes $s = s'\beta + \alpha \pmod{q}$ and obtains the final message-signature pair $(m, \sigma = (h, s))$.
4. BVerf. This verification algorithm computes $R'' = hQ + sP = (x_{R''}, y_{R''})$ and $h' = \mathcal{H}(m, x_{R''})$. The $\sigma = (h, s)$ is a valid signature of m if $h = h'$, otherwise, it is invalid.

Theorem 1. *Our proposed blind signature scheme can satisfy the correctness, unforgeability, blindness and untraceability.*

Proof. The correctness is obvious, that is, given a message/signature pair $(m, \sigma = (h, s))$ generated by BSign, it can pass the verification of BVerf. The correctness is described as follows.

$$\begin{aligned}
R'' = hQ + sP &= hxP + (s'\beta + \alpha)P \\
&= hxP + (k\beta - m'x\beta + \alpha)P \\
&= hxP + (k\beta - (h\beta^{-1} + \alpha)x\beta + \alpha)P \\
&= hxP + (k\beta - hx - \alpha x\beta + \alpha)P \\
&= k\beta P - \alpha\beta xP + \alpha P \\
&= \beta R' - \alpha\beta Q + \alpha P \\
&= R = (x_R, y_R), \\
h' = \mathcal{H}(m, x_R) &= h
\end{aligned}$$

Our proposed blind signature scheme has the unforgeability in the random oracle model if the one-more discrete logarithm problem is hard. Suppose that there exists a $\mathcal{PPT}$ adversary $\mathcal{A}_{unf}$ who can break the unforgeability of our proposed blind signature scheme, there will be another $\mathcal{PPT}$ adversary $\mathcal{B}_{omdl}$ can solve the one-more discrete logarithm problem with a non-negligible probability. Here, given $(\mathbb{G}, p, G)$ and two oracles $\mathcal{O}_{chal}$ and $\mathcal{O}_{DLog}$ as mentioned in Sect. 3.2, the $\mathcal{B}_{omdl}$ first invokes $\mathcal{O}_{chal}$ to obtain and then send Q to $\mathcal{A}_{unf}$. Then, $\mathcal{B}_{omdl}$ simulates the following oracles queried by $\mathcal{A}_{unf}$.

1. $\mathcal{O}_{sign1}$. To reply this oracle, the $\mathcal{B}_{omdl}$ invokes $\mathcal{O}_{chal}$ to obtain R'_i. Thus, this oracle will returns R'_i to $\mathcal{A}_{unf}$.
2. $\mathcal{O}_{\mathcal{H}}$. The $\mathcal{A}_{unf}$ randomly chooses α_i and β_i to compute $R_i = \alpha_i P + \beta R'_i - \alpha_i \beta_i Q = (x_{R_i}, y_{R_i})$. Then, it queries (m_i, x_{R_i}) to this oracle. The $\mathcal{B}_{omdl}$ randomly chooses $h_i \in \mathbb{Z}_q$ and sets $\mathcal{H}(m_i, x_{R_i}) = h_i$. Hence, the $\mathcal{A}_{unf}$ will obtain h_i after invoking this oracle.
3. $\mathcal{O}_{sign2}$. The $\mathcal{A}_{unf}$ computes $m'_i = h_i \beta_i^{-1} + \alpha_i$ and queries this oracle. Correspondingly, the $\mathcal{B}_{omdl}$ computes $S'_i = R'_i - m'_i Q$ to invokes $s'_i = \mathcal{O}_{DLog}(S'_i)$. It means that $\mathcal{A}_{unf}$ will obtain s'_i after the invocation.

Denote the times of $\mathcal{A}_{unf}$ invoking the above oracles as n_{s1}, n_h and n_{s2}, respectively. After the above invocations, $\mathcal{A}_{unf}$ will forge a valid message/signature pair $(m^*, (h_1^*, s_1^*))$, where $s_1^* = s_1'^* \beta^* + \alpha^* \pmod{q}$, $s_1'^* = (k^* - m_1^* x) \pmod{q}$ and $m_1^* = h_1^* \beta^{*-1} + \alpha^* \pmod{q}$. According to Forking Lemma [15,28], $\mathcal{B}_{omdl}$ can obtain the other valid forgery $(m^*, (h_2^*, s_2^*))$ via restarting the above simulation with setting the random oracle as $h_2^* = \mathcal{O}_{\mathcal{H}}(m^*, x_R^*)$, and now $s_2^* = s_2'^* \beta^* + \alpha^* \pmod{q}$, $s_2'^* = (k^* - m_2^* x) \pmod{q}$, $m_2^* = h_2^* \beta^{*-1} + \alpha^* \pmod{q}$.

This implies that $\mathcal{B}_{omdl}$ can compute $s_1^* - s_2^* = (s_1'^* - s_2'^*) \beta^* = (m_2^* - m_1^*) x \beta^* = (h_2^* - h_1^*) x \pmod{q}$ and hence obtains $x = (s_1^* - s_2^*)(h_2^* - h_1^*)^{-1} \pmod{q}$. $\mathcal{B}_{omdl}$ finally outputs $(x, Q), (s_1', S_1'), \ldots, (s'_{n_{s2}}, S'_{n_{s2}})$ as the $n_{s2} + 1$ solutions of one-more discrete logarithm problem with only querying $\mathcal{O}_{DLog}$ n_{s2} times. However, one-more discrete logarithm problem is hard for a $\mathcal{PPT}$ adversary, thus our proposed blind signature scheme meets the unforgeability.

As the blindness, in our proposal, two blinding factor α and β (both unknown to the signer) are utilized to blind the message $m' = \mathcal{H}(m, x_R) \beta^{-1} + \alpha \pmod{q}$. The signer is unable to obtain α, β or $\mathcal{H}(m, x_R)$, given m', thus our proposal can achieve blindness.

To prove the untraceability, we assume that the malicious signer has kept a signed list $L = \{R'_i, s'_i, m'_i\}$ for all the blinded messages. We also denote a revealed signature as $\{m_j, \sigma_j = (h_j, s_j)\}$. In our proposal, $m' = h\beta^{-1} + \alpha \pmod{q}$ and $s' = k - m'x \pmod{q}$, which breaks the linearity faced by Popescu's proposal [10]. Hence, the signer cannot recover the blinding factor α, β, and hence he/she fails to trace the targeted (R'_j, s'_j, m'_j) (corresponding to $\{m_j, \sigma_j = (h_j, s_j)\}$) from the list L.

7   Performance Analysis

In this section, we provide the performance analysis of our proposal via comparing it with other related schemes. The notations and corresponding executing time are listed in Table 1, which is executed on our personal computer (Dell with an i5-4210U 1.70-GHz processor, 4 GB memory and Window 7 OS) based on a popular cryptographic library (i.e. miracl library of version 7.0). The system security parameter is set as $\lambda = 128$ with using the Barreto-Naehrig (BN) [29] over the base field $\mathbb{F}$-256.

Table 1. Notations and executing time (in millisecond)

Notation	Description	Time
T_{pa}	A point addition in $\mathbb{G}$	0.0811
T_{sm}	A scale multiplication in $\mathbb{G}$	8.8517
T_h	A general hash function	0.00060
T_{mi}	A modular inversion in $\mathbb{Z}_q$	0.0471
T_{mm}	A modular multiplication in $\mathbb{Z}_q$	0.0097

Specifically, we count the number of cryptographic operations required by different algorithms (i.e. BKGen, BSign and BVerf) in our proposal and other existing schemes. The counted result is listed in Table 2. Furthermore, on basic of Table 1, we obtain the concrete time cost in Table 3.

Table 2. Number of cryptographic operations for different algorithms

Algorithm	Popescu [10]	Fuchsbauer et al. [30]	Hamid et al. [27]	Nayak et al. [31]	Our proposal
BKGen	T_{sm}	T_{sm}	T_{sm}	$2T_{sm}$	T_{sm}
BSign	$3T_{sm} + T_{pa} + T_h + T_{mi} + 3T_{mm}$	$3T_{sm} + 2_{pa} + T_h + T_{mm}$	$3T_{sm} + T_{pa} + T_{mi} + 4T_{mm} + T_h$	$5T_{sm} + T_{pa} + 2T_{mm} + T_h$	$4T_{sm} + 2T_{pa} + 4T_{mm} + T_{mi} + T_h$
BVerf	$2T_{sm} + T_{pa} + T_h$	$2T_{sm} + T_{pa} + T_h$	$2T_{sm} + T_{pa} + T_{mm} + T_h$	$T_{sm} + 2T_{pa} + T_h$	$2T_{sm} + T_{pa} + T_h$

From Table 3, one can find that the schemes proposed in [10, 27, 30] are more efficient than our proposal especially in BSign. However, all of them are faced with the problem of traceability. That is, the malicious signer can easily compute the blinding factors and then trace the blinded signature. On the other hand, the time cost of BVerf only requires 9.0145 ms in the recent untraceable solution (i.e. Nayak et al. [31]), which is less than that in our proposal (i.e. 17.7851 ms). But our proposal has a better efficiency in both KGen and BSign (i.e. 8.8517 and 35.6555 ms respectively) than Nayak et al. [31] (resp. 17.7034 and 44.3596 ms). Hence, our proposal can achieve a tradeoff between the security and efficiency.

Table 3. Time costs for different algorithms (in millisecond)

Algorithm	Popescu [10]	Fuchsbauer et al. [30]	Hamid et al. [27]	Nayak et al. [31]	Our proposal
BKGen	8.8517	8.8517	8.8517	17.7034	8.8517
BSign	26.713	26.7276	26.7227	44.3596	35.6555
BVerf	17.7851	17.7851	17.7948	9.0145	17.7851
Total	53.3498	53.3644	53.3692	71.0775	62.2923

8   Conclusion

To better support data privacy protection of smart grid during the data retransmission, we propose an improved blind signature scheme with untraceability. Specifically, we first prove that Popescu's proposal [10] cannot achieve untraceability, and then we provide a concrete construction with security analysis and performance analysis. The results show that our proposal can make a tradeoff between security (i.e. unforgeability, blindness and untraceability) and performance.

References

1. Maharjan, S., Zhu, Q., Zhang, Y., Gjessing, S., Basar, T.: Dependable demand response management in the smart grid: a stackelberg game approach. IEEE Trans. Smart Grid **4**(1), 120–132 (2013)
2. Saxena, N., Grijalva, S.: Efficient signature scheme for delivering authentic control commands in the smart grid. IEEE Trans. Smart Grid **9**(5), 4323–4334 (2018)
3. Si, G., Guan, Z., Li, J., Liu, P., Yao, H.: A comprehensive survey of privacy-preserving in smart grid. In: Wang, G., Ray, I., Alcaraz Calero, J.M., Thampi, S.M. (eds.) SpaCCS 2016. LNCS, vol. 10066, pp. 213–223. Springer, Cham (2016). https://doi.org/10.1007/978-3-319-49148-6_19
4. Wang, X., Yi, P.: Security framework for wireless communications in smart distribution grid. IEEE Trans. Smart Grid **2**(4), 809–818 (2011)
5. Zhang, Y., Rong, Yu., Nekovee, M., Liu, Y., Xie, S., Gjessing, S.: Cognitive machine-to-machine communications: visions and potentials for the smart grid. IEEE Netw. **26**(3), 6–13 (2012)
6. Gunduz, M.Z., Das, R.: Cyber-security on smart grid: threats and potential solutions. Comput. Netw. **169**, 107094 (2020)
7. Chaum, D.: Blind signatures for untraceable payments. In: Chaum, D., Rivest, R.L., Sherman, A.T. (eds.) Advances in Cryptology, pp. 199–203. Springer, Boston, MA (1983). https://doi.org/10.1007/978-1-4757-0602-4_18
8. Ra, G.-J., Seo, D., Bhuiyan, M.Z.A., Lee, I.-Y.: An anonymous protocol for member privacy in a consortium blockchain. In: Wang, G., Feng, J., Bhuiyan, M.Z.A., Lu, R. (eds.) SpaCCS 2019. LNCS, vol. 11611, pp. 456–464. Springer, Cham (2019). https://doi.org/10.1007/978-3-030-24907-6_34
9. Shen, J., Miao, T., Liu, Q., Ji, S., Wang, C., Liu, D.: S-SurF: an enhanced secure bulk data dissemination in wireless sensor networks. In: Wang, G., Atiquzzaman, M., Yan, Z., Choo, K.-K.R. (eds.) SpaCCS 2017. LNCS, vol. 10656, pp. 395–408. Springer, Cham (2017). https://doi.org/10.1007/978-3-319-72389-1_32

10. Popescu, C.: Blind signature schemes based on the elliptic curve discrete logarithm problem. Stud. Inf. Control **19**(4), 397–402 (2010)

11. Chaum, D., Fiat, A., Naor, M.: Untraceable electronic cash. In: Goldwasser, S. (ed.) CRYPTO 1988. LNCS, vol. 403, pp. 319–327. Springer, New York (1990). https://doi.org/10.1007/0-387-34799-2_25

12. Garman, C., Green, M., Miers, I.: Decentralized anonymous credentials. In: 21st Annual Network and Distributed System Security Symposium, NDSS 2014, San Diego, California, USA, 23–26 February 2014. The Internet Society (2014)

13. Kucharczyk, M.: Blind signatures in electronic voting systems. In: Kwiecień, A., Gaj, P., Stera, P. (eds.) CN 2010. CCIS, vol. 79, pp. 349–358. Springer, Heidelberg (2010). https://doi.org/10.1007/978-3-642-13861-4_37

14. Sun, G., Sun, S., Hongfang, Yu., Guizani, M.: Toward incentivizing fog-based privacy-preserving mobile crowdsensing in the internet of vehicles. IEEE Internet Things J. **7**(5), 4128–4142 (2020)

15. Pointcheval, D., Stern, J.: Provably secure blind signature schemes. In: Kim, K., Matsumoto, T. (eds.) ASIACRYPT 1996. LNCS, vol. 1163, pp. 252–265. Springer, Heidelberg (1996). https://doi.org/10.1007/BFb0034852

16. Juels, A., Luby, M., Ostrovsky, R.: Security of blind digital signatures. In: Kaliski, B.S. (ed.) CRYPTO 1997. LNCS, vol. 1294, pp. 150–164. Springer, Heidelberg (1997). https://doi.org/10.1007/BFb0052233

17. Camenisch, J., Koprowski, M., Warinschi, B.: Efficient blind signatures without random oracles. In: Blundo, C., Cimato, S. (eds.) SCN 2004. LNCS, vol. 3352, pp. 134–148. Springer, Heidelberg (2005). https://doi.org/10.1007/978-3-540-30598-9_10

18. Hazay, C., Katz, J., Koo, C.-Y., Lindell, Y.: Concurrently-secure blind signatures without random oracles or setup assumptions. In: Vadhan, S.P. (ed.) TCC 2007. LNCS, vol. 4392, pp. 323–341. Springer, Heidelberg (2007). https://doi.org/10.1007/978-3-540-70936-7_18

19. Fischlin, M.: Round-optimal composable blind signatures in the common reference string model. In: Dwork, C. (ed.) CRYPTO 2006. LNCS, vol. 4117, pp. 60–77. Springer, Heidelberg (2006). https://doi.org/10.1007/11818175_4

20. Abe, M., Ohkubo, M.: A framework for universally composable non-committing blind signatures. In: Matsui, M. (ed.) ASIACRYPT 2009. LNCS, vol. 5912, pp. 435–450. Springer, Heidelberg (2009). https://doi.org/10.1007/978-3-642-10366-7_26

21. Rückert, M.: Lattice-based blind signatures. In: Abe, M. (ed.) ASIACRYPT 2010. LNCS, vol. 6477, pp. 413–430. Springer, Heidelberg (2010). https://doi.org/10.1007/978-3-642-17373-8_24

22. Alkeilani Alkadri, N., El Bansarkhani, R., Buchmann, J.: BLAZE: practical lattice-based blind signatures for privacy-preserving applications. In: Bonneau, J., Heninger, N. (eds.) FC 2020. LNCS, vol. 12059, pp. 484–502. Springer, Cham (2020). https://doi.org/10.1007/978-3-030-51280-4_26

23. Kim, Y.S., Chang, J.K.: Provably secure proxy blind signature scheme. In: Eigth IEEE International Symposium on Multimedia (ISM 2006), San Diego, CA, USA, 11–13 December 2006, pp. 998–1003. IEEE Computer Society (2006)

24. Lysyanskaya, A., Ramzan, Z.: Group blind digital signatures: a scalable solution to electronic cash. In: Hirchfeld, R. (ed.) FC 1998. LNCS, vol. 1465, pp. 184–197. Springer, Heidelberg (1998). https://doi.org/10.1007/BFb0055483

25. Wang, H., Liu, X., Zhao, S., Huo, L.: Multi-authority e-voting system based on group blind signature. Int. J. Online Eng. **11**(9), 89–93 (2015)

26. Kong, W., Shen, J., Vijayakumar, P., Cho, Y., Chang, V.: A practical group blind signature scheme for privacy protection in smart grid. J. Parallel Distrib. Comput. **136**, 29–39 (2020)
27. Mala, H., Nezhadansari, N.: New blind signature schemes based on the (elliptic curve) discrete logarithm problem. In: International Econference on Computer and Knowledge Engineering (2013)
28. Bagherzandi, A., Cheon, J.H., Jarecki, S.: Multisignatures secure under the discrete logarithm assumption and a generalized forking lemma. In: Ning, P., Syverson, P.F., Jha, S. (eds.) Proceedings of the 2008 ACM Conference on Computer and Communications Security, CCS 2008, Alexandria, Virginia, USA, 27–31 October 2008, pp. 449–458. ACM (2008)
29. Barreto, P.S.L.M., Naehrig, M.: Pairing-friendly elliptic curves of prime order. In: Preneel, B., Tavares, S. (eds.) SAC 2005. LNCS, vol. 3897, pp. 319–331. Springer, Heidelberg (2006). https://doi.org/10.1007/11693383_22
30. Fuchsbauer, G., Plouviez, A., Seurin, Y.: Blind Schnorr signatures and signed ElGamal encryption in the algebraic group model. In: Canteaut, A., Ishai, Y. (eds.) EUROCRYPT 2020. LNCS, vol. 12106, pp. 63–95. Springer, Cham (2020). https://doi.org/10.1007/978-3-030-45724-2_3
31. Nayak, S.K., Majhi, B., Mohanty, S.: An ecdlp based untraceable blind signature scheme. In: International Conference on Circuits, pp. 829–834 (2013)
32. Verma, G.K., Singh, B.B.: Efficient message recovery proxy blind signature scheme from pairings. Trans. Emerg. Telecommun. Technol. **28**(11) (2017)

Author Index

Printed in the United States
By Bookmasters